Frommer's

Provence & the Riviera

4th Edition

by Darwin Porter & Danforth Prince

Here's what the critics say about Frommer's:

"Amazingly easy to use. Very portable, very complete."

—Booklist

"Detailed, accurate, and easy-to-read information for all price ranges."

—Glamour Magazine

"Hotel information is close to encyclopedic."

—Des Moines Sunday Register

"Frommer's Guides have a way of giving you a real feel for a place."

—Knight Ridder Newspapers

Wiley Publishing, Inc.

Published by:

Wiley Publishing, Inc.

111 River St.
Hoboken, NJ 07030

ISBN 0-7645-3824-1
ISSN 1094-7647

Editor: Myka Carroll
Production Editor: Bethany André
Cartographer: John Decamillis
Photo Editor: Richard Fox
Production by Wiley Indianapolis Composition Services

Front cover photo: *La vie Provençale*
Back cover photo: The lavender fields at Abbaye Notre-Dame de Sénanque near Gordes in Provence

For information on our other products and services or to obtain technical support, please contact our Customer Care Department within the U.S. at 800-762-2974, outside the U.S. at 317-572-3993 or fax 317-572-4002.

Wiley also publishes its books in a variety of electronic formats. Some content that appears in print may not be available in electronic formats.

Manufactured in the United States of America

5 4 3 2 1

Contents

List of Maps

An Invitation to the Reader

In researching this book, we discovered many wonderful places—hotels, restaurants, shops, and more. We're sure you'll find others. Please tell us about them, so we can share the information with your fellow travelers in upcoming editions. If you were disappointed with a recommendation, we'd love to know that, too. Please write to:

Frommer's Provence & the Riviera, 4th Edition
Wiley Publishing, Inc. • 111 River St. • Hoboken, NJ 07030

An Additional Note

Please be advised that travel information is subject to change at any time—and this is especially true of prices. We therefore suggest that you write or call ahead for confirmation when making your travel plans. The authors, editors, and publisher cannot be held responsible for the experiences of readers while traveling. Your safety is important to us, however, so we encourage you to stay alert and be aware of your surroundings. Keep a close eye on cameras, purses, and wallets, all favorite targets of thieves and pickpockets.

About the Authors

France and its southern tier are a second home to **Darwin Porter,** a native of North Carolina, and **Danforth Prince,** who lived in France throughout most of his 20s. Darwin, who has worked in television advertising and as a bureau chief for the *Miami Herald* and who hopes to someday create the perfect bouillabaisse, is the original author of *Frommer's France.* Dan worked for the Paris bureau of *The New York Times* between renovations of a historic building in the Loire Valley and bicycle trips through Provence and the Camargue. Both writers have made countless trips to southern France for work and R&R.

Frommer's Star Ratings, Icons & Abbreviations

Every hotel, restaurant, and attraction listing in this guide has been ranked for quality, value, service, amenities, and special features using a **star-rating system.** In country, state, and regional guides, we also rate towns and regions to help you narrow down your choices and budget your time accordingly. Hotels and restaurants are rated on a scale of zero (recommended) to three stars (exceptional). Attractions, shopping, nightlife, towns, and regions are rated according to the following scale: zero stars (recommended), one star (highly recommended), two stars (very highly recommended), and three stars (must-see).

In addition to the star-rating system, we also use **seven feature icons** that point you to the great deals, in-the-know advice, and unique experiences that separate travelers from tourists. Throughout the book, look for:

Finds	Special finds—those places only insiders know about
Fun Fact	Fun facts—details that make travelers more informed and their trips more fun
Kids	Best bets for kids and advice for the whole family
Moments	Special moments—those experiences that memories are made of
Overrated	Places or experiences not worth your time or money
Tips	Insider tips—great ways to save time and money
Value	Great values—where to get the best deals

The following **abbreviations** are used for credit cards:

AE	American Express	DISC	Discover	V	Visa
DC	Diners Club	MC	MasterCard		

Frommers.com

Now that you have the guidebook to a great trip, visit our website at **www.frommers.com** for travel information on more than 3,000 destinations. With features updated regularly, we give you instant access to the most current trip-planning information available. At Frommers.com, you'll also find the best prices on airfares, accommodations, and car rentals—and you can even book travel online through our travel booking partners. At Frommers.com, you'll also find the following:

- Online updates to our most popular guidebooks
- Vacation sweepstakes and contest giveaways
- Newsletter highlighting the hottest travel trends
- Online travel message boards with featured travel discussions

What's New in Provence & the Riviera

The area from the Languedoc-Roussillon region in western France to the string of Riviera towns in eastern France is the most dynamic part of the country. It is also the most fashionable, and trends change rapidly. Here is a preview of some of the major changes occurring in this sunny region.

ARLES This fabled old city used to be visited for its history and attractions, not its cuisine. But lately there has been considerable improvement in the fare, notably at **Brasserie Nord-Pinus,** place du Forum (✆ **04-90-93-44-44**), which is today one of the lightest and most sophisticated in town, employing top-notch chefs to prepare dishes based on the best of seasonal shopping. The menu of French and Provençal specialties changes frequently based on best market conditions. More and more discerning palates are discovering **La Gueule du Loup,** 39 rue des Arènes (✆ **04-90-96-96-69**), which also serves a hearty yet refined French and Provençal cuisine. The owners, the Allard family, take their food preparation seriously, and most diners are delighted with the results. See chapter 4.

ST. REMY-DE-PROVENCE Because of impressive media coverage, more discerning palates were pleased in 2003 at **L'Assiette de Marie,** 1 rue Jaume Roux (✆ **04-90-92-32-14**), with its French and Provençal cuisine. Even Princess Caroline of Monaco has been a frequent visitor. Marie-Ricco, the Corsican-Italian owner, handles her sudden popularity with style and grace, still sticking to menu items such as her goat cheese and homemade pastas that put her in the culinary map in the first place. Deliberately downgraded from a restaurant, **Charmeroy Maison de Gouts,** 51 rue Carnot (✆ **04-32-60-01-23**), has transformed itself into one of the most sought after tearooms of Provence. Charming and intimate, it is known for its mouth-watering pastries and "divine" teas. Madame Charmeroy, the owner, even named one of her best pastries after former resident Nostradamus and based it on a 16th-century recipe. See chapter 4.

BONNIEUX In this romantic hill town in the heart of Petit Luberon stands **Le Clos du Buis,** rue Victor Hugo (✆ **04-90-75-88-48**), in a restored stone-fronted Mediterranean villa from the 1700s. Though small, it's one of the most popular and affordable hotels in the area for those seeking its personalized charm. To cool you off, there's a pool. See chapter 4.

MARSEILLE There were predictions that **Chez Fonfon,** 140 rue du Vallon des Auffes (✆ **04-91-52-14-38**), would fall off after its legendary founder died in the late 1990s. But his great-nephew, Alexandre Pinna, took over and really came into his own in 2003. Pinna is a virtual media darling celebrated for his finely tuned French and Provençal cuisine that, if anything, seems better under new chefs than it was in its heyday when the likes of John Wayne showed up. See chapter 4.

ST-TROPEZ In the chic resort of St-Tropez, a man hailed as the world's greatest chef, Alain Ducasse, has opened **Spoon Byblos,** avenue Paul-Signac (✆ **04-94-56-68-00**), in the resort's swankiest hotel. Using produce mainly from the Mediterranean, Ducasse has inspired a French/international menu that has excited even the jaded palates of this fabled holiday center. Some of the recipes come from Morocco; others are from Andalusia or wherever. You never know with Ducasse. See chapter 5.

CANNES This resort, famed for its film festival, continues to open one hipster enclave after another. One of the latest is **Le Bâoli,** boulevard de la Croisette (✆ **04-93-43-03-43**), which has quickly earned a reputation for its artful French and Japanese cuisine. Dishes range from Gaul to Toyko, as evoked by such plates as lobster in citrus sauce or tappanyaki recipes prepared tableside. More media attention has focused on **La Tantra/Le Loft,** 13 rue du Dr. Monod (✆ **04-93-39-40-39**), now that it has introduced its new fusion menu of delectable French and Asian dishes in its Tao-inspired dining room. Expect lots of sushi, tempura, and even Kobe steak.

The hippest of the hip is the amusingly named **Le Harem,** 15 rue des Frères Pradignac (✆ **04-93-39-62-70**), serving a Mediterranean cuisine that is mainly "new Moroccan." Cinema stars frequent this chic enclave of fashion and good food. It's on the see-and-be-seen circuit but also delivers with its refined flavors and its slow-cooked *tagines* and other delights from North Africa. See chapter 5.

ST-PAUL-LE-VENCE This sleepy hill town over Nice has long been known for its swanky accommodations. Overnights have gotten even better with the opening of some small inns *de charme,* as the French say. **Hôtel Les Vergers de Saint-Paul,** 940 Route de la Colle (✆ **04-93-32-94-24**), is just as modern as the town is ancient, but is a small citadel of taste, luxury, and comfort, with a pool included. An even more charming rival is **Villa St. Maxime,** 390 Route de la Colle (✆ **04-93-32-76-00**), an extraordinary boutique hotel and a rare find that combines modern luxuries with antiquity. In beautifully landscaped grounds, the hotel is a nugget, with an Olympic-size pool. See chapter 6.

EZE This former fortified feudal center along the coast is today the setting for **Chateau Eza,** Moyene Corniche (✆ **04-93-41-12-24**), the former private Riviera estate where the royal family of Sweden once vacationed. It's a real pocket of posh and still fit for royalty, with its elegant rooms spread across a series of buildings that date from the Middle Ages. See chapter 6.

MONACO Alain Ducasse, hailed by some critics as the world's greatest chef, strikes again in the heart of Monaco with the opening of **Bar et Boeuf,** avenue Princess Grace (✆ **92-16-60-60**). This is Ducasse's take on a surf-and-turf restaurant, where the only fish served is sea bass and the beef is among the most desirable cuts in the land. Giving Ducasse some serious competition is the newly opened **Baccarat,** 4 bd. des Moullins (✆ **93-50-66-92**), one of Monaco's most elegant and upscale restaurants, specializing in refined Italian cuisine, and doing so exceedingly well. Come here for Monaco's most enticing and succulent pastas, among other dishes. See chapter 6.

1

The Best of Provence & the Riviera

Provence is one of the world's most evocative regions—both the western area, known as Provence, whose landscapes and magical light have seduced innumerable artists, and the eastern coastal area, known as the Riviera, whose beach resorts have seduced innumerable hedonists. Provence and the Riviera are beautiful, diverse, and culturally rich, offering everything from fabulous beaches to amazing art museums, to white-hot nightlife, to a distinctive cuisine that blends the best of the mountains and the sea.

As you're heading to the south of France to luxuriate in life along the sunny and sexy Mediterranean—not to exhaust yourself making difficult decisions—we've searched out the best deals and once-in-a-lifetime experiences for this book. What follows in this chapter is our roster of the best of the best, the kind of discoveries we'd share with our closest friends.

1 The Best Travel Experiences

- **Partying in the Land of Festivals:** Provence is called the Land of Festivals with good reason: It hosts some 500 with an astonishing 4,000 events. Of course, the ultimate example is the you-won't-believe-it-until-you've-seen-it Cannes Film Festival in May. July and August are the busiest months, as Aix-en-Provence, Toulon, and Nice host jazz festivals and Nîmes and Arles stage theater and dance performances. On May 16, St-Tropez's riotous *bravades* honor the saint in theory but are really just an excuse for revelry. Many festivals have deep roots in Provençal folklore, honoring the bounty of earth and sea: the wine harvest in numerous villages, the rice harvest in Languedoc's Camargue, and the apple harvest in Peyruis. Everything seems to end in a feast where the wine and pastis flow. Contact any tourist office for the free booklet *Provence—Terre de Festivals*. See "When to Go" in chapter 2.
- **Absorbing a Unique Lifestyle:** Provence and Languedoc share a uniquely Mediterranean lifestyle. Compared to the rest of France, the air here is drier, the sun beats down more strongly, and the light beloved by so many painters appears clearer. Nothing could be more typical than a game of boules played under shade trees on a hot afternoon in a Provençal village. This is a place that respects time-honored crafts; Picasso might have arrived here a painter, but he left a potter. And nothing is finer in life than to be invited into a Provençal kitchen—the heart of family life—and smell the aroma of herbs and wines cooking with the catch of the day. To walk in the gardens, filled with vegetables, flowers, and fruit trees, is reason enough to visit. Attend a harvest,

not just grapes, but perhaps linden blossoms. The dramatic landscape somehow seems at its most romantic when hit with the dreaded mistral winds blowing north from Africa. Discovering this land of ingrained traditions and making it your own is one of the great rewards of all European travel, especially if you go in the best months: May and September. See chapters 3 and 4.

- **Dining and Drinking Provence Style:** Many people flock to the south of France specifically to enjoy *cuisine Provençale,* a Mediterranean mix of bold flavors with an emphasis on garlic, olive oil, and aromatic local herbs like thyme and basil. The world's greatest bouillabaisse is made here, especially in Marseille; Provençal lamb is among the best in France; and the vegetables (such as asparagus, eggplant, tomatoes, and artichokes) will make you realize that this is France's market garden. The regional wines, though not equaling those of Bordeaux and Burgundy, are the perfect accompaniment, ranging from the warm, full-bodied Châteauneuf-du-Pape to the rare, choice Bellet, produced on Nice's hill slopes. See chapters 4 and 6.
- **Spending a Day in St-Rémy-de-Provence:** Our favorite town in Provence is St-Rémy. To wander St-Rémy's streets is to recapture Provence's essence, especially its Vieille Ville (Old Town). After exploring its alleys, pause on one of its immaculate leafy squares. Then go in search of an art gallery or two and perhaps reward yourself with a painting and a memory. See "St-Rémy-de-Provence" in chapter 4.
- **Following in the Footsteps of the Great Artists:** Modern art wasn't born in Provence, but artists from all over came here to paint its "glaring festive light." The good news is that most of them left behind fabulous legacies. Perhaps it all began when Monet arrived with Renoir in 1883. In time, they were followed by a host of others, including Bonnard, who took a villa in St-Tropez. Van Gogh arrived in Arles in 1888, and Gauguin showed up a few months later. Even the Fauves sought out this region, notably Matisse, whose masterpiece is his chapel at Vence. Not long afterward, Picasso arrived at Antibes. Deeply jealous of Picasso and Matisse, Chagall moved to Vence and was later infuriated that the street on which he lived was renamed avenue Henri-Matisse. He got over it and lived and painted on the Riviera until he died at 97. See chapters 4, 5, and 6.
- **Sunning and Swimming on the Riviera Beaches:** There are greater beaches but none more fabled, overcrowded though they are. Most of them are sandy, except those stretching from Antibes to the Italian frontier, including Nice's. These are shingled (covered with coarse gravel), but that doesn't stop the world from flocking to them. A beach mattress fits just fine on the shingles, and there are umbrellas to rent when you want to escape the relentless sun. Along the Riviera, topless is almost universally accepted. Legend has it that it began with Brigitte Bardot, who pulled off her bra and said, "Let's wake up sleepy St-Trop." There are also nudist beaches, notably at Cap d'Agde and Port Cros. If you decide not to go topless or bottomless, you can still wear your most daring bikini or thong. See chapters 5 and 6. Also see "The Best Beaches," below.

- **Having Fun Day and Night:** If nothing else, the Riviera is about the art of entertainment, both high and low. The Côte d'Azur offers not only beaches and racecars and yachts, but also fêtes and festivals and even bullfights, real Spanish-style ones where the animals are killed, in the old Roman arenas at Arles and Nîmes. Glittering casinos are seemingly everywhere—Monte Carlo, Cannes, Cassis, and Beaulieu, to name a few. Many cities have elegant restaurants and opera houses with resident companies. But mainly the Riviera offers white-hot nightclubs and dance clubs for all sexes and sexual orientations, especially in Cannes, Nice, Monte Carlo, and St-Tropez. See chapters 5 and 6.
- **Breaking the Bank at Monte Carlo:** Few other casinos can match the excitement generated at the Monte Carlo Casino. The world's wealthy flocked to Monaco when the casino was opened by Charles Garnier in 1878. But since 1891 much of the nonwealthy world has followed—even those who can't afford losses. During a 3-day gambling spree that year, Charles Deville Wells, an American, turned $400 into $40,000, an astonishing amount back then. His feat was immortalized in the song "The Man Who Broke the Bank at Monte Carlo." Even if you do no more today than play the slot machines, a visit to this casino will be a highlight of your trip as you bask amid the extravagant decor and under the gilded rococo ceilings. (Some not as lucky as Wells have leaped to their deaths from the casino windows or the "Suicide Terrace.") See "Monaco" in chapter 6.

2 The Best Romantic Getaways

- **Les Baux** (Provence): Les Baux stands in a spectacular position on a promontory of sheer rock ravines. In the distance across the plain, you can view the Val d'Enfer (Valley of Hell). After a turbulent history, the town today is one of the great escapes for the savvy French who can gaze from their windows on the thousands of olive trees (many planted by the Greeks) that produce the best oil in France. A pocket of posh, it has some of the country's grandest inns and finest cuisine. The most notable is **L'Oustau de Beaumanière,** Maussanel-les-Alpilles (✆ **04-90-54-33-07**)—after you and your loved one sample the ravioli with truffles, you'll understand why. See "Les Baux" in chapter 4.
- **Iles d'Hyères** (Provence): If an off-the-record weekend is what you have in mind, there's no better spot than what was known during the Renaissance as the "Iles d'Or" because of the golden glow of the island rocks in the sun. This string of enchanting little islands is 39km (24 miles) east-southeast of the port of Toulon. The largest and westernmost island is Ile de Porquerolles, thickly covered with heather, eucalyptus, and exotic shrubs. Ile de Port-Cros is hilly and mysterious, with spring-fed lush vegetation. The best spot for a romantic retreat is on this island—**Le Manoir** (✆ **04-94-05-90-52**), an 18th-century colonial-style mansion set in a park. See "Iles d'Hyères" in chapter 4.
- **Mougins** (Western Riviera): Only 8.1km (5 miles) north of Cannes, the once-fortified town of Mougins is a thousand years old, but never in its history has it been so popular as a place to enjoy the good life.

Picasso, who could afford to live anywhere, chose a place nearby, Notre-Dame-de-Vie, to spend his last years. The wonderful old town is known for its cuisine, and Roger Vergé reigns supreme at his elegant **Le Moulin de Mougins** (© **04-93-75-78-24**). However, you can live for less at more secluded and less publicized oases. See "Mougins" in chapter 5.

- **Peillon** (Eastern Riviera): Of all the "perched" villages *(villages perchés)* along the Côte d'Azur, this fortified medieval town on a craggy mountaintop 19km (12 miles) northeast of Nice, is our favorite. Peillon is the least spoiled of the perched villages and still boasts its medieval look, with covered alleys and extremely narrow streets. Tour buses avoid the place, but artists and writers flock there (we once spotted Françoise Sagan) to escape the mad carnival of the Riviera. For a cozy hideaway with your significant other, try the **Auberge de la Madone** (© **04-93-79-91-17**). Dinner for two on the terrace set among olive trees is the best way to start a romantic evening. See "Peillon" in chapter 6.
- **Roquebrune and Cap-Martin** (Eastern Riviera): Along the Grande Corniche, Roquebrune is one of the most charming of the Côte d'Azur's villages, and its satellite resort of Cap-Martin occupies a lovely wooded peninsula. Between Monaco and Menton, these two have long been romantic retreats. The best choice for hiding away with that certain someone is the **Hôtel Vista Palace,** Grande Corniche (© **04-92-10-40-00**), a modern luxury hotel clinging giddily to a cliff side over Monte Carlo. See "Roquebrune & Cap-Martin" in chapter 6.

3 The Most Dramatic Countryside Drives

- **From Carcassonne to Albi** (Languedoc-Roussillon): From the walled city of Carcassonne, D118 takes you north into the Montagne Noire (Black Mountains), which are both arid and lush in parts, marking the southeastern extension of the Massif Central. You can spend a full day here exploring the Parc Régional du Haut-Languedoc, crowned by the 1,110m (3,700-ft.) Pic de Noire. You can base yourself in the old wool town of Mazamet and have lunch here before continuing northwest on N112 to Castres, with its Goya Museum. Then you can continue exploring the surrounding area or head for Albi, 40km (25 miles) away, the hometown of Toulouse-Lautrec. See chapter 3.
- **From St-Rémy-de-Provence to Eygalières** (Provence): A 64km (40-mile) drive northeast of Arles takes you into some of the most dramatic and forlorn countryside in Provence, even to the Val d'Enfer (Valley of Hell). At the beginning of the tour, you pass Roman monuments before climbing into the hills, with their distant views of the Parc Naturel Régional de la Camargue and Mont Ventoux. The tour also takes you to Les Baux, the most dramatically situated town in Provence and today a gourmet citadel. After many turns and twists, you eventually reach the ancient village of Eygalières, with its medieval castle and church. See chapter 4.
- **Along the Ours Peak Road** (Western Riviera): The best driving tour in the area starts in St-Raphaël and lasts for only 56km (35 miles), but because the terrain is so rough

and torturous, allow at least 3 hours. The views are among the most dramatic along the Côte d'Azur, as you traverse a backdrop of the red porphyry slopes of Rastel d'Agay. Along the way, you'll go through the passes of Evèque and Lentisques. Eventually, hairpin bends in the road lead to the summit of Ours Peak (Pic de l'Ours), at 488m (1,627 ft.), and you're rewarded with a superb panorama. See chapter 5.

- **From Vence to Grasse** (Western and Eastern Riviera): After calling on the Matisse chapel in Vence, you can take D2210 through some of the most luxuriant countryside along the French Riviera, with views of the Gorges du Loup, and stop over in the artisans' village of Tourrettes-sur-Loup, where the main street is filled with the ateliers of craftspeople. As you continue, follow the signs to Point-du-Loup and you'll be rewarded with a panorama of waterfalls; later you will pass fields of flowers that eventually lead to the perfume center of Grasse. See chapter 6.
- **From Nice to Mont Chauve** (Eastern Riviera): The hilltops surrounding Nice have long been known for their colorful villages and rural scenery. In our view, the best countryside and the best panoramas unfold by driving to Mont Chauve (Bald Mountain) across a circuit that traverses 53km (33 miles). You can stop at several villages along the way, including Aspremont and Tourette-Levens. You'll even pass the Gorges du Gabres, with its sheer walls of limestone, before reaching the enchanting village of Falicon. Eventually you'll come to Mont Chauve. Allow at least 30 minutes to hike to the summit. See chapter 6.

4 The Best Beaches

Read below to discover the best beaches throughout Provence and the Riviera. See the chapters indicated to find out more about lodging, dining, and other activities in the general vicinity of these great strips of sand.

- **La Côte Vermeille** (Languedoc-Roussillon): In contrast to the eastern Riviera's pebbly beaches, the Côte Vermeille is filled with sand stretching toward Spain's Costa Brava. The best place for fun in the sun is the 11km (6-mile) beach between the resorts of Leucate-Plage and Le Barcarès in the Pyrénées-Orientales district near Perpignan. The "Vermilion Coast" takes its name from the red-clay soil studded with the ubiquitous olive groves. Henri Matisse was so taken with the light on this coast that he painted it. See chapter 3.
- **Beaches of Ile de Porquerolles** (Provence): These beaches lie 15 minutes by ferry from the Giens peninsula east of Toulon. One of the Iles d'Hyères, Porquerolles is only 8.1km (5 miles) long and some 2.4km (1½ miles) across and enjoys national park status. Its beaches, along the northern coast facing the mainland, get 275 days of sunshine annually. There are several white-sand beaches; the best are **Plage d'Argent, Plage de la Courtade,** and **Plage de Notre-Dame.** See "Iles d'Hyères" in chapter 4.
- **Plage de Tahiti** (St-Tropez, Western Riviera): And God created woman and man and all the other critters found on this sizzling sandy beach outside St-Tropez. Tahiti is France's most infamous beach, mainly because of all the

topless or bottomless action going on. Ever since the days of Brigitte Bardot, this beach has been a favorite of movie stars. It's very cruisy and very animated, with a French nonchalance about nudity. If you bother to wear a bikini, it should be only the most daring. See "St-Tropez" in chapter 5.

- **Plage Port Grimaud** (St-Tropez, Western Riviera): This long golden-sand beach is set against the backdrop of the urban architect François Spoerry's *cité lacustre,* facing St-Tropez. Spoerry created this 98-hectare (247-acre) marine village inspired by an ancient fishing village. The world has since flocked to Port Grimaud and its beach; homeowner Joan Collins comes here to hide from the paparazzi. Some of the Riviera's most expensive yachts are tied up in the harbor. This beach isn't as decadent as those at St-Trop, but it does pick up the "overflow" on the see-and-be-seen circuit. See "St-Tropez" in chapter 5.
- **The Beaches at Cannes** (Western Riviera): From the Palais des Festivals and west to Mandelieu, the beach at Cannes has real sand, not pebbles as at Nice. This beach resort offers a movable feast of high-fashion swimsuits. Ever since the 1920s, the word on the beach here has been: "Menton's dowdy. Monte's brass. Nice is rowdy. Cannes is class!" Along the fabled promenade, La Croisette, the white sands are littered with sun beds and parasols rented at the beach concessions. The beach is actually divided into 32 sections, our favorites being **Plages Gazagnaire, Le Zénith,** and **Waikiki.** Some of the beaches are privately run, but the best public beach is in front of the Palais des Festivals. See "Cannes" in chapter 5.
- **Monte-Carlo Beach** (at the Monaco border, Eastern Riviera): This beach, once frequented by Princess Grace, is actually on French soil. Of all the Riviera's beaches, this is the most fashionable, even though its sands are imported. The property adjoins the ultrachic **Monte-Carlo Beach Hotel,** 22 av. Princesse-Grace (✆ **92-16-25-25**). The great months to be here are July and August, when you never know who's likely to be sharing the sands with you—perhaps Luciano Pavarotti or Claudia Schiffer. The main topic on the beach? Both legal and funny money. See "Monaco" in chapter 6.

5 The Best Offbeat Experiences

- **Spending a Night in Aigues-Mortes** (Languedoc-Roussillon): St. Louis sailed from this port to fight in the Crusades to the east. He died in Tunis in 1270, but his successor, Philip III, held this port, the only stretch of the Mediterranean in French hands at the time. Great walls were built around the town, and ships all the way from Antioch used to anchor here. But beginning around the mid-14th century, Aigues-Mortes began to live up to its name of "dead waters," as the harbor filled with silt and the waters receded. Today it sits marooned in time and space right in the muck of the advancing Rhône delta. Nothing along the coast is as evocative of the Middle Ages as this town, where you can walk along its walls and slumber in one of its inns. See "Aigues-Mortes" in chapter 3.

- **Checking In and Stripping Down** (Cap d'Agde, Languedoc-Roussillon): Except in foul weather, it's compulsory to walk around nude in the holiday town on the outskirts of Cap d'Agde. You'll have to check your apparel at the gate. Along the Languedoc coast, between the Rhône delta and Béziers, Cap d'Agde was constructed like a pastiche of a local fishing village, similar to Port Grimaud near St-Tropez. At its outskirts is a town with supermarkets, nightclubs, a casino, and rooms for 20,000 bodies—nude bodies. See "Liberté, Egalité, Fraternité . . . Nudité" in chapter 3.
- **Exploring Massif des Calanques** (between Marseille and Cassis, Provence): At the old fishing port of Cassis, with its white cliffs and beaches that were a favorite of Fauve painters, you can rent a boat and explore the Calanques, small fjords along the rugged coast. Covered with gorse and heather, the white cliffs form a backdrop for this adventure. By car from Cassis, you can drive to the creek of Port Miou, with its rock quarries. To reach the Port Pin and En Vau creeks farther west, you must travel on foot (trails are well signposted). You can, however, take one of the boat excursions that leave regularly from Cassis. If you go on your own (not on the boat), you can take a picnic and spend the day skinny-dipping in these cool crystal waters. See "Exploring the Massif des Calanques" in chapter 4.

6 The Best Small Towns

- **Cordes-sur-Ciel** (Languedoc-Roussillon): Perched like an eagle's nest on a hilltop, Cordes is an arts-and-crafts town, its ancient houses on narrow streets filled with artisans plying their trades. Once fabled in France for the brilliance of its silks, today it's a sleepy town 25km (15½ miles) northwest of Albi, the city of Toulouse-Lautrec. Ideally, you should visit Cordes as a side trip from Albi, but you might become enchanted with the place and decide to stop over in this town of a hundred Gothic arches. See "Cordes-sur-Ciel" in chapter 3.
- **Uzès** (Provence): Uzès is a gem, a bit of a time capsule with lofty towers and narrow streets. Racine once lived here and was inspired by the town to write his only comedy, *Les Plaideurs.* André Gide also found a home in this "dream of the Middle Ages." Once Louis XIII called Uzès "the premier duchy of France." You can see why by staying at the stately 18th-century **Château d'Arpaillargues.** See "Uzès" in chapter 4.
- **Gordes** (Provence): One of the best known of Provence's hill villages, Gordes, east of Avignon, is deservedly called *le plus beau village de France.* Today an escape for in-the-know Parisians, it's a town of silk painters, weavers, and potters. The setting is bucolic, between the Coulon valley and the Vaucluse plateau. Houses built of golden stone rise to the Renaissance château crowning the top. The late artist Victor Vasarély lived here in a fortified château that has been turned into a museum displaying much of his work. See "Gordes" in chapter 4.
- **Roussillon** (Provence): Northeast of Gordes, Roussillon stands on a hilltop in the heart of "ocher country," where the earth is a bright red (*roussillon* means "russet"). This ancient village boasts

houses in every shade of burnt orange, dusty pink, and russet red—they take on a particular brilliance at sunset. Roussillon, however, is no longer the sleepy village described in Laurence Wylie's *A Village in the Vaucluse.* Artists, writers, and trendy Parisians have discovered its charms, and today many use it as their second home. See "Roussillon & Bonnieux" in chapter 4.

- **Roquebrune** (Eastern Riviera): This medieval hill village southwest of Menton is the finest along the Côte d'Azur. It has been extensively restored, and not even the souvenir shops can spoil its charm. Steep stairways and alleys lead up to its feudal castle crowning the village. But before heading here, take in rue Moncollet, flanked by houses from the Middle Ages. This castle, dating from the 10th century, is the oldest in France—in fact, it's the only Carolingian castle left standing. See "Roquebrune & Cap-Martin" in chapter 6.

7 The Best Châteaux & Palaces

- **Château d'If** (off Marseille, Provence): One of France's most notorious fortresses, this was the famous state prison whose mysterious guest was the Man in the Iron Mask. Alexandre Dumas *père*'s *Count of Monte Cristo* made the legend famous around the world. It doesn't really matter that the story was apocryphal: People flock here because they believe it, just as they go to Verona to see where Romeo and Juliet lived and loved and died. The château was built by François I in 1524 as part of the defenses of Marseille. To reach it, you take a boat in the harbor to the islet 3.2km (2 miles) offshore. See "Marseille" in chapter 4.
- **Palais des Papes** (Avignon, Provence): This was the seat of Avignon's brief golden age as the capital of Christendom. From 1352 to 1377, seven popes—all French—ruled here, a period called "the Babylonian Captivity." And they lived with pomp and circumstance, knowing "fleshly weaknesses." The Italian poet Petrarch denounced the palace as "the shame of mankind, a sink of vice." Even after Gregory XI was persuaded to return to Rome, some cardinals remained, electing their own pope or "anti-pope," who was finally expelled by force in 1403. See p. 128.
- **Château de la Napoule** (La Napoule, Western Riviera): The Riviera's most eccentric château is also the most fascinating. This great medieval castle was purchased in 1917 by American sculptor Henry Clews, heir to a banking fortune. He lived, worked, and was buried here in 1937. In this castle, Clews created his own grotesque menagerie—scorpions, pelicans, gnomes, monkeys, lizards, whatever came to his tortured mind. His view of feminism? A distorted suffragette depicted in his *Cat Woman.* He likened himself to Don Quixote. See p. 229.
- **Les Grands Appartements du Palais** (Monte Carlo, Monaco, Eastern Riviera): The world has known greater palaces, but this Italianate one on "The Rock" houses the man who presides over the tiny but incredibly rich principality of Monaco, Europe's second-smallest state. As head of the House of Grimaldi, Prince Rainier III sits on the throne, wondering whether his heir apparent, Prince Albert, will ever get married and

produce an heir. (Without a male heir, Monaco will revert back to France.) When the prince is here, a flag flies and you can watch the changing of the guard. The throne room is decorated with paintings by Holbein, Brueghel, and others, and in one wing of the palace is a museum devoted to souvenirs of Napoléon. See p. 325.

- **Villa Kérylos** (Beaulieu, Eastern Riviera): This villa is a faithful reconstruction of an ancient Greek palace, built between 1902 and 1908 by the archaeologist Théodore Reinach. Reinach, a bit of an eccentric, lived here for 20 years, preferring to take baths and eat and dress with his male friends (who pretended to be Athenian citizens), while segregating the women to separate suites. Designated a historic monument of France, with its white, yellow, and lavender Italian marble and its ivory and bronze copies of vases and mosaics, Kérylos is a visual knockout. The parties that went on here are legendary. See "Beaulieu" in chapter 6.

8 The Best Museums

- **Musée Toulouse-Lautrec** (Albi, Languedoc-Roussillon): This museum displays the world's greatest collection from this crippled genius, who immortalized cancan dancers, cafe demimonde, and prostitutes. In the brooding 13th-century Palais de la Berbie in the artist's hometown, the "red city" of Albi, this museum takes you into the special but tortured world of Toulouse-Lautrec. Particularly memorable are the posters that marked the beginning of an entirely new art form. When he died, his family donated the works remaining in his studio. See p. 79.
- **Musée Picasso** (Antibes, Western Riviera): After the bleak war years in Paris, Picasso returned to the Mediterranean in 1945. He didn't have a studio, so the curator of this museum offered him space. Picasso labored here for several months—it was one of his most creative periods. At the end of his stay, he astonished the curator by leaving his entire output on permanent loan to the museum, along with some 200 ceramics he produced at Vallauris. This museum reveals Picasso in an exuberant mood, as evoked by his fauns and goats in cubist style, his still lifes of sea urchins, and his masterful *Ulysses et ses Sirènes.* A much-reproduced photograph displayed here shows him holding a sunshade for his lover, Françoise Gilot. See p. 265.
- **Musée National Fernand-Léger** (Biot, Eastern Riviera): Ridiculed as a Tubist, Léger survived many of his most outspoken critics and went on to win great fame. This museum was built by Léger's widow, Nadia, after his death in 1955, and it became one of the first in France dedicated to a single artist. It owns some 300 of Léger's highly original works. You wander into a dazzling array of robotlike figures, girders, machines, cogs, and cubes. The museum allows you to witness how he changed over the years, dabbling first in Impressionism, as shown by his 1905 *Portrait de l'oncle.* Our favorite here—and one of our favorite artworks along the Riviera—is Léger's *Mona Lisa,* contemplating a set of keys with a wide-mouthed fish dangling at an angle over her head. See p. 270.
- **Fondation Maeght** (St-Paul-de-Vence, Eastern Riviera): One of

Europe's greatest modern art museums, this foundation is remarkable for both its setting and its art. Built in 1964, the avant-garde building boasts a touch of fantasy, topped by two inverted domes. The colorful canvases radiate with the joy of life. All your favorites are likely to be here: Bonnard, Braque, Soulages, Chagall, Kandinsky, and more. Stunningly designed is a terraced garden that's a setting for Calder murals, Hepworth sculptures, and the fanciful fountains and colorful mosaics of Miró. A courtyard is peopled with Giacometti figures that look like gigantic emaciated chessmen. See p. 275.

- **Musée des Beaux-Arts** (Nice, Eastern Riviera): In the former home of the Ukrainian Princess Kotchubey, the collection comes as an unexpected delight, with not only many Belle Epoque paintings but also modern works, including an impressive number by Sisley, Braque, Degas, and Monet, plus Picasso ceramics. There's whimsy, too, especially the sugar-sweet canvases by Jules Chéret, who died in Nice in 1932. Well represented also are the Van Loo family, a clan of Dutch descent whose members worked in Nice. The gallery of sculptors honors Rude, Rodin, and J. B. Carpeaux. See p. 290.
- **Musée Ile-de-France** (St-Jean-Cap-Ferrat, Eastern Riviera): Baronne Ephrussi de Rothschild left a treasure trove of art and artifacts to the Institut de France on her death in 1934. The Villa Ephrussi, the 1912 palace that contains these pieces, reveals what a woman with unlimited wealth and highly eclectic tastes can collect. It's all here: paintings by Carpaccio and other masters of the Venetian Renaissance; canvases by Sisley, Renoir, and Monet; Ming vases; Dresden porcelain; and more. An eccentric, she named her house after the ocean liner *Ile de France* and insisted that her 35 gardeners dress as sailors. See p. 311.

9 The Best Cathedrals & Churches

- **Basilique St-Sernin** (Toulouse, Languedoc-Roussillon): Consecrated in 1096, this is the largest and finest Romanesque church extant. It was built to honor the memory of a Gaulish martyr, St. Sernin, and was for a long time a major stop on the pilgrimage route to Santiago de Compostela in Spain. The octagonal bell tower is particularly evocative, with five levels of twin brick arches. Unusual for a Romanesque church, St-Sernin has five naves. The crypt, where the saint is buried, is a treasure trove of ecclesiastical artifacts, some from the days of Charlemagne. See p. 64.
- **Cathédrale St-Jean** (Perpignan, Languedoc-Roussillon): In 1324, Sancho of Aragón began this cathedral, but the consecration didn't come until its completion in 1509. Despite the different builders and architects over the decades, it emerged as one of Languedoc's most evocative cathedrals. The bell tower contains a great bell that dates from the 1400s. The single nave is typical of church construction in the Middle Ages and is enhanced by the altarpieces of the north chapels and the high altar, the work of the 1400s and the 1500s. See p. 90.
- **Cathédrale St-Just** (Narbonne, Languedoc-Roussillon): Though construction on this cathedral, begun in 1272, was never completed, it's an enduring landmark.

Construction had to be halted 82 years later to prevent breaching the city's ancient ramparts to make room for the nave. In High Gothic style, the vaulting in the choir soars to 130 feet. Battlements and loopholes crown the towering arches of the apse. The cathedral's greatest treasure is the evocative *Tapestry of the Creation,* woven in silk and gold thread. See p. 99.

- **Cathédrale Notre-Dame des Doms** (Avignon, Provence): Next to the Palais des Papes, this was a luminous Romanesque structure before baroque artists took over. It was partially reconstructed from the 14th through the 17th century. In 1859, it was topped by a tall gilded statue of the Virgin, which earned it harsh criticism from many architectural critics. The cathedral houses the tombs of two popes, John XXII and Benedict XII. You'd think this cathedral would be more impressive because of its role in papal history, but it appears that far more time and money went into the construction of the papal palace. Nevertheless, the cathedral reigned during the heyday of Avignon. See p. 130.
- **Basilique St-Victor** (Marseille, Provence): This is one of France's most ancient churches, first built in the 5th century by St. Cassianus to honor St. Victor, a 3rd-century martyr. The saint's church was destroyed by the Saracens, except for the crypt. In the 11th and 12th centuries, a fortified Gothic church was erected. In the crypt are both pagan and early Christian sarcophagi; those depicting the convening of the Apostles and the Companions of St. Maurice are justly renowned. See p. 182.

10 The Best Vineyards

Southern France is home to thousands of vineyards, many of which are somewhat anonymous agrarian bureaucracies known as *cooperatives.* Employees at these cooperatives tend to be less enthusiastic about showing off their product than those who work at true vineyards, where the person pouring your *dégustation des vins* might be the son or daughter of one of the owners. At least in southern France, don't assume that just because the word *château* appears in the name that there'll be a magnificent historic residence associated with the property. In some cases, the crenellated battlement you're looking for might be nothing more than a feudal ruin.

We selected the vineyards below because of the emotional involvement of their (private) owners, their degree of prestige, and, in many cases, their architectural interest. We've provided you with all of the information you need to visit the vineyards below, but see "A Taste of Provence" in the appendix for more information about the wines produced in these areas.

- **Château de Simone,** 13590 Meyreuil (✆ **04-42-66-92-58**): This well-respected vintner lies less than .5km (⅓ mile) north of Aix-en-Provence. The vineyards surround a small 18th-century palace that might have been transported unchanged from *La Belle du bois dormant.* You can't visit the interior, but you can buy bottles of the recent crops of reds, rosés, and whites for between 20.50€ and 23€ each. Because production at this vineyard is relatively small, you're limited to purchases of between 3 and 12 bottles, depending on the vintage. Advance notification is important. From Aix, take N7 toward Nice and then follow the signs to Trois Sautets.

- **Château Virant,** R.D. 10, 13680 Lançon-de-Provence (✆ **04-90-42-44-47;** www.chateauvirant.com): Set 23km (14 miles) west of Aix-en-Provence and 35km (22 miles) north of Marseille, and named after a nearby rock whose ruined feudal fortress is barely standing, this vineyard produces Appellation d'Origine Contrôlée–designated Coteaux d'Aix-en-Provence, as well as a translucent brand of olive oil from fruit grown on the property. The English-speaking Cheylan family showcases a labyrinth of cellars dating from 1630 and 1890. Tours and tastings can be arranged. The most expensive bottle here costs 7.50€. Ask for an explanation of their trademark *vin cuit* (cooked wine) *de Virant,* which is popular around these parts as a beverage at Christmastime. Notification in advance of your visit is wise.
- **Château de Calissanne,** R.D. 10, 13680 Lançon-de-Provence (✆ **04-90-42-63-03**): On the premises is a substantial 18th-century white-stone manor house sporting very old terra-cotta tiles and a sense of the *ancien régime.* Even older is the Gallo-Roman *oppidum Constantine,* a sprawling ruined fortress that you can visit if you obtain a special pass from the sales staff. Set amid the vineyards, it evokes old Provence. The white, rosé, and red Coteaux d'Aix-en-Provence and the two grades of olive oil produced by the property are sold in an outbuilding. Wine sells for less than 13€ per bottle. Advance reservations are vital. You'll find this place clearly signposted in Lançon-de-Provence, nearly adjacent to the above-mentioned Château Virant.
- **Château d'Aqueria,** Route de Roquemaure, 30126 Tavel (✆ **04-66-50-04-56**): Wines produced near the Provençal town of Tavel are considered some of the finest rosés in the world, and this vineyard is an expert at the fermentation of a brand that's sought after by wine lovers from as far away as Paris. There's an 18th-century château on the premises (it can be viewed only from the outside), and cellars and wine shops sell bottles of the famous pink wine at prices that rarely exceed 8.50€ a bottle. To reach it, drive 6km (4 miles) northwest of Avignon along the Route de Bagnols, following the signs to Tavel.
- **Château de Fonscolombe** (✆ **04-42-61-89-62**) and **Château de LaCoste** (✆ **04-42-61-89-88**), 13610 Le Puy Ste-Réparade: These vineyards are adjacent to each other, 20km (12½ miles) north of Aix-en-Provence. Fonscolombe has an exterior-only view of an 18th-century manor house and its garden, and offers tours of a modern facility that's of interest to wine-industry professionals. LaCoste is smaller and less state-of-the-art, but it offers an exterior view of a stone-sided villa that was built for a cardinal during the reign of the popes in Avignon. At either of these outfits, you can buy their red, white, and rosé wines, the most expensive of which sells for only 10€. Advance notification is required. From Aix, take the A51 in the direction of Sisteron, exiting at exit 12 toward Le Puy Ste-Réparade.
- **Domaine de Fontavin,** 1468 route de la Plaine, 84350 Courthézon (✆ **04-90-70-72-14;** www.fontavin.com): Set 10km (6 miles) north of Carpentras, this is one of the leading producers of the heady, sweet dessert wine known as Muscat des Baumes de Venise. Because the organization here dates only from 1989, there's

nothing particularly noteworthy in terms of architecture on-site. But oenophiles who come to this place appreciate its proximity to some of the most legendary grapevines in the French-speaking world. Bottles of the sweet elixir are sold at a price that rarely exceeds 12.80€ each. Follow the N7 from Carpentras in the direction of Orange and Courthézon.

- **Château de Coussin,** R.N. 7, 13530 Trets (✆ **04-42-61-20-00;** www.sumeire.com): This property, 16km (10 miles) east of Aix-en-Provence, is centered on a 16th-century manor whose stone facade bears geometric reliefs associated with Renaissance-era construction in Provence. The vineyards are scattered over three neighboring regions and have been owned by the same family for nearly a century. The château's interior (it contains a vaulted cloister) can be visited only with the hard-to-obtain permission of the owners, but the overview of the winemaking industry as seen within its bottling facility is worth the trip. Bottles sell for a maximum of 31.20€ each, and in some cases for much less.

  On a property that's almost immediately adjacent, an amiable competitor also offers wine tours to those who phone in advance: **Château de Grand'Boise,** 13530 Trets (✆ **04-42-29-22-95;** www.grandboise.com), whose venerable 19th-century château is the centerpiece of vineyards, olive groves, forests, and hunting preserves. The château itself, as well as the organization's cellars, can be visited if you phone in advance for an appointment. Bottles of red, white, and rosé sell for less than 10€ each.

- **Château de Capitoul,** Route de Gruissan, 1100 Narbonne (✆ **04-68-49-23-30;** www.chateau-capitoul.com): Set further to the west than most of the other vineyards mentioned within this survey, Château de Capitoul produces reds ("La Clape des Rocailles"), whites, and rosés that usually sell for 5.40€ to 7.50€ a bottle but, in some rare instances, go as high as 35€. Nestled amid its vineyards is an 19th-century manor house that can be visited if special permission is granted in advance from the owners. More easily accessible are the cellars, which lie within a nearby annex. Call in advance of your arrival. From Narbonne, drive 5km (3 miles) east, following the D32 (Route de Gruissan).

11 The Best Luxury Hotels

- **InterContinental Carlton Cannes** (Western Riviera; ✆ **04-93-06-40-06**): A World War II Allied commander issued orders to bombers to avoid hitting the Carlton "because it's such a good hotel." The 1912 hotel survived the attack and today is at its most frenzied during the annual film festival. Taste and subtlety aren't what the Carlton is about—it's all glitter, glitterati, and glamour, the most splendid of the area's architectural "wedding cakes." The white-turreted doyenne presides over La Croisette like some permanent sand castle. See p. 241.
- **Hôtel du Cap–Eden Roc** (Cap d'Antibes, Western Riviera; ✆ **04-93-61-39-01**): Looming large in F. Scott Fitzgerald's *Tender Is the Night,* this is the most stylish of the Côte's luxury palaces, standing at the tip of the Cap d'Antibes peninsula in its own manicured garden. The hotel reflects the opulence of a

bygone era and has catered to the rich and famous since it opened in 1870. See p. 265.

- **Hôtel Négresco** (Nice, Eastern Riviera; ✆ **04-93-16-64-00**): An aging Lillie Langtry sitting alone in the lobby, her once-great beauty camouflaged by a black veil, is but one of the many memories of this nostalgic favorite. Self-made millionaires and wannabes rub shoulders at this 1906 landmark. We could write a book about the Négresco, but here we'll give only two interesting facts: The carpet in the lobby is the largest ever made by the Savonnerie factory (the cost was about one tenth the cost of the hotel), and the main chandelier was commissioned from Baccarat by Tsar Nicholas II. See p. 294.
- **Grand Hôtel du Cap-Ferrat** (St-Jean-Cap-Ferrat, Eastern Riviera; ✆ **04-93-76-50-52**): The Grand Hôtel, built in 1908, competes with the Hôtel du Cap–Eden Roc as the Riviera's most opulent. Set in a well-manicured garden, it was once a winter haven for royalty. This pocket of posh has it all, including a private beach club with a heated seawater pool and a Michelin-starred restaurant utilizing market-fresh ingredients. See p. 312.
- **Hostellerie du Château de la Chèvre d'Or** (Eze, Eastern Riviera; ✆ **04-92-10-66-66**): In striking contrast to the palaces above, this gem of an inn lies in a medieval village 396m (1,300 ft.) above sea level. Following in the footsteps of former guests like Roger Moore and Elizabeth Taylor, you can stay in this artistically converted medieval château. All its elegant rooms open onto vistas of the Mediterranean. Everything here has a refreshingly rustic appeal rather than false glitter. As the paparazzi catch you sipping a champagne cocktail by the pool, you'll know you've achieved Côte d'Azur chic. See p. 319.
- **Hôtel de Paris** (Monte Carlo, Monaco, Eastern Riviera; ✆ **92-16-26-26**): The 19th-century aristocracy flocked here, and though the hotel isn't quite that fashionable anymore, it's still going strong. Onassis, Sinatra, and Churchill long ago checked out, but today's movers and shakers still pull up in limousines with tons of luggage. This luxury palace boasts two Michelin-starred restaurants, the more celebrated of which is Le Louis XV, offering the sublime specialties of Alain Ducasse. Le Grill boasts Ligurian-Niçois cooking, a retractable roof, and a wraparound view of the sea. See p. 330.

12 The Best Hotel Bargains

- **La Réserve** (Albi, Languedoc-Roussillon; ✆ **05-63-60-80-80**): La Réserve's design approximates a *mas provençal,* the kind of severely dignified farmhouse usually surrounded by scrublands, vineyards, olive groves, and cypresses. It's less expensive than many of the luxurious hideaways along the nearby Côte d'Azur and has the added benefit of lying just outside the center of one of our favorite fortified sites in Europe, the medieval town of Albi. See p. 80.
- **Hôtel Renaissance** (Castres, Languedoc-Roussillon; ✆ **05-63-59-30-42**): In the quaint town of Castres, with its celebrated Musée Goya, this hotel is a good introduction to the bargains awaiting you in provincial France. Built in the 1600s as a courthouse, it was

long ago converted from a dilapidated site into a hotel of discretion and charm—all at an affordable price, even if you opt for a suite. Some rooms have exposed timbers, and you'll sleep in grand but rustic comfort. See p. 83.

- **Hôtel Les Donjon–Les Ramparts** (Carcassonne, Languedoc-Roussillon; © **800/528-1234** in the U.S. and Canada, or 04-68-11-23-80): Built into the solid bulwarks of Carcassonne, one of France's most perfectly preserved medieval towns, is this small-scale hotel whose well-appointed furnishings provide a vivid contrast to the crude stone shell that contains them. A stay here truly allows you personal contact with a site that provoked bloody battles between medieval armies. See p. 86.
- **Hôtel des Croisades** (Aigues-Mortes, Languedoc-Roussillon; © **04-66-53-67-85**): Set within the medieval ramparts of this ancient city, a former private home from the late 19th century has been successfully converted to receive paying guests. Prices are still like those charged 30 years ago. You don't get grand luxury here, but you are assured of comfort and hospitality. See p. 102.
- **Hôtel du Palais** (Montpellier; Languedoc-Roussillon; © **04-67-60-47-38**): In the old town, in a labyrinth of narrow streets, this hotel dates from the late 18th century but has been successfully modernized to receive guests today at prices that are within the range of most travelers' budgets. The rooms are cozily arranged, and the hotel has a special French charm. It's one of the most historic hotels in town, and the bedrooms are relatively large, ideal for a short or even a long visit. See p. 108.
- **Hôtel Danieli** (Avignon, Provence; © **04-90-86-46-82**): Built during the reign of Napoléon, this 29-room gem is classified a historic monument. Small and informal, it has Italian flair but Provençal furnishings. The tile floors, chiseled stone, and baronial stone staircase add style in a town where too many budget hotels are bleak. See p. 135.
- **Hôtel d'Arlatan** (Arles, Provence; © **04-90-93-56-66**): At reasonable rates, you can stay in one of Provence's most charming cities at the former residence of the comtes d'Arlatan de Beaumont, built in the 15th century on the ruins of an old palace. Near the historic place du Forum, this small hotel has been run by the same family since 1920. The rooms are furnished with Provençal antiques, and the antique tapestries are grace notes. The best rooms overlook the garden. See p. 145.
- **Hôtel Clair Logis** (St-Jean-Cap-Ferrat, Eastern Riviera; © **04-93-76-51-81**): The real estate surrounding this converted 19th-century villa is among Europe's most expensive; nonetheless, the hotel manages to keep its prices under levels that really hurt. If you opt for one of the pleasant rooms (each named after a flower that thrives in the garden), you'll be among prestigious predecessors: Even General de Gaulle, who knew the value of a *centime* and *sou,* selected it for his retreats. See p. 313.

13 The Best Luxury Restaurants

- **Le Languedoc** (Carcassonne; Languedoc-Roussillon; © **04-68-25-22-17**): Acclaimed chef Didier Faugeras is the creative force behind this century-old dining room that serves some of the finest regional specialties in the area. Its most famous dish is *cassoulet au* *confit de canard,* a casserole with the duck meat cooked in its own fat. See p. 88.

- **Le Jardin des Sens** (Montpellier, Languedoc-Roussillon; ✆ **04-99-58-38-38**): Twins Laurent and Jacques Pourcel have set off a culinary storm in Montpellier. Michelin has bestowed two stars on them, the same rating it gives to Ducasse at his Monaco citadel. Postnouvelle reigns supreme, and both men know how to turn the bounty of Languedoc into meals sublime in flavor and texture. Though inspired by other chefs, they now feel free to let their imaginations roam. The results are often stunning, like the fricassée of langoustines and lamb sweetbreads. See p. 110.
- **Christian Etienne** (Avignon, Provence; ✆ **04-90-86-16-50**): In a house as old as the nearby papal palace, Etienne reigns as Avignon's culinary star. A chef of imagination and discretion, he has a magical hand, reinterpreting and improving French cuisine. He keeps a short menu so that he can give special care and attention to each dish. His menu is often themed—one might be devoted to the tomato. Save room for his chocolate/pine-nut cake, something of a local legend. See p. 135.
- **L'Oustau de Beaumanière** (Les Baux, Provence; ✆ **04-90-54-33-07**): This Relais & Châteaux occupies an old Provençal farmhouse. Founded in 1945 by the late Raymond Thuilier, the hotel's restaurant was once touted as France's greatest. It might long ago have lost that lofty position, but it continues to tantalize today's palates. Thuilier's heirs carry on admirably as they reinvent and reinterpret some of the great Provençal recipes. At the foot of a cliff, you dine in Renaissance charm, enjoying often flawless meals from the bounty of Provence. See p. 150.
- **Chantecler** (Nice, Eastern Riviera; ✆ **04-93-16-64-00**): The most prestigious restaurant in Nice, and the most intensely cultivated, Chantecler is currently in the hands of Alain Llorca, who's attracting the area's demanding gourmets and gourmands. You dine in a monument to turn-of-the-20th-century extravagance, and the menu is attuned to the seasons and to quality ingredients. A true taste of the country is evident in the fresh asparagus, black truffles, sun-dried tomatoes, and beignets of fresh vegetables—all deftly handled by a chef on the rise. See p. 302.
- **Le Louis XV** (Monte Carlo, Monaco; ✆ **92-16-30-01**): Maybe because he was spending too much time at his other restaurants in New York or Paris, the 2001 Michelin guide lowered chef Alain Ducasse's rating here from three stars to two stars. The good news is that even without Michelin's wholehearted approval, this restaurant is just as good as it's always been, whether Ducasse shows up or not. The kitchen specializes in the ultimate blending of the flavors of Liguria with the tastes and aromas of Provence and Tuscany. Yes, Ducasse dares grace the local macaroni gratin with truffles. See p. 334.

14 The Best Deals on Dining

- **Emile** (Toulouse; Languedoc-Roussillon; ✆ **05-61-21-05-56**): On one of the most beautiful old squares of Toulouse, this restaurant serves one of the finest regional cuisines in the area, all at an affordable price. The cassoulet Toulousain is hailed as the town's best. The flower-filled terrace is a magnet in the summer. See p. 72.

- **Le Bistro Latin** (Aix-en-Provence, Provence; ✆ **04-42-38-22-88**): The economic virtue of this Provençal restaurant lies in its fixed-price menus, whose composition is something of an art form. The prices are low, the flavors are sensational, and hints of Italian zest pop up frequently in such dishes as risotto with scampi. See p. 179.
- **L'Echalotte** (St-Tropez, Western Riviera; ✆ **04-94-54-83-26**): A reasonably priced restaurant in St-Tropez sounds like a contradiction, but this one is the most affordable and charming. Though the dining room is simple, it offers a tiny garden as a grace note. Post-modern never made it here, for the cuisine is solidly bourgeois—the chefs serve recipes presumably taught them by their mothers. Many of southwestern France's classic dishes, like magret of duckling, appear. But the true Côte devotee will opt for fresh fish, especially the delectable sea bass in a salt crust. See p. 216.
- **Le Monaco** (Cannes, Western Riviera; ✆ **04-93-38-37-76**): Restaurant tabs on La Croisette often resemble the annual budget of an Ivory Coast country. But believe it or not, pricey Cannes has working people who have to eat, and they often go to Le Monaco, a blue-collar eatery with great food served bistro style. You eat as the locals do, devouring couscous, roast rabbit with mustard sauce, and even grilled sardines. It's hearty and robust fare and completely affordable. See p. 250.
- **Le Safari** (Nice, Eastern Riviera; ✆ **04-93-80-18-44**): This ever-popular, ever-crowded brasserie overlooking the cours Saleya market soaks up every ray of Riviera sun. Dressed in jeans, waiters hurry back and forth, serving the habitués and visitors alike on the sprawling terrace. This place makes one of the best salade Niçoise concoctions in town, as well as a drop-dead spring lamb roasted in a wood-fired oven. See p. 306.

15 The Best Shopping Bets

- **Caves de l'Hôtel de France** (Auch, Languedoc-Roussillon; ✆ **05-62-61-71-71**): Southwestern France is fabled for its Armagnac brandies produced in the foothills of the Pyrénées since 1422, making them older than cognac. The best selection of this firewater, representing the output of some 100 distilleries, is found in this off-the-beaten-path shop. See "Auch" in chapter 3.
- **Centre Sant-Vicens** (Perpignan, Languedoc-Roussillon; ✆ **04-68-50-02-18**): This region of France is next door to Catalonia, whose capital is Barcelona. Catalan style, as long ago evoked by Antoni Gaudí, is modern and up-to-date here—at affordable prices. Textiles, pottery, and furnishings in forceful geometric patterns are displayed at this showcase. See "Perpignan" in chapter 3.
- **Les Indiens de Nîmes** (Avignon, Provence; ✆ **04-90-86-32-05**): Provence has long been celebrated for its fabrics, and one of the best, most original, and affordable selections is found here. Open since the early 1980s, this outlet went back into the attic to rediscover old Provençal fabrics and to duplicate them in a wide assortment. The fabric is sold by the

meter and can be shaped into everything from clothing to tableware. See "Avignon" in chapter 4.

- **Les Olivades Factory Store** (St-Etienne-du-Grès, Provence; ✆ **04-90-49-19-19**): About 12km (7½ miles) north of Arles on the road leading to Tarascon, this store features the region's most fully stocked showroom of art objects and fabrics inspired by the traditions of Provence. You'll find fabrics, dresses, shirts for men and women, table linen, and fabric by the yard. Part of the Olivades chain, this store has the widest selection and the best prices. See "Arles" in chapter 4.
- **Santons Fouque** (Aix-en-Provence, Provence; ✆ **04-42-26-33-38**): Collectors from all over Europe and North America purchase *santons* (figures of saints) in Provence. You'll find the best ones here, cast in terra cotta, finished by hand, and decorated with an oil-based paint. The figures are from models made in the 1700s. See "Aix-en-Provence" in chapter 4.
- **Verreries de Biot** (Biot, Eastern Riviera; ✆ **04-93-65-03-00**): Biot has long been known for its unique pottery, *verre rustique.* Since the 1940s, artisan glassmakers here have been creating this bubble-flecked glass in brilliant colors like cobalt and emerald. They're collector's items but sold at affordable prices on home turf. The Verreries de Biot is the oldest, most famous, and most frequently visited outlet. A half-dozen others are within a short distance of the town. If you arrive at this shop on any day except Sunday, you can actually see the glassmakers creating this unique product. See "Biot" in chapter 6.

16 The Best of Provence & the Riviera Online

- **www.sncf.fr**: This official website of the SNCF (French Rail) provides timetables and fares, plus sells seats online.
- **www.mappy.fr**: This useful site for motorists gives precise directions to town, toll prices, and the amount of time required to drive to towns and cities in France.
- **www.avignon-et-provence.com**: This site explores the papal city of the south, from museums to restaurants to outdoor fun, plus offers suggestions for the region itself.
- **www.nice-coteazur.org**: It could be more helpful, but this site does provide hotel data and a calendar of events.
- **www.cannes-on-line.com**: If you selected Cannes instead of Nice (see above), this is your site, with hotel data, a map of the resort, and a calendar of events.

2

Planning Your Trip to the South of France

In the pages that follow, we've compiled everything you need to know about the practical details of planning your trip: what documents you'll need, how to use French currency, how to find the best airfare, when to go, and more.

1 The Regions in Brief

LANGUEDOC-ROUSSILLON Languedoc might be a less popular destination than Provence, but it's compelling all the same and is also less frenetic and more affordable. Much of its landscape, cuisine, and lifestyle is similar to that of its neighbor, Provence. **Roussillon** is the rock-strewn arid French answer to ancient Catalonia, just across the Spanish border, linked more to Barcelona than to Paris. The **Camargue** is the name given to the steaming marshy delta formed by two arms of the Rhône River. Rich in bird life, it's famous for its flat expanses of tough grasses and for such fortified medieval sites as **Aigues-Mortes.** Also appealing are **Toulouse,** the bustling pink capital of Languedoc; and the "red city" of **Albi,** birthplace of Toulouse-Lautrec. **Carcassonne,** a marvelously preserved walled city with fortifications begun around A.D. 500, is the region's highlight.

PROVENCE This legendary region flanks the Alps and the Italian border along its eastern end and incorporates a host of sites that have long been frequented by the rich and reclusive. It's a land of gnarled olive trees, cypresses, umbrella pines, almond groves, lavender fields, and countless vineyards. The western section is more like Italy, its Mediterranean neighbor, than like France. Premier destinations are **Aix-en-Provence,** associated with Cézanne; **Arles,** "the soul of Provence," captured so brilliantly by van Gogh; **Avignon,** once the capital of Christendom during the 14th century; and **Marseille,** a port city established by the ancient Phoenicians (in some ways more North African than French). Special Provence gems are the small villages, like **Les Baux, Gordes,** and **St-Rémy-de-Provence,** birthplace of Nostradamus.

THE COTE D'AZUR (FRENCH RIVIERA) The strip of glittering coastal towns along Provence's southern edge is known as the Azure Coast. Long a playground of the rich and famous, the Riviera has become hideously overbuilt and spoiled by tourism. Even so, the names of its resorts still ring with excitement and evoke glamour: **Cannes, St-Tropez, Cap d'Antibes, St-Jean-Cap-Ferrat.** July and August are the most crowded times, but spring and fall can be a delight. **Nice** is the most affordable base for exploring the area. The principality of **Monaco,** the fabled piece of the Côte d'Azur, occupies less than a square mile. Don't expect sandy beaches—most are rocky. Topless bathing is common, especially in

St-Tropez. Glitterati and eccentrics have always been attracted to this narrow strip of real estate, but so have dozens of artists and their patrons, who have left behind a landscape of world-class galleries and art museums.

2 Visitor Information

REGIONAL INFORMATION

Your best source of information before you go is the **French Government Tourist Office;** visit its website at www.franceguide.com. In the United States, you can also call ✆ **410/286-8310** to request information. In Canada, call ✆ **514/288-4264;** in the United Kingdom, call ✆ **020/7399-3500;** in Ireland, call ✆ **01/679-0813;** and in Australia, call ✆ **02/9231-5244.** There's no representative in New Zealand, so you can call the Australian office.

INFORMATION ON MONACO

Information on travel to Monaco is available from the **Monaco Government Tourist and Convention Office** at www.visitmonaco.com. Most of its facilities (along with its consulate) are in New York at 565 Fifth Ave., 23rd Floor (✆ **800/753-9696** or 212/286-3330). In London, the office is at 3/18 Chelsea Garden Market, The Chambers, Chelsea Harbour, SW10 0XF (✆ **020/7352-9962**).

MORE INFORMATION ONLINE

Other helpful websites include Beyond the French Riviera (**www.provencebeyond.com**), Guide Web Provence (**www.provence.guideweb.com**), Relais & Châteaux (**www.relaischateaux.com**), FranceScape (**www.france.com/francescape**), and WebMuseum (**www.ibiblio.org/wm**).

3 Entry Requirements & Customs

ENTRY REQUIREMENTS

All foreign (non-French) nationals need a valid passport to enter France. Consult the following websites for more information: For U.S. citizens, **http://travel.state.gov**; Canadian citizens, **www.dfait-maeci.gc.ca/passport**; British citizens, **www.ukpa.gov.uk**; Irish citizens, **www.irlgov.ie/iveagh**; Australian citizens, **www.passports.gov.au**; and New Zealand citizens, **www.passports.govt.nz**.

The French government no longer requires visas for **U.S. citizens,** as long as they're staying in France for less than 90 days. For longer stays, U.S. visitors must apply for a long-term visa, residence card, or temporary-stay visa.

Tips **Museum Passes**

Carte Musée Côte d'Azur gives you entry to more than 60 museums and other attractions along the Riviera. A 1-day pass costs 8€, a 3-day pass costs 15€, and a 7-day pass costs 25€. For details, call ✆ **04-97-03-82-20** or visit www.cmca.net.

Nice, Marseille, Nîmes, and Toulouse are part of a cultural program offered by 13 French cities. The **Culture/Ville** 3-day pass costs 21€. It features a guided or audio tour in each city, including an entrance to one museum or one monument. Ask at the cities' tourist offices, or contact **the French Government Tourist Office** in the United States at ✆ **410/286-8310** (50¢ per minute) for the *Cities in France* brochure.

The South of France

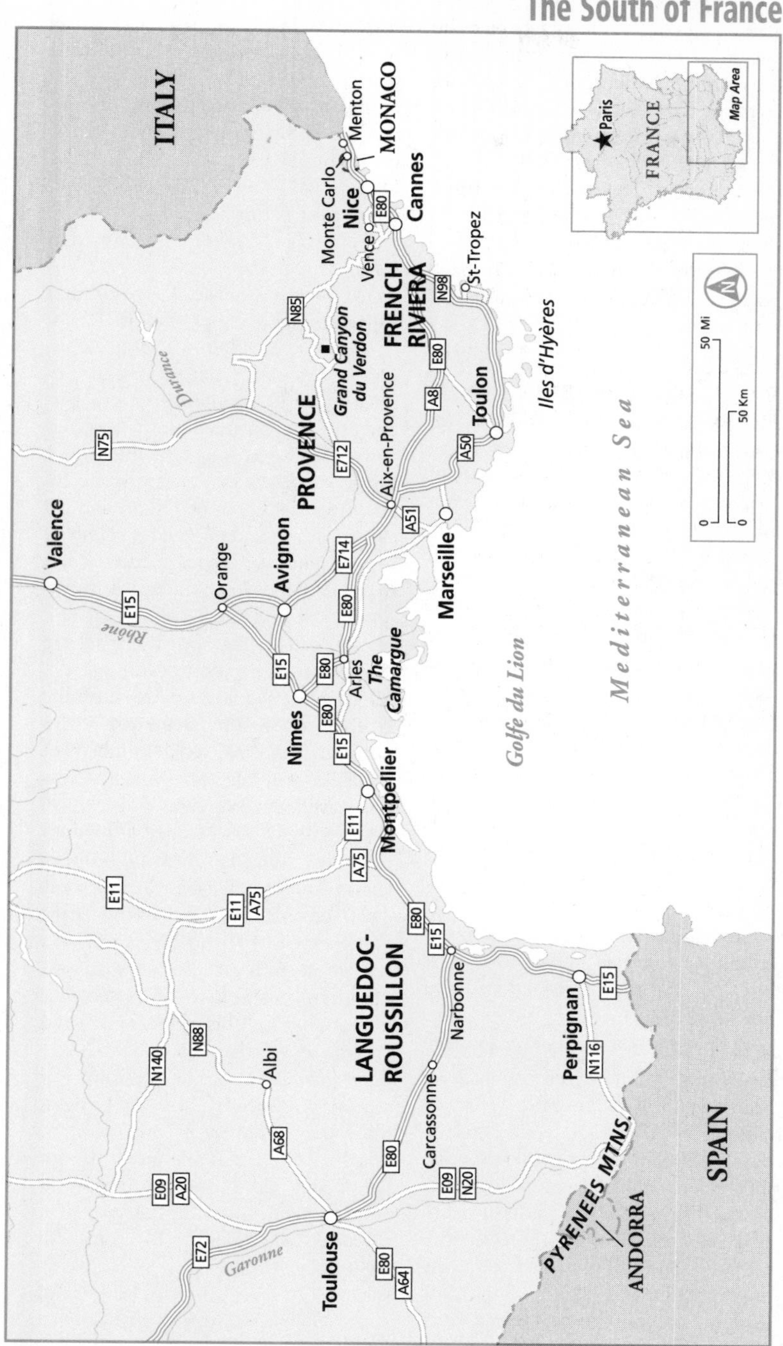

Each requires proof of income or a viable means of support in France and a legitimate purpose for remaining in the country. Applications are available from the Consulat-Général de France; check **www.france-consulat.org** for the location of the nearest office.

Document requirements for travel to Monaco are exactly the same as those for travel to France, and there are virtually no border patrols or passport formalities at the Monégasque frontier.

CUSTOMS

WHAT YOU CAN BRING INTO FRANCE Customs restrictions for visitors entering France differ for citizens of the European Union and for citizens of non-EU countries. **Non-EU nationals** can bring in duty-free 200 cigarettes, 100 cigarillos, 50 cigars, or 250 grams of smoking tobacco. You can also bring in 2 liters of wine, 1 liter of alcohol over 22 proof, and 2 liters of wine 22 proof or under; 50 grams of perfume; a quarter liter of eau de toilette; 500 grams of coffee; and 200 grams of tea. Visitors 15 and over can bring in other goods totaling 75€; for those 14 and under, the limit is 90€. (Customs officials tend to be lenient about general merchandise, realizing that the limits are unrealistically low.) **Citizens of EU countries** can bring in any amount of goods as long as these goods are intended for their personal use and not for resale.

WHAT YOU CAN BRING HOME Returning U.S. citizens who have been away for 48 hours or more are allowed to bring back, once every 30 days, $800 worth of merchandise duty-free. You'll be charged a flat rate of 4% duty on the next $1,000 worth of purchases. Be sure to have your receipts handy. On mailed gifts, the duty-free limit is $200. With some exceptions, you cannot bring fresh fruits and vegetables into the United States. For specifics on what you can bring back, download the invaluable free pamphlet *Know Before You Go* online at **www.customs.gov**, or contact the **U.S. Customs Service,** 1300 Pennsylvania Ave. NW, Washington, DC 20229 (✆ **877/287-8867**), and request the pamphlet.

For a clear summary of **Canadian** rules, write for the booklet *I Declare,* issued by the **Canada Customs and Revenue Agency** (✆ **800/461-9999** in Canada, or 204/983-3500; www.ccra-adrc.gc.ca). Canada allows its citizens a C$750 exemption once a year and only after an absence of 7 days, and you're allowed to bring back duty-free 1 carton of cigarettes, 1 can of tobacco, 40 imperial ounces of liquor, and 50 cigars. In addition, you're allowed to mail gifts to Canada valued at less than C$60 a day, provided that they're unsolicited and don't contain alcohol or tobacco (write on the package "Unsolicited gift, under $60 value"). All valuables should be declared on the Y-38 form before departure from Canada, including serial numbers of valuables you already own, such as expensive foreign cameras.

Citizens of the United Kingdom who are returning from a European Union country will go through a separate Customs Exit (called the "Blue Exit") especially for EU travelers. In essence, there is no limit on what you can bring back as long as the items are for personal use (this includes gifts) and you have already paid the necessary duty and tax. However, Customs law sets out guidance levels. If you bring in more than these levels, you might be asked to prove that the goods are for your own use. Guidance levels on goods bought in the EU for your own use are 3,200 cigarettes, 200 cigars, 400 cigarillos, 3 kilograms of smoking tobacco, 10 liters of spirits, 90 liters of wine, 20 liters of fortified wine (such as port or sherry), and 110 liters of beer. For more information, contact HM Customs & Excise at ✆ **0845/010-9000** (from outside the United Kingdom, 020/8929-0152), or consult the website www.hmce.gov.uk.

The duty-free allowance in **Australia** is A$400 or, for those under 18, A$200. Citizens can bring in 250 cigarettes or 250 grams of loose tobacco, and 1,125 milliliters of alcohol. If you're returning with valuables you already own, such as foreign-made cameras, you should file form B263. A helpful brochure available from Australian consulates or Customs offices is *Know Before You Go.* For more information, call the **Australian Customs Service** at ✆ **1300/363-263,** or log on to www.customs.gov.au.

The duty-free allowance for **New Zealand** is NZ$700. Citizens over 17 can bring in 200 cigarettes, 50 cigars, or 250 grams of tobacco (or a mixture of all three if their combined weight doesn't exceed 250g), plus 4.5 liters of wine and beer or 1.125 liters of liquor. New Zealand currency does not carry import or export restrictions. Fill out a certificate of export listing the valuables you are taking out of the country; that way, you can bring them back without paying duty. Request the free pamphlet *New Zealand Customs Guide for Travellers, Notice no. 4* from **New Zealand Customs,** The Customhouse, 17–21 Whitmore St., Box 2218, Wellington (✆ **04/473-6099** or 0800/428-786; www.customs.govt.nz).

4 Money

France, and especially the Riviera, is one of the world's most expensive destinations. But, to compensate, it often offers top-value food and lodging. Part of the problem is the value-added tax (VAT—called TVA in France), which tacks between 6% and 33% onto everything.

It's expensive to rent and drive a car in France (gasoline is costly, too), and flying within France costs more than flying within the United States. Train travel is relatively inexpensive, however, especially if you purchase a rail pass.

Prices in Provence and on the Riviera are higher than in the provinces. Three of the most touristed areas—Brittany, Normandy, and the Loire Valley—have reasonably priced hotels and many restaurants offering superb food at moderate prices.

It's a good idea to exchange some money—enough to cover airport incidentals and transportation to your hotel—before you leave so you can avoid the less favorable rates at airport currency exchange desks. Check with your local American Express or Thomas Cook office or your bank. American Express cardholders can order foreign currency by phone at ✆ **800/223-7373.**

It's best to exchange currency or traveler's checks at a bank, not a currency exchange desk, hotel, or shop.

CURRENCY

The **euro,** the new European currency, became the official currency of France and 11 other participating countries on January 1, 1999. The old currency, the French franc, disappeared into history on March 1, 2002, replaced by the euro, whose official abbreviation is EUR. Exchange rates of participating countries are locked into a common currency fluctuating against the dollar.

ATMS

ATMs are linked to a national network that most likely includes your bank at home. **Cirrus** (✆ **800/424-7787;** www.mastercard.com) and **Plus** (✆ **800/843-7587;** www.visa.com) are the two most popular networks; check the back of your ATM card to

Regarding the Euro

Since the euro's inception, the U.S. dollar and the euro have traded almost on par ($1 approximately equals 1€); therefore, all prices in this book are given in euros. However, at press time, 1€ was worth approximately $1.15 and was gaining in strength, so your dollars might not go as far as you'd expect. For up-to-date exact ratios between the euro and the dollar, check the currency converter website **www.xe.com/ucc**.

see which network your bank belongs to, and then call or check online for ATM locations at your destination.

Important note: Make sure that you have 4-digit PINs for your bankcards and credit cards (six digits won't work). Be sure to find out your daily withdrawal limit before you depart. Also keep in mind that many banks impose a fee every time a card is used at a different bank's ATM, and that fee can be quite high for international transactions (up to $5 or more).

TRAVELER'S CHECKS

Traveler's checks, though they have become less important since the advent of the ATM, still offer security to many travelers. If they are lost or stolen and you have a record of their serial numbers, they are easily replaced.

American Express offers traveler's checks in denominations of $10, $20, $50, $100, $500, and $1,000. You'll pay a service charge ranging from 1% to 4%. You can also get American Express traveler's checks over the phone by calling ✆ **800/721-9768.** By using this number, Amex gold and platinum cardholders are exempt from the fee.

Visa offers traveler's checks at Citibank locations nationwide, as well as at several other banks. The service charge ranges between 1.5% and 2%; checks come in denominations of $20, $50, $100, $500, and $1,000. Call ✆ **800/732-1322** for information. AAA members can obtain Visa checks without a fee at most AAA offices or by calling ✆ **866/339-3378. MasterCard** also offers traveler's checks. Call ✆ **800/223-9920** for a location near you.

CREDIT CARDS

Credit cards are a safe way to carry money and also provide a convenient record of all your expenses. You can also withdraw cash advances from your credit cards at any bank (though you'll start paying hefty interest on the advance the moment you receive the cash). At most banks, you don't even need to go to a teller; you can get a cash advance at the ATM if you know your PIN. (If you've forgotten your PIN or didn't even know you had one, call the phone number on the back of your credit card and ask the bank to send it to you. It usually takes 5 to 7 business days.) Keep in mind that credit card companies try to protect themselves from theft by limiting the funds someone can withdraw outside their home country, so notify your credit card company before you leave home.

If your wallet has been lost or stolen, notify your credit card companies immediately and file a report at the nearest police precinct. Your credit card company or insurer might require a police report number or record of the loss. Most credit card companies have an emergency toll-free number to call if your card is lost or stolen; they might be able to wire you a cash advance immediately or deliver an emergency credit card in a day or two. Visa's toll-free emergency number in France is ✆ **0800-90-1179.** American Express cardholders should call the company's U.S. hotline collect at ✆ **336/393-1111.** MasterCard holders should call ✆ **0800-90-1387.**

Tips How to Get Your VAT Refund

French sales tax, or **VAT (value-added tax),** is now a hefty 19.6%, but you can get most of that back if you spend 184€ or more at any participating retailer. The name of the refund is *détaxe,* meaning exactly what it says. You never really get the full 19.6% back, but you can come close.

After you spend the required minimum amount, ask for your détaxe papers; fill out the forms before you arrive at the airport and allow at least half an hour for standing in line. All refunds are processed at the final point of departure from the EU, so if you're going to another EU country, apply for the refund there.

Mark the paperwork to request that your refund be applied to your credit card so you aren't stuck with a check in francs that you can't cash. Even if you made the purchase in cash, you can get the refund put on a credit card. This ensures the best rate of exchange. While some airports will give you the refund in cash, you'll lose money unless you take the cash in French francs.

If you're considering a major purchase, especially one that falls between 184€ and 304€, ask the store policy before you get too involved—or be willing to waive your right to the refund.

5 When to Go

In terms of weather, the most idyllic months for visiting the south of France are May and June. Though the sun is intense, it's not uncomfortable. Coastal waters have warmed up by then, so swimming is possible, and all the resorts have come alive after a winter slumber but aren't yet overrun. The flowers and herbs in the countryside are at their peak, and driving conditions are ideal. In June, it remains light until around 10:30pm.

The most overcrowded times—also the hottest, in more ways than one—are July and August, when seemingly half of Paris shows up in the briefest of bikinis. Reservations are difficult to make, discos are blasting, and space is tight on the popular beaches. The worst traffic jams on the coast occur all the way from St-Tropez to Menton.

Aside from May and June, our favorite time is September and even early October, when the sun is still hot, at least during the day, and the great hordes have headed back north. This is also a good time for seeing the art museums along the Côte d'Azur and the cultural attractions in Avignon and other Provençal cities.

In November, the weather is often pleasant, especially at midday, though some of the restaurants and inns you'll want to visit might take a sudden vacation. It's the month that many chefs and hoteliers elect to go on their own vacations after a summer of hard work.

Winter hasn't been the fashionable season since the 1930s. In the early days of tourism, when Queen Victoria came to visit, all the fashionable people showed up in winter, deserting the Côte by April. Today it's just the reverse. However, winter on the Riviera is being rediscovered, and many visitors (particularly retired people or those with leisure time) elect to visit then. If you don't mind the absence of sunbathing and beach life, this could be a good time to show up. However, some resorts, like St-Tropez, become ghost towns when the cold weather comes, though Cannes, Nice, Monaco, and Menton remain active year-round.

WEATHER

The Mediterranean coast has the driest climate in France. Most rain falls in spring and autumn. Summers are comfortably dry—beneficial to humans but deadly to much of the vegetation, which (unless it's irrigated) often dries and burns up in the parched months.

Provence dreads *le mistral* (a cold, violent wind from the French and Swiss Alps that roars south down the Rhône Valley). It most often blows in winter, sometimes for a few days, but sometimes for up to 2 weeks.

Average Temperature & Rainfall in Provence & the Riviera

	Jan	Feb	Mar	Apr	May	June	July	Aug	Sept	Oct	Nov	Dec
Marseille												
Temp. (°F)	44	46	50	55	62	70	75	74	69	60	51	46
Temp. (°C)	6.7	7.8	10	13	17	21	24	23	21	16	11	7.8
Rainfall	1.9	1.6	1.8	1.8	1.8	1.0	0.6	1.0	2.5	3.7	3.0	2.3
Nice												
Temp. (°F)	48	49	52	55	62	68	74	74	70	62	54	50
Temp. (°C)	8.9	9.4	11	13	17	20	23	23	21	17	12	10
Rainfall	3.0	2.9	2.9	2.5	1.9	1.5	0.7	1.2	2.6	4.4	4.6	3.5

HOLIDAYS (JOURS FERIES)

In France, holidays are known as *jours feriés.* Shops and many businesses (banks and some museums and restaurants) close on holidays, but hotels and emergency services remain open.

The main holidays—a mix of secular and religious—include New Year's Day (Jan 1), Easter Sunday and Monday (early Apr), Labor Day (May 1), V-E Day in Europe (May 8), Whit Monday (mid-May), Ascension Thursday (40 days after Easter), Bastille Day (July 14), Assumption of the Blessed Virgin (Aug 15), All Saints' Day (Nov 1), Armistice Day (Nov 11), and Christmas (Dec 25).

PROVENCE CALENDAR OF EVENTS

January

Monte Carlo Motor Rally. The world's most venerable car race. For more information, call © **377-92-16-61-66.** Usually mid-January.

February

Fête de la Chandeleur (Candlemas), Basilique St-Victor, Marseille. A celebration in honor of the arrival in Marseille of the three Marys. A procession brings the Black Virgin up from the crypt of the abbey. For more information, call © **04-91-13-89-00.** Early February.

Carnival of Nice. Float processions, parades, confetti battles, boat races, street music and food, masked balls, and fireworks are part of this ancient celebration. The climax follows a 113-year-old tradition in which King Carnival is burned in effigy, an event preceded by Les Batailles des Fleurs (Battles of the Flowers), during which members of opposing teams pelt one another with flowers. Come with proof of a hotel reservation. For information or reservations, contact the **Nice Convention and Visitors Bureau,** at © **08-92-07-40-70,** or visit www.nicetourism.com. Mid-February to early March.

April

Féria Pascale (Easter Bullfighting Festival), Arles. This is a major bullfighting event that includes not only appearances by the greatest matadors, but also *abrivados* and *bodegas* (wine stalls). For more information, call ✆ **04-90-18-41-20.** Easter.

Procession des Pénitents (Procession of the Penitants). These marches are conducted in both **Arles** (✆ **04-68-39-11-99**) and **Collioure** (✆ **04-68-82-15-47**). Good Friday.

Procession du Christ Mort (Procession of the Dead Christ), on the French Riviera, is one of the most fascinating religious processions in **Roquebrune-Cap Martin** (✆ **04-93-35-62-87**). Good Friday.

May

La Fête des Gardians (Camargue Cowboys' Festival), Arles. This event features a procession of Camargue cowboys through the streets of town. Activities feature various games involving bulls, including Courses Camarguaises, in which competitors have to snatch a rosette from between the horns of a bull. For information, call ✆ **04-90-18-41-20.** May.

Cannes Film Festival. Movie madness transforms this city into the kingdom of the media-related deal, with daily melodramas acted out in cafes, on sidewalks, and in hotel lobbies. It's great for voyeurs. Reserve early and make a deposit. Getting a table on the Carlton terrace is even more difficult than procuring a room. Admission to some of the prestigious films is by invitation only. There are box-office tickets for the less important films, which play 24 hours. For information, contact the **Direction du Festival International du Film,** 99 bd. Malesherbes, 75008 Paris (✆ **01-53-59-61-00**). Two weeks before the festival, the event's administration moves en masse to the Palais des Festivals, esplanade Georges-Pompidou, 064 00 Cannes (✆ **04-93-39-01-01;** www.festival-cannes.fr). Mid-May.

Festival des Musiques d'Aujourd'hui, Marseille. This festival presents the works of very young French and European composers in music and dance. For more information, call **Experimental Music Groups of Marseille** at ✆ **04-96-20-60-10.** Mid-May.

Monaco Grand Prix. Hundreds of cars race through the narrow streets and winding corniche roads in a surreal blend of high-tech machinery and medieval architecture. For more information, call ✆ **01-42-96-12-23.** Mid-May.

Fête de la Transhumance (Move to Summer Grazing), St-Rémy. This event celebrates the now-abandoned custom of shepherds presenting their flocks to the public before moving them to higher ground for summer. In this mock event, the flocks move off as if really going up to the mountains. For more information, call ✆ **04-90-92-05-22.** Mid- to late May.

Le Pélerinage des Gitans (Gypsies' Pilgrimage), Stes-Maries-de-la-Mer. This festival is in memory of the two Marys for whom the town is named (Mary, the mother of James the lesser, and Mary Salome, the mother of James the greater and John). A model boat containing statues of the saints and a statue of St. Sarah, patron saint of Gypsies, is taken to the seashore and blessed by the bishop. For more information, call ✆ **04-90-97-82-55.** Last week of May.

June

Festival de la St-Eloi, Maussane-les-Alpilles. For this festival, wagons are decorated and raced in the Carreto Ramado, followed by Mass, a procession in traditional dress, and a benediction. Special events are held and local produce and handcrafts are sold. For more information, call ✆ **04-90-54-52-04.** Mid-June.

Festival Aix en Musique, Aix-en-Provence. Concerts of classical music and choral singing are held in historic buildings, such as the Cloisters of the Cathédrale St-Sauveur and the Hôtel Maynier d'Oppède. For more information, call ✆ **04-42-16-11-61.** Throughout June and July.

Festival d'Expression Provençale, Abbaye St-Michel de Frigolet, Tarascon. At this festival, homage is paid to the region's language with works by Provençal writers that are acted in French and Provençal. For more information, call ✆ **04-90-95-50-77.** Late June to early July.

Fête de la Tarasque, Tarascon. The town relives St. Martha's victory over the dragon known as the Tarasque, which was believed to live in the Rhône in the lst century. There's a procession of horsemen, an archery competition, historical events, a medieval tournament, a Tarasque procession, Novilladas (young bull-fighters), and an orchestral concert with fireworks. For more information, call ✆ **04-90-91-03-52,** or fax 04-90-91-22-96. Late June.

Feu de la St-Jean (St. John's Fire), Fontvieille. This event features folk troupes and Camargue cowboys who gather in front of the Château de Montauban. For more information, call ✆ **04-90-54-67-49.** June 25.

Reconstitution Historique, Salon-de-Provence. This pageant held in honor of Nostradamus includes a cast of 700 in historical costume and is followed by a son-et-lumière at the Château d'Empéri. For more information, call ✆ **04-90-56-27-60.** Late June to early July.

Festival de Marseille Méditerranée. This festival features concerts and recitals of music and song from the entire Mediterranean region. Theater and dance are also presented, along with special exhibitions in the city's main museums. For more information, call ✆ **04-91-13-89-00** or fax 04-91-13-89-20. Late June to late July.

July

St-Guilhem Music Season, St-Guilhem le Désert, Languedoc. This festival of baroque organ and choral music is held in a medieval monastery. For information, call ✆ **04-67-63-14-99.** Month of July.

La Fête des Pècheurs (Fishermen's Festival), Cassis. The local "Prud'-hommes" (members of the elected industrial tribunal) walk in procession wearing traditional dress, and a Mass is held in honor of St. Peter, followed by a benediction. For more information, call ✆ **04-42-01-71-17.** Early July.

Bastille Day. Celebrating the birth of modern-day France, the festivities in the south reach their peak in Nice with street fairs, pageants, fireworks, and feasts. The day begins with a parade down promenade des Anglais and ends with fireworks in the Vieille Ville. No matter where you are, by the end of the day you'll hear Piaf warbling "La Foule" (The Crowd), the song that celebrated her passion for the stranger she met and later lost in a crowd on Bastille Day. Similar celebrations also take place in Cannes, Arles, Aix, Marseille, and Avignon. July 14.

Nuit Taurine (Nocturnal Bull Festival), St-Rémy-de-Provence. At this festival, the focus is on the age-old allure of bulls and their primeval appeal to roaring crowds. *Abrivados* involve bulls in the town square as "chaperoned" by trained herders on horseback; *encierros* highlight a Pamplona-style stampeding of bulls through the streets. Music from local guitarists and flaming torches add drama. For more information, call ✆ **04-90-92-05-22.** Mid-July.

Nice Jazz Festival. This is the biggest, flashiest, and most prestigious jazz festival in Europe, with world-class entertainers. Concerts begin in early afternoon and go on until late at night (sometimes all night in the clubs) on the Arènes de Cimiez, a hill above the city. Reserve hotel rooms way in advance. For information, contact the Grand Parade du Jazz, c/o the tourist office of Nice (✆ **04-93-92-82-82**). Mid-July.

Festival d'Aix-en-Provence. This musical event par excellence features everything from Gregorian chant to melodies composed on computerized synthesizers. The audience sits on the sloping lawns of the 14th-century papal palace for operas and concertos. Local recitals are performed in the medieval cloister of the Cathédrale St-Sauveur. Make advance hotel reservations and take a written confirmation with you when you arrive. Expect heat, crowds, and traffic. For more information, contact the **Festival International d'Art Lyrique et de Musique,** Palais de l'Ancien Archévèche, 13100 Aix-en-Provence (✆ **04-42-17-34-34**). Throughout July.

Les Chorégies d'Orange, Orange. One of southern France's most important lyric festivals presents oratorios and choral works by master performers whose voices are amplified by the ancient acoustics of France's best-preserved Roman amphitheater. For more information, call ✆ **04-90-34-24-24.** Mid-July to early August.

Festival d'Avignon. One of France's most prestigious theater events, this world-class festival has a reputation for exposing new talent to critical acclaim. The focus is usually on avant-garde works in theater, dance, and music by groups from around the world. Make hotel reservations early. For information, call ✆ **04-90-27-66-50** or fax 04-90-27-66-83. Last 3 weeks of July.

Fête de la St-Eloi (Feast of St. Eloi), Gémenos. Some hundred draft horses draw a procession of traditional flower-decked wagons. Folk troupes also perform. For more information, call ✆ **04-42-32-18-44.** Late July.

August

Fêtes Daudet (Daudet Festival), Fontvieille. At this festival, Mass said in Provençal is held in the Avenue of Pine Trees. There's folk dancing outside Daudet's mill and a torchlight procession through the streets of town to the mill. For more information, call ✆ **04-90-54-67-49.** Mid-August.

Féria de St-Rémy, St-Rémy-de-Provence. This event features a 4-day celebration of bulls with *abrivado* and *encierro* (see the Nuit Taurine entry, above), branding, and Portuguese bull fighting (matadors on horseback). For more information, call ✆ **04-90-92-05-22.** Mid-August.

September

Féria des Prémices du Riz (Rice Harvest Festival), Arles. Bullfights are held in the amphitheater with

---

Tips **Tickets to the Avignon Festival**

Keith Prowse (also known as Global Tickets; ✆ **800/223-6108**) can order tickets to many of the musical or theatrical events at the Avignon festival, as well as other cultural events throughout France.

---

leading matadors, and a procession of floats makes its way along boulevard des Lices; there are also traditional events with cowboys and women in regional costume. For more information, call ✆ **04-91-13-89-00.** Early September.

Fête des Olives, Mouriès. A Mass is held in honor of the green olive. There's a procession of groups in traditional costume, an olive tasting, and sales of regional produce. For more information, call ✆ **04-90-47-56-58.** Mid-September.

Journée de l'Olivier en Provence, Salon-de-Provence. Another celebration of the olive, this event is attended by producers of olive oil, Marseille soap, olive-wood articles, booksellers, and pottery and earthenware makers. Special events are held in the history center. For more information, call ✆ **04-90-56-27-60.** Late September.

October

Perpignan Jazz Festival. Musicians from everywhere jam in what many visitors consider Languedoc's most appealing season. For more information, call ✆ **04-68-35-37-46.** Early October.

November

Marché aux Santons, Tarascon. For 4 days in late November craftspersons from throughout Provence congregate in this medieval village to sell their *santons* (carved representations of saints). For more information, call ✆ **04-90-91-22-96** or fax 04-90-91-03-52. This event is supplemented, sometimes with the same sellers, who move to the **Foire aux Santons** in Marseille, held between late November and Christmas. For more information, call ✆ **04-91-13-89-00** or fax 04-91-13-89-20.

December

Fête des Bergers (Shepherds Festival), Istres. This festival features a procession of herds on their way to winter pastures. There are cowboys, a Carreto Ramado, a blessing of the horses, an all-night Provençal party with shepherds and Provençal storytellers, and folk troupes. For more information, call ✆ **04-42-55-51-15.** First weekend in December.

Foire de Noël, Mougins. Hundreds of merchants, selling all manner of Christmas ornaments and gifts, descend on Mougins in Provence, to herald in the Christmas spirit. For more information, call ✆ **04-93-75-87-67.** Mid- to late December.

Midnight Mass, Fontvieille. A traditional midnight Mass, including the *pastrage* ceremony, the presentation of a newborn lamb. There's a procession of folk troupes, Camargue cowboys, and women in traditional costume from Daudet's mill to the church, followed by the presentation of the lamb. For more information, call ✆ **04-90-54-67-49.** December 24.

Noël Provençal, Eglise St-Vincent, Les Baux. The procession of shepherds is followed by a traditional midnight Mass, including the *pastrage* ceremony, traditional songs, and performance of a nativity play. For more information, call ✆ **04-90-54-34-39.** December 24.

Fête de St-Sylvestre (New Year's Eve), nationwide. Along the Riviera, it's most boisterously celebrated in Nice's Vieille Ville around place Garibaldi. At midnight, the city explodes. Strangers kiss strangers, and place Masséna and promenade des Anglais become virtual pedestrian malls. December 31.

6 Travel Insurance

Check your existing policies before you buy travel insurance for trip cancellation, lost luggage, medical expenses, or car rental insurance. You might have partial or complete coverage. But if you need more, ask your travel agent about a package. The cost of insurance varies, depending on the cost and length of your trip, your age and health, and the type of trip you're taking. Insurance for sports or adventure travel costs more than coverage for a European cruise. Some insurers provide packages for specialty vacations like skiing or backpacking. More dangerous activities might be excluded from basic policies.

TRIP-CANCELLATION INSURANCE Trip-cancellation insurance helps you get your money back if you have to back out of a trip, if you have to go home early, or if your travel supplier goes bankrupt. Allowed reasons for cancellation can range from sickness to natural disasters to the State Department declaring your destination unsafe for travel. (Insurers usually won't cover vague fears, though, as many travelers discovered when they tried to cancel their trips in October 2001 because they were wary of flying.) In this unstable world, trip-cancellation insurance is a good buy if you're getting tickets well in advance. Insurance policy details vary, so read the fine print—and especially make sure that your airline or cruise line is on the list of carriers covered in case of bankruptcy. For information, contact one of the following insurers: **Access America** (✆ 866/807-3982; www.accessamerica.com); **Travel Guard International** (✆ 800/826-4919; www.travelguard.com); **Travel Insured International** (✆ 800/243-3174; www.travelinsured.com); and **Travelex Insurance Services** (✆ 888/457-4602; www.travelex-insurance.com).

MEDICAL INSURANCE Most health insurance policies cover you if you get sick away from home—but check, particularly if you're insured by an HMO. With the exception of certain HMOs and Medicare/Medicaid, your medical insurance should cover medical treatment—even hospital care—overseas. However, most out-of-country hospitals make you pay your bills up front and send you a refund after you've returned home and filed the necessary paperwork. And in a worst-case scenario, there's the high cost of emergency evacuation. If you require additional medical insurance, try **MEDEX International** (✆ **800/527-0218** or 410/453-6300; www.medexassist.com) or **Travel Assistance International** (✆ **800/821-2828;** www.travelassistance.com; for general information on services, call the company's Worldwide Assistance Services, Inc., at ✆ **800/777-8710**).

LOST-LUGGAGE INSURANCE On international flights (including U.S. portions of international trips), baggage is limited to approximately $9.07 per pound, up to approximately $635 per checked bag. If you plan to check items more valuable than the standard liability, see if your valuables are covered by your homeowner's policy, get baggage insurance as part of your comprehensive travel-insurance package, or buy Travel Guard's BagTrak product. Don't buy insurance at the airport; it's usually overpriced. Be sure to take any valuables or irreplaceable items with you in your carry-on luggage because many valuables (including books, money, and electronics) aren't covered by airline policies.

If your luggage is lost, immediately file a lost-luggage claim at the airport detailing the luggage contents. For most airlines, you must report delayed, damaged, or lost baggage within 4 hours of arrival. The airlines are required to deliver luggage, once found, directly to your house or destination free of charge.

7 Health & Safety

THE HEALTHY TRAVELER

In general, France is viewed as a "safe" destination. You don't need to get shots, most food is safe, and the water in France is potable (though if you're concerned, order bottled water). It is easy to get a prescription filled in French towns and cities; Provence and the Riviera have some of the best medical facilities in Europe, and finding an English-speaking doctor is generally no problem in most of the top resorts of the Riviera or major cities in Provence such as Avignon.

If you get sick, consider asking your hotel concierge to recommend a local doctor—even his or her own. You can also try the emergency room at a local hospital; many have walk-in clinics for emergency cases that are not life-threatening. You might not get immediate attention, but you won't pay the high price of an emergency room visit.

BEFORE YOU GO

In most cases, your existing health plan will provide the coverage you need. But double-check; you might want to buy **travel medical insurance** instead. (See the section on insurance, above.) Bring your insurance ID card with you when you travel.

If you suffer from a chronic illness, consult your doctor before your departure. For conditions like epilepsy, diabetes, or heart problems, wear a **Medic Alert Identification Tag** (© **800/825-3785;** www.medicalert.org), which will immediately alert doctors to your condition and give them access to your records through Medic Alert's 24-hour hotline.

Pack **prescription medications** in your carry-on luggage, and carry prescription medications in their original containers, with pharmacy labels—otherwise they won't make it through airport security. Also bring along copies of your prescriptions in case you lose your pills or run out. Carry the generic name of prescription medicines, in case a local pharmacist is unfamiliar with the brand name. Don't forget an extra pair of contact lenses or prescription glasses.

Contact the **International Association for Medical Assistance to Travelers (IAMAT)** (© **716/754-4883,** or 416/652-0137 in Canada; www.iamat.org) for tips on travel and health concerns and lists of local English-speaking doctors. Any foreign consulate can also provide a list of area doctors who speak English. The United States **Centers for Disease Control and Prevention** (© **800/311-3435;** www.cdc.gov) provides up-to-date information on necessary vaccines and health hazards by region or country.

STAYING SAFE

Criminals frequent tourist attractions such as museums, monuments, restaurants, hotels, beaches, trains, train stations, airports, and subways. Purse snatching and pickpocketing occur throughout the south of France. Americans in Provence and Monaco should be particularly alert to pickpockets in train stations and subways. Passports should be carried on the body when necessary, and over-the-shoulder bags should not be used.

Crimes involving vehicles with nonlocal license plates are common. Thefts from cars stopped at red lights are also common, particularly in the Nice-Antibes-Cannes area and in Marseille. Car doors should be kept locked at all times while traveling to prevent incidents of "snatch and grab" thefts. In this type of scenario, the thief is usually a passenger on a motorcycle. Similar incidents have also occurred at tollbooths and rest areas. Special caution is advised when entering and exiting the car because that offers opportunity for purse-snatchings. There have also been a number of thefts at Nice Airport, particularly at car-rental parking lots where bags have been snatched as drivers have been loading luggage into rental cars.

Break-ins of parked cars are also frequent. Locking valuables in the trunk is not a safeguard. Valuables should not be left unattended in a car.

The loss or theft of a passport should be reported immediately to local police and your nearest embassy or consulate, where you can obtain information about passport replacement.

8 Specialized Travel Resources

FOR TRAVELERS WITH DISABILITIES

Facilities for travelers with disabilities are above average in France, and nearly all modern hotels in the south of France now provide rooms designed for persons with disabilities. However, older hotels (unless they've been renovated) might not have such important features as elevators, special toilet facilities, or ramps for wheelchair access.

The new high-speed **TGV trains** are wheelchair accessible; older trains have special compartments for wheelchair boarding. Guide dogs ride free. Be aware that some older stations don't have escalators or elevators.

Association des Paralysés de France, 17 bd. Auguste-Blanqui, 75013 Paris (✆ **01-40-78-69-00;** www.apf.asso.fr), is a privately funded organization that provides wheelchair-bound individuals with documentation, moral support, and travel ideas. In addition to the central Paris office, it maintains an office in each of the 90 *départements* of France and can help you find accessible hotels, transportation, sightseeing, house rentals, and (in some cases) companionship for paralyzed or partially paralyzed travelers. It's not, however, a travel agency.

Many travel agencies offer customized tours and itineraries for travelers with disabilities. **Flying Wheels Travel** (✆ **507/451-5005;** www.flyingwheelstravel.com) offers escorted tours and cruises that emphasize sports and private tours in minivans with lifts. **Accessible Journeys** (✆ **800/846-4537** or 610/521-0339; www.disabilitytravel.com) caters specifically to slow walkers and wheelchair travelers and their families and friends.

Organizations that offer assistance to travelers with disabilities include **MossRehab** www.mossresourcenet.org), which provides a library of accessible-travel resources online; the **Society for Accessible Travel and Hospitality** (✆ **212/447-7284;** www.sath.org; annual membership fees $45 adults, $30 seniors and students), which offers a wealth of travel resources for all types of disabilities and informed recommendations on destinations, access guides, travel agents, tour operators, vehicle rentals, and companion services; and the **American Foundation for the Blind** (✆ **800/232-5463;** www.afb.org), which provides information on traveling with Seeing Eye dogs.

In the United Kingdom, **RADAR** (Royal Association for Disability and Rehabilitation), Unit 12, City Forum, 250 City Rd., London ECIV 8AF (✆ **020/7250-3222;** www.radar.org.uk), publishes holiday "fact packs," which sell for £2 each or £5 for a set of all three. The first one provides general information, including planning and booking a holiday, insurance, finances, and useful organization and holiday providers. The second outlines transport and equipment, transportation available when going abroad, and equipment for rent. The third deals with specialized accommodations.

Another good resource is the **Holiday Care Service,** 2nd floor, Imperial Building, Victoria Road, Horley, Surrey

RH6 7PZ, UK (✆ **01293/774-535;** fax 01293/784-647; www.holidaycare.org.uk), a national charity that advises on accessible accommodations for the elderly and persons with disabilities. Once a member, you can receive a newsletter and access to a free reservations network for hotels throughout Britain and, to a lesser degree, Europe and the rest of the world.

FOR GAY & LESBIAN TRAVELERS

France is one of the world's most tolerant countries toward gays and lesbians, and no special laws discriminate against them. "The Gay Riviera" boasts a large gay population, with dozens of gay clubs and restaurants.

Gay Provence, 42 rue du Coq, Marseille (✆ **04-91-84-08-96;** www.gay-zprovence.org), is operated by a group of gays and lesbians, each native to Provence, who offer tours to American and European gays and lesbians. Various interests can be either preplanned or customized, and tours range from 1 day to 1 week. Participants are welcomed into the private homes of gay or gay-friendly locals—perhaps a cheese brunch at a goat farm or an evening in a private 18th-century castle. Attractions include such outdoor excursions as hiking, biking, or horseback riding, or cultural activities such as Mediterranean cooking lessons or meetings with artists and artisans.

The International Gay & Lesbian Travel Association (IGLTA) (✆ **800/448-8550** or 954/776-2626; www.iglta.org) is the trade association for the gay and lesbian travel industry, and offers an online directory of gay and lesbian friendly travel businesses.

Many agencies offer tours and travel itineraries specifically for gay and lesbian travelers. **Above and Beyond Tours** (✆ **800/397-2681;** www.abovebeyondtours.com) is the exclusive gay and lesbian tour operator for United Airlines. **Now, Voyager** (✆ **800/255-6951;** www.nowvoyager.com) is a well-known San Francisco–based gay-owned and operated travel service. **Olivia Cruises & Resorts** (✆ **800/631-6277** or 510/655-0364; www.olivia.com) charters entire resorts and ships for exclusive lesbian vacations and offers smaller group experiences for both gay and lesbian travelers.

The following travel guides are available at most travel bookstores and gay and lesbian bookstores, or you can order them from **Giovanni's Room** bookstore in Philadelphia (✆ **215/923-2960;** www.giovannisroom.com): ***Out and About*** (✆ **800/929-2268** or 415-644-8044; www.outandabout.com), which offers guidebooks and a newsletter 10 times a year packed with solid information on the global gay and lesbian scene; ***Spartacus International Gay Guide*** and ***Odysseus,*** both good, annual English-language guidebooks focused on gay men; the ***Damron*** guides, with separate annual books for gay men and lesbians; and, of course, ***Frommer's Gay & Lesbian Europe.***

FOR SENIORS

Many discounts are available for seniors—men and women of the "third age," as the French say. Contact the French Government Tourist Office (see "Visitor Information," earlier in this chapter).

At any rail station in France, seniors 60 and over (with proof of age) can get **A La Carte Senior.** The pass costs 45€ and is good for a 50% discount on unlimited rail travel throughout the year. The *carte* also offers reduced prices on some regional bus lines and half-price admission at state-owned museums. There are some restrictions—for example, you can't use it between 3pm Sunday and noon Monday and from noon Friday to noon Saturday.

Air France offers seniors a 10% reduction on its regular nonexcursion tariffs on travel within France. Some restrictions apply. Discounts of around 10% are offered to passengers 62 and over on selected Air France international flights. Be sure to ask for the discount when booking.

Members of **AARP** (© **800/424-3410** or 202/434-2277; www.aarp.org) get discounts on hotels, airfares, and car rentals. AARP offers members a wide range of benefits, including *AARP The Magazine* and a monthly newsletter. Anyone over 50 can join.

Many reliable agencies and organizations target the 50-plus market. **Elderhostel** (© **877/426-8056;** www.elderhostel.org) arranges study programs for those 55 and over (and a spouse or companion of any age). Most courses last 5 to 7 days in the United States and 2 to 4 weeks abroad, and many include airfare, accommodations in university dormitories or modest inns, meals, and tuition. **ElderTreks** (© **800/741-7956;** www.eldertreks.com) offers small-group tours to off-the-beaten-path or adventure travel locations, restricted to travelers 50 and older.

Recommended publications offering travel resources and discounts for seniors include the quarterly magazine ***Travel 50 & Beyond*** (www.travel50andbeyond.com); ***Travel Unlimited: Uncommon Adventures for the Mature Traveler*** (Avalon); ***101 Tips for Mature Travelers,*** available from Grand Circle Travel (© **800/221-2610** or 617/350-7500; www.gct.com); ***The 50+ Traveler's Guidebook*** (St. Martin's Press); and ***Unbelievably Good Deals and Great Adventures That You Absolutely Can't Get Unless You're Over 50*** (McGraw Hill).

FOR STUDENTS

If you're planning to travel outside the United States, you'd be wise to arm yourself with an **International Student Identity Card (ISIC),** which offers substantial savings on rail passes, plane tickets, and entrance fees. It also provides you with basic health and life insurance and a 24-hour help line. The card is available for $22 from **STA Travel** (© **800/781-4040,** and if you're not in North America, there's probably a local number in your country; www.statravel.com). If you're no longer a student but are still under 26, you can get an **International Youth Travel Card (IYTC)** for the same price from the same people, which entitles you to some discounts. (***Note:*** In 2002, STA Travel bought competitors **Council Travel** and **USIT Campus** after they went bankrupt. It's still operating some offices under the Council name, but it's owned by STA.) **Travel CUTS** (© **800/667-2887** or 416/614-2887; www.travelcuts.com) offers similar services for both Canadians and U.S. residents. Irish students should turn to **USIT** (© **01/602-1600;** www.usitnow.ie).

If you'd like to travel with other like-minded souls, check out the menu of trips offered by **Contiki** (© **800/CONTIKI;** www.contiki.com), the world's largest travel company for 18- to 35-year-olds. Popular tours include "The Best of France" and "Mediterranean Highlights."

You also might pick up a copy of ***Hanging Out in France,*** published by Frommer's (www.frommers.com/hangingout). It covers everything from adrenaline sports to the hottest club and music scenes.

9 Planning Your Trip Online

SURFING FOR AIRFARES

The "big three" online travel agencies, **Expedia.com, Travelocity.com,** and **Orbitz.com,** sell most of the air tickets bought on the Internet. (Canadian travelers should try Expedia.ca and

Travelocity.ca; U.K. residents can go to Expedia.co.uk and Opodo.co.uk.) Each has different business deals with the airlines and might offer different fares on the same flights, so it's wise to shop around. Expedia and Travelocity will also send you **e-mail notification** when a cheap fare becomes available to your favorite destination. Of the smaller travel agency websites, **Side-Step** (www.sidestep.com) has gotten the best reviews from Frommer's authors. It's a browser add-on that purports to "search 140 sites at once," but in reality it beats competitors' fares only as often as other sites do.

Also remember to check **airline websites.** Even with major airlines, you can often shave a few bucks from a fare by booking directly through the airline and avoiding a travel agency's transaction fee. But you'll get these discounts only by **booking online:** Most airlines now offer online-only fares that even their phone agents know nothing about. For the websites of airlines that fly to and from your destination, go to "Getting to the South of France," later in this chapter.

Great **last-minute deals** are available through free weekly e-mail services provided directly by the airlines. Most of these are announced on Tuesday or Wednesday and must be purchased online. Most are valid only for travel that weekend, but some (such as Southwest's) can be booked weeks or months in advance. Sign up for weekly e-mail alerts at airline websites, or check mega-sites that compile comprehensive lists of last-minute specials, such as **Smarter Living** (www.smarterliving.com). For last-minute trips, **site59.com** in the United States and **lastminute.com** in Europe often have better deals than the major-label sites.

If you're willing to give up some control over your flight details, use an **opaque fare service** like **Priceline** (www.priceline.com or www.priceline.co.uk) or **Hotwire** (www.hotwire.com). Both offer rock-bottom prices in exchange for travel on a "mystery airline" at a mysterious time of day, often with a mysterious change of planes en route. The mystery airlines are all major, well-known carriers, and the airlines' routing computers have gotten a lot better than they used to be. But your chances of getting a 6am or 11pm flight are pretty high. Hotwire tells you flight prices before you buy; Priceline usually has better deals than Hotwire, but you have to play its "name our price" game. If you're new at this, the helpful folks at **BiddingForTravel** (www.biddingfortravel.com) do a good job of demystifying Priceline's prices. Priceline and Hotwire are great for flights within North America and between the United States and Europe.

For much more about airfares and savvy air-travel tips and advice, pick up a copy of *Frommer's Fly Safe, Fly Smart* (Wiley Publishing, Inc.).

SURFING FOR HOTELS

Shopping online for hotels is much easier in the United States, Canada, and certain parts of Europe, including Provence, than it is in the rest of the world. Of the "big three" sites, **Expedia** might be the best choice, thanks to its long list of special deals. **Travelocity** runs a close second. Hotel specialist sites **hotels.com** and **hoteldiscounts.com** are also reliable. An excellent free program, **TravelAxe** (www.travelaxe.net), can help you search multiple hotel sites at once, even ones you might never have heard of.

Priceline and Hotwire are even better for hotels than for airfares; with both, you're allowed to pick the neighborhood and quality level of your hotel before offering up your money. Priceline's hotel product even covers Europe and Asia, though it's much better at getting luxury lodging for bargain prices than at finding anything at the bottom of the scale. ***Note:*** Hotwire overrates its hotels by one star.

Frommers.com: The Complete Travel Resource

For an excellent travel-planning resource, we highly recommend Frommers.com (www.frommers.com). We're a little biased, of course, but we guarantee that you'll find the travel tips, reviews, monthly vacation giveaways, and online-booking capabilities thoroughly indispensable. Among the special features are our popular **Message Boards,** where Frommer's readers post queries and share advice (sometimes even our authors show up to answer questions); **Frommers.com Newsletter,** for the latest travel bargains and insider travel secrets; and **Frommer's Destinations Section,** where you'll get expert travel tips, hotel and dining recommendations, and advice on the sights to see for more than 3,000 destinations around the globe. When your research is done, the **Online Reservations System** (www.frommers.com/book_a_trip) takes you to Frommer's preferred online partners for booking your vacation at affordable prices.

SURFING FOR RENTAL CARS

For booking rental cars online, the best deals are usually found at rental-car company websites, although all the major online travel agencies also offer rental-car reservations services. Priceline and Hotwire work well for rental cars, too; the only "mystery" is which major rental company you get, and for most travelers, the difference among Hertz, Avis, and Budget is negligible.

10 The 21st-Century Traveler

INTERNET ACCESS AWAY FROM HOME

Travelers have any number of ways to check their e-mail and access the Internet on the road. Of course, using your own laptop—or even a PDA (personal digital assistant) or electronic organizer with a modem—gives you the most flexibility. But if you don't have a computer, you can still access your e-mail and even your office computer from cybercafes.

WITHOUT YOUR OWN COMPUTER

It's hard nowadays to find a city that *doesn't* have a few cybercafes. Although there's no definitive directory for cybercafes—these are independent businesses, after all—three places to start looking are at **www.cybercaptive.com**, **www.netcafeguide.com**, and **www.cybercafe.com**.

Most major airports now have **Internet kiosks** scattered throughout their gates. These kiosks, which you'll also see in shopping malls, hotel lobbies, and tourist information offices around the world, give you basic Web access for a per-minute fee that's usually higher than cybercafe prices. The kiosks' clunkiness and high price means they should be avoided whenever possible.

To retrieve your e-mail, ask your **Internet service provider (ISP)** if it has a Web-based interface tied to your existing e-mail account. If your ISP doesn't have such an interface, you can use the free **mail2web** service (www.mail2web.com) to view and reply to your home e-mail. For more flexibility, you might want to open a free, Web-based e-mail account with **Yahoo! Mail** (http://mail.yahoo.com) or **Fastmail** (www.fastmail.fm). (Microsoft's Hotmail is another popular option, but Hotmail has severe spam problems.) Your home ISP might be able to forward your e-mail to the Web-based account automatically.

If you need to access files on your office computer, look into a service called **GoToMyPC** (www.gotomypc.com). The service provides a Web-based interface for you to access and manipulate a distant PC from anywhere—even a cybercafe—provided that your "target" PC is on and has an always-on connection to the Internet (such as with Road Runner cable). The service offers top-quality security, but if you're worried about hackers, use your own laptop rather than a cybercafe to access the GoToMyPC system.

WITH YOUR OWN COMPUTER

Major Internet service providers have **local access numbers** around the world, allowing you to go online by simply placing a local call. Check your ISP's website, or call its toll-free number and ask how you can use your current account away from home, as well as how much it will cost.

If you're traveling outside the reach of your ISP, the **iPass** network has dial-up numbers in most countries. You'll have to sign up with an iPass provider, who will then tell you how to set up your computer for your destination. For a list of iPass providers, go to www.ipass.com. One solid provider is **i2roam** (✆ **866/811-6209** or 920/235-0475; www.i2roam.com).

Wherever you go, bring a **connection kit** of the right power and phone adapters (see "Fast Facts: The South of France," below), a spare phone cord, and a spare Ethernet network cable.

Most business-class hotels throughout the world, including those in Provence, offer dataports for laptop modems, and a few thousand hotels in the United States and Europe now offer high-speed Internet access using an Ethernet network cable. You'll have to bring your own cables either way, so **call your hotel in advance** to find out what the options are.

USING A CELLPHONE

The three letters that define much of the world's **wireless capabilities** are GSM (Global System for Mobiles), a big seamless network that makes for easy cross-border cellphone use throughout Europe and dozens of other countries worldwide. In the United States, T-Mobile, AT&T

Online Traveler's Toolbox

Veteran travelers usually carry some essential items to make their trips easier. Following is a selection of online tools to bookmark and use.

- **Foreign Languages for Travelers** (www.travlang.com). Learn basic terms in more than 70 languages and click on any underlined phrase to hear what it sounds like.
- **Intellicast** (www.intellicast.com) and **Weather.com** (www.weather.com). Both sites give weather forecasts for cities around the world.
- **Travel Warnings** (http://travel.state.gov/travel_warnings.html, www.fco.gov.uk/travel, www.voyage.gc.ca, www.dfat.gov.au/consular/advice). These sites report on places where health concerns or unrest might threaten American, British, Canadian, and Australian travelers. Generally, U.S. warnings are the most paranoid; Australian warnings are the most relaxed.

Wireless, and Cingular use this quasi-universal system; in Canada, Microcell and some Rogers customers are GSM; and all Europeans and most Australians use GSM.

If your cellphone is on a GSM system and you have a world-capable phone, such as many (but not all) Sony Ericsson, Motorola, or Samsung models, you can make and receive calls across much of the globe. Just call your wireless operator and ask for "international roaming" to be activated on your account. Unfortunately, per-minute charges can be high—usually $1 to $1.50 in western Europe.

World-phone owners can bring down their per-minute charges with a bit of trickery. Call your cellular operator and say you'll be going abroad for several months and want to "unlock" your phone to use it with a local provider. Usually, they'll oblige. Then, in your destination country, pick up a cheap, prepaid phone chip at a mobile phone store and slip it into your phone. (Show your phone to the salesperson because not all phones work on all networks.) You'll get a local phone number in your destination country—and much, much lower calling rates.

Otherwise, **renting** a phone is a good idea. While you can rent a phone from any number of overseas sites, including kiosks at airports and at car-rental agencies, we suggest renting the phone before you leave home. That way, you can give loved ones your new number, make sure the phone works, and take the phone wherever you go—especially helpful when you rent overseas, where phone-rental agencies bill in local currency and might not let you take the phone to another country.

Phone rental isn't cheap. You'll usually pay $40 to $50 per week, plus airtime fees of at least a dollar a minute. In Europe, though, local rental companies often offer free incoming calls within their home country, which can save you big bucks. The bottom line: Shop around.

Two good wireless rental companies are **InTouch USA** (✆ **800/872-7626;** www.intouchglobal.com) and **Road-Post** (✆ **888-290-1606** or 905/272-5665; www.roadpost.com). Give them your itinerary, and they'll tell you what wireless products you need. InTouch will also advise you on whether your existing phone will work overseas for free; simply call ✆ **703/222-7161** between 9am and 4pm EST, or go to http://intouchglobal.com/travel.htm.

11 Getting to the South of France

FROM NORTH AMERICA

BY PLANE

Most airlines divide their year roughly into seasonal slots, with the lowest fares between November 1 and March 13. Shoulder season, between the high and low seasons, is only slightly more expensive and includes mid-March to mid-June and all of October. These can be ideal times to visit southern France.

THE MAJOR U.S. CARRIERS All major airlines fly to Paris from the U.S. cities listed below. Once you fly into Orly or Charles de Gaulle, you must take **Air France** (✆ **800/237-2747;** www.airfrance.com), to reach your destination in Languedoc, Provence, or the Riviera. From Orly and Charles de Gaulle, there are 20 flights per day to Marseille and to Nice, 16 to Toulouse, and 4 from Monday to Friday and 2 Saturday and Sunday to Avignon.

American Airlines (✆ **800/433-7300;** www.aa.com) offers daily flights to Paris from Dallas–Fort Worth, Chicago, Miami, Boston, and New York. **Delta Airlines** (✆ **800/241-4141;** www.delta.com) flies nonstop to Paris from Atlanta. Delta also operates daily nonstop flights from

Travel in the Age of Bankruptcy

At press time, two major U.S. airlines were flirting with bankruptcy and most of the rest weren't doing very well either. To protect yourself, **buy your tickets with a credit card**, as the Fair Credit Billing Act guarantees that you can get your money back from the credit card company if a travel supplier goes under (and if you request the refund within 60 days of the bankruptcy.) **Travel insurance** can also help, but make sure it covers against "carrier default" for your specific travel provider. And be aware that if a U.S. airline goes bust mid-trip, a 2001 federal law requires other carriers to take you to your destination (albeit on a space-available basis) for a fee of no more than $25, provided you rebook within 60 days of the cancellation.

both Cincinnati and New York. All these flights depart late enough in the day to permit transfers from much of Delta's vast North American network. Note that Delta is the only American airline offering nonstop service from New York to Nice.

Continental Airlines (✆ **800/525-0280;** www.continental.com) provides nonstop flights to Paris from Newark and Houston. Flights from Newark depart daily, while flights from Houston depart four to seven times a week, depending on the season. **US Airways** (✆ **800/428-4322;** www.usairways.com) offers daily nonstop service from Philadelphia to Paris.

THE FRENCH NATIONAL CARRIER **Air France** (✆ **800/237-2747;** www.airfrance.com) was formed from a merger combining three of France's largest airlines. The airline offers a daily nonstop flight between New York and Nice and also offers regular flights between Paris and such North American cities as Newark; Washington, D.C.; Miami; Atlanta; Boston; Cincinnati; Chicago; New York; Houston; San Francisco; Los Angeles; Montreal; Toronto; and Mexico City.

THE MAJOR CANADIAN CARRIER Canadians usually choose the **Air Canada** (✆ **888/247-2262** in the U.S. and Canada; www.aircanada.ca) flights to Paris from Toronto and Montreal that depart every evening. Two of Air Canada's flights from Toronto are shared with Air France and feature Air France aircraft.

Getting Through the Airport

With the federalization of airport security, security procedures at U.S. airports are more stable and consistent than ever. Generally, you'll be fine if you arrive at the airport **2 hours** before an international flight; if you show up late, tell an airline employee and he or she will probably whisk you to the front of the line.

Bring a **current, government-issued photo ID** such as a driver's license or passport, and if you've got an E-ticket, print out the **official confirmation page;** you'll need to show your boarding pass at the security checkpoint and show your ID at the ticket counter and the gate. (Children under 18 do not need photo IDs for domestic flights, but the adults checking in with them do.)

Security lines are often lengthy. If you have trouble standing for long periods of time, tell an airline employee; the airline will provide a wheelchair. Speed up security by **not wearing metal objects** such as big belt buckles or clanky earrings. If you've got metallic body parts, a note from your doctor can prevent a long chat with the security screeners. Keep in mind that only **ticketed passengers** are allowed past security, except for folks escorting passengers with disabilities or children.

Federalization has stabilized **what you can carry on** and **what you can't.** The general rule is that sharp things are out, nail clippers are okay, and food and beverages must be passed through the X-ray machine—but security screeners can't make you drink from your coffee cup. Bring food in your carry-on rather than checking it because explosive-detection machines used on checked luggage have been known to mistake food (especially chocolate, for some reason) for bombs. The Transportation Security Administration (TSA) has issued a list of restricted items; check its website at **www.tsa.gov** for details.

Flying for Less: Tips for Getting the Best Airfare

Passengers sharing the same airplane cabin rarely pay the same fare. Travelers who need to purchase tickets at the last minute, change their itinerary at a moment's notice, or fly one-way often get stuck paying the premium rate. Here are some ways to keep your airfare costs down.

- Passengers who can book their ticket **long in advance,** who can **stay over Saturday night,** or who **fly midweek** or **at less-trafficked hours** will pay a fraction of the full fare. If your schedule is flexible, say so, and ask if you can secure a cheaper fare by changing your flight plans.
- You can also save on airfares by keeping an eye out in local newspapers for **promotional specials** or **fare wars,** when airlines lower prices on their most popular routes. You rarely see fare wars offered for peak travel times, but if you can travel in the off-months, you might snag a bargain.
- Search **the Internet** for cheap fares (see "Planning Your Trip Online," above).
- **Consolidators,** also known as bucket shops, are great sources for international tickets. Start by looking in Sunday newspaper travel sections; U.S. travelers should focus on the *New York Times, Los Angeles Times,* and *Miami Herald.* But beware: Bucket shop tickets are usually nonrefundable or rigged with stiff cancellation penalties, often as high as 50% to 75% of the ticket price, and some put you on charter airlines with questionable safety records.

  One of the best agencies for trips to France is **Nouvelles Frontieres,** whose American subsidiary is **New Frontiers USA** (✆ **800/366-6387;** www.newfrontiers.com). It maintains that it can "beat published prices by 20% to 30%." Because of the company's massive buying power, rates in hotels from budget to first class can be slashed considerably. Value-packed travel packages, low-cost air fares across the Atlantic, and reduced car-rental rates continue to make New Frontiers a major player in the France-bound market.

  Several reliable consolidators are worldwide and available on the Net. **STA Travel** (✆ **800/781-4040;** www.statravel.com) is now the world's leader in student travel, thanks to its purchase of Council Travel. It also offers good fares for travelers of all ages. **Flights.com** (✆ **800/TRAV-800;** www.flights.com) started in Europe and has excellent fares worldwide, but particularly to that continent. It also has "local' websites in 12 countries. **Air Tickets Direct** (✆ **800/778-3447;** www.airticketsdirect.com) is based in Montreal and leverages the currently weak Canadian dollar for low fares; it'll also book trips to places that U.S. travel agents won't touch, such as Cuba.
- Join **frequent-flier clubs.** Accrue enough miles, and you'll be rewarded with free flights and elite

status. It's free, and you'll get the best choice of seats, faster response to phone inquiries, and prompter service if your luggage is stolen, if your flight is canceled or delayed, or if you want to change your seat. You don't need to fly to build frequent-flier miles—frequent-flier credit cards can provide thousands of miles for doing your everyday shopping.

FROM PARIS

BY PLANE

From Paris, if you're heading for the French Riviera, your connecting flight will probably land you in Nice's international airport, Aéroport Nice–Côte d'Azur. There are also airports at Avignon, Marseille, Montpellier, Nîmes, and Toulouse. If you have already been traveling in France before heading for the south, you can opt for Air France's **Euro-Flyer Pass,** a series of identically priced coupons for travel along intra-European air routes. If these coupons are purchased simultaneously with transatlantic passage to France from North America, they'll cost between $120 and $135 each, depending on the season. Call **Air France** at ✆ **800/237-2747** in the United States for information before you go.

BY TRAIN

With some 50 cities in France, including Marseille and Nice, linked by the world's fastest trains, you can reach the south of France by a trip of just a few hours. With 24,000 miles of track and about 3,000 stations, **SNCF** (French National Railroads) is fabled

Flying with Film & Video

Never pack film—developed or undeveloped—in checked bags, as the new, more powerful scanners can fog film. The film you carry with you can be damaged by scanners as well. X-ray damage is cumulative; the faster the film, and the more times you put it through a scanner, the more likely the damage. Film under 800 ASA is usually safe for up to five scans. If you're taking your film through additional scans, U.S. regulations permit you to demand hand inspections. In international airports, you're at the mercy of airport officials. On international flights, store your film in transparent baggies, so you can remove it easily before you go through scanners. Keep in mind that airports are not the only places where your camera may be scanned: Highly trafficked attractions are X-raying visitors' bags with increasing frequency.

Most photo supply stores sell protective pouches designed to block damaging X-rays. The pouches fit both film and loaded cameras. They should protect your film in checked baggage, but they also may raise alarms and result in a hand inspection.

An organization called **Film Safety for Traveling on Planes, FSTOP** (✆ **888/301-2665;** www.f-stop.org), can provide additional tips for traveling with film and equipment.

Carry-on scanners will not damage **videotape** in video cameras, but the magnetic fields emitted by the walk-through security gateways and handheld inspection wands will. Always place your loaded camcorder on the screening conveyor belt or have it hand-inspected. Be sure your batteries are charged, as you will probably be required to turn the device on to ensure that it's what it appears to be.

Tips **Have a Seat**

Remember that a train ticket itself does not guarantee you a seat; it merely gets you transportation from one place to another. On crowded trains and during busy times, you'll have to make a **seat reservation** (and pay for the privilege) if you want to be sure of sitting somewhere other than on top of your luggage. Seat reservations cost 8€ per person.

throughout the world for its on-time performance. You can travel first- or second-class by day as well as in a couchette or sleeper by night. Many trains carry dining facilities, which range from cafeteria-style meals to formal dinners.

The **TGV Méditerranée High-Speed Rail Line** (or TGV Med), which opened in June 2001, brought the south of France closer to Paris. Trip time between Paris and Marseille takes only 3 hours now instead of the usual 5. The high-speed track has been extended to the Provençal city of Avignon, where the track splits to go in one direction to Marseille and in the other direction to Nîmes. The link cost $3.25 billion and took 12 years to complete. Five hundred bridges and 20 viaducts were built between Valence and Marseille for the new tracks, with 1 million trees planted to meet environmental standards. New double-decker carriages on the trains, giving visitors a bird's-eye view of the lavender fields and vineyards of Provence, are being added.

INFORMATION If you plan much travel on European railroads, get the latest copy of the ***Thomas Cook European Timetable of Railroads.*** This comprehensive 500-plus-page book documents all Europe's mainline passenger rail services with detail and accuracy. It's available exclusively in North America from the **Forsyth Travel Library** (✆ **800/367-7984;** www.forsyth.com) at a cost of $28.95, plus $4.95 priority airmail postage to the United States, and US$6.95 for shipments to Canada.

For more information in the United States and to purchase rail passes (see below) before you leave, contact **Rail Europe** at ✆ **800/848-7245** or www.raileurope.com. In Canada, Rail Europe offices are at 2087 Dundas St. East, Suite 105, Mississauga, ON L4X 1M2 (✆ **800/361-7245** or 905/602-4195). In London, SNCF maintains offices at Rail Europe, 179 Piccadilly, London W1V OBA (✆ **0870/584-8848**).

For train information or to make reservations in Paris, call **SNCF** at ✆ **08-36-35-35-39** or check www.sncf.com. You can also go to any local travel agency, of course, and book tickets. A simpler way to book tickets is to take advantage of the *Billetterie* or ticket machines in every train station. If you know your PIN, you can use credit cards such as American Express, MasterCard, and Visa to purchase your ticket.

FRANCE RAIL PASSES Working cooperatively with SNCF, Air Inter Europe, and Avis, Rail Europe offers three flexible rail passes that can reduce travel costs considerably.

The **France Railpass** provides unlimited rail transport in France for any 4 days within 1 month, at $252 in first class and $218 in second. You can purchase up to 6 more days for an extra $32 per person per day. Children 4 to 11 travel for half price.

The **France Rail 'n' Drive Pass,** available only in North America, combines good value on both rail travel and Avis car rentals, and is best used by arriving at a major rail depot and then striking out to explore the countryside by car. It includes the France Railpass (see above) and use of a rental car. A 4-day rail pass (first class) and 2 days' use of the cheapest rental car (with unlimited mileage) is $245 per person (assuming two people traveling together). It's $215 per person for the second-class rail pass and the same car; you can upgrade to a larger car for a supplemental fee. Solo travelers pay from $315 for first class and $279 for second.

EURAILPASSES In-the-know travelers take advantage of one of Europe's greatest travel bargains: the **Eurailpass,** which permits unlimited first-class rail travel in any country in western Europe except the British Isles (good in Ireland). Passes are sold only in North America and are nontransferable. Check **www.eurail.com** for the most up-to-date prices; at press time, a Eurailpass cost $588 for 15 days, $762 for 21 days, $946 for 1 month, $1,338 for 2 months, and $1,606 for 3 months. Children 3 and under travel free, as long as they don't occupy a seat (otherwise they're charged half fare); children 4 to 11 are charged half fare.

If you're under 26, you can purchase a **Eurail Youthpass,** entitling you to unlimited second-class travel for $414 for 15 days, $534 for 21 days, $664 for 1 month, $938 for 2 months, and $1,160 for 3 months. Regardless of the pass, you'll have to pay an extra supplement for the high-speed TGV train anywhere in France.

Reservations are required on some trains (and cost an additional $9 per person). Many trains have *couchettes* (sleeping cars), which also cost extra. Obviously, the 2- or 3-month traveler gets the greatest economic advantages; the Eurailpass is ideal for extensive trips. You can visit all of France's major sights, from Normandy to the Alps, and then end your vacation in Norway, for example. Eurailpass holders are entitled to reductions on certain buses and ferries as well.

Travel agents and railway agents in such cities as New York, Montreal, and Los Angeles sell Eurailpasses. You can also purchase them at the North American offices of CIT Travel Service, the French National Railroads, the German Federal Railroads, and the Swiss Federal Railways. Check www.eurail.com for complete information.

Eurail Flexipass allows you to visit Europe with more flexibility. It's valid in first class and offers the same privileges as the Eurailpass. However, it provides a number of individual travel days that you can use over a longer period of consecutive days. That makes it possible to stay in one city for a while without losing days of rail travel. There are two passes: 10 days of travel in 2 months for $694, and 15 days of travel in 2 months for $914.

With many of the same qualifications and restrictions as the Flexipass is a **Eurail Youth Flexipass.** Sold only to travelers under 26, it allows 10 days of travel within 2 months for $488, and 15 days of travel within 2 months for $642.

FROM ELSEWHERE IN EUROPE

BY PLANE

From London, **Air France** (✆ **0845/084-5111;** www.airfrance.com) and **British Airways** (✆ **0845/773-3377;** www.britishairways.com) fly frequently to Paris, with a trip time of 1 hour. These airlines operate up to 17 flights daily from Heathrow. Many commercial travelers also use flights originating from the London City Airport in the Docklands. A ballpark figure for rates is London to Paris $42 one-way.

Direct flights to Paris also exist from other U.K. cities such as Manchester, Edinburgh, and Southampton. Contact Air France, British Airways, or **British Midland** (✆ **0870/607-0555;** www.flybmi.com). Daily papers often

Under the Channel

Queen Elizabeth and the late French president François Mitterrand opened the Channel Tunnel in 1994, and the ***Eurostar Express*** has daily passenger service from London to Paris and Brussels. The $15 billion tunnel, one of the great engineering feats of our time, is the first link between Britain and the Continent since the Ice Age. The 50km (31-mile) journey takes 35 minutes, with actual time spent in the Chunnel 19 minutes.

Eurostar tickets are available through **Rail Europe** (✆ **800/848-7245;** www.raileurope.com). In London, make reservations for Eurostar (or any other train in Europe) at ✆ **0870/584-8848.** In Paris, call ✆ **08-36-35-35-39.** Chunnel train traffic is competitive with air travel, if you calculate door-to-door travel time. Trains leave from London's Waterloo Station and arrive in Paris at Gare du Nord. London-Paris one-way passenger fare is $199 for second class and $279 for first class.

Fares are complicated and depend on a number of factors. The cheapest one-way fare is Leisure RT, requiring a purchase at least 14 business days before the date of travel and a minimum 2-night stay. A return ticket must be booked to receive this discounted fare. The most expensive passage is a one-way fare of $399 in first class.

The Chunnel accommodates not only trains, but also passenger cars, buses, taxis, and motorcycles, from $147 each way for a small car. **Le Shuttle,** a train carrying vehicles under the Channel (✆ **0870/535-3535** in the U.K.; www.eurotunnel.com), connects Calais, France, with Folkestone, England. It operates 24 hours a day, 365 days a year, running every 15 minutes during peak travel times and at least once an hour at night. Before boarding Le Shuttle, you stop at a toll booth to pay and then pass through Immigration for both countries at one time. During the ride, you travel in air-conditioned carriages, remaining in your car or stepping outside to stretch your legs. An hour later, in France, you simply drive off.

carry ads for cheap flights. The highly recommended **Trailfinders** (✆ **020/7937-5400;** www.trailfinders.com) sells discounted fares.

You can reach Paris from any major European capital. Your best bet is to fly on the national carrier, Air France, with more connections into Paris from European capitals than any other airline. From Dublin, try **Aer Lingus** (✆ **0818/365-000;** www.aerlingus.com), with the most flights to Paris from Ireland. From Amsterdam, the convenient choice is **KLM** (✆ **020-4-747-747;** www.klm.com).

If you don't want to go to Paris before flying to the south of France, you'll find a number of British flights going directly to the Nice–Côte d'Azur Airport, the Marseille-Provence Airport, and the Toulouse Airport. Daily flights are offered by British Airways, Air France, and British Midland.

BY TRAIN

From the United Kingdom, most passengers arrive in Paris before going the rest of the way by train to Provence. Passengers can take the **TGV Med** from the Gare de Lyon. The TGV

Med zips from Paris to Marseille in 3 hours, to Avignon in 2½ hours, and to Nice in 5½ hours. From the United Kingdom, call © **0990/848-848** or check www.raileurope.co.uk.

BY FERRY FROM ENGLAND

Ferries and hydrofoils operate day and night in all seasons, with the exception of last-minute cancellations during storms. Many crossings are timed to coincide with the arrival and departure of trains (especially those between London and Paris). Trains let you off a short walk from the piers. Most ferries carry cars, trucks, and freight, but some hydrofoils take passengers only. The major routes include at least 12 trips a day between Dover or Folkestone and Calais or Boulogne.

Hovercraft and hydrofoils make the trip from Dover to Calais, the shortest distance across the Channel, in just 40 minutes during good weather, while the ferries might take several hours, depending on the weather and tides. If you're bringing a car, it's important to make reservations because space below decks is usually crowded. Timetables can vary depending on weather conditions and many other factors.

The leading operator of ferries across the channel is **P&O Ferries** (© **0870/600-0611;** www.poferries.com). It operates car and passenger ferries between Portsmouth, England, and Cherbourg, France (three departures a day; 4¼ hr. each way during daylight hours, 7 hr. each way at night); between Portsmouth and Le Havre, France (three a day; 5½ hr. each way). Most popular is the route between Dover, England, and Calais, France (25 sailings a day; 75 min. each way), costing £28 one-way; children under 4 go free.

The shortest and most popular route across the Channel is between Calais and Dover. **Hoverspeed** runs at least 12 hovercraft crossings daily; the trip takes 35 minutes. It also runs a SeaCat (a catamaran propelled by jet engines) that takes just under 1 hour between Dover and Calais; the SeaCats depart about four times a day on the 55-minute voyage. For reservations and information, call Hoverspeed (© **800/677-8585** in North America, or 0870/240-8070 in the U.K.; www.hoverspeed.com). Typical one-way fares are £28 per person.

If you plan to transport a rental car between England and France, check with the company about license and insurance requirements and drop-off charges. Many forbid transport of their vehicles over the water between England and France. Transport begins at £95 each way. A better idea is to ask about a car exchange program (Hertz's is called "Le Swap"), in which you drop off a right-drive car and pick up a left-drive vehicle at Calais.

12 Package Deals & Escorted Tours

For package tours that offer adventure and activity, see "Special-Interest Trips," below.

Before you start your search for the lowest airfare, you might want to consider booking your flight as part of a travel package such as an escorted tour or a package tour. What you lose in adventure, you'll gain in time and money saved when you book accommodations, and maybe even food and entertainment, along with your flight.

PACKAGE VACATIONS

Packages are not the same thing as escorted tours. They are simply a way to buy airfare and accommodations at the same time. For popular destinations like the south of France, they are a smart way to go because they save you a lot of money. In many cases, a package that includes airfare, hotel, and transportation to and from the airport will cost you less than just the hotel alone would have, had you booked it yourself. That's because packages are sold in bulk to tour operators—who resell them to the public at a cost that drastically undercuts standard rates.

Packages, however, vary widely. Some offer flights on scheduled airlines, while others book charters. In some packages, your choice of accommodations and travel days might be limited. Some packages let you choose between escorted vacations and independent vacations; others allow you to add on just a few excursions or escorted day trips (also at lower prices than you could locate on your own) without booking an entirely escorted tour. Each destination usually has one or two packagers that are usually cheaper than the rest because they buy in even greater bulk. If you spend the time to shop around, you will save in the long run.

FINDING A PACKAGE DEAL

The best place to start your search is the travel section of your local Sunday newspaper. Also check the ads in the back of national travel magazines like *Travel & Leisure, National Geographic Traveler,* and *Condé Nast Traveler.*

Liberty Travel (✆ **888/271-1584** to be connected with the agent closest to you; www.libertytravel.com), one of the biggest packagers in the Northeast, often runs a full-page ad in the Sunday papers. **American Express Travel** (✆ **800/941-2639;** www.americanexpress.com) is another option. Check out its **Last Minute Travel Bargains** (www.lastminute.com) site, offered in conjunction with **Continental Airlines,** with discounted vacation packages and reduced fares that differ from the E-savers bargains Continental e-mails weekly to subscribers.

Another good resource is the airlines themselves, which often package their flights with accommodations. Check the offerings from **American Airlines Vacations** (✆ **800/321-2121;** www.aavacations.com) and **US Airways Vacations** (✆ **800/455-0123;** www.usairwaysvacations.com).

The **French Experience** (✆ **800/283-7262** or 212/986-3808; www.frenchexperience.com) offers inexpensive tickets to Paris on most scheduled airlines and arranges tours and stays in country inns, hotels, private châteaux, and B&Bs. In addition, it takes reservations for small hotels in Avignon, Aix-en-Provence, Cannes, and Nice.

ESCORTED TOURS

Escorted tours are structured group tours, with a group leader. The price usually includes everything from airfare to hotels, meals, tours, admission costs, and local transportation.

Many people derive a certain ease and security from escorted trips. Escorted tours let travelers sit back and enjoy their trip without having to spend lots of time behind the wheel. All the little details are taken care of, you know your costs up front, and there are few surprises. Escorted tours are particularly convenient for people with limited mobility.

On the downside, an escorted tour often requires a big deposit up front, and lodging and dining choices are predetermined. As part of a cloud of tourists, you'll get little opportunity for serendipitous interactions with locals. The tours can be jam-packed with activities, leaving little room for individual adventure—plus they often focus only on the heavily touristed sites, so you miss out on the lesser-known gems.

Before you invest in an escorted tour, ask about the **cancellation policy:** Is a deposit required? Can the company cancel the trip if it doesn't get enough people? Do you get a refund if the trip is canceled? If *you* cancel it? How late can you cancel if you are unable to go? When do you pay in full? ***Note:*** If you choose an escorted tour, think strongly about purchasing trip-cancellation insurance, especially if the tour operator asks you to pay up front.

BOOKING AN ESCORTED TOUR

The two largest tour operators conducting escorted tours of France and Europe are **Globus + Cosmos Tours** (✆ **800/338-7092;** www.globusandcosmos.com) and **Trafalgar** (www.trafalgartours.com). Both companies have first-class tours that run about $100 a day and budget tours for about $75 a day. The differences are mainly in hotel location and the number of activities. There's little difference in the companies' services, so choose your tour based on the itinerary and preferred date of departure. Brochures are available at travel agencies, and all tours must be booked through travel agents.

Tauck World Discovery (✆ **800/468-2825;** www.tauck.com) provides first-class, escorted coach grand tours of France as well as 1-week general tours of regions within France. Its 14-day tour of France covering the Normandy landing beaches, the Bayeux Tapestry, and Mont-St-Michel costs $3,760 per person, double occupancy (land only), while an 8-day trip beginning in Nice and ending in Paris costs $1,975 to $2,370 per person.

13 Special-Interest Trips

Provence and the Côte d'Azur are especially well organized for visitors looking for sports pursuits. Most clubs will accept temporary members, and activities are wide-ranging, from biking through the countryside to golfing on the pine-fringed fairways of Provence, to swinging a tennis racquet close to Mediterranean waters. If you like your activities offbeat, you can even go barging along the lowlands of the Camargue.

Of course, if you want to go really local, you'll take up boules and its local variant, *pétanque.* The game is relatively simple to learn—any local can teach you—and it's played with small metal balls on earth courts in every dusty village square.

BARGING

Before the advent of the railways, many of the crops, building supplies, raw materials, and other products were barged through a series of rivers, canals, and estuaries. Many of these are still graced with their old-fashioned locks and pumps, allowing shallow-draft barges easy passage through idyllic countryside.

Le Boat, 45 Whitney Road, Suite C-5, Mahwah, NJ 07430 (✆ **800/992-0291** or 201/560-1941; www.leboat.com), focuses on regions of France not covered by many other barge operators. The company's trio of barges are luxury craft of a size and shape that fit through the relatively narrow canals and locks of the Camargue, Languedoc, and Provence. Each 6-night tour accommodates no more than 10 passengers in 5 cabins outfitted with mahogany and brass, plus meals prepared by a Cordon Bleu chef. Prices depend on many factors and are highly variable, but call for information.

BICYCLING

A well-recommended company since 1979 is the California-based **Backroads,** 801 Cedar St., Berkeley, CA 94710 (✆ **800/462-2848** or 510/527-1555; www.backroads.com). Its well-organized tours of Provence last between 6 and 8 days and include stays in everything from Relais & Châteaux hotels to campgrounds where staff members prepare meals featuring local cuisine. All tours include an accompanying vehicle that provides liquid refreshments and assists in the event of breakdowns. A 6-day tour costs $2,798 per person, increasing to $3,698 for 8 days.

Holland Bicycling Tours, Inc., P.O. Box 6086, Huntington Beach, CA 92615 (✆ **800/852-3258;** www.hollandbicyclingtours.com), is the

North American representative of a Dutch-based company that leads a 10-day tour through Provence, past Roman ruins, van Gogh's sunflowers, and fields pungent with lavender, thyme, and basil. The trip begins in Avignon and concludes with a 2-day stay near Gordes, a charming town with vaulted passageways. The price is $2,100 per person. Occupants of single rooms pay a supplement of $350.

If you're interested in bicycling through selected regions of the south of France, the local tourist offices of each of the towns covered in this guide are, to an increasing degree, able to provide addresses, maps, and contacts for whatever a cyclist might need. In many cases, bikes can be rented within railway stations of any given town. For general advice on biking in France, contact the **Fédération Française du Cyclotourisme,** 8 rue Jean-Marie-Yégo, 75013 Paris (✆ **01-56-20-88-88;** www.ffct.org), or the **Fédération Française du Cyclisme,** 5 rue de Rome, 93561 Rosny-sous-Bois (✆ **01-49-35-69-00**).

FISHING

The Mediterranean provides a variety of fish and fishing methods. You can line fish from the rocks along the coast or from small boats known as *pointu.* Local fishers often take visitors along when fishing in the sea for tuna. The rivers provide sea trout, speckled trout, and silver eel, and the sandy shores of the Camargue offer the *tellina,* or sunset shell, which are small shellfish. For more information on regulations and access to fishing areas, contact the **Comité Régional PACA de la Fédération des Pècheurs en Mer** (✆ **04-91-72-63-96**).

GOLF

The area around Bouches-du-Rhône has many fine golf courses, with seven 18-hole courses, five 9-hole courses, and several practice courses in the Provence area. One excellent 18-hole course is **Golf de la Salette,** impasse des Vaudrans, 13011 Marseille (✆ **04-91-27-12-16**). One of the finest courses is **Golf de Valcros,** La Londe-Les Maures, 37km (23 miles) east of Toulouse off N98. Call ✆ **04-94-66-81-02** for more information.

Golf International, Inc., 14 East 38th St., New York, NY 10016 (✆ **800/833-1389** or 212/986-9176; www.golfinternational.com), offers the Golfing Epicurean package: a week-long trip based in the historic hilltop village of Mougins, a 10-minute drive from Cannes. Mougins is the golfing capital of the south of France and provides a wealth of fine dining opportunities. As part of this package, you spend 6 nights at the luxurious Les Mas Candille, a 200-year-old converted farmhouse in the village. The price includes golf on four of the best courses in the area: Royal Mougins, Cannes-Mougins, Valbonne, and Cannes-Mandelieu. Also included is a car rental with collision-damage waiver insurance and unlimited mileage. The cost is $2,475 to $2,937. You can request a copy of Golf International's *Complete Golfing Vacation Guide* by calling the number above.

For more information on the options available, contact the **Fédération Française de Golf,** 69 av. Victor-Hugo, 75116 Paris (✆ **01-41-40-77-00;** www.ffg.org).

GOURMET TOURS

Cuisine International, P.O. Box 25228, Dallas, TX 75225 (✆ **214/373-1161;** www.cuisineinternational.com), offers a 6-day culinary experience in Provence. Accommodations are in hotels and private homes, such as the one overlooking a lake in Provence that houses the school. Classes are arranged to allow time for sightseeing, and meals are eaten in restaurants and private homes. Rates are inclusive, except for airfare: The price is $2,200 to $3,000. A tour by **European Culinary Adventures,** 5 Ledgewood Way, no. 6, Peabody, MA 01960 (© **800/852-2625;** www.thefrenchkitchen.com), touts culinary vacations during which you stay in an 18th-century farmhouse (also the school) between Bordeaux and Toulouse. The price of a 6-day/5-night tour is $2,950 per person, including lodging, cooking classes, most meals, touring, and local transportation. In addition, four people can charter a 26m (85-ft.) barge for a week of cooking, dining, and touring.

HIKING

The Bouches-du-Rhône area is a walker's heaven, whether you enjoy a stroll or a strenuous long-distance hike or even mountain climbing. Walking challenges include the wetlands of the Camargue, the semiarid desert of La Crau, and the mountainous hills to the wild rocky inlets of Les Calanques. Long-distance hiking paths, **Sentiers de Grande Randonnée** (GRs), join the area's major places of interest. GR6 starts in Tarascon, runs along the foot of the Lubéron Hills, and crosses the Alpilles Hills. GR9 goes down the Lubéron, passes Mont Ste-Victoire, and ends in Ste-Baume. GR98 is an alternative path linking Ste-Baume with Les Calanques and ends in Marseille. GR51 links Marseille and Arles via La Crau. GR99A links GR9 to the highlands of the Var département.

Spring and autumn are the best for hiking; many of the paths are closed in summer because of forest fires. Be sure to check with the département before you begin your walk. For information, call the **Comité Départmental de Randonnée Pédestre (Bouches-du-Rhône Hiking Committee),** Paul Busti, 24 av. du Prado-Immeuble B, Bureau 401, 13008 Marseille (© **02-38-58-49-64**); or **Comité Départmental Mont-Alp-Escalade (Bouches-du-Rhône Mountaineering & Climbing Committee),** Daniel Gorgeon, 5 impasse du Figuier, 13114 Puyloubier (© **04-42-66-35-05**).

Adventure Center, 1311 63rd St., Suite 200, Emeryville, CA 94608 (© **800/227-8747** or 510/654-1879; www.adventurecenter.com), sponsors 8-day hiking/camping trips in Provence, beginning and ending in Nice. The cost of an outing, exclusive of airfare and other travel-related expenses, is $620 to $670 per person, 130€ of which is a local fee added in France. Included are 4 nights of campground accommodations. Eight evening meals are provided; the other seven are usually purchased in Provençal restaurants along the way. Campers are also expected to purchase three lunches. The company offers 16 trips per year, and though dates might vary, these include departures in May to September.

Another company known for its adventure trips is **Mountain Travel Sobek,** 1266 66 St., Suite 4, Emeryville, CA 94608 (© **888/687-6235;** www.mtsobek.com), which offers a tour package in summer. Trip dates vary but are offered four times a year between June and September. "Pleasures of Provence" ranges from $2,890 per person (travel not included), which covers a 6-day, 92km (57-mile) trek with accommodations provided in mostly luxury hotels. The fee also includes five dinners at fine restaurants, four lunches, and seven breakfasts. The hike starts and ends in Avignon.

HORSEBACK RIDING

One of the best ways to see the wildlife, salt swamps, and marshlands of the Camargue or the wooded hills around Alpilles, Ste-Baume, and Mont Ste-Victoire is on horseback. For more information, contact the **Sellerie Lou Mazet,** 13680 Lançon-de-Provence (© **04-90-42-89-38**), or the **Association Camarguaise de Tourisme Equestre** (Camargue Equestrian Tourism Association), Centre de Ginès-Pont de Gau, 13460 Stes-Maries-de-la-Mer (© **04-90-97-86-32**).

A clearinghouse for at least eight French stables is **Equitours** (Fun in the Saddle), P.O. Box 807, Dubois, WY 82513 (✆ **800/545-0019** or 307/455-3363; www.ridingtours.com). It can arrange 8-day cross-country treks through Provence and the Camargue regions, with prices starting from $1,695 per person.

LANGUAGE SCHOOLS

A clearinghouse for information on French-language schools is **Lingua Service Worldwide,** 75 Prospect St., Suite 4, Huntington, NY 11743 (✆ **800/394-LEARN** or 631/424-0770; www.linguaserviceworldwide.com). Its programs cover Antibes, Aix-en-Provence, Avignon, Cannes, Juan-les-Pins, Montpellier, and Nice. Courses can be long- or short-term, the latter with 20 lessons per week. They range from $500 to $1,200 for 2 weeks, depending on the city, the school, and the accommodations.

14 Getting Around the South of France

The most charming Provençal villages and best country hotels always seem to lie away from the main cities and train stations. You'll find that renting a car is usually the best way to travel once you get to the south of France, especially if you plan to explore in depth and not stick to the standard route along the coast.

If you're not driving, you'll find that the south of France has one of the most reliable bus and rail transportation systems in Europe. Trains connect all the major cities and towns, such as Nice and Avignon. Where the train leaves off, you can most often rely on the trusty local bus service.

BY CAR

Driving time in Europe is largely a matter of conjecture, urgency, and how much sightseeing you do along the way. The driving time from Marseille to Paris is a matter of national pride, and tall tales abound about how rapidly the French can do it. With the accelerator pressed to the floor, you might conceivably make it in 7 hours, but we always make a 2-day journey of it.

CAR RENTALS To rent a car, you'll need to present a passport, a driver's license, and a credit card. You'll also have to meet the minimum age requirement of the company. (For the least expensive cars, this is 21 at Hertz, 23 at Avis, and 25 at Budget. More expensive cars might require that you be at least 25.) It usually isn't obligatory within France, but certain companies have at times asked for the presentation of an International Driver's License, even though this is becoming increasingly superfluous in western Europe.

Note: The best deal is usually a weekly rental with unlimited mileage. All car-rental bills in France are subject to a 19.6% government tax. Though the rental company won't usually mind if you drive your car into, say, Germany, Switzerland, Italy, or Spain, it's often forbidden to transport your car by ferry, including across the Channel to England.

Unless it's factored into the rental agreement, an optional **collision-damage waiver (CDW)** carries an extra charge of 13€ to 21€ per day for the least expensive car. Buying this usually eliminates all but $250 of your responsibility in the event of accidental damage to the car. Because most newcomers aren't familiar with local driving customs and conditions, we recommend you buy the CDW, though you should check with your credit card company first to see if it will cover this automatically when you rent with its card. (It might cover damage but not liability, so make sure you understand this clearly.) At some companies, the CDW won't protect you against theft, so if this is the case, ask about buying extra theft protection. This cost is 9.10€ extra per day.

Automatic transmission is considered a luxury in Europe, so if you want it, you'll have to pay dearly.

Budget (www.budget.com) has numerous locations in southern France, including those in **Avignon** at the railway station (✆ 04-90-27-94-95) and at the airport (✆ 04-90-27-94-95); in **Marseille** at the airport (✆ 04-42-14-24-55), at 40 bd. de Plombières (✆ 04-91-64-40-03); in **Montpellier** at the airport (✆ 04-67-20-07-34); in **Nice** at the airport (✆ 04-93-21-42-51) and at 23 rue de Belgique, opposite the rail station (✆ 04-93-16-24-16); and in **Toulouse** at the airport (✆ 05-61-71-85-80) and at 49 rue Bayard (✆ 05-61-63-18-18).

For rentals of more than 7 days, in most cases cars can be picked up in one French city and dropped off in another, but there are additional charges. Still, Budget's rates are among the most competitive, and its cars are well maintained.

Hertz (www.hertz.com) is also well represented, with offices in **Avignon** at the airport (✆ 04-90-84-19-50) and at the train station (✆ 04-32-74-62-80); in **Marseille** at the airport (✆ 08-25-09-13-13) and at 15 bd. Maurice-Bourdet (✆ 04-91-14-04-24); in **Montpellier** at the airport (✆ 04-67-20-04-64); in **Nice** at the airport (✆ 08-25-34-23-43); and in **Toulouse** at the airport (✆ 05-61-71-27-09) and at the rail station (✆ 05-62-73-39-47). When making inquiries, be sure to ask about promotional discounts.

Avis (www.avis.com) has offices in **Avignon** at the airport (✆ 04-90-87-17-75) and at 160 bis av. Pierre-Senmard (✆ 04-90-87-17-75); in **Marseille** at the airport (✆ 04-42-14-21-67) and at 267 bd. National (✆ 04-91-50-70-11); in **Montpellier** at the airport (✆ 04-67-20-14-95) and at 900 av. des Prés d'Arènes (✆ 04-67-92-51-92); in **Nice** at the airport (✆ 04-93-21-36-33) and at place Massena, 2 av. des Phocéens (✆ 04-93-80-63-52); and in **Toulouse** at the airport (✆ 05-34-60-46-50) and at the train station (✆ 05-61-62-50-40).

National (www.nationalcar.com) is represented in France by Europcar, with locations in **Avignon** at the airport (✆ 04-90-84-01-48) and at the train station (✆ 04-90-27-30-07); in **Marseille** at the airport (✆ 04-91-05-90-86) and at the St-Charles train station, 96 blvd. Rabatau (✆ 04-91-83-05-05); in **Montpellier** at the airport (✆ 04-67-15-13-47); in **Nice** at the airport (✆ 04-93-21-80-90); and in **Toulouse** at the airport (✆ 05-61-30-00-01). You can rent a car on the spot at any of these offices, but lower rates are available by making advance reservations from North America.

Two United States–based agencies that don't have France offices but act as booking agents for France-based agencies are **Kemwel Holiday Auto** (✆ **800/678-0678;** www.kemwel.com) and **Auto Europe** (✆ **800/223-5555;** www.autoeurope.com). These can make bookings in the United States only, so call before your trip.

GASOLINE Known in France as *essence,* gas is expensive for those accustomed to North American prices. All but the least expensive cars usually require an octane rating that the French classify as *essence super,* the most expensive variety. Depending on your car, you'll need either leaded *(avec plomb)* or unleaded *(sans plomb).*

Beware the mixture of gasoline and oil called *mélange* or *gasoil* sold in some rural communities; this mixture is for very old two-cycle engines.

Note: Sometimes you can drive for miles in rural France without encountering a gas station, so don't let your tank get dangerously low.

DRIVING RULES Everyone in the car, in both the front and the back seats, must wear seat belts. Children under 12 must ride in the back seat. Drivers are supposed to yield to the car on their right, except where signs indicate otherwise, as at traffic circles.

If you violate the speed limit, expect a big fine. Those limits are about 130kmph (80 mph) on expressways, about 100kmph (60 mph) on major national highways, and 90kmph (56 mph) on country roads. In towns, don't exceed 60kmph (37 mph).

MAPS For France as a whole, most motorists opt for Michelin map 989. For regions, Michelin publishes a series of yellow maps that are quite good. Big travel-book stores in North America carry these maps, and they're commonly available in France (at lower prices). In this age of congested traffic, one useful feature of the Michelin map is its designations of alternative *routes de dégagement,* which let you skirt big cities and avoid traffic-clogged highways.

Another recommended option is *Frommer's Road Atlas Europe.*

BREAKDOWNS/ASSISTANCE A breakdown is called *une panne* in France. Call the police at ✆ **17** anywhere in France to be put in touch with the nearest garage. Most local garages offer towing. If the breakdown occurs on an expressway, find the nearest roadside emergency phone box, pick up the phone, and put a call through. You'll be connected to the nearest breakdown service facility.

BY PLANE

Regrettably, there are few competitors in the world of domestic air travel within France. **Air France** (✆ **800/237-2747**) serves about eight cities in France. Airfares tend to be much higher than for comparable distances in the United States, and discounts are few. Sample round-trip fares from Paris are $394 to Nice and $361 to Toulouse. Air travel time from Paris to most anywhere in France is about an hour.

BY TRAIN

Rail services between the large cities of Languedoc-Roussillon and Provence and the French Riviera are excellent. If you don't have a car, you can tour all the major hot spots by train. Of course, with a car you can also explore the hidden villages, such as the little Riviera hill towns, but for short visits with only major stopovers on your itinerary, such as Nice and Avignon, the train should suffice. Service is fast and frequent.

The major train hub for Languedoc is the city of Toulouse in southwestern France, which has frequent service from Paris and Lyon. Toulouse is also linked to Marseilles by 11 trains running every day. Montpellier is another major transportation hub for the Languedoc-Roussillon area. Eleven high-speed TGVs arrive daily from Paris, taking just 3½ hours. Montpellier also has good rail connections to Avignon. The ancient city of Nîmes, one of the most visited in the area, also is a major transportation rail terminus, a stop on the rail link between Bordeaux and Marseille.

Marseille, the largest city in the south of France, has rail connections with all major towns on the Riviera as well as with the rest of France. Seventeen high-speed TGVs arrive from Paris daily (trip time: 3 hr. 15 min.).

The major rail transportation hub along the French Riviera is Nice, although Cannes also enjoys good train connections. Nice and Monaco are linked by frequent service, and in summer about eight trains per day connect Nice with the rapid TGV train from Paris to Marseille. In winter, the schedule is curtailed depending on demand.

The most visited Riviera destination in the east, Monaco also has excellent rail links along the Riviera.

BY BUS

While the trains are faster and more efficient if you are traveling between major cities, both the towns and villages of Languedoc and Provence, including the French Riviera, are linked by frequent bus service. If you are not driving, you can use the network of buses that link the villages and hamlets with each other and the major cities to get off the beaten path.

Historic towns like Castres and Albi (of Toulouse-Lautrec fame) can be reached by bus from Toulouse; St-Paul-de-Vence from Nice; and Grasse, the perfume center, from Cannes.

Plan to take advantage of the bus services from Monday to Saturday when they run frequently; there are very few buses running on Sunday.

15 Tips on Accommodations

The French government rates hotels on a one- to four-star system. One-star hotels are budget accommodations, two-star lodgings are quality tourist hotels, three stars go to first-class hotels, and four stars are reserved for deluxe accommodations. In some of the lower categories, the rooms might not have private bathrooms; instead, many have what the French call a *cabinet de toilette* (hot and cold running water and maybe a bidet). In such hotels, bathrooms are down the hall. Not all private bathrooms have a shower/tub combination; ask in advance if it matters to you. Nearly all hotels in France have central heating, but, in some cases, you might wish the owners would turn it up a little on a cold night.

RELAIS & CHATEAUX Now known worldwide, this organization of deluxe and first-class hostelries began in France for visitors seeking the ultimate in hotel living and dining in a traditional atmosphere. Relais & Châteaux establishments (there are about 150 in France) are former castles, abbeys, manor houses, and town houses converted into hostelries or inns and elegant hotels. All have a limited number of rooms, so reservations are imperative. Sometimes these owner-run establishments have pools and tennis courts. The Relais part of the organization refers to inns called *relais,* meaning "post house." These tend to be less luxurious than zthe châteaux but are often charming. Top-quality restaurants are *relais gourmands.* Throughout this guide, we've listed our favorite Relais & Châteaux, but there are many more.

For a catalog of member establishments, send 9€ to **Relais & Châteaux,** 11 E. 44th St., Suite 707, New York, NY 10017. For information and reservations, call ✆ **800/735-2478** or 212/856-0115, or check out the website www.relaischateaux.com.

BED-AND-BREAKFASTS Called *gîtes-chambres d'hôte* in France, these might be one or several bedrooms on a farm or in a village home. Many offer one main meal of the day as well (lunch or dinner).

There are at least 6,000 of these listed with **La Maison des Gîtes de France et du Tourisme Vert,** 59 rue St-Lazare, 75439 Paris (✆ **01-49-70-75-75;** www.gites-de-france.fr). Sometimes these B&Bs aren't as simple as you might think: Instead of a bare-bones farm room, you might be in a mansion in the French countryside.

In the United States, a good source for this type of accommodation is **The French Experience,** 370 Lexington Ave., Room 511, New York, NY 10017 (✆ **800/283-7262** or 212/986-3800; www.frenchexperience.com), which also rents furnished houses for as short a period as 1 week.

Many Provence-bound visitors prefer to deal directly with a Stateside agency. The best is **Provence West,** P.O. Box 272884, Fort Collins, CO 80527 (✆ **970/226-5444;** www.provence west.com), run by Linda Posson. She has connections with some 80 of the best accommodations in the region, including such nuggets as a farmhouse 16km (10 miles) south of Avignon with three bedrooms. A 14-page booklet that describes the *gîte* experience is provided upon booking, with valuable tips including how to secure inexpensive car rentals. Another source is **France: Homestyle** (✆ **206/325-0132;** www.francehomestyle.com), run by Claudette Hunt. These lodgings are a bit fancier than a typical bare-bones *gîte.* Her repertoire in Provence includes more than 300 properties.

CONDOS, VILLAS, HOUSES & APARTMENTS If you can stay for at least a week and don't mind doing your own cooking and cleaning, you might want to rent a long-term accommodation. The local French Tourist Board might help you obtain a list of agencies that offer this type of rental (which is popular at ski resorts). In France, one of the best groups of estate agents is the **Fédération Nationale des Agents Immobiliers,** 106 rue de l'Université, 75007 Paris (✆ **01-47-05-44-36;** www.fnpc.fr).

In the United States, **At Home Abroad, Inc.,** 405 E. 56th St., Suite 6H, New York, NY 10022-2466 (✆ **212/421-9165;** www.athomeabroadinc.com), specializes in villas on the French Riviera and in the Dordogne as well as places in the Provençal hill towns. Rentals are usually for 2 weeks. For a $10 registration fee (applicable to any rental), you'll receive photographs of the properties and a newsletter.

A worthwhile competitor is **Vacances en Campagne,** British Travel International, P.O. Box 299, Elkton, VA 22827 (✆ **800/327-6097;** www.britishtravel.com). Its $5 directory contains information on more than 700 potential rentals across Europe, including France.

Barclay International Group, 3 School St., Glen Cove, NY 11542 (✆ **800/ 845-6636** or 516/759-5100; www.barclayweb.com), can give you access to about 3,000 apartments and villas throughout Languedoc, Provence, and the Riviera, ranging from modest modern units to those among the most stylish. Units rent from 1 night up to 6 months; all have color TVs and kitchenettes, and many have concierge staffs and lobby-level security. The least-expensive units cost $100 per night, double occupancy. Incremental discounts are granted for a stay of 1 week or 3 weeks. Rentals must be prepaid in U.S. dollars or by a major U.S. credit or charge card.

Hometours International, Inc., 1108 Scottie Lane, Knoxville, TN 37919 (✆ **866/367-4668** or 865/690-8484), offers beautiful Riviera villas, all with pools, at reasonable rates.

HOTEL ASSOCIATIONS

For budget travelers, **Hometours International, Inc.** (see above) offers a prepaid voucher program for the Campanile hotels, a chain of about 350 two-star family-run hotels throughout France. Rates begin as low as $90 per night double. This is an excellent alternative to B&B hotels because all chain members provide a buffet breakfast for only 6.50€ per person. B&B catalogs for $9 or apartment brochures for free are available from the address above.

Others wanting to trim costs might want to check out the **Mercure** chain, an organization of simple but clean and modern hotels offering attractive values throughout France. Even at the peak of the tourist season, a room at a Mercure in Provence rents for $111 to $185 per night. For more information on Mercure hotels and a copy of a 100-page directory, call **ACCOR** at ✆ **800/ 221-4542** in the United States.

Formule 1 hotels are bare bones and basic though clean and safe, offering rooms for up to three at around $30 per night. Built from prefabricated units, these air-conditioned, soundproof hotels are shipped to a site and assembled. (Formule 1, a member of the French hotel giant Accor, also owns the Motel 6 chain in the United States, to which Formule 1 bears a resemblance.)

While you can make a reservation at any member of the Accor group through the RESINTER number above, the chain finds that the low cost of Formule 1 makes it unprofitable and impractical to pre-reserve (from the United States) rooms in the Formule chain. So, you'll have to reserve your Formule 1 room on arrival in France. Be warned that Formule 1 properties have almost none of the Gallic charm for which some country inns are famous, but you can save money by planning your itinerary at Formule 1 properties. For a directory, contact **Formule 1/ETAP Hotels,** 6–8 rue du Bois Bernard, 91021 Evry CEDEX (✆ **01-69-36-75-00**).

Other worthwhile economy bets, sometimes with a bit more charm, are the hotels and restaurants belonging to the **Fédération Nationale des Logis de France,** 83 av. d'Italie, 75013 Paris (✆ **01-45-84-70-00;** www.logis-de-france.fr). This is a marketing association of 3,828 hotels, usually simple country inns especially convenient for motorists, most rated one or two stars. The association publishes an annual directory. Copies are available for $24.95 from the **French Government Tourist Office,** 444 Madison Ave., 16th Floor, New York, NY 10022 (✆ **212/838-7800**), and also from stores specializing in travel publications, including **Rand-McNally,** 150 East 52nd St., New York, NY 10022 (✆ **212/758-7488;** www.randmcnally.com), where virtually any travel guide currently in print, as well as a rich assortment of maps to virtually everywhere, either is stocked or can be ordered.

At the most inexpensive end, **Hostelling International USA,** 8401 Colesville Rd., Silver Springs, MD 20910 (✆ **202/783-6161;** www.hiayh.org), offers a directory of low-cost accommodations around the country.

16 Recommended Reading

GENERAL INTEREST

One obvious place to start is *A Year in Provence,* by Peter Mayle (Vintage Books, 1991). With its wit, warmth, and wicked candor, this foray into Provençal domesticity became an international best seller. It was called "part memoir, part homeowner's manual, and part travelogue." If you become addicted to Mayle, you can also read his *Hotel Pastis: A Novel of Provence* and *Toujours Provence.*

Artists and writers flocked to the Riviera in the 1920s and early 1930s, and this "hunt for happiness" is marvelously evoked by art critic and historian Xavier Girard in *French Riviera: Living Well Is the Best Revenge* (Assouline, 2002). You can witness first hand the lifestyles of the Riviera's most celebrated couple, Gerald and Sara Murphy, and all the "gang" that included everybody from Chanel to F. Scott Fitzgerald (whose *Tender Is the Night* is set on the Riviera). Edith Wharton's love affair with the Riviera, launched in 1919, is brilliantly glimpsed in *Edith Wharton on the Riviera* (Flammarion, 2002). She found the Riviera both a haven for writing and a "terrifying superficial world."

The Most Beautiful Villages of Provence (Thames & Hudson, 1994) proves successfully that Provence—"a land apart"—is best evoked by its villages. Brilliantly illustrated, the book includes more than 30 special villages to visit, many off the beaten track.

Robert Kanigel's *High Season: How One French Riviera Town Has Seduced*

Travelers for Two Thousand Years (Viking Press, 2002) is a love letter to Nice. The impressions of Yankee G.I.s to Russian royalty are combined to paint a memorable and ever-changing portrait of the French Riviera's capital city.

ART

Barbara Freed and Alan Halpern's *Artists and Their Museums on the Riviera* (Harry N. Abrams, 1998) is an intriguing book that follows the footsteps of celebrated artists who have lived and found inspiration on the Riviera, including Renoir, Picasso, Jean Cocteau, Chagall, and Matisse. From the private homes of the artists to museums or chapels they decorated, this book shows that the Riviera is a mecca for devotees of contemporary art.

Nina Athanassoglou-Kallmyer explores how Provence became a defining cultural force that shaped all aspects of the Cezanne's work, even his self-portraits, in *Cézanne and Provence: The Painter in His Culture* (University of Chicago Press, 2003). Lavishly illustrated, the book claims that Cézanne reconstructed a "modern French Arcadia."

CUISINE

Provence is celebrated for its cuisine, and Peter Johnson's *Provence: The Beautiful Cookbook* (Collins, 1993) is a beautifully illustrated book that sets a good table. Johnson takes us to the region where August Auguste Escoffier, the patron saint of French cooking, was born, and we learn much about how to make the most evocative dishes of the region. You'll even learn what specific herbs go to make up the celebrated Herbes de provence. It's also a walk down memory lane.

We also recommend *Patricia Wells at Home in Provence: Recipes Inspired by Her Farmhouse in France* (Scribner, 1996). This coffee-table book with its some 171 recipes is also useful. If you like fresh herbs and virgin olive oil, and everything they're used on, you can work your way through this wonderful compendium of country food.

FAST FACTS: The South of France

Auto Club An organization designed to help motorists navigate their way through breakdowns and motoring problems is **Club Automobile de Provence,** 149 bd. Rabatau, 13010 Marseille (© **04-91-78-83-00**).

Business Hours Business hours here are erratic, as befits a nation of individualists. Most banks are open Monday through Friday from 9:30am to 4:30pm. Many, particularly in smaller towns or villages, take a lunch break at varying times. Hours are usually posted on the door. Most museums close 1 day a week (often Tues), and they're generally closed on national holidays. Usual hours are from 9:30am to 5pm. Some museums, particularly the smaller and less-staffed ones, close for lunch from noon to 2pm. Most French museums are open on Saturday; many are closed Sunday morning but open Sunday afternoon. Again, refer to the individual museum listings.

Generally, offices are open Monday through Friday from 9am to 5pm, but always call first. In larger cities, stores are open from 9 or 9:30am (often 10am) to 6 or 7pm without a break for lunch. Some shops, particularly those operated by foreigners, open at 8am and close at 8 or 9pm. In some small stores, the lunch break can last 3 hours, beginning at 1pm.

Drugstores In France they are called *pharmacie.* Pharmacies take turns staying open at night and on Sunday; the local Commissariat de Police will tell you the location of the nearest one.

Electricity In general, expect 200 volts, 50 cycles, though you'll encounter 110 and 115 volts in some older establishments. Adapters are needed to fit sockets. Many hotels have two-pin (in some cases, three-pin) sockets for electric razors. It's best to ask your hotel concierge before plugging in any appliance.

Embassies & Consulates All embassies are in Paris. The **Embassy and Consulate of the United States** are at 2 rue St-Florentin (✆ **01-43-12-22-22;** Métro: Concorde), open Monday through Friday from 9am to 6pm. Passports are issued at the consulate; getting a passport replaced costs about $55. The United States also maintains a consulate in Marseilles at 12 bd. Paul-Peytral (✆ **04-91-54-92-00**).

The **Embassy of Canada** is at 35 av. Montaigne (✆ **01-44-43-29-00;** Métro: Franklin-D-Roosevelt), open Monday through Friday from 9am to noon and 2 to 5pm; the Canadian Consulate is at the same address. The **Embassy of the United Kingdom** is at 35 rue du Faubourg St-Honoré (✆ **01-44-51-31-00;** Métro: Concorde), open Monday through Friday from 9:30am to 1pm and 2:30 to 5pm; the U.K. consulate, 18 bis rue d'Anjou (✆ **01-44-51-31-02;** Métro: Concorde), is open Monday through Friday from 9am to noon and 2 to 5pm.

The **Embassy of Australia** is at 4 rue Jean-Rey, 15e (✆ **01-40-59-33-00;** Métro: Bir-Hakeim), open Monday through Friday from 9:15am to noon and 2:30 to 4:30pm. The **Embassy of New Zealand** is at 7 ter rue Léonard-de-Vinci (✆ **01-45-01-43-43;** Métro: Victor-Hugo), open Monday through Friday from 9am to 1pm and 2:30 to 6pm. The **Embassy of Ireland** is at 12 av. Foch, 16e (✆ **01-44-17-67-00;** Métro: Etoile). Hours are Monday through Friday from 9:30am to noon and 2:30 to 5:30pm.

Emergencies In an emergency while at a hotel, contact the front desk to summon an ambulance or do whatever is necessary. But for something like a stolen wallet, go to the police station in person. Otherwise, you can get help anywhere in France by calling ✆ **17** for the **police** or ✆ **18** for the **fire department** *(pompiers).* For roadside emergencies, see "Getting Around the South of France," earlier in this chapter.

Legal Aid The French government advises foreigners to consult their embassy or consulate (see above) in case of an arrest or similar problem. The staff can generally offer advice on how you can obtain help locally and can furnish you with a list of local attorneys. If you are arrested for illegal possession of drugs, the U.S. embassy and consular officials cannot interfere with the French judicial system. A consulate can advise you only of your rights.

Mail Most post offices in France are open Monday through Friday from 8am to 7pm, and Saturday from 8am to noon. Allow 5 to 8 days to send or receive mail from your home. Airmail letters to North America cost .65€ for 20 grams. Letters to the U.K. cost .45€ for up to 20 grams. An airmail postcard to North America or Europe (outside France) costs .65€.

You can exchange money at post offices. Many hotels sell stamps, as do local post offices and cafes displaying a red TABAC sign outside.

Newspapers & Magazines Most major cities carry copies of the *International Herald Tribune* and *USA Today,* and usually a major London paper or two. Nearly all big-city newsstands also sell copies of *Time* and *Newsweek.* The leading French newspapers are *Le Monde, Le Figaro,* and *La Libération.* The major French newsmagazines are *L'Express, Le Point,* and *Le Nouvel Observateur.*

Police Call ✆ **17** anywhere in France.

Restrooms If you're in dire need, duck into a cafe or brasserie. It's customary to make some small purchase if you do so. France still has many "hole-in-the-ground" toilets, so be forewarned.

Safety Those intending to visit the south of France, especially the Riviera, should exercise extreme caution—robberies and muggings here are commonplace. It's best to check your baggage into a hotel and then go sightseeing instead of leaving it unguarded in the trunk of a car, which can easily be broken into. Marseille is among the most dangerous cities.

Taxes *Watch it:* You could get burned. As a member of the European Union, France routinely imposes a value-added tax (VAT) on many goods and services. The standard VAT on merchandise is 19.6%. Refunds are made for the tax on certain goods, but not on services. The minimum purchase is 184€ for nationals or residents of countries outside the EU. See "How to Get Your VAT Refund," on p. 27, for more details.

Telephone The French also use a ***télécarte,*** a phone debit card, which you can purchase at rail stations, post offices, and other places. Sold in two versions, it allows you to use either 50 or 120 charge units (depending on the card) by inserting the card into the slot of most public phones. Depending on the type of card you buy, the cost is 7.45€ to 15€.

If possible, avoid making calls from your hotel; some French establishments double or triple the charges.

For tips on calling Monaco, which has its own phone system, see "Number, Please: Monaco's Telephone System," on p. 324.

Time The French equivalent of daylight saving time lasts from around April to September, which puts it 1 hour ahead of French winter time. Depending on the time of year, France is 6 or 7 hours ahead of U.S. Eastern Standard Time.

Tipping All bills, as required by law, are supposed to say *service compris,* which means that the tip has been included. Here are some general guidelines: For **hotel staff,** tip 1.05€ to 1.50€ for every item of baggage the porter carries on arrival and departure, and 1.50€ per day for the chambermaid. You're not obligated to tip the concierge (hall porter), doorperson, or anyone else—unless you use his or her services. In cafes, **waiter** service is usually included. For **porters,** there's no real need to tip extra after their bill is presented, unless they've performed some special service. Tip **taxi drivers** 10% to 15% of the amount on the meter. In theaters and restaurants, give **cloakroom attendants** at least .75€ per item.

Give **restroom attendants** about .30€ in nightclubs and such places. Give **cinema and theater ushers** about .30€. Tip the **hairdresser** about 15%, and don't forget to tip the person who gives you a shampoo or a manicure 2€. For **guides** for group visits to sights, .75€ to 1.50€ per person is a reasonable tip.

3

Languedoc-Roussillon & the Camargue

Languedoc, one of southern France's great old provinces, is a loosely defined area encompassing such cities as Nîmes, Toulouse, and Carcassonne. It's one of France's leading wine-producing areas and is fabled for its art treasures.

The coast of Languedoc—from Montpellier to the Spanish frontier—might be called France's "second Mediterranean," with first place naturally going to the Côte d'Azur. A land of ancient cities and a generous sea, it's less spoiled than the Côte d'Azur. An almost-continuous strip of sand stretches west from the Rhône and curves snakelike toward the Pyrénées. Back in the days of de Gaulle, the government began an ambitious project to develop the Languedoc-Roussillon coastline that has since become a booming success, as the miles of sun-baking bodies in July and August testify.

Ancient **Roussillon** is a small region of greater Languedoc, forming the Pyrénées-Orientales *département.* It includes the towns of Perpignan and Collioure within its borders. This is the French Catalonia, inspired more by Barcelona in neighboring Spain than by remote Paris. Over its long and colorful history, it has known many rulers. Legally part of the French kingdom until 1258, it was surrendered to James I of Aragón, and until 1344 it was part of the ephemeral kingdom of Majorca, with Perpignan as the capital. By 1463, Roussillon was annexed to France again. Then Ferdinand of Aragón won it back, but by 1659 France had it once again. In spite of some local sentiment for reunion with the Catalans of Spain, France still firmly controls the land.

The **Camargue** encompasses a marshy delta between two arms of the Rhône. Arles serves as the area's northern border, and the village Sète functions as a gateway to the region. South of Arles is cattle country, and here strong wild black bulls are bred for the arenas of Arles and Nîmes. The cattle is herded by *gardiens,* French cowboys, who wear wide-brimmed black hats and ride amazingly graceful small white horses, said to have been brought here by the Saracens. The whitewashed houses of the Camargue, plaited-straw roofs, pink flamingos that inhabit the muddy marshes, vast plains, endless stretches of sandbars—all this qualifies as "exotic" France.

1 Toulouse ★★★

705km (438 miles) SW of Paris; 245km (152 miles) SE of Bordeaux; 97km (60 miles) W of Carcassonne

The old capital of Languedoc and France's fourth-largest city, Toulouse (known as *la ville en rose,* or the city in pink) today is cosmopolitan in flavor. The major city of the southwest, it's the gateway to the Pyrénées mountain range. Toulouse might be a city with a distinguished historical past, but it is also a city of the future and the high-tech center of the aerospace industry in France. It is home to two huge aircraft makers—Airbus and Aérospatiale—and the National Center for Space Research has been headquartered here for more than 3 decades. The first regularly scheduled airline flights from France took off from the local airport in the 1920s. Today long-range passenger planes of the Airbus consortium, the most important rivals in the world to Boeing, are assembled in a gargantuan hangar in the suburb of Colombiers. In 1997, Toulouse launched an air and space museum (see the entry below for **La Cité de Espace**). Also making the city tick is its extraordinarily high population of students: some 100,000 in all, out of a population of 600,000.

An ancient city filled with gardens and squares, Toulouse has a stormy history. It has played many roles: Once it was the capital of the Visigoths and later the center of the *comtes de Toulouse* (counts of Toulouse; see the appendix for details). The city has 20 historic pipe organs, more than any other city in France, and hosts an annual international organ festival.

ESSENTIALS

GETTING THERE The **Toulouse-Blagnac International Airport** lies in the city's northwestern suburbs, 11km (7 miles) from the center; for flight information, call ✆ **05-61-42-44-00. Air France** (✆ **08-02-80-28-02;** www.airfrance.com) has about 25 flights a day from Paris and 2 per day from London. **British Airways** (✆ **08-02-80-29-02;** www.britishairways.com) also flies to Toulouse from London.

Nine high-speed TGV **trains** per day arrive from Paris (trip time: 5 hr.), 14 from Bordeaux (trip time: 2 hr.), and 11 from Marseille (trip time: 4½ hr.). For rail information and schedules, call ✆ **08-36-35-35-35.**

The **drive** to Toulouse from Paris takes 6 to 7 hours. Take A10 south to Bordeaux, connecting to A62 to Toulouse. The Canal du Midi links many of the region's cities with Toulouse by waterway.

VISITOR INFORMATION The **Office de Tourisme** is in the Donjon du Capitole, rue Lafayette near the Town Hall (✆ **05-61-11-02-22;** www.mairie-toulouse.fr).

SEEING THE SIGHTS

THE TOP ATTRACTIONS

Basilique St-Sernin ★★★ The city's major monument, consecrated in 1096, is the largest and finest Romanesque church extant in Europe; try to avoid touring it during Sunday morning Mass. An outstanding feature is the Porte Miègeville, opening onto the south aisle and decorated with 12th-century sculptures. The door to the south transept is the Porte des Comtes. Look for the Romanesque capitals surmounting the church's columns; the ones here depict the story of Lazarus. Nearby are the tombs of the comtes de Toulouse. Entering by the main west door, you can see the double side aisles that give the church five naves, an unusual feature in Romanesque architecture. An upper cloister forms a passageway around the interior.

In the axis of the basilica, 11th-century bas-reliefs depict *Christ in His Majesty.* The ambulatory leads to the crypt (ask the custodian for permission to enter), containing the relics of 128 saints, plus a thorn said to be from the Crown of Thorns. In the ambulatory, the old baroque altar shelves and shrine have been reset; the relics here are those of the Apostles and the first bishops of Toulouse.

Languedoc-Roussillon & the Camargue

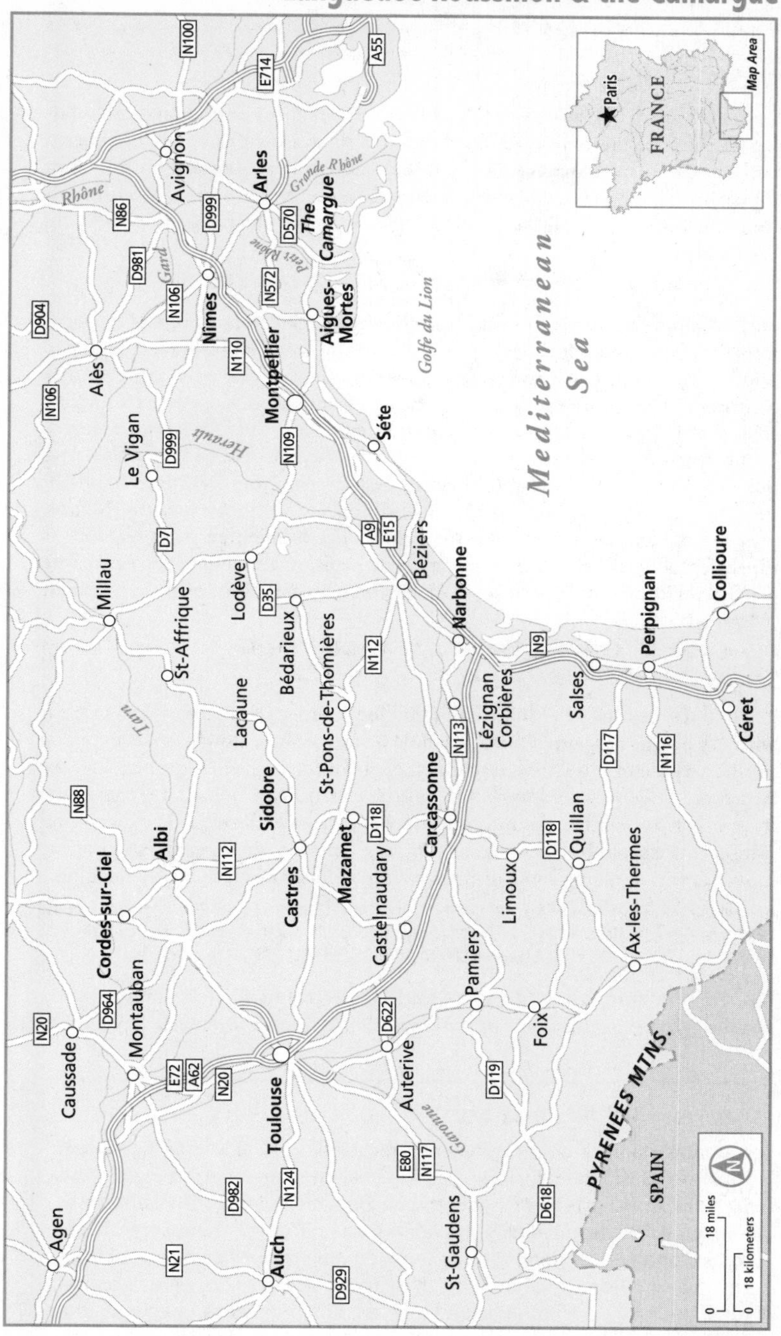

13 place St-Sernin. ✆ **05-61-21-80-45.** Free admission to the church; 2€ crypt. Church daily 8:30–11:30am and 2–5:30pm, but refrain from sightseeing during Sun morning Mass. Crypt Mon–Sat 10–11:30am and 2:30–5pm; Sun 2:30–5pm.

Cathédrale St-Etienne ★ This is the city's other major ecclesiastical building. Because of the time required to build it (it was designed and constructed between the 11th c. and the 17th c.), some critics scorn it for its mishmash of styles, yet it nonetheless conveys a solemn dignity. The rectangular bell tower is from the 16th century. It has a unique ogival nave to which a Gothic choir has been added.

Place St-Etienne, at the eastern end of rue de Metz. ✆ **05-61-52-03-82.** Daily 8am–7pm.

Fondation Bemberg Opened in 1995, this quickly became one of the city's most important museums. Housed in the magnificent Hôtel Assézat (built in 1555, with a 16th-c. courtyard), the museum offers an overview of 5 centuries of European art, with world-class paintings from the Renaissance to the late 19th century. The nucleus of the collection represents the lifelong work of collector extraordinaire Georges Bemberg, of a German-French family, who donated 331 works. The largest bequest was 28 paintings by Pierre Bonnard, including his *Moulin Rouge.* Bemberg also donated works by Pissarro, Matisse *(Vue d'Antibes),* and Monet, plus the Fauves. The foundation owns Canaletto's much-reproduced *Vue de Mestre* as well. The mansion also houses the **Académie des Jeux-Floraux,** which since 1323 has presented flowers made of wrought metal to poets.

Place d'Assézat, rue de Metz. ✆ **05-61-12-06-89.** Admission 4.60€. Tues–Sun 10am–12:30pm and 1:30–6pm; Thurs 10am–9pm.

La Cité de Espace ★ Some half a million visitors a year come here to learn what it's like to program a satellite's launch into orbit or how to maneuver one in space. Both an interactive teaching tool and a fun place to visit, here life-size structural models abound, including one of an astronaut riding an exercise bike in zero gravity. On the grounds outside you can walk through the Mir orbital station constructed by the Russians. The top floor focuses on exploration of the universe, with close-up shots of the moons of Jupiter taken by fly-by satellites.

Av. Jean Gonord. ✆ **05-62-71-48-71.** www.cite-espace.com. Admission 12€ adults, 10€ seniors over 60, 8€ children 6–17, free for children 6 and under; family tickets (2 adults, 2 children) 36€. Tues–Fri 9am–6pm; Sat–Sun 9am–7pm. Exit 17 of the E. Peripheral Route. Bus: 19 (Sat–Sun only).

Musée des Augustins/Musée des Beaux-Arts ★★ The museum was established within this convent in 1793, shortly after the French Revolution,

---

Fun Fact La Ville en Rose

Toulouse is a brick-built city, whereas most cities of the Middle Ages were constructed of stone. In Toulouse, the nearest stone quarries were some 50 miles away. Instead of stone, the builders of Toulouse learned to fashion red bricks from readily available Garonne clays. They were cheap, robust, and rosy, earning the city the nickname of *la ville en rose,* or "the city in pink." Because of the clay, these rose-colored bricks were lighter in tone than those in other cities such as Albi. For extra grandeur, the builders of Toulouse trimmed their bricks in white marble, giving the city an architectural touch of elegance and splendor.

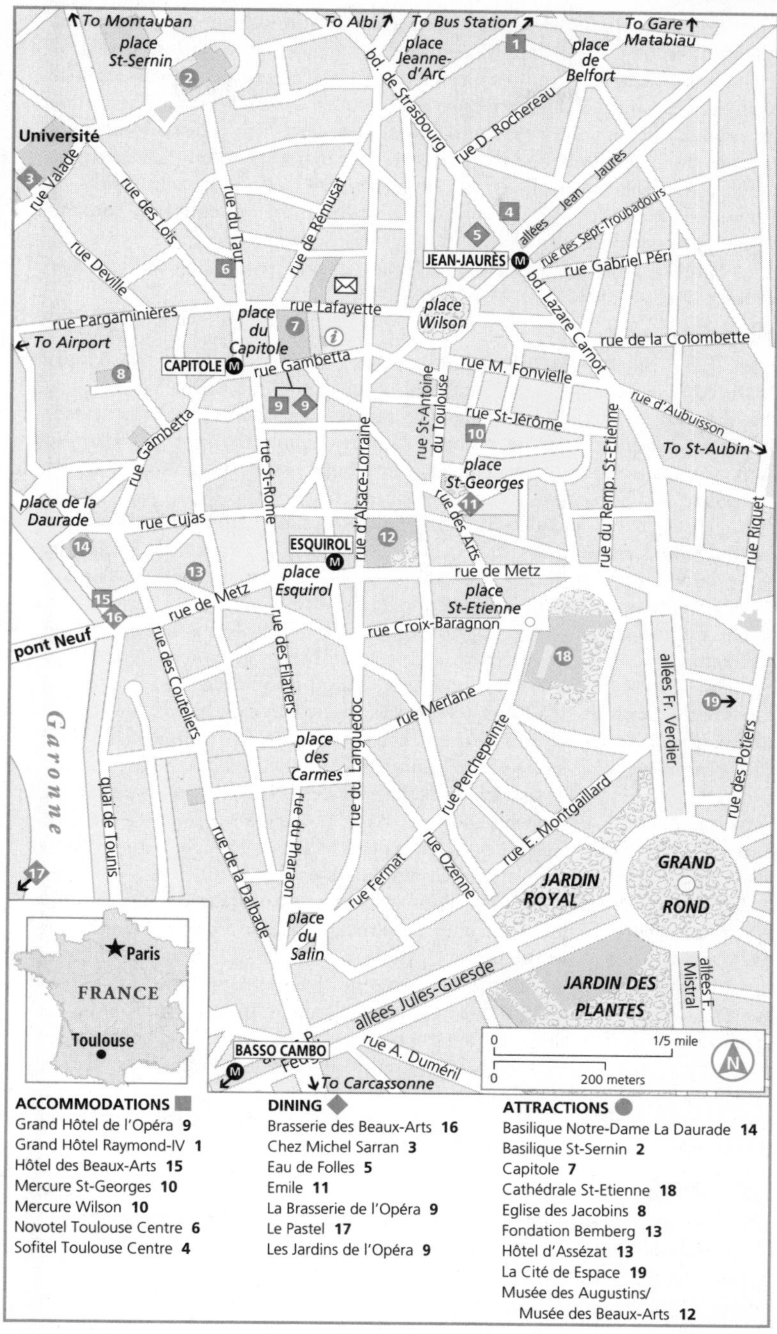
To Montauban
place St-Sernin
To Albi
To Bus Station
place Jeanne-d'Arc
To Gare Matabiau
place de Belfort
bd. de Strasbourg
rue D. Rochereau
Université
rue Valade
rue des Lois
rue du Taur
rue de Rémusat
allées Jean Jaurès
rue des Sept-Troubadours
JEAN-JAURÈS
rue Gabriel Péri
rue Deville
bd. Lazare Carnot
rue Pargaminières
place du Capitole
rue Lafayette
place Wilson
To Airport
rue de la Colombette
CAPITOLE
rue Gambetta
rue M. Fonvielle
rue d'Aubuisson
rue St-Antoine du Toulouse
rue St-Jérôme
rue Gambetta
rue St-Rome
rue d'Alsace-Lorraine
place St-Georges
rue du Remp. St-Etienne
To St-Aubin
place de la Daurade
rue Cujas
rue des Arts
rue Riquet
ESQUIROL
place Esquirol
rue de Metz
place St-Etienne
rue de Metz
pont Neuf
rue Croix-Baragnon
rue des Couteliers
rue des Filatiers
allées Fr. Verdier
Garonne
rue Merlane
rue Perchepeinte
place des Carmes
rue du Languedoc
rue des Potiers
quai de Tounis
rue du Pharaon
rue de la Dalbade
rue E. Montgaillard
rue Ozenne
rue Fermat
JARDIN ROYAL
GRAND ROND
place du Salin
Paris
FRANCE
Toulouse
allées Jules-Guesde
JARDIN DES PLANTES
allées F. Mistral
BASSO CAMBO
rue A. Duméril
To Carcassonne
0
1/5 mile
0
200 meters
N
ACCOMMODATIONS
Grand Hôtel de l'Opéra 9
Grand Hôtel Raymond-IV 1
Hôtel des Beaux-Arts 15
Mercure St-Georges 10
Mercure Wilson 10
Novotel Toulouse Centre 6
Sofitel Toulouse Centre 4
DINING
Brasserie des Beaux-Arts 16
Chez Michel Sarran 3
Eau de Folles 5
Emile 11
La Brasserie de l'Opéra 9
Le Pastel 17
Les Jardins de l'Opéra 9
ATTRACTIONS
Basilique Notre-Dame La Daurade 14
Basilique St-Sernin 2
Capitole 7
Cathédrale St-Etienne 18
Eglise des Jacobins 8
Fondation Bemberg 13
Hôtel d'Assézat 13
La Cité de Espace 19
Musée des Augustins/
Musée des Beaux-Arts 12

when revolutionary acts closed one of the city's most important monasteries and readapted it for public use. In addition to the fabulous paintings, a stroll through this place gives you the chance to view a 14th-century monastery in all its mystical splendor. This museum's 14th-century cloisters contain the world's largest and most valuable collection of Romanesque capitals. The sculptures and carvings are magnificent, and there are some fine examples of early Christian sarcophagi. On the upper floors is a large painting collection, with works by Toulouse-Lautrec, Gérard, Delacroix, and Ingres. The museum also contains several portraits by Antoine Rivalz, a local artist of major talent.

23 rue de Metz. ✆ **05-61-22-21-82.** Admission 3€, free for children 11 and under. Wed 10am–9pm; Thurs–Mon 10am–6pm. Closed May 1, Dec 25, and Jan 1.

MORE SIGHTS

The Gothic brick **Eglise des Jacobins** ★★, parvis des Jacobins (✆ **05-61-22-23-82**), is in Old Toulouse, west of place du Capitole along rue Lakanal. The convent, daring in its architecture, has been restored and forms the largest extant monastery complex in France. It's open daily throughout the year from 10am to 6pm. Entrance to most of the complex is free, but a visit to the cloisters is 2.50€ per person.

Small, charming, and dating mostly from the 18th century, the **Basilique Notre-Dame La Daurade** is at 7 quai de la Daurade (✆ **05-61-21-38-32**); its name derives from the gilding that covers some of its partially baroque exterior. It's open daily from 8am to 7pm. Admission is free.

The **Capitole** ★, place du Capitole (✆ **05-61-22-29-22**), is an outstanding achievement in civic architecture and one of the most potent symbols of Toulouse itself. Built in 1753, it houses the **Hôtel de Ville** (city hall), plus the **Théâtre du Capitole** (✆ **05-61-63-13-13**), where concerts, ballets, and operas are presented. Renovated in 1996, the theater is outfitted in an Italian-inspired 18th-century style in shades of scarlet and gold. In the Hotel de Ville, the only area that can be visited is the richly ornate **Salle des Illustres,** where you can see portraits of personalities who influenced the politics or culture of the city. Entrance is free. The Capitole complex is open Monday through Saturday from 9am to noon and 2 to 6pm (no afternoon hours on Sat).

The city has a number of fine old mansions, most of them dating from the Renaissance when Toulouse was one of the richest cities in Europe. The finest is the **Hôtel d'Assézat,** on rue de Metz. Built in 1555, it has an unaltered 16th-century courtyard. It houses the Académie des Jeux-Floraux (Academy of the Floral Games), whose purpose is to uphold the highest literary traditions of the region. Since 1323, it has presented to poets awards of flowers made of wrought metal. The mansion is also the headquarters of the above-mentioned Fondation Bemberg.

After all that sightseeing, head for the oval **place Wilson,** a showcase 19th-century square boasting fashionable cafes.

SHOPPING

The streets to attack during your shopping frenzy include **rue St-Rome** and **rue d'Alsace-Lorraine,** both of which are especially rich in clothing and housewares. This town has a great shopping mall, **Centre Commercial St-Georges,** rue du Rempart St-Etienne, where you can fill your suitcases with all kinds of glittery loot. But for upscale clothing boutiques, head for **rue Croix-Baragnon** and **rue des Arts,** and the **rue St-Antoine du T.**

The pearly gates of antiques heaven can be found on **rue Fermat.** More downmarket antiques are sprawled out each Sunday from 8am to noon during the weekly **flea market** that's conducted adjacent to the Basilique St-Sernin. In addition to that, there's a sale of knickknacks *(brocante)* on the first weekend (Fri–Sun 8am–1pm) of every month. Here, the contents of attics that have been undisturbed since the invasion of Normandy are disgorged, with trash and possible treasures as well, into the light of day.

In addition, **Violettes & Pastels,** 10 rue St-Pantaléon (✆ **05-61-22-14-22**), and **Péniche Maison de la Violette,** Canal du Midi, just in front of the rail station (✆ **05-61-90-01-30**), offer everything imaginable connected with violets, from violet-scented perfume to silk scarves patterned with the dainty purple flower.

WHERE TO STAY

EXPENSIVE

Grand Hôtel de l'Opéra ★★★ This is the most elegant and tranquil oasis in Toulouse. The owners of this opulent hotel have won several prestigious awards for transforming a 17th-century building (once a convent) into a sophisticated new address. The public rooms contain early-19th-century antiques, with Napoleonic-inspired tenting over the bars. Some of the spacious, stylish guest rooms have urn-shape balustrades overlooking formal squares, and all have high ceilings and modern luxuries. The comfortable beds are elegantly attired. Bathrooms include robes and deluxe toiletries.

1 place du Capitole, 31000 Toulouse. ✆ **05-61-21-82-66.** Fax 05-61-23-41-04. www.grand-hotel-opera.com. 57 units. 149€–211€ double; 252€–299€ suite. AE, DC, MC, V. Parking 12.50€. Métro: Capitole. **Amenities:** 2 restaurants; bar; health club; sauna; limited room service; laundry service; dry cleaning. *In room:* A/C, TV, minibar, hair dryer, safe.

Sofitel Toulouse Centre ★★ *Kids* Business travelers deem this eight-story hotel the best in town (though we still prefer the Grand Hôtel de l'Opéra as the choicest, most tranquil retreat). Adjacent to place Wilson, this Sofitel employs a charming bilingual staff and offers rooms for travelers with disabilities and suites big enough to fit an entire family or serve as an office away from the office. Rooms are furnished in an international chain format, and each unit comes with a first-rate tiled bathroom.

84 allées Jean-Jaurès, 31000 Toulouse. ✆ **05-61-10-23-10.** Fax 05-61-10-23-16. www.sofitel.com. 119 units. 200€–205€ double; 197€–297€ suite. AE, DC, MC, V. Parking 12.50€. Métro: Jean-Jaurès. **Amenities:** Restaurant; bar; health club; 24-hr. room service; babysitting; laundry service; dry cleaning. *In room:* A/C, TV, minibar, hair dryer.

MODERATE

Grand Hôtel Raymond-IV On a quiet street close to the town center and the train station, this antique building contains pleasantly decorated rooms with bland yet comfortable furniture. All units come with a modern, compact bathroom. The location means that you're within walking distance of the historic quarter and its theaters, shops, and nightclubs. Although breakfast is the only meal served, the English-speaking staff will direct you to nearby restaurants.

16 rue Raymond-IV, 31000 Toulouse. ✆ **05-61-62-89-41.** Fax 05-61-62-38-01. 38 units. 90€–145€ double. AE, DC, MC, V. Parking 10€. Métro: Jean-Jaurès or Capitole. *In room:* A/C in some units, TV, minibar.

Hôtel des Beaux-Arts ★ *Value* Occupying a dignified pink-brick villa built 250 years ago on the banks of the Garonne, this charming hotel is in the heart of town. Despite the historic facade, the well-equipped, soundproofed rooms are contemporary, refined, and comfortable, each decorated with an original piece of modern art. Bathrooms are clean and compact. Breakfast is the only meal served.

1 place du pont-Neuf, 31000 Toulouse. ✆ **05-34-45-42-42.** Fax 05-34-45-42-43. www.hoteldesbeauxarts.com. 19 units. 105€–151€ double; 175€ junior suite. AE, DC, MC, V. Parking 5€. **Amenities:** Nearby restaurant owned by hotel; limited room service; babysitting; dry cleaning. *In room:* A/C, TV, minibar, hair dryer, safe.

Mercure St-Georges Just a few paces from the Mercure Wilson (see below; the two share staff and management), this seven-story hotel is the less historic twin of the older and cozier-looking hotel. Decor here is rigidly standardized—bedrooms are identical, though comfortably modern, with small, clean bathrooms. Business travelers are the primary clientele at this location.

Rue St.-Jérome (place Occitaine), 31000 Toulouse. ✆ **05-62-27-79-79.** Fax 05-62-27-79-00. 148 units. 85€–120€ double; 160€–230€ suite. AE, DC, MC, V. Parking 15€. Métro: Capitole. **Amenities:** Restaurant; bar; limited room service; laundry service; dry cleaning. *In room:* A/C, TV, minibar, hair dryer, safe.

Mercure Wilson ★ This is the more appealing of the two Mercure hotels that stand almost adjacent to each other in the heart of Toulouse's historic central zone. Built around 1850, it's constructed of the distinctive pink-toned bricks cherished by local preservationists. In 1999, Mercure radically upgraded the hotel's interior, transforming it into one of the most up-to-date middle-bracket places in town. Most bedrooms are a comfortable size, and in spite of their chain format, furnishings are agreeable. There's no restaurant on the premises, but guests can easily migrate a few steps to the premises of the Mercure St-Georges (see above).

7 rue Labéda, 31000 Toulouse. ✆ **05-34-45-40-60.** Fax 05-34-45-40-61. 95 units. 115€–160€ double; 175€–200€ suite. AE, DC, MC, V. Parking 11€. Métro: Capitole. **Amenities:** Bar; lounge; laundry service; dry cleaning. *In room:* A/C, TV, minibar, hair dryer.

Novotel Toulouse Centre Set in the most verdant part of Toulouse's center, this modern and efficient hotel is a few paces from the city's Japanese gardens. The Matabiau train station is within a 5-minute walk, and the nerve center of the old city, place St-Sernin, is less than half a mile away. All rooms are alike, each with a single bed (which can be converted into a couch), a double bed, a long writing desk, and a roomy, fully equipped bathroom. In spite of the chain-style format, this is one of the best Novotel hotels, with larger than usual bedrooms and quality mattresses on the beds.

5 place Alfonse-Jourdain, 31000 Toulouse. ✆ **05-61-21-74-74.** Fax 05-61-22-81-22. 131 units. 103€ double; 142€ suite. AE, DC, MC, V. Parking 7€. Bus: 1 or 2. **Amenities:** Restaurant; bar; pool; limited room service; babysitting; laundry service; dry cleaning. *In room:* A/C, TV, minibar, hair dryer.

WHERE TO DINE

EXPENSIVE

Chez Michel Sarran ★★★ MODERN FRENCH The most stylish and consistently praised restaurant in Toulouse occupies two dining rooms in the heart of town, on two separate floors of a building near the Novotel Centre; one dignified and contemporary-looking dining room is upholstered with beige-toned linen from the popular Provençal upholsterer Soleiado. You'll enjoy the well-cultivated cuisine of rising star Michel Sarran. Your order might be taken by his wife, Françoise, who will suggest something from the very fresh, very creative array of dishes that have attracted diners as diverse as the prime minister of France and showbiz types like Sophie Marceau and Gilbert Becaud. Food seems designed to bring out the savors of southern and southwestern France, and is usually permeated with the pungency of fresh herbs and seafood. Examples include a salad of braised crawfish with crabmeat and a tapenade of olives, grilled snapper with caramelized tomatoes and sweet Basque tomatoes stuffed with anchovies, and grilled foie gras in a duck meat bouillon with sage and Parmesan. And dessert might be ravioli stuffed with creamed oranges and served with an aspic of sweet white Gaillac wine.

21 bd. Armand du Portal. ✆ **05-61-12-32-32.** www.michel-sarran.com. Reservations recommended. Main courses 25€–32€; fixed-price menus 70€–100€. AE, MC, V. Mon–Fri noon–2pm and 8–9:45pm. Closed Aug and 1 week around Christmas. Métro: Capitole.

Le Pastel ★★ MODERN FRENCH One of Toulouse's most luxurious and appealing restaurants occupies a stone-sided manor house built around 1850. Today the structure is the domain of Paris-trained chef and entrepreneur Gérard Garrigues. The setting is as restful as the cuisine is superb: Terraces ringed with flowers and a pair of dining rooms whose walls are accented with paintings by local artists (the works are for sale) contribute to the feeling of reflective calm and well-being. Menu items change about every 2 weeks, a policy that's tactfully explained by the mistress of the dining room, Marie-Noelle Garrigues. During our visit, the menu featured such game dishes as partridge cooked "in the Russian style," in a terrine with foie gras and puffy pastry, and sealed in with its own juices; filet of line-caught sea bass prepared in a minestrone of shellfish; caramelized turnips served as a *"tarte tatin"* and topped with pan-seared foie gras; and pigeon stuffed with pine nuts and dried fruit, served on a bed of braised cabbage. Wine choices are as comprehensive and sophisticated as anything else you're likely to find in Toulouse.

237 route de St-Simon. ✆ **05-62-87-84-30.** Reservations required. Main courses 22€–32€; fixed-price menus 29€–40€ lunch, 47€–74€ dinner. AE, DC, MC, V. Tues–Sat noon–2pm and 8–9:30pm. Métro: Basso-Cambo.

Les Jardins de l'Opéra ★★★ FRENCH The entrance to the city's best restaurant is in the 18th-century Florentine courtyard of the Grand Hôtel. The dining area is a series of intimate salons, several of which face a winter garden and a reflecting pool. You'll be greeted by the gracious Maryse Toulousy, whose husband, Dominique, prepares what critics have called the perfect combination of modern and old French cuisine. The outstanding menu listings are likely to include a salad of scallops and purple artichokes; tournedos of rabbit and fresh foie gras with a pepper sauce; and crawfish served in a mushroom-enriched puff pastry. His *vice versa de poivron rouge et calmar* is a tour de force: Calamari is stuffed with roasted red peppers in a red pepper sauce, and roasted red peppers are stuffed with calamari and flavored with squid ink. Desserts feature a sophisticated array of soufflés and tarts, some of which must be ordered at the beginning of the meal. A particularly luscious dessert—you can order it spontaneously, depending on how much appetite you have left at the end of the meal—is roasted figs stuffed with vanilla ice cream, drenched with Banyuls wine.

In the Grand Hôtel de l'Opéra, 1 place du Capitole. ✆ **05-61-23-07-76.** Reservations required. Main courses 29€–38€; fixed-price menus 40€–88€ lunch, 48€–92€ dinner. AE, DC, MC, V. Tues–Sat noon–2pm; Mon–Sat 8–10pm. Closed Jan 1–4 and July 28–Aug 29. Métro: Capitole.

MODERATE

Brasserie des Beaux-Arts TRADITIONAL FRENCH This turn-of-the-20th-century brasserie offers a pure and authentic Art Nouveau decor that's been enhanced because of its connection with the Jean Bucher chain. (They're the most successful directors of Art Nouveau French brasseries in the world, with at least a dozen similar places, some of which are classified as national historic monuments.) The carefully restored decor includes walnut paneling and many mirrors, and the cuisine emphasizes well-prepared seafood and all the predictable local dishes, including cassoulet, magrêt of duckling, lightly smoked salmon served with lentils and mussels, and confit of duckling. Try the foie gras or country-style sauerkraut, accompanied by the house Riesling, served in an earthenware pitcher. During warm weather, eat on the terrace. The staff here is likely to be hysterical during peak times, and when that happens, they tend to become less than suave.

1 quai de la Daurade. ✆ **05-61-21-12-12.** Reservations recommended. Main courses 15€–22€; fixed-price menus 22€–29€. AE, DC, MC, V. Daily noon–2:30pm and 7:30pm–1am. Métro: Esquirol.

Emile ★ *Finds* TOULOUSIEN In an old-fashioned house on one of the most beautiful squares of Toulouse, this restaurant offers the specialties of chef François Ferrier. In winter, meals are served one floor above street level in a cozy enclave overlooking the square; in summer, the venue moves to the street-level dining room and the flower-filled terrace. Menu choices include *cassoulet toulousain, magret de canard* (duck) traditional style, a medley of Catalonian fish, and grilled fish with a pungently aromatic cold sauce of sweet peppers and olive oil. The wine *carte* (menu) is filled with intriguing surprises.

13 place St-Georges. ✆ **05-61-21-05-56.** Reservations recommended. Main courses 16€–24€; fixed-price menus 20€–35€ lunch, 39€–45€ dinner. AE, DC, MC, V. Tues–Sat noon–2pm and 7–10:30pm (mid-May to Sept Mon 7–10:30pm). Métro: Capitole or Esquirol.

Le Brasserie de l'Opéra FRENCH Le Brasserie, in the most prestigious hotel in the city, evokes memories of the old Brasserie Lipp in Paris. It is warmly decorated with rich cove moldings, lots of burnished hardwood, shimmering glass, and cut flowers. Fresh shellfish is featured. Other specialties include filet of braised red snapper, duck stew, "butterfly oysters," and an array of *plats du jour,* or dishes of the day, based on traditional brasserie cuisine. Seasonal ingredients are used "with respect," in the words of one food critic.

In the Grand Hôtel de l'Opéra, 1 place du Capitole. ✆ **05-61-21-37-03.** Reservations recommended. Main courses 15€–23€; fixed-price lunch 22.50€. AE, DC, MC, V. Daily noon–11:30pm. Closed Aug 1–15. Métro: Capitole.

INEXPENSIVE

Eau de Folles *Value* TRADITIONAL FRENCH A relative newcomer to the restaurant scene in Toulouse, this restaurant's low prices and the variety of its menu promise to make it a long-term contender. Within a mostly white, *fin-de-siècle* setting that includes lots of mirrors, you'll be offered a fixed-price menu with a choice of 10 starters, 10 main courses, and 10 desserts. Menu items vary according to the inspiration of the chef, the availability of fresh ingredients, and whatever happens to be in stock on the day of your visit. You might begin with a marinade of fish, followed with strips of duck meat with green pepper sauce, and end it all with a homemade pastry such as a *tarte tatin* or a cup of rice pudding. Everything is very simple, served within a cramped but convivial setting.

14 allée du Président Roosevelt. ✆ **05-61-23-45-50.** Reservations recommended. Fixed-price menu 22€. No credit cards. Mon–Sat noon–1:30pm and 7–11pm. Métro: Capitole.

WHERE TO STAY & DINE NEARBY

Hôtel de Diane ★ *Finds* This hotel/restaurant surrounded by a 2-hectare (5-acre) park is the most tranquil retreat in the area. In a *fin-de-siècle* villa with comfortable, simple, yet refined rooms, it appeals to people who want to be away from the traffic and congestion of the inner city. Bedrooms are a standard motel size, and though bathrooms are not large, you'll find adequate space to spread out your stuff. The bungalow-style units are built side by side in a row facing the park; none has a kitchen, but each has a private terrace and private parking. The rustic atmosphere befits this getaway, where there are groves of pines and venerable hardwoods. The restaurant, Saint-Simon, offers a choice of meals in the garden or the Louis XV–style dining room. In spite of the attentive service and gracious welcome, the food is somewhat uneven—sometimes delicious, other times less so.

3 route de St-Simon, 31100 St-Simon. © **05-61-07-59-52.** Fax 05-61-86-38-94. 32 units, 13 bungalows. 68.60€–72€ double; 75€–78€ bungalow. AE, DC, MC, V. Free parking. Take D23 to exit 27, 8km (5 miles) SW from Toulouse. **Amenities:** Restaurant; bar; outdoor pool; room service during mealtimes; self-service laundry. *In room:* TV, minibar, hair dryer.

La Flanerie *Value* Set within a verdant, 6-acre garden that slopes down to the edge of the Garonne, this establishment is carved from an 1850 farm. Bedroom furnishings have been carefully selected and include a high level of style and, in some cases, canopied beds and some genuine antiques. These include fine marquetry desks, bronze lighting fixtures, and other remnants of *fin-de-siècle* France. A small bathroom comes with each unit. The hotel has a swimming pool and is permeated with a dignified air. For dining options, the owner directs guests to the nearby village of La Croix Salgarde, which has a number of little restaurants along its main street.

Route de Lacroix-Falgarde, 31320 Vieille-Toulouse. © **05-61-73-39-12.** Fax 05-61-73-18-56. 12 units. 67€–98€ double. AE, MC, V. Free parking. Bus: R. Take the D4 S of Toulouse for 8km (5 miles). Closed Feb 1–15. **Amenities:** Outdoor pool. *In room:* A/C, TV, minibar.

TOULOUSE AFTER DARK

The theater, dance, and opera in Toulouse are often on a par with that found in Paris. The best way to stay on top of the city's arts scene is to pick up a copy of the free monthly magazine *Toulouse Culture* from the Office de Tourisme.

One of the city's most notable theaters is the **Théâtre du Capitole,** place du Capitole (© **05-61-22-31-31**), which offers opera, operetta, and works from the classical French repertoire. The **Théâtre de la Digue,** 3 rue de la Digue (© **05-61-42-97-79**), presents ballet and works by local theater companies; and the **Halle aux Grains,** place Dupuy (© **05-61-62-02-70**), is the venue for many pop and classical concerts. Another contender is the **Théâtre Garonne,** 1 av. du Château d'Eau (© **05-61-48-56-56**), offering everything from works by Molière to 20th-century existentialist dramas. Yet another important entertainment venue is the **Théâtre Zenith,** 11 av. Raymond-Badiou (© **05-62-74-49-49**). Thanks to a large stage and a big seating capacity, it's usually the venue for rock concerts, variety acts, and musical comedies brought here from other European cities. A smaller competitor, with a roughly equivalent mix of music, theater, and entertainment, is the **Théâtre de la Cité,** 1 rue Pierre Baudis (© **05-34-45-05-00**).

The liveliest squares to wander after dark are place du Capitole, place St-Georges, place St-Pierre, and just off rue St-Rome and rue des Filatiers.

For bars and pubs, check out the Latin flair of **La Tantina de Bourgos,** 27 rue de la Garonette (© **05-61-55-59-29**), popular as a student scene; and the rowdier **Chez Tonton,** 16 place St-Pierre (© **05-61-21-89-54**), with its *après-*match frolicking atmosphere, complete with the winning soccer team boozing it up. A particularly popular bar with both live and recorded music is **Monsieur**

Carnaval, 34 rue Bayard (✆ **05-61-99-14-56**), the site of lots of jiving, rocking, and rolling *a la française.*

You'll find dozens of bars in the 18th-century neighborhood around the place Wilson, near Le Capitole, but a selection of some of the most charming include the mostly metal-sheathed **Les Deux G.,** Pont-Neuf (✆ **05-61-12-39-29**); **Bar Benachine,** 37 place des Carmes (✆ **05-61-55-57-59**), which is modern, blue-toned, and sometimes animated; and the very small, very intimate **Le Figue,** 6 place de la Colombette (✆ **05-61-99-61-87**).

Downtown Toulouse after dark can pulse with energy and, in some cases, abandon. A particularly popular disco is **Cockpit,** 1 rue du Puits-Vert (✆ **05-61-21-87-53**). Set near Le Capitol and the nocturnally animated place Wilson, it caters to a danceaholic clientele that incorporates, as any good disco does, a mixed clientele of males, females, straights, gays, and in-betweens.

Mostly heterosexuals migrate to **Disco La Strada,** 4 rue Gabrielle-Peri (✆ **05-34-41-15-65**), which begins to get animated every Wednesday through Saturday after 11pm; and a vaguely Iberian-looking establishment, **Bar La Bodega Bodega,** 1 rue Gabrielle-Peri (✆ **05-61-63-03-63**). With a scene that's more hip and fashionable than that of many of its competitors, it features recorded music and a venue where many friends seem to meet spontaneously over drinks.

As you enter **Le New Shanghai,** 12 rue de la Pomme (✆ **05-61-23-37-80**), you notice that this is a man's dance domain playing the latest in techno; venturing farther inside, you'll discover that it gives way to a darker, sexy cruise-bar environment with lots of hot men on the prowl. Plan on paying 8.50€ to get in on Friday and Saturday.

2 Auch ★

726km (451 miles) SW of Paris; 203km (126 miles) SE of Bordeaux; 64km (40 miles) W of Toulouse

The lively market town of Auch is on the west bank of the Gers in the heart of the ancient Duchy of Gascony, of which it was once the capital.

ESSENTIALS

GETTING THERE Five to 10 SNCF **trains** or **buses** per day run between Toulouse and Auch (trip time: 1½ hr.); 6 to 13 SNCF buses (✆ **05-62-05-73-37**) arrive in Auch daily from Agen (trip time: 1½ hr.). For rail information, call ✆ **08-36-35-35-35.** If you're **driving** to Auch, take N124 west from Toulouse.

VISITOR INFORMATION The **Office de Tourisme** is at place de la Cathédrale (✆ **05-62-05-22-89;** www.mairie-auch.fr).

EXPLORING THE TOWN

The town is divided into an upper and a lower quarter, connected by several flights of steps. In the old part of town in the upper quarter, the narrow streets, called *pousterles,* center on **place Salinis,** from which there's a good view of the Pyrénées. Branching off from here, the **Escalier Monumental** leads down to the Le Gers river and the lower quarter of town, a descent of 232 steps.

North of place Salinis is the **Cathédrale Ste-Marie** ★★, place de la Cathédrale (✆ **05-62-05-72-71**). Built between the 15th and 17th centuries, this is one of the handsomest Gothic churches in the south of France. It has 113 **Renaissance choir stalls** ★★★ made of carved oak, and a custodian will let you in for 1.50€. The stained-glass windows, also from the Renaissance, are impressive. Its 17th-century organ was one of the finest in the world at the time of Louis XIV. The cathedral is open daily from 8:30am to noon and 2 to 5pm (in winter, daily from 9:30am–noon and 2–5pm).

Next to the cathedral stands the 18th-century **archbishop's palace** with a 14th-century bell tower, the **Tour d'Armagnac,** which was once a prison. The tower and palace are not open to the public.

Most of the shops and boutiques are along **rue Dessoles** and **avenue Alsace.** You'll find everything from confectionery shops to clothing stores. Also consider visiting the **Caves de l'Hôtel de France** ★, rue d'Etigny (✆ **05-62-61-71-71**), for a bottle or two of Armagnac. It has the best selection of this firewater, with more than 100 distilleries represented.

WHERE TO STAY

Hôtel de France (Restaurant Jardin des Saveurs) ★ A lot has changed here since the 1970s, when the Hôtel de France was celebrated. This is no longer a mandatory stop in southern France for serious foodies, but the hotel is a solid and reliable choice even if long stripped of its Michelin stars. It was built around the much-modernized 16th-century core of an old inn. The rooms are comfortable, conservative, and furnished with traditional but somewhat nondescript pieces; some, however, are a bit dowdy. The cuisine here somewhat slavishly follows many of the culinary trends established by the since-retired founder, André Daguin, but with less panache. Today, with kitchens directed by Roland Garreau, the cuisine is "innovative within traditional boundaries." Menu choices include an assortment of preparations of foie gras from Gascony, brochette of oysters with foie gras, a duo of *magrêt de canard* cooked in a rock-salt shell and served with a medley of vegetables, and stuffed pigeon roasted with spiced honey.

Place de la Libération, 32003 Auch CEDEX. ✆ **05-62-61-71-84.** Fax 05-62-61-71-81. auchgarreau@intercom.fr. 29 units. 76€–90€ double; 195€–298€ suite. AE, DC, MC, V. Parking 10€. **Amenities:** Restaurant; bar. *In room:* A/C, TV, minibar.

Le Relais de Gascogne *Value* This hotel, the second best choice in town, offers economical accommodations and meals. The rooms were modernized in the 1990s and are comfortably furnished. Bathrooms are small and neatly organized.

5 av. de la Marne, 32000 Auch. ✆ **05-62-05-26-81.** Fax 05-62-63-30-22. 28 units. 44€–71€ double. MC, V. Parking 5.45€. Closed Dec 20–Jan 15. **Amenities:** Restaurant; limited room service. *In room:* TV.

WHERE TO DINE

Most people still head for the **Hôtel de France** (see above), if only for the memories. But gone are the days when this housed one of the great restaurants in the south of France.

Café Gascon SOUTHWESTERN FRENCH For access to very fresh produce, the owners of this restaurant have only to walk a few steps, into the Halles aux Herbes, a fruit and vegetable market that lies immediately next door. The setting is a stone-fronted 18th century, three-story house with space for the exposition of paintings and photographs, all arranged in a long corridor on the ground floor. There's a cave-like dining room on the street level, but most clients prefer to climb to the top of a wooden staircase to reach the main dining room on the second floor. Here, surrounded by decor that emulates what someone's grandmother might have crafted around the turn of the 20th century (the owners refer to it as *"une décoration bourgeoise"*), you'll be treated to very traditional service rituals (no one ever comes here just for a salad or just a main course). Everything is packaged as part of a three-course fixed-price menu, which might—depending on the inspiration of the chef—include elaborate salads. Two examples include *une* *salade folle* that's garnished with slices of foie gras and duck breast; and *une salade gaillard* that's accented with slices of chicken liver, a generous portion of Camembert, and mushrooms flambéed in Armagnac. Main courses include braised filets of veal with button mushrooms, and braised breast of duckling with a compote of red fruits.

5 rue Lamartine. ✆ **05-62-61-88-08.** Reservations recommended. 3-course fixed-price menus 15.25€–27€. MC, V. July–Aug Tues–Sun noon–2:30pm and 7–9:30pm; Sept–June Mon–Sat noon–2:30pm and Wed–Sat 7–9:30pm.

Le Daroles TRADITIONAL FRENCH Despite its much, much lower prices, this Parisian-style brasserie attracts many of the former clients of the Hôtel de France. Within an old-fashioned setting that includes mirrors, polished copper, mahogany paneling, and leather banquettes, you can enjoy a bustling, no-nonsense cuisine. Examples include strips of duckling with seasonal berries, scallops with herb and wine sauce, sauerkraut, foie gras, and pepper steak.

Place de la Libération. ✆ **05-62-05-00-51.** Fixed-price lunches and dinner 16€. DC, MC, V. Daily 7am–2am.

3 Cordes-sur-Ciel ★★

678km (421 miles) SW of Paris; 25km (15½ miles) NW of Albi

This site is remarkable—it's like an eagle's nest on a hilltop, above the Cérou valley. In days gone by, many celebrities, such as Jean-Paul Sartre and Albert Camus, considered this town a favorite hideaway.

The name Cordes is derived from the textile and leather industries that thrived here during the 13th and 14th centuries. Artisans working with linen and leather prospered, and the town also became known throughout France for its brilliantly colored silks. In the 16th century, however, plagues and religious wars reduced the city to a minor role. A brief renaissance occurred in the 19th century, when automatic weaving machines were introduced.

Today Cordes is an arts-and-crafts city, and many of the ancient houses on the narrow streets contain artisans plying their skills—blacksmiths, enamelers, graphic artists, weavers, engravers, sculptors, and painters.

You must park outside the city and then walk through an arch leading to the old town.

ESSENTIALS

GETTING THERE If you're **driving,** take N88 northwest from Toulouse to Gaillac, turning north on D922 into Cordes-sur-Ciel. **Trains** from Albi to Tessonnières and on to Vindrac run at the rate of two per day (trip time: 1 hr.). Once at Vindrac, you can take a Barrois minibus (✆ **05-63-56-14-80**) the rest of the 5km (3 miles) to Cordes. For train information and schedules, call ✆ **08-36-35-35-35.** For a taxi from Vindrac, call **Taxi Barrois** at ✆ **05-63-14-80.**

VISITOR INFORMATION The **Office de Tourisme** is in the Maison Fonpeyrouse, Grand-Rue Raymond VII (✆ **05-63-56-00-52**).

EXPLORING THE TOWN

Often called "the city of a hundred Gothic arches," Cordes contains numerous **maisons Gothiques** ★★, old houses built of pink sandstone. Many of the doors and windows are fashioned of pointed (broken) arches that still retain their 13th- and 14th-century grace. Some of the best-preserved line **Grand'Rue,** also called **"rue Droite."**

The **Musée d'Art et d'Histoire le Portail-Peint (Musée Charles-Portal),** Grand'Rue (no phone), is named after the archivist of the Tarn region who was also an avid historian of Cordes. The museum is in a medieval house, the foundations of which date from the Gallo-Roman era. It contains everyday artifacts of the textile industry of long ago, farming measures, samples of local embroidery, a reconstructed peasant home interior, and other medieval memorabilia. Official visiting hours are limited to the busiest seasons: In July and August, it's open daily from 11am to 12:30pm and 3:30 to 6:30pm; April through June and September and October, it's officially open only on Sunday and public holidays from 3 to 6pm. If you happen to arrive when the museum is closed, ask someone at the tourist office (see above) to accompany you for your visit; if they're not busy, they often will. Barring that, try to make an appointment for a visit later in the day. Admission is 2.30€ for adults and 1.10€ for children. For information, contact the tourism office (see above).

The **Maison du Grand-Fauconnier (House of the Falcon Master),** Grande'Rue, is named for the falcons carved into the stonework of the wall. A grandly proportioned staircase in the building leads to the **Musée Yves-Brayer** (✆ **05-63-56-00-40**). Yves Brayer moved to Cordes in 1940 and became one of its most ardent civic boosters. After watching Cordes fall gradually into decay, he renewed interest in its restoration. The museum contains minor artifacts relating to the town's history; the most interesting exhibits are rather fanciful scale models of the town itself. The museum is open daily from 10:30am to 12:30pm and 2 to 6pm. Admission costs 3€ for adults and 1.50€ for children 11 and under.

The **Eglise St-Michel,** Grande'Rue, dates from the 13th century, but many alterations have been made since. From the top of the tower you can view the surrounding area. Much of the lateral design of the side chapels was likely influenced by the cathedral at Albi. Before being shipped here, the organ (dating from 1830) was in Notre-Dame de Paris. The church can be visited only as part of guided visits arranged through the tourist office. With many exceptions, they're usually organized every day at 11am and 3pm, last for about an hour, and cost 3.80€ for adults and 1.50€ for students and children under 18.

WHERE TO STAY & DINE

Bistrot Tonin'ty *Value* FRENCH This is the least expensive, and the least fussy, of the several restaurants in Cordes that are owned and operated by Yves Thuriès, a celebrity chef whose recipes have been publicized, and praised, throughout France. (The most upscale of the restaurants in the group is Hôtel le Grand Ecuyer; see below.) During clement weather, you'll dine on aluminum furniture beneath a majestically gnarled 300-year-old wisteria vine whose blue-violet blossoms perfume the courtyard every spring. Otherwise, there's a mostly scarlet-toned dining room, with massive ceiling beams and smallish tables with immaculate napery. Menu items focus on the time-tested, the flavorful, and the traditional and include, among others, cassoulet, a croustade of magret of duckling layered with apples; foie gras that's redolent with spices; roasted salmon in the style of the chef; and a tempting array of sophisticated salads. Prices here are kept deliberately low, with all but a few of the main courses priced 7.50€ each.

The restaurant is the centerpiece of L'Hostellerie du Vieux Cordes; see the review below for more details.

Rue St-Michel, 81170 Cordes. ✆ **05-63-53-79-20.** www.thuries.fr. Reservations recommended. Main courses 7.50€–11.50€. Fixed-price menu (5 courses) 32€. AE, DC, MC, V. Open only Easter–Oct, daily noon–2:30pm and 7:30–9:30pm.

Hostellerie du Parc *Value* TRADITIONAL FRENCH This century-old stone house offers generous meals in a wooded garden or paneled dining room. Specialties of the house are unusual and, in many cases, charming, featuring such dishes as paté of pheasant garnished with foie gras, a ballotine of guinea fowl served with sweetbreads, and a confit of roasted rabbit with pink garlic from the nearby town of Lautrec.

The hotel offers 17 simply furnished rooms with private bathrooms. A double costs 60€ to 65€. Lessons in French cuisine are offered by the chef during your stay (in English).

Les Cabannes, 81170 Cordes. ✆ **05-63-56-02-59.** Fax 05-63-56-18-03. Reservations recommended. Main courses 12€–23€; fixed-price menus 22€–48€. AE, DC, MC, V. Apr–Oct daily noon–2pm and 7–10pm; Sun noon–2pm. Nov 15–Feb 15 closed Sun–Mon at dinner. Take route de St-Antonin (D600) for about 1km (¾ mile) west from the town center.

Hôtel le Grand Ecuyer ★★★ MODERN FRENCH The medieval monument that contains this restaurant (the 15th-c. hunting lodge of Raymond VII, comte de Toulouse) is classified as a national historic treasure. But despite its glamour and undeniable charm, the restaurant remains intimate and unstuffy. Chef Yves Thuriès prepares platters that have made his dining room an almost mandatory stop. Specialties include three confits of lobster, red mullet salad with fondue of vegetables, a confit of pigeon with olive oil and rosemary, and noisette of lamb in chicory sauce. The dessert selection is almost overwhelming.

The hotel contains 12 rooms and 1 suite, all with antiques and an undeniable sense of the Middle Ages blended with modern comforts. Doubles cost 120€ to 132€; the suite is 220€. The most-desired room, honoring former guest Albert Camus, has a four-poster bed and a fireplace.

Rue Voltaire, 81170 Cordes. ✆ **05-63-53-79-50.** Fax 05-63-53-79-51. www.thuries.fr. Reservations required. Main courses 27€–39€; fixed-price menus 32€–80€. AE, DC, MC, V. Easter–June Tues–Sun 7–9:30pm; July–Oct Wed–Sun noon–2pm and 7–9:30pm. Closed Oct 15 to Easter.

L'Hostellerie du Vieux Cordes This stylish and sophisticated inn is set midway along the length of the walled-in medieval city, within what was originally built in the 1200s as the monastery associated with the Eglise St-Michel, which sits immediately next door. Its centerpiece is its restaurant, a glamorous yet intimate affair (see Bistrot Tonin'ty, above). Public areas, including the scarlet-colored dining room, are more richly furnished than the bedrooms, which are outfitted with ceiling beams and massive wooden furniture that includes, in most cases, a bulky armoire. None of them is air-conditioned, but thanks to windows whose views sometimes sweep out over the valley, and ceiling fans, they're on the receiving end of welcome breezes. Each is accessed via a winding stone staircase that passes such atmosphere-inducing accessories as full suits of armor. Each room was renovated in the late 1990s or later, and each has a contemporary-looking tile-sheathed bathroom.

Rue St-Michel, 81170 Cordes. Tel. **05-63-53-79-20.** Fax 05-63-56-02-47. www.thuries.fr. 21 units. 45€–63€ double. AE, DC, MC, V. Free parking. Closed Jan. **Amenities:** Restaurant; bar; limited room service; babysitting; laundry service. *In room:* TV.

4 Albi

697km (433 miles) SW of Paris; 76km (47 miles) NE of Toulouse

The "red city" of Albi straddles both banks of the Tarn River. The cathedral and the bridges spanning the river are made of brick, as are most of the town's buildings, earning Albi its title—in the rosy glow of a setting sun, Albi often looks as if it were in flames, a spectacular sight.

The town is the birthplace of the famous painter Toulouse-Lautrec and contains an important museum of his works. The town's history has been stormy. The fortified cathedral that broods over the medieval center is a reminder of the bloody struggle between the Roman Catholic Church and the Cathars, a religious group the Church considered heretical. They were also called Albigenses after the town, which was an important center of their movement.

ESSENTIALS

GETTING THERE Fifteen **trains** per day link Toulouse with Albi (trip time: 1 hr.). There's also a Paris-Albi night train; for **rail** information, call ✆ **08-36-35-35-35.** If you're **driving** from Toulouse, take N88 northeast.

VISITOR INFORMATION The **Office de Tourisme** is in the Palais de la Serbie, place Ste-Cécile (✆ **05-63-49-48-80**).

SEEING THE SIGHTS

Cathédrale Ste-Cécile ★★★ Fortified with ramparts and parapets, this cathedral was built in 1282 by the lord bishop during the Albigensian Crusade, waged by the Church against the Cathars and the comte de Toulouse. The church contains frescoes and paintings; exceptional is the 16th-century rood screen with its unique polychromatic statues from the Old and New Testaments.

Opposite the north side of the cathedral is the **Palais de la Berbie** (Archbishop's Palace), another fortified structure dating from the late 13th century.

Near place du Vigan, in the medieval center of town. ✆ **05-63-43-23-43.** Cathédrale 2€; treasury 4€ adults, 3€ ages 12–25, free for ages 11 and under. June–Oct daily 8:30am–6:45pm; Nov–May daily 9am–noon and 2–6:30pm.

Musée Toulouse-Lautrec ★★ This is the world's most important collection of the artist's paintings—more than 600 specimens. His family bequeathed the works remaining in his studio. Toulouse-Lautrec was born in Albi on November 24, 1864, into a much-intermarried family of aristocrats whose ancestors can be traced back to Charlemagne. He was the only surviving child in a family probably genetically prone to pycnodysostosis, a form of dwarfism, and skeletal disorders. Despite his physical shortcomings, no one can debate the titanic dimensions of

Toulouse-Lautrec: Little Big Man

Although he spent most of his life in Paris, Toulouse-Lautrec is closely connected with Albi. He was born in Albi in the **Hôtel Bosc;** it's still a private home and cannot be toured, but there's a plaque on the wall of the building at 14 rue Toulouse-Lautrec in the historic town core.

You can visit the family's **Château de Bosc,** Camjac, 12800 Naucelle (✆ **05-65-69-20-83**), 29 miles from Toulouse. It was built in 1180 and renovated in the 1400s. The present owner, Mademoiselle de Céleran, and her team welcome visitors interested in Toulouse-Lautrec, but it's best to call ahead because tours are guided. It is usually open daily from 9am to 7pm. Admission is 4.55€ for adults, 3.05€ for children 8 to 14, and free for children 7 and under.

Toulouse-Lautrec's art. He is best known for his paintings, posters, and sketches of characters in music halls and circuses. The museum also owns paintings by Degas, Bonnard, Matisse, Utrillo, and Rouault.

Opposite the north side of the cathedral. ✆ **05-63-49-48-70.** Admission 4.50€ adults, 2.50€ students, free for children under 14. Apr–Sept daily 9am–6pm; Oct–Mar Wed–Mon 10am–noon and 2–5pm. Closed Dec 25 and Jan 1.

WHERE TO STAY

Hostellerie St-Antoine ★★ This 250-year-old hotel has been owned by the same family for five generations; today it's managed by Jacques and Jean-François Rieux. Their mother focused on Toulouse-Lautrec when designing the hotel, since her grandfather was a friend of the painter and was given a few of his paintings, sketches, and prints. Several are in the lounge, which opens onto a rear garden. The rooms have been delightfully decorated, with a sophisticated use of color, good reproductions, and occasional antiques. Units are generally spacious, furnished with French provincial pieces, and have midsize bathrooms.

Even if you're not staying at the hotel, the dining room is definitely worth a visit. The Rieux culinary tradition is revealed in the traditional yet creative cuisine, and everything tastes better washed down with Gaillac wines.

17 rue St-Antoine, 81000 Albi. ✆ **05-63-54-04-04.** Fax 05-63-47-10-47. www.saint-antoine-albi.com. 44 units. 100€–145€ double; 220€ suite. AE, DC, MC, V. Parking 6.50€. **Amenities:** Recommended restaurant; limited room service; babysitting; dry cleaning. *In room:* A/C, TV, minibar, hair dryer.

Hôtel Chiffre *Value* This hotel in the city center was built as lodgings for passengers on the mail coaches that hauled letters and people across southern France. Today, despite renovations, it maintains the original porch that sheltered carriages from the rain and sun. The rooms are outfitted with an artful kind of coziness, with upholstered walls in floral patterns, sometimes with views of the inner courtyard. The hotel restaurant, Bateau Ivre, is popular among locals because of its good-value fixed-price menus. The menu named for Toulouse-Lautrec consists of choices that were compiled after his death by his friends, who remembered the way he'd often prepare the dishes himself during his dinner parties, such as radishes stuffed with braised foie gras, supreme of sandre, and duckling roasted with garlic.

50 rue Séré-de-Riviéres, 81000 Albi. ✆ **05-63-48-58-48.** Fax 05-63-47-20-61. www.hotelchiffre.com. 37 units. 58€–74€ double. AE, DC, MC, V. Parking 6€. **Amenities:** Restaurant; bar; limited room service; laundry. *In room:* A/C, TV, hair dryer.

Hôtel George V This hotel offers a dignified kind of charm and a spartan, pleasingly old-fashioned setting at prices that are fair and reasonable. It was built around 1900 and is about a quarter mile from the town center. Bedrooms are high-ceilinged and generally spacious; bathrooms are small. They are simply decorated, in some cases with a bit of whimsy, with efficient furniture and excellent beds. Breakfast is the only meal served.

29 av. Maréchal-Joffre, 81000 Albi. ✆ **05-63-54-24-16.** Fax 05-63-49-90-78. www.hotelgeorgev.com. 9 units. 32€–42.50€ double. AE, MC, V. Free parking. *In room:* A/C, TV, minibar, hair dryer.

La Réserve ★★★ This country-club villa, 2km (1¼ miles) from Albi, is managed by the Rieux family, who also run the Hostellerie St-Antoine. It's in Mediterranean style, with tennis courts, a pool, and a fine garden in which you can dine. The rooms have charm and style, and contain imaginative decorations, each different from the next, linked to a certain historical era in France's past; upper-story rooms have sun terraces and French doors. Avoid those rooms over the kitchen, which can receive noise and fumes from below.

Route de Cordes à Fonvialane, 81000 Albi. ✆ **05-63-60-80-80.** Fax 05-63-47-63-60. www.relaischateaux.fr/reservealbi. 23 units. 130€–250€ double; 355€ suite. AE, DC, MC, V. Closed Nov–Apr. From the center of town, follow signs to Carmaux-Rodez until you cross the Tarn; then follow signs to Cordes. The hotel is adjacent to the main road leading to Cordes, 2km (1¼ miles) from Albi. **Amenities:** Restaurant; bar; outdoor pool; tennis courts; limited room service; babysitting; laundry service; dry cleaning. *In room:* A/C, TV, minibar, hair dryer, safe.

WHERE TO DINE

La Réserve (see "Where to Stay," above) boasts a wonderful restaurant.

Jardin des Quatre Saisons ★★ MODERN FRENCH The best food in Albi is served by Georges Bermond, who believes that menus, like life, should change with the seasons—and that's how the restaurant got its name. The setting is a modern, deceptively simple pair of dining rooms where the lighting has been subtly arranged to make everyone look as attractive as possible. Service is always competent and polite. Menu items have been fine-tuned and include delicious versions of a fricassée of snails garnished with strips of the famous hams produced in the nearby hamlet of Lacaune, ravioli stuffed with pulverized shrimp and served with a truffled cream sauce, and a gratinée of mussels in a compote of fish. Most delectable of all—an excuse for returning a second time—is a pot-au-feu of the sea that contains three or four species of fish garnished with a crawfish-flavored cream sauce. The wine selection is the finest in Albi.

19 bd. de Strasbourg. ✆ **05-63-60-77-76.** Reservations recommended. Main courses 15€–23€; fixed-price menus 21€–31€. AE, DC, MC, V. Tues–Sun noon–2:30pm; Tues–Sat 7–10pm.

Le Lautrec TRADITIONAL FRENCH Part of its charm derives from its associations with Toulouse-Lautrec—it lies across the street from his birthplace and is decorated with copies of his paintings. Also appealing is the rich patina of its interior brickwork. The skillfully prepared food items include a salad of fried scallops that come with rose oil and essence of shrimp, sweetbreads with morels, and roasted rack of lamb marinated in a brewed infusion of Provençal thyme. Most unusual of all is a medieval recipe for breast of duck "à Hippocrace," wherein cinnamon, rosewater, and honey are used.

13 rue Toulouse-Lautrec. ✆ **05-63-54-86-55.** Reservations recommended. Main courses 11.50€–14€; fixed-price lunch Tues–Fri 12.35€–37€; other fixed-price meals 15€–37€. DC, MC, V. Tues–Sat noon–2pm; Tues–Sat 7–9:30pm.

Le Moulin de la Mothe ★ MODERN FRENCH Although the building that contains this elegant restaurant was built in 1975, the site it occupies is immediately adjacent to a historic grain mill. Louis XII (Saint Louis) presented the mill to his soldiers for their success at a 12th-century battle that protected Albi from enemies at the gate. Today the Moulin de la Mothe sits only about 80m (267 ft.) from the cathedral and overlooks the river Tarn and a private park. You'll consume some of the best food in Albi here within a dining room awash with sunlight. Michel (the chef) and Marie-Claude (the maitre d'hotel) Pellaprat serve inventive regional cuisine that's been updated in an impressively sophisticated manner. Menu items change at least four times a year but might include a salad of crisp-broiled blood sausage with a confit of onions and apples, a "mosaic" of various sorts of duckling served with a slice of fried goose liver, and green asparagus roasted with thin-sliced cured ham. A light and airy dessert that has been a resounding success here for the past 20 years is a pear-flavored soufflé.

Rue de Lamothe. ✆ **05-63-60-38-15.** Reservations recommended. Main courses 19€–27€; fixed-price menus 28€–32€. AE, DC, MC, V. Thurs–Tues noon–2:30pm; Thurs–Sat and Mon–Tues 7:45–9:30pm. Closed 2 weeks in Feb and 1 week in Nov.

5 Castres ★

727km (452 miles) SW of Paris; 42km (26 miles) S of Albi

Built on the bank of the Agout River, Castres is the point of origin for trips to the Sidobre, the mountains of Lacaune, and the Black Mountains. Today the wool industry here, whose origins go back to the 14th century, has made Castres one of France's two most important wool-producing areas. The town was formerly a Roman military installation. A Benedictine monastery was founded here in the 9th century, and the town fell under the comtes d'Albi in the 10th century. With its acquisition of a number of 1st-century relics of St. Vincent, and its role as a stopover for pilgrimages to the tomb of St. James in Spain, Castres also held some religious significance. During the 16th-century Wars of Religion, the Protestant town was invaded by religious fanatics, who stole the relics from the basilica and dumped them into the river.

ESSENTIALS

GETTING THERE From Toulouse, there are eight **trains** per day (trip time: 1 hr., 15 min.); for rail information and schedules, call ✆ **08-36-35-35-35.** If you're **driving,** Castres is located on N126 east from Toulouse and along N112 south from Albi.

VISITOR INFORMATION The **Office de Tourisme** is at avenue de Roquecourbe (✆ **05-63-62-63-71;** www.ville-castres.fr).

THE TOP ATTRACTIONS

Eglise St-Benoît The town's most visible and important church is Castres's outstanding example of French baroque architecture. The architect Caillau began construction of the church in 1677, on the site of a 9th-century Benedictine abbey. The baroque structure was never completed according to its original plans. The painting at the church's far end, above the altar, was executed by Gabriel Briard in the 18th century.

Place du 8-Mai-1945. ✆ **05-63-59-05-19.** Free admission. Mon–Sat 9am–noon and 1:30–6:30pm; Sun 8:30am–12:30pm. Oct–May, except for religious services, the church is closed to casual visitors every Sun.

Le Centre National et Musée Jean-Jaurès This museum is dedicated to the workers' movements of the late 19th and early 20th centuries. Its collection contains printed material from the various Socialist movements in France during that period, as well as paintings, sculptures, films, and slides. See, in particular, an issue of *L'Aurore* containing Zola's famous *"J'accuse"* article about the Dreyfus case.

2 place Pélisson. ✆ **05-63-72-01-01.** Admission 1.50€ adults, .75€ children under 14. Apr–Sept daily 9am–noon and 2–6pm; Oct–Mar Tues–Sun 9am–noon and 2–5pm.

Musée Goya ★ The museum is in the town hall, an archbishop's palace designed by Mansart in 1669. The paintings of Francisco Goya y Lucientes were donated to the town in 1894 by Pierre Briguiboul, son of the Castres-born artist Marcel Briguiboul. *Les Caprices,* created in 1799 after the illness that left Goya deaf, fills nearly an entire room. A satire on Spanish society, the work is composed of symbolic images of demons and monsters. The museum collection also includes 16th-century tapestries and Spanish paintings from the 15th to the 20th centuries.

In the Jardin de l'Evêché. ✆ **05-63-71-59-30.** Admission 2.30€ adults, free for ages 17 and under. Apr–Sept Tues–Sat 9am–noon and 2–5pm, Sun 10am–noon and 2–6pm; Oct–Mar Tues–Sun 9am–noon and 2–5pm (July–Aug open Mon).

WHERE TO STAY

Hôtel de l'Europe ★ *Finds* This hotel exudes charm, especially in the bedrooms capped with ceiling beams, where the pinkish-gray masonry from the building's original construction during the 18th century still remains. Plus, each room has a view over the oldest part of the historic town. The hotel has great style, and its accommodations offer a certain glamour, some boasting canopy-draped beds. A number of the bathrooms are quite luxurious.

5 rue Victor-Hugo, 81100 Castres. ✆ **05-63-59-00-33.** Fax 05-63-59-21-38. 35 units. 60€ double. AE, MC, V. Parking 5€. **Amenities:** Restaurant; bar. *In room:* TV, minibar, hair dryer.

Hôtel Renaissance ★★ The Renaissance is the best hotel in Castres. It was built in the 17th century as the courthouse, and then functioned as a colorful but run-down hotel throughout most of the 20th century—until 1993, when it was discreetly restored. Today you'll see a severely dignified building composed of *colombages*-style half-timbering, with a mixture of chiseled stone blocks and bricks. Some rooms have exposed timbers; all are clean and comfortable, evoking the crafts of yesteryear.

17 rue Victor-Hugo, 81100 Castres. ✆ **05-63-59-30-42.** Fax 05-63-72-11-57. 20 units. 60€–67€ double; 80€ suite. AE, DC, MC, V. **Amenities:** Bar; laundry service; dry cleaning. *In room:* TV, hair dryer, iron.

WHERE TO DINE

In addition to those below, another worthy choice is **Le Victoria,** 24 place du 8-Mai-1945 (✆ **05-63-59-14-68**), where meals cost 18€ to 40€. A superb French cuisine is served, with regional products used whenever available.

Brasserie des Jacobins *Value* FRENCH/PROVENÇAL A likely bet for solid, well-seasoned, and conservative French and Provençal cuisine is this simple modern brasserie where the menu hasn't changed in many years and where most of the clients are local residents. Menu items include blanquettes of veal, cassoulet, and caramelized filets of pork with Provençal herbs. Decor is rustic, service is cordial, and many visitors find it especially suitable for a simple noontime meal.

1 place Jean-Jaurès. ✆ **05-63-59-01-44.** Reservations recommended. Main courses 8€–13€. AE, MC, V. Mon–Sat noon–2:30pm and 7–10:30pm.

La Mandragore ★ LANGUEDOCIEN On an easily overlooked narrow street, this restaurant occupies a small section of one of the many wings of the medieval château-fort of Castres. The decor is consciously simple, perhaps as an appropriate foil for the stone walls and overhead beams. Sophie Belaut (in the dining room) and Jean-Claude Belaut (in the kitchen) prepare a regional cuisine that's among the best in town, served with charm and tact. It might include artichokes with foie gras and truffle-flavored vinaigrette, roast pigeon stuffed with foie gras and served with gâteau of potatoes and flap mushrooms, filet of tuna with sweet peppers and cured ham, and magret of duckling with truffle oil and braised leeks.

1 rue Malpas. ✆ **05-63-59-51-27.** Reservations recommended. Main courses 13€–22€; fixed-price menu 14.50€–30€. DC, V. Mon 7–10pm; Tues–Sat noon–2pm and 7–10pm. Closed Jan.

6 Carcassonne ★★★

797km (495 miles) SW of Paris; 92km (57 miles) SE of Toulouse; 105km (65 miles) S of Albi

Evoking bold knights, fair damsels, and troubadours, the greatest fortress city of Europe rises against a background of the snow-capped Pyrénées. Floodlit at night, it captures a fairy-tale magic, but back in its heyday in the Middle Ages it was the target of assault by battering rams, grapnels, a mobile tower (inspired by the Trojan horse), catapults, flaming arrows, and the mangonel.

The city, which was used as a backdrop for the 1991 movie *Robin Hood, Prince of Thieves,* is overrun with hordes of visitors and tacky gift shops. The elusive charm of Carcassone comes out in the evening, when day-trippers depart and floodlights bathe the ancient monuments.

ESSENTIALS

GETTING THERE Carcassonne is a major stop for **trains** between Toulouse and destinations south and east. There are 24 trains per day from Toulouse (trip time: 50 min.), 14 trains per day from Montpellier (trip time: 2 hr.), and 12 trains per day from Nîmes (trip time: 2½ hr.). For rail information, call ✆ **08-36-35-35-35.** If you're **driving,** Carcassonne is on A61 south of Toulouse.

VISITOR INFORMATION The **Office de Tourisme** is at 15 bd. Camille-Pelletan (✆ **04-68-10-24-30**) and in the medieval town at Porte Narbonnaise (✆ **04-68-10-24-36**). You can also try the website at www.carcassonne.org.

SPECIAL EVENTS The town's nightlife sparkles with pizzazz during its summer festivals. From June 29 to July 29 is the **Festival de Carcassonne,** when instrumental concerts, modern and classical dance, operas, and theater shower the city. Tickets run 20€ to 50€ and can be purchased by calling ✆ **04-68-11-59-15.** For more information, contact the **Théâtre Municipal** at ✆ **04-68-25-33-13.** On the night of July 14 on **Bastille Day,** one of the best fireworks spectacles in France lights up the skies at 10:30pm. Over a period of 3 weeks in mid-August, the merriment and raucousness of the Middle Ages overtake the city during the **Spectacles Musicaux,** in the form of jousts, parades, food fairs, and street festivals. For information, contact the tourist office or the event's organizers, **Carlo Boxo, S.A.R.L.** (✆ **01-48-40-27-71**).

EXPLORING LA CITE

Carcassonne consists of two towns: **La Bastide St-Louis** (also known as **La Ville Basse,** or Lower City), and the older, more evocative medieval **Cité.** The former has little interest, but the latter is a major attraction, the goal of many a pilgrim. The fortifications of La Cité consist of a double line of **ramparts,** with inner and outer walls. The inner rampart was built by the Visigoths in the 5th century. Clovis, king of the Franks, attacked in 506 but failed. The Saracens overcame the city in 728 and held it until 752, when Pepin the Short (father of Charlemagne) drove them out. During a long siege by Charlemagne, when the populace of the walled city was starving and near surrender, Dame Carcas came up with an idea. According to legend, she gathered up the last remaining bit of grain, fed it to a sow, and then tossed the pig over the ramparts. It's said to have burst, scattering the grain. The Franks concluded that Carcassonne must have unlimited food supplies and ended their siege.

Carcassonne's walls were further fortified by the vicomtes de Trencavel in the 12th century and by Louis IX and Philip the Bold in the 13th century. However, by the mid–17th century, its importance as a strategic frontier fort ended and the ramparts were left to decay. In the 19th century, the builders of the Lower Town began to remove the stone for use in new construction. But a revival of interest in the Middle Ages led the government to order Viollet-le-Duc (who restored Notre-Dame in Paris) to repair and, where necessary, rebuild the walls. Reconstruction continued until very recently.

Walks along the outer ramparts are free and are possible year-round without restriction. Walks along the inner ramparts, however, are possible only as part of guided tours. Hour-long tours depart at 10-minute intervals in summer, daily between 9am and 7:30pm, and at 30-minute intervals in winter, daily between 9am and 5pm. Three of these per day in summer and one per day in winter are conducted in English. The cost is 5.45€ for adults and 3.50€ for persons 12 to 26; children 11 and under are free. For information, call the **Caisse Nationale des Monuments Historiques** at © **04-68-11-70-77.**

A small populace still resides within the walls. The **Basilique St-Nazaire** ★, La Cité (© **04-68-25-27-65**), dates from the 11th to 14th centuries and contains some beautiful stained-glass windows and a pair of rose medallions. The nave is in the Romanesque style, but the choir and transept are Gothic. The organ, one of the oldest in southwestern France, is 16th century. Note the well-preserved tomb of Bishop Radulph, dating from 1266. The cathedral is open daily: in July and August from 9am to 7:30pm, and off season from 9:30am to noon and 2 to 5:30pm. Mass is celebrated on Sunday at 11am. Admission is free.

Musée des Memoires du Moyen Age, Immeuble du Pont-Levis, Chemin des Anglais (© **04-68-71-08-65**), is set within the stone bulwarks that used to contain the drawbridge. This museum documents the traumatic battles, sieges, and feuds that marked life in Carcassonne during the Middle Ages. You'll be shown a video depicting a thousand years of medieval life in the town, and exhibitions that showcase the values and lifestyles of long ago. Entrance is 3.80€ for adults and 3.05€ for children and students. It is open from mid-June to mid-September daily from 10am to 8pm; from mid-September to mid-June, it's open daily from 10am to 6pm.

In the highest elevation of the Cité, at the uppermost terminus of La Rue Principale (rue Cros Mayrevielle) you'll find the **Château Comtal,** place du Château, (© **04-68-11-70-73**), a carefully restored 12th-century fortress that's open June through September every day from 9:30am to 7:30pm, and between October and May every day from 9:30am to 6pm. Entrance includes an obligatory 50-minute guided tour, in French and broken English. It costs 6€ for adults and 4€ for students and persons between 18 and 25. Entrance and participation in the tour is free for anyone under 18. Included in the tour is access to expositions that display the archaeological remnants that were discovered on-site, and access to an explanation of the 19th-century restorations that brought the site to its present condition. It's also the only way you'll be able to climb onto the city's inner ramparts, walls that during medieval days provided additional barriers against enemies that might have already penetrated the city's outermost fortifications.

SHOPPING

Carcassone, more than other French cities, is really two distinct shopping towns in one—the walled medieval city and the modern lower city. The whole of the medieval city is chock full of tiny stores and boutiques selling mostly gift items, antiques, and local arts and crafts. In the modern city, the major streets for shopping are **rue Clemenceau** and **rue de Verdun,** particularly if you're in the market for clothing. On the third Saturday of every month at the portail Jacobin, in the modern town center, a **flea market** sets up from 8am to 6pm.

Stores worth visiting include **Cellier des Vigneronnes,** 13 rue du Grand Puits (© **04-68-25-31-00**), where you'll find a wide selection of regional wines ranging from simple table wines to those awarded the distinction of Appellation d'Origine Controlée. Some antiques stores of merit include **Mme Fage-Nunez,**

4 place du Château (✆ **04-68-25-65-71**), for antique furniture; and **Antiquités Safi,** 54 rue de Verdun (✆ **04-68-25-65-71**), for paintings and art objects. For antique firearms, head for **Dominique Sarrante,** 13 Porte d'Aude (✆ **04-68-72-42-90**).

WHERE TO STAY

IN THE CITE

Hôtel de la Cité ★★★ Originally a palace for whatever bishop or prelate happened to be in power at the time, this has been the most desirable hotel in town since 1909. It's constructed in the actual walls of the city, adjoining the cathedral. The hotel was acquired in the '90s by the Orient-Express Hotel group and fluffed up to the tune of $3 million. You enter a long Gothic corridor/gallery leading to the lounge. Many rooms open onto the ramparts and a garden, and feature antiques or reproductions. A few accommodations contain wooden headboards and four-posters. The most ideal unit is no. 308 because it opens onto the most panoramic view of the city. Modern equipment has been discreetly installed throughout, including bathrooms of generous size. The hotel is renowned for its restaurant, La Barbacane (p. 88).

Place de l'Eglise, 11000 Carcassonne. ✆ **04-68-71-98-71.** Fax 04-68-71-50-15. www.hoteldelacite.orient-express.com. 61 units. 250€–312€ double; 430€–620€ suite. AE, DC, MC, V. Parking 15€. Closed Dec 3–Jan 15. **Amenities:** 3 restaurants; bar; outdoor pool; limited room service; laundry. *In room:* A/C, TV, minibar, hair dryer.

Hôtel des Remparts An abbey in the 12th century, this building at the edge of a stone square lies in the town center. It was converted into a charming hotel in 1983 after major repairs to the masonry and roof. The rooms contain no-frills furniture and acceptably comfortable mattresses. Most were renovated, or at least repainted, in the late 1990s. Bathrooms are just large enough. The owners are proud of the massive stone staircase that twists around itself. Make reservations at least a couple of months ahead if you plan to stay here during summer.

3–5 place du Grand-Puits, 11000 Carcassonne. ✆ **04-68-11-23-00.** Fax 04-68-25-06-60. 61 units. 120€–140€ double. AE, DC, MC, V. Parking 10€. **Amenities:** Restaurant; bar; laundry service; dry cleaning. *In room:* A/C, TV, minibar, hair dryer, safe.

AT THE ENTRANCE OF THE CITE

Hôtel Les Donjon–Les Ramparts ★ *Finds* This little hotel is big on charm and the best value in the moderate range. Built in the style of the old Cité, it has a honey-colored stone exterior with iron bars on the windows. The interior is a jewel, reflecting the sophistication of the owner, Christine Pujol. Elaborate Louis XIII–style furniture graces the reception lounges. A newer wing contains additional rooms in a medieval architectural style, and the older rooms have been renewed. Their furnishings are in a severe style that's consistent with the artfully medieval look of the nearby ramparts. Each unit comes with a compact tiled bathroom. The hotel also runs a restaurant nearby, the Brasserie du Donjon. In summer the garden is the perfect breakfast spot.

2 rue du Comte-Roger, 11000 Carcassonne. ✆ **800/528-1234** in the U.S. and Canada, or 04-68-11-23-00. Fax 04-68-25-06-60. www.hotel-donjon.fr. 62 units. 74€–100€ double; 130€–170€ suite. AE, DC, MC, V. Parking 5€. **Amenities:** Restaurant; bar; limited room service; laundry service. *In room:* A/C, TV, minibar, hair dryer.

LA BASTIDE ST-LOUIS

Grand Hôtel Terminus Built in 1914, with frequent renovations ever since, this is an old-style, very grand hotel. It functioned as the Nazi local headquarters between 1941 and 1943. Bedrooms are high-ceilinged, comfortable, and rather charmingly old-fashioned, thanks to the presence of most of the original furnishings as well as Art Deco pieces added during the 1920s and 1930s. Rooms come in many shapes and sizes—some quite spacious, others a bit cramped. The furnishings are comfortable, especially the inviting beds, most often doubles or twins. The hotel lies in the heart of *la Ville Basse,* adjacent to the railway station and the Canal du Midi, about 3.2km (2 miles) from the medieval Cité. On the premises is a hardworking management team staffed by members of the same family.

2 av. du Maréchal-Joffre, 11001 Carcassonne. ✆ **04-68-25-25-00.** Fax 04-68-72-53-09. 91 units. 49€–115€double; 125€ suite. MC, V. Parking 8€. Bus: 4. Closed Nov–Mar. **Amenities:** Restaurant; bar; lounge; 24-hr. room service. *In room:* TV.

Hôtel Du Pont Vieux *Value* One of the best and most reasonably priced hotels in Carcassonne, this rustic boardinghouse lies at the foot of the medieval city. It has been completely restored without losing its provincial French charm. From the elegantly furnished lounge to the quiet reading room, it's cozy and inviting. The medium-size rooms have traditional furnishings and double-glazed windows to cut down on the noise. An indoor garden provides a retreat from the crowds.

32 rue Trivalle, 11000 Carcassonne. ✆ **04-68-25-24-99.** Fax 04-68-47-62-71. www.hoteldupontvieux.com. 19 units. 55€–65€ double; 68€–89€ suite. Rates include breakfast. AE, DC, V. Parking 7.25€. **Amenities:** Restaurant; limited room service; babysitting; laundry service. *In room:* TV, minibar, hair dryer, safe.

Hôtel Montségur ★ *Value* This stately town house, built around 1887 with a mansard roof and dormers, has a front garden that's screened from the street by trees and a high wrought-iron fence. Didier and Isabelle Faugeras have furnished the hotel with antiques, avoiding that institutional look. Modern amenities include an elevator. The rooms are cheaper than you'd imagine from the looks of the place. Michelin ignores it, but this is a good and decent choice. A continental breakfast is available; Didier is the chef at the highly recommended Le Languedoc across the street (p. 88).

27 allée d'Iéna, 11000 Carcassonne. ✆ **04-68-25-31-41.** Fax 04-68-47-13-22. www.hotelmontsegur.com. 21 units. 53€–84€ double. AE, DC, MC, V. Free parking. **Amenities:** Restaurant; bar; 24-hr. room service; laundry service. *In room:* A/C, TV, hair dryer.

STAYING NEARBY

Domaine d'Auriac ★★★ Carcassonne's premier address for both food and lodging is this moss-covered 19th-century manor house located about 2.5km (1½ miles) west of the Cité. It was built around 1880 as a cube-shape building, with about a half-dozen stone-sided annexes (site of many of the bedrooms) on the ruins of a medieval monastery, some of whose ceiling vaults are still visible within the cellars. Each bedroom has a photo-magazine aura, with lots of flowered fabrics, a range of decorative styles, and, in many cases, massive and sometimes sculpted ceiling beams. The tiled bathrooms are first-rate. Bernard and Anne-Marie Rigaudis are the experienced owners, assisted by their grown children Marie-Hélène and Pierre. Part of the allure of this Relais & Châteaux member are the well-crafted and well-conceived meals that, during clement weather, are served beside the pool on flowering terraces. Fixed-price menus, priced at from 40€ to 64€ each, change several times each season but always demonstrate a sophisticated twist, making local recipes more glamorous and interesting. The hotel is one of the few in the region with its own golf course, from which sweeping panoramas are available over the surrounding countryside.

Route St-Hilaire, 11009 Carcassonne. ✆ **04-68-25-72-22.** Fax 04-68-47-35-54. www.relaischateaux.fr/auriac. 26 units. 130€–285€ double; 250€–420€ suite. AE, DC, MC, V. Free parking. Closed Jan and Apr 29–May 6.

Take D104 W 2.5km (1½ miles) from Carcassonne. Pets accepted for a fee. **Amenities:** Restaurant; bar; outdoor pool; 18-hole golf course; tennis court; secretarial service; 24-hr. room service, babysitting; laundry service; dry cleaning. *In room:* A/C, TV, minibar, hair dryer, safe.

WHERE TO DINE

Au Jardin de la Tour TRADITIONAL FRENCH Part of the charm of this restaurant derives from the location of its verdant garden adjacent to the western foundation of the château, providing a green space that's very much appreciated in the midst of the city's closely built-up medieval core. The building dates from the early 1800s, although wide-ranging renovations have brought it up-to-date. The decor features rustic finds from local antique fairs. You can order from a large selection of salads, filet of beef with morels, cassoulet, terrines of foie gras, and all kinds of grilled fish. The cookery is consistently good, relying on fresh ingredients deftly handled by a talented kitchen staff.

11 rue Porte-d'Aude. ✆ **04-68-25-71-24.** Reservations recommended in summer. Main courses 12€–30€; set menus 18€–26€. MC, V. Tues–Sat 8:30–11pm. Closed Nov 15–Apr 15.

La Barbacane ★ FRENCH Named after the medieval neighborhood (La Barbacane) where it sits, this restaurant enjoys equal billing with the celebrated Hôtel de la Cité, which contains it. The soothing-looking dining room, with walls upholstered in fabric with gold fleur-de-lis on a cerulean blue background, features the cuisine of the noted chef Franck Putelat. Menu items are based on seasonal ingredients, with just enough zest. Examples are green ravioli perfumed with *seiche* (a species of octopus) in its own ink, a fraîcheur of Breton lobster with artichoke hearts and caviar, and organically fed free-range chicken stuffed with truffles. A particularly succulent dessert is chestnut parfait with malt-flavored cream sauce and date-flavored ice cream.

In the Hôtel de la Cité, place de l'Eglise. ✆ **04-68-71-98-71.** Reservations recommended. Main courses 23€–55€; fixed-price menus 60€–80€. AE, DC, MC, V. Daily 7:30–10pm. Closed Dec–Mar.

Le Languedoc ★★ TRADITIONAL FRENCH Acclaimed chef Didier Faugeras is the creative force behind the inspired cuisine here. The high-ceilinged century-old dining room is filled with antiques; a brick fireplace contributes to the warm Languedoc atmosphere. The specialty is *cassoulet au confit de canard* (the famous stew made with duck cooked in its own fat). It has been celebrated as a much-perfected staple here since the early 1960s. The *pièce de résistance* is tournedos Rossini, with foie gras truffles and Madeira sauce. A smooth dessert is flambéed crepes Languedoc. In summer you can dine on a pleasant patio or in the air-conditioned restaurant. (Faugeras and his wife, Isabelle, are the owners of the worthy Hotel Montségur, just across the street.)

32 allée d'Iéna. ✆ **04-68-25-22-17.** Reservations recommended. Main courses 15€–25€; fixed-price menus 22€–40€. AE, DC, MC, V. Sept–June Tues–Sun noon–2pm,Tues–Sat 7:30–9:30pm; July–Aug daily noon–1:30pm, Mon–Sat 7:30–9pm. Closed Dec 20–Jan 20 and the last week of June.

DINING NEARBY

Château St-Martin ★ FRENCH One of Languedoc's most successful chefs operates out of this 16th-century château at Montredon, 4km (2½ miles) northeast of Carcassonne. Ringed by a wooded park, the restaurant serves the superb cuisine of co-owners Jean-Claude and Jacqueline Rodriguez. Dine inside or on the terrace. Recommended dishes are turbot with fondue of baby vegetables, sea bass with scallop mousseline, sole in tarragon, and *confit d'oie carcassonnaise* (goose meat cooked in its own fat and kept in earthenware pots). Two other specialties are cassoulet languedocienne and *boullinade nouvelloise* (made with different sorts of fish that include scallops, sole, turbot, and most definitely not a rascasse or hogfish). On the premises are 15 simple, relatively new hotel rooms; doubles rent for 80€.

Montredon, 11090 Carcassonne. ✆ **04-68-71-09-53.** Reservations required. Main courses 13€–25€; fixed-price menus 28€–50€. AE, DC, MC, V. Thurs–Tues noon–1:45pm and 7:30–9:45pm. Restaurant is 4km (2½ miles) northeast of La Cité. Follow the signs pointing to Stade Albert Domec.

CARCASSONNE AFTER DARK

Carcassonne nightlife is centered on **rue Omer-Sarraut** (in La Bastide) and **place Marcou** (in La Cité). **La Bulle,** 115 rue Barbacane (✆ **04-68-72-47-70**), explodes with techno and rock dance tunes for an under-30 crowd that keeps the energy pumping and the place hopping till 4am Wednesday through Sunday. The cover charge begins at 9€ per person. Another enduringly popular disco, 4km (2½ miles) southwest of town, is **Le Black Bottom,** route de Limoux (✆ **04-68-47-37-11**), which rocks to every conceivable kind of dance music every Thursday through Sunday beginning at 11pm. Entrance costs 10€ per person.

7 Perpignan ★★

904km (562 miles) SW of Paris; 369km (229 miles) NW of Marseille; 64km (40 miles) S of Narbonne

At Perpignan you might think you've crossed the border into Spain, for it was once Catalonia's second city after Barcelona. Even earlier it was the capital of the kingdom of Majorca. But when the Roussillon—the French part of Catalonia—was finally partitioned off, Perpignan became permanently French by the Treaty of the Pyrénées in 1659. However, Catalan is still spoken here, especially among the country people.

Legend has it that Perpignan derives its name from Père Pinya, a plowman who followed the Tèt River down the Pyrénées mountains to the site of the town today, where he cultivated the fertile soil while the river kept its promise to water the fields.

Today Perpignan is content to rest on its former glory, its residents—some 110,000 in all—enjoying the closeness of the Côte Catalane and the Pyrénées-Orientales to their north. The pace is decidedly relaxed. You'll have time to smell the flowers that grow here in great abundance.

This is one of the sunniest places in France, but summer afternoons in July and August can be a cauldron. That's when many of the locals take the 10km (6-mile) ride to the beach to cool off. There's a young, vibrant scene here, especially along the quays of the Basse River, site of impromptu nighttime concerts, beer drinking, and the devouring of endless tapas, a tradition inherited from nearby Barcelona.

Our favorite time to visit this area is the grape harvest in September after temperatures have dropped. If you come then, you might want to drive through the Rivesaltes district bordering the city to the west and north.

ESSENTIALS

GETTING THERE Four **trains** per day arrive from Paris (trip time: 6–10 hr.) after stopping first at Montpellier. There are also at least three conventional trains that pull into Perpignan from Nice (trip time: 6 hr.). For rail information and schedules, call ✆ **08-36-35-35-35.** If you're **driving** from the French Riviera, drive west along A9 to Perpignan.

VISITOR INFORMATION The **Office Municipal du Tourisme** is within the Palais des Congrès, place Armand-Lanoux (✆ **04-68-66-30-30;** www.perpignantourisme.com).

SPECIAL EVENTS During all 4 weeks of every very hot July, **Les Estivales** causes the city to explode with a medley of music, expositions, and theater. For information, call ✆ **04-68-35-01-77** or go to www.estivales.com. Our favorite time to visit this area is during the **grape harvest** in September. If you visit at this time, you might want to drive through the Rivesaltes district bordering the city to the west and north. Temperatures have usually dropped by then.

Perpignan is host to one of the most widely discussed celebrations of photojournalism in the industry. Established in the late 1980s, it's the **Festival International de Photo-Journalisme,** also called **Le Visa pour l'Image.** From late August until mid-September, at least 10 sites of historic, usually medieval, interest are devoted to the exposition of photojournalistic expositions from around the world. Entrance to all the expositions is free, and an international committee awards prizes. For more information, call ✆ **04-68-66-18-00.**

SEEING THE SIGHTS

A 3-hour guided **walking tour** is a good way to see the attractions in the town's historic core. Some tour leaders even lace their commentary with English. Tours are conducted at 3pm daily from mid-June to mid-September, and also daily at 3pm for 2 weeks around Christmas. The rest of the year, they are offered only Wednesday and Saturday at 2:30pm. They depart from the sidewalk in front of the tourist office and are priced at 4€ per person. For more details, contact the tourist office (see above).

Castillet/Musée des Arts et Traditions Populaires Catalans ★ The Castillet is one of the chief sights of Perpignan. The machicolated and crenellated redbrick building from the 14th century is a combination gateway and fortress. It houses the museum, also known as La Casa Païral, which contains exhibitions of Catalan regional artifacts and folkloric items, including typical dress. Part of the charm of the Castillet derives from its bulky-looking tower, which you can climb for a good view of the town.

Place de Verdun. ✆ **04-68-35-42-05.** Admission 4€ adults, 2€ students and children 17 and under. May–Sept Wed–Mon 10am–7pm; Oct–Apr Wed–Mon 11am–5:30pm.

Cathédrale St-Jean ★ The cathedral dates from the 14th and 15th centuries and has an admirable nave and interesting 17th-century retables. Leaving via the south door, you'll find on the left a chapel with the *Devout Christ,* a magnificent wood carving depicting Jesus contorted with pain and suffering—his head, crowned with thorns, drooping on his chest.

Place Gambetta/rue de l'Horloge. ✆ **04-68-51-33-72.** Free admission. Daily 9am–noon and 3–7pm.

Palais des Rois de Majorque At the top of the town, the Spanish citadel encloses the Palace of the Kings of Majorca. A structure from the 13th and 14th centuries, built around a court encircled by arcades, it has been restored by the government. You can see the old throne room with its large fireplaces and a square tower with a double gallery; from the tower there's a fine view of the Pyrénées.

Rue des Archers. ✆ **04-68-34-48-29.** Admission 4€ adults, 2€ students, free for children 7 and under. June–Sept daily 10am–6pm; Oct–May daily 9am–5pm.

A MAJOR HISTORIC SITE NEARBY

Château de Salses ★ This important historic site is in the hamlet of Salses, 25km (15 miles) north of the city center. Since the days of the Romans, this fort

Finds Céret: Birthplace of Cubism

Driving 31km (19 miles) southwest of Perpignan, you reach this enchanting little town, long a mecca for artists. A group of avant-garde artists was drawn here when Manolo (1873–1945), the Catalonian sculptor, let fellow artists in on a secret: **Céret** is a little gem. In time, Picasso and Braque arrived, making Céret the capital of cubism.

In the center of town, you can visit **Musée d'Art Moderne** ★★, 8 bd. Maréchal-Joffre (✆ **04-68-87-27-76**), with one of the finest collections of art in the southwest. The museum is dedicated to the painters who have lived in and around Céret, if only briefly. Of course, most visitors come here to see works by Picasso, which include paintings, sculptures, and sketches. Also displayed are works by Chagall, Braque, Matisse, Maillol, and Miró, plus four paintings by Pierre Brune, founder of the museum. On the second floor, the space is devoted to floating exhibits by contemporary French artists. July through September, museum hours are daily from 10am to 7pm; May through June and in October, hours are daily from 10am to 6pm; and November through April, hours are Wednesday through Monday from 10am to 6pm. Admission is 5.50€ for adults, 3.50€ for students, and free for ages 15 and under.

Information about the town is found at the **Office de Tourisme,** 1 ave Clemenceau (✆ **04-68-87-00-53**). **Car Inter 66** (✆ **04-68-39-1-96**) runs one bus per hour (trip time: 45 min.) from Perpignan to Céret during the day; a one-way fare costs 5.30€.

has guarded the main road linking Spain and France. Ferdinand of Aragón erected a fort here in 1497 to protect the northern frontier of his kingdom. Even today, Salses marks the language-barrier point between Catalonia in Spain and Languedoc in France. This Spanish-style fort, designed by Ferdinand himself, is a curious example of an Iberian structure in France. In the 17th century, it was modified by the French military engineer Vauban to look more like a château. After many changes of ownership, Salses fell to the forces of Louis XIII in September 1642, and its Spanish garrison left forever. Less than 2 decades later, Roussillon was incorporated into France. There's a small-scale gift shop dispensing film and cold drinks on the premises.

In the town of Salses. ✆ **04-68-38-60-13.** Admission 5.50€ adults, 3.50€ youths under 25, free for children under 17. Apr–May and Oct daily 9:30am–12:30pm and 2–6pm; June and Sept daily 9:30am–6:30pm; July–Aug daily 9:30am–7pm; Nov–Mar daily 10am–noon and 2–5pm.

SHOPPING

With its inviting storefronts and pedestrian streets, Perpignan is a good town for shopping. Catalan is the style indigenous to the area, and it's reflected in textiles and pottery in strong geometric patterns and sturdily structured furniture. For one of the best selections of Catalan pottery, furniture, and carpets, and even a small inventory of antiques, visit the **Centre Sant-Vicens,** rue Sant-Vicens (✆ **04-68-50-02-18**), site of about a dozen independent merchants. You'll find it 4km (2½ miles) south of the town center, following the signs pointing to Enne and Collioures. In the town center, **La Maison Quinta,** 3 rue des Grands-des-Fabriques (✆ **04-68-34-41-62**), offers Catalan-inspired items for home decorating.

WHERE TO STAY

Hôtel de la Loge This beguiling little place dates from the 16th century but has been renovated into a modern hotel. It's located right in the heart of town, near Loge de Mer, the town hall, from which it takes its name, and the Castillet. The cozy rooms are attractively furnished, all with a sense of warmth and hospitality. The tiled bathrooms are small but offer adequate shelf space.

1 rue des Fabriques d'en-Nabot, 66000 Perpignan. ✆ **04-68-34-41-02.** Fax 04-68-34-25-13. www.hotelde laloge.fr. 22 units. 45.50€–57.50€ double. AE, DC, MC, V. **Amenities:** Lounge. *In room:* A/C, TV, minibar, hair dryer.

La Villa Duflot ★★★ This is the area's greatest hotel, yet its prices are reasonable for the luxury offered. Tranquillity, style, and refinement reign supreme. When this hotel opened, the mayor proclaimed, "Now we have some class in Perpignan." Located in a suburb, La Villa Duflot is a Mediterranean-style dwelling surrounded by a large park of pine, palm, and eucalyptus. The hotel has an appealing, almost family touch to it and isn't the least bit intimidating. You can sunbathe in the gardens surrounding the pool and order drinks at any hour at the outside bar. The guest rooms are situated around a patio planted with century-old olive trees. All are spacious and soundproof, with solid marble bathrooms and Art Deco interiors.

Rond Point Albert Donnezan, 66000 Perpignan. ✆ **04-68-56-67-67.** Fax 04-68-56-54-05. www.little-france.com/villa.duflot. 24 units. 105€–175€ double; half-board 93.50€–128.50€ per person double occupancy. AE, MC, V. To get here from the center of town, follow the signs to Perthus-Le Belou and the A9 autoroute, and travel 3km (2 miles) south of Perpignan's center. Just before you reach A9, you'll see the hotel. **Amenities:** Restaurant (see review below); 2 bars; outdoor pool; limited room service; laundry service. *In room:* A/C, TV, minibar, hair dryer.

Park Hotel ★ This four-story hotel facing the Jardins de la Ville offers well-furnished, soundproofed rooms. Although the Park is solid and reliable, it is the town's second choice, having none of the glamour of Villa Duflot. Midsize to spacious bedrooms are comfortably furnished with taste but not much flair; each comes with an average-size bathroom.

The restaurant, Le Chapon Fin, serves up first-class Mediterranean cuisine. The food, made from prime regional produce, is some of the finest in the area. Post-nouvelle choices include roast sea scallops flavored with succulent sea urchin velouté, various lobster dishes, and penne with truffles. As an accompaniment, try one of the local wines—perhaps a Collioure or Côtes du Roussillon. The restaurant is open for lunch Monday through Saturday and for dinner Monday through Friday. The hotel also houses Le Bistrot du Park, a less expensive eatery specializing in seafood.

18 bd. Jean-Bourrat, 66000 Perpignan. ✆ **04-68-35-14-14.** Fax 04-68-35-48-18. 68 units. 65€–95€ double; 260€ suite. AE, DC, MC, V. Parking 8.50€. **Amenities:** Restaurant; bar; 24-hr. room service; laundry service. *In room:* A/C, TV, minibar, hair dryer.

WHERE TO DINE

Côté Théâtre ★ MEDITERRANEAN This restaurant is housed within a severely dignified stone building. It was constructed in the 15th century as the home of the Catholic Inquisition's grand inquisitor. It attracts a quietly conservative crowd who dine beneath an elaborately crafted wooden ceiling that is designated a historic monument in its own right. The cuisine is traditional, earthy, and completely unafraid of strong, even gutsy flavors and old-fashioned traditions. Menu items include calamari or octopus salad with herbs and vinaigrette; braised sea scallops with shallots; a variety of different fish hauled from local waters, sometimes prepared with flap mushrooms; and deboned and stuffed pigs' feet prepared the old-fashioned way.

7 rue du Théâtre. ✆ **04-68-34-60-00.** Reservations recommended. Main courses 17€–27€; fixed-price menus 27€–62€ lunch Mon–Fri, 40€–57€ dinner and Sat lunch. AE, DC, MC, V. Tues–Sat noon–2pm; Mon–Sat 7:30–10:30pm. Closed 2 weeks late July to early Aug.

La Villa Duflot ★★ Slightly removed from the city center, this *restaurant avec chambres* is the most tranquil oasis in the area (see hotel review above). André Duflot, the owner, employs top-notch chefs who turn out dish after dish with remarkable skill and professionalism. Try, for example, a salad of warm squid or a platter of fresh anchovies marinated in vinegar. Sample the excellent foie gras of duckling. Two new specialties include gratin of lobster and a succulent magret of duckling with figs. The dessert sensation is fresh peaches in Banyuls wine. On the premises is an American bar.

109 av. Victor Dalbiez, 66000 Perpignan. ✆ **04-68-56-67-67.** Fax 04-68-56-54-05. Reservations required. Main courses 17€–21€; fixed-price menu 35€ Sat–Sun only. Daily noon–2:30pm and 8–11pm. AE, MC, V. Take N9 from the town center leading to autoroute, exiting at Perpignan Sud (south) heading toward Argeles.

Le Bistrot Gourmand ★ *Finds* FRENCH/CATALONIAN Set in the heart of Perpignan's oldest neighborhood, this informal and charming bistro serves excellent cuisine to a clientele that tends to congregate in greater numbers at lunch than at dinner, partly because of the noon meal's good value and partly because it's a lunch favorite of local workers and shop owners. Menu items include mussels in cream sauce, medallions of sea bass with a sweet white wine sauce, and filet of beef drenched in a heady Banyuls wine. One particular dish that's not to be missed if you crave strong Mediterranean flavors is an *anchoiade* (a paste of grilled anchovies) served with a medley of grilled Languedocien red peppers.

40 rue de la Fusterie. ✆ **04-68-51-21-14.** Reservations recommended. Main courses 11.10€–16.50€; fixed-price lunch 12€; fixed-price dinners 15.60€–19.50€. V. Mon–Sat noon–2pm and 7–10pm. Closed for dinner July–Aug.

PERPIGNAN AFTER DARK

Unlike the towns up north, Perpignan is permeated by Spanish and Catalan influences. This is especially evident at night, when a round of tapas and late-night promenades are among the evening's activities. The streets radiating from **place de la Loge** offer a higher concentration of bars and clubs than any other part of town.

Hot and sometimes overheated Perpignan offers lots of diversions to amuse its visitors during the welcome cool of the night. The accepted scheduling of an evening on the town involves a drink and a dialogue in one of the *bars de nuit,* followed by a drop-in at one of the discos. You might begin your bar crawl at **Le Habana-Club,** 5 rue Grande-des-Fabriques (✆ **04-68-34-11-00**), where recorded salsa and merengue play against a backdrop of sunset-colored cocktails. Suds with an Irish accent are offered at **Le Shannon Bar,** 3 rue de l'Incendie (✆ **04-68-35-12-48**), where a small community of Irish expatriates (and Celtic wannabes) wax nostalgic in a publike atmosphere.

Discos in Perpignan universally open their doors around 11pm and include **Le Napoli,** 3 rue place de Catalonia (✆ **04-68-35-55-88**), a modern, mirror-sheathed space that might remind you of an airport waiting lounge, but without the chairs. (Yes, you'll have to stand up and either mingle or dance at this place, since there's virtually nowhere to sit.) Another option for dancing is the **Uba-Club,**

5 bd. Mercader (✆ **04-68-34-06-70**), where there are (thankfully) some sofas and chairs, a modern decor, and a smallish dance floor. One of the largest discos in town is **Le Milord,** 20 rue Jules-Verne (✆ **04-68-55-40-77**), where a convivial crowd of persons ages 30 to 50 gather on either of two floors for dancing, playing billiards, flirting, and reminiscing.

Perpignan has two gay bars of note, neither of which has a listed phone number. Noted for its bar life (there's no dancing) is **Le Sept,** rue Grande-des-Fabriques, close to the harbor in the oldest part of town. Many of the region's gay men and women gravitate between it and **Le Soft,** 6 rue des Abreuvoirs, near the cathedral. Intimate and shadowy, Le Soft has a mirror-sheathed cellar, a dance floor, and a clientele that seems to have known one another for a very long time.

During summer, the nearby resort complex of **Canet-Plage,** 12km (7½ miles) east of Perpignan's historic core, contains a beachfront strip of seasonal bars and dance clubs that come and go with the tides and with midsummer tourism.

8 Collioure ★★

929km (577 miles) SW of Paris; 27km (17 miles) SE of Perpignan

You might recognize this port and its sailboats from the Fauve paintings of Lhote and Derain. It's said to resemble St-Tropez before it was spoiled. In the past, it attracted Matisse, Picasso, and Dalí. Collioure is the most authentic and alluring port of Roussillon, a gem with a vivid Spanish/Catalan image and flavor. Some visitors believe it's the most charming village on the Côte Vermeille.

ESSENTIALS

GETTING THERE Collioure is serviced by frequent **train** and bus connections, especially from Perpignan, at the rate of 15 trains per day (trip time: 20 min.). For train information and schedules, call ✆ **08-36-35-35-35.** Many visitors **drive** along the coastal road (RN 114) leading to the Spanish border.

VISITOR INFORMATION The **Office de Tourisme** is on place du 18-Juin (✆ **04-68-82-15-47**).

SPECIAL EVENTS The annual **Salon des Antiquaires** takes place on a 3-day weekend around November 1. Antiques dealers from throughout southern France set up shop for wholesalers and retailers. For more information, contact the tourist office.

EXPLORING THE TOWN

The town's sloping, narrow streets; charming semifortified church; antique lighthouse; and eerily introverted culture make it worth an afternoon stopover. This is the ideal small-town antidote to the condo-choked Riviera, and out of season, things around here are relatively calm.

The two curving ports are separated from each other by the heavy masonry of the 13th-century **Château Royal,** place du 8-Mai-1945 (✆ **04-68-82-06-43**). The château, now a museum of painting and folkloric artifacts, is open daily June through September from 10am to 6pm, and October through May from 9am to 5pm (closed Jan 1, May 1, and Dec 25). Admission is 3€ for adults and 2€ for children; free for children under 7. Also try to visit the **Musée Jean-Peské,** route de Port-Vendres (✆ **04-68-82-10-19**), with its collection of works by artists who migrated here to paint. It's open in July and August daily from 10am to noon and 3 to 7pm, and September through June Wednesday through

Monday from 10am to noon and 2 to 6pm. Admission is 1.85€ for adults, 1.20€ for children 12 to 16, and free for children under 12.

WHERE TO STAY

Casa Païral ★ This is a small-scale, family-operated place, not too businesslike, but sort of charming. On sunny days, the most alluring part of this 150-year-old house is an outdoor swimming pool in the shadow of century-old trees. The small to medium-size bedrooms are comfortable and filled with charming old antiques alongside more modern pieces; bathrooms are small. The best doubles have a petit salon plus a small balcony. Only breakfast is served, but there are many restaurants nearby. The hotel lies 150m (492 ft.) from the port and the beach.

Impasse des Palmiers, 66190 Collioure. ✆ **04-68-82-05-81.** Fax 04-68-82-52-10. www.roussillhotel.com. 28 units. 90€–117€ double; 150€–165€ suite. AE, MC, V. Parking 8€. Closed Nov 2–Mar 29. **Amenities:** Outdoor pool. *In room:* A/C, TV, minibar, hair dryer.

Hôtel Princes de Catalogne This is a relatively modern hotel of little architectural interest, but its position is in the town center and it has a hardworking and cooperative staff. Bedrooms contain simple, angular furniture with touches of traditional Provençal upholsteries, a writing table, and comfortable beds; they are a bit more spacious than you might have expected. The tidy bathrooms are tiled and small. Guests gather in the evening to enjoy tapas at the bar and live piano music, but this activity usually doesn't go on late enough to disturb the early-to-bed guests.

Rue des Palmiers, 66190 Collioure. ✆ **04-68-98-30-00.** Fax 04-68-98-30-31. 29 units. 68€ double; 102€ suite. AE, MC, V. Free parking. **Amenities:** Bar. *In room:* A/C, TV, minibar, hair dryer, safe.

Le Bon Port Built during the 1940s, this stucco-sided hotel perches beside the port, across the water from the town center, which lies within a 5-minute walk. It offers comfortable, appealingly simple bedrooms with summery furniture, tile floors, and flowered upholsteries; some have shared bathrooms. Accommodations are scattered within three separate buildings, the smallest of which is a two-unit cabana set beside the swimming pool. Staff is soft-spoken and charming, and knows what's going on within Collioure.

12 route de Port-Vendres, 66190 Collioure. ✆ **04-68-82-06-08.** 24 units, 8 with shared bathrooms. 57€–77€ double. MC, V. **Amenities:** Bar; pool; babysitting. *In room:* TV.

Les Caranques *Value* Constructed around the core of a private villa built after World War II and enlarged twice since then, this hotel is comfortably furnished, personalized, and one of the best bargains in town. The rooms are a bit small but neatly maintained. Set on the perimeter of Collioure, away from the crush (and the charm) of the center, the hotel features a terrace that opens onto a view of the old port. The terrace stretches from the hotel to the sea, where guests can swim directly from the rocks.

Route de Port-Vendres, 66190 Collioure. ✆ **04-68-82-06-68.** Fax 04-68-82-00-92. www.les-caranques.com. 22 units. 70€–75€ double. AE, MC, V. Free parking. Closed Oct 15–Mar. **Amenities:** Lounge.

Les Templiers ★ *Finds* The most charming and atmospheric hotel in the town center maintains its headquarters about 15m (50 ft.) inland from the port, in a *fin-de-siècle* house whose ground floor is devoted to a recommended bar and restaurant (see "Where to Dine," below). Part of the charm of the place derives from the clusters of mature local men playing cards at tables in the bar and conversing (and, in some cases, according to the staff, "cheating") in Catalan. The hotel consists of four separate buildings, each within a short walk from one another. The most atmospheric, most comfortable, and most lavishly decorated of the four is the hotel's headquarters, site of registration for the annexes, which do not employ receptionists or check-in staffs of their own. In the main building, expect at least 2,000 paintings—so many that most of the wall surfaces are completely covered with them—and a bar that's artfully sculpted to resemble a boat, complete with a sculpture at one end of a mermaid comforting (or seducing) a much smaller depiction of a sailor. Bedrooms in the main building have polychrome (i.e., painted) Catalan-style furniture and views of the town's chateau and, in some cases, the sea; those in the annexes have traditional but less lavish decors and less inspiring views.

12 Quai de l'Amirauté, 66190 Collioure. ✆ **04-68-98-31-10.** Fax 04-68-98-01-24. www.hotel-templiers.com. 55 units. 46€–75€ double in main building; 34€–50€ double in annexes. AE, DC, MC, V. Closed Jan to mid-Feb. **Amenities:** Restaurant; bar; limited room service (main building only); babysitting; laundry service. *In room:* A/C, TV.

Relais des Trois Mas et Restaurant La Balette ★★ This is not only the town's premier hotel, but also the restaurant of choice. This hotel was established more than 20 years ago by connecting a trio of older homes (Provençal farmhouses) into a new construction. In the decor of its beautiful rooms, the hotel honors the famous artists who lived at Collioure. The rooms, which lead to spacious bathrooms with Jacuzzis, open onto water views. Even if you aren't a guest, you might want to take a meal in the dining room, with its vistas of the harbor. Jose Vidal is the best chef in town. His cooking is inventive—often simple but always refined.

Route de Port-Vendres, 66190 Collioure. ✆ **04-68-82-05-07.** Fax 04-68-82-38-08. 23 units. 105€–275€ double; 230€–440€ suite. Half-board 75€ extra per person (obligatory June–Sept). MC, V. Parking 15€. Closed Nov 15–Dec 15. **Amenities:** Restaurant; bar; pool; limited room service. *In room:* A/C, TV, minibar, hair dryer.

WHERE TO DINE

Note that the **Restaurant La Balette** (see above) is the best dining room in town.

L'Andalou ★ *Value* FRENCH/SPANISH Situated at the edge of Collioure's historic core, this cozy bistro and tavern is the creative statement of Manuel Fernandez; his wife, Caroline; and extended members of their family. It's decorated with a hanging collection of flamenco dresses and depictions of the surrounding landscape. The menu offers succulent, well-prepared testimonials to the old-fashioned, savory seafood that fed many generations of Catalonians. Look for such Spanish-style dishes as a *parillade* of seafood; a spicy, garlic-laced *soupe de poissons* (fish soup); or perhaps a portion of yellow Manchego cheese in a style you expect in Madrid. A particularly attractive bargain is the house *paella,* priced at 10€ for one person and at 27€ for a full-blown celebration of the dish. A roster of French and Spanish wines (especially *riojas*) can accompany your meal.

10 rue de la République. ✆ **04-68-82-32-78.** Reservations recommended. Main courses 11.50€–18.20€. AE, MC, V. Thurs–Tues noon–2:30pm and 7pm–midnight.

La Pêcherie SEAFOOD Simple, hearty, and completely unpretentious, this seafood restaurant lies a short walk from the town's most interesting hotel, Trois Mas, within a stone-sided, thick-beamed 19th-century house. The richly atmospheric interior showcases pleasant aromas of spicy seafoods bubbling away beneath ceiling beams, near walls of exposed masonry. Expect generous portions and cheap prices for grilled fish (sea bass, red mullet, and sea wolf are especially popular), a spicy version of fish soup, a local and savory version of bouillabaisse, and a wine list featuring the vintages of the region.

54 rue de la Democratie. ✆ **04-68-82-20-23.** Reservations recommended. Main courses 22€–30€ for most fish dishes and up to 52€ for some shellfish. MC, V. Daily noon–1:30pm and 7–10:30pm. Closed Nov.

Les Templiers CATALAN Part of its charm derives from a bar whose every inch of wall surface is covered with paintings, and a well-established role as the town's most popular card-playing venues for retired Catalan-speaking local gents. After an aperitif in the bar, you'll be prepared for a meal in the dining room, where stone vaults, more paintings, and the possibility of sitting at a table on the pavement in front add to the allure. Menu items are entirely based on old-fashioned Catalan traditions. An excellent starter is a circular platter of grilled anchovies, artfully arranged like spokes on a wheel, and drizzled with olive oil and sprinkled with parsley and other herbs. Other options include a platter of fried fish that incorporates whatever was hauled in from the Mediterranean that day, a savory bouillabaisse, fresh codfish served with a "caviar" of mashed eggplant, shoulder of Pyrénéen lamb with a spicy onion jam, and seafood paella. Dessert might include a time-tested crème Catalane or an unusual form of ice cream: Flavored with steamed and pulverized fennel, it's served with spice bread and saffron sauce.

12 Quai de l'Amirauté, 66190 Collioure. ✆ **04-68-98-31-10.** Reservations recommended in midsummer. Main courses 15€–25€; fixed-price menu (3 courses) 19€. AE, DC, MC, V. Wed–Mon noon–3pm and Wed–Sun 7–10:30pm (June–Sept daily). Closed Jan to mid-Feb.

Le Trémail CATALAN/SEAFOOD Set on a narrow, cobble-covered alleyway in the oldest part of Collioure, this is a rustic and authentically Catalan restaurant. It functioned for many generations as the family home of the owner, Jean-Paul Fabre. Surrounded by stone walls, hand-painted Spanish tiles, and dangling fish nets, less than 18m (60 ft.) from the edge of the sea, it specializes in grilled fish *(à la plancha),* invariably served with olive oil and herb-enriched vinaigrette. Examples include grilled anchovies with braised onions and peppers, a succulent version of whatever the day's catch from the local fishing fleet might be, and desserts like *crème Catalán* or a homemade pastry. A limited number of "noble fish"—sole and turbot—might be on hand, along with a limited roster of meat. Particularly succulent are *rondelles* of calamari with red wine.

16 bis rue Mailly. ✆ **04-68-82-16-10.** Reservations recommended. Main courses 14-27€; set menu 21€. DC, MC, V. Tues–Sun noon–2:15pm and 7:15–10:30pm; mid–June and mid–Sept also Mon. Closed Jan.

9 Narbonne ★

845km (525 miles) SW of Paris; 61km (38 miles) E of Carcassonne; 93km (58 miles) S of Montpellier

Medieval Narbonne was a port to rival Marseille in Roman days, with its "galleys laden with riches." It was the first town outside Italy to be colonized by the Romans, but the Mediterranean, now 8km (5 miles) away, left it high and dry. It's an intriguing place, steeped in antiquity.

After Lyon, Narbonne was the largest town in Gaul. Even today you can see evidence of the town's former wealth. Too far from the sea to be a beach town, it attracts history buffs to its memories of a glorious past. Some 50,000 Narbonnais live in what is really a sleepy backwater. However, many locals are trying to make a go with their vineyards. Caves are open to visitors in the surrounding area (the tourist office will advise). If you want to go to the beach, you'll have to head to the nearby sands at the village of **Gruisson** and the beach (Gruisson-Plage) that adjoins it, or to the suburb of **St-Pierre la Mer** and its adjoining beach (Narbonne-Plage). Both lie 14km (9 miles) south of Narbonne. Buses from the town center are frequent, marked with their respective destinations.

ESSENTIALS

GETTING THERE Narbonne has rail, bus, and highway connections with other cities on the Mediterranean coast and with Toulouse. Rail travel is the most popular way to get here, with 14 **trains** per day arriving from Perpignan (trip time: 70 min.), 13 per day from Toulouse (trip time: 1½ hr.), and 12 per day from Montpellier (trip time: 1 hr.). For rail information, call ✆ **08-36-35-35-35.** If you're **driving,** Narbonne is at the junction of A61 and A9, easily accessible from either Toulouse or the Riviera.

VISITOR INFORMATION The **Office de Tourisme** is on place Roger-Salengro (✆ **04-68-65-15-60;** www.mairie-narbonne.fr).

Finds Liberté, Egalité, Fraternité . . . Nudité

The municipality known as **Agde,** 40km (25 miles) northeast of Narbonne and 50km (31 miles) southwest of Montpellier, operates like every other *commune* in France, with one startling exception: its flourishing nudist colony. In the 1970s, the community's founder/matriarch, Mademoiselle Geneviève Oltha, had the idea of promoting a simple pine grove beside the sea as a place for an escape from the stresses of urban life. Within less than 25 years, the site burgeoned into the largest nudist colony in Europe, with a roster of about 100 midwinter residents and a midsummer population usually approaching 50,000.

Don't expect everyone in Agde to be nude, since the town's four major subdivisions (Cité d'Agde, Cap d'Agde, Grau d'Agde, and La Tamarissière) offer options for the clothed as well. However, in the clearly signposted and, for the most part, fenced-in **Quartier Naturiste Cap d'Agde** ★ (✆ **04-67-26-00-26**), nudity is required on the beaches and encouraged elsewhere. Stores, restaurants, and shops (most selling everything except—you guessed it—clothing) are part of the setup. Those who arrive on foot at the compound's gate pay 3€ for entrance; motorists with as many passengers as can be crammed into their cars pay 9€. The **Agde Office de Tourisme,** Espace Molière, Centre Ville (✆ **04-67-94-29-68**), or its satellite branch, the **Office Municipal de Tourism,** Cap d'Agde, Les Plages (✆ **04-67-01-04-04**), long ago became accustomed to answering questions for the clothed, the unclothed, and the clothing indecisive.

Conveniently close to but not within the nudist zone are two museums. The **Musée Agathois,** rue de la Fraternité (✆ **04-67-94-82-51**), is noted for the homage it pays to (clothed) cultural models of the city's 19th-century fishing tradition and the region's handcrafts. The **Musée Ethèbe,** Mas de la Clape, Cap d'Agde (✆ **04-67-94-69-60**), showcases the artifacts dredged up by marine explorations of the nearby sea bottom. Its star exhibit and namesake is the nearly life-size **l'Ethèbe,** a graceful-looking Greek statue from the 6th century B.C. Admission to both museums costs 3.80€.

EXPLORING THE TOWN

The town's sights are concentrated in the medieval Vielle Ville (Old City), a massive central labyrinth of religious and civic buildings.

THE CENTRAL COMPLEX

A ***billet global,*** good for 3 days, allows entrance into all the museums in the archbishop's palace plus the Musée Lapidaire. It costs 4.55€ for adults and 1.50€ for students and youth ages 12 to 18. The museums are free for children 11 and under.

The neo-Gothic **Hôtel de Ville** (town hall) in the complex was reconstructed by Viollet-le-Duc, the 19th-century architect who refurbished Notre-Dame in Paris between 1845 and 1850.

Cathédrale St-Just ★★ The cathedral's construction began in 1272, but it was never finished. Only the transept and a choir were completed. The choir is 39m (130 ft.) high, built in the bold Gothic style of northern France. At each end of the transept are 58m (194-ft.) towers from 1480. There's an impressive collection of Flemish tapestries. The cathedral is connected to the archbishop's palace by 14th- and 15th-century cloisters.

Place de l'Hôtel-de-Ville (enter on rue Gauthier). ✆ **04-68-32-09-52.** Free admission. May–Sept daily 10am–7pm; Oct–Mar daily 9am–noon and 2–6pm.

Donjon Gilles-Aycelin If you happen to visit between mid-June and mid-September, you might want to participate in one of the occasional hikes up the steep steps of the watchtower. A watchtower and prison in the late 13th century, it has a lofty observation platform with a view of the cathedral, the surrounding plain, and the Pyrénées.

Place de l'Hôtel-de-Ville. ✆ **04-68-90-30-30.** 1.50€ adults, .70€ students and ages 11–18. Apr–Sept daily 11am–7pm; Oct–Mar daily 10am–noon and 2–5pm.

Palais des Archevêques (Archbishop's Palace, or Vieux-Palais) The palace was conceived as part fortress, part pleasure residence. It has three military-style towers from the 13th and 14th centuries. The Old Palace on the right dates from the 12th century, and the so-called "New Palace" on the left dates from the 14th. It's said that the old, arthritic, and sometimes very overweight archbishops used to be hauled up the interior's monumental Louis XIII-style stairs on mules.

Today the once-private apartments of the former bishops contain three museums. The **Musée Archéologique** ★ contains prehistoric artifacts, Bronze Age tools, 14th-century frescoes, and Greco-Roman amphorae. Several of the sarcophagi date from the 3rd century, and some of the mosaics are of pagan origin. The **Musée d'Art et d'Histoire de Narbonne** is located three floors above street level in the archbishop's once-private apartments (the rooms where Louis XII resided during his siege of Perpignan). Their coffered ceilings are enhanced with panels depicting the nine Muses. A Roman mosaic floor and 17th-century portraits are on display. There's also a collection of antique porcelain, enamels, and a portrait bust of Louis XIV. In the **Horreum Romain,** you'll find a labyrinth of underground passageways, similar to catacombs but without burial functions, dug by the Gallo-Romans and their successors for storage of food and supplies during times of siege.

Place de l'Hôtel-de-Ville. ✆ **04-68-90-30-30,** or 04-68-90-30-54 for museum information. Billet global or 5€. Apr–Sept daily 9:30am–12:15pm and 2–6pm; Oct–Mar Tues–Sun 10am–noon and 2–5pm.

MORE SIGHTS

Basilique St-Paul-Serge This early Gothic church was built on the site of a 4th-century necropolis. It has an elegant choir with fine Renaissance woodcarvings and some ancient Christian sarcophagi. The chancel, from 1229, is admirable. The north door leads to the Paleo-Christian Cemetery, part of an early Christian burial ground.

Rue de l'Hôtel-Dieu. ✆ **04-68-32-68-98.** Free admission. Apr–Sept daily 9am–7pm; Oct–Mar daily 9am–noon (plus Mon–Sat 2–6pm).

Musée Lapidaire Located in the 13th-century Notre-Dame de Lamourguier, this museum contains an important collection of Roman artifacts—broken sculptures and Latin inscriptions—as well as relics of medieval buildings. While it has no major exhibits, it does offer a vast array of classical busts, Roman lintels, and ancient sarcophagi that will satisfy all but the most feverish archaeologists. It takes less than an hour to see it all. You can enter with your general admission ticket to the museums of the archbishop's palace.

Place Lamourguier. ✆ **04-68-65-53-58.** Billet global or 2.50€. July–Aug daily 9:30am–12:15pm and 2–6pm; rest of year by arrangement with tourist office.

WHERE TO STAY

Hôtel du Languedoc Although there is a cookie-cutter chain hotel in town, the Novotel, and a motel on the outskirts, the Languedoc remains the traditional favorite because of its old-fashioned ambience and nostalgic feel of the province. It bravely keeps up with the times, however, and has a welcoming atmosphere because of a very helpful staff. It offers well-equipped rooms with acceptably comfortable mattresses. As is typical of an old hotel of this era, rooms come in various shapes and sizes.

Even if not a guest, consider a visit to its well-respected restaurant, which features an array of regionally inspired dishes. Try such specialties as grilled salmon served with anchovy butter or tender lamb from the hills cooked with broad beans. Fresh oysters are often on the menu. Also on site is the town's best wine bar, Le Bacchus, specializing in the many esoteric vintages grown nearby and willing to serve wine by the glass.

22 bd. Gambetta, 11100 Narbonne. ✆ **04-68-65-14-74.** Fax 04-68-65-81-48. www.hoteldulanguedoc.com. 40 units. 40€–72€ double; 79€ suite. AE, DC, MC, V. Parking 6.10€. **Amenities:** Restaurant; bar/Breton-style creperie. *In room:* TV.

La Résidence ★ Our favorite hotel in Narbonne is near the Cathédrale St-Just. The 19th-century La Résidence, converted from the premises of a once-stately villa, is decorated with antiques. Bedrooms are fitted with doubles or twins and fine linen. Bathrooms are small but neat. The hotel doesn't have a restaurant but offers breakfast and a gracious welcome.

6 rue du 1er-Mai, 11100 Narbonne. ✆ **04-68-32-19-41.** Fax 04-68-65-51-82. 25 units. 68€–76€ double. AE, DC, MC, V. Parking 6.50€. Closed Jan 16–Feb 17. *In room:* A/C, TV, minibar, hair dryer.

WHERE TO DINE

L'Alsace FRENCH/ALSATIAN Across from the train station, L'Alsace is the most reliable restaurant within Narbonne. The comfortable dining room is done in English style, with wood paneling and a glass-enclosed patio. In spite of the restaurant's name, the cuisine isn't from Alsace-Lorraine, but is typical of southwestern France, with a focus on seafood. The Sinfreus, who own the place, offer a fry of red mullet, a savory kettle of bourride, and magret of duck with flap mushrooms. Especially delectable is this restaurant's specialty: sea wolf or other whole fish baked in a salt crust, a method that usually produces a delightfully pungent and flaky product.

2 av. Pierre-Sémard. ✆ **04-68-65-10-24.** Reservations recommended. Main courses 20.25€–22.50€; fixed-price menus 18€–32.50€. AE, DC, MC, V. Mon noon–2:30pm; Wed–Sun noon–2:30pm and 7:30–10pm.

La Table St-Crescent ★★★ FRENCH/LANGUEDOCIENNE This is one of the region's most respected restaurants. It's just east of town, beside the road leading to Perpignan, in a complex of wine-tasting boutiques established by a local syndicate of wine growers. The foundations of this place date, it's said, from the 8th century, when it functioned as an oratory (small chapel) and prayer site. Today it's outfitted with nondescript modern furniture that's obviously little more than a foil for the cuisine of master chef Claude Giraud. He delivers a refined, brilliantly realized repertoire, with sublime sauces and sophisticated herbs and seasonings. Menu items change four times a year based on seasonality of ingredients and the inspiration of the owners. Main courses include sea bass marinated with olives, beef filet with foie gras and truffles, and a lasagna of grilled eggplant with a confit of tomatoes and oil of pistou. Especially succulent is roasted shoulder of lamb with crispy noodles and sweet garlic-and-sage sauce. Wine steward Sabrine Giraud (the chef's wife) will help you select the perfect accompaniment to your meal. The most unusual dessert is a platter piled high with four confections, each of which uses some variation on the olive.

In the Palais des Vins, route de Perpignan. ✆ **04-68-41-37-37.** Reservations recommended. Main courses 15€–36€; fixed-price menus 30€–52€ (Tues–Fri at lunch, 19€). AE, DC, MC, V. Tues–Fri and Sun noon–2:30pm; Mon–Sat 7–9:30pm.

NARBONNE AFTER DARK

The city has some routine dance clubs—nothing special. Check out the action, if any, at **Le Cassiopée,** chemin Rochegrise (✆ **04-68-41-75-61**), or at **Dancing GM Palace,** Centre Commercial Forum Sud, Route de Perpignan (✆ **04-68-41-59-71**).

10 Aigues-Mortes ★★

750km (466 miles) SW of Paris; 63km (39 miles) NE of Sète; 40km (25 miles) E of Nîmes; 48km (30 miles) SW of Arles

South of Nîmes, you can explore much of the Camargue by car, mainly on the roads of the **Parc Regional de Carmargue.** The most rewarding target is Aigues-Mortes, the city of the "dead waters." It is France's most perfectly preserved walled town. In the middle of dismal swamps and melancholy lagoons, Aigues-Mortes stands on four navigable canals. Although it is now 6km (4 miles) from the sea, it was once a thriving port, the first in France on the Mediterranean. Louis IX and his crusaders set forth from here on the Ninth Crusade.

ESSENTIALS

GETTING THERE Four **trains** and five **buses** per day connect Aigues-Mortes and Nîmes. Trip time is about an hour. For information and schedules, call ✆ **08-36-35-35-35.** If you're **driving** to Aigues-Mortes, take D979 south from Gallargues, or A9 from Montpellier or Nîmes.

VISITOR INFORMATION The **Office de Tourisme** is at Porte de la Gardette (✆ **04-66-53-73-00;** www.ot-aiguesmortes.fr).

EXPLORING THE TOWN

The main allure in Aigues-Mortes is the city itself. A sense of medievalism still permeates virtually every building, every rampart, and every cobbled street, and the town is still enclosed by **Ramparts** ★★ that were constructed between 1272 and 1300. The **Tour de Constance** ★★ (✆ **04-66-53-61-55**), which looks out on the marshes, is a model castle of the Middle Ages. At the top, which you can reach by elevator, a panoramic view unfolds. Admission is 5.50€ for adults, 3.50€ for youths ages 18 to 25, and free for children 17 and under. The monument is open every day May through August from 9:30am to 8pm, September from 9:30am to 7pm, October through January from 10am to 5pm, and February through April from 10am to 6pm.

The city's religious centerpiece is the **Eglise Notre-Dame des Sablons,** rue Jean-Jaurès (✆ **04-66-53-86-73**). Originally constructed of wood in 1183, it was rebuilt in stone in 1246 in the ogival style. Its stained-glass windows are modern, having been installed in 1980 as replacements for the badly damaged and weather-beaten originals. The church is open daily from 8:30am to 6pm.

WHERE TO STAY

Note that the **Restaurant Les Arcades** (see below) also rents rooms.

Hostellerie des Remparts Established about 300 years ago, this weather-worn inn lies at the foot of the Tour de Constance, adjacent to the medieval fortifications. Popular and often fully booked (especially in summer), it evokes the Middle Ages with charm and a sense of nostalgia. The rooms with simple furniture are accessible via narrow stone staircases. Each comes with a rather thin but reasonably comfortable mattress and a small bathroom. Breakfast is the only meal served.

6 place Anatole-France, 30220 Aigues-Mortes. ✆ **04-66-53-82-77.** Fax 04-66-53-73-77. 19 units. 43€–70€ double. AE, DC, V.

Hôtel des Croisades ★ Set within 25m (83 ft.) of the medieval ramparts, adjacent to the canal ("le Chenal maritime") and the marina, this is a cozy, well-maintained hotel that's under the care of Mireille and Robert Thiers. It was originally built as a private home in the late 1800s and was transformed in 1987 into

---

The Legacy of Roman Blood & Gore

Bullfighting is alive and well in the Camargue. Bullfighters usually come in from Spain, but these high-energy odes to high jinx and high testosterone are conducted in ways that aren't completely *espagnol.* Sometimes the bull is killed and sometimes it will mangle a local youth during a bullring celebration. Most *gardiens* are too shrewd to participate in a head-on confrontation with a bull, though there are likely to be at least one or two on horseback in or near the ring during the contest.

Although there are some minor bullfights in July and August in small arenas in the Camargue, the best ones are staged in Arles at the **Amphitheater (Les Arénes;** p. 112). Tickets range in price from 9.10€ to 76€. In modern times, the most avid aficionado of the bullfights in Arles was Picasso, who, in gratitude for the blood and gore, donated 70 of his drawings to the city of Arles. The corridas staged here Easter through September have been called "as bloody as anything presented to the Romans."

Fun Fact **Birth of the American Cowboy**

Many historians believe that the first real cowboys of North America were *gardiens,* imported from the Camargue to Louisiana to tend the flocks of the New World.

the simple but decent and dignified hotel you'll see today. Bedrooms are well proportioned and clean, often with reproduction furniture that evokes old France, including oversize armoires and deep colors like bordeaux and terra cotta. Rooms 11, 12, 14, and 15 have the most panoramic views over the walled city and the marina. Breakfast is the only meal served.

2 rue du Port, 30220 Aigues-Mortes. © **04-66-53-67-85.** 15 units. 48€ double. MC, V. Free parking. **Amenities:** Breakfast room. *In room:* A/C, TV.

Hôtel Les Templiers ★ The town's leading inn is a gem of peace and tranquillity, along with luxurious comfort. Protected by the ramparts built by Saint Louis, king of France, this 17th-century residence has been tastefully converted to receive guests in all the comfort of a private home. The small to medium-size guest rooms are decorated in a homey Provençal style. You'll find fine linen on a comfortable French bed, plus a compact and tidy private bathroom. You can relax in the courtyard, where you can also enjoy breakfast. Arrangements can be made to take half board at the Le Maguelone restaurant across the street.

23 rue de la République, 30220 Aigues-Mortes. © **04-66-53-66-56.** Fax 04-66-53-69-61. 10 units. 90€–125€ double. AE, DC, V. Closed Nov–Jan. **Amenities:** Restaurant; bar. *In room:* A/C, TV, hair dryer.

Hôtel St-Louis Though not grand in any way or as fine as Hôtel Les Templiers, this is the town's second-place choice for lodgings. An inn near place St-Louis, it offers small but comfortably furnished bedrooms, each with a tiled and compact bathroom.

Many locals come here to enjoy the regional meals served in the hotel's restaurant, L'Archére, your best bet for steak and fresh fish. The area, of course, is known for its beef, and this dining room (open to nonresidents) serves some of the most tender and juicy steaks in the area. It also has a good bounty of seafood brought in daily from the nearby coast. Chefs are skilled in the kitchen, turning out an array of the local favorites along with homemade desserts prepared fresh every day.

10 rue de l'Amiral-Courbet, 30220 Aigues-Mortes. © **04-66-53-72-68.** Fax 04-66-53-75-92. 22 units. 56€–97€ double. AE, DC, MC, V. Parking 12€. Closed Jan to Mar 10. **Amenities:** Restaurant; bar; limited room service. *In room:* TV, minibar.

WHERE TO DINE

Restaurant Les Arcades ★★ TRADITIONAL FRENCH There's no contest: This is the area's finest dining choice. This restaurant has several formal sections with beamed ceilings or intricately fitted stone vaults. Almost as old as the nearby fortifications, the place is especially charming on sultry days, when the thick masonry keeps the interior cool. Good food is served at reasonable prices and is likely to include warm oysters, fish soup, pot-au-feu with three different meats, roasted monkfish in red-wine sauce, lobster fricassée, and grilled duckling.

The owner also rents 10 large, comfortable rooms, each with air-conditioning, TV, and phone. A double is 83€ to 106€, with breakfast included.

23 bd. Gambetta, 30220 Aigues-Mortes. ✆ **04-66-53-81-13.** Reservations recommended. Main courses 9€–28€; fixed-price menus 29€–38€. AE, DC, MC, V. Tues 7:30–9:30pm; Wed–Sun noon–2pm and 7:30–9:45pm (also open Mon night July–Aug). Closed 2 weeks in Mar and 2 weeks in Oct.

A SIDE TRIP FROM AIGUES-MORTES

LES GARDIENS OF THE CAMARGUE ★

Steamy, sweaty, and as flat as the plains of Nebraska, the marshy delta of the Rhône has been called a less fertile version of the Nile delta. The waterlogged flatlands encompassing the Grand and Petit Rhône were scorned by conventional farmers throughout the centuries because of their high salt content and root-rotting murk.

However, the area was considered a fit grazing ground for the local black-pelted longhorn cattle, so a breed of cowpokes and cowboys evolved on these surreal flatlands, whose traditions will make you think of Dodge City combined with primal hints of ancient Celtic lore. These French cowboys, caretakers of the cattle that survive amid the flamingos, ticks, hawks, snakes, and mosquitoes of the hot, salty wetlands, are known and loved by schoolchildren as *les gardiens.*

Moments A Day in the Life of a Camargue Cowboy

If observing unique wildlife or riding a horse through France's hottest and most legendary wetlands attracts you, you will enjoy a stay in France's cowboy country. Both hotels below will arrange a *ballade* on horseback for you, excursions that focus on the ecology and panorama of the marshlands. With equipment included, the cost is 25€ for 2 hours. A full-day equestrian excursion that includes lunch is priced at 80€.

At **L'Etrier Camarguais,** chemin bas des Launes, 13460 Les-Stes-Maries-de-la-Mer (✆ **04-90-97-81-14;** fax 04-90-97-88-11), about a mile north of Les-Stes-Maries-de-la-Mer, you'll find 28 rooms (with minibar, air-conditioning, and TV) costing 130.50€ to 150.95€ for a double, with half board included. In a compound surrounded by marshland, it resembles a combination log cabin/terra-cotta-and-stone farmhouse. The bar is decorated with saddles from around the world, the staff is accommodating, and the comfortably unpretentious rooms are outfitted in the Provençal style.

Offering a Camargue holiday on a somewhat grander scale is **Mas de la Fouque,** route d'Aigues-Mortes, 13460 Les-Stes-Maries-de-la-Mer (✆ **04-90-97-81-02;** fax 04-90-97-96-84). About 3km (2 miles) west of Les-Stes-Maries-de-la-Mer (about 6km/3½ miles by car because of the meandering roads), its rooms face southern views over the marshy Etang des Launes. It's more appealing and has more amenities than its less expensive competitor. The 14 rooms (12 with air-conditioning, and all with TV and minibar) cost 372.40€ for a double, with half board included. The restaurant offers respite even for nonguests, with elegant fixed-price lunches and dinners for between 40€ and 65€. A tennis court and swimming pool are on the premises, and if you like nature, the hotels will help arrange guides for wildlife-watching safaris during the autumn and winter.

The tradition of *les gardiens* originated in the 1600s, when local monasteries began to disintegrate and large tracts of cheap land were bought by private owners. Wearing their traditional garb of leather pants and wide-rimmed black hats, the *gardiens* present a fascinating picture as they ride through the marshlands on their sturdy horses. Their terrain isn't the romantic wide, open spaces of America's West, but consists instead of monotonous stretches whose highest point might be a mound of debris left from a medieval salt flat. The *gardiens* tend not to be overly communicative to outsiders; in speaking to one another, they use a clipped, telegraphic form of Provençal whose syntax would make Académie Française members shudder. Motor homes and caravans are beginning to appear in the area today, but once *les gardiens* lived in distinctive, single-story *cabanes* with thatched roofs and without windows. Bull's horns were positioned above each building's entrance as a means of driving away evil spirits.

An ally in the business of tending cattle is the strong, heavy-tailed Camargue horse, probably a descendant of Arabian stallions brought here by Moorish invaders after the collapse of the Roman Empire. Brown or black at birth, these horses develop a white coat, usually after their fourth year. Traditionally, they had no sheltered stables but were left to fend for themselves during the stifling summers and bone-chilling winters.

Today, in the world of modern tourism, the *gardiens* have become living symbols of an antique tradition that hasn't changed much—the cattle still run semiwild, identified by the brand of their *manadier,* or owner. However, today you can expect to see fewer *gardiens* than in the past. They seem willing to participate in tourism only up to a point. Many reminders of their traditions remain in the form of felt-sided cowboy hats as well as commemorative saddles and boots whose style resembles that of cowherds on the faraway plains of Spain.

11 Montpellier ★★

758km (471 miles) SW of Paris; 161km (100 miles) NW of Marseille; 50km (31 miles) SW of Nîmes

The capital of Mediterranean (or Lower) Languedoc, this ancient university city is still renowned for its medical school, founded in the 13th century. Nostradamus qualified as a doctor here, and even Rabelais studied at the school. Petrarch came to Montpellier in 1317 and stayed for 7 years.

Today Montpellier is a bustling metropolis, one of southern France's fastest-growing cities, thanks to an influx of new immigrants. Except for some dreary suburbs, the city has a handsomely laid-out core, with tree-flanked promenades, broad avenues, and historic monuments. Students are about a quarter of the population, giving the city a lively, animated aura. In recent years, many high-tech corporations, including IBM, have settled in Montpellier.

ESSENTIALS

GETTING THERE Some 10 **trains** per day arrive from Avignon (trip time: 1 hr.), 10 from Marseille (trip time: 1¾ hr.), 11 trains from Toulouse (trip time: 2½ hr.), and 13 from Perpignan (trip time: 1½ hr.). Trains arrive hourly from Paris's Gare de Lyon, requiring between 8 and 10 hours, depending on the train, and, in most cases, requiring a change of equipment in Lyon. One TGV (very fast) train arrives from Paris every day, taking less than 4 hours, without any changes of equipment en route. For rail information, call ✆ **08-36-35-35-35.** Two **buses** a day arrive from Nîmes (trip time: 1¾ hr.).

If you're **driving,** Montpellier lies off A9, heading west.

VISITOR INFORMATION The **Office de Tourisme** is at 30 av. Jean de Lattre de Tassigny (© **04-67-60-60-60;** www.ot-montpellier.fr).

SPECIAL EVENTS From late June to early July, an array of classical and modern dance performances cascade into town for the **Festival International Montpellier Danse.** Tickets sell for 6€ to 45€ and can be purchased through the organization's box office, **Montpellierdanse,** 18 rue Ste-Ursule (© **08-00-60-07-40**). In late July, the **Festival de Radio France et de Montpellier** presents a variety of orchestral music, jazz, and opera. Tickets run 10€ to 32€; call © **04-67-02-02-01** or contact the **Théâtre Le Corum,** esplanade Charles de Gaulle (© **04-67-61-67-61**).

EXPLORING THE TOWN

Called the Oxford of France because of its academic community, Montpellier is a city of young people, as you'll notice if you sit at one of the cafes on the heartbeat **place de la Comédie,** with its 18th-century Fountain of the Three Graces. It's the living room of Montpellier, the ideal place to chat, people-watch, or cruise.

Paul Valéry met André Gide in the **Jardin des Plantes,** 163 rue Auguste-Broussonnet (© **04-67-63-43-22**), and you might begin here, as it's the oldest such garden in France. It's reached from boulevard Henri-IV. This botanical garden, filled with exotic plants and a handful of greenhouses, was opened in 1593. Admission is free. It's open April through September, Tuesday through Sunday from 10am to 7pm, and October through March, Monday through Friday from 10am to 5pm.

Nearby is the town's spiritual centerpiece, the **Cathédrale St-Pierre,** on place St-Pierre (© **04-67-66-04-12**), founded in 1364. This is hardly one of the grand cathedrals of France, and it suffered badly in centuries of religious wars and revolutions. For a long time after 1795, it wasn't a cathedral at all, but was occupied by a medical school. Today the cathedral lacks pretension; its greatest architectural achievement is its unusual canopied porch, supported by two conical turrets. The best artworks inside are 17th-century canvasses in the transepts—notably the work of a Huguenot, Montpellier-born Sébastien Bourdon, who painted himself among the "heathen" in *The Fall of Simon Magnus.* Also moving is Jean Troy's *Healing of the Paralytic.* In theory, the church can be visited daily from 9am to noon and 2:30 to 7pm.

Before leaving town, take a stroll along the 17th-century **promenade du Peyrou** ★★, a terraced park with views of the Cévennes and the Mediterranean. This

---

Moments Oenophilia

If bending an elbow while holding a glass of wine is, in your opinion, a sport, consider a wine-lover's tour of one of the architectural oddities of Montpellier's wine district. Take a half-day exploration of the cellars and vineyards of the 18th-century **Château de Flaugergues,** in the hamlet of Flaugergues (© **04-99-52-66-37**). Positioned within a 10-minute drive east of Montpellier, on the road leading to the seacoast, it accepts visitors who appreciate the nuances of the region's rough-and-ready reds, rosés, and whites. Appointments should be made in advance for visits that are usually scheduled any afternoon between 2:30 and 6:30pm. The castle's elaborate architecture is viewed by locals as one of the local "follies" (folies) of the region.

Finds Exploring the Port Town of Séte

Séte, reached after a 34km (21-mile) drive southwest of Montpellier, boasts the largest fishing port on the Mediterranean and was once the principal link to France's colonies in North Africa. Even today a car-ferry transports passengers to and from the coasts of North Africa. You can almost picture Marlene Dietrich leaving the port bound for Morocco in a 1930s movie.

In an architectural blend of Art Deco and Second Empire, Séte was built on a limestone rock on the slopes of Mont Saint-Clair and is connected to the mainland by two sand pits. This city of canals sprawls across two islands and a network of estuaries connected and crisscrossed by bridges. These canals evoke comparison with Venice.

If you're staying over and want to dine, your best bet is **Le Grand Hotel,** 17 quai Maréchal de Lattre de Tassigny (✆ **04-67-74-71-77;** fax 04-67-74-29-77), at the center of the port, near the intersection of the two canals. Try for a front bedroom with its view of the moored boats. The limestone facade of the hotel is accented with elaborate corbels and bas-reliefs, some of which are designed like the prows of boats. The hotel's grandeur dates from the 1880s, with potted palms, a skylit atrium, and wickered armchairs. Today the place still retains much of its original beaux-arts charm, and the bedrooms are generally roomy, well furnished, and modernized. Rooms are air-conditioned, containing minibars, TV, and safes. Doubles rent for 115€.

At the same address is the restaurant **La Rotonde** (✆ **04-67-74-86-14**), which takes up two impressive ground-floor rooms of the hotel and is under separate management. The chef specializes in seafood, as would be predicted, and dishes are fresh and full of flavor. The restaurant is open for lunch Sunday through Friday from noon to 2:30pm, and dinner Monday through Saturday from 7 to 9:30pm. Full meals range in price from 25.50€ to 54.20€; reservations are recommended.

For information about Séte and the area, stop in at the **Office de Tourisme,** 60 Grand'Rue (✆ **04-67-74-71**). Trains arrive every hour during the day from Montpellier (trip time: 20 min.), at a one-way fare of 5.50€.

is a broad esplanade constructed at the loftiest point of Montpellier. Opposite the entrance is an Arc de Triomphe, erected in 1691 to celebrate the victories of Louis XIV. In the center of the promenade is an equestrian statue of Louis XIV and, at the end, the **Château d'Eau,** a pavilion with Corinthian columns that serves as a monument to 18th-century classicism. Water is brought here by a conduit, nearly 14km (9 miles long), and an aqueduct.

Musée Fabre ★★ One of France's great provincial art galleries, this museum occupies the former Hôtel de Massilian, where Molière once played for a season. The origins of the collection were an exhibition of the Royal Academy that was sent to Montpellier by Napoléon in 1803. The most important works of the collection, however, were given by François Fabre, a Montpellier painter, in 1825. After Fabre's death, many other paintings from his collection were donated to the gallery. Several of these he painted himself, but the more important works were ones he had acquired—including Poussin's *Venus and Adonis* and paintings from the Italian Renaissance. This generosity was followed by donations from others, notably Valedau, who in 1836 left the museum his collection of Rubens, Gérard Dou, and Téniers.

39 bd. Bonne-Nouvelle. ✆ **04-67-14-83-00.** Admission 4.50€ adults, 2€ students and persons 20 and under. Tues–Fri 9:30am–5:30pm; Sat–Sun 10am–5:30pm.

SHOPPING

Stroll down **place de la Comédie,** with its ultramodern Polygone shopping center, site of more than 120 independent boutiques, and **rue Jean-Moulin.** This town has a plethora of name-brand boutiques and department stores. For traditional regional delicacies, visit **Au Gourmets,** 2 rue Clos-René (✆ **04-67-58-57-04**), or visit **Pâtissier Schoeller,** 121 av. de l'Odàve (✆ **04-67-75-71-55**), for a plentiful supply of Ecusson de Montpellier (a chocolate praline with Grand Marnier wrapped in chocolate).

WHERE TO STAY

Note that **Le Jardin des Sens** (see below) also rents rooms.

IN MONTPELLIER

Expensive

Holiday Inn Montpellier ★ In the heart of Montpellier, this 1898 monument adjacent to the town's railway station stands behind an entrance with a soaring portal set into a dignified stone facade. In 1998, it underwent a radical renovation that retained the charming interior garden and the original detailing. The well-furnished, contemporary-looking bedrooms range in size from medium to spacious and are fitted with fine linens; the marble-sheathed bathrooms are roomy.

3 rue Clos-Rene, 34000 Montpellier. ✆ **04-67-12-32-32.** Fax 04-67-92-13-02. www.holiday-inn.com. 80 units. 170€ double; 180€–220€ suite. AE, DC, MC, V. Parking 8€. **Amenities:** Restaurant; bar; fitness center; limited room service; babysitting; laundry service; dry cleaning. *In room:* A/C, TV, minibar, coffeemaker, hair dryer, safe, iron.

Sofitel Montpellier Antigone ★ In the heart of Montpellier, this modern hotel is a favorite with businesspeople. However, in summer it does quite a trade with visitors as well. It's particularly distinguished for its pool, which, along with a bar and breakfast room, occupies most of the top floor. The rooms are chain format but first class. The best accommodations are on a floor known as Privilège, where you get such extras as an all-marble bathroom. It's a winning choice, with the most efficient staff in the city. Of the hotel's two bars, the Botanica, is one of the coziest hideaways in town.

11 rue Pertuisanes, 3400 Montpellier. ✆ **04-67-99-72-72.** Fax 04-67-65-17-50. www.sofitel.com. 90 units. 175€–213€ double; 315€ suite. AE, DC, MC, V. Valet parking 14€. Pets accepted. **Amenities:** 2 bars; outdoor pool; health club; car-rental desk; limited room service; laundry service; dry cleaning; nonsmoking rooms. *In room:* A/C, TV, hair dryer.

Moderate

Hôtel du Palais ★ One of the most historic hotels in town, the Palais is in the town center, amid a labyrinth of narrow streets. Built in the late 1700s, it has the kind of grandly symmetrical design associated with the *ancien régime.* Much of the decor dates from a restoration in 1983. Lots of fabrics, big curtains, and walls painted to resemble marble adorn the public rooms. Rooms are relatively large, cozy, and appealing; each features antique reproductions and a compact bathroom. Breakfast is the only meal served.

3 rue du Palais, 34000 Montpellier. ✆ **04-67-60-47-38.** Fax 04-67-60-40-23. 26 units. 61€–68€ double. AE, DC, MC, V. Parking 6€. *In room:* A/C, TV, minibar.

Hôtel du Parc ★ *Finds* One of the town's more charming moderately priced hostelries, this cozy hotel lies in the heart of the city near the Palais des Congrès. It was a Languedocian residence in the 18th century but has been turned into a hotel with a lot of grace notes and French provincial charm. Rooms have been carefully decorated and are accompanied by streamlined bathrooms. A garden and flowering terrace are available for breakfast outside. Numerous restaurants surround the hotel.

8 rue Achille-Bège, 34000 Montpellier. ✆ **04-67-41-16-49.** Fax 04-67-54-10-05. www.hotelduparc-montpellier.com. 19 units. 56€–64€ double. AE, MC, V. Free parking. **Amenities:** Lounge; limited room service. *In room:* A/C, TV, minibar, hair dryer.

La Maison Blanche ★★ This hotel seems to have worked hard to create a French Créole ambience: It's set in a modern clapboard motel whose balconies drip with ornate gingerbread and whose verdant gardens are bordered with lattices. The rooms are stylishly furnished in rattan and wicker and offer comfortable beds. Parts of the interior, especially the dining room, might remind you more of the France of Louis XIII than Old Louisiana, but overall the place is charming and unusual. The hotel is a 5-minute drive northeast of Montpellier's center.

1796 av. de la Pompignane, 34000 Montpellier. ✆ **04-99-58-20-70.** Fax 04-67-79-53-39. 38 units. 64€–87€ double; 125€ suite. AE, DC, MC, V. Free parking. Take bd. d'Antigone east until you reach the intersection with av. de la Pompignane, and head north until you see the hotel on your right. **Amenities:** Restaurant; bar; outdoor pool; limited room service; laundry service. *In room:* A/C, TV, hair dryer.

Le Guilhem Contained within a pair of interconnected stone-fronted 16th-century town houses, which needed to be almost completely rebuilt when the hotel was established in the 1950s, this is a well-managed hideaway with lots of (French) southern charm. There's a tastefully antique-looking lobby area, a polite staff, and conservatively contemporary bedrooms outfitted in monochromatic tones of mostly yellow or blue or, to a lesser degree, pink. Many overlook the well-established trees of a substantial garden, and many contain the quirky angles and idiosyncratic dimensions of the building's original designs. Other than breakfast, no meals are served, but considering the hotel's location near l'Arc de Triomphe, in Montpellier's historic core, there are many dining options nearby.

18 rue Jean-Jacques Rousseau, 34000 Montpellier. ✆ **04-67-52-90-90.** Fax 04-67-60-67-67. 76€–140€ double. Parking 4€. **Amenities:** 24-hr. room service (drinks and snacks only); babysitting (with prior notice); laundry service. *In room:* A/C, minibar, TV.

Inexpensive

Les Arceaux It's basic and most acceptable, and the price is right. A hotel has stood at this prime location, right off the renowned promenade du Peyrou, since the turn of the 20th century. The small to medium-size rooms are pleasantly but simply furnished, with compact bathrooms. A shaded terrace adjoins the hotel. Breakfast is the only meal served.

33–35 bd. des Arceaux, 34000 Montpellier. ✆ **04-67-92-03-03.** Fax 04-67-92-05-09. 18 units. 50€–58€ double. MC, V. *In room:* TV, minibar.

Ulysse ★ *Value* One of the city's better bargains, Ulysse delivers a lot for the price. It's simple, but the owners have worked hard—on a budget—to make the hotel as stylish as possible, with individually decorated rooms. The furnishings are functional but possess a certain flair. Bathrooms are fully equipped. The housekeeping is first rate, even though the prices are not.

338 av. de St-Maur, 34000 Montpellier. ✆ **04-67-02-02-30.** Fax 04-67-02-16-50. www.hotelulysse.com. 30 units. 48€–53€ double. AE, DC, V. From bd. d'Antigone, head north along av. Jean-Mermoz to rue de la Pépinière; continue right for a short distance and take a sharp left at the first intersection, which leads to av. de St-Maur. **Amenities:** Limited room service; nonsmoking rooms. *In room:* TV, minibar, safe.

NEAR MONTPELLIER

Demeure des Brousses ★★ *Finds* This 18th-century country house stands in a large, impressive park. The house was built by Monsieur and Madame Brousse, who made their fortune as *épiciers,* or spice merchants. A tranquil choice, it has been skillfully converted for guests. Rooms range from medium-size to spacious, each individually decorated in such 19th-century styles as French Empire. Public rooms are decorated like those of a gracious French country house, including loads of antiques, making this an intimate retreat. It's about a 10-minute drive from the heart of Montpellier.

Route de Vauguières, 34000 Montpellier. ✆ **04-67-65-77-66.** Fax 04-67-22-22-17. www.demeure-desbrousses.com. 17 units. 80€–90€double. AE, DC, MC, V. Free parking. Take D-172E 2 miles east of the town center. **Amenities:** Restaurant; bar; limited room service; laundry service; dry cleaning. *In room:* TV, hair dryer.

WHERE TO DINE

EXPENSIVE

Le Chandelier ★ MODERN FRENCH This is the most dramatic modern restaurant in Montpellier, with superb food as prepared by Gilbert Furland, excellent service as choreographed by Jean-Marc Forest, and a sweeping view over an upscale residential neighborhood (l'Antigone). Located on the seventh floor of a modern office building, the restaurant's large terrace becomes the main attraction during clement weather. The staff searches for "temptations of the palate," which means that you'll be presented with some unusual flavor combinations. Examples include a sophisticated version of calamari fried with fresh thyme, an escalope of foie gras in orange sauce, an award-winning ragout of lobster, and sautéed pigeon in a Provençal pistou. A particularly scrumptious dessert is a crispy *tarte* with caramelized mango.

Place Zeus, 3967 rue Léon-Blum. ✆ **04-67-15-34-38.** Reservations recommended. Main courses 20€–37€; fixed-price menus 38€–67€ lunch, 50€–67€ dinner. AE, DC, MC, V. Tues–Sat noon–1:30pm; Mon–Sat 8–10pm.

Le Jardin des Sens ★★★ *Finds* MODERN FRENCH If we could award more than three stars, we'd grant five to this citadel of fine cuisine. The chefs—the biological twins Laurent and Jacques Pourcel—have taken Montpellier by storm. Post-nouvelle reigns here; the rich bounty of Languedoc is served in preparations designed to enhance its natural flavor. The seemingly flawless meals could be almost anything, depending on where the chefs' imaginations roam. An appropriate starter might be ravioli stuffed with foie gras of duckling and flap mushrooms, floating in chicken bouillon fortified with truffles, broad beans, and crispy potatoes. A main course of note involves crisp-fried crawfish tails, served with a confit of pigeon and a fricassée of green peas with slices of Bayonne ham. A *tarte fine* with tomatoes, roasted monkfish, and essence of thyme is memorable, as is a filet of pigeon stuffed with pistachios. A dessert specialty is a gratin of limes with slices of pineapple *en confit.*

The Jardin des Sens also rents 12 deluxe guest rooms and 2 suites, designed in cutting-edge modernism by Bruno Borrione, a colleague of Philippe Starck.

11 av. St-Lazare. ✆ **04-99-58-38-38.** Fax 04-67-72-13-05. www.jardindessens.com. Reservations required. Main courses 39€–51€; fixed-price menus 46€ lunch (Mon–Fri), 90€–122€ dinner. AE, MC, V. Tues and Thurs–Sat noon–2pm; Mon–Sat 7:30–10pm.

MODERATE

La Réserve Rimbaud ★ FRENCH This memorable restaurant is located in a bulky manor house built in 1875 by a prosperous local family, the Rimbauds. It offers only about 30 seats in a setting that might've been plucked from the early 1900s. Menu items, prepared and presented by the English-speaking Tarrit family, change with the season but are likely to include truffle-studded chicken croquettes, monkfish with local herbs, curried crayfish, baked sea wolf with local herbs, stuffed calamari, warm foie gras with apples, fricassée of sole with baby vegetables, and chocolate cake with orange mousse and Grand Marnier sauce.

820 av. de St-Maur. ✆ **04-67-72-52-53.** Reservations recommended. Main courses 12€–28€; fixed-price menus 40€–58€. AE, DC, MC, V. Tues–Sat noon–2pm and 8–10pm; Sun noon–2pm. Closed Jan–Mar. Take N113 (av. de Nîmes) northeast toward Nîmes, follow it to the intersection with av. St-Lazare, and turn left; the restaurant is on the right.

L'Olivier ★ *Finds* MODERN FRENCH No restaurant, with the exception of Le Jardin des Sens, has improved more than L'Olivier has. Chef Michel Breton, assisted by his wife, Yvette, is seeing his name become linked with talk of the south of France. Don't even dream of showing up here without a reservation: The establishment holds places for only 20 diners at a time. The subdued, rather bland-looking modern space is painted a clear yellow and accented with contemporary paintings. But you don't come here for background—you want to try Breton's "creative statements." Some dishes that might appear regularly are salmon with oysters, fricassée of lamb with thyme, warm monkfish terrine, frogs' legs with wild mushrooms, haunch of rabbit stuffed with wild mushrooms, and salad of lamb sweetbreads with extract of truffles. The welcome is warm-hearted and sincere.

12 rue Aristide-Olivier. ✆ **04-67-92-86-28.** Reservations required. Main courses 20€–27€; fixed-price menus 38€. AE, MC, V. Tues–Sat noon–2pm and 7:30–9:30pm. Closed Aug and holidays.

MONTPELLIER AFTER DARK

After the sun sets, head for **place Jean-Jaurès, rue de Verdun,** and **rue des Ecoles Laïques,** or take a walk down **rue de la Loge** for its carnival atmosphere of talented jugglers, mimes, and musical artists.

Rockstore, 20 rue de Verdun (✆ **04-67-06-80-00**), with its 1950s rock memorabilia and live concerts, draws lots of students. Then walk up a flight of stairs to its disco, which pounds out techno and rock. The cover for the disco is 10€. An exotic cocktail bar is **Viva Brazil,** 7 rue de Verdun (✆ **04-67-58-63-33**), where you chop your way through the lush rain-forest vegetation and friendly natives to reach the mirrored sanctuary of the dance floor. For the best jazz and blues in town, check out **JAM,** 100 rue Ferdinand-de-Lesseps (✆ **04-67-58-30-30**). In a noisy, smoky, and even gritty space, its regular concerts attract jazz enthusiasts from miles around. Concert tickets average 50€.

A more recently inaugurated disco, modern, noisy, convivial, and known throughout the region, is **Toto Loco,** route de Carnon, in the hamlet of Lattes (✆ **04-99-52-23-74**), 5km (3 miles) south of the center of Montpellier. Populated with a crowd of drinkers and dancers ages 23 to 40, and open every Thursday through Sunday beginning around 10:30pm, it charges a 7€ or 8€ cover on Friday and Saturday nights, which includes the first drink. Gays and lesbians gather at the town's most animated bar/disco, **La Villa Rouge,** route de Palavas (✆ **04-67-06-52-15**).

Le Corum (✆ **04-67-61-67-61**), the most up-to-date theater in town, is the site of many plays, dance recitals, operas, and symphonic presentations. It lies within the Palais des Congrès, esplanade Charles-de-Gaulle, in the heart of town. For complete ticket information and schedules, contact the Corum directly or an organization that's instrumental in its management, the **Opéra Comédie,** place de la Comédie (✆ **04-67-60-19-99**).

12 Nîmes ★★★

708km (440 miles) S of Paris; 43km (27 miles) W of Avignon

Nîmes, the ancient Nemausus, is a great place to view some of the world's finest Roman remains. The city grew to prominence during the reign of Caesar Augustus (27 B.C. to A.D. 14). Today it possesses one of the best-preserved Roman amphitheaters in the world and a near-perfect Roman temple. The city of 135,000 is more like Provence than Languedoc, and there's a touch of Pamplona (Spain) here in the festivals of the *corridas* (bullfights) at the arena. The Spanish image is even stronger at night, when the bodegas fill, usually with students drinking sangría and listening to the sounds of flamenco.

ESSENTIALS

GETTING THERE Ten TGV trains on the TGV Méditerranée High-Speed Rail Line arrive each day from Paris (trip time: 3 hr.); tickets are from 75.90€ each way. For rail information and schedules, call ✆ **877/2TGVMED** or check www.raileurope.com. The bus station, **Gare Routière,** is just behind the railway station, on the rue Ste-Félicité (✆ **04-66-29-52-00**).

If you're **driving,** Nîmes can be reached from Lyon along A7 south to the town of Orange, connecting here to A9 into Nîmes.

VISITOR INFORMATION The **Office de Tourisme** is at 6 rue Auguste (✆ **04-66-58-38-00**).

EXPLORING THE CITY

THE TOP SIGHTS

Amphithéâtre Romain ★★★ The elliptically shaped amphitheater is a better-preserved twin to the one at Arles and is far more complete than the Colosseum of Rome. It's two stories high, each floor having 60 arches, and was built of huge stones painstakingly fitted together without mortar. One of the best preserved arenas from ancient times, it once held more than 20,000 spectators, who came to see gladiatorial combats and wolf or boar hunts. Today it's used for everything from ballet recitals to bullfights.

Place des Arènes. ✆ **04-66-76-72-77.** Admission 4.45€ adults, 3.20€ students and children 15 and under. Apr–Oct daily 9am–6:30pm; Nov–Mar daily 9am–5:30pm.

Carré d'Art/Musée d'Art Contemporain Across the square stands the modern-day twin of the Maison Carrée, a sophisticated research center and exhibition space that contains a library, a newspaper kiosk, and an art museum. Its understated design from 1993 was inspired by (but doesn't overpower) the ancient monument nearby. The museum's permanent expositions are often supplemented

---

Fun Fact **Denim de Nîmes**

By 1860, the togas of Nîmes's citizenry had given way to denim, the cloth de Nîmes. An Austrian immigrant, Leví-Strauss, started to export this heavy fabric to California for use as material to make work pants for gold diggers in those boomtown years. The rest, as they say, is history.

Nîmes

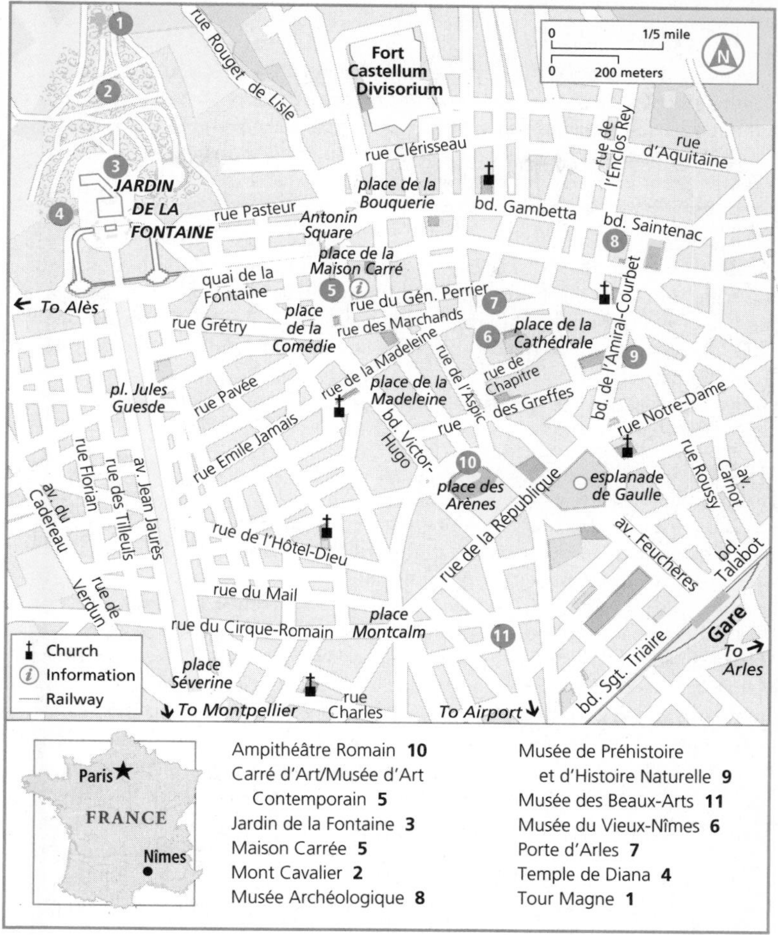

with temporary exhibits of contemporary art. ***Note:*** The view from this modern building's terrace allows you to rise above the roaring traffic and presents a panorama of ancient monuments and medieval churches.

Place de la Maison Carré. ✆ **04-66-76-35-35.** Admission 4.45€ adults, 3.20€ students and children 14 and under. Apr–Oct Tues–Sun 10am–6pm; Nov–Mar Tues–Sun 11am–6pm.

Maison Carrée ★★★ The pride of Nîmes, this is one of the most beautiful, and certainly one of the best-preserved, Roman temples of Europe. It was built during the reign of Caesar Augustus. Set on a raised platform with tall Corinthian columns, it inspired Thomas Jefferson as well as the builders of La Madeleine in Paris. A changing roster of cultural and art exhibits is presented beneath an authentically preserved roof that the city of Nîmes repaired in 1996.

Place de la Comédie. ✆ **04-66-36-26-76.** Free admission. Nov–Mar daily 9am–5pm; Apr–Oct daily 9:30am–6:30pm.

Tips **Your Lucky Ticket**

If you want to explore the city's monuments and museums, you can buy a ***billet global,*** sold at the ticket counter of any of the local museums and monuments. It provides access to all the cultural sites over a 3-day period and costs 9.55€ for adults and 4.80€ for students and children 15 and under. Entrance is free for children under 10.

Musée des Beaux-Arts The city's largest museum contains French paintings and sculptures from the 17th to the 20th centuries, as well as Flemish, Dutch, and Italian works from the 15th to the 18th centuries. Seek out in particular one of G. B. Moroni's masterpieces, *La Calomnie d'Apelle,* and a well-preserved Gallo-Roman mosaic.

Rue Cité-Foulc. ✆ **04-66-67-38-21.** Admission 4.50€ adults, 3.20€ students and children 14 and under. Tues–Sun 11am–6pm.

MORE SIGHTS

Jardin de la Fontaine, at the end of quai de la Fontaine, is a gorgeous garden that was laid out in the 18th century, using the ruins of a Roman shrine as an ornamental centerpiece. It was planted with rows of chestnuts and elms, adorned with statuary and urns, and intersected by grottos and canals—making it one of the most beautiful gardens in France. Adjoining it is the ruined **Temple de Diana** and the remains of some Roman baths. Within a 10-minute walk north of the town center, **Mont Cavalier,** a low but rocky hill, is topped by the sturdy bulk of the **Tour Magne,** the city's oldest Roman monument. You can climb it for a panoramic view over Nîmes and its environs. Admission to the tower is 2.40€ for adults and 1.90€ for students and children 14 and under. It's open daily April through October from 9:30am to 6:30pm, and November through March from 9am to 4:30pm.

Nîmes is home to a great number of museums. If time allows, visit the **Musée du Vieux-Nîmes,** place de la Cathédrale (✆ **04-66-76-73-70**), housed in an episcopal palace from the 1700s. It's rich in antiques. The museum charges 4.50€ for adults and 3.20€ for children. From April to September, hours are Tuesday through Sunday from 10am to 6pm; October through March, hours are Tuesday through Sunday from 11am to 6pm.

One of the city's busiest thoroughfares, **boulevard de l'Amiral-Courbet,** leads to the **Porte d'Arles**—the remains of a gate built by the Romans during the reign of Augustus. Farther south, in the same stately building at 13 bis bd. l'Amiral-Courbet, are the **Musée de Préhistoire et d'Histoire Naturelle** (✆ **04-66-76-73-45**) and the **Musée Archéologique** ★ (✆ **04-66-76-74-80**). For a combined admission of 4.50€ for adults and 3.20€ for children, you're admitted to both museums. From April to September, hours are Tuesday through Sunday from 10am to 6pm; from October to March, hours are Tuesday through Sunday from 11am to 6pm.

A FAMOUS ROMAN BRIDGE

Outside the city, 23km (14 miles) to the northeast, the well-preserved, much-photographed **pont du Gard** ★ spans the Gard River. Consisting of three tiers of arches arranged into gracefully symmetrical patterns, its huge stones are held together without mortar. It dates from about 19 B.C. and is a vivid reminder of the technical know-how of the ancient Romans. Frédéric Mistral, the national poet of Provence and Languedoc, recorded a medieval legend that the devil constructed the bridge with the proviso that he could claim the soul of the first person to go across it. Take Highway N86 from Nîmes to a point 3km (2 miles) from the village of Remoulins, where signs are prominently posted.

In April 2001, the appeal of the pont du Gard was increased with the construction of a new museum, **La Grande Expo du Pont du Gard,** B.P. 7, 30210 Vers Pont du Gard (✆ **04-66-37-50-99**). Inside, four exhibits detail its construction, its role throughout the Middle Ages in the development of the region, and insights into its symbolism as an enduring symbol of the architectural savvy of ancient Rome. There's also a restaurant and cafe, and a gift shop. From November to Easter, it's open daily from 10am to 6pm; from Easter to mid-June and during September and October, it's open daily from 9:30am to 7pm; and from mid-June to August, it's open daily from 9:30am to 9:30pm. Admission is 11€ for adults and 9€ for students and persons under 25.

SHOPPING

If you'd rather concentrate on shopping, head to the center of town and **rue du Général-Perrier, rue des Marchands, rue du Chapître,** and the pedestrian **rue de l'Aspic** and **rue de la Madeleine.** A Sunday market runs from 8am to around 1pm in the parking lot of the **Stade des Costières,** site of most of the town's football (soccer) matches, adjacent to the southern edge of the boulevard Périphérique that encircles Nîmes.

To appease your sweet tooth, go to just about any pastry shop in town and ask for the regional almond-based cookies called ***croquants villaret*** and ***caladons.*** They're great for a burst of energy or for souvenirs. One of the best purchases you can make in Nîmes, especially if you're not continuing east into Provence, is a ***santon.*** These wood or clay figurines are sculpted into a cast of characters from Provençal country life and can be collected together to create a uniquely country-French nativity scene. For a selection of *santons* in various sizes, visit the **Boutique Provençale,** 10 place de la Maison Carré (✆ **04-66-67-81-71**), or **Au Papillon Bleu,** 15 rue du Général-Perrier (✆ **04-66-67-48-58**).

WHERE TO STAY

EXPENSIVE

Imperator Concorde ★★★ This is the largest hotel in town and a member of the well-managed Concorde chain. Set behind the town's ancient Roman monuments, with a pale pink Italianate facade, it was much improved by renovations in the late 1990s. Bedrooms are artful and cozy, each outfitted in a monochromatic, jewel-toned color scheme of pink, ochre, or navy blue. Furniture is traditional French *ancien régime,* with fluted or cambriole details; beds are comfortable.

Quai de la Fontaine, 30000 Nîmes. ✆ **04-66-21-90-30.** Fax 04-66-67-70-25. www.concorde-hotels.com. 62 units. 143€–183€ double; 304€–319€ suite. AE, DC, MC, V. Parking 14€. **Amenities:** Restaurant; bar; limited room service; laundry service; dry cleaning. *In room:* A/C, TV, minibar, hair dryer.

MODERATE

Hôtel Vatel ★ This modern seven-story hotel, 3km (2 miles) north of the town center, is part of a group of buildings that include a technological university and a large hospital. Its student staff from the local hotel school work on-site as part of their on-the-job training. Rooms are streamlined, tasteful, and modern, and include marble-sheathed bathrooms. The upholstery is richly patterned, and beds are comfortable. In all, the modern format of this hotel provides levels of comfort that older hotels, in more historic settings, simply can't match.

140 rue Vatel, B.P. 7128, 30913 Nîmes CEDEX. ✆ **04-66-62-57-57.** Fax 04-66-62-57-50. 46 units. 93€ double; 183€ suite. AE, DC, MC, V. From the A4 autoroute, exit at NIMES OUEST. **Amenities:** 2 restaurants; bar; pool; health club; sauna. *In room:* A/C, TV, minibar, hair dryer.

New Hôtel La Baume ★★ Our favorite hotel in Nîmes sits behind a facade of chiseled stone in the heart of the city's oldest section, within a 10-minute walk from the Roman arena and within a 5-minute walk from the Maison Carrée. Built in the 17th century as a private home, it's constructed around a spacious interior courtyard studded with flowering plants and accented with small tables and a magnificent stone staircase that's an architectural treasure in its own right. (Access to any bedrooms is possible via elevator from the reception area, but frankly, it's a lot more glamorous to ascend the staircase instead.) Overall, the setting represents a winning combination of modern and traditional, with great attention paid to the preservation of the building's original architectural heritage. Each of the bedrooms is outfitted in a nostalgic Provençal style, each with a unique monochromatic color scheme (blues, greens, ochres, or soft oranges). Whereas the toilets within each unit are set within private enclosures (with doors), the shower/tub combination within each is partially open to view, allowing for stylish displays of nudity, which you, in a style that's very French, can enjoy with a companion.

21 rue Nationale, 30000 Nîmes. ✆ **04-66-76-28-42.** Fax 04-66-76-28-45. www.new-hotel.com. 33 units. 100€ double; 130€ suite. AE, DC, MC, V. Parking 7.60€. **Amenities:** Bar; limited room service (breakfast only); laundry service; dry cleaning. *In room:* A/C, TV, minibar, hair dryer.

Novotel Atria Nîmes Centre Opened in mid-1995, this cost-conscious member of a nationwide chain occupies a desirable site in the heart of Nîmes, adjacent to the ancient arena. Its six floors wrap around a carefully landscaped inner courtyard. Each room contains a double bed, a single bed (which converts into a sofa), a well-equipped bathroom, and a wide writing desk. All the rooms were recently renovated, although still in a rather sterile chain format.

5 bd. de Prague, 3000 Nîmes. ✆ **04-66-76-56-56.** Fax 04-66-76-56-59. www.accor-hotels.com. 119 units. 103€ double; 142€ suite. AE, DC, MC, V. Parking 8€. **Amenities:** Restaurant; bar; limited room service; laundry service; dry cleaning. *In room:* TV, minibar.

INEXPENSIVE

Hôtel de Milan The three-story Hôtel de Milan is just across the street from the railway station and is especially convenient for Eurailpass holders on a tight budget. Rooms have all just been totally renovated in a basic Provençal style. They are a bit small but reasonably comfortable and a good value for the price; bathrooms, however, are cramped. The only meal served on the premises is breakfast, but the staff will direct you to several restaurants within the neighborhood.

17 av. Feuchères, 30000 Nîmes. ✆ **04-66-29-29-90.** Fax 04-66-29-05-31. 33 units. 46€ double; 61€ triple. DC, MC, V. **Amenities:** Lounge; limited room service. *In room:* TV.

Hôtel l'Amphithéâtre The core of this small-scale, old-fashioned hotel dates from the 18th century—it has functioned as a hotel for longer than anyone remembers. A stay here involves trekking to your room up steep flights of creaking stairs and navigating your way through a labyrinth of upper corridors. Small bedrooms are outfitted in a deliberately old-fashioned way, usually with antiques or antique reproductions, wall-to-wall carpeting, and creaky but comfortable mattresses. Bathrooms are cramped but tidy affairs. The hotel and staff are less than perfect, but at these prices, who's complaining?

4 rue des Arènes, 30000 Nîmes. ✆ **04-66-67-28-51.** Fax 04-66-67-07-79. 16 units. 44€–53.35€ double. AE, MC, V. Parking 8.50€. Closed Jan 2–20. *In room:* TV.

WHERE TO DINE

The dining room at the **New Hôtel La Baume** (see above) is also a good choice.

EXPENSIVE

Alexandre ★★★ TRADITIONAL FRENCH The most charming, amusing, and competent restaurant around is on the outskirts of Nîmes, 9km (5½ miles) south of the center. In its verdant setting, you'll discover the elegant but rustic domain of Michel Kayser, an exceptional chef who adheres to classic tradition, with subtle improvements. He's assisted in the dining room by his charming wife, Monique. Menu items are designed to amuse as well as delight the palate: Examples are a medley of truffles and cèpes, roasted pigeon stuffed with purée of vegetables and foie gras, and the region's most sophisticated version of an old country recipe, local roast pigeon with apricot chutney. Especially appealing is the cheese trolley loaded with esoteric goat cheeses from the region and worthy cheeses from other parts of France. The dessert trolley is incredibly hard to resist.

Route de l'Aéroport de Garons. ✆ **04-66-70-08-99.** Reservations required. Main courses 28€–42€; fixed-price menus 49€–61€ lunch, 35€–80€ dinner. AE, MC, V. July–Aug Tues–Sun noon–1:30pm and 8–9:30pm; Sept–June Tues–Sun noon–1:45pm, Tues and Thurs–Sat 8–9:45pm. Closed 2 weeks in Feb. From the town center, take rue de la République southwest to av. Jean-Jaurès; then head south and follow the signs to the airport in the direction of Garons.

MODERATE

Chez Jacotte PROVENÇAL At least some of the charm of this restaurant derives from its setting on a narrow, traffic-free street in the old town, with outdoor tables overlooking a small, shaded, medieval-looking square. During harsher weather, opt for a table inside the ochre and russet-colored dining room, beneath crisscrossed ceiling vaults that were built, according to the charming owner, "in stages between the Middle Ages and the 18th century." The restaurant's owner and namesake, Jacotte Friand, will greet you in the dining room and recommend one of the dishes prepared by the sophisticated chef, Marc Maloyan. Cuisine here is redolent with the flavors and perfumes of France's "Deep South" and is entirely based on very fresh ingredients and produce. Examples include several different variations of local lamb, usually roasted in its own juices and served with fresh vegetables; a rich and pungent version of *aïoli de morue* (codfish and garlic stew); crisp-skinned mullet in basil-flavored olive oil; goat cheese and fig gratin; and an old-fashioned version of *brandade de morue* (codfish) prepared in a style that many local residents remember from their childhoods.

15 rue Fresque (impasse). ✆ **04-66-21-64-91.** Reservations recommended. Main courses 14€–17€. MC, V. Tues–Fri noon–2pm and Tues–Sat 7–10pm.

Restaurant au Chapon Fin ALSATIAN/LANGUEDOCIENNE This tavern/restaurant stands on a little square behind St-Paul's. It has beamed ceilings, small lamps, and a black-and-white stone floor. You'll find both Alsatian and Languedocienne specialties. From the a la carte menu, you can order foie gras with truffles, a casserole of roasted lamb and eggplant, *coq au vin* (chicken with wine), and entrecôte flambéed with morels. A new specialty is an *estouffade de Saint-Gilles,* a form of beef boiled in red wine and served with onions and pickles, whose recipe originated in Saint Gilles, a hamlet not far from Nîmes.

3 rue du Château-Fadaise. ✆ **04-66-67-34-73.** Reservations required. Main courses 14€–16€; fixed-price lunch 10.50€–16€. AE, DC, MC, V. Mon–Fri noon–2pm and 7:30–10pm; Sat 7:30–10pm.

San Francisco Steak House STEAK/FRENCH Near place de la Couronne, this popular theme restaurant is patterned on California. It serves the best steaks and seafood in Nîmes, always in generous portions with plenty of flavor, as well as succulent veal and lamb chops. Two trendy dishes are grilled ostrich steak and grilled bison steak. There is a full gamut of traditional beef dishes, including steak tartare. Begin your meal with a shrimp-stuffed avocado or a tender salad of grapefruit and crawfish segments.

33 rue Roussy (near place de la Couronne). ✆ **04-66-21-00-80.** Reservations required. Main courses 14€–27€. AE, DC, MC, V. Mon–Fri noon–2pm; Mon–Sat 7:30pm–midnight. Bus: 3 or 5.

Wine Bar Chez Michel *Value* TRADITIONAL FRENCH This place has mahogany panels and leather banquettes like those you might have found in a turn-of-the-20th-century California saloon. An array of salads and platters is served, and at lunch you can order a "quick menu," including an appetizer, a garnished main course, and two glasses of wine. Typical dishes are magret of duckling and contrefilet of steak with Roquefort sauce. You can now enjoy lunch on the terrace in the newly renovated courtyard. A restaurateur extraordinaire, Michel Hermet also makes his own wine; his vineyards that have been associated with his family for many generations. There are more than 300 other varieties of wine to choose from, by the glass or the pitcher.

11 place de la Couronne. ✆ **04-66-76-19-59.** Main courses 12€–25€; fixed-price menus 14€–23€ at lunch, 17€–25€ at dinner. AE, DC, MC, V. Tues–Sat noon–2pm; Mon–Sat 7pm–midnight.

NIMES AFTER DARK

Once the warm weather hits, all sorts of activities take place at the arena, including concerts and theater under the stars. The Office de Tourisme has a complete listing of events and schedules. Otherwise, for popular events like football (soccer), bullfights, and rock concerts, you can contact the **Bureau de Location des Arènes,** 4 rue de la Violette (✆ **04-66-02-80-80**). Tickets for more highbrow events, such as symphonic or chamber-music concerts, theater, and opera performances, are sold through **Le Théâtre Municipal (Le Théâtre de Mîmes),** 1 place de la Calade (✆ **04-66-36-65-00**).

If you like hanging out with a mix of French students and soldiers, head to **Café Le Napoléon,** 46 bd. Victor-Hugo (✆ **04-66-67-20-23**). Popular with the intelligentsia is the **Haddock Cafe,** 13 rue de l'Agau (✆ **04-66-67-86-57**), with its weekly live rock concerts.

The town's jazz aficionados know that **Le Diagonal,** 41 bis rue Emile-Jamais (✆ **04-66-21-70-01**), hosts the area's best jazz and blues concerts every Saturday. The sexy and hip **La Comédie,** 28 rue Jean-Reboul (✆ **04-66-76-13-66**), is the hands-down best for dancing and attracts a pretty crowd of youthful danceaholics. A little less flashy but a lot more fun, **Lulu Club,** 10 impasse de la Curaterie (✆ **04-66-36-28-20**), is the gay and lesbian stronghold in Nîmes.

A contender for the nightlife attentions of the city's young and restless is **Le Cococlub,** 20 rue de l'Etoile (✆ **04-66-21-59-22**). Open every Wednesday through Saturday, beginning after 11pm, it rocks and rolls to music from Los Angeles and London.

Streets to explore for a dose of nocturnal good times on virtually any night of the week include **place de la Maison Carrée** and **boulevard Victor-Hugo.** From June to September, locals flock to the beach to patronize one of the summer shanty restaurants and bars. Bus no. 6 will take you to the **plage de la Corniches** for this nighttime venue for partying and drinking.

4

Provence

Provence has been called a bridge between the past and the present, where yesterday blends with today in a quiet, often melancholy way. Peter Mayle's best-selling *A Year in Provence, Toujours Provence,* and *Encore Provence* have played no small part in the burgeoning popularity this sunny corner of southern France has enjoyed during recent years.

The Greeks and Romans filled the landscape with cities boasting Hellenic theaters, Roman baths, amphitheaters, and triumphal arches. These were followed in medieval times by Romanesque fortresses and Gothic cathedrals. In the 19th century, Provence's light and landscapes attracted illustrious painters like Cézanne and van Gogh. Despite the changes over the years, the howling mistral, the legendary bone-chilling wind that blows through each winter, will forever be heard through the broad-leaved plane trees.

Provence has its own language and its own customs. The region is bounded on the north by the Dauphine, on the west by the Rhône, on the east by the Alps, and on the south by the Mediterranean. We'll focus in the next chapters on the part of Provence known as the glittering French Riviera or Côte d'Azur.

1 Orange ★★

658km (409 miles) S of Paris; 55km (34 miles) NE of Nîmes; 26km (16 miles) S of Avignon

Orange gets its name from the days when it was a dependency of the Dutch House of Orange-Nassau, not because it's set in a citrus belt. Actually, the last orange grove departed 2,000 years ago. The juice that flows in Orange today comes from its fabled vineyards, which turn out a Côtes du Rhône vintage. Many *caves* (vineyards) are spread throughout the district, some of which offer *dégustations* (wine tastings) to paying customers. The tourist office (see "Essentials," below) will provide you with a list.

Overlooking the Valley of the Rhône, today's Orange, with a somewhat sleepy population of about 30,000, tempts visitors with Europe's third-largest extant triumphal arch and best-preserved Roman theater. Louis XIV, who toyed with the idea of moving the theater to Versailles, said, "It is the finest wall in my kingdom." UNESCO has placed the arch on its World Cultural and Natural Heritage List in the hopes that it can be preserved "forever."

ESSENTIALS

GETTING THERE Orange sits on some major rail and highway arteries, making arrivals by train, bus, or car convenient. Some 20 **trains** per day arrive from Avignon (trip time: 20 min.), for around 4.70€ one-way. From Marseille, there are 5 trains per day (trip time: 1¼ hr.), for 17.10€ one-way. From Paris (trip time: 3½ hours), there are two daily TGV trains into Orange; a one-way fare is 62.50€. For rail information, call ✆ **08-36-35-35-35.** For information on bus routes, contact the **Gare Routière** (✆ **04-90-34-15-59**), on place Pourtoules, behind the Théâtre Antique.

If you're **driving** from Paris, take A6 south to Lyon; then connect with A7 to Orange. The drive takes 5½ to 6½ hours.

VISITOR INFORMATION The **Office de Tourisme** is at 5 cours Aristide-Briand (✆ **04-90-34-70-88**).

SPECIAL EVENTS From early July to early August, a drama, dance, and music festival called **Les Chorégies d'Orange** takes place at the Théâtre Antique, one of the most evocative ancient theaters in Europe. For information or tickets, visit the office, 18 place Sylvain, adjacent to the theater; call ✆ **04-90-11-04-04** or go to www.choregies.asso.fr.

SEEING THE SIGHTS

In the southern part of town, the **Théâtre Antique** ★★★, place des Frères-Mounet (✆ **04-90-34-24-24**), dates from the days of Augustus. Built into the side of a hill, it once held 8,000 spectators in tiered seats. Carefully restored, the nearly 105m (350-ft.) long, 38m (125-ft.) high theater is noted for its acoustics. It's open daily April through September from 9am to 6:30pm, and October through March from 9am to noon and 1:30 to 5pm. Admission is 4.75€ for adults and 4€ for students and those under 18.

To the west of the theater stood a huge temple, which, with a gymnasium, formed one of the greatest buildings in the empire. Across the street, the **Musée Municipal d'Orange,** place du Théâtre-Antique (✆ **04-90-34-70-88**), displays fragments of the temple. Your ticket to the theater also admits you to the museum, which is open daily April through September from 9:30am to 6:30pm, and October through March from 9:30am to noon and 1:30 to 5pm.

Even older than the theater is the **Arc de Triomphe** ★★, on avenue de l'Arc-de-Triomphe. It has decayed, but its decorations and other elements are still fairly well preserved. Built to honor the conquering legions of Caesar, it rises 22m (72 ft.) and is nearly 21m (70 ft.) wide. Composed of a trio of arches held up by Corinthian columns, it was used as a dungeon for prisoners in the Middle Ages.

Before leaving Orange, head for the park, **Colline St-Eutrope,** adjacent to the Théâtre Antique, for a view of the valley with its mulberry plantations.

After exploring the town itself, you can drive south for 13km (8 miles) along A9 to **Châteauneuf-du-Pape,** where you can have lunch (any day but Mon) at the **Hostellerie du Château des Fines-Roches,** route d'avignon (✆ **04-90-83-70-23**). Although the Hostellerie was built in the 19th century, it looks feudal, thanks to its medieval features. If you're pressing on to Avignon, it's only another 13km (8 miles) south along any of three highways (each marked AVIGNON).

WHERE TO STAY

Hôtel Louvre et Terminus *Value* Surrounded by a garden terrace, this conservatively decorated Logis de France offers a good value, housed in a much-renovated building begun around 1900. Don't expect grandeur: Everything is simple, efficient, and rather brusque. Bedrooms, ranging from small to medium in size, have all the basic necessities and either double or twin beds; the tiled bathrooms are small.

89 av. Frédéric-Mistral, 84100 Orange. ✆ **04-90-34-10-08.** Fax 04-90-34-68-71. 32 units. 60€–90€ double; 120€ suite. AE, DC, MC, V. Parking 8€ in garage. **Amenities:** Restaurant; lounge. *In room:* A/C, TV, minibar, hair dryer.

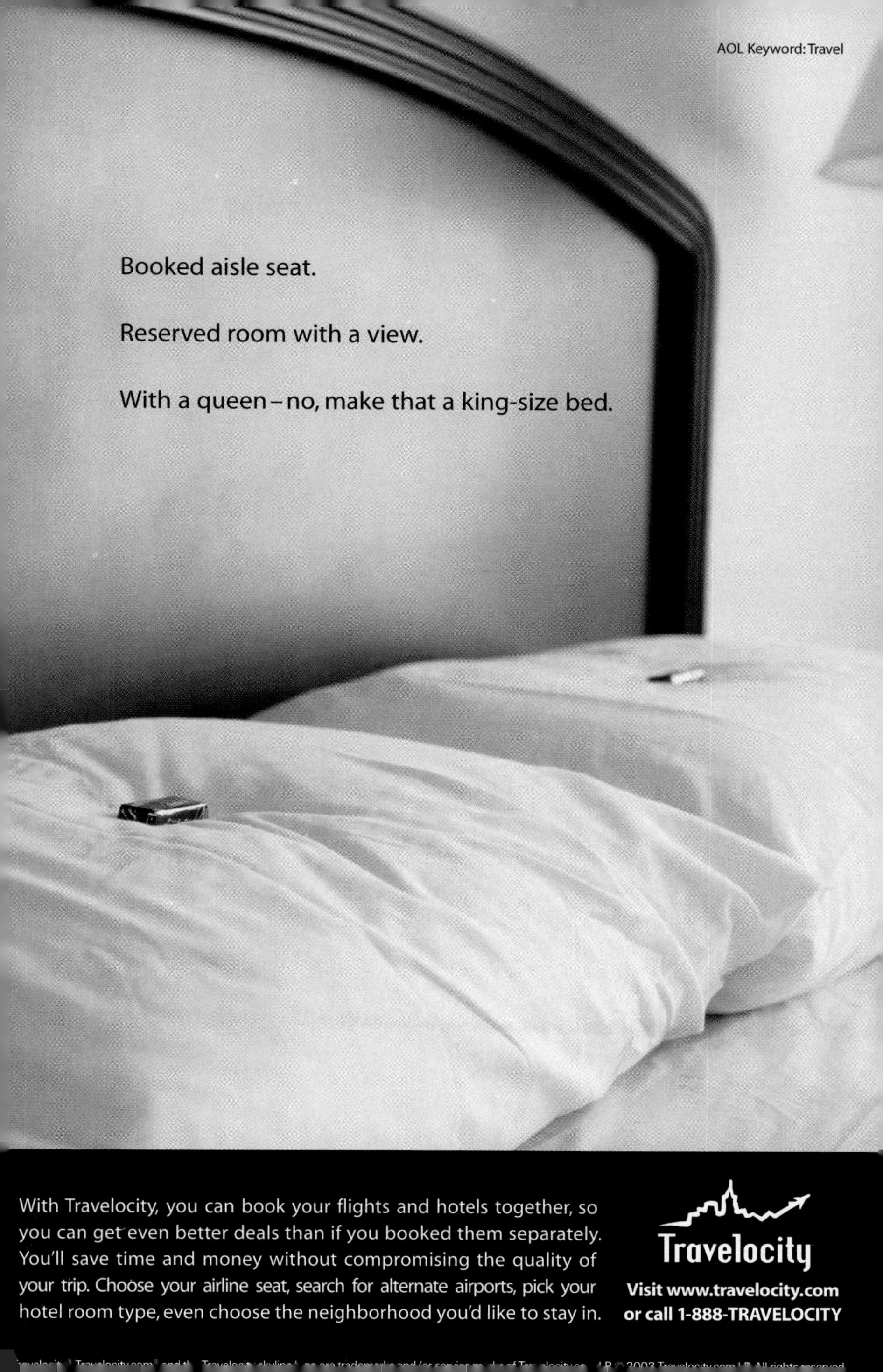

AOL Keyword: Travel
Booked aisle seat.
Reserved room with a view.
With a queen – no, make that a king-size bed.
With Travelocity, you can book your flights and hotels together, so you can get even better deals than if you booked them separately. You'll save time and money without compromising the quality of your trip. Choose your airline seat, search for alternate airports, pick your hotel room type, even choose the neighborhood you'd like to stay in.
Travelocity
Visit www.travelocity.com
or call 1-888-TRAVELOCITY

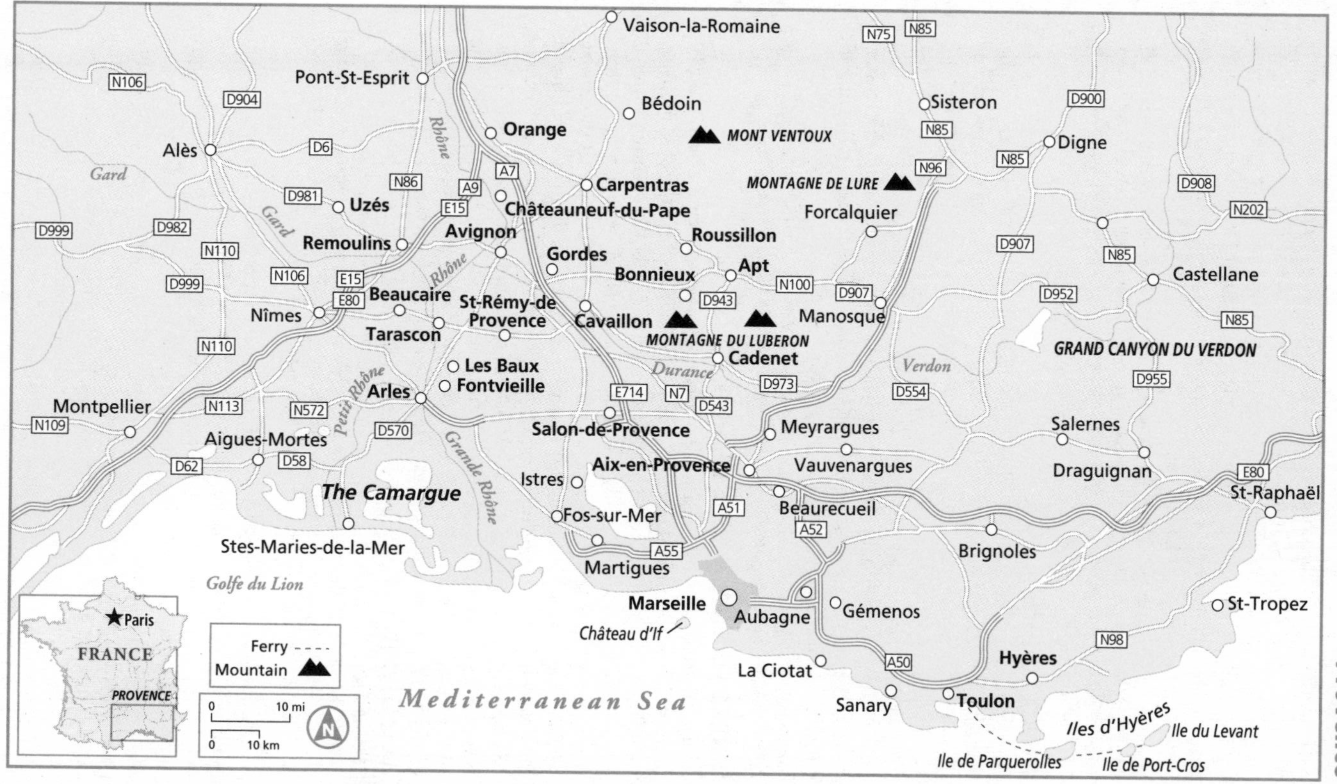
Vaison-la-Romaine
Pont-St-Esprit
Bédoin
Sisteron
Orange
MONT VENTOUX
Digne
Alès
Gard
Carpentras
MONTAGNE DE LURE
Uzès
Châteauneuf-du-Pape
Forcalquier
Avignon
Remoulins
Roussillon
Gordes
Apt
Bonnieux
Castellane
Beaucaire
St-Rémy-de Provence
Nîmes
Cavaillon
Manosque
Tarascon
MONTAGNE DU LUBERON
GRAND CANYON DU VERDON
Les Baux
Cadenet
Fontvieille
Arles
Durance
Verdon
Montpellier
Meyrargues
Salon-de-Provence
Salernes
Aigues-Mortes
Petit Rhône
Grande Rhône
Rhône
Aix-en-Provence
Vauvenargues
Draguignan
Istres
The Camargue
Beaurecueil
St-Raphaël
Fos-sur-Mer
Stes-Maries-de-la-Mer
Brignoles
Martigues
Golfe du Lion
Marseille
Aubagne
Gémenos
St-Tropez
Château d'If
Paris
FRANCE
PROVENCE
Ferry
Mountain
La Ciotat
Hyères
Mediterranean Sea
Sanary
Toulon
Iles d'Hyères
Ile du Levant
Ile de Parquerolles
Ile de Port-Cros
0
10 mi
10 km
N
N106
D904
D6
N86
D981
D982
D999
N110
N106
E15
E80
A9
A7
N75
N85
N96
D900
D908
N202
D907
D952
D943
N100
N113
N572
D570
E714
N7
D543
D973
D554
D955
N109
D62
D58
A51
A52
A55
A50
N98
E80

Mercure Orange This comfortable modern hotel lies about a kilometer west of the city, in a 20-year-old building whose wings curve around a landscaped courtyard. Its well-furnished rooms are arranged around a series of gardens. This is your best bet for general overnight comfort far from the crowds. It was completely renovated in 1999, with an upgrade of many of the bedrooms and mattresses. Bathrooms are small but neat.

80 route de Caderousse, 84100 Orange. ✆ **04-90-34-24-10.** Fax 04-90-34-85-48. www.accorhotels.com. 99 units. 85€–118€ double. AE, DC, MC, V. Free parking. Drive about a kilometer (half-mile) west of the city center, following directions to Caderousse. **Amenities:** Restaurant; bar; pool; limited room service; laundry service. *In room:* A/C, TV, minibar.

WHERE TO DINE

Le Parvis *Kids* TRADITIONAL FRENCH Jean-Michel Berengier sets the best table in Orange, though the dining room is rather austere. He bases his cuisine on well-selected vegetables and the best ingredients from "mountain or sea." Try his escalope of braised sea bass with fennel or asparagus or his lamb with a garlic cream sauce. A can't-miss dish is the foie gras, which could be flavorfully followed by fresh seafood, whose preparation varies according to the season. (The staff prides itself on dozens of preparations.) The service is efficient and polite. A special children's menu is offered for 9.50€.

55 cours Pourtoules. ✆ **04-90-34-82-00.** Reservations required. Main courses 12€–19€; fixed-price menus 22€–42€. AE, MC, V. Tues–Sun noon–2:30pm; Tues–Sat 7:30–9:15pm. Closed 3 weeks in Nov.

WHERE TO STAY & DINE NEARBY

Château de Rochegude ★★ This Relais & Châteaux property stands on 10 hectares (25 acres) of parkland. The stone castle is at the edge of a hill, surrounded by Rhône vineyards. Throughout its history this 12th-century turreted residence has been renovated by a series of distinguished owners, ranging from the pope to the dauphin. The current owners have made many 20th-century additions, but ancient touches still survive. Each room is done in a traditional Provençal style, with elegant fabrics and furniture influenced by the region's 18th- and 19th-century traditions. As befits a château, bedrooms come in many shapes and sizes, some quite spacious. Bathrooms are tiled or clad in marble. The food and service are exceptional. You can enjoy meals surrounded by flowering plants in the stately dining room. There are also sunny terraces where refreshments are served.

26790 Rochegude. ✆ **04-75-97-21-10.** Fax 04-75-04-89-87. www.chateauderochegude.com. 29 units. 230€–335€ double; 400€–534€ suite. AE, DC, MC, V. Free parking. The hotel is 13km (8 miles) north of Orange; take D976, following signs toward Gap and Rochegude. **Amenities:** Restaurant; bar; outdoor pool; tennis court; limited room service; laundry service. *In room:* A/C, TV, minibar, hair dryer.

Hostellerie Le Beffroi ★ *Finds* This charming hotel from 1554 boasts ocher walls and original detailing on the exterior, and flowered wallpaper, heavy ceiling beams, plaster detailing, and fireplaces in the rustic interior. The elegantly furnished rooms display 19th-century antiques. Bedrooms offer fine linen on a comfortable French bed, most often a double or twins. Bathrooms are small but neat. There's a garden with a view of the town where you can order meals under a giant fig tree. For your convenience, the hotel, across from the chiseled fountain in the Haute-Ville sector, maintains a limited number of parking spaces.

The town itself is worth exploring, for it contains some fascinating reminders of its former Roman occupation, including Les Ruines Romaines, two areas that've been excavated—the Quartier Puymin and Quartier Villasse.

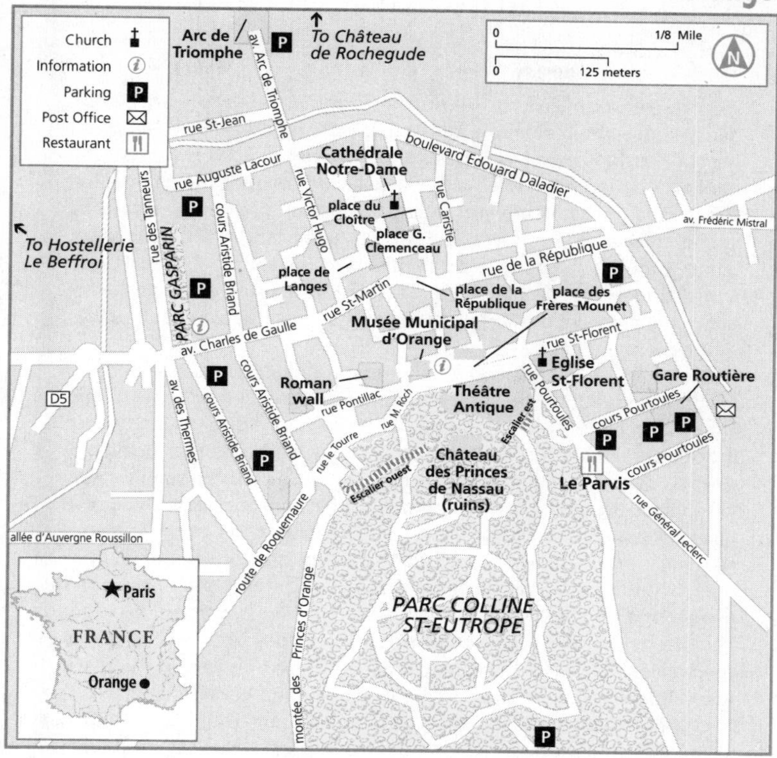

Rue de l'Evèché, 84110 Vaison-la-Romaine. © **04-90-36-04-71.** Fax 04-90-36-24-78. www.vaison-la-romaine.com. 22 units. 85€–120€ double. AE, DC, MC, V. Parking 8€. Closed Feb–Mar. From Orange, drive 34km (21 miles) northeast, following the signs to Vaison-la-Romaine. The hotel is in Vaison's medieval core (Cité Médiévale). **Amenities:** 2 restaurants; lounge; pool; laundry service; dry cleaning. *In room:* TV, minibar, hair dryer.

2 Châteauneuf-du-Pape

671km (417 miles) S of Paris; 19km (12 miles) N of Avignon; 13km (8 miles) S of Orange

Near Provence's north border, the Château du Pape was built as the Castelgandolfo, the country seat of the French popes of Avignon, during the 14th-century reign of Pope John XXII. Now in ruins, it overlooks the vast acres of vineyards that the popes planted, the start of a regional industry that today produces some of the world's best reds as well as an excellent white.

ESSENTIALS

GETTING THERE There's no rail station in Châteauneuf, so train passengers must get off at Sorgues (7km/4½ miles south) or Orange (13km/8 miles north). For **rail information,** call © **08-36-35-35-35.** About three buses a day arrive from both towns. Buses from Avignon are also a possibility. Bus passengers are deposited and retrieved in place de la Bascule, behind Châteauneuf's post office. The tourist office (below) is the best source for schedules and information about bus access.

Driving Les Routes de la Lavande

As characteristic of Provence as heather is of the Yorkshire moors, lavender has played a major role here for hundreds of years. When it was part of the Roman Empire, Provence produced the flowers to scent the public baths. In the Middle Ages, villages burnt piles of the plant in the streets, the prevalent medical theory being that disease was spread by vapors in the air. But it was during the Renaissance that the current industry took root, linked to the Médicis, who padded their wealth with a brisk trade in the distillation of the flower's essential oils. Today lavender production and distillation are more than just trades—they're a way of life for many families.

The heart of lavender production lies in Provençal fields stretching from the foothills of the Vercors mountains to the Verdon canyons and from Buech to the Luberon range. Plants grown and distilled in this area are sold under the Haute-Provence label, renowned for its quality. A drive through the region is most scenic just before the midsummer harvest, when the countryside is a purplish hue from the blossoms of the lavender plants, spread out in seemingly endless rows to the horizon. Not only can you take in the sight and scent of the flowers, but you can also tour the distilleries and farms. Some of these facilities are open only during summer, when the year's harvest is undergoing distillation. Those that are open year-round offer tours. They also sell the plants themselves, as well as the essential oils and dried flowers of the plant (used in Provençal cooking), perfumes, honey, and herbal teas.

One of the best places to visit lavender farms and distilleries is **Nyons,** 42km (26 miles) northeast of Orange. From Orange, take A7 northwest for 3km (1¾ miles) to Route 976 and drive northeast for 13km (8 miles) to St-Cécile-les-Vignes, where the road becomes Route 576. Continue northeast for 6km (3¾) miles to Tulette, turn right onto Route 94, and go 22km (13½ miles) northeast to Nyons. Stop at the **Office de Tourisme,** place Libération (✆ **04-75-26-10-35**), to pick up the brochure *Les Routes de la Lavande,* offering a brief explanation and history of lavender production and a map of the region and its production facilities, with addresses, phone numbers, and hours.

If you're **driving** from Avignon, head north on A7 to the intersection with Route 17, at which point you continue northwest following the well-posted signs into Chateauneuf-du-Pape.

VISITOR INFORMATION The **Office de Tourisme** is at place du Portail (✆ **04-90-83-71-08**).

A SPECIAL EVENT Since the Middle Ages, the annual **Fête de la Véraison** has been held in early August. See below for details.

WINE LURE & LORE

What makes the local wines distinctive is the blending of 13 varieties of grapes, grown on vines surrounded by stones that reflect heat onto them during the day and keep them warm in the cool night. As a result, the wines produced in the

On the outskirts of Nyons, start out at the **Jardin des Arômes (Garden of Scents),** promenade de la Digue (✆ **04-75-26-04-30**), with its collection of aromatic plants and lavenders; it's open around the clock throughout the year and charges no admission. To reach it from Nyons, follow the road signs pointing to Gap. After viewing and enjoying the scent of the living plants close by, go to **Bleu Provence,** 58 promenade de la Digue (✆ **04-75-26-10-42**), a family-owned distillery founded in 1926, for thyme, rosemary, lavender, and "every other spice that's Provençal." There's a shop on the premises where you can find the essential oils, soaps, and unguents, as well as staff that will take you on a guided English or French-language tour. If you walk around the premises on your own, the visit is free; to participate in the 45-minute guided tours, the cost is 2.50€ per person. It's open daily except Monday morning, from 9:30am to 12:15pm and 2:30 to 6:30pm (till 7pm June–Sept).

In St-Nazaire-le-Desert, northeast of Nyons, you can visit **Gérard Blache,** in the village center next to the Auberge du Desert (✆ **04-75-27-51-08**), place de la Fontaine, a shop that sells all things lavender in July and August daily from 10am to 7:30pm. From here, head southeast to **Rosans,** where the distillery of the Cooperative des Producteurs de Lavande des Alpes (Lavender Cooperative of the Alps), on D94 west of Rosans (✆ **04-92-66-60-30**), offers short guided tours and sales of essential oils from mid-June to August daily from 10am to noon and 2 to 6pm. Southwest of here is **Buis-les-Baronnies,** where the Shop Bernard Laget, in the village center on place aux Herbes (✆ **04-75-28-12-01**), includes lavender products among its medicinal and aromatic plants; it's open Tuesday through Sunday from 9:30am to noon and 3:30 to 7pm. Finally, head southeast of Buis to **Savoillan,** where the Ferme St-Agricole (St. Agricol Farm) (✆ **04-75-28-86-57**) boasts botanical paths leading through an experimental garden, a species preservation garden, and a greenhouse. The farm is open daily from June 15 to September 15 from 10:30am to 1pm, and from September 16 to June 14 from 10:30am to 1pm and 2 to 6pm. Admission is 3.05€.

district's vineyards are among the most potent in France, with an alcohol content of at least 12.5% and, in many instances, as high as 15%. The region played a central role in the initiation of the Appellation d'Origine Contrôlée, France's strict quality-control system. This was formed when the late Baron Le Roy de Boiseaumarie, the most distinguished of the local vintners, initiated geographical boundaries and minimum standards for the production of wines given the Châteauneuf-du-Pape label. In 1923, local producers won exclusive rights to market their Côtes du Rhônes under that label, and thus paved the way for other regions to identify and protect their distinctive wines. You'll see a plaque devoted to his memory in the town's place de la Renaissance.

To learn about the town's wine-related lore, there are two major *associations de vignerons,* each representing a consortium of individually owned vineyards whose owners pool their marketing, advertising, and bottling programs. Open Monday through Friday from 8am to noon and 2 to 6pm, **Syndicat Reflets,** 3 chemin du Bois de la Ville (© **04-90-83-71-07**), represents six vintners, and **Prestige et Tradition,** 3 rue de la République (© **04-90-83-72-29**), represents 10. They offer *dégustations* and sales.

Another useful source is **La Vinothèque,** 9 rue de la République (© **04-90-83-74-01**). A sales and marketing outlet for Madame Carre, matriarch of the Comtes d'Argelas vineyards, it's open for wine tastings and sales daily from 10am to 7pm. On the premises is La Boutique de la Vinothèque, where wine accessories (corkscrews, racks, decanters) are sold.

TOURING & TASTING THE WINES

A map posted in the village square, place du Portail (but called place de la Fontaine by just about everyone), pinpoints 22 wineries open for touring and tasting. The best known is **Domaine de Mont-Redon,** on D68 about 5km (3 miles) north of the town center (© **04-90-83-72-75**). It offers samplings of recent vintages of red and white wines and sales of *eau-de-vie,* a clear grape liqueur produced in a limited batch of 2,000 bottles annually. A noteworthy competitor is **Clos des Papes,** avenue Le Bienheureux Pierre de Luxembourg, in the town center (© **04-90-83-70-13**), where humidified cellars produce what many connoisseurs consider the region's best wine. Both establishments prefer advance notice before your arrival.

The town's only museum devotes all its exhibition space to winemaking. The **Musée des Vieux Outils de Vignerons of the Caves du Père-Anselme,** avenue Le Bienheureux Pierre de Luxembourg (© **04-90-83-70-07**), contains the history and artifacts of local wine production, including a 16th-century winepress, winemakers' tools, barrel-making equipment, and a tasting cellar. It's open daily from mid-June to mid-September from 9am to 7pm, and the rest of the year from 9am to noon and 2 to 6pm. Admission and tastings are free.

A WINE FESTIVAL During 3 days in early August, the village hosts the annual **Fête de la Véraison** ★, a medieval fair. It includes tasting stalls set up by local winemakers, actors impersonating Provençaux troubadours, bear-baiters (who are much kinder to their animals than their medieval counterparts), falconers with their birds, lots of merchants selling locally made handcrafts, battered flea market kiosks, and food. Don't expect dancing—what you'll get is a festival where the antique fountain on place du Portail spurts out wine, and vast amounts of that beverage are consumed. If you attend, you can drink all the wine you want for the price of a *verre de la Véraison.* This souvenir glass, filled on demand at any vintner who participates, costs 3.05€ and is sold at strategically positioned kiosks around town.

Finds Wine & Chocolates

One of the newest industries in Châteauneuf is the **Chocolaterie Castelain,** whose factories and showrooms lie on the Route d'Avignon (© **04-90-83-54-71**), about 3km (2 miles) south of town. They've become known for a popular type of black chocolate *(la ganache)* flavored with a distilled version *(vieu marc de Châteauneuf)* of the red wine produced in local vineyards. The brand name of their chocolates is **Palet des Pâpes.** The chocolates taste extremely good when consumed with any of the local vintages.

WHERE TO STAY

Hostellerie du Château des Fines-Roches ★★ This medieval-inspired manor house is from late in the 19th century. Named for the smooth rocks *(fines roches)* found in the soil of the nearby vineyards, the château devotes its huge cellars to the storage of thousands of bottles of local wines. The guest rooms on the upper floors of this charming hotel were renovated in 1997 and include Provençal styling with a scattering of antiques. The bathrooms are small but well organized.

We highly recommend taking a meal in the restaurant here. Menu items, carefully crafted and full of flavor, include filets of red mullet prepared with aromatic herbs and garnished with its own liver marinated in vinaigrette, barigoule of crawfish tails with artichokes, filet of bull from the Camargue marinated in a particular vintage *(syrah)* of strong red wine, and roast rack of local lamb with a gratin of eggplant and sheep's cheese. The wine list focuses on local vintages, particularly those from the village.

Rte. d'Avignon, 84230 Châteauneuf-du-Pape. ✆ **04-90-83-70-23.** Fax 04-90-83-78-42. www.chateaufinesroches.com. 6 units. 160€–180€ double. AE, DC, MC, V. From the center of town, drive 3km (2 miles) south, following the signs to Avignon. **Amenities:** Restaurant; bar. *In room:* A/C, TV, minibar, hair dryer.

WHERE TO DINE

La Mère Germaine ★ PROVENÇAL Named after the matriarch who established this place several generations ago, La Mére Germaine contains both a restaurant gastronomique and a simple bistro. Both enjoy sweeping panoramas from terraces where tables are set out in the summer months. Cuisine in both establishments is based on the traditions of Provence. In the bistro, you're likely to find simple platters of grilled fish, stews, casseroles, and grilled meats, but in the restaurant, cuisine is more elaborate, intricate, and tuned to the seasons. Dishes in the restaurant include zucchini flowers stuffed with mushrooms and drizzled with ratatouille juice, roasted rabbit stuffed with black-olive tapenade and fresh tomatoes, filet of turbot with *barigoule* (Provençal vinaigrette), and crispy rack of lamb scented with herbs from the surrounding *garrigue* (scrubland).

Eight simple, well-scrubbed bedrooms are available on the premises. None has a phone or elaborate amenities, but for a comfortable sojourn after a meal in the restaurant, they all offer good value and a sense of comfort and efficiency.

Place de la Fontaine, 84230 Châteauneuf-du-Pape. ✆ **04-90-83-54-37.** Fax 04-90-83-50-27. Reservations recommended. In the bistro, platters 15.20€–24€; in the restaurant, fixed-price menus 25.50€–66.50€. AE, DC, MC, V. Thurs–Tues noon–2:30pm and 7–9:30pm.

3 Avignon ★★★

684km (425 miles) S of Paris; 80km (50 miles) NW of Aix-en-Provence; 106km (66 miles) NW of Marseille

In the 14th century, Avignon was the capital of Christendom—the popes lived here instead of in Rome. The legacy left by their "court of splendor and magnificence" makes Avignon one of the most interesting and beautiful of Europe's medieval cities.

The popes are long gone, but life goes on exceedingly well. Today this walled city of some 100,000 residents reaches its peak celebration time during the famous Festival d'Avignon, a 3-week stint of music, art, and theater when bacchanalia reigns in the streets. Avignon at any time of the year is a major stopover on the route from Paris to the Mediterranean. Lately, it has become well known as a cultural center. Artists and painters in increasing numbers have been moving here. Experimental theaters, painting galleries, and art cinemas have brought diversity to the inner city, especially rue des Teinturiers.

ESSENTIALS

GETTING THERE The fastest and easiest way is to take a 1-hour **flight** from Paris's Orly Airport to Aéroport Avignon-Caumont (✆ **04-90-81-51-51**), located 8km (5 miles) southeast of Avignon. Taxis from the airport to the center cost 15€ to 20€. From Paris, **TGV trains** depart from gare de Lyon, taking 2 hours and 38 minutes. A one-way fare costs 101€ in first class and 79.20€ in second class. Trains arrive frequently from Marseille, taking 70 minutes and costing 15€; from Arles, the trip takes 30 minutes and costs 5.60€. For train information and reservations, call ✆ **08-36-35-35-39.**

Eurostar's high-speed trains now bridge the gap between London's Waterloo Station and Avignon. This route is offered every Saturday between July 20 and September 7; the journey, excluding one stop in Ashford in Kent, lasts 6 hours. For information or to purchase tickets, which must be reserved at least 14 days in advance, call **Rail Europe** at ✆ **800/387-6782** or visit www.raileurope.com.

If you're **driving** from Paris, take A6 south to Lyon; then take A7 south to Avignon. If you'd like to explore the area by **bike,** go to **Cycles Peugeot,** 80 rue Guillaume-Puy (✆ **0490-86-32-49**), which rents all sorts of bikes for around 16€ to 19€ per day, including 10-speed road bikes and mountain bikes. A deposit of 152€ is required, in the form of either cash or a credit-card imprint.

VISITOR INFORMATION The **Office de Tourisme** is at 41 cours Jean-Jaurès (✆ **04-32-74-32-74;** www.ot-avignon.fr).

SPECIAL EVENTS The biggest celebration is the **Festival d'Avignon,** held during 3 weeks in July and the first week in August. The international festival focuses on avant-garde theater, dance, and music. Part of the fun is the bacchanalia that takes place nightly in the streets. The prices for rooms and meals skyrocket, so make reservations far in advance. For information on dates, tickets, and venues, contact the **Bureaux du Festival,** 8 bis rue de Mons, 84000 Avignon (✆ **04-90-27-66-50;** www.festival-avignon.com). Tickets cost 12€ to 33€.

EXPLORING THE CITY

THE PAPAL PALACE

Palais des Papes ★★★ Dominating Avignon from a hill is one of the most famous (or notorious, depending on your point of view) palaces in the Christian world. Headquarters of a schismatic group of cardinals who came close to toppling the authority of the popes in Rome, it is part fortress, part showplace. It all began in 1309, when Pope Clement V fled to Avignon to escape political infighting in Rome. His successor, John XXII, chose to stay in Avignon. The third Avignon pope, Benedict XII, was the one responsible for the construction of this magnificent palace. Avignon became, for a time, the Vatican of the north. During the period, dubbed "the Babylonian Captivity" by Rome, the popes held extravagant court in the palace; art and culture flourished—and so did prostitution and vice. When Gregory XI was persuaded to return to Rome in 1376, Avignon proceeded to elect its own rival pope, and the Great Schism split the Christian world. The real struggle, of course was about the wealth and power of the papacy. The reign of popes in Rome and antipopes in Avignon finally ended in 1417 with the election of Martin V, and the papal court here was disbanded.

Chapelle St-Jean is known for its beautiful frescoes, attributed to the school of Matteo Giovanetti and painted between 1345 and 1348. The frescoes present scenes from the life of John the Baptist and John the Evangelist. More Giovanetti frescoes can be seen above the Chapelle St-Jean in the **Chapelle St-Martial.** The frescoes here depict the miracles of St. Martial, patron saint of Limousin.

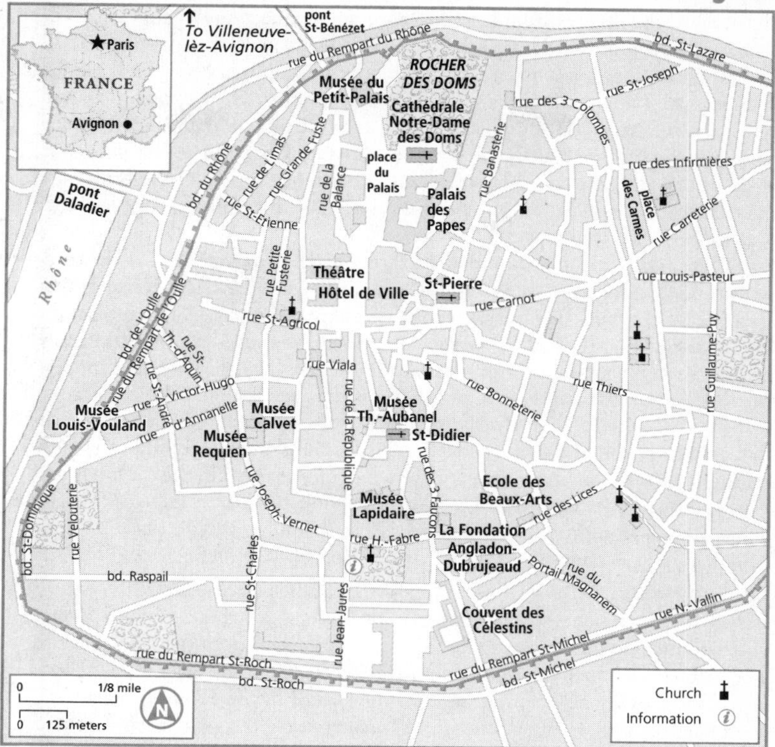

Grand Tinel (Banquet Hall) is about 41m (135 ft.) long and 9m (30 ft.) wide, and the pope's table stood on the southern side. The **pope's bedroom** is on the first floor of the Tour des Anges. Its walls are entirely decorated in tempera with foliage on which birds and squirrels perch; birdcages are painted in the recesses of the windows. In a secular vein, the **Studium (Stag Room)**—study of Clement VI—was frescoed in 1343 with hunting scenes. Added under the same Clement, who had a taste for grandeur, the **Grande Audience (Great Audience Hall)** contains frescoes of the prophets; these are also attributed to Giovanetti and were painted in 1352.

Between two and four French-language guided tours are offered every day at schedules that vary widely according to the season and day of the week. Tours usually last 50 minutes, and aside from the exceptions mentioned above, they are somewhat monotonous, since most of the rooms have been stripped of their once-legendary finery. Self-guided tours in English, using a handheld audio mechanism, are available anytime during opening hours.

Place du Palais. ✆ **04-90-27-50-00.** Admission (including tour with guide or cassette recording) 9.50€ adults, 7.50€ students and seniors, free for ages 7 and under. Daily Nov–Mar 9:30am–5:45pm; Apr–June and Aug–Oct daily 9am–7pm; July daily 9am–8pm.

MORE ATTRACTIONS

Even more famous than the papal residency is the ditty *"Sur le pont d'Avignon, l'on y danse, l'on y danse."* Ironically, **pont St-Bénézet** ★★ was far too narrow for the *danse* of the rhyme. Spanning the Rhône and connecting Avignon with Villeneuve-lèz-Avignon, the bridge is now a ruin, with only 4 of its original 22 arches. According to legend, it was inspired by a vision that a shepherd named Bénézet had while tending his flock. The bridge was built between 1177 and 1185 and suffered various disasters from then on. (In 1669, half the bridge fell into the river.) On one of the piers is the two-story **Chapelle St-Nicolas**—one story in Romanesque style, the other in Gothic. The remains of the bridge are open daily from 9am to 6:30pm. Admission is 3.50€ for adults, 3€ for students and seniors, and free for ages 7 and under.

It's worth at least an hour to walk through the **Quartier de La Balance,** where the Gypsies lived in the 1800s. Over the years, La Balance had grown seedy, but since the 1970s, major renovations have taken place. Start at place du Palais, going along rue de La Balance, detouring, if possible, into the historically evocative rue de la Grande Fusterie and the rue des Grottes. The main interest here is the restoration of the old town houses with their renewed elegant facades, many graced with mullioned windows. In the district are some of the ramparts that used to surround Avignon, stretching for 4km (2¾ miles). Built in the 14th century by the popes, these ramparts were partially restored in the 19th century by that busy restorer of medieval monuments, Viollet-le-Duc. The most intriguing section is along rue du Rempart-du-Rhône, leading east to place Crillon. After a look, you can return to place de l'Horloge via rue St-Etienne.

Cathédrale Notre-Dame des Doms ★ Near the palace is the 12th-century cathedral, containing the Flamboyant Gothic tomb of some of the apostate popes. Crowning the top is a gilded statue of the Virgin from the 19th century. The cathedral's hours vary according to whatever religious ceremony is scheduled, but generally it's open during the hours noted below. From the cathedral, enter the promenade du Rocher-des-Doms to stroll through its garden and enjoy the view across the Rhône to Villeneuve-lèz-Avignon.

Place du Palais. ✆ **04-90-86-81-01.** Free admission. Hours vary according to religious ceremonies but are generally daily 9am–noon and 2–6pm.

La Fondation Angladon-Dubrujeaud ★ This museum, opened in 1995, contains the magnificent art collection of Jacques Doucet, renowned Parisian haute couture designer and Belle Epoque dandy and dilettante. Doucet cultivated a number of young artists, among them Picasso, Braque, Max Jacob, Marcel Duchamp, and Guillaume Apollinaire, and began to collect their early works. For decades, Doucet's heirs kept the treasure trove a relative secret and lived in quiet splendor amid canvases by Cézanne, Sisley, Derain, Degas, and Modigliani. Today you can wander through Doucet's former abode, which is also filled with rare antiques and art objects that include 16th-century Buddhas and Louis XVI chairs designed by Jacob. Doucet died in 1929 at the age of 76, his own fortune so diminished that his nephew paid for his funeral. But his rich legacy lives on here.

5 rue Laboureur. ✆ **04-90-82-29-03.** Admission 5€ adults, 3€ students and youths 14–18, 1.50€ children 7–13. Tues–Sun 1–6pm.

Musée Calvet ★ An extensive collection of ancient silver is housed in this lovely 18th-century neoclassical mansion. The museum displays works of Vernet, David, Corot, Manet, and Soutine. Our favorite oil is by Brueghel the Younger, *Le Cortège nuptial (The Bridal Procession).*

65 rue Joseph-Vernet. ✆ **04-90-86-33-84.** Admission 6€ adults, 2.30€ students, free for children 17 and under. Wed–Mon 10am–1pm and 2–6pm.

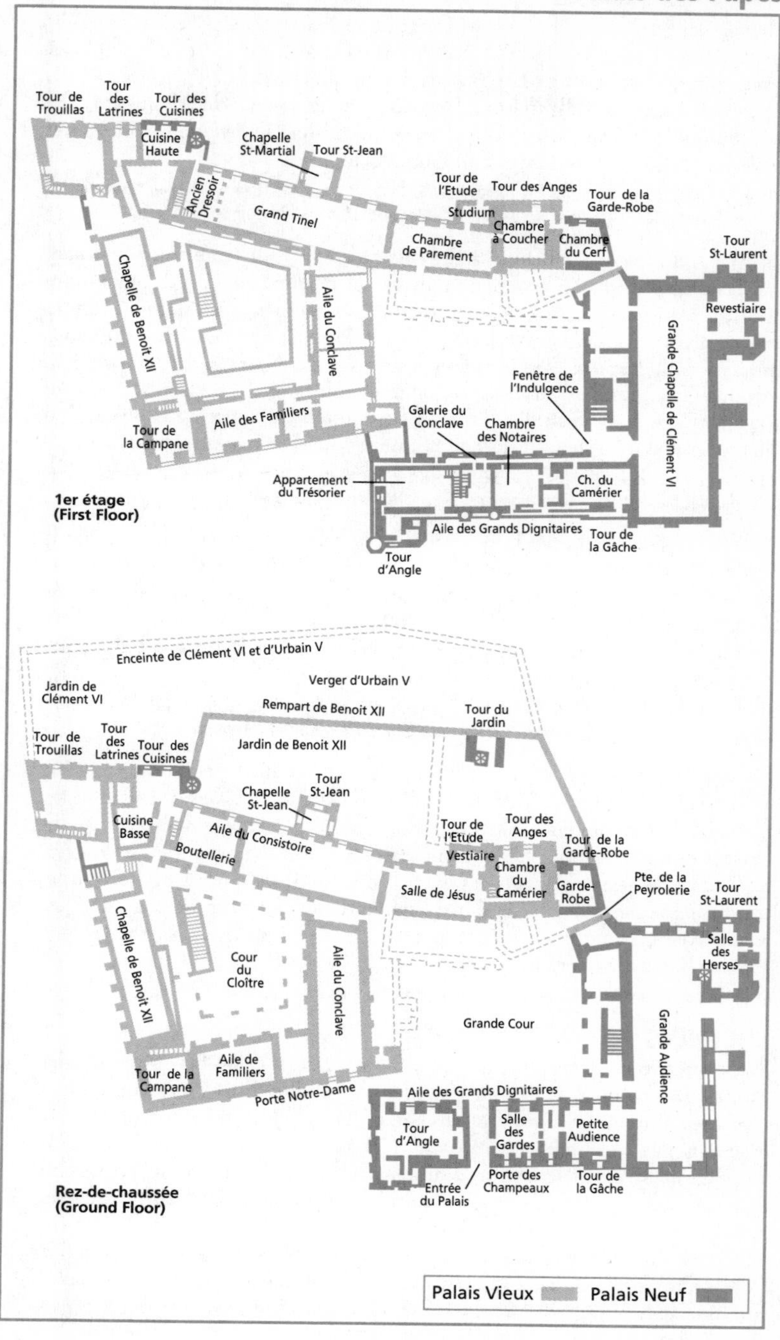
Tour de Trouillas
Tour des Latrines
Tour des Cuisines
Cuisine Haute
Chapelle St-Martial
Tour St-Jean
Ancien Dressoir
Grand Tinel
Tour de l'Etude
Tour des Anges
Tour de la Garde-Robe
Studium
Chambre à Coucher
Chambre du Cerf
Chambre de Parement
Tour St-Laurent
Chapelle de Benoit XII
Aile du Conclave
Revestiaire
Grande Chapelle de Clément VI
Fenêtre de l'Indulgence
Galerie du Conclave
Chambre des Notaires
Aile des Familiers
Tour de la Campane
Appartement du Trésorier
Ch. du Camérier
Aile des Grands Dignitaires
Tour de la Gâche
Tour d'Angle
1er étage
(First Floor)
Enceinte de Clément VI et d'Urbain V
Jardin de Clément VI
Verger d'Urbain V
Rempart de Benoit XII
Tour du Jardin
Tour de Trouillas
Tour des Latrines
Tour des Cuisines
Jardin de Benoit XII
Tour St-Jean
Chapelle St-Jean
Cuisine Basse
Aile du Consistoire
Boutellerie
Tour de l'Etude
Tour des Anges
Vestiaire
Tour de la Garde-Robe
Chambre du Camérier
Garde-Robe
Pte. de la Peyrolerie
Tour St-Laurent
Salle de Jésus
Salle des Herses
Chapelle de Benoit XII
Cour du Cloître
Aile du Conclave
Grande Cour
Grande Audience
Tour de la Campane
Aile de Familiers
Porte Notre-Dame
Aile des Grands Dignitaires
Tour d'Angle
Salle des Gardes
Petite Audience
Porte des Champeaux
Tour de la Gâche
Entrée du Palais
Rez-de-chaussée
(Ground Floor)
Palais Vieux
Palais Neuf

Musée du Petit-Palais This was the bishop's palace where the first two Avignon popes lived until Benedict XII constructed Palais des Papes. It holds an important collection of paintings from the Italian schools of the 13th to 16th centuries, including works from Florence, Venice, Siena, and Lombardy. In addition, salons display 15th-century paintings done in Avignon, and several galleries are devoted to Roman and Gothic sculptures.

Place du Palais. ✆ **04-90-86-44-58.** Admission 6€ adults, 3€ students, free for children 12 and under. June–Sept Wed–Mon 10am–1pm and 2–6pm; Oct–May Wed–Mon 9:30am–1pm and 2–5:30pm.

Musée Lapidaire ★ Behind a baroque facade, a 17th-century Jesuit church has been turned into an intriguing museum of mainly Gallo-Roman sculptures that can be viewed in less than an hour. In the museum you can trace the history of the various civilizations that have cultivated Provence. Some of the exhibitions are scary, including a man-eating monster discovered at Noves called *Tarasque.* Fascinating Greco-Roman statues are on exhibition, including a magnificent copy of Praxiteles' *Apollo the Python Killer* ★. A large number of ancient sarcophagi and funery art is also on show, including an unusual series of masks from Vaison.

18 rue de la République. ✆ **04-90-85-75-38.** Admission 3€ adults, 1.50€ students 12–18, free for children 11 and under. May–Oct daily 10am–noon and 2–6pm; Nov–Apr daily 2–6pm.

Musée Louis-Vouland In a 19th-century mansion opening onto a lovely garden, Avignon's treasure trove of lavish 17th- and 18th-century antiques and objets d'art is displayed. The collection includes Sèvres porcelain, the comtesse du Barry's tea set, great tapestries from Aubusson and Gobelins, glittering chandeliers, and commodes to equal those at Versailles. Our favorites are the Louis XV inkpots with silver rats holding the lids.

17 rue Victor-Hugo. ✆ **04-90-86-03-79.** Admission 4€ adults, 2.50€ students. May–Oct Tues–Sat 10am–noon and 2–6pm, Sun 2–6pm; Nov–Apr Tues–Sun 10am–noon and 2–6pm.

Musée Requien For aficionados only, this offbeat museum can easily take up an hour of your time. Located next to the Musée Calvet, it was named after the naturalist Espirit Requien (1788–1851), who was largely responsible for the nucleus of the collection. The museum houses one of the most important natural history libraries in France but is most often visited from its **herbarium** ★, containing some 200,000 specimens gathered by botanists from around the world. To round out the collection is a parade of exhibits that trace the geology, zoology, and botany of Provence.

61 rue Joseph-Vernet. ✆ **04-90-82-43-51.** Free admission. Tues–Sat 9am–noon and 2–6pm.

SHOPPING

Since the 1960s, **Antiquités Bourret,** 5 rue Limas (✆ **04-90-86-65-02**), has earned a reputation as a repository for 18th- and 19th-century Provençal antiques. The idea behind **Les Indiens de Nîmes,** 4 rue Joseph-Vernet (✆ **04-90-86-32-05**), is to duplicate 18th- and 19th-century Provençal fabric patterns. They're sold by the meter and are available in clothing for men, women, and children. In addition, you can buy kitchenware and furniture inspired by Provence and the steamy wetlands west of Marseille.

The clothing at **Souleiado,** place de l'Eglise (✆ **04-90-92-45-90**), derives from a Provençal model, and even the Provençal name (meaning "first ray of sunshine after a storm"). Most, but not all, of the clothing is for women. Fabrics are also sold by the meter.

Hervé Baume, 19 rue Petite Fusterie (✆ **04-90-86-37-66**), is for those who yearn to set a table like that encountered in Provence. This place is stocked with merchandise such as handblown crystal hurricane lamps. The place is piled high with a little bit of everything—from Directoire dinner services to French folk art.

Jaffier-Parsi, 42 rue des Fourbisseurs (✆ **04-90-86-08-85**), is known for its copper saucepans shipped from the Norman town of Villedieu-les-Poêles, which has been making them since the Middle Ages.

If you seek new points of view on Provençal pottery, go to **Terre è Provence,** 26 rue de la République (✆ **04-90-85-56-45**). You can pick up wonderful kitsch—perhaps terra-cotta plates decorated with three-dimensional cicadas.

Most markets in Avignon are open from 7am to 1pm. The big covered market is Les Halles on place Pie, open Tuesday through Sunday. Other smaller food markets are on rampart St-Michel on Saturday and Sunday, and on place Crillon on Friday. The flower market is on place des Carmes on Saturday, which becomes a flea market on Sunday. A more upscale antiques market fills up rue des Teinturiers all day on Saturday.

WHERE TO STAY

VERY EXPENSIVE

La Mirande ★★★ In the heart of Avignon (behind the Palais des Papes), this restored 700-year-old town house is one of France's grand little luxuries. The hotel treats you to 2 centuries of decorative art: From the 1700s Salon Chinois to the Salon Rouge, its striped walls were in Rothschild red. In 1987, Achim and Hannelore Stein transformed it into a citadel of opulence. Room no. 20 is the most sought-after, its lavish decor opening onto the garden. But all the rooms are stunning, with exquisite decor, hand-printed fabrics on the walls, antiques, bedside controls, and huge bathtubs. The restaurant is among the finest in Avignon; Chef Daniel Hébet has a light, sophisticated touch.

4 place Amirande, 84000 Avignon. ✆ **04-90-85-93-93.** Fax 04-90-86-26-85. www.avignon-et-provence.com/la-mirande. 20 units. 300€–430€ double; 614€–875€ suite. AE, DC, V. Parking 15€. **Amenities:** Restaurant; bar; limited room service; babysitting; laundry service; dry cleaning. *In room:* A/C, TV, minibar, hair dryer, safe.

EXPENSIVE

Hôtel d'Europe ★★★ Though slightly cheaper, this deluxe hostelry is almost the equal of the Mirande. The vine-covered Hôtel d'Europe has been in operation since 1799. You enter through a courtyard, where tables are set in the warmer months. The grand hall and salons boast tastefully arranged antiques. The good-size guest rooms have handsome decorations, period furnishings, and tile or marble bathrooms with deluxe toiletries and thick towels. Three suites perched on the roof have views of the Palais des Papes. In some twin-bedded rooms, the beds are a bit narrow but are comfortable overall. The restaurant, La Vieille Fontaine, is one of the most distinguished in Avignon. Meals are served in elegant dining rooms or a charming inner courtyard. The wine list is impressive but celestial in price.

12 place Grillon, 84000 Avignon. ✆ **04-90-14-76-76.** Fax 04-90-85-43-66. www.hotel-d-europe.fr. 45 units. 125€–400€ double; 480€–670€ suite. AE, DC, MC, V. Parking 14€. **Amenities:** Restaurant; bar; tennis by arrangement; business services; 24-hr. room service; laundry service; dry cleaning. *In room:* A/C, TV, minibar, hair dryer.

MODERATE

Clarion Hotel Cloître Saint-Louis ★ This unusual hotel is in a former Jesuit school, built in the late 1580s. It's not far from the railroad station, and the venerable building has a grandly baroque facade, wraparound arcades, and soaring ceiling vaults. While public areas retain many original features, bedrooms are more functional. Their decor is rather dull and severe; some have sliding glass doors overlooking the patio. A newer wing has been added, however, designed by world-class architect Jean Nouvel; these rooms display sleek modern lines and twin or double beds. The staff is hardworking, and maintenance is tidy.

20 rue Portail Boquier, 84000 Avignon. ✆ **800/CLARION** in the U.S., or 04-90-27-55-55. Fax 04-90-82-24-01. www.cloitre-saint-louis.com. 80 units. 113€–275€ double; 275€ suite. AE, MC, V. Parking 8€. **Amenities:** Restaurant; bar; outdoor pool; limited room service; dry cleaning. *In room:* A/C, TV, minibar, hair dryer, safe.

Hôtel Bristol In the center of Avignon, on one of the principal streets leading to the landmark place de l'Horloge and the Palais des Papes, the Bristol is one of the town's better bets. A traditional hotel, it offers comfortably furnished well-maintained rooms, most recently renovated in the early 1990s. Most bedrooms contain twin beds. Three units are suitable for persons with disabilities. Bathrooms are compact and tiled. Breakfast is the only meal served. Though it's not the most atmospheric place in Avignon, it offers good, solid value in an expensive city.

44 cours Jean-Jaurès, 84009 Avignon. ✆ **04-90-16-48-48.** Fax 04-90-86-22-72. 67 units. 85€–161€ double. Rates include breakfast. AE, DC, MC, V. Parking 10€. Closed Feb. **Amenities:** Bar; limited room service; laundry service; dry cleaning. *In room:* A/C, TV, minibar, hair dryer, safe.

Hôtel du Palais des Papes From the twin terraces of this simple but well-established hotel, you'll enjoy views of both the clock tower (overlooking the place de l'Horloge) and the Palais des Papes. Few other hotels boast as central a location, and only a handful are able to combine construction that was completed in series between the 15th century and the 1920s. You'll access the three floors of this place via a corkscrew-shape stone staircase that, in addition to exposed stone walls, massive ceiling beams, and wrought-iron bedsteads, evoke a modern twist on the Middle Ages that, fortunately, includes neatly tiled bathrooms. There are two dining rooms in this hotel, one medieval-looking, with a big fireplace, and the other with a beamed ceiling but slightly more modern. Cuisine is Provençal and French, flavorful, and served in generous portions. The hotel and its restaurant have been operated for many previous generations by the Donche-Gay family, members of whom are almost always on hand.

1 rue Gérard Philippe, 84000 Avignon. ✆ **04-90-86-04-13.** Fax 04-90-27-91-17. 26 units. 85€–132€ double. AE, MC, V. Parking 8€ per night in a nearby municipal parking lot. **Amenities:** Restaurant; bar; limited room service; babysitting; laundry service. *In room:* TV, minibar.

Hôtel Mercure Cité-des-Papes Nearly adjacent to the Palais des Papes, this five-story modern building offers bedrooms that offer solid comfort, though they are not particularly stylish. Views from many of its windows extend over the place de l'Horloge. In 1999, its management added another dozen on the upper floors by taking over the premises of a next-door restaurant. The restaurant, La Table de Provence, is expected to close in 2004.

1 rue Jean-Vilar, 84000 Avignon. ✆ **04-90-80-93-00.** Fax 04-90-80-93-01. 85 units. 110€–125€ double. 3rd and 4th occupants 12.15€ each. AE, DC, MC, V. Parking 8€. **Amenities:** Laundry service; dry cleaning. *In room:* A/C, TV, minibar, hair dryer, safe.

INEXPENSIVE

Hôtel d'Angleterre *Value* In the heart of Avignon, this Art Deco structure from around 1929 is the city's best budget hotel. The small rooms are comfortably but basically furnished, with adequate mattresses. All except one come with a small bathroom. Breakfast is the only meal served.

29 bd. Raspail, 84000 Avignon. ✆ **04-90-86-34-31.** Fax 04-90-86-86-74. www.hoteldangleterre.fr. 40 units, 39 with private bathroom. 55€–74€ double. MC, V. Parking 7€. Closed Dec 20–Jan 20. **Amenities:** Laundry service; dry cleaning. *In room:* TV.

Hôtel Danieli ★ This hotel's Italian influence is clear in its arches, chiseled stone, tile floors, and baronial stone staircase. Built during the reign of Napoléon I, it's classified as a historic monument in its own right. Its small, informal public rooms are outfitted mostly in antiques acquired by the history-conscious owner. The guest rooms, however, have painted bamboo furnishings and acceptably comfortable mattresses. Tiled bathrooms are compact and efficiently organized. Unless special arrangements are made for a group (and this hotel accepts many), breakfast is the only meal served.

17 rue de la République, 84000 Avignon. ✆ **04-90-86-46-82.** Fax 04-90-27-09-24. 29 units. 68€–98€ double. MC, V. Parking 7€. **Amenities:** Lounge; laundry service; dry cleaning. *In room:* TV.

Hôtel de Blauvac ★ *Finds* Named after its original owner and builder, the early-17th-century Marquis de Blauvac, this hotel occupies a converted two-story town house whose neoclassical facade and interior stonewalls and ceiling beams have been carefully preserved. Inside, amid Provençal fabrics and accessories, you'll find a cozy and appealing collection of public rooms and bedrooms. Each is high-ceilinged and charming, with an unpretentious decor—usually with a large old-fashioned armoire and other antique touches—that you'll almost never find in large chain-motif hotels. Bathrooms are small but tidy.

11 rue de la Bancasse, 84000 Avignon. ✆ **04-90-86-34-11.** Fax 04-90-86-27-41. www.hotel-blauvac.com. 16 units. 57€–68.50€ double. AE, DC, MC, V. Parking 8.60€ per night in a nearby public lot. *In room:* TV, minibar.

Hôtel le Médiéval About 3 blocks south of the Palais des Papes, this hotel is in a three-story town house from the late 1600s. It is clean, simple, and uncomplicated. Under beamed ceilings, most rooms are medium to spacious in size, each offering good comfort and generally large beds. The rooms that are the most quiet and peaceful overlook the small inner courtyard, with its pots of flowers and flowering shrubs. Others that overlook a congested medieval street corner might be a bit noisier but are not without a rough-and-ready charm of their own. Bathrooms are tiled and a bit small but still have adequate shelf space. Don't look for either a bar or a restaurant on the premises. Breakfast is served in the bedrooms.

15 rue Petite Saunerie, 84000 Avignon. ✆ **04-90-86-11-06.** Fax 04-90-82-08-64. hotel.medieval@wanadoo.fr. 34 units. 45€–62€ double. Extra bed 8€. AE, DC, MC, V. *In room:* TV.

WHERE TO DINE

EXPENSIVE

Brunel PROVENÇAL In the historic heart of Avignon, this elegant, flower-filled, air-conditioned restaurant is managed by the Brunel family. It offers such specialties as warm paté of duckling and breast of duckling with apples. The chef prepares a superb plate of ravioli stuffed with wild mushrooms served with roasted foie gras. Grilled John Dory is accompanied by artichoke hearts, and even the lowly pigs' feet emerge with a sublime taste. Desserts are excellent and prepared fresh daily. House wines can be ordered by the carafe.

46 rue de La Balance. ✆ **04-90-85-24-83.** Reservations required. Main courses 20€–32€; fixed-price menus 28€. AE, MC, V. Mon–Sat noon–1:30pm; Tues–Sat 7:30–9:30pm.

Christian Etienne ★★★ PROVENÇAL The stone house containing this restaurant is from 1180, built around the same time as the Palais des Papes (next door). Owner Christian Etienne continues to reach new culinary heights. His dining room contains early-15th-century frescoes honoring the marriage of Anne de Bretagne to the French king in 1491. Several of the fixed-price menus present specific themes: Two feature seasonal tomatoes, mushrooms, or vegetables; one offers preparations of lobster; and the priciest relies on the chef's discretion *(menu confiance)* to come up with unique combinations. In summer, look for a vegetable menu in which every course is based on ripe tomatoes; the main course is a mousse of lamb, eggplants, tomatoes, and herbs. A la carte specialties include filet of red snapper with black-olive coulis, rack of lamb with fresh thyme and garlic essence, and a dessert of fennel sorbet with saffron-flavored English cream sauce. Note for strict vegetarians: The vegetable menus aren't completely vegetarian; they're flavored with small amounts of meat or fish or, sometimes, meat drippings.

10 rue Mons. ✆ **04-90-86-16-50.** Reservations required. Main courses 25€–30€; fixed-price menus 26€–70€. AE, DC, MC, V. Mon–Sat noon–2:30pm and 8–10:30pm.

Hiély-Lucullus ★★ FRENCH Before the arrival of Christian Etienne (see above), this Relais Gourmand reigned supreme in Avignon. The town's most fabled chef, Pierre Hiély, has retired, though he drops in occasionally to check on his former sous chef, André Chaussy. He's doing fine and continues to offer reasonable fixed-price menus (no a la carte). Try one of his appetizers, like *petite marmite du pêcheur,* a savory fish soup ringed with black mussels. A main-dish specialty is *pintadeau* (young guinea hen) with peaches. The pièce de résistance is *agneau des Alpilles grillé* (grilled alpine lamb). Dessert might be vanilla-bourbon cream in puff pastry. Carafe wines include Tavel Rosé and Châteauneuf-du-Pape.

5 rue de la République. ✆ **04-90-86-17-07.** Reservations required. Fixed-price menus 24€–38€. MC, V. Thurs–Mon 12:30–2pm and 7:30–9:30pm. Closed 1 week in Feb and 1 week in June.

MODERATE

La Fourchette *Value* FRENCH Creative cooking at a moderate price is offered here in two dining rooms, one like a summerhouse with walls of glass, the other a tavern with oak beams. You might begin with fresh sardines flavored with citrus, or a parfait of chicken livers with a spinach flan and a confiture of onions. For a main course we recommend the blanquette of monkfish with endives, or the daube of beef prepared in the local style with a gratin of macaroni.

7 rue Racine. ✆ **04-90-85-20-93.** Main courses 15€–24€; fixed-price dinner 27€. MC, V. Mon–Fri noon–2:30pm and 7:30–10pm. Bus: 11.

Piedoie ★ *Finds* MODERN FRENCH In an intimate yellow-and-ochre-colored dining room behind the city ramparts, this place is the creative statement of its namesake, Thierry Piedoie, a chef who takes his food seriously. Menu items change with the seasons and availability of ingredients, but are likely to include a warm tartlet of asparagus tips and Serrano ham; a platter with smoked Scottish salmon, black Provençal olives, and herb salad; sweetbreads with glazed ginger and a confit of lemons; and filet of sole served with sesame seeds and grapefruit segments.

26 rue des Trois-Faucons. ✆ **04-90-86-51-53.** Reservations recommended. Main courses 13.50€–20.75€; fixed-price menus 16.90€–29€ lunch, 25€–42.50€ dinner. MC, V. Thurs–Tues noon–2pm and 7–9:30pm. Closed 2 weeks in Feb and 2 weeks in Nov.

NEARBY ACCOMMODATIONS & DINING

Auberge de Cassagne ★★ This could be your best bet for food and lodging in the greater Avignon area. The hotel, set in a park, is an enchanting little Provençal inn with country-style rooms. Rooms, most of which are connected by the pleasant, tree-studded inner courtyard, have been recently renovated and boast fine Provençal linens and tile flooring. The roomy bathrooms are handsomely maintained, with generous shelf space and deluxe toiletries. The cuisine is exceptionally good, much of it in the style of Paul Bocuse. You can enjoy your meals in an elegantly rustic dining room or at a table in the garden. The kitchens feature dishes like a duo of turbot and salmon served with a ragout of mushrooms, foie gras braised in port wine, and tagliatelle with a confit of tomatoes and olive oil.

450 allée de Cassagne, Rte. de Vèdene (D62), Le Pontet, 84130 Avignon. ✆ **04-90-31-04-18.** Fax 04-90-32-25-09. 40 units. 120€–300€ double; 315€–475€ suite. AE, DC, MC, V. Free parking. Take N7 and D62 for 6km (4 miles) northeast. **Amenities:** Restaurant; outdoor pool; nearby golf course; tennis court; health club; Jacuzzi; sauna; limited room service; babysitting; laundry service; dry cleaning. *In room:* A/C, TV, minibar, hair dryer, safe.

Hostellerie de l'Abbaye de la Celle ★★ One of France's most famous chefs, Alain Ducasse, whose five-star Michelin ratings have been the source of endless jealously and competition, is the owner of this idyllic Provençal inn. It lies in the hamlet of La Celle, midway between Nice and Avignon, on rocky, rolling land, a short walk from an 18th-century monastery that's the architectural highlight of the village. Within its premises, Ducasse set out to create an inn that lives up to one's fantasy of Provence. The components that go into this include a dining room featuring simple and delicious cooking, and individually decorated rooms that evoke what you might have found within a distinguished Mediterranean villa. Five of them are within an annex that Ducasse commissioned in 1999; the others are within an ocher-sided manor house that was built in 1745 as one of the outbuildings of the nearby monastery. Bathrooms are roomy and luxurious.

Place du Général-de-Gaulle, 83170 La Celle. ✆ **04-98-05-14-14.** Fax 04-98-05-14-15. www.abbaye-celle.com. 10 units. 235€–320€ double. AE, DC, MC, V. From Avignon, take the A8 Autoroute in the direction of Toulon, then exit at Brignoles, and follow the signs to La Celle. It's a total distance of 35km (22 miles) and takes about 40 min. each way. **Amenities:** Restaurant; bar; pool; babysitting. *In room:* TV, minibar, safe.

AVIGNON AFTER DARK

Near the Palais des Papes is **Le Grand Café,** La Manutention (✆ **04-90-86-86-77**), a restaurant/bar/cafe that might become your favorite watering hole. The dance-club standby is **Les Ambassadeurs,** 27 rue Bancasse (✆ **04-90-86-31-55**), which is more animated than its competitor, **Piano Bar Le Blues,** 25 rue Carnot (✆ **04-90-85-79-71**); the cover at both is 4€. Near Le Blues is a restaurant, **Red Zone,** 27 rue Carnot (✆ **04-90-27-02-44**), whose bar area is the site of live performances by whatever band happens to be in town.

Winning the award for having the most unpronounceable name is **Le Woolloomoolloo** (it means "Black Kangaroo" in an Aboriginal dialect of Australia), 16 bis rue des Teinturiers (✆ **04-90-85-28-44**). The bar and cafe complement a separate room devoted to the cuisine of France and a changing roster of cuisines from Asia, Africa, and South America. An alternative is **Bokao's Café,** 9 quai St-Lazare (✆ **04-90-82-47-95**), which offers both a restaurant and a disco as diversions during long sultry nights in Avignon. The most viable option for lesbians and gays is **L'Esclav,** 12 rue de Limas (✆ **04-90-85-14-91**), a bar and disco that are the focal point of the city's gay community.

VISITING VILLENEUVE-LEZ-AVIGNON ★

The modern world is impinging on Avignon, but across the Rhône at Villeneuve-lèz-Avignon, the Middle Ages slumber on. When the popes lived in exile at Avignon, his cardinals built palaces *(livrées)* across the river. Many visitors prefer to stay or dine here rather than in Avignon. This satellite town lies just across the

Rhône from Avignon and is most easily accessed via bus no. 11, which transits across the larger of the two (relatively modern-day) bridges, the **Pont Daladier.**

For information about the town, contact the **Office de Tourisme,** 1 place David (© **04-90-25-61-33**).

In addition, you might visit the **Eglise Notre-Dame,** place Meissonier (© **04-90-25-61-33**), founded in 1333 by Cardinal Arnaud de Via. Other than its architecture, the church's proudest possession is an antique copy (by an unknown sculptor) of Enguerrand Charonton's *Pièta,* the original of which is in the Louvre. It's open April through September Tuesday through Sunday from 10am to 12:30pm and 3 to 7pm. From October to January and March, it is open Tuesday through Sunday from 10am to 12:30pm and 2 to 5:30pm. Admission is free.

Chartreuse du Val-de-Bénédiction France's largest Carthusian monastery (or charterhouse), and once the country's most powerful, was built in 1352. The complex contains a church, three cloisters, and rows of cells that housed the medieval monks. The Centre National d'Ecritures et du Spectacle that now occupies the premises offers artists and writers the opportunity to live and work rent-free in the monastic cells for up to a year. Exhibitions of photography and painting are presented throughout the year.

Pope Innocent VI, whose tomb is here, founded this charterhouse. Don't miss the chapel that contains a remarkable *Coronation of the Virgin* by Enguerrand Charonton—the section of the 1453 masterpiece that depicts the denizens of hell is Bosch-like in its horror. The 12th-century graveyard cloister is lined with cells where the former fathers prayed and meditated.

60 rue de la République. © **04-90-15-24-24.** Admission 5.50€ adults, 3.50€ students, free for ages 17 and under. Apr–Sept daily 9am–6:30pm; Oct–Mar daily 9:30am–5:30pm.

Tour Philippe le Bel Constructed by Philippe the Fair in the 13th century, when Villeneuve became a French possession, the tower served as a gateway to the kingdom. If you have the stamina, you can climb to the top for a panoramic view of Avignon and the Rhône Valley.

Rue Montée-de-la-Tour. © **04-32-70-08-57.** Admission 1.60€ adults, .90€ students and children 12–17. Apr–Sept daily 10am–12:30pm and 2–7:30pm; Oct–Jan and Mar Tues–Sun 10am–12:30pm and 3–7pm.

WHERE TO STAY & DINE IN VILLENEUVE-LEZ-AVIGNON

Best Western La Magnaneraie ★★ One of the most charming accommodations in the region is this 15th-century country house on a hectare of gardens, under the direction of Gérard and Eliane Prayal. Tastefully renovated, the place is furnished with antiques and good reproductions. Bathrooms are neatly arranged. Many guests who arrive for only a night remain for many days to enjoy the good food and atmosphere, garden, tennis court, and landscaped pool. Madame Prayal's cuisine is excellent: Menu items might include zucchini flowers stuffed with mushroom-and-cream purée, feuilleté of foie gras and truffles, croustillant of red snapper with basil and olive oil, and rack of lamb with thyme. Dessert might be gratin of seasonal fruits with sabayon of lavender-flavored honey.

37 rue Camp-Bataille, 30400 Villeneuve-lèz-Avignon. © **04-90-25-11-11.** Fax 04-90-25-46-37. www.bestwestern.com. 32 units. 118€–168€ double; 300€–450€ suite. AE, DC, MC, V. **Amenities:** Restaurant; bar; pool; 24-hr. room service; babysitting; laundry service; dry cleaning. *In room:* A/C, TV, minibar, hair dryer, safe.

Hôtel de l'Atelier *Value* Villeneuve's budget offering is this 16th-century village house that has preserved much of its original style. Inside is a tiny duplex lounge with a large stone fireplace. Outside, a sun-filled rear garden, with potted orange and fig trees, provides fruit for breakfast. The immaculate accommodations are comfortable and informal, though a bit dowdy. Bathrooms are small but nicely arranged. In the old bourgeois dining room, a continental breakfast is the only meal served.

5 rue de la Foire, 30400 Villeneuve-lèz-Avignon. © **04-90-25-01-84.** Fax 04-90-25-80-06. hotel-latelier@libertysurf.fr. 23 units. 53€–80€ double. AE, DC, MC, V. Parking 6€ in nearby garage, free on street. **Amenities:** Lounge. *In room:* TV.

Le Prieuré ★★★ This small, charming, well-managed property was converted from a 1322 cardinal's residence. Roger Mille purchased it in 1943, and three generations of his family have been running it. Adjacent to the village church, it has an ivy-covered stone exterior, along with green shutters, a tiled roof, and a series of rustic but plush public rooms. There is a choice of bedrooms. Those in the main house, the actual old priory, are a bit smallish but filled with antique charm. Those in the modern annex by the swimming pool are much more spacious and offer better views. Whatever your assignment, you'll be rewarded with grand style and luxe living. One of the finest Relais & Châteaux properties in the south of France, "The Priory" remains the first choice for those with traditional taste who demand the very best wherever they travel.

Tables at the in-house restaurant are eagerly booked, as Le Prieure has long been known for the excellence of its cuisine and the charm of its setting. June through September, lunches, which feature an array of dishes, especially freshly made salads, are served on a luxurious terrace adjacent to the pool.

7 place du Chapitre, 30400 Villeneuve-lèz-Avignon. © **04-90-15-90-15.** Fax 04-90-25-45-39. www.leprieure.fr. 36 units. 95€–215€ double; 245€–295€ suite. AE, DC, MC, V. Free parking. Closed Nov–Mar. **Amenities:** Restaurant; bar; lounge; outdoor pool; 2 tennis courts. *In room:* A/C, TV, minibar, hair dryer, safe.

4 Uzès ★

682km (424 miles) S of Paris; 39km (24 miles) W of Avignon; 51km (31½ miles) NW of Arles

This scenically beautiful village is set on a limestone plateau that straddles the line between Provence and the Garrigues region, the severe though charming countryside along the foot of the ancient Massif Central. It is famous for the long-standing House of Uzès, home of France's highest-ranking ducal family, who still live in the ducal palace of Le Duché that dominates the town.

Jean Racine lived here in 1661, sent by his family to stay with an uncle, the vicar general of Uzès, in hopes that his dramatic ambitions might be dispelled. They weren't, and he went on to claim his place as one of France's great dramatists/poets. More recently, Uzès was the setting of Jean-Paul Rappeneau's version of *Cyrano de Bergerac,* in which Gérard Depardieu played the part of the soldier-poet.

In 1962, the village was named one of France's 500 *villes d'art* and has since taken good advantage of preservation funds set aside for restoration of its historic district. However, the designation has been viewed as a mixed blessing since many visitors, notably Parisians taking a break from city life, have since discovered the charms of the village.

ESSENTIALS

GETTING THERE There's no rail station in Uzès. **Train** passengers must get off at Avignon or Nîmes (both are a 1-hr. bus ride away). For rail information and schedules, call © **08-36-35-35-35.** There are about eight **buses** a day from both places. For bus information, contact the **Gare Routière d'Uzès,** avenue de la Libération (© **04-66-22-00-58**). By **car** from Avignon, take N100 west to the intersection with D981, following the road signs northwest into Uzes.

VISITOR INFORMATION The **Office de Tourisme** is on place Albert-1er (✆ **04-66-22-68-88**).

SPECIAL EVENTS The well-attended **Nuits Musicales d'Uzès** draws musicians of many stripes and talents from all over the world to a series of musical concerts performed at various venues throughout the town. The event takes place during the second half of July, with tickets costing from 8€ to 35€ per performance, depending on seating arrangements. Tickets for these events along with announcements of concerts are available at the tourist office.

SEEING THE SIGHTS

In the old part of town, every building is worth a moment or two of consideration. A pleasant square for a stroll, the asymmetrical **place aux Herbes** is defined by the medieval homes and sheltered walkways along its edges. The **Cathédrale St-Théodorit,** place de l'Evêché (✆ **04-66-22-13-26**), still utilizes its original 17th-century organ, a remarkable instrument composed of 2,772 pipes. The cathedral is open daily from 9am to 6:30pm. If you're lucky enough to be here during the last 2 weeks of July, you can attend one of the organ concerts that highlight the Nuits Musicales d'Uzès festival (see above). Adjacent is the circular six-story **Tour Fenestrelle,** all that remains of the original 12th-century cathedral that was burnt down by the Huguenots. It's closed to the public.

Le Duché ★ The palace is in a massive conglomeration of styles, the result of nearly continuous expansion of the residence in direct correlation to the rising wealth and power of the duke and duchess. The Renaissance facade blends Doric, Ionic, and Corinthian elements. Easily seen from below is the Tour de la Vicomté, a 14th-century watchtower recognizable by its octagonal turret.

Large segments of the compound, most notably its sprawling annex, are occupied by the comte and comtesse de Crussol d'Uzès and cannot be visited. You can climb the winding staircase in the square 11th-century Tour Bermonde for a sweeping view over the countryside from its elevated terrace. The 11th-century cellar, noted for its huge dimensions and vaulted ceilings, contains casks of wine from the surrounding vineyards. Tours of the site end with a *dégustation* of the reds and rosés of the Cuvée Ducale. The building's showcase apartments include a dining room with Louis XIII and Renaissance furnishings, a great hall (Le Grand Hall) done in the style of Louis XV, a large library that includes family memoirs, and the 15th-century Chapelle Gothique. Visits are usually part of an obligatory French-language tour, but you can follow the commentary in an English-language pamphlet.

Place du Duché. ✆ **04-66-22-18-96.** 10€ adults, 6.50€ students and teens 12–16, 4€ children 7–11, free for children 10 and under. June–Sept daily 10am–6:30pm; Oct–May daily 10am–noon and 2–6pm.

WHERE TO STAY

Hôtel d'Entraigues ★ *Value* The core of this hotel is a 15th-century manor house, expanded into two separate buildings, and much of it still looks as it did 300 years ago. It's nestled in a Mediterranean garden adjacent to the cathedral. Room furnishings vary from comfortably old-fashioned to modern contemporary. Like Marie d'Agoult, d'Entraigues is imbued with the charm of yesterday, but the comfort isn't as lavish here; Marie d'Agoult also has far greater amenities such as a pool and tennis courts. D'Entraigues's strongest selling point is its remarkable prices.

8 rue de la Calade, 30700 Uzès. ✆ **04-66-22-32-68.** Fax 04-66-22-57-01. www.lcm.fr/savry. 34 units. 70€–152€ double. AE, DC, MC, V. Parking 10€. **Amenities:** Restaurant; bar; limited room service. *In room:* TV, minibar, hair dryer.

Hôtel Marie d'Agoult (Château d'Arpaillargues) ★★ The foundations of this place are believed to date from a 3rd-century fortress, making it as old as the Gallo-Roman occupation of Provence. The combination of rough and chiseled stone construction you see today is from the late 1600s and early 1700s, and was a site where silkworms were raised when this area was a silk-making center. The hotel is named for a former occupant, Marie d'Agoult, mistress of Franz Liszt and mother of Richard Wagner's wife, Cosima. The place offers a sleepy insight into a way of life of long ago. The rooms, on the ground floor, have vaulted ceilings with exposed brick, and bathrooms are small but tidy.

Arpaillargues, 30700 Uzès. ✆ **04-66-22-14-48.** Fax 04-66-22-56-10. 27 units. 130€–183€ double; 206€–229€ suite. AE, MC, V. Closed Nov–Mar. Drive 4km (2½ miles) west of Uzès, following the signs to Andouze-Arpaillargues. **Amenities:** Restaurant; bar; pool; tennis courts; limited room service. *In room:* A/C in most units, TV, minibar, hair dryer, safe.

WHERE TO DINE

If you'd like to dine in town, consider the **Jardins de Castille,** the restaurant of the Hôtel d'Entraigues (see above). However, the area's best place to dine is in the hamlet of **St-Maximin,** 6km (3½ miles) southeast of Uzès. To reach it from Uzès, follow the signs to St-Maximin.

Les Fontaines MEDITERRANEAN In a 12th-century building in the heart of Uzès, you can enjoy thoughtful service and a well-seasoned roster of mostly Mediterranean dishes. Examples include chicken with garlic and goat cheese, a Moroccan *tagine* of lamb garnished with dried fruits, eggplant caviar, and a huge array of fresh-caught grilled fish, including a succulent version of monkfish with a pistous served over the top. The courtyard contains a scattering of summertime tables and a pair of verdant fig trees.

6 rue Entre les Tours. ✆ **04-66-22-41-20.** Reservations recommended. Main courses 12.50€–14.90€; set menus 17€–21.50€. MC, V. Mar–June and Sept–Jan Fri–Tues noon–2:30pm and 7–10pm; July–Aug daily.

5 Arles ★★★

724km (450 miles) S of Paris; 35km (22 miles) SW of Avignon; 89km (55 miles) NW of Marseille

Arles has been called "the soul of Provence," and art lovers, archaeologists, and historians are all attracted to this town on the Rhône. Many of the scenes painted so luminously by van Gogh remain to delight. The great Dutch painter left Paris for Arles in 1888. He was to paint some of his most celebrated works in this Provençal town.

The Greeks are said to have founded Arles in the 6th century B.C. Julius Caesar established a Roman colony here in 46 B.C. Under Roman rule, Arles prospered. Constantine the Great named it the second capital in his empire in A.D. 306, when it was known as "the little Rome of the Gauls." It wasn't until 1481 that Arles was incorporated into France.

Though Arles isn't quite as lovely as it was when van Gogh came here, it has enough antique charm to keep the appeal alive. Its first-rate museums, excellent restaurants, and summer festivals (such as the early June international photography festival) make a visit rewarding.

ESSENTIALS

GETTING THERE **Trains** leave from Paris's Gare de Lyon and arrive at Arles's **Gare S.N.C.F.** (avenue Paulin-Talabot), a short walk from the town center. One high-speed direct TGV travels from Paris to Arles each day (4½-hr. journey; 92€

for first class, 68€ for second). For other trains, you must change in Avignon. There are hourly connections between Arles and Avignon (30 min.; 8.40€ for first class; 5.60€ for second), Marseille (1 hr.; 17€ for first class, 11.40€ for second), and Aix-en-Provence (1¾ hr., change in Marseille; 22€ for first class, 14€ for second). For rail schedules and information, call ✆ **08-36-35-35-39.**

There are about four **buses** per day from Aix-en-Provence (trip time: 1¾ hr.). For bus information, call ✆ **04-90-93-74-90.**

If you're **driving,** head south along D570 from Avignon.

VISITOR INFORMATION The **Office de Tourisme,** where you can buy a *billet global* (see below), is on the esplanade Charles-de-Gaulle (✆ **04-90-18-41-20**).

GETTING AROUND If you'd like to get around by bicycle, head for a kiosk immediately adjacent to the town's tourist information office, a site that doubles as a bike rental outfit: **Europbike,** kiosk à Journaux Le Provençal, esplanade Charles de Gaulle (✆ **04-90-49-54-69**). A six-speed road bike, the only kind they have, rents for 14€ per day and requires a deposit of 260€. **Cycles Peugeot,** 15 rue du Pont (✆ **04-90-96-03-77**), rents bikes at comparable rates.

EXPLORING THE TOWN

Arles is full of monuments from Roman times. The general vicinity of the old Roman forum is occupied by **place du Forum,** shaded by plane trees. Once the Café de Nuit, immortalized by van Gogh, stood on this square. You can see two columns in the Corinthian style and pediment fragments from a temple at the corner of the Hôtel Nord-Pinus. South of here is **place de la République,** the principal plaza, dominated by a 15m (50-ft.) blue porphyry obelisk. On the north is the impressive Hôtel de Ville (town hall) from 1673, built to Mansart's plans and surmounted by a Renaissance belfry.

Eglise St-Trophime ★ On the east side of the square, this church's 12th-century portal is one of the finest achievements of the southern Romanesque style. In the pediment, Christ is surrounded by the symbols of the Evangelists. Frederick Barbarossa was crowned king of Arles on this site in 1178. The cloister, in both the Gothic and Romanesque styles, is noted for its medieval carvings. Be warned that the hours listed below are sometimes unpredictable; hours can change at the whim of the custodial staff.

On the east side of place de la République. ✆ **04-90-49-33-53.** Free admission to church; cloister 3.05€ adults, 2.30€ students and ages 12–18, free for ages 11 and under. Church daily 8:30am–6:30pm; cloister mid-June to mid-Sept daily 9am–12:30pm and 2–7pm.

Les Alyscamps ★ This is one of the most famous necropolises of the western world. Its fame began when Genesius, a Roman civil servant, refused to write down an edict calling for persecution of Christians. For this, he was beheaded in 250; later he was made a saint when it was said that miracles began to happen on this site. In time, the fame of Les Alyscamps spread throughout the Christian world; more of the faithful wanted to be buried here, and coffins were shipped down the Rhône for burial. By the 10th century, the legend spread that the heroes of Roncevaux—Roland and Olivier—were also entombed here, which brought the place even more fame. Dante even mentioned it in his *Inferno.*

In the Middle Ages, there were 19 churches and chapels on the site. After the Renaissance, the graveyard was desecrated: Tombs were removed and stones were taken to construct other buildings. For an evocative experience, walk down L'Allée des Sarcophages, where 80 generations have been buried over 2,000 years. The lane is lined with sarcophagi under tall poplar trees.

Arles

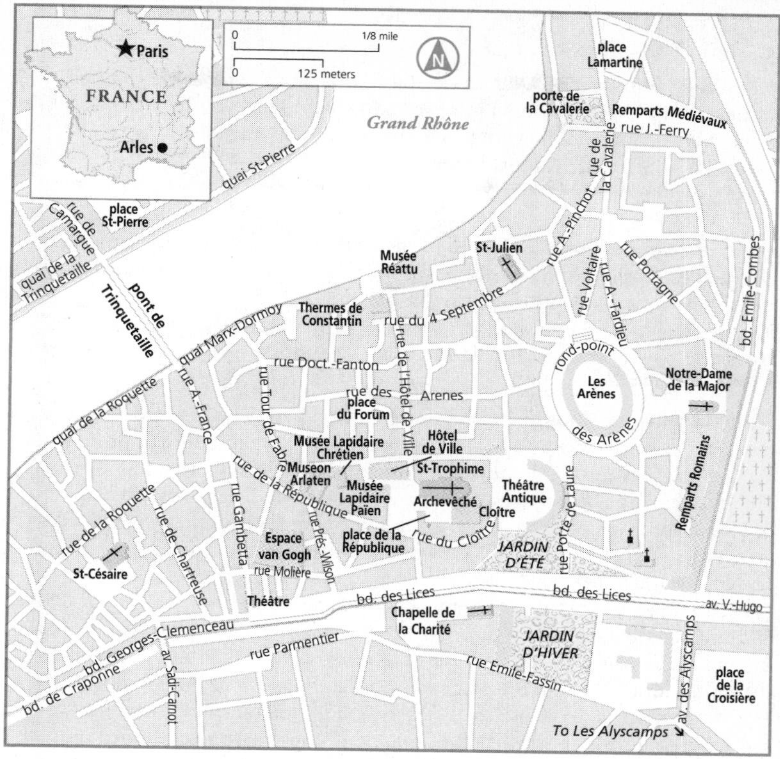

Rue Pierre-Renaudel. ✆ **04-90-49-36-87.** Admission 3.50€ adults, 2.60€ ages 12–18, free for ages 11 and under. Mid-Sept to mid-June daily 9am–12:30pm and 2–7pm; mid-June to mid-Sept daily 9am–7pm.

Musée de l'Arles Antique ★★ Opened in 1995, the museum holds one of the world's most famous collections of Roman Christian sarcophagi as well as a rich ensemble of sculptures, mosaics, and inscriptions from the Augustinian period to the 6th century A.D. Eleven detailed models show ancient monuments of the region as they existed in the past. Allow 1 hour to view the museum's holdings.

Presqu'île du Cirque Romain. ✆ **04-90-18-88-88.** Admission 5.35€ adults, 1€ students and children under 12. Feb 11–Nov 1 daily 9am–7pm; Nov 2–Feb 10 daily 10am–5 pm.

Musée Réattu ★ The town's museum is named for the rather mediocre local painter Jacques Réattu, but it contains more important works—etchings and drawings by Picasso, and paintings by Alechinsky, Dufy, Léger, Henri Rousseau, and Zadkine. Note the Arras tapestries from the 16th century.

10 rue du Grand-Prieuré. ✆ **04-90-49-37-58.** Admission 4€ adults, 3€ students and ages 12–18, free for children under 12. Apr–Sept daily 9am–7pm; Oct–Mar daily 10am–4:30pm.

Museon Arlaten ★ The museum was founded by Frédéric Mistral, the Provençal poet who led a movement to establish modern Provençal as a literary language, using the money from his Nobel Prize for Literature in 1904. This is really a folklore museum, with regional costumes, portraits, furniture, dolls, a

Tips **The *Billet Global***

Before heading out in Arles, go to the tourist office, where you can purchase a *billet global,* the all-inclusive pass that admits you to the town's museums, Roman monuments, and all the major attractions, at a cost of 10€ for adults and 5€ for children.

music salon, and a room devoted to mementos of Mistral. Among its curiosities is a letter (in French) from President Theodore Roosevelt to Mistral, bearing the letterhead of the Maison Blanche in Washington, D.C.

29 rue de la République. ✆ **04-90-96-08-23.** Admission 4€ adults, 2.70€ students and children under 18. July–Aug 9:30am–1pm and 2–6:30pm; Oct–Mar 9:30am–12:30pm and 2–5pm; Apr, May, and Sept 9:30am–12:30pm and 2–6pm.

Théâtre Antique/Amphitheatre (Les Arènes) ★★ These are the city's two great classical monuments. The Roman theater, begun by Augustus in the 1st century, was mostly destroyed and only two Corinthian columns remain. Here the famous *Venus of Arles* was discovered in 1651. A copy of a masterpiece of Hellenistic statuary, it was broken into three pieces and armless when discovered. Arles offered it to Louis XIV, who had it restored, and today it is in the Louvre. To reach the theater, take rue de la Calade from the city hall.

Nearby, also built in the 1st century, the Amphitheater seats almost 25,000 and still hosts bullfights in summer. The government warns you to visit the old monument at your own risk, since the stone steps are uneven and much of the masonry is worn down to the point where it might be a problem for older travelers or for those with disabilities. For a good view, you can climb the three towers that remain from medieval times when the amphitheater was turned into a fortress. Note that the theater and Les Arènes maintain the same hours and the same fluid scheduling as Eglise St-Trophime.

Théâtre Antique: Rue du Cloître. ✆ **04-90-49-36-25.** Amphitheatre: Rond-pont des Arènes. ✆ **04-90-49-36-86.** Admission to each site 3€ adults, 2.20€ students and youth age 18 and under. Daily 9am–7pm (hours can be unpredictable).

Thermes de Constantin Near the banks of the Rhone is found the entrance to some 4th-century Roman baths, which have been partially restored with characteristic bands of brickwork. The baths or thermae are all that remain of a once grand imperial palace that stood here, Palais Constantin. These baths are the largest that remain in Provence. Dating from Constantine's era, the ruins of the baths measure 98m by 45m (322 ft. by 148 ft.). You enter by the tepidarium, going through the caldarium, with its remaining hypocaust. Allow about half an hour to inspect the ruins.

Rue Dominique-Maisto. ✆ **04-90-49-35-40.** 3€ adults, 2€ children. Daily 9am–7pm.

WHERE TO STAY

EXPENSIVE

Grand Hotel Nord Pinus ★★ Few hotels in Arles manage to evoke Provence's 19th-century charm as effectively as this one. Sprawled across one entire edge of the central square in Arles, it evokes the Belle Epoque of France better than almost any other building in town. Its real fame originated in the 1950s, when a professional circus performer from the Cirque de Medrano (Monsieur Nello and his wife, Germaine) bought it and transformed it into a bastion of hip for such clients as Picasso, Jean Cocteau, Simone Signoret, and Yves Montand. Occupying an antique town house on a tree-lined square in the heart of town, it has public rooms filled with antiques and an ornate staircase lined with graceful wrought-iron balustrades. Bedrooms are glamorous, even theatrical, filled with rich upholsteries, with thick curtains artfully arranged around the oversize French doors. All have neat tiled bathrooms. Many bullfighters and artists have stayed here—you'll see their photographs and framed artworks in many of the public areas.

Place du Forum, 13200 Arles. ✆ **04-90-93-44-44.** Fax 04-90-93-34-00. www.nord-pinus.com. 25 units. 137€–275€ double; 412€ suite. Rates include breakfast. AE, MC, V. Parking 13€ per night. Closed Feb. **Amenities:** Restaurant; bar; limited room service; laundry service; dry cleaning. *In room:* A/C, TV, minibar.

Hôtel Jules César et Restaurant Lou Marquês ★★★ This 17th-century Carmelite convent is now a stately country hotel with the best restaurant in town. Although it's in a noisy neighborhood, most rooms face the unspoiled cloister. You'll wake to the scent of roses and the sounds of birds singing. Throughout you'll find a blend of antique neoclassic architecture and modern amenities. The decor is luxurious, with antique Provençal furnishings found at auctions throughout the countryside. The interior rooms are the most tranquil and also the darkest, though enlivened by bright fabrics. Most of the downstairs units are spacious, and although the upstairs rooms are small, they have a certain old-world charm. The rooms in the modern extensions are comfortable but lack character.

9 bd. des Lices, 13200 Arles CEDEX. ✆ **04-90-52-52-52.** Fax 04-90-52-52-53. www.hotel-julescesar.fr. 58 units. 120€–215€ double; 345€–375€ suite. AE, DC, MC, V. Parking 13€. Closed Nov 12–Dec 24. **Amenities:** 2 restaurants; bar; limited room service; laundry service. *In room:* TV, minibar, hair dryer.

MODERATE

Hôtel d'Arlatan ★★ This hotel occupies the former residence of the comtes d'Arlatan de Beaumont, near place du Forum. It has been managed by the same family since 1920. It was built in the 15th century on the ruins of an old palace begun by Constantine—in fact, there's still a wall from the 4th century. Rooms are furnished with Provençal antiques and reproductions, with the walls covered in patterned wallpaper and, in some rare instances, tapestries in the style of Louis XV and Louis XVI. The most appealing rooms overlook the garden. This was a former private residence, so accommodations range from small (on the upper floors) to more spacious on the ground floor.

26 rue du Sauvage, 13361 Arles. ✆ **04-90-93-56-66.** Fax 04-90-49-68-45. www.hotel-arlatan.fr. 51 units. 95€–160€ double; 160€–245€ suite. AE, MC, V. Parking 12.50€. Closed Jan. **Amenities:** Dining room; laundry service. *In room:* A/C, TV, minibar, hair dryer.

Finds Les Olivades

In a somewhat isolated position 12km (7½ miles) north of Arles, **Les Olivades Factory Store,** chemin des Indienneurs, St-Etienne-du-Grès (✆ **04-90-49-19-19**), stands beside the road that's signposted to Tarascon and Avignon. Because of the wide array of art objects and fabrics inspired by the traditions of Provence, it's worth your while to make a trek out here. Fabrics, dresses, shirts for men and women, table linens, and fabric by the yard are all available at retail outlets of the Olivades chain throughout Provence, but here the selection is a bit cheaper and more diverse.

INEXPENSIVE

Hôtel Calendal ★ *Value* Because of its reasonable rates, the Calendal is a bargain hunter's favorite. On a quiet square near the arena, it offers renovated rooms with bright colors, high ceilings, and a sense of spaciousness. Most have views of the hotel's garden, filled with palms and palmettos. The restaurant has a limited menu featuring omelets, soups, and platters.

5 rue Porte de Laure, 13200 Arles. ✆ **04-90-96-11-89.** Fax 04-90-96-05-84. www.lecalendal.com. 38 units. 45€–71€ double. AE, DC, MC, V. Parking 10€. Bus: 4. **Amenities:** Restaurant; laundry service.

Hôtel de la Muette A short walk from the city's ancient Roman arena, this hotel occupies an old building that has been an inn since the 1100s. Extensively renovated and restored, it presents a severe-looking stone facade to the outside world and an interior that retains the ancient ceiling beams and rough-textured masonry walls. Cheerfulness is added in the form of many coats of white paint and traditional Provençal fabrics in sunny colors of maize, red, and blue. Overall, the place is comfortable, if a bit cramped, representing good value for the money. Bathrooms are small, with barely adequate shelf space.

15 rue des Suisses, 13200 Arles. ✆ **04-90-96-15-39.** Fax 04-90-49-73-16. 18 units. 48€–53€ double. AE, MC, V. Parking 7€. **Amenities:** Lounge; 24-hr. room service (for drinks and snacks). *In room:* TV, hair dryer.

Hôtel Le Cloître *Value* This hotel, between the ancient theater and the cloister, is a great value. Originally part of a 12th-century cloister, it still has its original Romanesque vaultings. Throughout you'll find a richly Provençal atmosphere, pleasant rooms with high ceilings, and subtle references to the building's antique origins. Bedrooms are lean on amenities except for phones and small bathrooms. Some units have TVs available for a supplement of 3.50€ per day. There's also a TV lounge and a breakfast salon.

16 rue du Cloître, 13200 Arles. ✆ **04-90-96-29-50.** Fax 04-90-96-02-88. hotel_cloitre@hotmail.com. 30 units. 43€–63€ double. AE, MC, V. Parking 4.55€. Closed mid-Nov to Mar 15. Bus: 4.

Hôtel Mirador Just a minute's walk north of Arles' Roman arena, this is a pleasant family-run hotel in a central location. Bedrooms are slightly cramped but well maintained and cozy, with adequate bathrooms. Public areas are outfitted in a *faux-antique* decor of exposed wood and flower-patterned fabrics. You'll be happiest here if you don't expect grandeur, but accept small inconveniences with a sense of humor.

3 rue Voltaire, 13200 Arles. ✆ **04-90-96-28-05.** Fax 04-90-96-59-89. www.hotel-mirador.com. 15 units. 30€–41€ double. AE, MC, V. Parking 6.10€. Closed Feb. **Amenities:** Lounge. *In room:* TV.

WHERE TO DINE

For a truly elegant meal, consider dining at the **Restaurant Lou Marquês** at the Hôtel Jules César (see "Where to Stay," above).

MODERATE

Brasserie Nord-Pinus FRENCH/PROVENÇAL It has accoutrements not duplicated in any other hotel: Terraces that surround it on all sides, an ancient Roman column (part of the ancient Temple of Constantine) that rises from one edge of the terrace, a collection of photos in its bar (the Corrida Bar) of the grand painters of the 1950s who made it their hangout, and a collection of valuable photos of African wildlife taken by Peter Beard, a long-ago friend of Karen Blixen, that are artistically and historically important. Some visitors compare its high-ceilinged, lush, and artfully decadent brown, gold, and white interior to a Batista-era hotel in old Havana: It's hot, artsy, sensual, a bit imperial, comfortable, and very grand. The decor of the restaurant is vaguely baroque, filled with paneling and mirrors, with a '50s-era decor that's grand and elegant and that no one wants to change. The cuisine is one of the lightest and most sophisticated in town, employing top-notch chefs to prepare dishes based on the best of seasonal shopping. The menus change frequently but are generally a delight. The food is colorful, spicy, and artfully arranged on platters.

Place du Forum. ✆ **04-90-93-44-44.** Reservations recommended. Main courses 15€–18€; fixed-price menus 35€–40€. AE, DC, MC, V. Thurs–Mon 12:30–2pm; Wed–Mon 8–10:30pm.

La Gueule du Loup FRENCH/PROVENÇAL Named after its original founder, who, according to local legend, grew to resemble a wolf as he aged, this cozy and well-managed restaurant occupies a stone-fronted antique house in the historic core of Arles, near the ancient Roman arena. Today it's owned by members of the Allard family, who prepare serious, gourmet-style French food that's more elaborate than what's served by many of its competitors. The best examples include a hearty filet of bull braised in red wine, brandade of codfish, warm goat cheese with marinated beets, breast of duck with mashed potatoes, squid and monkfish in saffron sauce, and crème brulée with essence of orange blossoms. Reservations are important, since the cozy interior has room for only 30 diners at a time.

39 rue des Arènes. ✆ **04-90-96-96-69.** Reservations highly recommended. Main courses 19€–22€; fixed-price menu 25€. DC, MC, V. Easter to Oct Tues–Sat noon–2:30pm, Mon–Sat 7–9:30pm. Closed Mon night Nov to Easter.

L'Olivier ★ PROVENÇAL/FRENCH On the western edge of the old town is one of the most charming restaurants in Arles, occupying a house whose foundations date from the 12th century. Inside you'll find a pair of dining rooms with beamed ceilings, fireplaces, terra-cotta tiles, ladder-backed chairs, and the kind of antiques your French grandmother might have had in her home. Menu items vary with the season, but the best examples include fresh local asparagus garnished with sweetbreads on a bed of roasted tomatoes, fava bean soup with garlic croutons and saffron-flavored rouille, codfish steak with a bouillon of garlic and fresh herbs, and baby pigeon roasted with foie gras-flavored butter.

1 bis rue Réattu. ✆ **04-90-49-64-88.** Reservations recommended. Main courses 15€–25€; set menus 28€–55€. MC, V. Tues–Sat noon–2:30pm and 7:30–9:30pm.

INEXPENSIVE

El Quinto Toro PROVENÇAL/SPANISH Set within a few steps of the place de Forum, and outfitted with a decor inspired by the *corrida* (bullfights) that are held in and around Arles, this is a well-managed restaurant with no more than 30 seats and a following of local fans. Some of the best food is grilled over live coals that waft aromas from the busy kitchens into the dining rooms. You might begin with a platter of Spanish tapas and then follow with generous slabs of duck breast or fresh fish, both grilled and both succulent. A noteworthy specialty, not widely available, is a slab of wood-grilled bull steak from the Camargue. The owners pride themselves on the earthy simplicity of their cuisine and don't provide fancy sauces, preferring instead to emphasize the natural juices and flavors of the meat or fish. A wide selection of French and Spanish wines and beers accompanies your meal.

12 rue de la Liberté. ✆ **04-90-49-62-29.** Reservations recommended in summer. Main courses 8.50€–14€. AE, V. Thurs–Tues noon–2:30pm and 7–10:30pm.

ARLES AFTER DARK

Because of its relatively small population (around 50,000), Arles doesn't offer as many nightlife options as Aix-en-Provence, Avignon, Nice, or Marseille. The town's most appealing choice is the bar/cafe/music hall **Le Cargo de Nuit,** 7 av. Sadi-Carnot, route pour Barriol (© **04-90-49-55-99**). It's open only on Friday and Saturday nights. On those nights, there's a supper club, followed by live music—salsa, jazz, rock and roll, whatever, and then disco dancing until 3am. The cover ranges from 6.50€ to 12€.

The town's most animated cafe, where most of the singles go, is **Le Café van Gogh,** 11 place du Forum (© **04-90-96-44-56**). Overlooking an attractive plaza, it features live music and an ambience that the almost young and the restless refer to as *super-chouette,* or "super cool."

6 Les Baux ★★★

715km (444 miles) S of Paris; 19km (12 miles) NE of Arles; 80km (50 miles) N of Marseille and the Mediterranean

Cardinal Richelieu called Les Baux a "nesting place for eagles." In its lonely position high on a windswept plateau overlooking the southern Alpilles, Les Baux seems to be part of the mysterious, shadowy rock formations.

Once it was the citadel of the powerful seigneurs of Les Baux, who ruled with an iron fist and sent their conquering armies as far as Albania. In medieval times, the flourishing culture of Les Baux attracted troubadours from all over Europe to the "court of love." Later, Les Baux was ruled by the notorious "Scourge of Provence," Raymond de Turenne, who sent his men throughout the land to kidnap people. If a victim's friends and family could not pay ransom, the poor wretch was forced to walk a gangplank over the cliff's edge.

When Les Baux became a Protestant stronghold in the 17th century, Richelieu, fed up with its constant rebellion against Louis XIII, commanded his armies in 1632 to destroy the "eagle's nest." Today the castle and ramparts are a mere shell, though you can see remains of great Renaissance mansions.

With its dramatic situation, Les Baux is one of the most visited sites in southern France. More than a million visitors come here every year.

ESSENTIALS

GETTING THERE There's no rail station in Les Baux, so most **train** passengers get off at Arles, where there are four **buses** daily that stop at Les Baux (trip time: 25 min.) and more that stop in Maussane-les-Alpilles, 3km (2 miles) south. The bus makes fewer runs between November and March. For information, call Ste. Ceyte Tourism Mediterranée at © **04-90-93-74-90** in Arles.

By **car** from Avignon, take D-942 northeast to D938 to the intersection to D938, at which point you head northeast to D131 leading into Les Baux.

VISITOR INFORMATION The **Office de Tourisme** is on Maison du Roy, near the northern entrance to the old city (© **04-90-54-34-39**).

EXPLORING THE AREA

Les Baux has two aspects: the inhabited and carefully preserved medieval village and the evocative ruins of its fortress, the "dead" village. Visitors enter the city through the 19th-century **Port Mage,** but in medieval times, the monumental Porte Eyguières was the only entrance to the fortified city.

From place St-Vincent are sweeping views over the Vallon de la Fontaine. This is the site of the 12th-century **Eglise St-Vincent** (no phone), with its beautiful campanile, called La Lanterne des Morts (Lantern of the Dead). The stained-glass

Tips A Hiker's Warning

Because of the danger of brush fires during the simmering dry heat of midsummer, all of the footpaths and hiking trails in the region of the Alpilles are either closed or severely limited between mid-June and mid-September. For more information, contact any of the local tourist offices.

windows were a gift from Rainier of Monaco, in his capacity as the marquis des Baux. They are modern, based on designs of French artist Max Ingrand. The church is open November through March daily from 10am to 5:30pm.

Yves Brayer Museum, at the intersection of rue de la Calade and rue de l'Eglise (✆ **04-90-54-36-99**), holds a retrospective collection of the works of Yves Brayer (1907–90), a figurative painter and Les Baux's most famous native son (he's buried in the village cemetery). He painted scenes of Italy, of Morocco, and, in Spain, of many bullfights, working mainly in shades of red, ocher, and black. Brayer also decorated the restored 17th-century La Chapelle des Pénitents Blancs, which stands close to the Church of St. Vincent, with frescoes of the Annunciation, the Nativity, and Christ in Majesty. The museum is open April through September daily from 10am to 12:30pm and 2 to 6pm, and the rest of the year from Wednesday through Monday 10am to 12:30pm and 2 to 5:30pm. Admission is 4€ for adults and 10€ for students and children.

The Renaissance-era **Hôtel de Manville,** rue Frédéric-Mistral, functions today as the Mairie (Town Hall). Only its courtyard can be visited. The town's ancient town hall on place Louis Jou now contains the **Musée des Santons** (no phone), a collection of antique crèche figures. It's open April through October daily from 7am to 7pm, and November through March from 10am to 6:30pm.

In the Renaissance-era Hôtel Jean-de-Brion, rue Frédéric-Mistral (✆ **04-90-69-88-03** or 04-90-54-34-17), is the **Fondation Louis Jou,** which can be visited only by special arrangement. It has engravings and serigraphs by the artist. The 1569 **Hôtel des Porcelles** contains a collection of contemporary artists who have worked in Les Baux and in Provence.

Château des Baux The grounds of the chateau encompass a complex of evocative, mostly ruined buildings, which were carved out of the rocky mountain peak. Also called *la ville morte* (the "ghost village") or La Citadelle, the Château des Baux is at the upper (northern) end of Les Baux. It's accessible via the rue du Château, at the Hôtel de la Tour du Brau, which contains a small archaeological and lapidary museum. Inside the compound is the ruined château des Baux with its tower-shaped *donjon* and surrounding ramparts, and the two towers, Tour Paravel and Tour Sarascenes. The collection of replicated medieval siege engines were built from the original plans. The ruined chapel of St-Blaise houses a little museum devoted to the olive. The site of the former castle covers an area at least five times that of the present village of Les Baux. As you stand here you can look out over the "Valley of Hell" and even glimpse the Mediterranean in the distance.

North end of Les Baux, via the rue de Château. ✆ **04-90-54-55-56.** Admission 6.50€ adults, 5€ students and 3.50€ ages 7–17. Mar daily 9am–6:30pm; July–Aug daily 9am–8:30pm; Sept–Oct daily 9am–5pm.

WHERE TO STAY

Note that **La Riboto de Taven** (see "Where to Dine," below) has two rooms for rent.

VERY EXPENSIVE

L'Oustau de Beaumanière ★★★ This Relais & Châteaux property is one of southern France's most legendary hotels. On the premises of a Provençal *mas* (farmhouse) bought in 1945 by the late Raymond Thuilier, it became a rendezvous for the glitterati in the 1950s and 1960s, and continues today, in a less spectacular kind of glamour, under the founder's grandson, Jean-André Charial. The hotel consists of three stone houses draped in flowering vines at the base of the rocky hill on which the fortified town rises. The plush guest rooms evoke the 16th and 17th centuries. All contain large sitting areas and sumptuous marble bathrooms, but no two are exactly alike. Most beds are twins or queen size. The hotel has three annexes with comparable comfort but less style—Le Manor is the most appealing. In the stone-vaulted dining room, the chef serves specialties like ravioli of truffles with leeks, and *rossini* (stuffed with foie gras) of veal with fresh truffles. The award-winning *gigot d'agneau* (lamb) *en croûte* has become this place's trademark and is particularly succulent. For dessert, consider a soufflé of red fruits. Reservations are essential.

Les Baux, 13520 Maussane-les-Alpilles. ✆ **04-90-54-33-07.** Fax 04-90-54-40-46. 27 units. 250€–275€ double; 400€–430€ suite. AE, DC, MC, V. Closed Jan 3–Mar 4. Restaurant closed Wed Oct–Apr 1. **Amenities:** Restaurant; bar; outdoor pool; 24-hr. room service; laundry service; dry cleaning. *In room:* A/C, TV, minibar, hair dryer.

EXPENSIVE

La Cabro d'Or ★★★ This is the less celebrated sibling of the Oustau de Beaumanière, located about a kilometer (half-mile) away. It was built in the 1700s as a farmhouse and consists of about five low-slung stone structures. The decor in these very comfortable accommodations evokes old-timey Provence.

Moments A Drive Through Hell

Below Les Baux is a jagged and irregular gorge, **Val d'Enfer (Valley of Hell).** You can access the valley by D27 and D78G and drive through this bleak and rugged scenery. Centuries ago, caves in the gorge were inhabited by humans. The gorge is the source of many Provençal legends—witches, sprites, and fairies are said to live in the caves.

On your way to the valley, you can stop at the **Cathédrale d'Images** ★★ (✆ **04-90-54-38-65**), off Route duVal d'Enfer (D27), a kilometer (half-mile) north of the village, in a former quarry. Photographer Albert Plecy converted this dark, cavernous space of large, square limestone columns and high-arched ceilings into a three-dimensional palette for an interactive experience with frescoes of the Italian Renaissance. Forty-eight strategically placed projectors splash images from the frescoes in all directions: You might walk across a projection of a full fresco, while on the wall next to you a close-up of an infant's face from the scene is enlarged and displayed, and above you the dueling men in the back of the fresco are plucked out and brought into focus. The moving display, in synchronization with well-chosen musical pieces from the era, is 30 minutes long, though you can stay longer and watch the loop replay. It's open daily in summer from 10am to 7pm but is closed from mid-November to early March. Admission is 7€ for adults and 4.10€ for children under 18.

Some have sweeping views over the surrounding countryside, and all have unusual art and, in most cases, recently upgraded bathrooms with deluxe toiletries. The in-house restaurant is in a barn from the 1800s with massive ceiling beams that are works of art in their own right. It's flanked with a vine-covered terrace that overlooks an ornamental pond and garden, with a farther view of a rocky, barren landscape that has been compared to the surface of the moon.

13520 Les Baux de Provence. ✆ **04-90-54-33-21.** Fax 04-90-54-45-98. www.lacabrodor.com. 31 units. 160€–225€ double; from 340€ suite. Off-season rates about 25% lower. Half board 75€ extra per person. AE, DC, MC, V. **Amenities:** Restaurant (closed Mon Oct–Apr); bar; pool; 2 tennis courts; laundry service. *In room:* A/C, TV, minibar, hair dryer.

MODERATE

Auberge de la Benvengudo ★ This auberge is a tastefully converted 19th-century farmhouse surrounded by sculptured shrubbery, towering trees, and parasol pines. Rooms are almost equally divided between the original building above the restaurant, and an attractive stone-sided annex. Bedrooms are sunny, clean, and recently renovated. Each has a private terrace or balcony and, in some cases, an antique four-poster bed. The inn serves a delectable cuisine, with menu items that include a filet of hogfish with saffron, filet of red mullet with a concasse of tomatoes, grilled lamb chops with ratatouille, and osso buco Provençal. Extras include an expansive terrace redolent of lavender and thyme.

Vallon de l'Arcoule, route d'Arles, 13520 Les Baux. ✆ **04-90-54-32-54.** Fax 04-90-54-42-58. 24 units. 135€–155€ double; 185€ suite. AE, MC, V. Closed late Jan to Mar 20. Take RD78 for 1.5km (1 mile) southwest of Les Baux, and follow signs to Arles. **Amenities:** Restaurant; bar; outdoor pool; tennis court; babysitting. *In room:* TV, hair dryer.

Mas de L'Oulivié ★★ This picturesque salmon-colored complex of traditional Provençal buildings, capped with terra-cotta roofs, is about a mile from town. Lounges have beamed ceilings, terra-cotta floor tiles, and comfortable provincial furnishings. The high-ceilinged bedrooms have casement doors that open onto the garden. The units vary in size and shape—some are quite spacious—with a corresponding wide difference in price. Bathrooms are tiled and roomy. Breakfast and lunch are the only meals served.

13520 Les Baux de Provence. ✆ **04-90-54-35-78.** Fax 04-90-54-44-31. www.masdeloulivie.com. 27 units. 115€–230 double; 400€ suite. AE, DC, MC, V. Closed Nov–Mar. **Amenities:** Restaurant; bar; pool; babysitting; laundry service; dry cleaning. *In room:* A/C, TV, minibar, hair dryer, safe.

INEXPENSIVE

Hostellerie de la Reine-Jeanne *Value* Set in the heart of the village of Les Baux, this warm, well-scrubbed inn is the best bargain in Les Baux. You enter through a typical provincial French bistro. All the bedrooms are spartan but comfortable, and three have terraces; bathrooms are cramped. The chef prepares fixed-price menus.

Grand-Rue, 13520 Les Baux. ✆ **04-90-54-32-06.** Fax 04-90-54-32-33. 10 units. 47€–62€ double. MC, V. Free parking. Closed Nov 15–Feb 15 (open during the Christmas holidays). **Amenities:** Restaurant.

Hôtel Bautezar The entrance of this inn takes you down a few steps into the large medieval vaulted dining room, where you'll find Provençal furnishings and cloth tapestries hanging from the white stone walls, and a terrace with a view of the Val d'Enfer. The well-maintained guest rooms are decorated in Louis XVI style. Bathrooms are small but tidy.

Rue Frédéric-Mistral, 13520 Les Baux. ✆ **04-90-54-32-09.** Fax 04-90-54-51-49. 11 units. 61€–77€ double. MC, V. Closed Jan–Mar 15. **Amenities:** Restaurant; bar; lounge.

WHERE TO DINE

Two cafes near place St-Vincent offer refreshments and panoramic views: the **Hostellerie de la Reine Jeanne,** rue Frédéric-Mistral (© **04-90-54-32-06**), and the **Café/Restaurant Bautezar,** rue Frédéric-Mistral (© **04-90-54-32-09**). Note also that **L'Oustau de Beaumanière** (see above) boasts an excellent dining room.

La Riboto de Taven ★★★ Known for its flawless cuisine and market-fresh ingredients, this is one of the great restaurants of the area, a rival of Cabro d'Or. This 1835 farmhouse with a pool outside the medieval section of town has been owned by two generations of the Novi family. In summer, you can sit outdoors. Menu items might include sea bass in olive oil, fricassée of mussels flavored with basil, and lamb en croûte with olives—plus homemade desserts. The cuisine is a personal statement of Jean-Pierre Novi, whose cookery is filled with brawny flavors and the heady perfumes of Provençal herbs.

You can also stay in one of seven rooms large enough to be suites, for 235€, breakfast included. All but two of the units have air-conditioning; the two that don't have natural cooling because of the very thick stone walls of the original *mas Provençal.*

Le Val d'Enfer, 13520 Les Baux. © **04-90-54-34-23.** Fax 04-90-54-38-88. www.riboto-de-taven.fr. Reservations required. Fixed-price menu 48€. AE, DC, MC, V. Wed–Mon 7:30–9:30pm.

7 St-Rémy-de-Provence ★

705km (438 miles) S of Paris; 26km (16 miles) NE of Arles; 19km (12 miles) S of Avignon; 13km (8 miles) N of Les Baux

We're not alone in our enthusiasm for St-Rémy, for we've spotted Princess Caroline here several times. Nostradamus, the famous French physician/astrologer, was born here in 1503. In 1922, Gertrude Stein and Alice B. Toklas found St-Rémy after "wandering around everywhere a bit," as Ms. Stein wrote to Cocteau. But mainly St-Rémy is associated with Vincent van Gogh: He committed himself to an asylum here in 1889 after cutting off his left ear. His "cell" was later occupied by an interned German during World War I—Albert Schweitzer. Between moods of despair, van Gogh painted such works as *Olive Trees* and *Cypresses.*

Come to sleepy St-Rémy today not only for its memories and sights, but for an experience of Provençal small-town living that you won't find in Aix or Avignon. It's a market town of considerable charm and attracts the occasional celebrity who "hides out" here away from the hordes.

ESSENTIALS

GETTING THERE Local **buses** from Avignon (between four and nine per day) take 45 minutes and cost 5.35€ one-way. In St-Rémy, buses pull into the place de la République, in the town center. For bus information, call © **04-90-82-07-35.**

The nearest **train station** is Avignon Gare. For more information about schedules, call © **08-36-35-35-39.**

If you're **driving,** head south from Avignon along D571.

VISITOR INFORMATION The **Office de Tourisme** is on place Jean-Jaurès (© **04-90-92-05-22**).

SEEING THE SIGHTS

The cloisters of the asylum at the 12th-century **Monastère de St-Paul-de-Mausolée ★★**, avenue Edgar-le-Roy (© **04-90-92-77-00**), were made famous by van Gogh's paintings. Now a psychiatric hospital, the former monastery is east

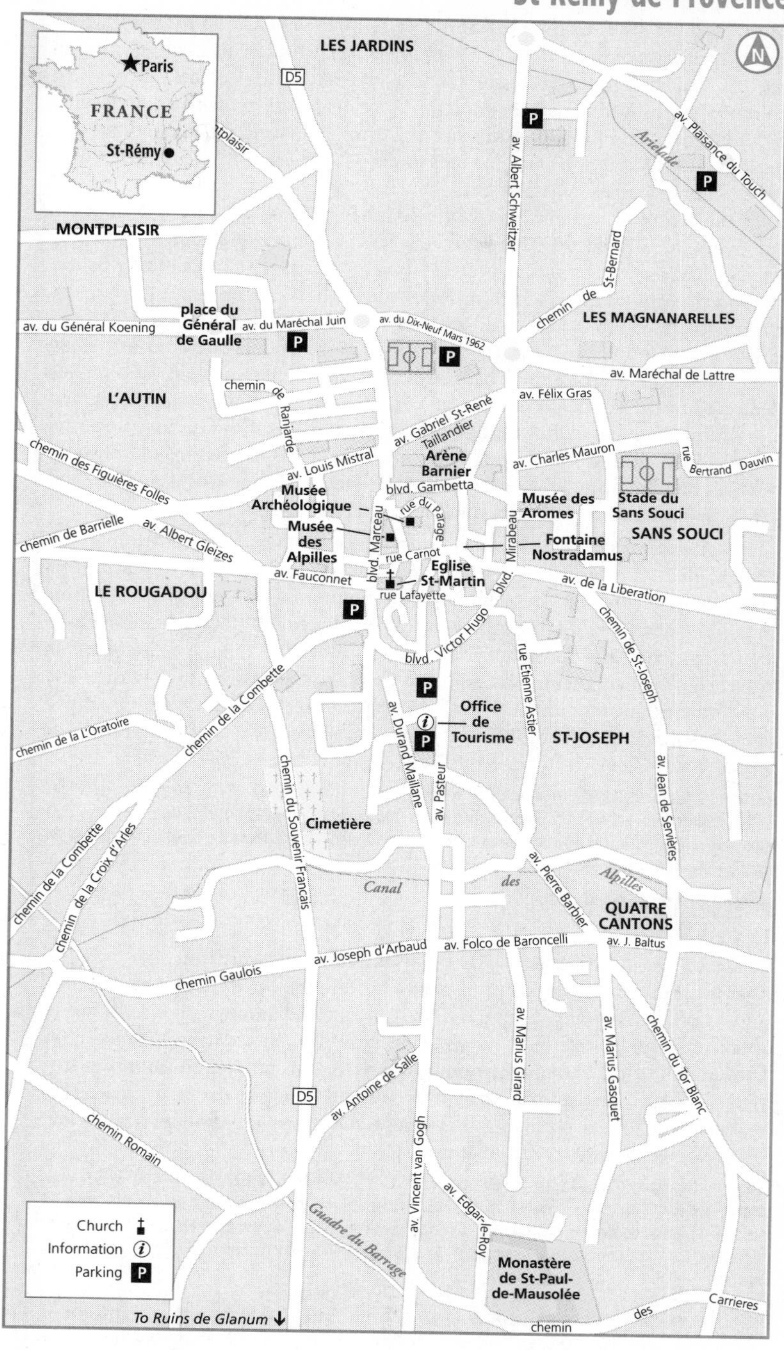

FRANCE
Paris
St-Rémy
LES JARDINS
D5
MONTPLAISIR
place du Général de Gaulle
av. du Général Koening
av. du Maréchal Juin
av. du Dix-Neuf Mars 1962
av. Albert Schweitzer
av. Plaisance du Touch
Arielade
chemin de St-Bernard
LES MAGNANARELLES
av. Maréchal de Lattre
av. Félix Gras
L'AUTIN
chemin de Ranjarde
av. Gabriel St-René Taillandier
Arène Barnier
av. Charles Mauron
rue Bertrand Dauvin
chemin des Figuières Folles
av. Louis Mistral
blvd. Gambetta
Musée Archéologique
rue du Parage
Musée des Aromes
Stade du Sans Souci
SANS SOUCI
chemin de Barrielle
av. Albert Gleizes
Musée des Alpilles
blvd. Marceau
rue Carnot
Fontaine Nostradamus
blvd. Mirabeau
Eglise St-Martin
av. Fauconnet
rue Lafayette
av. de la Liberation
LE ROUGADOU
blvd. Victor Hugo
chemin de St-Joseph
rue Étienne Astier
chemin de la Combette
chemin de la L'Oratoire
Office de Tourisme
av. Durand Maillane
ST-JOSEPH
av. Jean de Servières
chemin du Souvenir Francais
av. Pasteur
Cimetière
chemin de la Combette
chemin de la Croix d'Arles
Canal des Alpilles
av. Pierre Barbier
QUATRE CANTONS
av. Joseph d'Arbaud
av. Folco de Baroncelli
av. J. Baltus
chemin Gaulois
av. Marius Girard
av. Marius Gasquet
chemin du Tor Blanc
D5
av. Antoine de Salle
chemin Romain
av. Vincent van Gogh
av. Edgar-le-Roy
Guadre du Barrage
Monastère de St-Paul-de-Mausolée
chemin des Carrieres
Church
Information
Parking
To Ruins de Glanum

of D5, a short drive north of Glanum (see below). You can't visit the cell where this genius was confined from 1889 to 1890, but it's still worth coming here to see the Romanesque chapel and the cloisters with their circular arches and columns and beautifully carved capitals. The cloisters are open Tuesday through Saturday from 9am to 7pm. Admission is 2€ for adults and 1€ for students and persons ages 12 to 16. It's free for kids under 12. Adjacent to the church, you'll see a commemorative bust of van Gogh.

In the center of St-Rémy, the **Musée Archéologique,** in the Hôtel de Sade, rue du Parage (✆ **04-90-92-64-04**), displays sculptures and bronzes from the ancient Roman excavations at nearby Glanum. There is an outstanding collection on the ground floor, which includes votive altars, sarcophagi, obelisks, and fragments of columns and cornices from the temples of pagan gods. In the courtyard are found the ruins (fragmented) of baths from the 4th century, along with ruins from a 5th-century baptistery. Upstairs are fragments from a temple dedicated to the goddess Valetudo, an evocative statue of a captured Gaul, and a beautiful low relief with the effigy of Fortuna and Hermes. There is also a prehistoric collection of items from bones to flints. It's open year-round Tuesday through Sunday from 11am to 5pm (except Jan 1, May 1, Nov 1 and 11, and Dec 25). Entrance costs 2.50€ for adults; it's free for ages 17 and under.

Site Archéologique de Glanum (Ruins de Glanum) A Gallo-Roman settlement thrived here during the final days of the Roman Empire. Its historic monuments include an Arc Municipal, a triumphal arch dating from the time of Julius Caesar, and a cenotaph called the Mausolée des Jules. Garlanded with sculptured fruits and flowers, the arch dates from 20 B.C. and is the oldest in Provence. The mausoleum was raised to honor the grandsons of Augustus and is the only extant monument of its type. Entire streets and foundations of private residences from the 1st-century town can be seen. Some of the remains are from a Gallo-Greek town from the 2nd century B.C.

Av. Vincent-van-Gogh (1km/½-mile south of St-Rémy on D5). ✆ **04-90-92-23-79.** Admission 5€ adults, 3.50€ students and ages 12–25, free for children 17 and under. Apr–Sept daily 9am–7pm, Oct–Mar daily 9am–noon and 2–5pm. Closed Jan 1, May 1, Nov 1 and 11, and Dec 25. From the town center, follow the signs to Les Antiques/Les Baux.

WHERE TO STAY

EXPENSIVE

Domaine de Valmouriane ★★ This is a country-house hotel that occupies what was built at least a century ago as a farmhouse. Set on rocky, sun-flooded land, it offers charming, antiques-dotted accommodations, each with flowered upholsteries and a reference to whatever Provençal writer it was named after. Throughout, there's a sense of nostalgia for bygone eras and enormous charm. Madame Capel, the German-born owner, attends to dozens of small details. The establishment's focal point is a flowering terrace near the dining room, where Pierre Walter prepares spectacular meals.

Petite rte. Des Baux (D27), 13210 St-Rémy-de-Provence. ✆ **04-90-92-44-62.** Fax 04-90-92-37-32. www.valmouriane.com. 160€–240€ double. AE, DC, MC, V. From St-Rémy, drive 5km (3 miles) from the center, following the signs to Beaucaire/Tarascon, and then, after reaching the D27, follow signs to Les Baux. **Amenities:** Restaurant; bar-cum-tearoom; pool; tennis court; Jacuzzi; babysitting; laundry service. *In room:* TV, minibar, hair dryer, safe.

Hôtel Château des Alpilles ★★ When she converted this mansion in 1980, Françoise Bon wanted to create a "house for paying friends." When it was built in 1827 by the Pichot family, it housed Chateaubriand and a host of other luminaries. To reach it, you pass beneath the 300-year-old trees that surround the neoclassic exterior. Inside the château, the spacious rooms have combined the best of an antique framework with plush upholstery, rich carpeting, and vibrant colors. Modern units, lacking the warmth of the main house, are found in a renovated annex, Le Ferme, which was originally built in 1840 as a greenhouse. Madame Bon has installed an elevator, but you might prefer to descend the massive stone staircase. In 2001, all the travertine-trimmed bathrooms were rebuilt, with up-to-date plumbing added. A separate apartment is available in a converted chapel on the grounds.

Ancienne route du Grès, 13210 St-Rémy-de-Provence. ✆ **04-90-92-03-33.** Fax 04-90-92-45-17. chateau.alpilles@wanadoo.fr. 15 units. 160€–220€ double; 242€–350€ suite. Breakfast 17€. AE, DC, MC, V. Closed Nov 15–Feb 15. **Amenities:** Restaurant; outdoor pool; 2 tennis courts; sauna; limited room service; laundry service. *In room:* TV, minibar, hair dryer, safe.

Vallon de Valrugues ★★★ Surrounded by a park, this Mediterranean hotel is the fanciest in the area, although its major rival, the Château des Alpilles, appears more friendly and inviting. Nonetheless, Vallon is one of the most tranquil hotels in Provence, with graceful terraces overlooking the olive groves or the Alpilles. Bedrooms are immaculately kept and handsomely furnished, like magazine advertisements for graceful Provençal living. For those who can afford it, a suite is offered that's like a little country house sitting on the roof, with panoramic views in all directions and its own little swimming pool.

The dining terrace is so pleasant it almost competes with the cuisine, which is winning praise for innovative light dishes such as John Dory with truffles and frozen nougat with a confit of fruits. The cellar has the best selection of regional wines of all the hotels in St. Rémy.

Chemin Canto-Cigalo, 13210 St-Rémy-de-Provence. ✆ **04-90-92-04-40.** Fax 04-90-92-44-01. 53 units. 175€–270€ double; 410€–880€ suite. AE, MC, V. Free parking. Closed Jan 27–Feb 23. **Amenities:** Restaurant; bar; pool; putting green; 2 tennis courts; gym; sauna; horseback riding; limited room service; laundry service. *In room:* Minibar, hair dryer, safe.

MODERATE

Château de Roussan ★ *Finds* Although there are more lavish château hotels in the district, this one is more evocative of another time and place. This château's most famous resident, the Renaissance seer Nostradamus, lived in a rustic outbuilding a few steps from the front door. An archway of 300-year-old trees leads to the 1701 neoclassical facade of softly colored local stone. Most bedrooms are spacious, with mattresses that are well worn but still comfortable enough. Bathrooms have old-fashioned plumbing that still works. As you wander around the grounds, you'll be back in history, especially when you come upon the baroque sculptures lining the basin, fed by a stream. The restaurant is open daily for lunch and dinner. Be warned that the staff here can be off-putting, but the sense of mysticism and the historical importance of the place usually compensates for Gallic crabbiness.

Route de Tarascon, 13210 St-Rémy-de-Provence. ✆ **04-90-92-11-63.** Fax 04-90-92-50-59. 21 units. 70€–120€ double. Half board 30€. AE, MC, V. **Amenities:** Restaurant; bar; laundry service. *In room:* Hair dryer.

Les Antiques This moderately priced, stylish 19th-century villa is in a large park with a pool. It contains an elegant reception lounge, which opens onto several salons, all furnished in Napoléon III. Some accommodations are in a private modern pavilion, with direct access to the garden. The rooms are handsomely furnished, usually in pastels with flowered wallpapers. Those in the modern pavilion are more comfortable and larger, but have less character. Bathrooms are small but well maintained, with fair shelf space and luxury toiletries. In summer you're served breakfast (the only meal) in what used to be the Orangerie.

15 av. Pasteur, 13210 St-Rémy-de-Provence. ✆ **04-90-92-03-02.** Fax 04-90-92-50-40. 27 units. 60€–133€ double. AE, DC, MC, V. Closed Oct 29–Apr 13. **Amenities:** Pool. *In room:* TV.

Mas de Cornud ★ *Finds* The setting is a severely dignified, carefully renovated Provençal farmhouse, built 250 years ago and converted between 1985 and 1993 into a well-managed inn you'll see today. American-born David Carpita (formerly a banker) and his Egyptian-born wife, Nito, maintain a building that's loaded with regional memorabilia and antiques, along with artifacts from the rest of the world. Accommodations are cozy, high-ceilinged, and charming, with many yards of cheerful fabrics, a whimsical sense of nostalgia, and sometimes antique ceiling beams. The Carpitas maintain a high-caliber on-site cooking school, whose participants sometimes fill the hotel to capacity. This occurs during weeklong sojourns at four scattered moments throughout the year.

Rte. De Mas-Blanc, 13210 St-Rémy-de-Provence. ✆ **04-90-92-39-32.** Fax 04-90-55-99. www.mascornud.com. 6 units. 130€–160€ double; 220€–240€ suite. Rates include breakfast. No credit cards. Closed Nov–Mar. From St-Rémy, follow D99 to the D27 and then D31, following the signs to Mas de Cornud, driving 3km (2 miles) west of St-Rémy. **Amenities:** Restaurant; honor bar; outdoor pool; *pétanque* court; babysitting; laundry service. *In room:* No phone.

INEXPENSIVE

Hôtel de Soleil There's something wonderfully appealing about the masses of ivy that cascade down the facade of this hotel, which is only a 4-minute walk south of the town center. It's set in a pleasant garden with venerable trees and a wrought-iron gazebo. Inside the rich assortment of ceiling beams and Provençal accessories evokes the region around you. Bedrooms are simple but convenient, with tasteful settings and comfortable beds, plus small tiled bathrooms. Breakfast is the only meal served here.

35 av. Pasteur, 13210 St-Rémy-de-Provence. ✆ **04-90-92-00-63.** Fax 04-90-92-61-07. 24 units. 52€–66€ double. AE, DC, MC, V. Free parking. Closed Nov to mid-Mar. **Amenities:** Pool. *In room:* TV, hair dryer, safe.

Hôtel van Gogh Set 20m (67 ft.) east of the town's historic center, beside the highway leading to Cavaillon, this is a low-slung and pleasant hotel covered with ivy. Built in 1974 and renovated several times since then, it offers reception areas with a fireplace, parquet floors, and traditional furniture; clean bedrooms with a minimum of furniture; and small bathrooms. Breakfast, which takes place on a backyard veranda with a striped canopy, is the only meal served.

1 av. Jean Moulin, 13210 St-Rémy de Provence. ✆ **04-90-92-14-02.** Fax 04-90-92-09-05. www.alpilles.com. 21 units. 55€–65€ double. MC, V. Free parking. **Amenities:** Bar; lounge; pool; limited room service; babysitting. *In room:* TV, hair dryer, safe.

WHERE TO DINE

A great dining choice is the restaurant at **Vallon de Valrugues** (see above).

Charmeroy Maison de Gouts TEA/PASTRIES Charming, intimate, and restful, this is a well-managed and attractive tearoom where doses of rest and relaxation are dispensed along with savory cups of some genuinely unusual teas. Operated with flair and imagination by a bilingual local resident, Madame Fabienne Charmeroy, it's within a small-scale stone-fronted house in the heart of town, close to the fountain of Nostradamus. You'll find tea tables nestled amid displays that sell almost everything to do with the tea-drinking and tea-brewing ritual, including teapots, tea caddies, and tea cozies.

The pastries sold here are usually linked in some way to the herbs and fruits of the region, with an emphasis on using whatever Provençal products are fresh at the time. Especially tempting are the tarts layered with slices of pear, prune, apricots, and lemon slices. But if you think the pastries are unusual, wait till you check out the teas: Many are custom-blended by Madame Charmeroy to reflect some aspect of Provence. Examples include a version named after Nostradamus, based on a 16th-century recipe, using grapes and cinnamon, that might have been consumed by the psychic himself. Other versions combine raspberries, orange blossoms, herbs from the Alpilles, edible orchids, white grapes, vanilla, figs, and apples into blends with names like Chung Hao, Fancy Oolang Black Dragon, and Gunpowder Green.

51 rue Carnot. ✆ **04-32-60-01-23.** Pots of tea 3.70€ each; pastries 5.50€ each. Daily 10am–noon and 3:15–7pm. Closed mid-Nov to mid-Dec and mid-Jan to mid-Mar.

La Maison Jaune ★★ FRENCH/PROVENÇAL The pair of dining rooms in this 18th-century mansion are among the most popular in town. The cuisine is prepared and served with flair by François and Catherine Perraud. In good weather, you can dine on an outdoor terrace overlooking the Hôtel de Sade. Menu items include pigeon roasted in wine from Les Baux, grilled sardines served with candied lemon and raw fennel, artichoke hearts marinated in white wine and offered with tomatoes, and a succulent version of roasted rack of lamb served with a tapenade of black olives and pulverized anchovies.

15 rue Carnot. ✆ **04-90-92-56-14.** Reservations required. Prix-fixe menus for lunch and dinner 29€, 44€, and 52€. Apr–Dec noon–2:30pm and 7–9:30pm. Closed Jan–Mar.

L'Assiette de Marie FRENCH/PROVENÇAL Everything about this restaurant emulates the kind of cuisine and clutter that you'd have expected within the home of a French grandmother with roots in the Edwardian Age. It occupies a stone-fronted 200-year-old house in the center of St-Rémy, within a dining room whose walls are so densely covered with bric-à-brac (old mirrors, old paintings, old porcelain, and memorabilia from at least three of the last French governments) that, in the words of the staff, "There's not even room to hang another painting." Even the plates used at table are artfully mismatched and antique, the kind of thing you'd find within a slightly junky but endlessly fascinating antiques store.

Marie Ricco, the Corsican-Italian owner, and her polite staff offer only one dining choice: A 29€ three-course fixed-price menu whose components change with the season and the inspiration of the chef. Menu items might include *une assiette de Marie* (Marie's platter), loaded with the Provençal equivalent of antipasti (grilled and marinated peppers, tapenade of olives, and miniportions of brandade de morue) and warm cheese from local goats, resting on a bed of either mache or wild field greens. Pastas, served as main courses, are always made fresh and on-site, and might include ravioli stuffed with seasoned cod, cannelloni stuffed with ewe's cheese and fresh spinach, and an excellent version of lasagna made with magret de canard; a cassoulette of lamb; and roasted rack of rabbit. The dessert choices always include flan. If you opt to dine here, you won't be alone: Diners who preceded us have included Pamela Anderson, Princess Caroline of Monaco, and Rod Stewart.

1 rue Jaume Roux. ✆ **04-90-92-32-14.** Reservations recommended. Fixed-price menu 29€. MC, V. Wed–Mon noon–2pm and 7–10pm; June–Sept daily.

Le Jardin de Frédéric ★ TRADITIONAL FRENCH Charming, with a good-humored atmosphere, this restaurant occupies a green-painted villa that was built on the site of a garden where Frédéric Mistral, "national poet" of Provence, wrote part of his opus. Menu items are innovative and reflect culinary techniques from both local sources and the grand restaurants of faraway Paris. Savor the seductive, succulent soufflé of codfish, served with saffron and garlic sauce, or carpaccio of duckling with foie gras. Try the tender rack of Sisteron lamb with a creamy garlic sauce, or filet of sea bass with basil sauce. Dessert might be a chocolate mousse with vanilla sauce. In summer, the dining room expands, perhaps in a style that would have been appreciated by Mistral himself, outside into the open air.

8 bd. Gambetta. ✆ **04-90-92-27-76.** Reservations required. Main courses 16€–19.90€; fixed-price menus 22.50€–29€. MC, V. Thurs–Tues noon–2pm and 7:30–9:30pm. Closed Feb.

8 Gordes ★

713km (443 miles) SE of Paris; 35km (22 miles) E of Avignon; 16km (10 miles) NE of Cavaillon; 64km (40 miles) N of the Marseille airport

Gordes is a colorful village whose twisted narrow cobblestone streets circle a rocky bluff above the Imergue Valley. By the turn of the 20th century, as its residents migrated toward cities and factory jobs, it suffered from the kind of attrition that was affecting agrarian communities all over Europe.

The 12th-century village was saved by modern art. Cubist painter André Lhote discovered the hamlet in 1938, and renowned artists like Marc Chagall began visiting and summering here. The late Victor Vasarély, one of the founders of op art, became its most famous full-time resident.

ESSENTIALS

GETTING THERE There's no rail station in Gordes. **Trains** arrive at nearby Cavaillon, where taxis wait at the railway station; the trip into Gordes costs around 22.80€. For rail information and schedules in Cavaillon, call ✆ **08-36-35-35-35.** There are no local buses. By **car** from Avignon, take Route 100 east to the intersection to D2, at which point you head north following the signs into Gordes. The village itself is closed to cars, but large parking lots are along its edge.

VISITOR INFORMATION The **Office de Tourisme** is in the Salle des Gardes du Château, place du Château (✆ **04-90-72-02-75**).

SEEING THE SIGHTS

Dominating the skyline, the **Château de Gordes** is a fortified 12th-century structure whose dramatic silhouette contributed to the town's nickname as "the Acropolis of Provence." The château was really a fortress with crenellated bastions and round towers in each of its four corners. This is home to a museum, **Musée du Château de Gordes** (✆ **04-90-72-02-89**), site of a collection of works by Flemish-born painter Pol Mora. This collection might or might not be replaced with the *oeuvres* of other painters during the lifetime of this edition of our guide, including some by surrealist and geometric master Vasarély. It's open Wednesday through Monday from 10am to noon and 2 to 6pm. Adults pay 4€ admission; students and persons ages 11 to 18 pay 3.50€. Entrance is free for children under 10.

Some 4km (2½ miles) south of the village, surrounded by a rocky, arid landscape that supports only stunted olive trees and gnarled oaks (the Provençaux refer to this type of terrain as *la garrigue*), stands the **Moulin des Bouillons,** route de St-Pantaléon (✆ **04-90-72-22-11**), an olive-oil mill so ancient it was mentioned in the 1st-century writings of Pliny the Elder. It's now owned by the stained-glass artist Frédérique Duran, and its interior boasts the original Roman floors and the base of the olive press. The complex is open Wednesday through Monday from 10am to noon and 2 to 6pm. A ticket granting admission to the mill costs 4.50€.

Cousin to the *trullis* of Italy are the reconstructed bories in the **Village des Bories,** Les Savournines (✆ **04-90-72-03-48**), 3km (2 miles) southwest of town. These mysterious stone beehive structures are composed of thin layers of stone that spiral upward into a dome. The substantial buildings were constructed without mortar and are surrounded by stone boundary walls of similar construction. Their origin and use is a mystery—some sources claim they're Neolithic. What is known is that they were inhabited until the early 1800s. Their form suggests they were developed by shepherds and goat herders as shelter for themselves and their flocks. To get here, take D15, veering right beyond a fork at D2. A sign marks another right turn toward the village, where you must park and walk for about 45 minutes to visit the site. The village is open daily from 9am to dusk. Admission is 5.50€ for adults and 3€ for children.

Founded in 1148, the **Abbaye Notre-Dame de Sénanque** ★, a Cistercian monastery 4km (2½ miles) north of Gordes on D15/D177 (✆ **04-90-72-05-72;** www.senanque.fr), sits in isolation surrounded by lavender fields. It was abandoned during the revolution, reopened in the 19th century, closed again in 1969, and reopened yet again (by the Cistercians) in 1988. The influential 20th-century writer and Catholic theologian Thomas Merton can be counted among those who found peace here. One of Provence's most beautiful medieval monuments, it's open Monday through Saturday from 10am to noon and 2 to 6pm, and Sunday from 2 to 6pm. Admission costs 5€ for adults and 2€ for persons ages 12 to 18. It's free for persons under 12. Be aware that this is a working monastery, not merely a tourist site. You can attend any of five Masses per day, buy religious souvenirs and texts in the gift shop, and generally marvel at a medieval setting brought back to life.

WHERE TO STAY

Hôtel La Bastide de Gordes ★★ This manor house dates from the 17th century. After World War II, it was enlarged to become the headquarters for the town's gendarmerie, and in 1988, it was transformed into a tasteful hotel, in a building staggered uphill near the town's summit. Some rooms have views over the valley of the Luberon. Bedrooms are luxurious and tasteful, with contemporary, antique, and reproduction furnishings and soft colors. Known for its inventive and creative cuisine, the on-site restaurant, Michel Del Burgo, is named for its chef and is a worthy choice even if you're not a guest of the hotel. Against a backdrop of old-fashioned Provençal elegance, market-fresh ingredients concocted into sublime dishes are served to an appreciative clientele with discerning palates.

Le Village, 84220 Gordes. ✆ **04-90-72-12-12.** Fax 04-90-72-05-20. www.bastide-de-gordes.com. 29 units. 167€–323€ double; 350€–498€ suite. AE, MC, V. Free parking. Closed Nov 4–Mar 14. **Amenities:** Restaurant; bar; pool; health club; sauna; limited room service; babysitting; laundry service; dry cleaning. *In room:* A/C, TV, minibar, hair dryer, safe.

Hôtel La Gacholle *Value* Built in the 1960s in the form of an earth-toned Provençal *mas,* this inn combines stone walls, wooden beams, a tiled roof, brick floors, and flagstone terraces into an intimate setting. It stands in a grove of holm oak, offering a great view over the Luberon valley from its pool and dining terrace.

The guest rooms are cozy, comfortable, and designed for a maximum of peace and quiet. In 1998, the entire place was renovated, repainted, and redecorated by hard-working new owners. Improvements have been made to the quality of both the bedroom mattresses and the neatly kept bathrooms.

The restaurant, containing a blazing fireplace, is flanked with rough-hewn stone and accented with elegant linen, crystal, and china. You'll enjoy dishes that include pan-fried foie gras with figs and honey, crisp-fried local fish served with a "caviar" of eggplant and fresh Provençal herbs, and a ragout of Provençal lamb. In season, the fresh asparagus, prepared either hot or cold in a variety of ways, is heavenly.

Route de Murs, 84220 Gordes. ✆ **04-90-72-01-36.** Fax 04-90-72-01-81. www.lagacholle.com. 11 units. 107€–125€ double. MC, V. Closed Jan 10–Feb 28. From town, drive 1.2km (3/4 mile) northeast, following the only road with signs for Murs. **Amenities:** Restaurant; bar; pool; tennis court; babysitting. *In room:* TV, minibar, hair dryer, safe.

Hotel le Gordos Set within a prosperous-looking residential neighborhood, about a kilometer southwest of the town center, this hotel was established in the early 1990s within the stone-sided shell of what was originally built several hundred years ago as a Provençal *mas.* Surrounded by shrubbery and capped with the kind of terra-cotta tiles you might have noticed throughout the region, it's a less expensive version of its plusher sibling, Hôtel Le Bastide de Gordes. Inside you'll find a smooth and seamlessly comfortable decor that's light, airy, and traditional. Bedrooms are simple but appealing, with lights of sunlight, pale colors, and tiled bathrooms. The establishment's social center is a swimming pool that's set into the garden. There's no restaurant on-site, but many appropriate dining choices lie within a short walk or drive.

Route de Cavaillon, 84220 Gordes. ✆ **04-90-72-00-75.** Fax 04-90-72-07-00. www.hotel-le-gordos.com. 19 units. 104€–175€ double. AE, MC, V. Free parking. From the center of Gordes, follow the signs to Cavaillon and travel a kilometer (half-mile) southwest. **Amenities:** Pool; tennis court; babysitting. *In room:* TV.

Hôtel Les Bories ★★★ This is Gordes's best accommodation, a modern hotel clad in rough stone and built around the core of an old Provençal *mas.* It takes advantage of its hillside setting, offering vistas from the dining terrace, outdoor pool and terrace, glass-fronted lobby, and indoor pool. The garden ties into the valley with olive, holm oak, and lavender. The decor was inspired by high-tech Milanese design, with streamlined furniture, tile floors, and Oriental rugs in both public spaces and the spacious guest rooms. The cozy dining room is in a nook rising into a craggy stone vault, and the matching fireplace is topped by a mantle of massive rugged beams.

Route de l'Abbaye de Sénanque, 84220 Gordes. ✆ **04-90-72-00-51.** Fax 04-90-72-01-22. 30 units. 314€–340€ double; 390€–964€ suite. AE, DC, MC, V. Closed mid-Jan to mid-Feb. From town, drive 2.4km (1 1/2 miles) north, following the signs to Abbaye de Sénanque or Venasque. **Amenities:** Restaurant; bar; 2 pools; health club; sauna; limited room service; babysitting; laundry service; dry cleaning. *In room:* A/C, TV, minibar, hair dryer, safe.

WHERE TO DINE

The area's best cuisine is served at the **Hôtel Les Bories.** Also excellent is the restaurant at the **Hôtel La Gacholle** (see above).

Comptoir des Arts ★ PROVENÇAL An especially appealing restaurant in Gordes occupies what was originally built in the 1850s as the town's *épicerie* (food market). Today Justine Cairel manages a kitchen staff and a limited number (only 26) of seats within a restaurant noted for its coziness and Provençal charm. Additional seating is offered on either of two outdoor terraces, set against the front and back of the restaurant, respectively. Expect furniture that's crafted from old wine cases, and a changing array of paintings by local artists, many of which are for sale. Menu items focus on regional ingredients and time-tested recipes that many local residents might remember from their childhoods. Your meal might begin with a platter of stuffed baby vegetables or a chilled slab of fresh-made foie gras. Roasted rack of lamb with Provençal herbs is an excellent choice, or perhaps a garlicky version of aïoli of codfish. Desserts here are best showcased as part of an *assiette gourmande,* wherein a selection of the pastry chef's most appealing creations are artfully arranged on the same dessert platter.

Place du Château. ✆ **04-90-72-01-31.** Reservations recommended. Main courses 15€–23€; fixed-price menu 32.50€. No credit cards. Sun–Thurs noon–2:30pm, Sat–Thurs 7–9:30pm; July–Aug daily. Closed Nov to mid-Dec and mid-Jan to Easter.

Le Mas Tourteron PROVENÇAL On the outskirts of the village of Les Imberts, this restaurant occupies an 18th-century Provençal *mas* whose cherry trees and vines still produce good fruit. There's just one dining room, a sun-flooded space, with additional seating that spills over into the verdant garden. Menu items are based on fresh ingredients and include cassolette of asparagus and herbs with a medley of other (strictly seasonal) ingredients, charlotte of lamb with Provençal herbs, and a *tarte à l'envers* (upside-down tart) of roast rabbit with black-olive tapenade. Things here are small-scale and just a wee bit fussy, but overall, the food is very good and the staff is friendly.

Chemin de St-Blaise, Les Imberts. ✆ **04-90-72-00-16.** Fixed-price lunch Wed–Fri 25€; other times, set menus 32.50€–46.20€. AE, MC, V. Wed–Sun noon–2pm; Tues–Sat 7:30–9:30pm. Closed mid-Nov to mid-Feb. Take D2 for 6km (4 miles) southwest of Gordes.

9 Roussillon & Bonnieux ★

These villages lie so close to each other that you can visit both in a long morning or afternoon.

ROUSSILLON

45km (28 miles) E of Avignon; 10km (6 miles) E of Gordes

Color—17 shades of ocher, to be more precise—has proven to be this village's lifeblood. From as far back as Roman times, the area's rich deposits of ocher have been valued. Beginning in the late 1700s, Roussillon's ocher powders were shipped around the world from nearby Marseille. Though the mining industry has dried up, hordes of artists and visitors still flock here to marvel and be inspired by the gorgeous ranges of the vibrant warm tones. Roussillon also served as a giant laboratory of sorts for the famous American sociologist Laurence William Wylie, who packed up his family and moved here for a year to study the village's complex life of work and play, love and family feuds, and simple day-to-day existence. He published his study as *A Village in the Vaucluse* in 1957.

ESSENTIALS

GETTING THERE From Avignon, drive east on N7 to D973 and then to D22. Finally, turn north on D149 and follow the signs to Roussillon. The trip takes about 45 minutes. There's no train or bus service.

VISITOR INFORMATION The **Office de Tourisme** is on place de la Poste (✆ **04-90-05-60-25**).

SEEING THE SIGHTS

Take time to explore the narrow, steep streets, soaking in the rusts, reds, and ochers of the stone used in the construction of the houses. From the **Castrum,** at the high point along rue de l'Eglise, you'll see a magnificent vista. Face north and gaze across the Vaucluse plateau and to Mont Ventoux. Turn south to see the Coulon valley and the Grand Luberon.

You can reach the **old ocher quarries,** with their sunburned exposed rocks, by taking a 40-minute scenic walk east of the village. Paths to the quarries start at the tourist office (see "Essentials," above). Another panorama is the huge red cliffs of **Chaussée des Géants.** To view them, take the path southeast of the tourist office. The walk is about 45 minutes and includes a great look back at Roussillon.

About 5km (3 miles) south of town on D149 is the **pont Julien.** Built more than 2,000 years ago, this three-arched Roman engineering feat of precisely hewn stone spans the Calavon River without the use of any mortar. It's thought to have been named in honor of the nearby Roman town of Apta Julia, known today as Apt.

WHERE TO STAY

Le Clos du Buis ★ *Finds* Set on the northern outskirts of the small town of Bonnieux, within a garden that's centered on a copse of small trees *(les buis)* with pale green leaves, this is a small-scale and intensely personalized bed and breakfast hotel that's housed within a late-18th-century stone-fronted Mediterranean-style villa. There are very few amenities within this hotel, other than a small swimming pool in the garden that functions as the single most gregarious spot on-site. Bedrooms are simple but comfortable, often with rough-hewn ceiling beams, sweeping views over the Luberon countryside, white walls, and splashes of jewel-toned color. Life here is simple, old-fashioned, and charming. Whereas there's no on-site restaurant, guests who request it in advance can arrange an evening fixed-price meal (22€ per person), whose makeup and presentation varies with the availability of raw ingredients, the season, and the number of other diners eating in that night.

Rue Victor Hugo, 84480 Bonnieux. ✆ **04-90-75-88-48.** Fax 04-90-75-88-57. www.leclosdubuis.com. 7 units. 75€–92€ double. Rates include breakfast. MC, V. Free parking. Closed mid-Nov to mid-Feb. **Amenities**: Outdoor pool; laundry service. *In room:* No phone.

Le Mas de Garrigon This sprawling country estate house is now an inviting inn with an authentic Provençal feel. The well-scrubbed rooms are spacious, with dark exposed beams, warm-colored walls, and beautiful contrasting fabrics. All have private south-facing terraces that look out onto the Luberon; the bathrooms are small but neatly organized. There's a well-stocked library with comfortable armchairs, a sitting room with a large terra-cotta mantel and fireplace, and an intimate dining room with rustic antique furniture, where excellent meals are served. Staff here is not particularly well informed, but it's well-meaning nonetheless.

Route de St-Saturnin d'Apt, 84220 Roussillon. ✆ **04-90-05-63-22.** Fax 04-90-05-70-01. www.masdegarrigon-provence.com. 9 units. 260€–280€ double; 360€ suite. AE, DC, MC, V. **Amenities:** Restaurant; bar; pool; limited room service; laundry service; dry cleaning. *In room:* A/C, TV, minibar, hair dryer.

Le Mas de la Tour The history of this *mas* on the outskirts of town dates back some 800 years. In 1985, it was completely renovated, with all modern amenities added, including a large enticing pool. The rooms run the gamut from matchbox-size to palatial. The smaller ones have exterior entrances and are somewhat reminiscent of those found in simple motels; the larger ones have bathtubs and terraces. Each has a firm, comfortable mattress.

84400 Gargas. ✆ **04-90-74-12-10.** Fax 04-90-04-83-67. 31 units. 101€–144€ double. MC, V. Closed Oct–Mar. From Gargas, drive 3km (2 miles) south, following the signs to Apt. **Amenities:** Restaurant; bar; pool. *In room:* TV, minibar, hair dryer.

WHERE TO DINE

David PROVENÇAL The town's most popular restaurant, it creates a pleasurable experience with its airy dining area and panoramic views of the red cliffs and hills of the Vaucluse. In the warmer months, dining is *en plein air* on the flowered terrace. The talented chef/owner Jean David is a traditional restaurateur who takes pride in his art, which he's been practicing since the 1950s. He works alongside his wife, son, and daughter in this family-run place. Menu items include a rice casserole of scallops and spinach, grilled country lamb flank rubbed with rosemary and served with an assortment of seasonal vegetables, and a tender beef filet with dark morel sauce. The light homemade fruit sorbets are a perfect end to a satisfying meal.

Place de la Poste. ✆ **04-90-05-60-13.** Reservations recommended. Main courses 14€–22€; fixed-price menus 24.30€–44.50€. AE, MC, V. Tues–Sun noon–2pm and 7:30–9pm. Closed mid-Nov to mid-Mar.

Le Bistro de Roussillon PROVENÇAL Here's a place where the vibrancy of a fast-paced Paris bistro collides with relaxed Provençal *savoir-vivre.* The result is a superlative ambience of hearty meals, intriguing chatter, and festive, friendly service. The bistro has one intimate dining room and two terraces—one with a vista of valley and hills and the other facing the square. Menu items vary from light salads to regional fare like *daube* (a traditional beef-and-vegetable stew often served over pasta), roast rack of pork with honey and spices, and grilled filet of hogfish.

Place de la Mairie. ✆ **04-90-05-74-45.** Reservations recommended. Main courses 13.40€–15€; fixed-price menu 25€. MC, V. Daily noon–2:30pm and 7–9pm. Closed Jan and mid-Nov to mid-Dec.

BONNIEUX

11km (7 miles) S of Roussillon; 45km (28 miles) N of Aix-en-Provence

This romantic hill town, nestled in the heart of the Petit Luberon, commands views of nearby Roussillon, the whole Coulon Valley, and the infamous Château de Lacoste, whose ruins bear testament to the life of its disturbed owner, Donatien Alphonse François, comte de Sade (also known as the marquis de Sade), who lived there in the 1770s. The celebrated marquis, who gave us the term *sadism,* died in a lunatic asylum. Because of the danger of falling stones, the ruins of the château cannot be visited—even by the most devoted aficionados of de Sade—but merely admired from afar.

Strategically located between Spain and Italy, Bonnieux has had a bloody history of raids and battles since its beginnings in Roman times, when it stood closer to the valley floor. To better defend itself, the town was moved farther up the hill during the 1200s, when it also received sturdy ramparts and sentry towers. In the 16th century, Bonnieux grew into a Catholic stronghold and often found itself surrounded by Protestants who were suspicious and jealous of its thriving economy. Since its streets were lined with mansion after mansion belonging to prominent bishops, allegations swirled around that the town received particular "favors" to bolster its standing. Envy and zeal got the best of the Protestants, and they eventually laid siege to the town, killing approximately 3,000 of the 4,000 inhabitants. Even though Bonnieux is the largest hill town in the area, its population never truly recovered and continues to hover around 1,500.

ESSENTIALS

GETTING THERE From Roussillon, **drive** south along D149 directly to Bonnieux. The trip takes about 15 minutes. There's no train or bus service.

The Libertine Trail of the Marquis de Sade

Denounced by some and a cult figure to others even today, Donatien Alphonse François, comte de Sade (1740–1814), is, of course, better known as the "marquis de Sade." The word *sadism* was coined from his name, and this "freest spirit who ever was" led a life devoted to an unleashed libido. By 1764, a police alert advised brothel madams to "refrain from providing the marquis with girls to go to any private chambers with him." Because of his prolonged sexual orgies that combined various kinds of torture (willing or unwilling), and especially because he recorded his controversial ideas for public consumption, he was often in and out of prison.

The marquis and his wife, the very plain but very wealthy Renée-Pélagie de Montreuil, hated Paris and court life and sought a secluded place in the country for their family of three. His wife, who was at first totally devoted to him, apparently overlooked his "deviant behavior," and so he was supposedly a "happily married man."

The marquis grew up in the area around Lacoste. Banished from home because of his violent rages, he spent 6 years of his childhood with his uncle, the noted cleric/scholar Abbé de Sade (who also happened to be a libertine) at the Abbé's castle at Saumane-de-Vaucluse, halfway between Lacoste and Mazan.

This crenellated fortress was a gift from the popes at Avignon, and it still stands in the hilltop village of Saumane-de-Vaucluse, to the west of Lacoste. The castle has been restored, and you can visit it. It is believed that the fictional Château de Silling, depicted in *The 120 Days of Sodom,* was based on this castle, where "all that the cruelest art and most refined barbarity could invent in the way of atrocity" was concealed for orgies and torture.

When the marquis returned to Paris, he attended the prestigious Lycée Louis Le Grand, where flagellation was the school's accepted form of punishment. He related to this on an erotic level, and the experience was the catalyst for his lifelong obsession with the exploration of the pain of pleasure and the pleasure of pain.

De Sade country really begins some 40km (25 miles) east of Avignon and not far from Ménerbes. The little village of Lacoste, surmounted by the marquis's ancestral castle, exists in a kind of time pocket, with a population that is about the same as it was back in the days of history's most articulate libertine. The château itself (not open to the public) isn't in good shape—just a moat, a few walls, some ramparts, and a scattering

VISITOR INFORMATION The **Office de Tourisme** is at 7 place Carnot (© **04-90-75-91-90**).

SEEING THE SIGHTS

You'll most likely want to work with gravity and not against it when exploring this steep village. Start at the summit with the **Vieille Eglise (Old Church)** and its cemetery. The grounds of stately cedars surrounding this Romanesque of rooms. More interesting is the panoramic view—on a clear day, you can even see Bonnieux. As you stand here, it's easy to imagine the marquis's world of tortured damsels and debauched noblemen coming alive again in such a remote spot in a foreboding landscape.

Though he spent 1771 worrying about "garden, farmyard, cheeses, and firewood," in 1772 the marquis found himself deep in trouble. His manservant, Latour, had arranged for four girls to meet with the marquis. De Sade had prepared some sweets whose sugar had been soaked in extract of Spanish fly (an actual aphrodisiac); later, some of the girls complained to the police that they'd been poisoned and accused Latour and de Sade of homosexual sodomy. The marquis fled but in *absentia* was found guilty of poisoning and sodomy. The punishment under law was decapitation—de Sade and Latour were later executed in effigy at Aix-en-Provence.

In 1778, de Sade's days of indulgence came to an end. His mother-in-law, outraged at his behavior, had him legally imprisoned for life. He wrote his novels, including *Justine* and the *120 Days of Sodom,* in prison. Freed in 1790 following the onset of the Revolution, he found that his wife had finally abandoned him forever. Napoléon ordered that the marquis be placed in a mental institution, where he died in 1814 at age 74, leaving scores of unpublished manuscripts that were not to see print for more than a century.

In time, this "abominable assemblage of all crimes and obscenities" won an adoring public. Sadists looked to him as the father of their cult. Foreigners attracted to the marquis's reputation have turned Lacoste into a lively place. An American art school was founded here in the 1970s, and—surprise, surprise—many locals are proud of their hometown boy. A small theater has been built in a stone quarry just below the château, and so the marquis's long-cherished wish to make Lacoste into a mecca for thespians has come true. **Théâtre de Lacoste** now draws some 1,600 patrons at a time, equaled in size in the region only by Avignon's outdoor theater. Believe it or not, one recent production dramatized a fictional love affair between the marquis and St. Theresa of Avila. Don't expect comfort or even high-tech acoustics when you come to a production at this theater: Seats are lined up on stone ledges, and the audience is subject to the vagaries of wind and weather. For information about tickets and performances, contact the Mairie (Town Hall) of Lacoste at ✆ **04-90-75-82-04.**

church, which dates from the 1100s, provide the best vantage point from which you can view the valley's hill towns. Hours of this church are erratic, corresponding to the whims of the priest who performs Mass here at irregular intervals. Farther down the incline is the **Musée de la Boulangerie,** 12 rue de la République (✆ **04-90-75-88-34**), dedicated to the authentic portrayal of the art of French breadmaking. Exhibits show all stages of the process, from planting and harvesting the grain to the final mixers and ovens that turn the flour, water, salt, and yeast mixture into warm, crusty loaves. The museum is open April through September Wednesday through Monday from 10am to noon and 3 to 6:30pm, in October Saturday and Sunday from 10am to 12:30pm and 2:30 to 6pm. It's closed throughout the rest of the year. Admission is 3.50€ for adults and 1.50€ for children 12 and under.

At the lower extreme of town, clearly signposted from the center, is the **Eglise Neuve (New Church),** from the late 1800s. Many people find the architecture of this church to be less than inspiring. You visit it, however, to admire the four beautiful panels from the Old Church. They date from the 1500s and are painted in the brightly colored German style to show the intensity of the Passion of Christ. It's open daily from 9am to 6pm.

WHERE TO STAY

Auberge de l'Aiguebrun ★ *Finds* To relax in one of the most tranquil settings in Provence and soak up that special surreal sunlight, come here. Artists and lovers seek out this remarkable 19th-century manor house enclosed by the Luberon hills and a mountain river. The intimate guest rooms look out over the river or the hills. They are individually decorated in the Provençal style with tawny colors and have bathrooms with up-to-date accessories. In the public rooms, attention is lovingly paid to every detail, from the crackling fire on cooler evenings to the soft and classical music wafting from room to room. The hotel also has a superb restaurant with its own garden; it's open Wednesday through Monday (closed Wed at lunchtime).

Off D943, 84480 Bonnieux. ✆ **04-90-04-47-00.** Fax 04-90-04-47-01. 134€–164€ double; 234€ suite. MC, V. Free parking. Closed Dec–Feb. From town, drive 6km (4 miles) southeast, following the signs to Lourmarin. **Amenities:** Restaurant; bar; pool; babysitting. *In room:* TV, hair dryer.

Hostellerie du Prieuré Protected in the shadows of Bonnieux's medieval ramparts, this is an 18th-century abbey turned hotel. The bedrooms are individually furnished in a simple, dignified manner befitting the style of the building and overlook the hotel garden or the ramparts. Depending on the weather and the season, breakfast is served either inside, next to the blazing fireplace, or in the verdant, lushly landscaped garden. The in-house restaurant serves such dishes as a chartreuse of lamb with a confit of eggplant, red snapper filets with pistou, and a dessert *fondant* of bitter chocolate. The restaurant is closed Wednesday all day and Thursday at lunchtime.

Rue J.-B.-Aurard, 84480 Bonnieux. ✆ **04-90-75-80-78.** Fax 04-90-75-96-00. 12 units. 100€–180€ double. MC, V. On-street parking free, in garage 12€. Closed Nov–Mar. **Amenities:** Restaurant; bar; limited room service; laundry service; dry cleaning. *In room:* Hair dryer.

WHERE TO DINE

You can also consider dining at the two inns listed above.

Le Fournil PROVENÇAL Charming and completely without pretension, this restaurant occupies the premises of a clean, dry, well-swept cave opening on a small-scale square graced with a 12th-century fountain. The inventive chefs, Guy Malbec and Jean-Christophe Lèche, have given recipes of long standing a new and livelier taste. The menu varies with the season and the inspiration of the chefs but might include crispy-skinned supreme of stuffed guinea fowl with baby vegetables, a confit of fruit, and parsley sauce; a platter of roasted and grilled baby goat, featuring two cooking techniques on one platter, with a confit of lemon; and filet of monkfish with sweet garlic and served with a purée of potatoes and olive oil. The wine list contains 35 to 40 selections, mainly regional choices like Côtes du Rhône and Côte de Luberon.

5 place Carnot. ✆ **04-90-75-83-62.** Reservations recommended. Main courses 14.20€–16.20€; fixed-price menus 24.50€–33.60€. MC, V. Sept–June Tues 7:30–9:30pm, Wed–Sun 12:15–2pm and 7:30–9:30pm; July–Aug Tues–Sun 12:30–1:45pm and 7:30–9:30pm, Sat 7:30–9:30pm. Closed Jan to mid-Feb and mid-Nov to mid-Dec.

10 Apt

52km (32 miles) W of Avignon; 52km (32 miles) N of Aix-en-Provence; and 726km (451 miles) S of Paris

Known as *Colonia Apta Julia,* this was an important Gallo-Roman city and today is a large, bustling market town. Ignore the modern industrial area and head for the Vieille Ville to capture the beauty of Apt. Here you can walk long, narrow streets that wind between old houses where every nook and cranny offers something waiting to be discovered.

Apt is known for its wines—it's a region of the Rhône Valley where the grapes that go into Côte de Luberon and Côtes de Ventoux are grown. It is also known for its basket- and wickerwork and has been a producer of hats since the 17th century. Others know it as the capital of crystallized fruit or *fruit-confits,* so beloved in Provence.

The old Roman city faded into history and was eventually deserted and covered by silt from the river and the hillsides. Roman remains are still buried around 5m to 10m (16 ft.–33 ft.) below the current town.

ESSENTIALS

GETTING THERE Apt has no railway station. From Avignon, five **buses** per day make the 75-minute trek to Apt; a one-way ticket is around 8€. Bus passengers are deposited in a parking lot beside the **Route de Digne** (✆ **04-90-74-20-21**), at the eastern periphery of town.

The best way to reach Apt is by **driving;** follow the N100 east from Avignon.

VISITOR INFORMATION The **Office de Tourism** is at 20 av. Philippe-de-Girard (✆ **04-90-74-03-18**).

EXPLORING THE AREA

Apt, capital of Le Luberon, proclaims itself "the world capital of crystallized fruits." The town is filled with Les Confiseurs selling this treat (see "Shopping," below). The best time to visit Apt is for its Saturday morning market centered on **place de la Bouquerie,** voted one of the 100 most appealing village markets in France. The streets are literally packed with market stalls and lined with temporary shops. Lavender growers, purveyors of goat cheese, potters, local beekeepers, and craftspeople who look like leftovers from the 1960s invade the town to peddle their wares. The Tour de l'Horloge, dating from the 1500s and straddling the rue des Marchands, is a particularly active area for the Saturday market. On market days, the town fills with jazz musicians, barrel organ players, stand-up comics, and what one local merchant calls "assorted freaks."

Cathédrale Ste-Anne This major monument is known for its ancient two-level crypt. According to legend, the bones of the legendary Ste-Anne, mother of the Virgin Mary, were miraculously discovered in this crypt in the 8th century, occasioning the building of the cathedral. Her life is depicted in a beautiful set of 14th-century stained-glass windows at the end of the apse. Her shroud is also displayed among the reliquaries of the treasury. Scholars speculate that Anne was not the biblical figure, but a dim memory of the primeval pan-European mother goddess sometimes known as Ana or Anna Perenna to the Romans.

Tips Outdoors in Luberon National Park

The information office for the **Luberon National Park** is in an 18th-century house, La Maison du Parc, 1 place Jean-Jaurès (✆ **04-90-04-42-00**). The office provides maps, details of hiking trails in the park, and other outdoor activities in the area. Much of the land in the Luberon area is privately owned, but trails in the park are open to the public. In summer there are tastings of the regional produce here. On-site is a small **Museum of Paleontology,** of only specialist interest. Admission is 1.50€, and it's open May through October Monday through Saturday from 8:30am to noon, and the rest of the year Monday through Friday from 1:30 to 6pm.

In the 13th century, the present church was enlarged, and in the 18th century, the floor was raised and the broken barrel vault turned into a higher ogee vault. The oldest part of the cathedral is the tower crypt, which still has a funerary monument honoring a priest in the time of Apia Julia and Carolingian flagstones. The church and its treasury are filled with rare ecclesiastical artifacts. In the chapel of St. John the Baptist, you can see an early Christian marble sarcophagus from the Pyrenees. Among the treasures in the sacristy are 11th- and 12th-century manuscripts, elaborate vestments, and an 11th-century Arab standard brought back from the First Crusade. The nave is adorned with scenes from the life of Christ, painted by Pierre and Christophe Delpech in the 18th century.

To see the Sacristy, you must ask Claude Pion, the church caretaker. She is constantly on-site during open hours (see below) and will open it according to the schedule of daily Masses or the priorities of the priests. If she does, a donation to the maintenance of the church is appreciated.

Vieille Ville. No phone. Free admission. Mon–Sat 10am–noon and 4–6pm; Sun 10am–noon. Ask the caretaker for entrance to the Sacristy.

Hôtel Colin d'Albertas The lavish 17th-century baroque interior of this building was opened for hour-long daily guided tours in 1999. It contains some of the most spectacular plaster- and stuccowork in the region and is a museum in its own right.

Rue de la République. ✆ **04-90-74-02-40.** Tours 5.50€ adults, 4€ students. June–Sept daily 3 and 6pm.

Musée Archéologique The town's major museum contains Roman objects found in local excavations, including pieces of mosaics, sarcophagi, coins, and even oil lamps from the 2nd century B.C. It also displays sacred and decorative art by faience makers from the 17th and the 19th centuries.

Place Carnot. ✆ **04-90-04-76-65.** 2€ for adults, 1€ for students and children. June–Sept Wed–Mon 10am–noon and 2:30–5:30pm; Oct–May Wed–Mon 10am–noon and 2:30–4:30pm.

SHOPPING

The large town is filled with confiseurs selling candied fruits. The best are **Confiserie Marcel Richaud,** 48 quai de la Liberté (✆ **04-90-74-13-56**), and **Confiseur Le Coulon/Jean Ceccon,** 24 quai de la Liberté (✆ **04-90-74-21-90**).

WHERE TO STAY & DINE

Auberge de la Loube ★ *Finds* PROVENÇAL Small, personalized, and charming, this is the century-old domaine of Provençal chef and entrepreneur Maurice de la Loube. Isolated on the outskirts of an agrarian hamlet known for its rolling hills and authentic Luberon flavor, it offers delicious cuisine and a look at a slower, more relaxed lifestyle that's envied by many French urbanites. The stone-fronted house has a terrace in front, with dining tables and views that sweep out over the countryside. Main courses, often focusing on local lamb that's perfectly roasted with just the right amount of Provençal seasoning, are succulent and generous, but the real culinary charm of the place might lie in the flavor and variety of Monsieur de la Loube's starters. Several of these will be carried to your table in a wicker basket and laid out with fanfare on your table. Collectively, they represent the best of traditional Provence. Depending on the configuration of your meal, they're likely to include poached asparagus in vinaigrette sauce, tapenade of local olives, brandade of codfish, braised carrots with a garlicky aïoli, and eggplant "caviar."

The dining room is charming, outfitted with mirrors, small lamps that cast warm glows on the thick ochre-colored walls, and vases of flowers. Ask (either before or after your meal) to view the approximately 19 antique carriages, many of them made in the United States and imported here during the early 20th century, that are stored in a nearby outbuilding. Collecting them is the personal hobby of Monsieur de la Loube and a source of enormous personal pride.

Quartier de la Loube, Buoux. ✆ **04-90-74-19-58.** Reservations recommended. Main courses 15€–17€; fixed-price menus 21€–30€. MC, V. Fri–Tues noon–1:30pm and 8–9:30pm. Closed Feb. Located 8km (4½ miles) south of Apt; from Apt, follow signs to Buoux.

Auberge du Luberon TRADITIONAL FRENCH Though mainly a restaurant, this place is also a hotel. It's in the heart of the city's historic center, in a century-old building. The menu reflects old-fashioned culinary virtues and style. Specialties include foie gras with a confit of fruits, in the style that Apt is famous for; a charlotte of lamb with eggplant; John Dory with artichoke hearts *barigoules;* and a trolley laden daily with 13 different desserts.

There are 14 bedrooms, about half in a nearby annex. Doubles without air-conditioning cost 52€; those with air-conditioning cost 84€.

8 place Faubourge du Ballet, 84400 Apt. ✆ **04-90-06-69-49.** Fax 04-90-04-79-49. www.auberge-luberon-peuzin.com. Reservations recommended. Main courses 17€–30€; fixed-price menus 26€–84€. AE, DC, MC, V. Oct–June Tues–Sun noon–1:45pm, Tues–Sat 7:30–9:30pm; July–Sept Tues–Sun noon–1:45pm, daily 7:30–9:30pm. AE, MC, V. Closed Nov 6–Dec 26.

Relais de Roquefure *Value* Lying 6km (3½ miles) north of the center, this Logis de France country hotel in the Luberon Nature Reserve is the finest place to stay in the area. It offers good food and a good night's sleep, all at a fair price. Georges and Jeannine Rousset, the owners, are hospitable hosts. Rooms are small but comfortable, with fine, soft beds and small bathrooms. In summer, guests can sit under the shade trees. The food is some of the best in the area, emphasizing regional produce.

Along N000, 84400 Apt. ✆ **04-90-04-88-88.** Fax 04-90-74-14-86. www.relaisderoquefure.com. 15 units. 58€–110€ double. Half board 97€–117€ double. MC, V. Closed Dec–Jan. **Amenities:** Restaurant; bar; pool; bike rental; laundry service; dry cleaning. *In room:* Hair dryer.

11 Salon de Provence

47km (29 miles) SE of Avignon; 37km (23 miles) NW of Aix-en-Provence; 53km (33 miles) NW of Marseille

The hometown of Nostradamus is centered between Aix-en-Provence and Avignon, and makes an excellent stopover between these towns. Today a busy modern town, it grew up as a fortified hilltop fortress centering on Château de l'Empéri. With a population of some 35,000, it has been a center of the olive oil industry since the 15th century, although it owes much of its prosperity to the French Air Force's officer training school centered here.

Salon-de-Provence was the birthplace of Adam de Craponne (1527–76), creator of the famous canal, bearing his name today, that irrigates the region of Crau.

ESSENTIALS

GETTING THERE **Train** connections, about seven a day from Avignon, are the best and most direct (40 min. each way). For information and schedules, contact the local tourist office. From Aix-en-Provence, there are about seven daily **buses** (trip time: between 30 and 45 min.) to downtown Salon de Provence's place Morgan. For information on bus travel into and around Salon de Provence, contact the **Gare Routière** in Aix-en-Provence (✆ **04-42-27-17-91**). Train connections from Aix are less convenient and require a transfer in Marseille.

If you're **driving,** Salon de Provence is strategically located at the junction of highways connecting Avignon with Aix-en-Provence (N7), and Marseille with Arles and Nîmes (N113), as well as the A7 and A54 autoroutes.

VISITOR INFORMATION The **Office de Tourisme** is at 56 cours Gimon (✆ **04-90-56-27-60**).

EXPLORING THE TOWN

A major attraction in the town is the **Fontaine Moussue** on the place Crousillat just outside the Porte de l'Horloge. Covered by a thick mound of moss, this much-photographed fountain dates from the 18th century. It is surrounded by plane trees planted to commemorate events over the centuries. One was planted in 1799 to mark the end of the Revolution; another was planted in 1919 to mark the end of World War I.

Château de l'Empéri This château is surrounded by ancient circular walls. You can enter through the 17th-century Porte de l'Horloge or the Porte Bourg Neuf. The château dates from the 10th century and is one of the most beautiful in Provence, with its courtyards, towers, and walls. Once this was the residence of the archbishops of Arles, lords of Salon. Both François I, in 1516, and Marie de Médici, in 1600, visited and stayed here. From 1831, it was used as a barracks and was severely damaged in an earthquake in 1909. Over the years it, has been gradually and attractively restored.

The château houses the Musée de Art et d'Histoire Militaire, with a collection of more than 10,000 artifacts, including military uniforms, weapons, waxwork figures, and military flags. The museum covers the era from Louis XIV, the Sun King, up to France's entry into World War II.

Montée du Puech. ✆ **04-90-56-22-36.** 3.05€ adults, 2.30€ children 7–18, free for ages 6 and under. Wed–Mon 10am–noon and 2:30–6pm.

Musée Nostradamus *Overrated* Nostradamus (1503–66), who was born in St-Rémy-de-Provence, spent the last 19 years of his life at this little house close to the château. It's now a museum devoted to him and his famous enigmatic predictions of the future. A series of fairly unconvincing tableaux depicts scenes from his life, with a rambling commentary on portable CD players.

Nostradamus was born into a family of converted Jews and trained as a doctor in Montpellier. He treated plague victims in Lyon and Aix. He married a woman from Salon in 1547 and settled here, where he studied astrology, publishing almanacs and inventing new recipes for cosmetics. Written in the future tense, his *Centuries* in rhyming quatrains was published in 1555, bringing him instant celebrity. Nostradamus is buried in the interesting 14th-century Eglise St-Laurent, which lies just to the north of the town center.

11 rue Nostradamus. © **04-90-56-64-31.** 3.05€. Mid-June to mid-Sept daily 10am–noon and 3–8pm. Rest of year daily 10am–noon and 2–6pm.

Musée Grevin de la Provence In this wax museum, lifelike tableaux attempt to re-create 2,600 years of the history of Provence. That history is re-created in part in the exhibition of some 15 historical paintings, one of which depicts the fabled marriage of Gyptis and Protis. Their marriage sealed the union of the Phocaeans with the Celtic-Ligurians. The exhibits go up to the 20th century, including scenes from the cinema. The museum is hardly Madame Tussaud's and it's a bit kitschy, but families with children in tow might find it worth a half-hour or so of viewing time.

Place du Puits de Jacob. © **04-90-56-36-30.** 3.05€. Mid-June to mid-Sept daily 10am–noon and 3–8pm. Rest of year daily 10am–noon and 2–6pm.

SHOPPING

Despite the vast amounts of soap and detergent sold by large corporations in France today, Salon de Provence maintains two small-scale artisans that continue to make soap the old-fashioned way, in limited batches, by hand. They are **Rampal,** 71 rue Félix Pyat (© **04-90-56-07-28**), and **Marius Fabre,** Avenue Paul Bourrat (© **04-90-53-24-77**). Visits to the first are conducted only by prior appointment; visits to the second are possible only on Monday and Thursday at 10:30am.

WHERE TO STAY

Abbaye de Sainte-Croix ★★ No hotel in the region can boast origins as authentic and charming as this ancient one-time monastery from the 1100s, 4km (2½ miles) north of the city center. A Relais & Châteaux hotel, it lies behind thick stone walls, with most of its original arches and vaults, and a severely dignified, sometimes forbidding kind of grandeur evocative of the Middle Ages. The generally spacious bedrooms feature a simple elegance: lovely old furniture, terra-cotta floors, and sometimes spectacular views over fields of lavender and rugged hills. The place is more famous as a restaurant than as a hotel—see "Where to Dine," below.

Val de Cuech, 13300 Salon de Provence. © **04-90-56-24-55.** Fax 04-90-56-31-12. www.hotels-provence.com. 25 units. 165€–295€ double; 410€ suite. AE, DC, MC, V. Free parking. Closed Nov to mid-Mar. **Amenities:** Restaurant; bar; pool; limited room service; babysitting; laundry service; dry cleaning. *In room:* A/C, TV, minibar, hair dryer, safe.

Hôtel d'Angleterre Set on the northwestern fringe of the peripheral boulevard (Cours Carnot) that flanks the edge of town (a 10-min. walk from the center), this is a conservative, not particularly exciting three-story hotel with roots in British tourism during the early 1900s. Everything has been radically modernized from its original turn-of-the-20th-century charm, with touches of kitsch and an overwhelming sense of bourgeois, and somewhat tense propriety. One of the few appealing touches is the circular skylight in the breakfast room. Come here for the relatively low rates, as bedrooms are spartan and not particularly cozy. They range from small to medium and are reasonably comfortable; bathrooms are a bit cramped.

98 Cours Carnot, 13300 Salon de Provence. © **04-90-56-01-10.** Fax 04-90-56-71-75. 26 units. 43.50€–49.50€ double. MC, V. Closed Dec 24–Jan 2. **Amenities:** Lounge. *In room:* A/C, TV, hair dryer, safe.

WHERE TO DINE

Abbaye de Sainte-Croix ★★★ FRENCH/PROVENÇAL In the hotel of the same name recommended above, this restaurant serves the best food in the region. Part of its appeal comes from its architecture of medieval soaring vaults and high perpendicular lines. From its terrace is a view over the low hills of the Alpilles. Menu items change with the season and the inspiration of the chef, and include such delectable items as lobster salad with a walnut oil vinaigrette; sliced sea wolf with a fondant of green and red peppers, basil, and locally produced olives and olive oil; thin-sliced roasted lamb with truffles from the Luberon in clarified butter; turbot with morels; and aiguillette of duck with a tapenade of olives.

Val de Cuech, 13300 Salon-de-Provence. ✆ **04-90-56-24-55.** Reservations recommended. Main courses 25.20€–33.60€; fixed-price menus 52.60€–65.20€ lunch, 73€–97€ dinner. AE, MC, V. Closed Nov to mid-Mar.

Mas du Soleil (Restaurant Francis Robin) ★ FRENCH/MEDITERRANEAN In an 1850s stone-sided farmhouse, the ocher-colored facade of this inn is a 5-minute walk from the center of town. The critically acclaimed cuisine of Francis Robin changes according to the season and the availability of the ingredients. Menu items include such treats as a rosemary-infused rack of lamb for two, filet of beef layered with escalope of foie gras, warm salad of filet of red snapper, and a medley of grilled Mediterranean fish. One tempting main course that the chef is particularly proud of is a *civet* (stew) of lobster. Dining room windows overlook a swimming pool in the garden.

An upper floor contains 10 well-maintained bedrooms outfitted with flowered wallpaper and traditional furniture. Each has a bay window overlooking the garden and terrace or a private patio.

38 chemin St-Côme, Salon-de-Provence. ✆ **04-90-56-06-53.** Reservations recommended. Main courses 13€–45€. Fixed-price menus 30€–87€. AE, DC, MC, V. Tues–Sun noon–2pm; Tues–Sat 7:30–9pm.

12 Aix-en-Provence ★★

755km (469 miles) S of Paris; 80km (50 miles) SE of Avignon; 32km (20 miles) N of Marseille; 175km (109 miles) W of Nice

The most charming center in all Provence, this faded university town was once a seat of aristocracy, its streets walked by counts and kings. Founded in 122 B.C. by a Roman general, Caius Sextius Calvinus, who named it *Aquae Sextiae* after himself, Aix (pronounced "ex") has been, in turn, a Roman military outpost, a civilian colony, the administrative capital of a province of the later Roman Empire, the seat of an archbishop, and the official residence of the medieval comtes de Provence. After the union of Provence with France, Aix remained until the Revolution a judicial and administrative headquarters.

The celebrated son of this old capital city of Provence, Paul Cézanne immortalized the countryside nearby. Just as he painted it, Montagne Ste-Victoire looms over the town today, though a string of high-rises has now cropped up on the landscape.

The Université d'Aix has been attracting international students since 1413. Today absinthe has given way to pastis in the many cafes scattered throughout the town.

This city of some 150,000 is reasonably quiet in winter, but active and bustling when the summer hordes pour in. Summer brings frequent cultural events, ranging from opera to jazz, June through August. Increasingly, Aix is becoming a "bedroom community" for urbanites fleeing Marseille after 5pm.

Aix-en-Provence

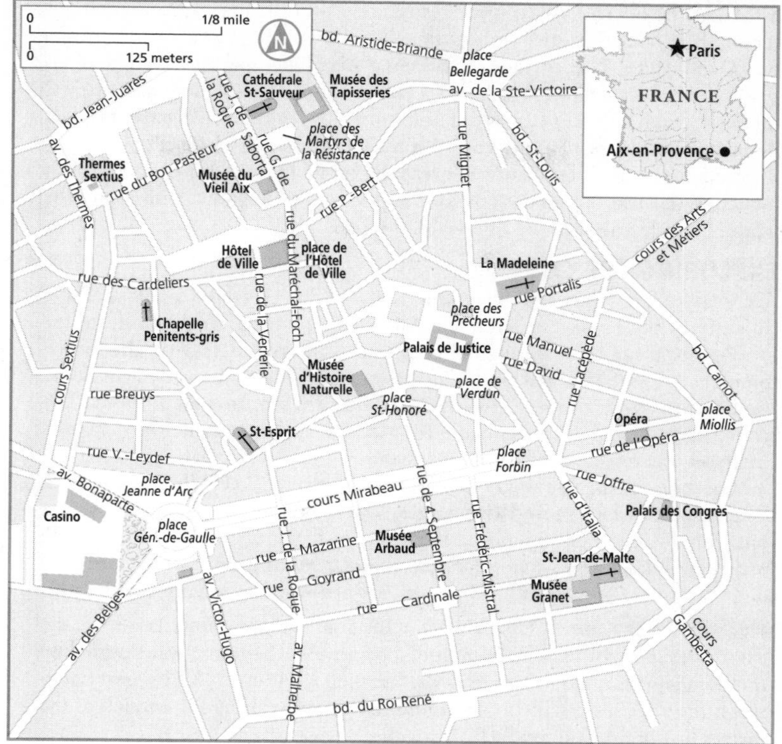

ESSENTIALS

GETTING THERE The city is easily accessible, with 21 **trains** arriving from Marseille, taking 35 minutes and costing 5.70€ one-way. Eight trains arrive from Nice; the trip takes 3 to 4 hours and costs 27.60€ one-way. There are also eight trains per day from Cannes, taking 3½ hours and costing 25.10€ one-way. A newer train station designed for the high-speed TGV trains is at Vitroll, 5.5km (9 miles) to the west of Aix.

There are **bus** links, costing 3.60€ one-way, into the center of Aix. For more information, call ✆ **08-36-35-35.** Buses from Marseille arrive at the rate of one every 10 minutes, or else five per day from Avignon, plus two per day from Nice. For more information, call ✆ **04-42-91-26-80.**

If you're **driving** to Aix from Avignon or other points north, take A7 south to RN7 and follow it into town. From Marseilles or other points to the south, take A51 north into town.

If you'd like to explore the region by bike, head for **Cycles Zammit,** 27 rue Mignet (✆ **04-42-23-19-53**), a very short walk northeast of the cours Mirabeau. Here you can rent either 10-speed racing bikes or more durable mountain bikes for 12.20€ per day. As deposit, they'll want to hold on to either your passport, your driver's license, or cash worth the value of the bike you rent, usually around 350€.

VISITOR INFORMATION The **Office de Tourisme** is at 2 place du Général-de-Gaulle (✆ **04-42-16-11-61;** www.aixenprovencetourism.com).

SPECIAL EVENTS Aix is more geared toward music than any other city in the south of France. It offers at least four summer festivals that showcase music, opera, and dance. They include the **Saison d'Aix** (June–Aug), which focuses on symphonic and chamber music, and a **Jazz Festival** (end of July) that attracts musicians from all over the world. For information, call the **Office des Fêtes et de la Culture,** Espace Forbin, cours Gambetta (✆ **04-42-63-06-75**).

Also noteworthy is the **Festival International de Danse** (July–Aug 3 weeks), attracting classical and modern dance troupes from throughout Europe and the world. For information, call ✆ **04-42-96-05-01.**

EXPLORING THE CITY

Aix's main street, **cours Mirabeau** ★★, is one of Europe's most beautiful. Plane trees stretch their branches across the top like an umbrella, shading it from the hot Provençal sun and filtering the light into shadows that play on the rococo fountains below. Shops and sidewalk cafes line one side of the street; sandstone *hôtels particuliers* (mansions) from the 17th and 18th centuries fill the other. The street begins at the 1860 fountain on place de la Libération, which honors Mirabeau, the revolutionary and statesman.

After touring Aix, you might consider a side trip on D10 15km (9 miles) to the east to the **Château de Vauvenarges,** site of Pablo Picasso's last home. You can't visit the château's interior, but Picasso and one of his wives, Jacqueline Roche, are buried nearby. Stop for a meal at **Au Moulin de Provence,** rue des Maquisards (✆ **04-42-66-02-22**), which lies across the road from the château.

Atelier de Cézanne Outside town is the studio of the painter who was the major forerunner of cubism, surrounded by a wall. The house was restored by American admirers. It remains much as Cézanne left it in 1906: "his coat hanging on the wall, his easel with an unfinished picture waiting for a touch of the master's brush," as Thomas R. Parker wrote.

9 av. Paul-Cézanne (outside town). ✆ **04-42-21-06-53.** Admission 3.80€ adults, 2.75€ students and children. Apr–Sept Wed–Mon 10am–noon and 2:30–6pm; Oct–Mar Wed–Mon 10am–noon and 2–5pm. Closed Jan 1, May 1, and Dec 25.

Cathédrale St-Sauveur ★ The architecture of the cathedral covers many eras: Notable is the baptistery, which dates from the 4th or 5th centuries; Romanesque and Gothic stand side by side in a double nave. Its greatest treasure is the brilliant 15th-century triptych by Nicolas Froment, *The Burning Bush.* It shows Good King René and his second wife, Jeanne de Laval, kneeling before the Virgin, who is poised above the burning bush. The delicate oil and tempera painting is usually closed to the public—for a tip, the custodian might open it for you.

Place des Martyrs de la Résistance. ✆ **04-42-23-45-65.** Free admission. Daily 9am–noon and 2–6pm.

Chapelle Penitents-gris (Chapelle des Bourras) This 16th-century chapel honoring St. Joseph was built on the ancient Roman Aurelian road linking Rome and Spain. The chapel was restored by Herbert Maza, founder and former president of the Institute for American Universities. Visits can be prearranged with Monsieur Borricand, rector of a group of local ecclesiastics.

15 rue Lieutaud. ✆ **04-42-26-26-72.** Free admission (donations welcome). July–Aug Sat 4:30–6pm; Sept–June Sat 2:30–4:30pm.

Musée des Tapisseries ★ This museum is in a former archbishop's palace. Lining its gilded walls are three series of tapestries from the 17th and 18th centuries, collected by the archbishops to decorate the palace: *The History of Don*

Quixote, by Natoire; *The Russian Games,* by Leprince; and *The Grotesques,* by Monnoyer. In addition, the museum exhibits rare furnishings from the 17th and 18th centuries.

28 place des Martyrs de la Résistance. ✆ **04-42-23-09-91.** Admission 2€ adults, free for ages 25 and under. Wed–Mon 10–11:45am and 2–5:45pm. Closed Jan 1, May 1, and Dec 25.

Musée Granet (Musée des Beaux-Arts) A former director once claimed that the walls of this museum "would never be sullied by a Cézanne." Fortunately, that's not true—the museum owns eight paintings by Cézanne, none of them major. The great painter had a famously antagonistic relationship with the people of Aix. The museum is housed in the former center of the Knights of Malta and contains works by Van Dyck, Van Loo, and Rigaud; portraits by Pierre and François Puget; and an interesting *Jupiter and Thetis* by Ingres. Ingres also did an 1807 portrait of the museum's namesake, François Marius Granet. Granet's own works abound.

Place St-Jean-de-Malte (up rue Cardinale). ✆ **04-42-38-14-70.** Admission 2€ adults, free for ages 24 and under. Wed–Mon 10am–noon and 2:30–6pm. Closed Jan 1, May 1 and 21, July 14, Aug 15, Nov 1 and 11, and Dec 25 and 31.

SHOPPING

For the best selection of art objects and fabrics inspired by the traditions of Provence, head to **Les Olivades,** 15 rue Marius-Reinaud (✆ **04-42-38-33-66**). It sells fabrics, shirts for women and men, fashionable dresses, and table linens.

Opened a century ago, **Bechard,** 12 cours Mirabeau (✆ **04-42-26-06-78**), is the most famous bakery in town. It takes its work so seriously that it refers to its underground kitchens as a *laboratoire* (laboratory). The pastries are truly delectable—in most cases, made fresh every day.

La Boutique du Pays d'Aix, in the Office de Tourisme, 2 place du Général-de-Gaulle (✆ **04-42-16-11-61**), carries a wide selection of *santons* (carved figurines inspired by the Nativity of Jesus), locally woven textiles and carvings, and *calissons* (sugared confections made with almonds and a confit of melon).

Founded in 1934 on a busy boulevard just east of the center of town, **Santons Fouque,** 65 cours Gambetta, route de Nice (✆ **04-42-26-33-38**), stocks the largest assortment of *santons* in Aix. More than 1,800 figurines are cast in terra cotta, finished by hand, and painted according to 18th-century models. Each of the trades practiced in medieval Provence is represented, including shoemakers, barrel makers, coppersmiths, and ironsmiths, poised to welcome the newborn Jesus. Figurines range in price from 11€ to 900€.

WHERE TO STAY

IN AIX

Very Expensive

Villa Gallici ★★★ This elegant inn is relentlessly chic. It has been stylishly decorated by its creators (architects and interior designers Messrs Dez, Montemarco, and Jouve). It was originally hailed as "divinely over the top." Each room has an individualized charming decor; some boast a private terrace or garden. Beds are hung with "waterfalls" of sprigged and striped cotton, mattresses are decadently comfortable, and towels are predictably plush. The villa sits in a large enclosed garden in the heart of town, close to one of the best restaurants, Le Clos de la Violette (see below), and a 5-minute walk from the town center. Despite its grand reputation as a place that requires ironbound advance reservations and where famous people bask in sybaritic anonymity, some of the staff are not as well informed as they might be. But that is only a minor distraction in an otherwise well-orchestrated symphony.

Av. de la Violette (impasse des Grands Pins), 13100 Aix-en-Provence. ✆ **04-42-23-29-23.** Fax 04-42-96-30-45. www.villagallici.com. 22 units. 270€–500€ double; 550€–600€ suite. AE, DC, MC, V. **Amenities:** Restaurant; bar; pool; 24-hr. room service; babysitting; laundry service. *In room:* A/C, TV, minibar, hair dryer, safe.

Expensive

Hôtel des Augustins ★ Converted from the 12th-century Grands Augustins Convent, this hotel has been beautifully restored, with ribbed-vault ceilings, stained-glass windows, stone walls, terra-cotta floors, and Louis XIII furnishings. The reception desk is in a chapel, and oil paintings and watercolors decorate the public rooms. Before its transformation into a hotel in 1892, this site won a place in history by sheltering an excommunicated Martin Luther on his return from Rome. The spacious soundproof guest rooms—two with terraces—all have automatic alarm-call facilities. They are outfitted in a severe kind of monastic dignity, with dark-grained wooden furniture and high ceilings. Touches of luxury, however, appear with the firm, very comfortable mattresses (a lot cozier than what was used by the monks of long ago) and big bathrooms. There's no full-fledged restaurant on the premises; consequently, breakfast is the only meal served.

3 rue de la Masse, 13100 Aix-en-Provence. ✆ **04-42-27-28-59.** Fax 04-42-26-74-87. 29 units. 107€–229€ double. AE, DC, V. Nearby parking in private garage 12€. **Amenities:** Laundry service; dry cleaning. *In room:* TV, minibar, hair dryer.

Hôtel Pigonnet ★★ This pink-sided Provençal mansion on the edge of town is surrounded by gardens and memories of Paul Cézanne, who used to visit there. Many renovations were completed here during 1998. The high-ceilinged bedrooms contain antique and reproduction French provincial furnishings, elaborate curtains, and a pervasive sense of country elegance. Breakfast is served on a colonnaded veranda overlooking a reflecting pool in the courtyard. In summer, the in-house restaurant expands outward into the garden, featuring such dishes as a terrine of house-made foie gras, roasted Provençal lamb in a honey-flavored rosemary sauce, and a roulade of chicken with crawfish in shellfish sauce.

5 av. du Pigonnet, 13090 Aix-en-Provence. ✆ **04-42-59-02-90.** Fax 04-42-59-47-77. www.hotelpigonnet.com. 52 units. 180€–250€double; 450€ suite. AE, DC, MC, V. Free parking. **Amenities:** Restaurant; bar; pool; limited room service; babysitting; laundry service; dry cleaning. *In room:* A/C, TV, minibar, hair dryer, safe.

Mercure Paul-Cézanne ★ *Overrated* The refined interior of this place is more tasteful than you'd expect in a member of a nationwide chain. Since being sold by its former owner, however, it has lost its top position to the much more stylish and tranquil Gallici, and there have been increasing complaints about a less than cooperative staff. The lounge seems more like a private sitting room than a hotel lobby. Many of the rooms have mahogany Victorian furniture, Louis XVI chairs, marble-top chests, gilt mirrors, and oil paintings. Bedroom mattresses, while not exactly plush, are at least comfortable. The bathrooms have hand-painted tiles. Breakfast is served in a small room opening onto a rear courtyard.

40 av. Victor-Hugo, 13100 Aix-en-Provence. ✆ **04-42-91-11-11.** Fax 04-42-91-11-10. 55 units. 115€–131€ double; 160€ suite. AE, DC, MC, V. Parking 10€. **Amenities:** Bar; lounge; babysitting; laundry service; dry cleaning. *In room:* A/C, TV, minibar, hair dryer.

Moderate

Grand Hôtel Nègre Coste This hotel, a former 18th-century town house, is so popular with the dozens of musicians who flock to Aix for the summer festivals that it's usually difficult to get a room at any price. Such popularity is understandable. Outside, flowers cascade from jardinières, and windows are surrounded with 18th-century carvings. Inside there's a wide staircase, marble portrait busts, and a Provençal armoire. The soundproof rooms contain interesting antiques and recently renovated bathrooms. The higher floors overlook cours Mirabeau or the old city.

33 cours Mirabeau, 13100 Aix-en-Provence. ✆ **04-42-27-74-22.** Fax 04-42-26-80-93. 37 units. 65€–125€ double. AE, DC, V. Parking 10€. *In room:* A/C, TV.

Résidence Rotonde A contemporary hotel in the town center, the Rotonde provides cheerful, streamlined accommodations. Occupying part of a residential building, it has an open spiral cantilevered staircase and molded-plastic and chrome furniture. The rooms have ornate wallpaper, Nordic-style beds, and adequately comfortable mattresses. Bathrooms are a bit small but adequate for the job, with suitable shelf space. There's no restaurant, but breakfast is served.

15 av. des Belges, 13100 Aix-en-Provence. ✆ **04-42-26-29-88.** Fax 04-42-26-29-98. 41 units. 72€–82€ double; 90€–150€ suite. AE, DC, MC, V. Parking 9€. **Amenities:** Bar; lounge. *In room:* A/C, TV, minibar.

Inexpensive

Hôtel des Quatre Dauphins This hotel is in an 18th-century five-story former town house, a short walk from the place des Quatre Dauphins and the Cours Mirabeau. Despite frequent modernization, some of the original motifs remain. The bedrooms were recently refurbished in a simplified Provençal style. Some have painted ceiling beams and casement windows that overlook the street outside. Space is not overly abundant, but mattresses are comfortable, and many clients find the blue-and-white color schemes soothing. Bathrooms are just adequate for the job, with tidy maintenance. Breakfast is served in your bedroom or within a small breakfast salon.

54 rue Roux Alphéran, 13100 Aix-en-Provence. ✆ **04-42-38-16-39.** Fax 04-42-38-60-19. 12 units. 59€–76€ double. MC, V. *In room:* TV.

Hôtel La Caravelle *Value* A 3-minute walk from the center is this conservatively furnished hotel with a bas-relief of a three-masted caravelle on the stucco facade. The hotel is run by Monsieur and Madame Henri Denis in a continuing tradition of warm hospitality. The majority of the rooms were restored between 1995 and 1998; they have double-glazed windows to help muffle the noise. Mattresses are relatively comfortable. Breakfast is served in the stone-floored lobby.

29 bd. du Roi-René (at cours Mirabeau), 13100 Aix-en-Provence. ✆ **04-42-21-53-05.** Fax 04-42-96-55-46. lacaravelle@mail.com. 30 units. 58€–66€ double. AE, DC, MC, V. *In room:* A/C, TV.

IN MEYRARGUES

Château de Meyrargues ★★ This 12th-century château is one of France's oldest fortified sites, having been a Celtic outpost in 600 B.C. Once the lords of Les Baux lived here, but now it's an award-winning holiday retreat. The entrance is imposing, with twin stone towers flanking a sweeping set of balustraded steps. From its terraces and rooms you can enjoy a panoramic view of the valley of the Durance. The spacious accommodations feature canopied beds, fabrics inspired by Provençal designs and colors, worthy antiques, and tiled bathrooms with showers equipped with floods of hot water. The hotel was completely renovated and upgraded between 1994 and 1995.

Meals are served in a baronial-looking dining room with a large fireplace, near a bar with a private terrace. Fixed-price menus tend to emphasize grilled fish and roasted versions of Provençal lamb. There are 4.8 hectares (12 acres) of private terrain around the château, wherein patches of verdant gardens are interspersed with a swimming pool and lots of rocky outcroppings.

13650 Meyrargues. ✆ **04-42-63-49-90.** Fax 04-42-63-49-92. www.chateau-de-meyrargues.com. 11 units. 115€–200€ double; 305€ suite. AE, MC, V. From Aix, take A51 for 17km (10½ miles) northeast, following the signs for Sisteron and Pertuis; get off at Exit 14, and then follow the signs to the château. **Amenities:** Restaurant; bar; pool; limited room service; babysitting. *In room:* A/C, TV, minibar, hair dryer.

IN BEAURECUEIL

Mas de la Bertrande ★ This charming hotel has a setting that looks like a Cézanne canvas, at the foot of Montaigne Ste-Victoire. The former stable has ceiling beams, a country fireplace, and plush furniture. The hotel's staff is very attentive, and rooms are cozily outfitted with Provençal furniture. Bathrooms are well equipped and tidily maintained.

The cuisine is one of the primary reasons for a stop here. The chef's innovative specialties are served on the terrace or in the dining room, both ringed with flowers. Specialties are herb-flavored lamb, stuffed sole, bisque of mussels, truffled chicken, rockfish soup, foie gras of the region, and an excellent tarte Tatin. The cheese board has selections from all over France.

13100 Beaurecueil. ✆ **04-42-66-75-75.** Fax 04-42-66-82-01. 10 units. 122€–144€ double. AE, V. Closed Feb 15–Mar 15. From Aix, drive 10km (6 miles) southeast, following the signs to Trets. **Amenities:** Restaurant; bar; pool; limited room service; laundry service; dry cleaning. *In room:* TV, minibar.

WHERE TO DINE

EXPENSIVE

Le Clos de la Violette ★★★ MODERN FRENCH Le Clos de la Violette is in an elegant residential neighborhood that is best reached by taxi. The restaurant's creative and innovative cuisine is usually much better than the attention span of its sometimes inexperienced waitstaff. The imposing Provençal villa has an octagonal reception area and several modern dining rooms. Menu items are stylish and seasonal, richly tuned to the flavors of Provence. Examples include local goats' cheese in puff pastry with a confit of fresh celery, braised sea wolf with beignets of fennel, warm onion brioche with a fig-flavored vinaigrette and balsamic vinegar, and roasted Provençal lamb in puff pastry. An absolutely superb dessert might be a "celebration" of Provençal figs—an artfully arranged platter containing a galette of figs, a tart of figs, a parfait of figs, and a sorbet of figs.

10 av. de la Violette. ✆ **04-42-23-30-71.** Reservations required. Main courses 30€–45€; fixed-price lunch 54€; tasting menu 117€. AE, V. Apr–Oct Tues and Thurs–Sat noon–1:30pm, Tues–Sat 7:30–9:30pm; Nov–Mar Tues–Sat noon–2:30pm and 7:30–10pm. Closed late Dec to early Jan, Feb, and early Aug.

MODERATE

Antoine Côte Cour PROVENÇAL/ITALIAN This popular trattoria occupies an 18th-century town house a few steps from place Rotonde. Patrons include Emanuel Ungaro as well as many other film and fashion types, who mingle smoothly with old-time "Aixers." Despite the grandeur of the setting, the ambience is unpretentious, even jovial. Crusty bread and small pots of aromatic purées (anchovy and basil) are placed at your table before your order is taken. A simple wine, such as Côtes du Rhône, will go nicely with the kind of hearty Mediterranean food that's de rigueur. Examples are a memorable version of *pastis* (pasta Romano flavored with calves' liver, flap mushrooms, and tomato sauce), *osso buco* (veal shank layered with salty ham), a selection of *légumes farcies* (such as eggplant and zucchini stuffed with minced meat and herbs), and at least half a dozen kinds of fresh fish.

19 rue Mirabeau. ✆ **04-42-93-12-51.** Reservations recommended. Main courses 17€–29€. DC, MC, V. Tues–Sat noon–2:30pm; Mon–Sat 7:30pm–midnight.

Chez Maxime GRILL/PROVENÇAL This likeable restaurant reflects the skills and personality of its owner/namesake, Felix Maxime. It's in the pedestrian zone with a terrace on the sidewalk. The most important element here is the cuisine. Redolent with the flavors of Provence, a *tian*—layers of eggplant, peppers, and Mediterranean herbs in a terra-cotta pot, infused with garlic, aromates, and olive oil, and baked until bubbly—is a superb beginning. Another fine appetizer is *rillettes* (like a roughly textured paté) of sea wolf with a garlicky rouille mayonnaise. Specialties include as many as 19 kinds of grilled meat or fish cooked over an oak-burning fire, and several preparations of lamb. A staff member will dress your cut of meat next to your table. The wine list features more than 500 vintages, including many esoteric bottles from the region.

12 place Ramus. ✆ **04-42-26-28-51.** Reservations recommended. Main courses 15€–24.10€; fixed-price menus 16€ lunch, 22€ dinner. MC, V. Tues–Sat noon–2:30pm; Mon–Sat 7:30–10pm. Closed 2 weeks in Jan.

INEXPENSIVE

Brasserie Royale TRADITIONAL FRENCH Located on a tree-lined boulevard, the informal Brasserie Royale offers excellent, unpretentious regional cooking at reasonable prices. It's a modernized, animated, and invariably crowded place with an interior dining room and a popular glass-enclosed, canopied section on the sidewalk. You're served such hearty fare as tripe Provençal, daube Provençal (a favorite dish here), and *bourride Provençale.* The daube consists of succulent chunks of beef braised in a rich red wine stock, enriched with various fresh vegetables, and well seasoned with herbs. The bourride is a savory fish stew richly spiced with garlic and a bouquet garni and served in a tureen on slices of fresh bread with the fish on the side. Gigot of tender alpine lamb is another specialty; the meat is perfumed with the fresh herbs of Provence. The chef is known for his *plats du jour,* which on our last visit included *lapin* (rabbit) chasseur, paella, osso buco, and couscous. If you're dining light, you might enjoy one of the omelets. Wines of Provence come by the half or full bottle. The brasserie is also a *glacier* during the afternoon, serving several different ice-cream specialties, milk shakes, and Irish coffee.

17 cours Mirabeau. ✆ **04-42-26-01-63.** Main courses 9.50€–14€; fixed-price menus 12€–24.70€. MC, V. Daily noon–2pm and 7pm–1am.

Le Bistro Latin ★ *Value* PROVENÇAL The best little bistro in Aix-en-Provence (for the price) is run by Bruno Ungaro and his partner, Gilles Holtz, who pride themselves on their fixed-price menus. They offer two intimate dining rooms, a street-level room and another in the cellar decorated in Greco-Latin style. The staff is young and enthusiastic, and Provençal music plays in the background. Try the chartreuse of mussels, one of the meat dishes with spinach-and-saffron/cream sauce, or crepe of hare with basil sauce. We've enjoyed the classic cuisine on all our visits, particularly the scampi risotto.

18 rue de la Couronne. ✆ **04-42-38-22-88.** Reservations recommended. Main courses 16€–21€; fixed-price menus 15€ lunch, 14€–17€ dinner. MC, V. Mon–Sat noon–2pm and 7–10:30pm.

AIX AFTER DARK

Aix is one of Provence's largest towns (after Marseille and Nice) and a university town to boot, making it a hotspot for animated nightlife.

Rockers go to **Le Mistral,** 3 rue Frédéric-Mistral (✆ **04-42-38-16-49**), where techno and house music blare long and loud. The cover is 16€. Its slightly more subdued competitor, **Le Richelm,** 24 rue de la Verrerie (✆ **04-42-23-49-29**), plays the same music but sometimes dips into 1970s and 1980s disco. Nearby is **The Red Clover**, 30 rue de la Verrerie (✆ **04-42-23-44-61**), where the good times roll, especially at happy hour from 6 to 8pm.

Less competitive and favored by those over 30 is the **Scat Club,** 11 rue de la Verrerie (✆ **04-42-23-00-23**), where a pianist and jazz trio provide music. It's open Tuesday through Saturday from 11pm, with live music beginning at 12:30am. It shuts down at 6am. The cover charge of 13€ includes your first drink.

13 Marseille ★★★

771km (479 miles) S of Paris; 187km (116 miles) SW of Nice; 31km (19 miles) S of Aix-en-Provence

Bustling Marseille, with more than a million inhabitants, is the second-largest city in France (its population surpassed that of Lyon in the early 1990s) and France's premier port. It's been called France's New Orleans. A crossroads of world traffic—Dumas called it "the meeting place of the entire world"—the city is ancient, founded by Greeks from the city of Phocaea, near present-day Izmir, Turkey, in the 6th century B.C. Marseille is a place of unique sounds, smells, and sights. It has seen wars and much destruction, but trade has always been its raison d'être.

Perhaps its most common association is with the national anthem of France, "La Marseillaise." During the Revolution, 500 volunteers marched to Paris, singing this rousing song along the way. The rest is history.

Although in many respects Marseille is big and sprawling, dirty and slumlike in many places, there's much elegance and charm here as well. The Vieux Port, the old harbor, is especially colorful, compensating to an extent for the dreary industrial dockland nearby. Marseille has always symbolized danger and intrigue, and that reputation is somewhat justified. However, the city is experiencing somewhat of a renaissance, and because it is now so easily reached by train from Paris, there is much hope for its future economy. Since the 1970s, a great deal of that economy has revolved around thousands upon thousands of North and sub-Saharan Africans who have poured into Marseille, creating a lively medley of races and creeds. One quarter of the present population of Marseille is of North African descent. These Africans have flocked here to find a better life than what they had in their own shattered lands.

Marseille today actually occupies twice the amount of land space as Paris, and its age-old problems remain, including a declining drug industry, smuggling, corruption (often at the highest levels), the Mafia, and racial tension. Unemployment, as always, is on the rise. But in spite of all these difficulties, it's a bustling, always fascinating city unlike any other in France. A city official proclaimed recently that "Marseille is the unbeloved child of France. It's attached to France, but has the collective consciousness of an Italian city-state, like Genoa or Venice."

ESSENTIALS

GETTING THERE The **airport** (✆ **04-42-14-14-14**), 28km (17 miles) northwest of the center, receives international flights from all over Europe. From the airport, blue-and-white minivans *(navettes)* make the trip to Marseille's St-Charles rail station, near the Vieux-Port, for a fee of 8€. The minivans run daily at 20-minute intervals, from 5:30am to 9:50pm.

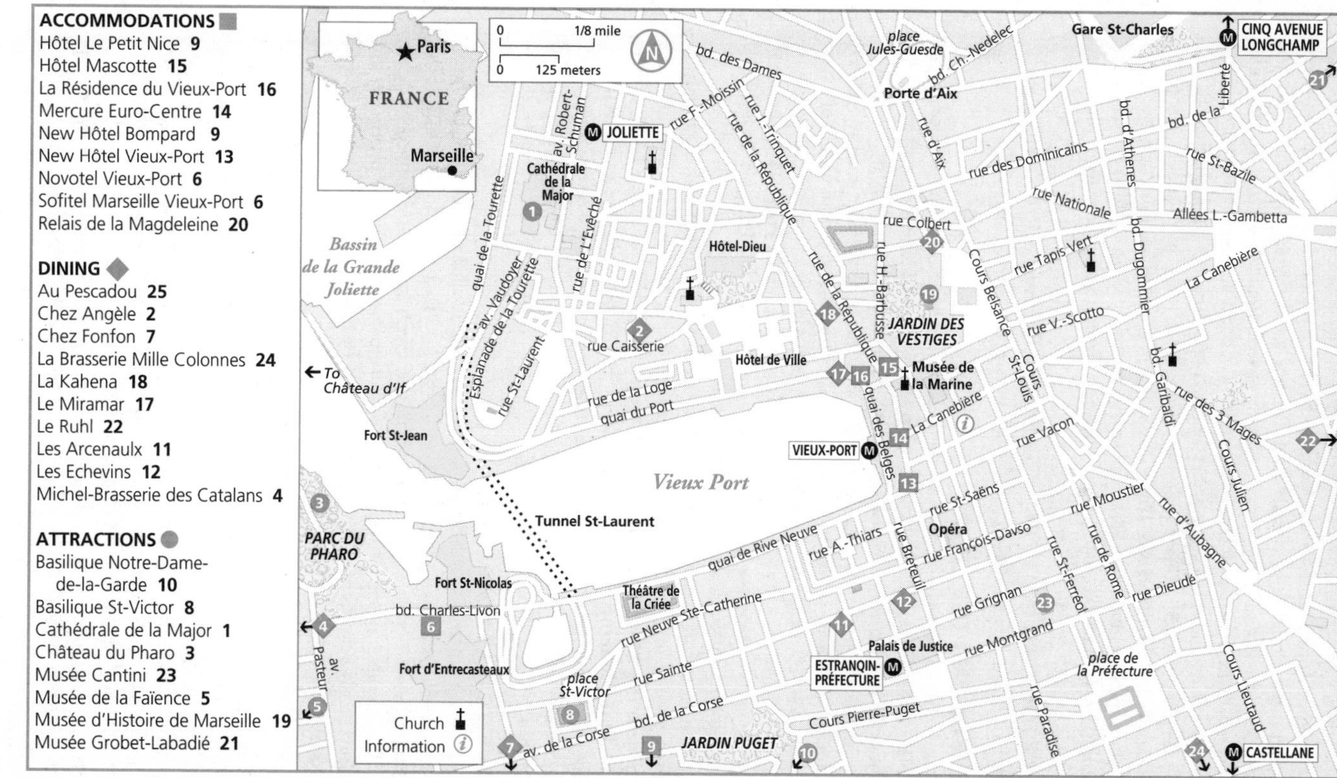
ACCOMMODATIONS
Hôtel Le Petit Nice 9
Hôtel Mascotte 15
La Résidence du Vieux-Port 16
Mercure Euro-Centre 14
New Hôtel Bompard 9
New Hôtel Vieux-Port 13
Novotel Vieux-Port 6
Sofitel Marseille Vieux-Port 6
Relais de la Magdeleine 20
DINING
Au Pescadou 25
Chez Angèle 2
Chez Fonfon 7
La Brasserie Mille Colonnes 24
La Kahena 18
Le Miramar 17
Le Ruhl 22
Les Arcenaulx 11
Les Echevins 12
Michel-Brasserie des Catalans 4
ATTRACTIONS
Basilique Notre-Dame-de-la-Garde 10
Basilique St-Victor 8
Cathédrale de la Major 1
Château du Pharo 3
Musée Cantini 23
Musée de la Faïence 5
Musée d'Histoire de Marseille 19
Musée Grobet-Labadié 21
Church
Information
FRANCE
Paris
Marseille
0 1/8 mile
0 125 meters
N
Bassin de la Grande Joliette
To Château d'If
Fort St-Jean
PARC DU PHARO
Fort St-Nicolas
Fort d'Entrecasteaux
bd. Charles-Livon
av. Pasteur
Vieux Port
Tunnel St-Laurent
Théâtre de la Criée
place St-Victor
JARDIN PUGET
av. de la Corse
bd. de la Corse
rue Sainte
rue Neuve Ste-Catherine
quai de Rive Neuve
Cours Pierre-Puget
ESTRANQIN-PRÉFECTURE
Palais de Justice
rue A.-Thiars
rue Breteuil
rue Grignan
rue Montgrand
rue Paradise
place de la Préfecture
rue St-Ferréol
rue François-Davso
Opéra
rue St-Saëns
rue de Rome
rue Dieudé
rue Moustier
rue d'Aubagne
Cours Lieutaud
CASTELLANE
Cours Julien
rue des 3 Mages
bd. Garibaldi
La Canebière
Allées L.-Gambetta
bd. Dugommier
bd. d'Athenes
rue St-Bazile
bd. de la Liberté
CINQ AVENUE LONGCHAMP
Gare St-Charles
rue Nationale
rue des Dominicains
rue Tapis Vert
rue V.-Scotto
Cours St-Louis
rue Vacon
Cours Belsance
rue d'Aix
Porte d'Aix
place Jules-Guesde
bd. Ch.-Nedelec
rue Colbert
rue H.-Barbusse
JARDIN DES VESTIGES
Musée de la Marine
quai des Belges
VIEUX-PORT
rue de la République
Hôtel de Ville
Hôtel-Dieu
rue J.-Trinquet
bd. des Dames
rue F.-Moissin
JOLIETTE
av. Robert-Schuman
Cathédrale de la Major
rue de L'Evêche
rue Caisserie
rue de la Loge
quai du Port
rue St-Laurent
Esplanade de la Tourette
av. Vaudoyer
quai de la Tourette

Marseille has **train** connections from hundreds of European cities, with especially good connections to and from Italy. The city is the terminus for the TGV bullet train, which departs daily from Paris's Gare de Lyon (trip time: 3 hr., 16 min.). Some Parisians now day-trip to the Mediterranean beaches at Marseille and return to the City of Light for dinner. Local trains leave Paris almost every hour, making a number of stops before reaching Marseille. For information, call ✆ **08-36-35-35-35. Buses** pull into Marseille at the Gare Routière, on place Victor Hugo (✆ **04-91-08-16-40**), adjacent to the St-Charles railway station.

If you're **driving** from Paris, follow A6 south to Lyon then continue south along A7 to Marseille. The drive takes about 7 hours. From towns in province, take A7 south to Marseille.

VISITOR INFORMATION The **Office de Tourisme** (Métro: Vieux-Port) is at 4 La Canebière (✆ **04-91-13-89-00;** www.marseille-tourisme.com).

EXPLORING THE CITY

Many visitors never bother to visit the museums, preferring to absorb the unique spirit of the city as reflected by its busy streets and at its sidewalk cafes, particularly those along the main street, **La Canebière.** Known as "can of beer" to World War II GIs, it's the spine and soul of Marseille, but the seediest main street in France. Lined with hotels, shops, and restaurants, the street is filled with sailors of every nation and a wide range of foreigners, especially Algerians, some of whom live in souklike conditions. La Canebière winds down to the **Vieux Port** ★★, dominated by the massive neoclassical forts of St-Jean and St-Nicholas. The port is filled with fishing craft and yachts and ringed with seafood restaurants.

Motorists can continue along to the **corniche Président-J.-F.-Kennedy,** a promenade running for about 5km (3 miles) along the sea. You pass villas and gardens along the way and have a good view of the Mediterranean. To the north, the **Port Moderne** (also known simply as "La Joliette," or "the gateway to the East") is a man-made labyrinth of nautical engineering. Its construction began in 1844, and a century later, the Germans destroyed it. Today it's one of the busiest ports in the Mediterranean.

THE TOP ATTRACTIONS

Basilique Notre-Dame-de-la-Garde This landmark church crowns a limestone rock overlooking the southern side of the Vieux-Port. It was built in the Romanesque-Byzantine style popular in the 19th century and topped by a 9m (30-ft.) gilded statue of the Virgin. Visitors come here not so much for the church as for the view—best seen at sunset—from its terrace. Spread out before you are the city, the islands, and the sea.

Rue Fort-du-Sanctuaire. ✆ **04-91-13-40-80.** Free admission. Daily 7am–7pm. Métro: Vieux-Port. Bus: 60.

Basilique St-Victor ★ For a city as ancient as Marseille, antique monuments are few, thanks to the waves of building that have always reflected this city's role as a major commercial center. This semifortified basilica is one of the most noteworthy. It was built above a crypt from the 5th-century foundation of the church and abbey founded by St. Cassianus. You can visit the crypt, which also reflects work done in the 10th and 11th centuries.

Place St-Victor. ✆ **04-96-11-22-60.** Admission to crypt 2€. Crypt daily 10am–7pm. Church daily 9am–7pm. Head west along quai de Rive-Neuve (near the Gare du Vieux-Port). Métro: Vieux-Port.

Cathédrale de la Major This was one of the largest cathedrals (some 135m/450 ft. long) built in Europe in the 19th century. Its interior is adorned

Moments Exploring the Massif des Calanques

You can visit the **Massif des Calanques,** a wild and rugged terrain, from either Marseille or Cassis. This craggy coastline lies between the two ports, directly south of Marseille and to the west of Cassis. With its highest peak at 555m (1,850 ft.), the Calanques stretch for some 20km (12½ miles) of dazzling limestone whiteness. This is one of France's great natural beauty areas.

Exactly what is a *calanque?* The word comes from the Provençal *cala,* meaning "steep slopes." Nature has cut steep coastal valleys into solid rock, creating rivers. Most of these gorges extend less than a kilometer inland from the Mediterranean. They're similar to fjords, created by glaciers, but these gorges have been created by the raging sea. The needlelike rocks and cliff faces overhanging the sea attract rock climbers and deep-sea divers.

In July and August, the **Société des Excursionnistes Marseillais,** 16 rue de la Rotonde (✆ **04-91-84-75-52**), conducts free walking tours of the Calanques twice a week. Call for information, since the days of these walking tours can vary depending on weather. This outfit also conducts boat trips daily in summer, leaving from quai des Belges in Marseille and costing 15€. Trips are conducted in a combination of French and English, and last for about 2½ hours.

The highlight of the Calanques is **Sormiou,** with its beach, seafood eateries, and small harbor. Sormiou is separated from another small but enchanting settlement at Morgiou by **Cap Morgiou,** which offers a panoramic belvedere with splendid views of both the Calanques and the eastern side of the massif. At **Morgiou** there are tiny creeks for swimming.

with mosaic floors and red-and-white marble banners, and the exterior is in a bastardized Romanesque-Byzantine style. The domes and cupolas might remind you of Istanbul. This vast pile has almost swallowed its 12th-century Romanesque predecessor (originally a baptistery) built on the ruins of a Temple of Diana.

Place de la Major. ✆ **04-91-13-49-80.** Free admission. Hours vary. Métro: Vieux-Port.

Musée des Beaux-Arts ★ One of the most scenic sights is Palais Longchamp, with its spectacular fountain and colonnade, built during the Second Empire. This museum, housed in a northern wing of the palace, displays a vast array of paintings from the 16th to the 19th century. They include works by Corot, Millet, Ingres, David, and Rubens. Some 80 sculptures and objets d'art were bequeathed to the museum as well; particularly interesting is a gallery of Pierre Puget sculpture. One salon is devoted to Honoré Daumier, born in Marseille in 1808.

In Palais Longchamp, on place Bernex. ✆ **04-91-14-59-30.** Admission 2€ adults, 1€ students and children 12–18. June–Sept Tues–Sun 11am–6pm; Oct–May Tues–Sun 10am–7pm. Métro: Cinq av. Longchamp or Réformés.

Musée Cantini ★ The temporary exhibitions of contemporary art staged here are often as good as the permanent collection. This museum is devoted to modern art, with masterpieces by Derain, Marquet, Ernst, Masson, Balthus, and others. It also owns a selection of works by important young international artists.

19 rue Grignan. ✆ **04-91-54-77-75.** Admission 3€ adults, 1.50€ students, free for seniors and ages 10 and under. Oct–May Tues–Sun 10am–5pm; June–Sept Tues–Sun 11am–6pm.

Musée de la Faïence This museum contains one of the largest collections of porcelain in France. Its collections date from Neolithic times to the present. Especially numerous are the delicate and richly ornate ceramics that graced the tables of local landowners during the 18th and 19th centuries. The museum is about 5km (3 miles) south of the center of Marseille, in a stately manor house (Château Pastré) that was built by a local ship owner in 1864.

In the Château Pastré, 157 av. de Montredon. ✆ **04-91-72-43-47.** 2€ adults, 1€ students and ages 11–18, free for children under 11. June–Sept Tues–Sun 11am–6pm; Oct–May Tues–Sun 10am–5pm.

Musée d'Histoire de Marseille You're allowed to wander through an archaeological garden where excavations are still going on, as scholars attempt to learn more about the ancient town of Massalia, founded by Greek sailors. Of course, many of the exhibits, such as old coins and fragments of pottery, only suggest their former glory. To help you more fully realize the era, you're aided by audiovisual exhibits and a free exhibition room. A medieval quarter of potters has been discovered, and the Louis XIV town is open to the public. You can also see what's left of a Roman wreck that was excavated from the site.

Centre Bourse, square Belsunce. ✆ **04-91-90-42-22.** Admission 2€ adults, 1€ students and children 11–18. Mon–Sat noon–7pm. Métro: Vieux-Port.

Musée d'Histoire Naturelle If you have the time to spare and you are already visiting Palais Longchamp, consider ducking into this museum for a half-hour or so. It is usually visited jointly with a visit to the more important Musée des Beaux-Arts. The museum lies in the right wing of the Palais Longchamp and offers a parade of the fossilized remains of the animals of Provence. The museum illustrates 400 million years of the natural history of Provence in its exhibits, including a safari section that shows the diversity of animals throughout the world. Of special interest to botany lovers is a gallery showcasing regional flora and fauna. On the lowest level, a Mediterranean aquarium is devoted to fish from the five continents.

In the Palais Longchamp, place Bernex. ✆ **04-91-14-59-50.** 3€ adults, 1.50€ students and ages 12–18, free for children under 12. Mid-June to Sept Tues–Sun 10am–5pm; Oct to mid-June Tues–Sun 11am–6pm.

Musée Grobet-Labadié ★ This private collection, bequeathed to the city in 1919, includes exquisite Louis XV and Louis XVI furniture, as well as an outstanding collection of medieval Burgundian and Provençal sculpture. Other exhibits are 17th-century Gobelin tapestries; 15th- to 19th-century German, Italian, French, and Flemish paintings; and 16th- and 17th-century Italian and French faience.

140 bd. Longchamp. ✆ **04-91-62-21-82.** Admission 2€ adults, 1€ students and children 11–18. Oct 1–May 31 Tues–Sun 10am–5pm; June 1–Sept 30 Tues–Sun 11am–6pm. Closed public holidays. Métro: Réformés.

PANORAMIC VIEWS

Basilique Notre-Dame-de-la-Garde, rue Fort-du-Sanctuaire (✆ **04-91-13-40-80**), crowns a limestone bluff overlooking the southern flank of the Vieux Port. Built in 1864 in the Romanesque-Byzantine style, and capped with a 9m (30-ft.)

gilded statue of the Virgin, it sits atop the foundations of a fortress that was commissioned during the Renaissance by French monarch François I. Although the architecture shows France's gilded age at its most evocative, visitors come here not so much for the church as for the view—best seen at sunset—from its terrace. Spread out before you are the city, the islands, and the sea. The church is open daily from mid-June to mid-September from 7am to 8pm, and the rest of the year from 7am to 7pm.

Another vantage point for a panoramic view is the **Parc du Pharo,** a promontory facing the entrance to the Vieux Port. Most people visit this park to escape the urban congestion of Marseille, but if you're in the mood for some history, check out the gray-stone facade of the **Château du Pharo** (✆ **04-91-14-64-95**). Built in the 1860s by Napoléon III for his empress, Eugénie (who is reputed not to have liked it and seldom visited), it's owned and maintained by the city of Marseille as a convention center and—less frequently—as a concert hall. The building has no regular hours, but if nothing is going on, you can enter the lobby and ask for a quick glance at the Salon des Génies.

BOATING TO CHATEAU D'IF ★★

From quai des Belges at the Vieux Port, you can take a ride to the infamous **Château d'If.** Boats leave the quai about every 60 to 90 minutes, depending on the season, for the 20-minute ride costing 8€. Contact the **Groupement des Armateurs Côtiers;** its office on quai des Belges (✆ **04-91-55-50-09**) is open daily from 7am to 7pm.

On the sparsely vegetated island of Château d'If (✆ **04-91-59-02-30**), François I built a fortress to defend Marseille and its port. The site later housed a state prison; carvings by Huguenot prisoners can still be seen inside some of the cells. Alexandre Dumas used the château as a setting for his novel *The Count of Monte Cristo.* The château is open Tuesday through Sunday April through September from 9am to 7pm, and October through March from 9am to 5:30pm. Admittance to the island costs 3.80€ for adults and 2.30€ for students and children 12 to 18. It's free for children under 12.

SHOPPING

Only Paris and Lyon can rival Marseille in breadth and diversity of merchandise. Your best bet is a trip to the Vieux Port and the streets surrounding it for a view of the folkloric objects that literally pop out of the boutiques.

ART & ANTIQUES The sunlight of Provence has always been cited by artists for its luminosity, and so Marseille has a handful of well-respected art galleries. The most internationally minded of the lot is **Galerie Roger-Pailhas,** 61 cours Julien (✆ **04-91-54-02-22**). Antiques from around Provence are sold at **Antiquités François-Décamp,** 302 rue Paradis (✆ **04-91-81-18-00**).

FASHION You don't normally think of Marseille as a place to go to shop for fashion, but the local fashion industry is booming. The fashion center is found along **Cours Julien,** where you'll find dozens of boutiques and ateliers. Much of the clothing reflects North African influences, although there is a vast array of French styles as well.

For hats, at **Felio,** 4 place Gabriel-Péri (✆ **04-91-90-32-67**), you'll find large-brimmed numbers that would've thrilled ladies of the Belle Epoque or guests at a stylish wedding inspired in the 1920s by Lanvin. There's a selection of *casquettes Marseillaises* (developed for men as protection from the *soleil du Midi*) and berets that begin at 22.80€.

FOLKLORE & SOUVENIRS Especially popular are the ***santons*** (carved wooden crèche figurines). The best place for acquiring these artifacts is just above the Vieux Port, behind the Théâtre National de la Criée. At **Ateliers Marcel Carbonel,** 47 rue Neuve-Ste-Catherine (© **04-91-54-26-58**), more than 600 figures, available in half a dozen sizes, sell at prices beginning at 9.80€.

All the souvenir shops along the pedestrian **rue St-Féréol,** running perpendicular to La Canebière, sell folkloric replicas of handcrafts from Old Provence, including the cream-colored or pale-green bars of the city's local soap, **savon de Marseille.** Infused with a healthy dollop of olive oil, it's known for its kindness to skin dried out by the sun and mistral. A large selection is available at **La Savonnerie du Sérail,** 50 bd. Anatole de la Forge (© **04-91-98-28-25**).

FOOD & CHOCOLATE At **Amandine,** 69 bd. Eugène-Pierre (© **04-91-47-00-83**), a photograph or a work of graphic art can be reproduced in various shades of chocolate on top of a delicious layer cake in any flavor you specify in advance. If you don't happen to have your scrapbook with you, you can buy a cake emblazoned with scenes of the Vieux Port or whatever. More traditional pastries and chocolates are found at **Puyricard,** 25 rue Francis-Davso (© **04-91-54-26-25**), with another location at 155 rue Jean-Mermoz (© **04-91-77-94-11**). The treats available here include chocolates stuffed with almond paste *(paté d'amande)* or *confits de fruits,* along with a type of biscuit called *une Marseillotte.*

Since medieval times, Marseille has thrived on the legend of Les Trois Maries—three saints named Mary who, assisted by awakened-from-the-dead St. Lazarus, reportedly came ashore at a point near Marseille to Christianize ancient Provence. In commemoration of their voyage, small boat-shaped cookies called ***les navettes*** are flavored with secret ingredients (that include orange zest, orange-flower water, and sugar); they are forever associated with Marseille. They're sold throughout the city, notably at **Le Four des Navettes,** 136 rue Sainte (© **04-91-33-32-12**). It opened in 1791 and is dedicated to perpetuating the city's most cherished medieval myth and ferociously guarding the secret of how the pastries are made. The boat-shaped cookies are sold for 6.80€ per dozen.

One of the city's most sophisticated emporiums for takeout food is **La Fromagerie Marrou,** 2 bd. Baille (© **04-91-78-17-68**). Established in 1902 and known as one of the most comprehensive upscale food stores in Marseille, it sells more than just cheeses: meats, baked goods, deli items, wines, liqueurs, foie gras, and caviar. With a main branch at 2 bd. Baille, the shop maintains secondary branches at 475 rue Paradis and 15 place Castellane.

A MARSEILLE MALL Looking for something that approximates, with a Provençal accent, a sun-flooded mall in California? Head for the most talked-about real-estate development in the city's recent history, **L'Escale Borély,** avenue Mendès-France. Within a 25-minute transit (take the Métro to rond-point du

---

Tips **A Day at the Beach**

Bus no. 83 leaves from the Vieux-Port heading for the public beaches outside Marseille. This bus will take you to both **plage du Prado** and **plage de la Corniche,** the best bets for swimming and sunning. The sands are a bit gray and sometimes rocky, but the beaches are wide and the water is generally clear. These beaches are set against a scenic backdrop of the cliffs of Marseille.

Prado and then transfer to bus no. 19) south of Marseille, it incorporates shops, cafes, bars, and restaurants. Note the newest fad from your seat on a terrace as you sip pastis: in-line skating. For more on L'Escale Borély, see "Marseille After Dark," below.

WHERE TO STAY

VERY EXPENSIVE

Sofitel Marseille Vieux-Port ★★★ This hotel lacks the glamour and style of Petit Nice, but it is the highest government-rated hotel in the city center, a seven-story palace standing above the embankments of the old port. Some of the guest rooms have panoramic views of the port of Old Marseille; others look out on the boulevard. All are fairly generous in size, up-to-date, comfortable, and furnished in Provençal style. In 1987, its owner, the Accor hotel giant, turned over 90 rooms to a new Novotel (see below). Today two entrances, staffs, and dining facilities coexist in the same building.

36 bd. Charles-Livon, 13007 Marseille. ✆ **04-91-15-59-00.** Fax 04-91-15-59-50. www.sofitel.com. 130 units. 195€–335€ double; 645€–975€ suite. AE, DC, MC, V. Parking 14€. Métro: Vieux-Port. **Amenities:** Restaurant; bar; 24-hr. room service; laundry service; dry cleaning. *In room:* A/C, TV, minibar, hair dryer.

EXPENSIVE

Hôtel Le Petit Nice ★★★ This is the best in Marseille, with the finest restaurant. The Résidence opened in 1917 when the Passédat family joined two villas. The narrow approach takes you past what looks like a row of private villas, in a secluded area below the street paralleling the beach. Rooms are decorated with tasteful fabrics and quality carpeting, and all come equipped with fine beds. Units in the main house are modern and even avant-garde—four units were inspired by Cubism and have geometric appointments and bright colors. The spacious Marina Wing across from the main building offers individually decorated rooms in the antique style, opening onto sea views. Marble bathrooms are quite sumptuous and come with deluxe toiletries.

The beautiful glass-enclosed restaurant has a view of the shore and the rocky islands off the coast. In summer, dinner is served in the garden facing the sea. It's run by Gerald Passédat, whose imaginative culinary successes include sliced sea wolf in the style of the Passédat family matriarch, Lucy; vinaigrette of *rascasse* (hogfish); and sea devil with saffron and garlic.

Corniche Président-J.-F.-Kennedy/Anse-de-Maldormé, 13007 Marseille. ✆ **04-91-59-25-92.** Fax 04-91-59-28-08. www.relaischateaux.com. 16 units. 119€–260€ double; 610€–790€ suite. AE, DC, MC, V. Free parking. Closed 3 weeks in Nov. Métro: Vieux-Port. **Amenities:** Restaurant; bar; pool; limited room service; laundry service. *In room:* A/C, TV, minibar, hair dryer, safe.

MODERATE

La Résidence du Vieux-Port Old-fashioned, with a touch of raffish charm and an unbeatable location directly beside the harbor, this eight-story hotel's guest rooms have loggia-style terraces opening onto the port. They are simple but serviceable, with comfortable mattresses. A restoration was completed in 1997. The conscientious staff tends to guests appropriately.

18 quai du Port, 13001 Marseille. ✆ **04-91-91-91-22.** Fax 04-91-56-60-88. 41 units. 115.50€–152€ double; 169€–199€ suite. AE, DC, MC, V. Parking 6€. Métro: Vieux-Port. **Amenities:** Cafe, bar; limited room service; laundry service. *In room:* A/C, TV, minibar.

Mercure Euro-Centre One of the most modern hotels in town, this bronze building looks out over the Greco-Roman ruins of the Jardin des Vestiges, a 2-minute walk from the Old Port and near a collection of boutiques, the Centre

Bourse. The well-kept rooms are furnished in a functional chain-style format, with twin or double beds. Tiled bathrooms are compact but have adequate shelf space. There is a restaurant on the grounds where many of Marseille's shoppers go. Many staff members speak English.

Rue Neuve-St-Martin, 13001 Marseille. ✆ **04-97-17-22-22.** Fax 04-91-56-24-57. 199 units. 82€–123.50€ double; 160€–229€ suite. AE, DC, MC, V. Parking 10€. Métro: Colbert. **Amenities:** Restaurant; bar; limited room service; laundry service. *In room:* A/C, TV, minibar, hair dryer.

New Hôtel Vieux-Port *Value* Located close to the port, in a six-story turn-of-the-20th-century building that was completely renovated between 1994 and 1997, this hotel offers comfortable rooms and a hardworking, English-speaking staff. Rooms that overlook the port are outfitted in a traditional way; the more contemporary-looking accommodations look out over the commercial neighborhood nearby. This hotel offers exceptional value for Marseille, although most of the accommodations are small. Each comes with a firm mattress on twin or double beds; bathrooms are compact but well cared for.

3 bis rue Reine-Elisabeth, 13001 Marseille. ✆ **04-91-99-23-23.** Fax 04-91-90-76-24. www.newhotelvieuxport.activehotels.com. 47 units. 115€–135€ double. Children under 11 stay free. Parking 15€. Bus: 83. Metro: Vieux-Port. **Amenities:** Restaurant; bar; lounge; steam room; health club; spa; laundry service; dry cleaning. *In room:* A/C, TV, minibar, hair dryer.

Novotel Vieux-Port *Value* In the same building as the more upscale Sofitel (see above), this Novotel dates from 1987. Bedrooms are outfitted in a chain-hotel format—services are less extensive, amenities are less plush, and spaces a bit more cramped than those at the Sofitel, but this is one of the most reasonably priced, good-value hotels in town. Each room contains both a double and a single bed (which also serves as a couch) and a desk, and has an efficiently designed bathroom. The rooms overlooking the old port tend to fill up first. The lattice-decorated restaurant (Côte Jardin) serves solid and basic meals.

36 bd. Charles-Livon, 13007 Marseille. ✆ **04-96-11-42-11.** Fax 04-96-11-42-20. H0911@accor-hotels.com. 90 units. 120€–150€ double. AE, DC, MC, V. Parking 10€. Métro: Vieux-Port. **Amenities:** Restaurant; bar; limited room service; laundry service. *In room:* A/C, TV, minibar.

INEXPENSIVE

Hôtel Mascotte Everything about this hotel evokes the tenuous grandeur of 19th-century port life in Marseille. It's less than 2 blocks from the inner sanctums of the Vieux-Port, behind a battered beaux-arts facade whose ornate corbels and cornices have seen the sun and mistrals of many, many seasons. Inside, a series of renovations have stripped the bedrooms of some of their old-fashioned charm but have left behind clean, efficient, soundproofed spaces that are sometimes larger than you might expect. Each accommodation is well maintained and equipped, with twin or double beds. Bathrooms are small but tidily kept. Breakfast is the only meal served, but considering the many dining options in the surrounding neighborhood, no one seems to care.

5 la Canebière, 13001 Marseille. ✆ **04-91-90-61-61.** Fax 04-91-90-95-61. 45 units. 78€–88€ double. AE, DC, MC, V. Parking in nearby public lot 12€. *In room:* A/C, TV.

New Hôtel Bompard *Finds* This tranquil retreat is set atop a cliff along the corniche, about 2.5km (1½ miles) east of Vieux Port. Partly because of its elegant garden, it might remind you of a well-appointed private home. Bedrooms have conservatively traditional furniture, tasteful and subdued color schemes, and balconies or terraces overlooking the grounds. Comfortable beds are fitted with firm mattresses and quality linen. The small bathrooms have just adequate shelf space. There's a bistro on the premises, Le Lautrec, which serves a pleasant meal.

2 rue des Flots-Bleus, 13007 Marseille. ✆ **04-91-99-22-22.** Fax 04-91-31-02-14. www.new-hotel.com. 48 units. 85€–108€ in main building; 170€–200€ in Provençal *mas.* Free parking. Bus: 61 or 83. *In room:* A/C, TV, minibar.

WHERE TO DINE

EXPENSIVE

Chez Fonfon ★ *Finds* PROVENÇAL/FRENCH This is one of the legendary restaurants of Marseille, with a clientele of famous actors and cinemas that included John Wayne and Yves Montand in the 1950s and 1960s, and a bevy of newer, mostly French stars during the late 1990s. Its founder, a formidable but funny chef named Fonfon, died in 1998, and since then, the place has been capably handled by his great-nephew, Alexandre Pinna. Expect a location directly fronting the Port du Vallon des Auffes, a harbor for fishing boats that's within a 20-minute walk east of the more famous Vieux Port; a decor inspired by the furnishings and colors (ochres and russets) of the midsummer Provençal landscape; and the kind of earthy, savory cuisine that many Marseillais remember from their childhoods. Examples include filet of bull braised in red wine; a savory bouillabaisse; all kinds of fish, sometimes grilled, sometimes baked in a salt crust and served on a slab of hot stone; and different variations of Provençal lamb. Appropriate starters for a meal here include fish soup, a medley of stuffed vegetables *(les petits farcis),* and fresh baby octopus, either grilled or fried.

140 rue du Vallon des Auffes, Port du Vallon des Auffes. ✆ **04-91-52-14-38.** Reservations recommended. Main courses 20€–45€; fixed-price menus 32€–50€. AE, DC, MC, V. Tues–Sat noon–2pm; Mon–Sat 7:15–10pm. Metro: Vieux-Port.

Le Miramar ★★★ SEAFOOD Since the mid-1960s, aficionados of bouillabaisse have been flocking here for a taste of the famous savory fish soup. When you try it here, you might exclaim, "Ah, bouillabaisse!" Savoring the delights of this fine restaurant will be one of the culinary highlights of your trip. It's hard to imagine that bouillabaisse was once a rough-and-tumble recipe favored by local fisherfolk. It was actually devised as a way of using the least desirable portion of their catch. Actually, it's two dishes—beginning with a saffron-tinted soup followed by the various fish poached in the soup. It's consumed with a large dollop of *rouille,* a sauce of red chilies, garlic, olive oil, egg yolk, and cayenne. For the version served here, the chef considers rascasse or hogfish essential but views lobster as a "silly frill that adds nothing to the soup but plenty to the bill." The setting is a large, big-windowed room with frescoes of underwater life, linked to an outdoor terrace that overlooks Marseille's most famous church, Notre-Dame-de-la-Garde.

12 quai du Port. ✆ **04-91-91-10-40.** Reservations recommended. Main courses 31€–48€; bouillabaisse 65€ per person (minimum 2 persons). AE, DC, MC, V. Tues–Sat noon–2:30pm and 7–9:30pm. Closed 2 weeks in Jan and 3 weeks in Aug. Métro: Vieux-Port/Hôtel de Ville.

Michel-Brasserie des Catalans ★ SEAFOOD Although it's decorated with shellacked lobsters and starfish, this restaurant serves a fine bouillabaisse. Just beyond the Parc du Pharo, next to the Old Port, it's one of the best old-time restaurants in town. The cooking emphasizes the taste of the seafood rather than fancy sauces. In addition to the bouillabaisse, it offers a good *bourride* (fish stew with aïoli sauce). The waiter brings you an array of fresh fish from which you make your selection. There's a kind of raffish insouciance here that you might find very appealing.

6 rue des Catalans. ✆ **04-91-52-30-63.** Reservations recommended. Main courses 32.20€–43€. AE, DC, MC, V. Daily noon–2pm and 7:30–10pm. Bus: 81 or 83.

MODERATE

Au Pescadou ★ SEAFOOD This is one of Marseille's finest seafood restaurants. It's now run by the three multilingual sons of the original owner, Barthélémy Mennella. The venue is rough-edged but civil. Beside a busy traffic circle downtown, it overlooks a fountain and a sidewalk display of fresh oysters. For an appetizer, try almond-stuffed mussels or "hors d'oeuvres of the fisherman." Main-dish specialties are bouillabaisse, *gigot de lotte* (monkfish stewed in cream sauce with fresh vegetables), and scallops cooked with morels.

Adjacent to the main restaurant, and under the same management, is an informal newcomer, **La Brasserie Mille Colonnes,** 21 place Castellane (✆ **04-91-78-18-10**). Bustling and gregarious, it serves platters of grilled fish as well as blanquettes of veal, steak *(a bac),* and pastas. Full meals, without wine, rarely exceed 24.50€; *plats du jour* cost from 7.25€ to 10.20€.

19 place Castellane. ✆ **04-91-78-36-01.** Reservations recommended. Main courses 12.75€–19.50€; bouillabaisse 38€ per person; fixed-price menus 25€–32.50€. AE, DC, MC, V. Mon–Sat noon–2pm and 7–11pm; Sun noon–2pm. Closed July–Aug. Métro: Castellane.

Le Ruhl ★★ *Finds* SEAFOOD Since 1940, this restaurant has offered two versions of bouillabaisse that have wowed gastronomes with their flavor. Set about 3km (2 miles) east of the Vieux-Port, across the boulevard from a rocky stretch of seacoast, it offers two blue-and-white dining rooms, lots of varnished mahogany and polished brass, and seats that never come without some kind of sea view. Alex Galligani, the owner, recently drafted the *Charte de la Bouillabaisse Marseillaise,* which stipulates that a proper bouillabaisse must contain at least four types of fish, including guarnard, John Dory, anglerfish, chapon, conger, and scorpion fish. All of these are present within the standard-issue "bouillabaisse de pecheur" served here, and within the "bouillabaisse homard" you'll get chunks of lobster meat as well. The other distinctive specialty of this place is grilled fish, almost every kind that lives in the Mediterranean, a display of whose raw ingredients greets you near the restaurant's entrance.

269 Corniche Président-J.-F.-Kennedy. ✆ **04-91-52-01-77.** Reservations recommended. Main courses 17.20€–24.50€; bouillabaisse 37.50€–47.50€. AE, V. Daily noon–2:30pm and 8–10pm. Metro: Vieux-Port, then take bus for 3km (2 miles) east.

Les Arcenaulx ★ *Finds* PROVENÇAL These bulky stone premises were built by the navies of Louis XIV. Close to the water near the Vieux Port, they contain this restaurant and two bookstores (one for French classics, one for modern titles), all directed by the hardworking and charming sisters Simone and Jeanne Laffitte. Look for authentic and hearty Provençal cuisine with a Marseillais accent. Dishes include a *baudroie à la Raimu*—a kettle of seasonal fish, named for a popular 20th-century actor (similar to bouillabaisse). Equally tempting are artichokes *barigoule* (loaded with aromatic spices and olive oil), a charlotte of crabs, and a worthy assortment of *petites légumes farcies* (Provençal vegetables stuffed with chopped meat and herbs).

25 cours d'Estienne d'orves. ✆ **04-91-59-80-30.** Reservations recommended. Main courses 20€–32€; fixed-price menus 24€–48€. AE, DC, MC, V. Mon–Sat noon–2pm and 8–10:30pm. Métro: Vieux-Port.

Les Echevins PROVENÇAL/SOUTHWESTERN FRENCH On the opposite side of the building from Les Arcenaulx (see above), this restaurant occupies what was once a dorm for the prisoners forced to row the ornamental barges of Louis XIV during his inspections of Marseille's harbor. Today it contains chandeliers, plush carpets, antiques, and massive rocks and thick beams. You'll get a lot for your money, as the owners charge relatively reasonable prices and use very fresh ingredients. Provençal dishes include a succulent version of baked sea wolf prepared as simply as possible—with herbs and olive oil. There's also roast codfish with aïoli and a delicious *baudroie* (a simpler bouillabaisse). Desserts usually include roasted figs served with sweet dessert wine.

44 rue Sainte. ✆ **04-96-11-03-11.** Reservations recommended. Main courses 15€–42€; fixed-price menus 32€–45€. AE, DC, MC, V. Mon–Fri noon–2:30pm and 7:30–11:30pm; Sat 7:30–11:30pm. Métro: Vieux-Port.

INEXPENSIVE

Chez Angèle PROVENÇAL/PIZZA A local friend guided us here, and though most of Marseille's cheap eating places aren't recommendable, this one is worthwhile if you're watching your euros. Small and unpretentious, with a raffish kind of amiability on the part of the owner, it's a pizzeria-restaurant, with a menu more comprehensive than usual. Pizza (the best are pistou, fresh seafood, or cèpes), well-prepared ravioli, tagliatelle, osso buco, and grilled shrimp, squid, and daurade Provençal style are available. For something really ethnic, ask for Francis's version of *pieds et paquets,* a country recipe savored by locals—equal portions of grilled sheep's foot and sheep's intestines stuffed with garlic-flavored bread crumbs, herbs, and chopped vegetables. Note that this place lies on the route between Marseille and Aix.

50 rue Caisserie. ✆ **04-91-90-63-35.** Reservations recommended. Pizzas, pastas, and salads 8.20€–16€; fixed-price menu 22.50€. MC, V. Mon–Fri noon–2:30pm and daily 7–11pm. Closed July 20–Aug 20. Métro: Vieux-Port.

La Kahena TUNISIAN This is one of the busiest and most-respected Tunisian restaurants in a city that's loaded with worthy competitors. Established in 1976 and set close to the Old Port, it's a two-room enclave of savory North African aromas: minced or grilled lamb, tomatoes, eggplant, herbs, and couscous, so beloved by Tunisian expatriates. The menu lists 10 varieties of couscous, including versions with lamb, chicken, fish, the savory sausages known as *merguez,* and a "complete" version that includes a little bit of each of those ingredients. Also look for *méchoui,* a succulent version of roasted lamb. The restaurant's name, incidentally, derives from a 6th-century B.C. Tunisian princess who was legendary for uniting all the Berber tribes of North Africa.

2 rue de la République. ✆ **04-91-90-61-93.** Reservations recommended. Main courses 10.70€–16€. MC, V. Daily noon–2:30pm and 7:30–11pm. Métro: Vieux-Port.

NEARBY ACCOMMODATIONS & DINING

Relais de la Magdeleine ★ *Finds* In a stone-sided, early-18th-century country mansion at the foot of the Ste-Baume mountain range, this hotel is surrounded by large homes, open fields, and woodlands, while still near the beach. It's near the venerated spot where, according to medieval legend, Mary Magdalene is believed to have died. The inn has striking architectural details; note a carving of St. Roch, with his dog above the entrance. The decor is upscale, with antiques and worthy reproductions. Guest rooms are individually furnished, in Directoire, Provençal, and Louis styles. Bathrooms are neatly kept.

The relais also serves savory and well-prepared meals. Specialties include lamb cooked with Provençal honey and thyme, and filet of sole Beau with red wine butter and a fondue of leeks.

Route d'Aix, 13420 Gemenos. ✆ **04-42-32-20-16.** Fax 04-42-32-02-26. www.relais-magdeleine.com. 24 units. 95€–185€ double; 190€–215€ suite. AE, MC, V. Free parking. Closed Dec–Mar 15. Head east of Marseille for 24km (15 miles) along A50. **Amenities:** Restaurant; bar; lounge; pool; nearby golf course; nearby tennis courts; laundry service; dry cleaning. *In room:* TV, hair dryer.

MARSEILLE AFTER DARK

You can get an amusing (and relatively harmless) exposure to the town's saltiness during a walk around the **Vieux-Port,** where a medley of cafes and restaurants angle their sightlines for the best view of the harbor.

Escale Borély, avenue Mendès-France, is a modern-day equivalent of the Vieux-Port. It's a waterfront development south of the town center, only 20 minutes away by bus no. 83. About a dozen cafes as well as restaurants of every possible ilk present a wide choice of cuisines, plus views of in-line skaters on the promenade in front and the potential for dialogues with friendly strangers.

Unless the air-conditioning is powerful, Marseille's dance clubs produce a lot of sweat. The best of them is the **Café de la Plage,** in the Escale Borély (© **04-91-71-21-76**), where a 35-and-under crowd dances in an environment that's safer and healthier than many of the competitors'. Closer to the Vieux-Port, you can dance and drink at the **Metal Café,** 20 rue Fortia (© **04-91-54-03-03**), where 20- to 50-year-olds listen to music that's been recently released in London and Los Angeles; or try the nearby **Trolley Bus,** 24 quai de Rive-Neuve (© **04-91-54-30-45**), best known for its techno, house, hip-hop, jazz, and salsa. Also very appealing, if only because people here seem to have more fun than at the usual run-of-the-mill pastis dive, is **Pêle-Mêle,** 8 place aux Huiles (© **04-91-54-85-26**), a many-faceted bar/disco/cafe and host of occasional live music.

If you miss free-form modern jazz and don't mind taking your chances in the less than completely savory neighborhood adjacent to the city's rail station (La Gare St-Charles—a taxi here and back is recommended), consider dropping into **La Cave à Jazz,** rue Bernard-du-Bois (© **04-91-39-28-28**).

A cabaret that presents sexy performers, broad humor, and occasional political satire is **Le Chocolat Théâtre,** 59 cours Julien (© **04-91-42-19-29**), which also involves a restaurant. The venue and hours change weekly, so phone in advance.

The gay scene here isn't as interesting as it is in Nice, though there are a number of gay bars. **MP Bar,** 10 rue Beauveau (© **04-91-33-64-79**), is *le gay bar* in Marseille. It's open nightly from 6pm to sunrise. A rival gay bar, **L'Enigme,** 22 rue Beauvau (© **04-91-33-79-20**), attracts a clientele mainly of young men, with an occasional lipstick lesbian showing up. On Friday and Saturday nights there is house, techno, and dance music played by hip, hot DJs. Action goes on daily until 5am. The youth-conscious **New Can Can,** 3–5 rue Sénac (© **04-91-48-59-76**), is an enormous venue that is everybody's favorite dance spot Thursday through Sunday from around 11pm to dawn. On Friday it's free before midnight; after that, a 13€ cover charge is imposed. On Saturday there's an 8€ cover charge, rising to 14€ after midnight.

14 Toulon

835km (519 miles) S of Paris; 127km (79 miles) SW of Cannes; 68km (42 miles) E of Marseille

This fortress and modern town is the principal naval base of France: the headquarters of the Mediterranean fleet, with hundreds of sailors wandering the streets. With its beautiful harbor, it's surrounded by hills and crowned by forts. A large breakwater protects it on the east, and the great peninsula of Cap Sicié is on the west. Separated by the breakwater, the outer roads are known as the Grande Rade, and the inner roads are the Petite Rade. On the outskirts is a winter resort colony. Like Marseille, the population of Toulon has grown because of the large influx of people from North Africa, especially French-speaking Algeria, which was once a part of France before it broke away.

Toulon

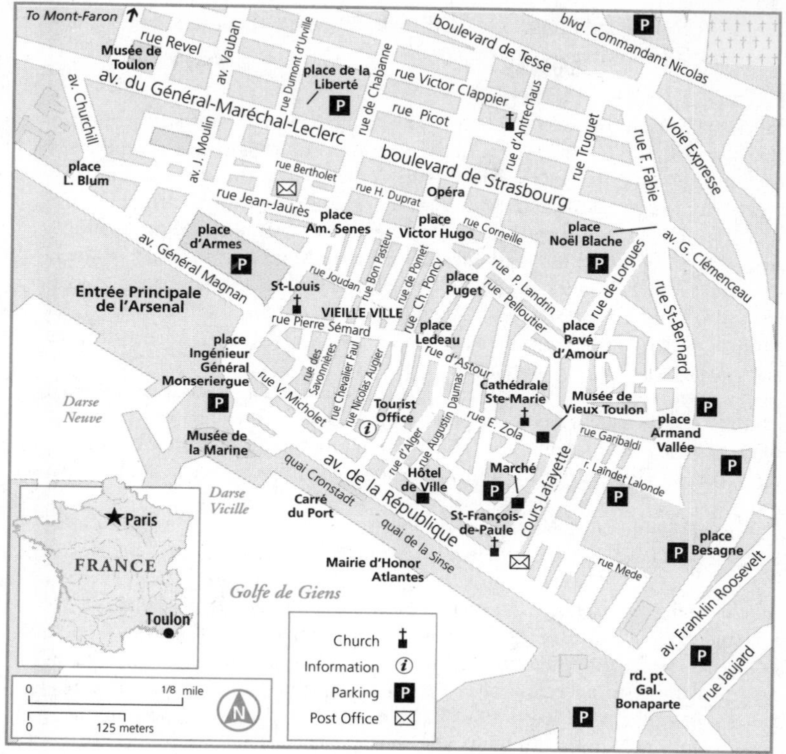

Note that there's racial tension here, worsened by the closing of the shipbuilding yards. There are no particular dangers to tourists that one wouldn't find in any Mediterranean port, be it Barcelona or Genoa. However, caution at night is always advised, especially in the immediate port area.

Park your vehicle underground at place de la Liberté; then go along boulevard des Strasbourg, turning right onto rue Berthelot. This will take you into the pedestrian zone in the core of the old city, centered on the rue d'Alger. This area is filled with shops, hotels, restaurants, and cobblestone streets but can be dangerous at night. The best beach, Plage du Mourillon, is 2km (1¼ miles) east of the heart of town.

ESSENTIALS

GETTING THERE & GETTING AROUND **Trains** arrive from Marseille about every 30 minutes (trip time: 1 hr.). If you're on the Riviera, frequent trains arrive from Nice (2 hr.) and Cannes (80 min.). For rail information and schedules, call © **08-36-35-35-35.**

Three **buses** per day arrive from Aix-en-Provence (trip time: 75 min.). For information, call Ste. Comet at **04-42-91-26-80.**

If you're **driving** from Marseille, take A50 east to Toulon. When you arrive, park your car and get around on foot, as the *vieille ville* (old town) and most attractions are easy to reach. A municipal **bus** system serves the town as well. A bus map is available at the tourist office. For information, call **04-94-03-87-03.**

VISITOR INFORMATION The **Office de Tourisme** is at place Raimu (✆ **04-94-18-53-00;** www.toulontourisme.com).

EXPLORING THE TOWN

In **Vieux Toulon,** between the harbor and boulevard des Strasbourg (the main axis of town), are many remains of the port's former days. The site where the city's raffish and gutsy style might best be appreciated is the open-air fruit and vegetable market, **Le Marché,** which spills over onto the narrow, plantain-lined streets around cours Lafayette every morning from 7:30am till around 2:30pm. Also in Old Toulon is the **Cathédrale Ste-Marie-Majeure (St. Mary Major),** rue Emile Zola (✆ **04-92-92-28-91**), which was built in the Romanesque style in the 11th and 12th centuries and then much expanded in the 17th century. Its badly lit nave is Gothic, and the belfry and facade are from the 18th century. It's open daily from 8am to noon and 2 to 6pm.

In contrast to the cathedral, tall modern buildings line **quai Stalingrad,** opening onto Vieille d'Arse. On **place Puget,** look for the atlantes (caryatids), figures of men used as columns. These interesting figures support a balcony at the Hôtel de Ville (city hall) and are also included in the facade of the naval museum.

The **Musée de la Marine,** place du Ingénieur-Général-Monsenergue (✆ **04-94-02-02-01**), contains many figureheads and ship models. It's open Wednesday through Monday July and August from 10am to 6pm, and September through June from 9:30am to noon and 2 to 6pm. Admission is 4.60€ for adults and 3€ for students. The **Musée de Toulon,** 113 bd. du Général-Maréchal-Leclerc (✆ **04-94-36-81-00**), shows works from the 16th century to the present. There's a particularly good collection of Provençal and Italian paintings, as well as religious works. The latest acquisitions include New Realism pieces and minimalist art. It's open daily from 1 to 6pm; admission is free.

Somewhat less interesting is the **Musée du Vieux Toulon,** 69 cours Lafayette (✆ **04-94-62-11-07**), which is not to be confused with the above-mentioned Musée de Toulon. Its exhibits pertain to the role of commerce, shipbuilding, and the French military during the development of Toulon, with a tableaux of the historic figures who either protected or fostered its growth from medieval times to the present. It's open Monday through Saturday from 2 to 6pm. Entrance is free.

PANORAMAS & VIEWS

We suggest taking a drive, an hour or two before sunset, along the **corniche du Mont-Faron.** It's a scenic boulevard along the lower slopes of Mont Faron, providing views of the busy port, the town, the cliffs, and, in the distance, the Mediterranean.

For a panoramic view over the dry, sun-flooded landscapes, consider boarding a **funicular** (✆ **04-94-92-68-25** for information), which departs from a point on the boulevard l'Amiral Vence near the Hotel La Tour Blanche. The *téléphérique* (cable car) operates daily from 9 to 11:45am and 2:15 to 6:30pm, costing 5.80€ for adults and 4€ for children round-trip. Once you get to the top, enjoy the view and then visit the **Memorial du Débarquement en Provence,** Mont Faron (✆ **04-94-88-08-09**), which, among other exhibits, documents the Allied landings in Provence in 1944. It's open in summer daily from 9:30 to 11:45am and 2:30 to 5:45pm; in winter, it's open Tuesday through Sunday from 9:30 to 11:30am and 2 to 4:30pm. Admission is 3.80€ for adults, 1.50€ for children 5 to 12, and free for children 4 and under.

WHERE TO STAY

Hôtel La Corniche An attractive hotel near the town's beaches, with an interior garden, La Corniche offers a pleasant staff, two restaurants, and comfortable accommodations. Those at the front have sea views and loggias, and are more expensive. Room decoration is in Provençal style. The more formal of the two restaurants is the Bistro; it features a trio of pine trees growing upward through the roof and a large bay window overlooking the port. The simpler restaurant is the cramped but cozy Rôtisserie, which is under a different management. Both emphasize fish among their offerings. A fairly good but limited wine list complements the food, which is perfectly adequate and much improved in recent years. You'll find this place in the neighborhood known as Le Mourillon, a 15-minute walk from the congested commercial center of Toulon.

17 Littoral Frédéric-Mistral (at Le Mourillon), 83000 Toulon. ✆ **800/528-1234** in the U.S., or 04-94-41-35-12. Fax 04-94-41-24-58. www.hotel-corniche.com. 23 units. 78€–115€ double; 105€–185€ suite. AE, DC, MC, V. Parking 9€. Bus: 3, 13, or 23. **Amenities:** 2 restaurants; bar; limited room service; laundry service. *In room:* A/C, TV, minibar, hair dryer.

Hôtel Maritima The most decent bargain hotel in Toulon stands near the railway station and Jardin Alexandre-1er. Built in the late 1800s, it has been frequently renovated and altered over the years. Furnishings are blandly traditional but serviceable; it's modest but well maintained. The mattresses have slept many guests but are still reasonably comfortable. Bathrooms are small and short on shelf space, and have rather thin towels but are tidily maintained. There's no restaurant, although several lie right outside the door. Only breakfast is served on-site.

9 rue Gimelli, 83000 Toulon. ✆ **04-94-92-39-33.** 35 units, 5 with shared bathrooms. 24€ double without bathroom, 37.50€ double with bathroom. No credit cards. Bus: 3. **Amenities:** Lounge. *In room:* TV.

New Hôtel Tour Blanche ★ With excellent modernized accommodations, attractive gardens with terraces, and a pool, this seven-story hotel is the best in Toulon. In the rocky hills about a kilometer north of the town center, it has sweeping views from even the lower floors out over the town to the port and the sea. Many bedrooms, especially those overlooking the bay, have balconies, and each is simply outfitted in an international modern style. Bathrooms are tiled and compact. The restaurant, Les Terrasses, offers a panoramic view, and food and wine whose selection is inspired by the culinary traditions of Provence and the Midi.

Bd. de l'Amiral-Vence, 83000 Toulon. ✆ **04-94-24-41-57.** Fax 04-94-22-42-25. www.new-hotel.com. 91 units. 76€–98€ double. AE, DC, MC, V. Free parking. Bus: 40. From the town center, follow signs to the Mont Faron téléphérique, and you'll pass the hotel en route. **Amenities:** Restaurant; bar; outdoor pool; limited room service; laundry service. *In room:* A/C, TV, minibar, hair dryer.

WHERE TO DINE

La Chamade ★ SOUTHERN FRENCH The cuisine here is memorable, and the restaurant the finest for miles. It's in the town center, in a nondescript building whose thick walls hint at its age. The chef offers diners a fixed-price menu that includes a choice of three appetizers, three main courses, and three desserts. Menu items change with the seasons but might include foie gras of duckling with salty caramel sauce, eggplant with roasted lamb served with coriander sauce, and a dessert confection consisting of semibaked, ultramoist chocolate cake with mint-flavored cream sauce.

25 rue Denfert-Rochereau. ✆ **04-94-92-28-58.** Reservations recommended. Main courses 12€–17€; fixed-price menu 37€. AE, MC, V. Mon–Fri noon–2:30pm and 7–9:30pm; Sat 7–9:30pm. Closed Aug 1–25. Bus: 1 or 21.

TOULON AFTER DARK

A town that's the temporary home of thousands of sailors is bound to have a nightlife scene that's earthier, and a bit raunchier, than those of equivalent-size towns elsewhere. A rough-and-ready bar that sports stiff drinks, live music, and a complete lack of pretension is **Le Bar 113,** 113 av. de Infanterie de la Marine (✆ **04-94-03-42-41**). **Bar à Thym** is at 32 bd. Cuneo (✆ **04-94-41-90-10**), where everybody seems to drink beer, gossip, and listen to live music. Toulon is also home to one of the Azure Coast's best-known gay discos, **Boy's Paradise,** 1 bd. Pierre-Toesca (✆ **04-94-09-35-90**), near the city's train station.

Adjacent to the port is the gay **Bar La Lampa,** Port de Toulon (✆ **04-94-03-06-09**), where tapas and live music accompany lots of beer and wine or whiskey.

If you want more resorty outlets, you might be happy at Hyère, about 26km (16 miles) east of Toulon, where there's an upscale disco, **Le Fou du Roy,** in the Casino des Palmiers (✆ **04-94-12-80-80**). About 15km (9 miles) west of Toulon, in the port town of Sanary, **Mai-Tai,** route de Bandol (✆ **04-94-74-23-92**), appeals to dancers under age 30.

15 Hyères ★

852km (529 miles) S of Paris; 100km (62 miles) SE of Aix-en-Provence; 122km (76 miles) SW of Cannes; 18km (11 miles) E of Toulon

The broad avenues of Hyères, shaded by date palms, still evoke the lazy Belle Epoque. The full name of the town is Hyères-les-Palmier, as it is known for its production of palm trees. Believe it or not, many of these trees are exported to the Middle East.

Hyères is the oldest resort along the Côte d'Azur, having once been frequented by the likes of Queen Victoria, Napoléon, Leo Tolstoy, and Robert Louis Stevenson. It was particularly popular with the British before 1939. It has changed so little from its heyday that many French film directors, including Jean-Luc Godard *(Pierrot le Fou)* and François Truffaut, who shot his last film here (*Vivement Dimanche,* released as *Confidentially Yours* in the United States), have used it as locations for period pieces. Today it lives off its past glory and its memories.

As a visitor, you'll find the most interesting section of Hyères to be the Vieille Ville, which lies 5km (3 miles) inland from the sea on a hill. Try to arrive early to attend a bustling morning market around place Massillon. The more modern town and the nucleus of the 19th-century resort stretch toward the sea.

ESSENTIALS

GETTING THERE **Flights** from Paris arrive at the Toulon-Hyères airport, which lies between the town center and the beach. For flights, call ✆ **04-42-14-14-14.** Rail connections are fairly easy, as Hyères lies on the main Nice-Lyon-Paris line. Nine local **trains** a day connect Hyères with Toulon; a one-way ticket costs 8.50€. There are two **buses** per day from Toulon, Cannes, and Nice. For information about bus and rail schedules, call Phoceens Car, 2 place Massena in Nice at ✆ **04-93-85-66-61.**

If you're **driving,** A5 goes through Toulon to Marseille and points north and west; A57 goes northeast to join A8, the autoroute between Nice and Aix-en-Provence.

VISITOR INFORMATION The **Office de Tourisme,** at 3 av. Ambroise Thomas (✆ **04-94-01-84-50**), dispenses information about the town and the area.

EXPLORING THE AREA

The land lying between the city and the sea is unattractive, and the beaches are a bit polluted, but there are some swimming possibilities here, notably at **Hyères-Plage.** There is also a yacht marina at **Port d'Hyères.** We find the parks and old town of Hyères more interesting than its beachfront.

Heading into town from the beach, go along the wide **avenue Gambetta** shaded by double rows of palms. At the end of Gambetta, continue along rue Rabaton to **place Massillon,** the beginning of the old town and the site of many good terrace cafe-restaurants. The daily market also takes place here. The 12th-century **Tour St-Blaise,** which stands on the square, was once a command post of the Knights Templar.

Above place Massillon is a warren of intriguing old streets climbing the hillside. Many are cobblestoned and bordered by stone walls, with an abundance of flowers in summer. Look for the medieval arched *portes.* Most of the Vieille Ville houses have been restored, often painted in lovely Mediterranean pastels with contrasting shutters and doors.

Part of the ramparts have survived, although most of them have been torn down; they date from the 12th century. All that remains of the south "curtain wall" are **Porte-St-Paul,** next to the Collegiate Church, and **Porte Baruc.** A trio of lovely old towers has survived from the north curtain wall.

Steep narrow streets lead up behind Tour St-Blaise to the 18th-century **Le Collegiale St-Paul,** place St-Paul (© **04-94-65-83-30**). In the Romanesque narthex are 400 fragments from the Church of Notre-Dame-de-Consolation, destroyed in bombing raids in 1944. The Gothic nave dates from the 15th and 16th centuries. The church is flanked by an elegant turreted Renaissance house constructed above one of the medieval city gates. The church is open Wednesday through Saturday April through October from 10am to noon and 3:30 to 6pm. November through March, it is open Wednesday through Saturday from 3 to 5pm.

Artifacts left behind by the Greeks and Romans can be examined at the **Musée Municipal,** place Lefebvre (© **04-94-00-78-80**). The museum is often the venue for special exhibitions. Entrance is free, and it is open Monday, Wednesday, Thursday, and Friday from 10am to noon and 3 to 6pm. If there's a special exhibition, it is also open Saturday and Sunday from 3 to 6pm.

The main attraction of the town is **Parc St-Bernard,** 20km (12½ miles) east of Toulon by N98, on the hill above Hyères. It is open year-round daily from 8am to 6:30pm. To reach the park, go up rue Saint Esprit to where it becomes rue Barbacane. Charles and Marie-Laure de Noailles, great patrons of the arts, commissioned a modern Cubist-style villa here in 1924 and brought in garden designer Gabriel Guevrekian, who created an extensive garden in the shape of an isosceles triangle, pointing away from the end of the villa. The Noailles played a role in nurturing the avant-garde artists of the Jazz Age, including F. Scott Fitzgerald. Edith Wharton was a devoted friend of the family. The villa is currently being restored, but you can visit the terraced gardens where olives and pines provide shade, and there are benches for sitting. Also in the park are the ruins of **Château d'Hyères,** above the medieval old town. Signposts and arrows lead visitors on a self-guided walk through the ruins, which have unrestricted access.

WHERE TO STAY

Hôtel du Soleil The foundations of this hotel date from the 11th century, when they were lodgings for the guards who defended the once-formidable fortress of Hyères. What you'll see, however, dates from around 1900—a boxy-looking *bastide* (masonry building) atop the old foundations. Over the years, a sheathing of ivy has softened the angles a bit, and the interior has been kept up-to-date with frequent modernizations. Bedrooms are cozy, if somewhat small, with Provençal furniture and casement windows; from the back are views of the sea, and in front are views of upscale villas on a nearby hill. Breakfast is the only meal served, although there are several places to eat (including the Bistrot de Marius, below) within a 3-minute walk.

Rue du Rempart (place Clemenceau), 83400 Hyères. ✆ **04-94-65-16-26.** Fax 04-94-35-46-00. www.hoteldusoleil.com. 27 units. 34€–84€ double. AE, DC, MC, V. **Amenities:** Breakfast room. *In room:* TV.

Ibis Thalasse This hotel is located between the coastal road and the beach, on the eastern edge of the land bridge that stretches between the French mainland and the Gien peninsula. Designed in a horseshoe shape, with the open end of the U facing the beach, the hotel places emphasis on resort life. Bedrooms are a decent size and decorated in a standardized format that includes one double bed and one single bed, a writing table, and a soothing color scheme of blue-gray. Bathrooms are motel standard, with tidy maintenance. There is also a downtown Ibis hotel.

Allée de la Mer, La Capte, 83400 Hyères-Plage. ✆ **04-94-58-00-94.** Fax: 04-94-58-09-35. 96 units. 97€–108€ double. AE, DC, MC, V. **Amenities:** Restaurant; bar; pool; health club; spa; babysitting. *In room:* A/C, TV, hair dryer.

WHERE TO DINE

Bistrot de Marius PROVENÇAL/SEAFOOD Set almost adjacent to the Tour des Templiers, this restaurant dates from 1910, when it was established in a building whose foundations date from the 13th century. Its trio of dining rooms (one is upstairs) has exposed stone and paneling, and a sense of historic charm. Fish, especially grilled sea bass, monkfish, dorado, and tuna, are specialties here, along with mussels and oysters. Sauce choices include *marchand de vin* (a red wine–based sauce), and lemon-butter and basil-flavored vinaigrette. A succulent version of bouillabaisse, priced at 31.15€, is a meal in itself, and there is a limited selection of chicken, veal, and beef.

1 place Massillon. ✆ **04-94-35-88-38.** Reservations recommended. Main courses 11€–18€; fixed-price menus 16€–30€. AE, DC, MC, V. Sept–June Wed–Mon noon–3:30pm and 7–11:30pm; July–Aug daily noon–3:30pm and 7–11:30pm.

Crèche Provençale ★ PROVENÇAL In a century-old inn with exposed structural beams and stone, you can order time-tested Provençal dishes. Tables are elaborately laid with rich naperies, porcelain, and crystal. Dishes include a terrine of leeks with a confit of tomatoes; roasted red snapper with thyme-flavored cream sauce, a tapenade of black olives, and paper-thin slices of cured ham; and deboned pigeon with braised cabbage and balsamic vinegar.

15 route de Toulon. ✆ **04-94-65-30-28.** Reservations required. Main courses 15€–25€; fixed-price lunches 27€–39.50€; fixed-price dinners 32.50€–42.50€. AE. Tues–Fri and Sun noon–2:30pm; Tues–Sun 7–9:30pm.

16 Iles d'Hyères ★

39km (24 miles) SE of Toulon; 119km (74 miles) SW of Cannes

Off the Riviera in the Mediterranean is a little group of islands enclosing the southern boundary of the Hyères anchorage. During the Renaissance they were called the Iles d'Or, from a golden glow sometimes given off by the rocks in the sunlight. Nothing in the islands today will remind you of the turbulent time when they were attacked by pirates and Turkish galleys, or even of the Allied landings here in World War II.

Mass tourism has arrived on these sun-baked islands, with some of the tackiness that goes with it. Cars are forbidden on all three major islands, and they cannot be transported on any of the ferryboats. Expect a summer holiday spirit not unlike a Gallic version of Nantucket, with thousands of midsummer day-trippers arriving, often with children, for a day of sun, sand, and people-watching.

Which island is the most appealing? Ile des Porquerolles is the most beautiful. Thinking of heading to Le Levant? You might want to steer clear—only 25% of the island is accessible to visitors, as three-quarters of it belongs to the French army, and it is used frequently for testing missiles.

ESSENTIALS

GETTING THERE **Ile de Porquerolles** Ferryboats leave from at least three points along the Côte d'Azur. The most frequent, most convenient, and shortest trip sails from the harbor of La Tour Fondue on the peninsula of Gien, a 32km (20-mile) drive east of Toulon. Depending on the season, there are 4 to 20 departures a day for a 15-minute crossing. Round-trip fares are 14.30€. For information, call the **Transports Maritimes et Terrestres du Littoral Varois,** La Tour Fondue, 83400 Giens (✆ **04-94-58-21-81**). The next-best option is the ferryboat from Toulon. There are infrequent boats (usually only twice a day, Apr–Sept) from the ports of Le Lavandou and Cavalaire. For information on rides from these ports and from Toulon, call **Trans-Med 2000,** quai Stalingrad, 83000 Toulon (✆ **04-94-92-96-82**).

Ile de Port-Cros The most popular ferry route to this island is the 35-minute crossing from Le Lavandou, departing four to six times daily, depending on the season. (Between Nov and Mar, there are only three per week.) For information, call the **Compagnie Maritime des Vedettes "Iles d'Or,"** 15 quai Gabriele-Peri, 83980 Le Lavandou (✆ **04-94-71-01-02**). Round-trip fares are 21€ for adults and 13.80€ for children 4 to 11. The same company also offers less convenient and longer crossings from Cavalaire, but only April through September. For no additional fee, you can be dropped off at the military installations at Le Levant.

VISITOR INFORMATION Other than temporary, summer-only kiosks without phones that distribute brochures and advice near the ferry docks of Porquerolles and Port-Cros, there are no tourist bureaus on the islands. Consequently, the mainland tourist offices in Toulon and Hyères try to fill in the gaps. Contact the **Office de Tourisme,** 3 av. Ambroise Thomas, Hyères (✆ **04-94-01-84-50**); or the **Office de Tourisme,** place Raimu, Toulon (✆ **04-94-18-53-00**).

ILE DE PORQUEROLLES ★

This is the largest and westernmost of the Iles d'Hyères. It has a rugged south coast, but the north strand, facing the mainland, is made up of sandy beaches bordered by heather, scented myrtles, and pine trees. The island is about 8km (5 miles) long and 2km (1¼ miles) wide, and is 5km (3 miles) from the mainland.

The population is only 400. The island is said to receive 275 days of sunshine annually. It's a land of rocky capes, pine forests twisted by the mistral, sun-drenched vineyards, and pale ocher houses. The "hot spots," if there are any, are the cafes around **place d'Armes** where everybody gathers.

The island has had a violent history of raids, attacks, and occupation by everybody from the Dutch, English, and Turks to the Spaniards. Ten forts, some in ruins, testify to a violent past. The most ancient is **Fort Ste-Agathe,** built in 1531 by François I. In time it was a penal colony and a retirement center for soldiers of the colonial wars.

The French government in 1971 purchased the largest hunk of the island and turned it into a national park and botanical garden.

WHERE TO STAY & DINE

Le Relais de la Poste On a small square in the heart of the island's main settlement, this pleasant and unpretentious hotel is the oldest on the island—it opened "sometime in the 19th century" and is today managed by the good-natured sixth generation of its founding family. It offers Provençal-style rooms with loggias. Most rooms are small to medium in size, but each comes with a comfortable mattress and fine linens on a twin or double bed. In-room amenities are lean except for a phone. Bathrooms are compact and well organized. The hotel has a billiard table and a crêperie that sells only sugared snack-style dessert crepes and fresh fruit juices.

Place d'Armes, 83540 Porquerolles. ✆ **04-98-04-62-62.** Fax 04-94-58-33-57. 30 units. 75€–109€ double. No credit cards. Closed late Oct to Easter. **Amenities:** Bar; lounge; bike rental.

Mas du Langoustier ★★ In a large park on the island's western tip, this tranquil resort hotel is actually an old Provençal *mas* with a view of a lovely pine-ringed bay. Employees greet guests in a covered wagon by the jetty. In an antique Provençal style, bedrooms are the most elegantly decorated on the island; bathrooms are roomy. If you visit only for a meal, the menu is the finest in the islands, mainly seafood in a light nouvelle style. Try the *loup* (sea bass) with Noilly Prat in puff pastry or tender kid with dried tomatoes roasted in casserole. The house wine is an agreeable rosé. You can drink and dine on the terraces.

83400 Porquerolles. ✆ **04-94-58-30-09.** Fax 04-94-58-36-02. www.langoustier.com. 50 units. 214€–281€ double. Rates include half board. AE, DC, MC, V. Closed mid-Oct to Apr 25. **Amenities:** 2 restaurants; bar; tennis courts; limited room service; babysitting; laundry service; dry cleaning. *In room:* TV, minibar, hair dryer, safe.

ILE DE PORT-CROS ★

Lush subtropical vegetation reminiscent of a Caribbean island makes this a green paradise, 5km (3 miles) long and 2km (1¼ miles) wide. The most mountainous of the archipelago, Port-Cros has been a French national park since 1963. Although a fire in 1892 devastated the island, it has bounced back with pine forests and ilexes. Bird-watchers flock here to observe nearly 100 different species. There are many marked trails, mainly for day-trippers. The most popular and scenic is ***sentier botanique;*** the more adventurous and athletic take the 10km (6-mile) ***circuit historique,*** but bring a packed lunch for this one. Divers follow a 30m (100-ft.) trail from Plage de la Palud to the islet of Rascas, where a plastic guide sheet identifies the underwater flora. Thousands of pleasure craft call here annually, which does little to help the island's fragile environment.

WHERE TO STAY & DINE

Le Manoir ★ This is the only bona-fide hotel on the island, but despite lack of competition, its owners work hard to make their guests as comfortable as possible. It consists of an 18th-century manor house, plus an annex that holds most of the guest rooms. Accommodations are simple and clean. Chef Sylvain Chaduteau serves lobster-and-fish terrine, several seasoned meats, and fresh local fish with baby vegetables, as well as regional goat cheese and velvety mousses.

83400 Ile de Port-Cros. ✆ **04-94-05-90-52.** Fax 04-94-05-90-89. 22 units. 150€–180€ double; 190€–220€ duplex apt for 2. Rates include half board. MC, V. Closed Oct–Apr. **Amenities:** Restaurant; bar; pool; limited room service; babysitting; laundry service; dry cleaning. *In room:* A/C, hair dryer.

17 Grand Canyon du Verdon ★

Trigance: 72km (45 miles) S of Digne-les-Baines; 20km (12½ miles) W of Castellane; 43km (27 miles) NW of Draguignan; 85km (53 miles) E of Manosque

La-Palud-sur-Verdon: 64km (40 miles) S of Digne-les-Bains; 25km (15½ miles) W of Castellane; 60km (37 miles) NW of Draguignan; 66km (41 miles) E of Manosque

Over the centuries, the Verdon River, a tributary of the Durance, has cut Europe's biggest canyon into the surrounding limestone plateau. The canyon runs from pont de Soleils to Lac Ste-Croix, a distance of 21km (13 miles) east to west. The upper section of the gorge, to the east, is between 210m and 1605m (700 ft. and 5,350 ft.) wide; the lower section narrows to between 6m and 105m (20 ft. and 350 ft.). All along its length, the cliffs rise and fall. The gorge's depth varies from 263m (875 ft.) at one point to 750m (2,500 ft.).

Vertiginous roads wind along both rims of the canyon, giving you the opportunity to pull over at any of several scenic belvederes. Among the best of these is the Balcon de la Mescla, the first stop traveling west from Trigance on the canyon's south side, where the sheer cliffs drop 270m (900 ft.) to the river. A short distance away is Falaise de Cavaliers (Horseman's Cliff), dropping 323m (1,075 ft.) and signaling the beginning of the Corniche Sublime, where the gorge plunges to 428m (1,425 ft.) along a stretch running west to Aiguines. In between these scenic stops, you can actually drive across the canyon on the dramatic pont de l'Artuby, a single-arched, 120m (400-ft.) long span, 638m (2,125 ft.) above the river.

Ancient villages cling to rocky outcroppings along the two rim roads. At Aiguines, a private castle flanked by four turrets and covered in polished variegated tiles dominates the skyline. On Route 19, 9km (5½ miles) north of the canyon on its western end, sits Moustiers-Ste-Marie, a medieval village of potters who sell their wares—but beware, prices here are celestial, especially in July and August, when tourist dollars are easy to come by.

ESSENTIALS

GETTING THERE From the Riviera, follow A85 for 84km (52 miles) northwest from Cannes to Castellane; then take Route 952 west to the intersection with Route 955 and proceed along 955 south to Trigance, about 20km (12½ miles). From here, continue south to Route 71, 3km distant, and take a left to travel west along the southern edge of the canyon. At Les-Salles-sur-Verdon, on the banks of Lac St-Croix, turn right on D957 and drive north, crossing the Verdon where it flows into Lac St-Croix; then, just south of Moustiers-Ste-Marie, turn right again on Route 952 to trace the north side of the canyon back to the east.

VISITOR INFORMATION Information about accommodations, activities, and events is available from the **Verdon Accueil,** 83630 Aiguines (✆ 04-94-70-21-64) or rue Nationale, 04120 Castellane (✆ 04-92-83-67-36); the **Office de Tourisme de Castellane,** 04120 Castellane (✆ 04-92-83-61-14); or the **Office de Tourisme d'Esparron,** 04800 Esparron (✆ 04-92-77-15-45).

EXPLORING THE CANYON

Activities available in the canyon include guided hikes from the **Bureau des Guides,** 04120 La-Palud-sur-Verdon (✆ 04-92-77-32-02), and the **Office de Tourisme d'Esparron,** 04800 Esparron (✆ 04-92-77-15-45). Canoeing and kayaking are available through the **Aqua Vivae Est,** La Piscine, 04120 Castellane

(✆ 04-92-83-75-74), and the **Club Nautique,** 04800 Esparron (✆ 04-92-77-15-25). Rafting trips are conducted by **Acti Raft,** 04120 Castellane (✆ 04-92-83-76-64).

A deservedly popular walk in the area is a 2-hour round-trip trek launched at the parking lot at Samson Corridor. The route is clearly marked as it bends its way to a tunnel after Point Sublime. Continue your trek to a footbridge spanning the Baou River. After crossing it, go straight ahead through another two tunnels until you reach a belvedere with a panoramic sweep of the Trescaïre Chaos. For the tunnels, carry along a flashlight.

A more strenuous 6- to 8-hour walk starts at the Chalet de la Maline on the Crest Road and goes for about 15km (9.5 miles) to Point Sublime. The footpath is marked with arrows. Again, you'll need a flashlight, but this trek is so long that food and water are also recommended. Before heading out, you can call ✆ **04-92-83-65-38,** 04-92-77-31-16, or 04-92-83-65-34 for a taxi company that will pick you up at a designated time when you reach Point Sublime.

WHERE TO STAY

Auberge Point-Sublime This hotel offers simple, unpretentious rooms, each with congenially battered, old-fashioned (but not antique) furniture. Bedrooms are small and without particular style, although each has a comfortable mattress, plus a somewhat cramped bathroom. You do get views over the gorge and a location that's convenient, 2km (1¼ miles) south of the Couloir Samson, the point where many trekkers exit from hikes in the nearby gorge. The restaurant serves all-Provençal fixed-price meals. Specialties are civets of both rabbit and lamb, a truffle-studded omelet, and crawfish with truffles. Staff here is unusually bossy, insisting that residents consume at least one meal a day on-site.

04120 Point Sublime, Rougon. ✆ **04-92-83-60-35.** Fax 04-92-83-74-31. 14 units. 44€–53€ double, including half board. MC, V. Closed Nov 3–Mar. From Castellane, drive 19km (12 miles) north toward Moustiers-Ste-Marie; it's beside the road on the distant outskirts of Rougon. **Amenities:** Restaurant; bar; lounge. *In room:* TV.

Château de Trigance ★ This Relais & Châteaux property is the district's best hotel, rising on a rocky spur above a hamlet of fewer than 120 full-time inhabitants; it occupies the core of a 9th- and 10th-century fortress. There's no room for a garden, but there are views from virtually every window over the Provençal plain. The rooms contain strong hints of their medieval origins—baldaquin-style beds with comfortable mattresses. Modern extras that were added in 1969 include tiled bathrooms.

The dining room is unusual; originally used to store weapons, it has a vaulted ceiling that was, in accordance with the era's techniques, built without groins or a central key. A wooden form was constructed and carefully chiseled stones were fitted into position on top. When complete, the form was burnt away and the vaulting remained—somewhat precariously until it was shored up with additional mortar. The fare is intensely cultivated: "Marbled" foie gras of duckling with artichoke hearts; pressed leeks with smoked salmon, crawfish, and sweet-and-sour sauce; and roasted leg of lamb "en surprise" with a "spaghetti" of zucchini and cream of garlic *en confit*. There's a parking lot near the entrance of the hotel, thereby saving you the arduous hike up the medieval-looking steps that were once the only route of access.

83840 Trigance, Var. ✆ **04-94-76-91-18.** Fax 04-94-85-68-99. www.chateau-de-trigance.fr. 10 units. 105€–180€ double. AE, DC, MC, V. Free parking. Closed Nov 1–Mar 20. **Amenities:** Restaurant; bar; limited room service; laundry service; dry cleaning. *In room:* TV.

Grand Canyon du Verdon

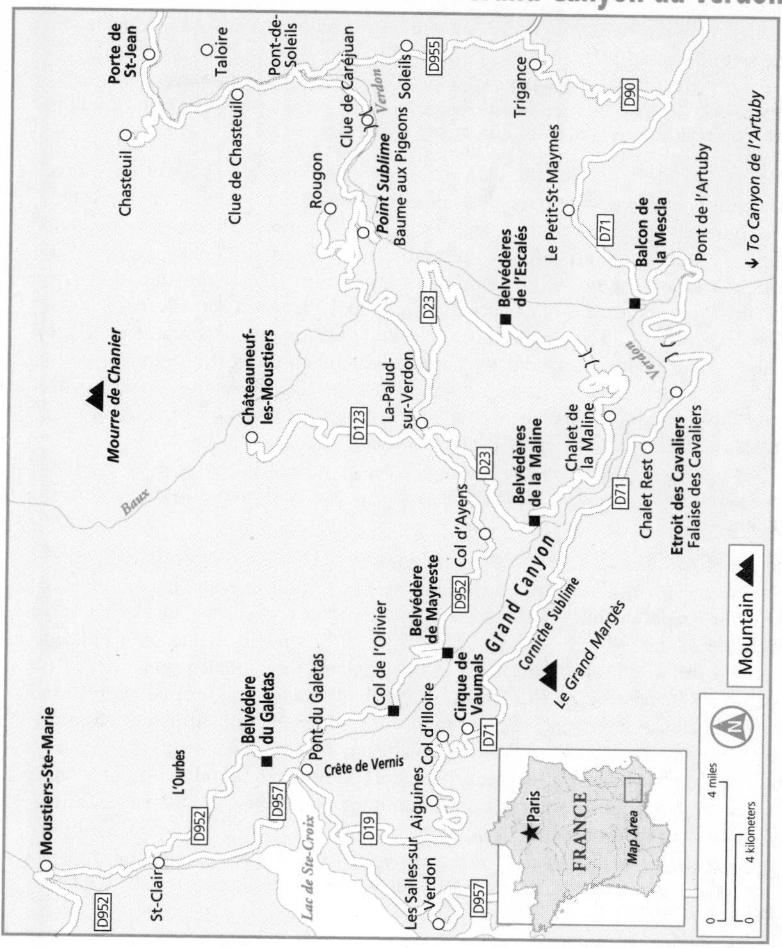

Hôtel Les Gorges du Verdon This hotel is inspired by an earth-toned Provençal *mas.* It's in the heart of La-Palud-sur-Verdon (pop. 250, alt. 914m/3,000 ft.), about 6km (4 miles) west of the canyon edge. Though you won't be able to see the canyon from the windows, views over the rugged countryside stretch out on virtually every side. The rooms were upgraded in 1998, with elaborate curtains added that soften their modern angularity. Tiles were installed in many of the bathrooms, adding a glossy kind of modern comfort. Overall, the rooms aren't exactly plush, but they have good mattresses, and since most guests opt to spend their days in the great outdoors, no one really seems to care. Most have a private terrace or balcony overlooking a scenic landscape. Some are entered from a landing with a staircase leading down into the room, creating a mezzanine effect.

Half board is obligatory in midsummer. Nonresidents often stop for meals here. Well-prepared menu items include duck thigh stuffed with mushrooms, grilled whole sea bass with anise-flavored butter, and Provençal lamb chops with tarragon-flavored butter sauce.

04120 La-Palud-sur-Verdon. ✆ **04-92-77-38-26.** Fax 04-92-77-35-00. 31 units. 105€–145€ double. MC, V. Free parking. Closed late Oct to late Mar. **Amenities:** Restaurant; bar; pool; tennis court; limited room service; babysitting; laundry service; dry cleaning. *In room:* TV, hair dryer, safe.

Hôtel Le Vieil Amandier At the edge of town, this hotel offers clean, uncomplicated guest rooms and a dining room with straightforward but thoughtfully prepared cuisine. Half the rooms face the pool and get southern light; the remainder are just as comfortable but without views. The largest is the rustic and woodsy no. 6; nos. 3 and 4 are more Provençal, and the others are blandly international. Your hosts are Cécile and Bernard Clap (Bernard is the hamlet's mayor). They maintain a pleasant, unpretentious restaurant where lunch and dinner are served daily. Cuisine is artful and flavorful, featuring good value for the money. Menu items include profiteroles of goat cheese with chives and olive oil, duckling with myrtle leaves and garlic, and rack of lamb in puff pastry served with fine-textured ratatouille.

83840 Trigance, Var. ✆ **04-94-76-92-92.** Fax 04-94-85-68-65. 12 units. 50€–76€ double. AE, DC, MC, V. Free parking. Closed Nov 3–Apr 1. **Amenities:** Restaurant; bar; pool; laundry service; dry cleaning. *In room:* TV, hair dryer.

Inter Hôtel Grand Canyon de Verdon *Finds* This is the most charming and interesting hotel along the south bank of the Verdon canyon. It's on a rocky outcropping above the precipice, vertiginously close to the edge, and exists only because of the foresight of the grandfather of the present owner. In 1946, on holiday in Provence from his home in the foggy northern French province of Pas de Calais, he fell in love with the site, opened a brasserie, and secured permission to build a hotel here. In 1982, his grandson, Georges Fortini, erected the present two-story hotel. Rooms are simple, small, but comfortable, with light-grained wood and off-white walls. Set on a 4-hectare (10-acre) tract on the Corniche Sublime, the hotel features a glassed-in restaurant overlooking a 322m (1,075-ft.) drop to the canyon bottom.

Falaise des Cavaliers, 83630 Aiguines. ✆ **04-94-76-91-31.** Fax 04-94-76-92-29. 15 units. 50€–80€ double. Rates include half board. AE, DC, MC, V. Closed Oct–Apr. **Amenities:** Restaurant; bar. *In room:* TV, minibar, hair dryer.

WHERE TO DINE

Many of the inns recommended under "Where to Stay," above, are also the finest places to dine—notably the **Château de Trigance.**

Les Santons ★ FRENCH/PROVENÇAL One of the region's most charming restaurants occupies a stone-sided 12th-century house adjacent to the village church. You'll find a cozy dining room filled with 19th-century paintings and antique pottery, reminders of Old Provence, and fewer than 20 seats. A terrace, lined with flowering plants, doubles the seating space during clement weather. André Abert is the sophisticated chef who makes as much use as possible of fresh local ingredients. These include truffles and honey. Examples are homemade noodles studded with truffles and chunks of foie gras, chicken roasted with lavender-scented honey and Provençal spices, and Sisteron lamb roasted with honey and spices and served with an herb-scented ratatouille and *gratin dauphinoise* (potatoes with grated cheese).

Place de l'Eglise, 04360 Moustiers-Ste-Marie, Alpes-de-Haut-Provence. ✆ **04-92-74-66-48.** Reservations recommended. Main courses 27€–32€; fixed-price menus 24€–53€. AE, MC, V. Mon noon–2pm; Wed–Sun noon–2pm and 7:30–9:30pm. Closed mid-Nov to mid-Dec and mid-Jan to mid-Feb.

5

The Western Riviera: From St-Tropez to Cannes to Cap d'Antibes

The western part of the **Côte d'Azur** begins at glittering St-Tropez and ends at the even more elegant Cap d'Antibes. In between are mostly middle-class resort towns, like St-Raphaël, scattered along a coast that also features the wild and desolate landscape of the Massif de l'Estérel.

Ste-Maxime and Fréjus offer some of the area's best budget accommodations, having been taken over by French families in search of a holiday getaway on the once-exclusive coast.

The area does, of course, embrace Cannes, the most famous resort in the region because of the glitz and glamour surrounding its film festival, which overflows into the upscale La Napoule-Plage, home of the Clews Museum.

Inland, the terrain climbs away from the coast to the hillside communities of Grasse, with its perfume distilleries, and Mougins, a charming old village and culinary center that makes for a romantic retreat. Food also lures gastronomes to Golfe-Juan, which features one of the region's best restaurants, Chez Tétou, a stop for a rich bowl of bouillabaisse.

Nightlife is the focus of neighboring Juan-les-Pins, attracting spirited adventurers to its all-night jazz clubs and discos. Nearby Vaullaris hosts Galerie Madoura, a pottery firm with exclusive rights to reproduce Picasso's earthenware designs. Antibes also profits from its association with Picasso by the museum dedicated to his life and work. This largely middle-class resort gives way to Cap d'Antibes, the peninsular resort that's as tony today as when F. Scott Fitzgerald used it as the setting for his novel *Tender Is the Night.*

1 St-Tropez ★★

874km (543 miles) S of Paris; 76km (47 miles) SW of Cannes

Sun-kissed lasciviousness is rampant in this carnival town, but the true Tropezian resents the fact that the port has such a bad reputation. "We can be classy, too," one native has insisted. Creative people in the lively arts along with ordinary folk create a volatile mixture. One observer said that St-Tropez "has replaced Naples for those who accept the principle of dying after seeing it. It's a unique fate for a place to have made its reputation on the certainty of happiness."

St-Tropez—this palimpsest of nostalgia—was popularized by sex symbol Brigitte Bardot in *And God Created Woman,* but it had attracted the famous for a long time. Colette lived here for many years. Even the late diarist Anaïs Nin, confidante of Henry Miller, posed for a little cheesecake on the beach here in

1939 in a Dorothy Lamour–style bathing suit. Earlier St-Tropez was visited by Matisse, Signac, and Bonnard, and even Maupassant before he died of syphilis.

Artists, composers, novelists, and the film colony come to St-Tropez in summer. Trailing them is a line of humanity unmatched anywhere else on the Riviera for sheer flamboyance. Chic people anchor their yachts here in summer but disappear long before the dreaded mistral of winter.

In 1995, Bardot pronounced St-Tropez dead—"squatted by a lot of no-goods, drugheads, and villains"—and swore she'd never go back, at least in summer. But 1997 saw her return, as headlines in France flashed the news that St-Tropez was "hot once again." Not only Bardot, but other celebrities have been showing up, including Oprah Winfrey, Don Johnson, Quincy Jones, Barbra Streisand, Jack Nicholson, Robert DeNiro, Sean "P. Diddy" Combs, and even Elton and Sly (not together!).

ESSENTIALS

GETTING THERE The nearest rail station is in St-Raphaël, a neighboring resort; at the Vieux Port, four or five **boats** per day between April and October leave the **Gare Maritime de St-Raphaël,** rue Pierre-Auble (✆ **04-94-95-17-46**), for St-Tropez (trip time: 50 min.), costing 10€ each way. Year-round, between 10 and 15 Sodetrav **buses** per day leave from the Gare Routière in St-Raphaël (✆ **04-94-97-88-51**) and go to St-Tropez, taking 1½ to 2¼ hours, depending on the bus and the traffic, which during midsummer is usually horrendous. A one-way ticket costs 8.30€. Buses run directly to St-Tropez from Toulon and Hyères. Buses also run directly to St-Tropez from the nearest airport at Toulon-Hyères, 56km (35 miles) away.

If you **drive,** note that parking in St-Tropez is very difficult, especially in summer. In 1998, the situation was slightly relieved with the construction of a **Parc des Lices** (✆ **04-94-97-34-46**), beneath place des Lices, whose entrance is on avenue Paul-Roussel. Designed for 471 cars, this parking lot charges 2€ to 3.50€ per hour, depending on the season. Many visitors with expensive cars prefer this site because it's more carefully guarded than any other lot. If you don't use it, you'll have to squeeze your car into tiny parking spaces wherever you can find them. To get here from Cannes, drive southwest along the coastal highway (RD98), turning eastward when you see the signs pointing to St-Tropez.

VISITOR INFORMATION The **Office de Tourisme** is on quai Jean-Jaurès (✆ **04-94-97-45-21;** www.ot-saint-tropez.com).

OUTDOOR PURSUITS

A DAY AT THE BEACH

The hottest Riviera beaches are at St-Tropez. The best for families are closest to the center, including the **Plage de la Bouillabaisse** and **Plage des Graniers.** The more daring are the 9.5km (6-mile) crescents at **Plage des Salins** and **Plage de Pampelonne,** some 3km (2 miles) from the town center and best reached by bike (see below) if you're not driving. At Pampelonne there are about 35 businesses on a 4.8km (3-mile) stretch, located about 10km (6⅓ miles) from St-Tropez. You'll need a car, bike, or scooter to get from town to the beach. Parking is about 3.50€ for the day. Famous hedonistic spots along Pampelonne include the cash-only club **La Voile Rouge** (✆ **04-94-79-84-39**), which features bawdy spring break–style entertainment. Also thriving is **Le Club,** 55 bd. Patch, Plage de Pampelonne (✆ **04-94-55-55-55**), and **Nikki Beach,** Plage de Pampelonne (no phone). Maintained by an American from Miami, it's wild, frenetic, uninhibited, and about as Floridian a

The French Riviera

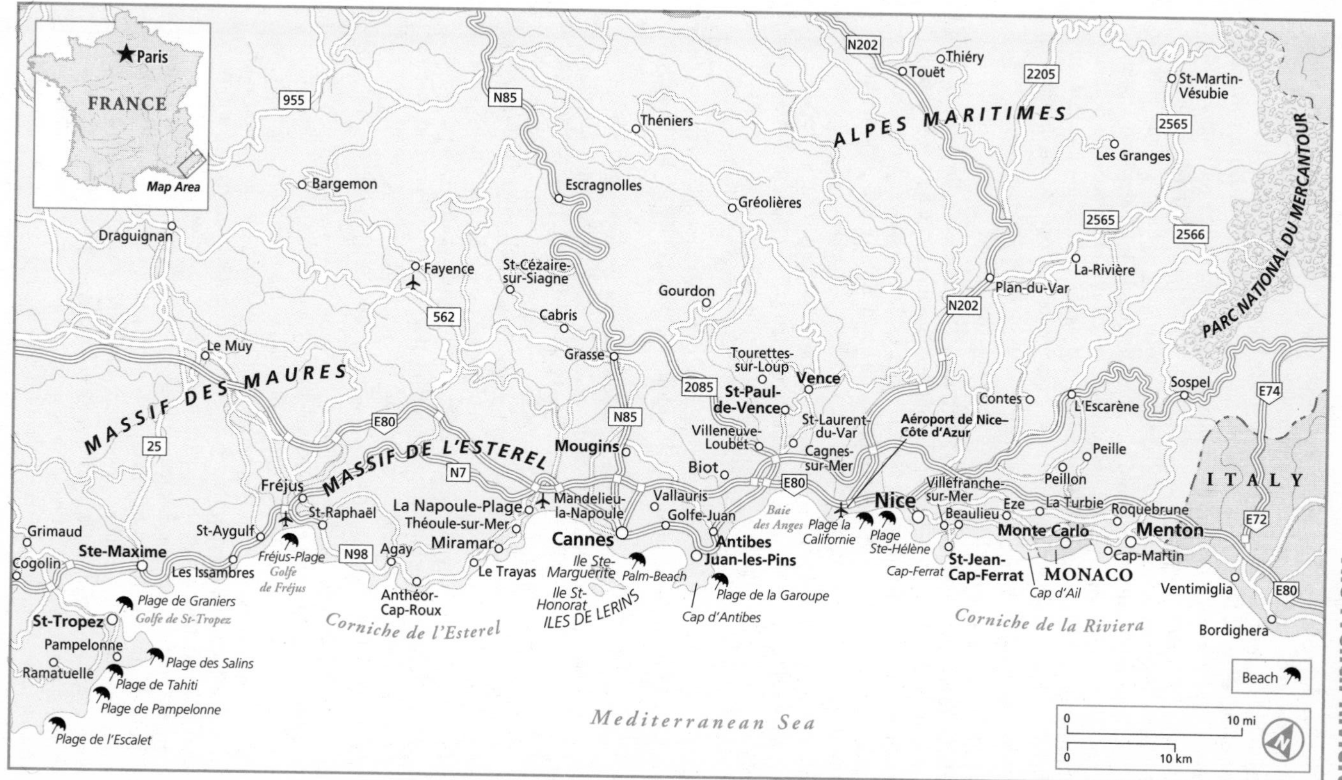

venue as you're likely to find in the south of France. **Plage des Jumeaux** (✆ **04-94-79-84-21**) is another actively patronized beach spot, but with a large percentage of families with young kids because it has playground equipment. **Marine Air Sports** (✆ **04-07-22-43-97;** www.marine-air-sport.com) rents boats; **Team Water Sports** (✆ **04-94-79-82-41**) rents jet-skis, scooters, water-skiing equipment, and boats.

Called "notoriously decadent," **Plage de Tahiti** occupies the north end of the 5.5km (3½-mile) long Pampellone, lined with concessions, cafes, and restaurants. It's a strip of golden sand long favored by exhibitionists wearing next to nothing (or nothing) and cruising shamelessly. If you ever wanted to go topless, this is the place to do it. Gay men tend to gravitate to **Coco Beach** in Ramatuelle, about 6.5km (4 miles) from the center of St-Tropez.

STAYING ACTIVE

BICYCLING & MOTOR-SCOOTERING The largest outfitter for bikes and motor scooters is **Louis Mas,** 5 rue Josef-Quaranta (✆ **04-94-97-00-60**). You'll be required to leave a deposit of 153€ to 229€, payable with a major credit card, plus 8€ to 12€ per hour for a bike and 30€ to 45€ per hour for a motor scooter, depending on its size.

BOATING The highly recommended **Suncap Company,** 15 quai de Suffren (✆ **04-94-97-11-23**), rents boats from 5.5 to 12m (18–40 ft.) long. The smallest can be rented to qualified sailors without a captain, but the larger ones come with a captain at the helm. Prices begin at 475€ per day.

GOLF The nearest golf course, at the edge of Ste-Maxime, across the bay, is the **Golf Club de Beauvallon,** boulevard des Collines (✆ **04-94-96-16-98**), a popular 18-hole course.

Sprawling over a rocky, vertiginous landscape that requires a golf cart and a lot of exertion is the Don Harradine–designed **Golf de Ste-Maxime-Plaza,** route du Débarquement, Ste-Maxime (✆ **04-94-55-02-02**). Built in 1991 with the four-star Plaza de Ste-Maxime, it welcomes nonguests; phone to reserve tee times. Greens fees at both golf courses range from 50€ to 65€ for 18 holes per person, depending on the season, but if your tee-off begins 3 hours or less before sunset, you'll pay discounted rates of between 35€ and 45€ per person for 18 holes, depending on the season. Rental of an electric golf cart, suitable for two passengers, costs around 24€ for 18 holes, regardless of the season.

SCUBA DIVING A team of dive enthusiasts who are ready, willing, and able to show you the azure-colored depths off the coast of St-Tropez operate from the ***Octopussy I*** and ***II.*** Both are aluminum-sided, yellow-painted dive boats built in the 1990s. They're based year-round in St-Tropez's Nouveau Port, although the outfit's corporate headquarters lie on the outskirts of town, at the address noted below. Experienced divers pay from 30€ to 44€ for a one-tank "exploration" dive, depending on how much of their own equipment they use, and novices are charged 45€ for a *baptême* that includes one-on-one supervision and a descent to a depth of around 5m (15 ft.). Except for people who sign up for the *baptême,* where supervision for neophyte divers is enhanced and where you'll be expected to show strong swimming skills in advance, you have to have a license to participate in any of the conventional dives. For reservations and information, call or write *Les Octopussys,* quartier de Bertaud, Gassin, 83900 St-Tropez (✆ **04-94-56-53-10;** fax 04-94-56-46-59). And for a look at the actual boats, head down to the Nouveau Port, where, whenever they're not out on the open sea, they're usually moored to the wharves.

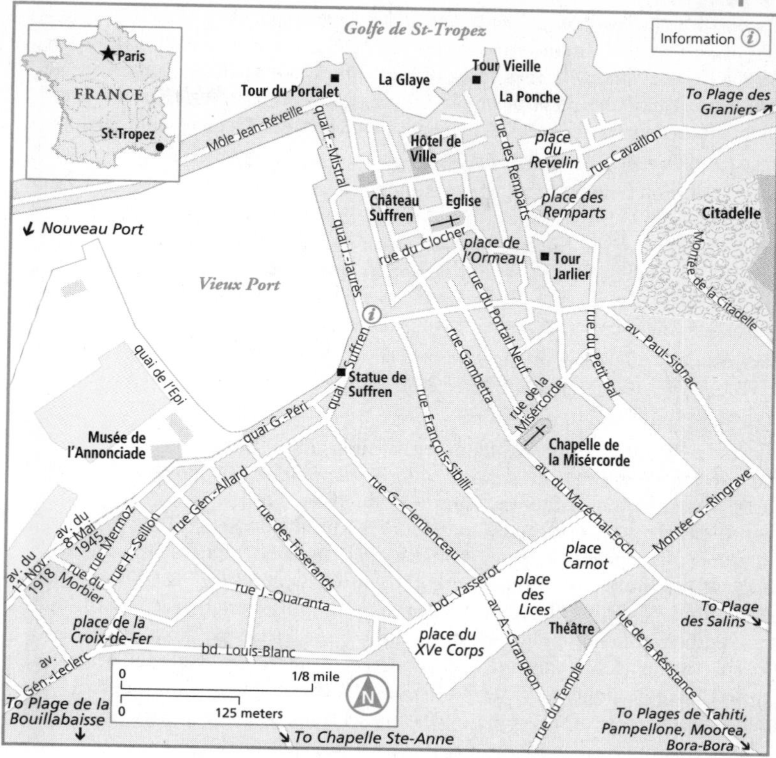

TENNIS Anyone who phones in advance can use the eight courts (both artificial grass and "Quick," a form of concrete) at the **Tennis-Club de St-Tropez,** route des Plages, in St-Claude (✆ **04-94-97-80-76**), about a kilometer from the resort's center. Open year-round, the courts rent for 15€ per hour from 10am to 5pm, and 20€ per hour after 5pm.

SEEING THE SIGHTS

Château Suffren is east of the port at the top end of quai Jean-Jaurès. Home to occasional art exhibits, it was built in A.D. 980 by Comte Guillame I of Provence.

Near the junction of quai Suffren and quai Jean-Jaurès stands the bronze **Statue de Suffren,** paying tribute to Vice-Admiral Pierre André de Suffren. This St-Tropez native became one of the greatest sailors of 18th-century France, though he's largely forgotten today. In the Vieille Ville, one of the most interesting streets is **rue de la Misércorde.** It's lined with stone houses with boutiques. This street evokes medieval St-Tropez better than any other in town. At the corner of rue Gambetta is the **Chapelle de la Misércorde,** with a blue, green, and gold tile roof.

Three kilometers (2 miles) east of St-Tropez, **Port Grimaud** ★ makes an interesting outing. From St-Tropez, drive 4km (3 miles) west on A98 to Route 98, and then 1.5km (1 mile) north to the Port Grimaud exit. If you approach the village at dusk, when it's bathed in Riviera pastels, it looks like a hamlet from the 16th century. But this is a mirage. Port Grimaud is the dream of its promoter, François

Spoerry, who carved it out of marshland and dug canals. Flanking these canals, fingers of land extend from the square to the sea. The homes are Provençal style, many with Italianate window arches. Boat owners can anchor at their doorsteps. One newspaper called the port "the most magnificent fake since Disneyland." Most shops and restaurants in Port Grimaud are closed between October and March.

Musée de l'Annonciade (Musée St-Tropez) ★★ Near the harbor, installed in the former chapel of the Annonciade, this museum is a legacy from the artists who loved St-Tropez. Opened in 1955, it is one of the finest modern art collections on the Riviera. The collection includes such works as Van Dongen's yellow-faced *Women of the Balustrade* and paintings and sculpture by Bonnard, Matisse, Braque, Dufy, Utrillo, Seurat, Derain, and Maillol. Many of the artists, including Paul Signac, depicted the port of St-Tropez.

Place Grammont. ✆ **04-94-97-04-01.** Admission 5.35€ adults, 3.10€ children. June–Sept Wed–Mon 10am–noon and 3–7pm; Oct and Dec–May Wed–Mon 10am–noon and 2–6pm.

SHOPPING

There's a high density per capita of stylish shops in St-Tropez, but since there's no street that's specifically designated as a shopping street, most of them are tucked away in out-of-the-way corners of the old town. Expect to have instant brand-name recognition, and a sometimes predictable sense of Gallic grandeur, in names that include Hermès, Sonia Rykiel, and Dior. One of the less predictable inventories, sometimes with a lot of whimsy and fun, is **Choses,** quai Jean-Jaurès (✆ **04-94-97-03-44**), a women's clothing store that is typical (but stocked better than some) of the many middle-bracket shops along the Riviera. Its specialty is clingy and often-provocative T-shirt dresses. **Galeries Tropéziennes,** 56 rue Gambetta (✆ **04-94-97-02-21**), crowds hundreds of unusual gift items—some worthwhile, some silly—into its showrooms near place des Lices. The inspiration is Mediterranean, breezy, and sophisticated.

In a resort that's increasingly loaded with purveyors of suntan lotion, touristy souvenirs, and T-shirts, **Jacqueline Thienot,** 12 rue Georges-Clemenceau (✆ **04-94-97-05-70**), maintains an inventory of Provençal antiques prized by dealers from as far away as Paris. The one-room shop is in a late-18th-century building that shows the 18th- and 19th-century antiques to their best advantage. Also sold are antique examples of Provençal wrought iron and rustic farm and homemaker's implements.

Olives and wood from the trees that produce them have always been prized in Provence. For access to carvings made from the wood, head for **Autour de l'Olivier,** 2 place de l'Ormeau (✆ **04-94-97-64-31**), where large inventories of kitchen utensils, bread boards, carved crucifixes, trays and platters, ornaments, and gift items are carved from the yellow-and-brown wood.

The fish, vegetable, and flower market is located down a tiled alley (place aux Herbes) behind the tourist office. It operates daily from 8am to noon in summer and Tuesday through Sunday from 8am to noon in winter. On Tuesday and Saturday mornings on place des Lices, there's an outdoor market with food, clothes, and brocante (flea-market finds). This is one of the best Provençal markets in the south of France, with more than 100 vendors selling everything from tableware to homemade bread.

WHERE TO STAY

VERY EXPENSIVE

Hôtel Byblos ★★★ The builder said he created "an antihotel, a place like home." That's true if your home resembles a palace in Beirut with salons decorated with Phoenician gold statues from 3000 B.C. On a hill above the harbor, this complex boasts intimate patios and courtyards, and retreats filled with antiques and rare objects like polychrome carved woodwork, marquetry floors, and a Persian-rug ceiling. Every room is unique. Unusual features might be a fireplace on a raised hearth or a bed recessed on a dais. The rooms range from medium to spacious, often with high ceilings and antiques or reproductions, and each with an elegant French bed. Some units have such special features as four-posters with furry spreads or sunken whirlpool baths. Le Hameau contains 10 duplex suites built around a small courtyard with an outdoor spa. Some rooms have balconies overlooking an inner courtyard; others open onto a terrace of flowers.

You can dine by the pool enjoying Provençal food. Later you can dance on a circular floor surrounded by bas-relief columns in the hotel's nightclub, **Caves du Roy.**

Av. Paul-Signac, 83990 St-Tropez. ✆ **04-94-56-68-00.** Fax 04-94-56-68-01. www.byblos.com. 98 units, 10 duplex suites. 430€–510€ double; from 790€–1,550€ suite. AE, DC, MC, V. Parking 24€ in garage. Closed Oct 15 to mid-Apr. **Amenities:** 2 restaurants; 2 bars; pool; spa; 24-hr. room service; massage; laundry service; dry cleaning. *In room:* A/C, TV, minibar, hair dryer, safe.

Hôtel Le Yaca ★ Life here is called *la dolce vita.* Built in 1722 off a narrow street in the old part of town, this was the first hotel in St-Tropez. Colette lived here in 1927, and before that, it was the home of pre-Impressionists like Paul Signac. In time it attracted such lovers as Jean Marais and Jean Cocteau, Tyrone Power and Linda Christian, Rita Hayworth (with two different lovers on two different occasions: Orson Welles and Prince Ali Khan), and even Greta Garbo, who arrived alone. Errol Flynn stayed in his room with a young French starlet for 3 days before reappearing. In time, some of the biggest stars in France stayed here, including Bardot herself along with Alain Delon and Charles Aznavour. The high-ceilinged reception area boasts a view of an inner courtyard filled with flowers, over which many of the rooms look as well. Each bedroom was renovated in 2000. Some are on the upper floor, with handmade terra-cotta floor tiles and massive ceiling timbers. Each has a comfortable bed, dignified and utilitarian furniture, and high ceilings, plus a roomy bathroom.

1 bd. d'Aumale, 83900 St-Tropez. ✆ **04-94-55-81-00.** Fax 04-94-97-58-50. www.hotel-le-yaca.fr. 27 units. 250€–520€ double; 500€–1,100€ suite. AE, DC, MC, V. Parking 20€. Closed mid-Oct to mid-Apr. **Amenities:** Restaurant; bar; pool; 24-hr. room service; massage; babysitting; laundry service; dry cleaning. *In room:* A/C, TV, minibar, hair dryer, safe.

Hotel Villa Belrose ★★ *Finds* Small-scale and *luxe,* this is a pocket of posh that's set within a sloping garden in Gassin, an upscale residential neighborhood that's within a 10-minute drive northwest of downtown St-Tropez. It was built in 1997 in an ochre-and-white-walled replica of a rambling private villa, with views that sweep from most of the bedrooms out over the gulf of St-Tropez. Much of the establishment's identity derives from its elegant restaurant, open daily for lunch and dinner to nonresidents who reserve a table in advance. Chef Thierry Thiercelin prepares fixed-price menus that focus on Mediterranean cuisine that's as chic as St-Tropez itself. Bedrooms in this hideaway are lavishly and opulently accessorized with fine linens and lots of upscale toiletries in the bathrooms, but there's no disguising the fact that they fall midway along the spectrum of being either cozy or cramped, depending on your point of view. In many cases, glass doors open onto private terraces, a well-landscaped garden with plenty of botanical surprises and charm, and those magnificently ethereal views.

Gassin, St-Tropez. ✆ **04-94-55-97-97.** Fax 04-94-55-97-98. www.villabelrose.com. 38 units. 530€–670€ double; 1,600€–2,300€ suite. Half-board 95€ extra per person per day. AE, DC, MC, V. Outdoor parking free;

indoor parking 20€. Closed Nov to mid-Mar. **Amenities:** Restaurant; poolside grill; pool; exercise room; spa; 24-hr. room service; babysitting; laundry service; dry cleaning. *In room:* A/C, TV, minibar, hair dryer, safe.

La Bastide de St-Tropez ★★★ Near the landmark place des Lices, this tile-roofed replica of a Provençal manor house looks deliberately severe, but the interior is opulent. It contains a monumental staircase leading from a sun-filled living room to the upper floors. The guest rooms are named according to their individual decor: Rose of Bengal, Fuchsia, or Tangerine Dawn. Each has a terrace or private garden, and some have Jacuzzis. Several, however, are quite small. The soft beds under fine quilting with matching draperies are among the most luxurious in St-Tropez. The well-appointed bathrooms have deluxe toiletries. The hotel is noted for its restaurant, L'Olivier.

Rte. des Carles, 83990 St-Tropez. ✆ **04-94-55-82-55.** Fax 04-94-97-21-71. www.bastide-saint-tropez.com. 26 units. 320€–425€ double; 675€–1,195€ suite. AE, DC, MC, V. Closed Jan. **Amenities:** Restaurant; bar; pool; 24-hr. room service; babysitting; laundry service; dry cleaning. *In room:* A/C, TV, minibar, hair dryer, safe.

Résidence de la Pinède ★★★ This deluxe palace is just a grade below Byblos but, to compensate, offers even finer cuisine. This Relais & Châteaux hotel was built in the 1950s around a rustic stone-sided tower once used to store olives. Jean-Claude and Nicole Delion are the owners of this luxury place on the seaside. The airy, spacious rooms open onto balconies or terraces with a view over the bay of St-Tropez. The stylish but offhand staff seems constantly overburdened. The hotel is St-Tropez's only rival to the Byblos, and, though just as luxurious, it tends to have a more serious and staid clientele. Rooms are stylish and plush, accompanied by neatly kept bathrooms.

Plage de la Bouillabaisse, 83990 St-Tropez. ✆ **04-94-55-91-00.** Fax 04-94-97-73-64. www.relaischateaux.fr/pinede. 40 units. 255€–660€ double; 700€–820€ suite. AE, DC, MC, V. Free parking. Closed mid-Oct to Mar. **Amenities:** Restaurant; bar; pool; 24-hr. room service; babysitting; laundry service; dry cleaning. *In room:* A/C, TV, minibar, hair dryer, safe.

EXPENSIVE

Hôtel La Mandarine ★ La Mandarine is built in the Provençal style with strong angles, thick stucco walls, a tile roof, and patios. Rooms are luxuriously furnished and open onto one or more terraces; some of the suites offer as many as three terraces. Fine linens and elegant fabrics grace the comfortable beds. Beautifully maintained bathrooms are tiled and equipped with luxury toiletries. You definitely get glamour here.

Rte. de Tahiti, 83990 St-Tropez. ✆ **04-94-79-06-66.** Fax 04-94-97-33-67. www.hotellamandarine.com. 42 units. 180€–345€ double; from 385.50€ suite. Rates include continental breakfast. AE, MC, V. Closed Oct 15–Mar 15. Take the road leading to Plage de Tahiti; it's just off the road, a kilometer southeast of the center. **Amenities:** Restaurant; bar; pool; limited room service; massage; babysitting; laundry service; dry cleaning. *In room:* A/C, TV, minibar, safe.

Hôtel La Ponche ★ *Finds* Overlooking the old fishing port, this is a long cherished address, run by the same family for more than half a century. It is named for the famous beach where part of Brigitte Bardot's classic *And God Created Woman* was filmed. The hotel is filled with the original airy paintings of Jacques Cordier, which adds to the elegant atmosphere. Each room has been newly redecorated and is well equipped, opening onto views of the sea. Sun-colored walls with subtle lighting evoke a homey feeling. The bathrooms are midsize to large.

3 rue des Remparts, 83990 St-Tropez. ✆ **04-94-97-02-53.** Fax 04-94-97-78-61. www.laponche.com. 18 units. 210€–310€ double; 220€–480€ suite. AE, MC, V. Parking 18€. Closed Nov to mid-Feb. **Amenities:** Restaurant; bar; limited room service; laundry service; dry cleaning. *In room:* A/C, TV, minibar, hair dryer, safe.

L'Hotel des Lices ★ One consistently reliable bet for lodgings in St-Tropez is this modern hotel in its own small garden, close to place des Lices. The tastefully furnished rooms are tranquil, overlooking either the pool or the garden; their rates vary widely according to season, size, and view. Each unit is designed for comfort, from the quality mattresses to the well-appointed bathrooms. Breakfast is the only meal served, although afternoon snacks are provided beside the pool.

135 av. Augustin-Grangeon, 83900 St-Tropez. ✆ **04-94-97-28-28.** Fax 04-94-97-59-52. 42 units. 130€–241€ double. AE, V. Free parking. Closed Jan 7 to Easter and Nov 11–Dec 26. **Amenities:** Restaurant; bar; pool; 24-hr. room service; babysitting; laundry service; dry cleaning. *In room:* A/C, TV, safe.

MODERATE

Hôtel Ermitage ★ *Value* This hotel is attractively isolated amid the rocky heights of St-Tropez. It was built in the 19th century as a private villa. Today its red-tile roof and green shutters shelter a plush hideaway. A walled garden is illuminated at night, and a cozy corner bar near a wood-burning fireplace takes the chill off blustery evenings. The guest rooms offer good value for St-Tropez. They are pleasantly but simply furnished, with efficiently organized and well-maintained bathrooms. Breakfast is the only meal served.

Av. Paul-Signac, 83990 St-Tropez. ✆ **04-94-97-52-33.** Fax 04-94-97-10-43. 26 units. 95€–155€ double. AE, DC, MC, V. **Amenities:** Bar; limited room service; babysitting; laundry service; dry cleaning. *In room:* TV, hair dryer.

Hôtel La Tartane This small-scale hotel is midway between the center of St-Tropez and the Plage des Salins, about a 3-minute drive from each. There are attractive public rooms with terra-cotta floors and an attentive management that works hard to keep everything pulled together. The guest rooms are well-furnished bungalows centered on the pool. They range from small to medium in size, but each comes with a fine mattress on a double bed or twins. Bathrooms are small and a bit cramped, with minimum shelf space, but they are well maintained.

Route des Salins, 83990 St-Tropez. ✆ **04-94-97-21-23.** Fax 04-94-97-09-16. www.latartane.com. 27 units. 137€–213€ double. AE, DC, V. Closed Oct–Mar 15. **Amenities:** Restaurant; bar; pool; babysitting; laundry service; dry cleaning. *In room:* A/C, TV, hair dryer, minibar, safe.

Hôtel Le Levant On the road leading from the old town of St-Tropez to the beach at Les Salins, this hotel stands behind a screen of cypresses and palmettos. Designed like a low-slung Provençal *mas* (farmhouse), it has thick stucco walls and a tile roof. The recently redecorated rooms, in Provençal motifs, have big windows and white walls, as well as private entrances overlooking the garden and its pool. Each has comfortable double or twin beds. Tiled bathrooms are small but efficiently organized.

Rte. des Salins, 83990 St-Tropez. ✆ **04-94-97-33-33.** Fax 04-94-97-76-13. www.hotel-le-levant.com. 28 units. 106€–142€ double. AE, MC, V. Closed mid-Oct to Mar 15. **Amenities:** Bar; pool; limited room service; babysitting. *In room:* A/C, TV, minibar.

Hôtel Sube If you want to be right on the port, this should be your first choice. A way station and hotel for the French postal services in the 1800s, it was renamed around 1900 for its then-owner. It's directly over the Café de Paris in the center of a shopping arcade. The two-story lounge has a beamed ceiling and a glass front, allowing a great view of the harbor activity. The lounge is furnished with a 3m (10-ft.) high fireplace, a wall torchère, and provincial chairs. The bedrooms are very small and decorated in a provincial style; bathrooms are modest. The maids keep everything clean and tidy.

15 quai Suffren, 83900 St-Tropez. ✆ **04-94-97-30-04.** Fax 04-94-54-89-08. www.nova.fr/sube. 28 units. 120€–250€ double. AE, MC, V. Parking nearby 30€ in summer, free in winter. **Amenities:** Restaurant/cafe; bar; limited room service. *In room:* A/C, TV.

INEXPENSIVE

Hôtel Lou Cagnard ★ *Value* This pleasant roadside inn, with a tile roof and green shutters, offers quiet rooms in the rear overlooking the garden. Monsieur and Madame Yvon have recently taken over and improved the hotel considerably, for it's fresher and more inviting than ever. They extend a warm welcome to their international guests. Although there is nothing grand about the bedrooms, they are comfortable, with fine mattresses and well-maintained bathrooms with adequate shelf space. Continental breakfast is available. This hotel is a bargain in pricey St-Trop.

Av. Paul-Roussel, 83990 St-Tropez. ✆ **04-94-97-04-24.** Fax 04-94-97-09-44. 19 units. 51€–92€ double. MC, V. Closed Nov 4–Dec 26. **Amenities:** Lounge. *In room:* TV, safe.

WHERE TO DINE

The restaurant at the **Résidence de la Pinède** (p. 212) serves flavor-filled Provençal dishes.

EXPENSIVE

Bistrot des Lices ★ PROVENÇAL Don't let the *bistrot* in the name fool you. This is a first-class restaurant, with the most celebrated cuisine in St-Tropez; a glamorous clientele; a world-class inventory of cigars, dessert wines, and after-dinner drinks; and an amused and bemused staff. There's turn-of-the-20th-century decor that subtly evokes the gaslight era, and tables set amid the manicured hedges and flowering shrubs of a garden in back. Chef Christophe Jourdren, who has worked in the kitchens of many stylish and expensive hotels of Provence, is known for his creative use of local produce at its most fresh—both vegetarians and meat-eaters are pleased by its originality. Examples include a risotto of fresh vegetables served with an essence of parsley; a salad of crawfish tails roasted with fresh thyme; codfish served in a basil-flavored crust, with essence of tomatoes and fresh garlic; and filets of young rabbit served with spice bread. Hearty appetites appreciate the filet of beef "Rossini," with foie gras and essence of truffles.

3 place des Lices. ✆ **04-94-55-82-82.** Reservations required in summer. Main courses 18€–35€; fixed-price menus 18€ lunch, 28€ dinner. AE, MC, V. Daily noon–2:30pm and 7:30–11:30pm.

La Ramade PROVENÇAL We consider this courtyard-style restaurant an appealing antidote to St-Tropez's congestion and commercialism. It's designed for maximum exposure to the Provençal night, thanks to tables beneath the trees. Despite the charming, slightly disorganized service, you'll appreciate the seafood-based specialties that emerge amid clouds of herb-infused steam from the tiny kitchens. Examples include savory versions of both *bourrides* and bouillabaisses, as well as a platter of sea wolf slow-roasted over charcoal flames.

3 rue du Temple. ✆ **04-94-97-00-15.** Reservations recommended. Main courses 25€–50€. AE, DC, MC, V. Daily 8pm–midnight. Closed mid-Oct to Easter.

Le Bar à Vin ★ FRENCH/PROVENÇAL This appealing and reasonably priced bistro is close to place des Lices. In summer, the guests tend to be Europeans in their 20s and 30s on holiday. The crowd is mixed, though heavily gay. Things are calmer in winter, when the diners are usually locals. Managed by a bilingual entrepreneur, Bertrand Bertrand, it boasts a red-tile floor by the ceramic artist Alain Vagh. The menu items are designed to accompany a choice selection of wines. Provençal and Mediterranean flavors predominate: sardines *en escabèche* (grilled sardines marinated in olive oil, herbs, and vinegar and served cold); gratin of eggplant with goat cheese; and grilled beefsteak, veal, and lamb.

13 rue des Feniers. ✆ **04-94-97-46-10.** Reservations recommended. Main courses 23€–39€. MC, V. May–Sept daily 7pm–1am; Oct–Apr Wed–Mon 7pm–1am. Closed Jan.

Le Girelier PROVENÇAL The Rouets own this portside restaurant whose blue-and-white color scheme has become its own kind of trademark. Filled with rattan furniture and boasting a large glassed-in veranda, it serves well-prepared grilled fish in many versions, as well as bouillabaisse, served for two only. Also available is brochette of monkfish, a kettle of mussels, and *pipérade* (a Basque omelet with pimentos, garlic, and tomatoes).

Quai Jean-Jaurès. ✆ **04-94-97-03-87.** Main courses 25€–80€; fixed-price menu 35€. AE, DC, MC, V. Daily noon–2pm and 7–11pm. Closed Jan–Mar and Nov 11–Dec 15.

Les Mouscardins ★★★ FRENCH/PROVENÇAL At the end of St-Tropez's harbor, this restaurant wins awards for culinary perfection. The dining room is in formal Provençal style with an adjoining sunroom under a canopy. The menu includes classic Mediterranean dishes; as an appetizer, we recommend *moules* (mussels) *marinières.* The two celebrated fish stews of the Côte d'Azur are offered: bourride Provençale and bouillabaisse. The fish dishes are excellent, particularly the sauté of monkfish, wild mushrooms, and green beans. The dessert specialties are soufflés made with Grand Marnier or Cointreau.

1 rue Portalet. ✆ **04-94-97-29-00.** Reservations required. Main courses 25€–50€; fixed-price menu 65€ at lunch, 50€ at dinner. AE, DC, MC, V. June–Sept Mon–Sat noon–2pm and 7:30–10pm; Oct–May Tues–Sat noon–2pm and 7:30–9:30pm.

Spoon Byblos ★★ FRENCH/INTERNATIONAL This is one of the latest statements of Alain Ducasse, considered by some the world's greatest chef—at least the most acclaimed. Originally launched in Paris, Spoon has now traveled to everywhere from London to the Riviera. Within the swanky Hotel Byblos, Spoon serves the cuisines of many cultures with produce mainly from the Mediterranean. Special inspiration is drawn from the food of Catalonia, Andalusia, and Morocco, and there are more than 300 wines from around the world. Music plays in the background, ranging from hip-hop to the hits of the '70s.

The restaurant opens onto a circular bar of blue-tinted glass and polished stainless steel. The menu will have you salivating before you even take a bite. Dig into the shrimp and squid consommé with a hint of jasmine and orange, or the spicy king prawns on a skewer. A lamb couscous is served, and it's delectable; you also might enjoy spit-roasted John Dory. You might top off a meal with the chef's favorite cheesecake.

In the Hotel Byblos, av. Paul-Signac. ✆ **04-94-56-68-00.** Reservations required. Main courses 30€–38€. Summer daily 8pm–2am; off season daily 7:30pm–12:30am.

MODERATE

Chez Joseph TRADITIONAL FRENCH Chic, yet casual and friendly, this restaurant is a fixture on the St-Tropez restaurant scene. The cozy bar is outfitted with photos of the rich and famous (Elton John, George Michael, Michael Bolton); the crowd is heavily gay and fashionable. Glasses of champagne are served to an animated crowd that seems to remain in place until 6am the next morning. Adjacent to the bar is a restaurant with about 35 tables, giving you lots of opportunities for people gazing. Menu items are consciously artful: lobster salad, an adventurous tartare of salmon and lobster (advisable only for the strong and the brave), tournedos Rossini, grilled jumbo shrimp, and fricassée of scallops. Except for one or two costly seafood dishes, most prices are quite reasonable.

Place de la Mairie. ✆ **04-94-97-01-66.** Reservations recommended. Main courses 12.50€–48.95€. AE, MC, V. May–Sept daily 1–3pm and 8pm–midnight; Oct–Apr Thurs–Tues 1–3pm and 8pm–midnight. Closed Nov 15–Dec 15.

Chez Maggi PROVENÇAL/ITALIAN Across from Chez Joseph (above), this restaurant retains the name it was given by two women during its earlier incarnation as a lesbian bar. Since its acquisition by the present owners, it has emerged as St-Tropez's most flamboyant gay restaurant/bar. At least half its floor space is devoted to a very busy bar, where patrons tend to range from ages 25 to 35, and whose turf extends out onto the pavement in front. There are no tables and chairs in front, however, so cruising at Chez Maggi, in the words of loyal patrons, is "très crazee" and seems to extend for blocks in every direction, spilling over into Chez Joseph.

Meals are served in an adjoining dining room. Menu items include chicken salad with ginger, *petits farcis Provençaux* (local vegetables stuffed with minced meat and herbs), brochettes of sea bass with lemon sauce, and a well-recommended chicken curry with coconut milk, capers, and cucumbers.

7 rue Sibille. ✆ **04-94-97-16-12.** Reservations recommended. Main courses 14€–27€; fixed-price menu 30€. MC, V. Restaurant daily 7pm–midnight; bar daily 7pm–3am. Closed Oct to mid-Mar.

L'Echalotte ★ TRADITIONAL FRENCH This charming restaurant, with a tiny garden and simple but clean dining room and tables on a veranda (weather permitting), serves consistently good food for moderate prices. Because of demand, reservations might be difficult to get, especially in peak summer weeks. The cuisine is solidly bourgeois, including grilled veal kidneys, crawfish with drawn-butter sauce, filet of turbot with truffles, and classic dishes of southwestern France, such as three preparations of foie gras and magret of duckling. The menu includes several species of fish; daurade royale can be cooked in a salt crust.

35 rue Allard. ✆ **04-94-54-83-26.** Reservations recommended in summer. Main courses 13€–30€; fixed-price menu 18€–26€. AE, MC, V. Daily noon–2pm and 7–9pm. Closed Thurs lunch in season and closed Thurs all day off season.

ST-TROPEZ AFTER DARK

On the lobby level of the Hôtel Byblos, **Les Caves du Roy,** avenue Paul-Signac (✆ **04-94-56-68-00;** www.lescavesduroy.com), is the most self-consciously chic nightclub in St-Tropez. Entrance is free, but drink prices begin at a whopping 18€. It's open nightly from 11:30pm till dawn, but only from May to late September. **Le Papagayo,** in the Résidence du Nouveau-Port, rue Gambetta (✆ **04-94-97-76-70**), is one of the largest nightclubs in town. The decor was inspired by the psychedelic 1960s. Entrance is 17€ and includes the first drink.

Immediately adjacent to Le Papagayo is a club whose upscale male-and-female clients might be equally at home in Les Caves du Roy, **Le VIP Room,** in the Résidence du Port (✆ **04-94-97-14-70**); they pay about 16€ per cocktail for the chance to (demurely or not) whoop it up in sleepy old St-Tropez. Expect an active bar area, a dance floor, and the kind of social posturing and preening that can be either amusing or not, depending on your point of view.

Le Pigeonnier, 13 rue de la Ponche (✆ **04-94-97-84-26**), rocks, rolls, and welcomes a crowd that's mostly gay, male, and between the ages of 20 and 50.

Most of the socializing revolves around the long, narrow bar, where menfolk from all over Europe seem to enjoy chitchatting. There's also a dance floor. For another gay hotspot, check out the action at **Chez Maggi** (see "Where to Dine," above).

Below the Hôtel Sube, the **Café de Paris,** sur le Port (✆ **04-94-97-00-56**), is one of the most consistently popular hangouts. An attempt has been made to glorify a utilitarian room with early-1900s globe lights, an occasional 19th-century bronze artifact, masses of artificial flowers, and a long zinc bar. The crowd is irreverent and animated. It's open daily. The reporter Leslie Maitland aptly captured the kind of crowd attracted to **Café Sénéquier,** sur le Port (✆ **04-94-97-00-90**): "What else can one do but gawk at a tall, well-dressed young woman who appears *comme il faut* at Sénéquier's with a large white rat perched upon her shoulder, with which she occasionally exchanges little kisses, while casually chatting with her friends."

Le Bar du Port, sur le Port, adjacent to the Café de Paris (no phone), is breezy, airy, and almost obsessively hip. This cafe/bar attracts one of the most consistently young clienteles on the port. Expect lots of table-hopping, stylishly skimpy clothing, recorded music that might make you want to get up and dance, and insights into what's really going on in the minds of French 20-somethings.

If your idea of a night out is sitting in a cafe drinking wine, you can "hang out" at such joints as **Kelly's Irish Pub,** sur le Port (✆ **04-94-54-89-11**), which draws mostly a foreign crowd at the end of Vieux Port. The tavern is casual, not chic. If you're nostalgic for a St-Germain-des-Prés atmosphere, head for the old-fashioned **Café des Arts,** place des Lices (✆ **04-94-97-02-25**), with its zinc bar, one of the most famous in St-Tropez.

2 Ste-Maxime

24km (15 miles) SW of St-Raphaël; 61km (38 miles) SW of Cannes

Ste-Maxime is just across the gulf from glitzy St-Tropez, but its atmosphere is much more sedate. Young families are the major vacationers here, though an occasional refugee from across the water will come over to escape the see-and-be-seen crowd. The town is surrounded by the red cliffs of the Massif des Maures, protecting it from harsh weather. However, the wide stretches of sand and the cafe-lined promenades lure travelers to spend their days basking in the sun. More active vacationers might want to try windsurfing or water-skiing in the calm waters, or even golfing. A 16th-century fort, built by the monks of Lérins (who also named the port), houses a museum. The best thing about Ste-Maxime is the price—though the town isn't as in vogue as St-Tropez, it's fun and affordable.

ESSENTIALS

GETTING THERE The nearest train service is at St-Raphaël. Call **Sodetrav** buses (✆ **04-94-95-24-82**) for bus information from St-Raphaël. Buses also

---

Tips **Wheeling around Ste-Maxime**

A great way to explore Ste-Maxime is on two wheels with some wind in your hair. Consider visiting **Rent Bike,** 13 rue Magali (✆ **04-94-43-98-07**), which rents bikes and mopeds. Mountain bikes are 12€ per day, with a 150€ deposit; mopeds are 17€, with a 380€ deposit.

---

travel to Ste-Maxime from St-Tropez for a fare of 6€ each way. **Transports Maritimes MMG,** quai L.-Condroyer (© **04-94-96-51-00**), provides a boat service from St-Tropez to Ste-Maxime April through October (trip time: 20 min.). Tickets cost 6€ one-way—only slightly more than bus fare, and for a much more pleasant ride.

VISITOR INFORMATION The **Office de Tourisme** is on promenade Simon-Lorière (© **04-94-55-75-55**).

A DAY AT THE BEACH

Beaches are the main attraction here. There are at least four nearby. Two are an easy walk from the town center: Across the road from the casino is **Plage du Casino**—we advise avoiding it because of the fumes from the nearby roadway, the narrow sands, and the hordes of sunbathers. A better bet is **Plage de la Croisette,** a wider, nominally less-congested expanse that's a 2-minute walk west of Plage du Casino. The most appealing are **Plage de la Nartelle** and the adjacent **Plage des Eléphants,** broad expanses of clean, fine-textured light-beige sand about 1¼ miles west of town. To reach them, follow signs along the coastal road pointing to St-Tropez. Here you can rent a mattress for sunbathing from any of several concessionaires for around 20€.

SEEING THE SIGHTS

Start with the 16th-century **Tour Carrée des Dames (Dames Tower)** at place des Aliziers. It was originally a defensive structure; today it's home to the **Musée des Traditions Locales,** place de l'Eglise (© **04-94-96-70-30**), with exhibits on the area's history and tradition. The museum is open Wednesday through Monday April through October from 10am to noon and 3 to 6pm, and November through March from 3 to 6pm only. Admission is 3€ for adults and 1€ for children.

Facing the tower is the **Eglise Ste-Maxime,** place des Niziers (© **04-94-55-74-60**), with a green marble altar from the former Carthusian monastery of La Verne in the Massif des Maures. The choir stalls date from the 15th century.

St-Maxime hosts various markets, including a daily **flower-and-food market** on rue Fernand-Bessy Monday through Saturday from 6am to 1pm and 4:30 to 8pm. On Thursday, a **crafts market** is held on and around place du Marché; on Friday, vendors sell a variety of **knickknacks** on place Jean-Mermoz. In the pedestrian streets of the old town, an **arts-and-crafts fair** takes place daily in summer from 4 to 11pm.

Outside town are several worthy sights. About 10km (6 miles) north on the road to Muy is the **Musée du Phonographe et de la Musique Méchanique** (© **04-94-96-50-52**). This extensive display of audio equipment is the result of one woman's 40-year obsession. Sometimes she gives personal tours. In the museum is one of Edison's original "talking machines" and an audiovisual pathegraphe used to teach foreign language in 1913. The museum is open Easter through October only, Wednesday through Sunday from 10am to noon and 3 to 6pm. Admission is 3€ for adults and 1.50€ for children 5 to 12 years.

If you're a nature lover, follow the signs along boulevard Bellevue for 1.5km (1 mile) north of town to the little town of **Sémaphore.** Here you'll find a panoramic view of the mountains and oceans from an altitude of 120m (400 ft.). There are also many hiking trails that wind along the coast or into the mountains. The tourist office has maps, or you can head for the Sentier du Littoral (Chemin des Douaniers), a trail that meanders along the coast toward St-Tropez and has access to the sea at almost all points along the way.

WHERE TO STAY

Although hotels are less expensive here than in the neighboring towns, you might find that you must pay for half board in July and August. Most places are closed in winter, but May, June, and September are good times to find a good deal.

VERY EXPENSIVE

Hotel Le Beauvallon ★★★ At long last, Ste-Maxime offers a *luxe* palace as worthy as some of the plush joints of its rival, St-Tropez. Overlooking the St-Tropez Bay and enclosed by landscaped gardens, this is a plush choice with palatial elegance and a grand cuisine. Bedrooms are spacious and sumptuously furnished in grand comfort, and modern bathrooms contain luxurious toiletries, deep tubs, and power showers. It's an ideal choice for a romantic escape and shelters you from the tacky world of the heavily built-up waterfront, with its apartments, condos, and hotels. The resort is so all-encompassing that you might find it tempting not to leave the grounds. Guests dine at three venues, including on the fine white sands of the hotel's private beach. Golfers can play on the adjacent 18-hole course.

Baie de St-Tropez, Beauvallon Grimaud 83120 Ste-Maxime. ✆ **04-94-55-78-88.** Fax 04-94-55-78-78. www.lebeauvallon.com. 69 units. 320€–610€ double; from 670€–2,200€ suite. AE, DC, MC, V. **Amenities:** 3 restaurants; 2 bars; golf; private spas; 24-hr. room service; babysitting; laundry service; dry cleaning. *In room:* A/C, TV, minibar, hair dryer, safe.

EXPENSIVE

Hôtel La Belle Aurore ★★ La Belle Aurore is on its own private beach and is one of the finest addresses in the area for the cost. If it has a serious challenger, it's Les Santolines (see below). Though the well-furnished guest rooms aren't air-conditioned, each has a terrace overlooking the sea; the breezes keep the inside temperature comfortable. Tiled bathrooms are small and tidy.

4 bd. Jean-Moulin, 83120 Ste-Maxime. ✆ **04-94-96-02-45.** Fax 04-94-96-63-87. 17 units. 214€–250€ double; 404€–550€ suite. AE, DC, MC, V. Closed Oct 15–Mar 15. **Amenities:** Restaurant; lounge; pool; limited room service; babysitting; laundry service; dry cleaning. *In room:* A/C, TV, minibar, hair dryer, safe.

MODERATE

Hôtel La Croisette ★ This charming hotel is surrounded by its own lush garden and has an intimate aura, lying 200m (656 ft.) from the beach. Room rates vary according to view—those with a balcony and sea view are most expensive; those that open onto the garden are less. Homey and cozy, they are decorated in a provincial southern style; the tiled bathrooms are tidy. Maintenance here is high quality.

2 bd. des Romarins, 83120 Ste-Maxime. ✆ **04-94-96-17-75.** Fax 04-94-96-52-40. www.hotel-la-croisette.com. 19 units. 109€–165€ double; 284€ suite. AE, MC, V. Closed Nov–Mar 15. **Amenities:** Bar; limited room service; babysitting; laundry service; dry cleaning. *In room:* A/C, TV, minibar, hair dryer, safe.

Hôtel Les Santolines ★★ This is an excellent choice for those who want to remove themselves from the crowds. Les Santolines is 10 minutes from the busy center area but still close to the beach. The building is arranged around a grassy courtyard that has a pool and the town's most inviting *jardin fleuri* (flower garden). Rooms are comfortable and private; most have balconies. The look is very French provincial. Some bathrooms are rather dramatically tiled in sea blue; all have double basins.

Quartier de la Croisette, 83120 Ste-Maxime. ✆ **04-94-96-31-34.** Fax 04-94-49-22-12. www.hotel-les-santolines.com. 13 units. 109€–125€ double. AE, MC, V. **Amenities:** Bar; pool; babysitting. *In room:* A/C, TV, minibar, hair dryer.

Hôtel Montfleuri ★ *Finds* This hotel on a hillside in a quiet residential neighborhood opens onto a superb view of the Gulf of St-Tropez. The large guest rooms come with balconies. Each has a comfortable mattress and fine linen, twin or double beds, and a small bathroom. The hotel restaurant serves "family cooking" Provençal style in a pleasant garden.

3 av. Montfleuri, 83120 Ste-Maxime. ✆ **04-94-55-75-10.** Fax 04-94-49-25-07. 30 units. 85€–230€ double. AE, DC, MC, V. Closed Nov 5–Dec 26 and Jan 5–Mar 1. **Amenities:** Restaurant; bar; pool; laundry service; dry cleaning. *In room:* A/C, TV, minibar, hair dryer, safe.

INEXPENSIVE

Hôtel de la Poste This modern hotel's location in the town center, convenient to the beach and shopping, makes up for what it lacks in personality. With a recent head-to-toe renovation, the inside is cool and comfortable, with a quiet lounge and a pleasant bar. Guest rooms are clean, well maintained, and comfortably furnished. Bathrooms are small but well maintained. There's a friendly staff, always happy to help you decide how to spend your day. There's no restaurant in the hotel, but you're not far from a wide selection.

11 bd. Frédéric-Mistral, 83120 Ste-Maxime. ✆ **04-94-96-18-33.** Fax 04-94-55-88-63. 28 units. 75€–115€ double. AE, DC, MC, V. **Amenities:** Lounge; bar; pool; limited room service; babysitting; laundry service; dry cleaning. *In room*: A/C, TV, minibar, hair dryer, safe.

Hôtel Le Chardon Bleu Situated 10m (33 ft.) from the beach, Le Chardon Bleu is also close to the pedestrian area and the casino. The hotel has a garden where you can enjoy a meal amid the aroma of the flowers. The well-maintained rooms are comfortable and inviting, though the furnishings are standard; all have small balconies. Bathrooms are tiled and compact.

20 rue de Verdun, 83120 Ste-Maxime. ✆ **04-94-55-52-22.** Fax 04-94-43-90-89. 25 units. 46€–79€ double. AE, DC, MC, V. **Amenities:** Lounge. *In room:* A/C, TV, minibar, safe.

WHERE TO DINE

Le Gruppi FRENCH/PROVENÇAL Earthy and amusing, this restaurant thrives on the promenade adjacent to the sea and has done so ever since the Lindermanns opened it in the 1960s. Bay windows illuminate dining rooms on two floors, decorated in bright green and salmon with rattan furnishings. The deluxe version of the establishment's savory bouillabaisse must be ordered a day in advance; otherwise, you get a simplified version, which the chefs refer to as a *soupe de poisson.* Other menu items are seafood platters; herbed and roasted lamb from Sisteron; and veal, chicken, and all the vegetarian bounty of Provence. If you opt for fish, a staff member will carry a basket filled with the best of the day's catch for your inspection and advise you on their respective merits. One particularly succulent example is braised sea wolf in champagne sauce.

82 av. Charles-de-Gaulle. ✆ **04-94-96-03-61.** Reservations recommended. Main courses 20€–30€; fixed-price menus 23€–34€. AE, MC, V. Apr–Sept daily noon–2:30pm and 7–10pm; Oct–Mar Tues noon–2:30pm, Thurs–Mon noon–2:30pm and 7–10pm. Closed 2 weeks in Dec.

Restaurant Sans Souci FRENCH/PROVENÇAL Philippe Sibilia's Italian-born grandfather opened this place in 1953, and since then it's been always reliable, always good. In a turn-of-the-20th-century building next to the church, it has a Provence-inspired decor with ceiling beams and old-time accessories. Menu items prepared by the good-humored owner are concocted from fresh ingredients and years of practice. Examples are pan-fried Provençal veal, sea wolf with fennel, octopus salad, filet of hake with basil, and one of our favorite dishes anywhere, noisettes of lamb with a tapenade of olives that's enhanced with pulverized anchovies and a hint of fresh cream.

58 rue Paul-Bert. ✆ **04-94-96-18-26.** Reservations recommended. Main courses 12.50€–16.20€; fixed-price menus 16€–25€. V. Feb–Oct daily noon–2pm and 7–10:30pm.

3 Fréjus ★

3km (2 miles) W of St-Raphaël; 14km (9 miles) NE of St-Tropez

Fréjus was founded by Julius Caesar in 49 B.C. as Forum Julii; later, under Augustus's rule, it became a key naval base. The warships with which Augustus defeated Antony and Cleopatra at the battle at Actium were built here in 31 B.C. By the Middle Ages, however, the port had declined. It began to silt up from disuse and was eventually filled in. Today the port lies more than 3km (2 miles) inland.

The Vieille Ville still boasts remnants from Roman times, including parts of an arena and a theater. There's also an interesting section dating to medieval times called the "Cité Episcopale." The baptistery is one of France's oldest ecclesiastical buildings.

In more recent times, Fréjus has again expanded toward the water. The beach area, Fréjus Plage, tends to blend into St-Raphaël. The two towns are often considered a single holiday destination, though serious beachgoers often opt to stay in St-Raphaël, where the hotels are closer to the water and cheaper.

ESSENTIALS

GETTING THERE From the main station at St-Raphaël, several **trains** a day arrive at a small train station in Fréjus on rue Martin-Bidoure (✆ **08-36-35-35-35**). The beach is a shorter walk (about 15 min.) from the St-Raphaël station than from the Fréjus station.

Estérel (✆ **04-94-53-78-46**) runs a bus service between the two towns every 30 minutes. Buses arrive at the **Fréjus Gare Routière,** place Paul-Vernet (✆ **04-94-82-16-88**), at the east end of the town center. One-way tickets cost 2€. **Sodetrav** buses (✆ **04-94-95-24-82**) en route to St-Tropez from St-Raphaël stop along the coast in Fréjus.

GETTING AROUND You can rent mopeds at **Location 2 Roues,** 83 Le Méditerranée-Nouveau Port (✆ **04-94-40-76-20**). Prices range from 25€ to 40€. Credit-card deposits are required. **Holiday Bikes,** 93 av. de Provence (✆ **04-94-52-30-65**), rents the pedal-powered version of two-wheeled transportation. Expect to pay 9€ to 17.50€, plus a security deposit.

VISITOR INFORMATION The **Office de Tourisme** is at 325 rue Jean-Jaurès (✆ **04-94-51-83-83**).

SPECIAL EVENTS The **Fête des Plantes** is held annually in the park of the Villa Aurélienne (see below), during a 9-day period in late March and April. For information, call ✆ **04-94-52-90-41** or contact the local tourist office.

EXPLORING THE TOWN

THE TOP SIGHTS

The best way to see the Roman ruins is to hop on one of the town's sightseeing **Trains du Soleil** (see above).

The best preserved of the ruins is the **Amphithéâtre** ★, rue Henri-Vadon (✆ **04-94-51-34-31**). In Roman times, it held up to 10,000 spectators. The upper levels of the galleries have been reconstructed with the same greenish stone used to create the original building. Today it's used as a venue for rock concerts

Tips Touring Fréjus by *le Petit Train*

For an overview of Fréjus's rich assortment of ancient and medieval monuments, take the municipally funded blue-and-white **Trains du Soleil** (also known as *"le petit train"*). Electrically powered and rubber wheeled, they operate hourly between 2:20 and 6:20pm daily in July and August, and Tuesday through Saturday the rest of the year. Tickets cost 5.50€ for adults and 3.75€ for children 3 to 9. Tours originate from parking lot Kennedy, midway between Fréjus and St-Raphaël adjacent to the Pont d'Arcole. Call © **04-93-41-31-09** for more details.

and the city's two annual Spanish-style *corridas* (bullfights). Ask the tourist office for dates and details. It's open Wednesday through Monday April through September from 9:30am to noon and 2 to 6:30pm, and October through March from 9am to noon and 2 to 4:30pm. Admission is free.

A half-kilometer north of town on rue du Théâtre-Romain, the **Théâtre Romain** (© **04-94-51-34-31**), not to be confused with the amphitheater, has been largely destroyed. However, one wall and a few of the lower sections remain and are used as a backdrop for occasional summer concerts. The site is open 24 hours, and visits, which aren't monitored, are free. Northwest of the theater, you can see a few soaring arches as they follow the road leading to Cannes. These are the remaining pieces of the 40km (25-mile) aqueduct that once brought fresh water to Fréjus's water tower.

Cité Episcopale ★★ The town's most frequently visited site is its fortified cathedral in the heart of the Vieille Ville. At its center is the **Cathédrale St-Léonce,** completed in the 16th century after many generations of laborers had worked on it. It was begun in the 10th century, and parts of it date from the 12th and 13th centuries. Its most striking features are Renaissance—ornately carved walnut doors depicting scenes from the Virgin's life and tableaux inspired by Saracen invasions. The 5th-century **baptistery** ★★ is one of the oldest in France. Octagonal like many paleo-Christian baptisteries, it features eight black granite columns with white capitals. Most interesting are the two doors, which are different sizes. Catechumens would enter by the smaller of the two; inside, a bishop would wash their feet and baptize them in the center pool. The baptized would then leave through the larger door; this signified their enlarged spiritual stature.

The most beautiful of all the structures in the Episcopal quarter is the 12th-century **cloister** ★★. The colonnade's two slender marble pillars are typical of the Provençal style. Inside, the wooden ceiling is divided into 1,200 small panels decorated with animals, portraits, and grotesques by 15th-century artists. A bell tower rises above the cloister, its steeple covered with colored tiles. In the building is the **Musée Archéologique,** which features a collection of Roman finds from the area. Roman sculptures dominate, but the small Greek vases that Romans used during their travels are some of the most attractive pieces. Be sure to see the two-headed bust of Hermes; since its discovery in 1970, it has come to be the town's symbol.

Rue de Fleury. © **04-94-51-26-30.** Admission includes entrance to all sites, the museum, and (optional) guided tour of cloister and baptistery: 4.60€ adults, 3.10€ students under 25 and children. Apr–Sept daily 9am–7:30pm; Oct–Mar daily 9am–noon and 2–7pm.

MORE SIGHTS

The small, round **Chapelle Cocteau,** avenue Nicola (✆ **04-94-53-27-06**), was designed by the artist, film director, social gadfly, and *prince des poètes* Jean Cocteau. It was built between 1961 and 1965, and was decorated by Cocteau himself. Its octagonal shape, low-slung with small windows, might remind you of an African thatch-covered hut. It's open Wednesday through Monday April through September from 2 to 6pm, and October through March from 2 to 5pm. Admission is free.

Just outside Fréjus are two curiosities that reflect the cultural mixture of France's early-20th-century empire. The **Pagode Hong-Hien** (✆ **04-94-53-25-29**), still used as a Buddhist temple, is about 2km (1¼ miles) northeast on R.N. 7. It was built in 1919 by soldiers conscripted from Indochina as a shrine to their fallen comrades. It's open daily from 9am to noon and 2 to 6pm; admission is 1.25€. Off D4, leading to Bagnols, you can see the purple-red exterior of the **Mosquée Soudanaise** (no phone), built by Muslim soldiers conscripted from the French colony of Mali. It's controlled by the French Ministry of Defense and is off-limits to casual visitors.

The grand neoclassical **Villa Aurélienne,** avenue du Général-d'Armée Calliès (✆ **04-94-52-90-41**), was originally a holiday home for an English industrialist in the 1880s. It's the venue of a widely varied series of temporary art exhibitions. Call for information. The park surrounding the villa hosts occasional festivals (see "Special Events," above).

Parc Zoologique, Le Capitou (✆ **04-98-11-37-37**), is off A8 about 5.5km (3½ miles) north of the center of Fréjus. The safari park is home to more than 250 species of animals and is open daily May through September from 10am to 6pm, and October through April from 10am to 5pm. Admission is 10€ for adults and 6€ for children 3 to 10.

WHERE TO STAY

Hôtel L'Aréna ★★ This hotel in the center of the Vieille Ville is created from a former bank. Beautifully restored in bright Provençal colors, L'Aréna is an appropriately informal beach town retreat. Each of the small but comfortable rooms opens onto a garden area where tropical plants give the air a sweet smell. Furnishings and mattresses are comfortable and simple, but not at all plush. Likewise, bathrooms are small and tidy, with minimal equipment. The staff is friendly, and the hotel is a good value for the area.

145 rue du Général-de-Gaulle, 83615 Fréjus. ✆ **04-94-17-09-40.** Fax 04-94-52-01-52. 36 units. 95€–145€ double. AE, DC, MC, V. Closed Dec 15–Jan 16. **Amenities:** Restaurant; bar; pool; 24-hr. room service; babysitting; laundry service; dry cleaning. *In room:* A/C, TV, hair dryer.

WHERE TO DINE

Les Potiers ★ *Finds* FRENCH/PROVENÇAL The town's smallest and most charming restaurant is midway between the town hall and the ancient arena. Staffed only by chef Hubert Guillard and his wife, Jeanne, it occupies a century-old stone house and has only 15 seats. Menu items change with the seasons but usually include rabbit à la Provençal; goat served with fruit salad and warm asparagus; filet of lamb marinated in thyme, olive oil, and garlic and served with a sauce miroir concocted from cream of Cassis and red Bandol wine; and filet of sea wolf with a rosemary-cream sauce. For dessert, how about a thin slice of apple tart with cinnamon-flavored ice cream?

135 rue des Potiers. ✆ **04-94-51-33-74.** Reservations required. Main courses 13.50€–21€; fixed-price menus 22€–31€. MC, V. Wed–Mon noon–1:45pm and 7:30pm–9:15pm.

4 St-Raphaël

3km (2 miles) E of Fréjus; 43km (27 miles) SW of Cannes

Between the red lava peaks of the Massif de l'Estérel and the densely forested hills of the Massif des Maures, St-Raphaël was first popular during Roman times, when rich families came to the large resort here. Barbaric hordes and Saracen invasions characterized the Middle Ages; it wasn't until 1799, when a proud Napoléon landed at the small harbor beach on his return from Egypt, that the city once again drew attention.

Fifteen years later, that same spot in the harbor was the point of embarkation for the fallen emperor's journey to exile on Elba. In 1864, Alphonse Karr, a journalist and ex-editor of *Le Figaro,* helped reintroduce St-Raphaël as a resort. Dumas, Maupassant, and Berlioz came here from Paris on his recommendation. Gounod also came; he composed *Romeo et Juliet* here in 1866. Unfortunately, most of the Belle Epoque villas and grand hotels were destroyed during World War II when St-Raphaël served as a key landing point for Allied soldiers.

Today some of the mansions have been rebuilt and others have been replaced by modern resorts and buildings. However, the city still offers the wide beaches, good restaurants and hotels, and coastal ambience of other Côte d'Azur resorts—at a fraction of the price. This is why St-Raphaël, one of the richest towns on the coast, draws more families than couture-clad Parisians.

ESSENTIALS

GETTING THERE Reaching St-Raphaël is easier than ever. The town sits directly on the rail lines running parallel to the coast between Marseille in the west and the Italian border town of Ventimiglia in the east. Within some 3 hours you can take a fast **TGV train** from Paris to Marseille. For rail information and schedules, call ✆ **877/2TGVMED** or check www.raileurope.com. Once at Marseilles, it is another 1¾ hours by train to St-Raphaël. Trains leave Marseille every hour during the day, costing 20€ one-way. Trains from Cannes head east to St-Raphaël every 30 minutes during the day (25-min. trip); one-way fare costs 6.50€.

The bus station behind the train station provides both local and regional service. **Estérel-Forum Autocars** (✆ **04-94-95-16-71**) links directly with Fréjus, charging around 2€ each way for buses that run at 30-minute intervals, and around 6.50€ for service from Nice, a 60-minute transit. **Sodetrav** (✆ **04-94-95-24-82**) links St-Raphaël with St-Tropez (trip time: 70–90 min.); fares are around 9€ each way. Buses from Nice arrive every hour. Another option for local bus service into nearby hills and hamlets is provided by **Beltrame** (✆ **04-94-95-95-16**).

Between April and October, **Les Bateaux Bleus** (✆ **04-94-95-17-46**) provides waterborne transit—about a half-dozen boats per day—between a point near the railway station of St-Raphaël and St-Tropez for around 10€ each way.

By car from St. Tropez in the west, take D98A northwest to N98, at which point you drive east toward St-Raphaël. From Cannes, head west along N98.

GETTING AROUND Normally, taxis line up at the bus station; if you can't find one, call ✆ **04-94-95-04-25.** You can rent bikes and scooters from **Patrick Moto,** 260 av. du Général-Léclerc (✆ **04-94-53-87-11**). Bikes rent for 8.50€, with a 130€ deposit; mountain bikes rent for 15€, with a 300€ deposit; and scooters go for 20€, with a 400€ deposit. MasterCard and Visa can be used for the deposit.

VISITOR INFORMATION The **Office de Tourisme** faces the train station on rue Waldeck-Rousseau (✆ **04-94-19-52-52**).

SPECIAL EVENTS The **Competition Internationale de Jazz de New Orleans** is held during 3 days in early July, when Dixieland-style musicians from around the world congregate to display their talent. Call ✆ **04-94-19-88-47,** or contact the tourist office, for exact dates and musical venues. In mid-August, the **Festival St-Pierre des Pêcheurs** is conducted in and around the town center. Honoring the fishers who helped feed the town throughout most of its existence, it features a night of fireworks, a brief medieval-style procession to and from the village church, music, dancing on platforms built beside the port, and a series of *jutes* (mock naval battles between competing boat teams) where everyone gets soaking wet.

A DAY AT THE BEACH

Of course, most visitors come here to have fun on the beaches. The best ones (some rock, some sand) are between the Vieux Port and Santa Lucia; stands rent equipment for watersports on each beach.

The closest to the town center is the **Plage du Veillat,** a long stretch of sand that's crowded and family friendly. Within a 5-minute walk east of the town center is **Plage Beau Rivage,** whose name is misleading because it's covered with a smooth and even coating of light-gray pebbles that might be uncomfortable to lie on without a towel. History buffs will enjoy a 7km (4½-mile) excursion east of town to the **Plage du Débarquement,** a partly pebble and partly sand stretch that was hurled into world headlines on August 15, 1945, when Allied forces overran the southern tier of occupied France, bringing World War II to a more rapid conclusion. Today expect relatively uncrowded conditions, except during the midsummer crush.

St-Raphaël's answer to the decadence of nearby St-Tropez is most visible in the municipality's official nude beach, the **Plage de St-Ayguls,** 10km (6 miles) west of the town center. Surrounded by thick screens of reeds that thrive along the marshy seafront, it's a short, clearly signposted walk from the heart of the simple fishing village of St-Ayguls.

SEEING THE SIGHTS

St-Raphaël is divided in half by railroad tracks. The historically interesting **Vieille Ville** (old city) lies inland from the tracks. Here you'll find St-Raphaël's only intact ancient structure, the **Eglise des Templiers,** place de la Vieille Eglise, Quartier des Templiers (✆ **04-94-19-25-75**). The 12th-century church is the third to stand on this site; two Carolingian churches underneath the current structure have been revealed during digs. A Templar watchtower sits atop one of the chapels, and at one time, watchers were posted to look out over the sea for ships that might pose a threat. The church served as a fortress and refuge in case of pirate attack. In the courtyard are fragments of a Roman aqueduct that once brought water from Fréjus. You can visit the church June through September every Tuesday through Saturday from 10am to noon and 2 to 5:30pm. Ironically, there are no Masses conducted in this church on Sunday—it's a consecrated church, but one that's been relegated to something akin to an archaeological rather than religious monument.

St-Raphaël's other major church, **Notre-Dame-de-la-Victoire,** boulevard Félix-Martin (✆ **04-94-19-81-29**), was completed in 1887, an ostentatious monument to the gilded age of commerce that helped finance its construction.

May through September, it's open daily from 7:30am to 10pm; October through April, it's open daily from 7am to 8pm. Entrance is free.

Near the Eglise des Templiers, the **Musée d'Archéologie Sous-Marine (Museum of Underwater Archaeology),** rue des Templiers (✆ **04-94-19-25-75**), displays amphorae, ships' anchors, ancient diving equipment, and other interesting items recovered from the ocean's depths. At one time, rumors circulated about a "lost city" off the coast of St-Raphaël. Jacques Cousteau came to investigate; instead of a sunken city, he discovered a Roman ship that had sunk while carrying a full load of building supplies. October through May, the museum is open Tuesday through Saturday from 10am to noon and 2 to 5:30pm. June through September, it's open Tuesday through Saturday from 9am to noon and 3 to 6:30pm. Admission costs 3.50€ for adults and 2€ for students and children 17 and under.

You'll also find **flower and fruit markets** in the old city. Stall owners open every morning. On the second Saturday of each month, vendors selling a variety of odds and ends also appear. Also check out the **Marché Alimentaire de St-Raphaël,** where carloads of produce, fish, meat, wines, and cheeses are sold daily from 8am to 1pm at two sites—place Victor-Hugo and place de la République—a 5-minute walk apart.

The seafront's broad **promenades,** dotted with statues dedicated to Félix Martin (a 19th-century mayor and tireless promoter of the resort) and Alphonse Karr (a 19th-century artist and local luminary), wind between the beaches and hotels. Near the old port, a **pyramid** commemorating Napoléon's return to France from Egypt stands on avenue du Commandant-Guilbaud.

WHERE TO STAY

There are plenty of accommodations in St-Raphaël, but during summer even the less-than-desirable places fill up fast. Reserve well in advance.

Hôtel Bleu Marine This hotel overlooking the yacht basin harbor at Santa Lucia provides comfortable accommodations in a setting that's a bit removed from the crowded beaches. All the well-furnished rooms have private balconies; the tiled bathrooms are tidily organized. The restaurant boasts well-prepared regional food, which can be served on a sunny terrace that overlooks the sailboats and yachts.

Nouveau Port Santa Lucia, 83700 St-Raphaël. ✆ **04-94-95-31-31.** Fax 04-94-82-21-46. 100 units. 115€–125€ double. AE, DC, V. Parking 9€. **Amenities:** Restaurant; bar; pool; health club; limited room service; massage; babysitting; laundry service; dry cleaning. *In room:* A/C, TV, minibar, hair dryer, safe.

Hôtel Continental *Value* The Continental is a good choice for a cost-conscious beach vacation. Rooms come in a wide variety, ranging from compact (relatively cramped) to spacious, with rates charged according to view (seascape or urban). Some have balconies; all have comfortable mattresses and clean, tiled bathrooms. No meals are served other than breakfast, but many well-recommended restaurants lie within a short walk.

100 promenade du Président-René-Coty, 83700 St-Raphaël. ✆ **04-94-83-87-87.** Fax 04-94-19-20-24. 44 units. 94€–193 double. AE, V. Parking 10€. **Amenities:** Lounge; babysitting; laundry service; dry cleaning. *In room:* A/C, TV, minibar, hair dryer, safe.

Hôtel Excelsior This hotel, on the beachfront promenade, is a charming family-run place—the best address at St-Raphaël. The small to medium-size guest rooms are comfortably appointed, with tidy bathrooms; most have views of the ocean. A sand beach is directly across the street.

193 promenade du Président-René-Coty, 83700 St-Raphaël. ✆ **04-94-95-02-42.** Fax 04-94-95-33-82. www.excelsior-hotel.com. 40 units. 50€–165€ double. AE, DC, MC, V. **Amenities:** Restaurant; pub; lounge; limited room service; laundry service; dry cleaning. *In room:* A/C, TV, minibar, hair dryer, safe.

WHERE TO DINE

L'Arbousier ★ FRENCH/PROVENÇAL Thanks to the charm and humor of Christien Roncy, director of the dining room, and the cuisine of her husband, Philippe, this restaurant is a success story that deserves to be better known than it already is. In their own words, the architecture of the building "isn't particularly pretty," although lots of money was spent in 1998 making it cozier and more Provençal-looking. But there's something innately stylish and even fun about this place that keeps clients coming back again and again. Flavors are rich, sunny, and sometimes earthy; typical dishes are green asparagus and lobster served with lemon-flavored butter; cannelloni-shaped filets of red snapper and squid served with hearts of artichokes, chopped onions and peppers, and white wine; and a sophisticated version of roasted pigeon in a stewpot, accompanied by ravioli stuffed with the pigeon's by-products, served with sherry sauce and pepper. Hearty appetites usually appreciate the roasted rabbit with dried plums and garnished with foie gras of duckling. Dessert might be a delectable crystallized version of local strawberries served with a pepper-flavored mint sauce.

6 av. de Valescure. ✆ **04-94-95-25-00.** Reservations recommended. Main courses 24€–30.20€; fixed-price lunches 24€–50€; fixed-price dinners 33€–50€. AE, DC, MC, V. Tues–Sun noon–2:30pm; Tues–Sat 7:30–10:30pm.

Restaurant Pastorel FRENCH Across from the town hall, this restaurant has been a fixture since 1922, when it was founded by the mother (Madame Pastorel) of the present owner, Charles Floccia. In two dining rooms plus an outdoor terrace, you can enjoy traditional Provençal recipes such as *bourride* (a close approximation of the bouillabaisse served in Marseille), marinated sardines, rack of lamb with Provençal herbs and parsley, a medley of stuffed baby vegetables, and ragout of rabbit in red-wine sauce. The signature dish is a succulent pot of stewed fish flavored with garlic and a medley of vegetables.

54 rue de la Liberté. ✆ **04-94-95-02-36.** Reservations recommended. Fixed-price menus 30€–33€. AE, MC, V. Tues–Sat noon–2pm and 7–10pm; Sun noon–2pm.

ST-RAPHAEL AFTER DARK

Because this is a family vacation spot, the after-dark scene is a little sparse. Of course, there's the **Grand Casino,** square de Grand (✆ **04-94-95-10-59**), with slot machines and gambling, plus a nightly dance party in summer featuring an upbeat orchestra. The slot machines are open daily from 11am to 4am; gambling begins at 8pm, and the dance club opens at 10pm. In summer, the entire place stays open to 4am.

One of our favorite bars is **Le Coco Club,** Port Santa Lucia (✆ **04-94-95-95-56**), where live music and stiff drinks contribute to a kind of gregarious, often flirtatious conviviality. Alternative choices include **La Réserve** (✆ **04-94-95-02-02**), a popular disco with a punk-rock crowd between 16 and 25. Another disco, with less emphasis on youth culture, is **Le Kilt,** rue Jules-Barbier (✆ **04-94-95-29-20**). Gay people, both men and women, tend to congregate at **Le Pipeline,** 16 rue Charabois (✆ **04-94-95-93-98**), where there's disco music and a long-standing reputation as a dance palace that can be animated and fun for everyone. For more information, contact the town's tourist office.

5 Massif de l'Estérel ★★★

3km (2 miles) NE of Fréjus; 8km (5 miles) SE of Cannes

Stretching for 39km (24 miles) of coast from La Napoule to St-Raphaël, this mass of twisted red volcanic rock is a surreal landscape of dramatic panoramas. Forest fires have devastated all but a small section of cork oak, adding barrenness to an already otherworldly place. This was once the stamping ground of a colorful 19th-century highwayman, Gaspard de Besse, who hid in the region's many caves and terrorized local travelers until, at age 25, he was hanged and then decapitated by military authorities in the main square at Aix-en-Provence.

Following the path of the ancient Roman Aurelian Way, N7 traces the area's northern edge, running through the Estérel Gap between Fréjus and Cannes. To get to the massif's summit, **Mont Vinaigre** (elevation 589m/1,962 ft.), turn right at the Testannier crossroads 11km (7 miles) northeast of Fréjus. A parking area allows you to leave your car and make the final 15 minutes of the ascent on foot, climbing to the observation deck of a watchtower for a view stretching from the Alps to the Massif des Maures. At La Napoule, turn around to follow the southwesterly trail of N98 back to Fréjus.

This route offers the massif's most stunning vistas, first turning inland just beyond Le Trayas at **Pointe de l'Observatoire,** where you can ascend to the **Grotte de la Ste-Baume** for the views that inspired the medieval hermit St. Honorat, who once dwelt in the cave. Farther along N98, at **Pointe de Baumette,** is a memorial to the French writer/aviator Antoine de St-Exupéry. At Agay, turn inland again to reach the rocky **Gorge du Mal-Infernet,** a twisted rut in the earth, offering a contrast to the surrounding peaks with their overview of the region. Continuing along this inland route leads you to **Pic du Cap-Roux,** at 431m (1,438 ft.), and **Pic de l'Ours,** at 488m (1,627 ft.), both offering sweeping views of land and sea. Although the park is administered by the **Office National des Forets** (✆ **04-94-44-16-45**), the local tourist offices noted within this chapter are much better sources of information about diversions within its borders.

ESSENTIALS

GETTING THERE Both of the area's twisted boundary roads run from Cannes to Fréjus, with N7 tracing the northern boundary and the southerly N98 following a route along the coast.

VISITOR INFORMATION You can get additional information on sights, routes, and accommodations at the **Offices de Tourisme** in St-Raphaël, rue Waldeck-Rousseau (✆ **04-94-19-52-52**); Fréjus, 325 rue Jean-Jaurès (✆ **04-94-51-83-83**); Les-Adrets-de-l'Estérel, place de la Mairie (✆ **04-94-40-93-57**); and Agay, boulevard de la Plage (✆ **04-94-82-01-85**).

WHERE TO STAY

Note that the **Auberge des Adrets** (see below) also rents rooms.

L'Estirado des Andrets & Auberge Panoramique ★ *Finds* In the heart of Estérel, this is a combined hotel and restaurant that's worth a detour. A stay, or even a stopover for lunch, is like a journey back in old-time Provence. Everything is traditional in style, with cozy, well-furnished bedrooms with a private bathroom or shower. On a hot summer day in Provence, guests congregate at the swimming pool or else lounge in the sun against a scenic backdrop of forested hills. The food at Auberge Panoramique is among the best in the area, highlighting a Provençal and French cuisine that changes with the seasons. Dining can be in the shade of a straw hut in summer or else close to a roaring fireplace in winter. Between sea and hills, the location is in the village of Les Andrets between Cannes and St. Raphaël.

83600 Les Andrets de l'Esterel. ✆ **04-94-40-90-64.** Fax 04-94-40-98-52. www.estirado.com. 24 units. 52€–71€ double; 93€–111€ suite. MC, V. **Amenities:** Restaurant; lounge; pool; limited room service; babysitting; laundry service; dry cleaning. *In room:* TV, hair dryer, safe.

WHERE TO DINE

Auberge des Adrets ★★ PROVENÇAL/FRENCH Despite an official mailing address that places this medieval inn in Fréjus, it lies only 2km (1½ miles) east of Les-Adrets-de-l'Estérel. Records of its existence go back to A.D. 824, when troubadours sang and horses rested here after treks across a landscape even rougher and more arid than other points nearby. In 1653, the site was designated a Relais de Poste, where travelers and their horses could find lodging. Today it focuses on upscale versions of Provence's rural dishes, as interpreted by Xavier Charaux. He presides over an antiques-filled dining room that spills out onto a large terrace overlooking arid landscapes and the faraway Baie de Cannes. Menu items are likely to include warm foie gras sautéed with roughly textured bread, magret of duckling roasted with a honey-flavored sesame sauce, and aromatic rack of lamb with an olive tapenade. Dessert might be a hot soufflé with black chocolate.

The hotel also offers 10 carefully decorated rooms, each with air-conditioning, some kind of ornate (usually baldaquin) bed, and views over a garden. Doubles cost 151€ to 214€ in high season; breakfast is 12€ extra.

R.N. 7, 83600 Fréjus. ✆ **04-94-82-11-82.** Fax 04-94-82-11-80. Main courses 12€–20€; fixed-price menu 36€. AE, DC, MC, V. Tues–Sat noon–2pm and 7:30–10pm; Sun noon–2pm; July–Aug daily. Closed Nov.

6 La Napoule-Plage ★

901km (560 miles) S of Paris; 8km (5 miles) W of Cannes

This secluded resort is on the sandy beaches of the Golfe de la Napoule. In 1919, the once-obscure fishing village was a paradise for the eccentric sculptor Henry Clews, son of a New York banker, and his wife, Marie, an architect. Clews fled America's "charlatans," whom he believed had profited from World War I. His house is now a museum.

ESSENTIALS

GETTING THERE La Mandelieu Napoule-Plage lies on the **bus** and **train** routes between Cannes and St-Raphaël. For information and schedules, call ✆ **08-36-35-35-35.** If you're **driving,** take A8 west from Cannes.

VISITOR INFORMATION The **Office de Tourisme** is on avenue de Cannes (✆ **04-93-49-95-31;** www.ot-mandelieu.fr).

THE MAIN ATTRACTION

Château de la Napoule/Musée Henry-Clews ★★ An inscription over the entrance to this fairy-tale–like château reads: ONCE UPON A TIME. The château, a brooding, medieval-looking fortress whose foundations begin at the edge of the sea, was rebuilt from the ruins of a real medieval château. Clews covered the capitals and lintels with his own grotesque menagerie—scorpions, pelicans, gnomes, monkeys, lizards—the revelations of a tortured mind. Women and feminism are recurring themes in the sculptor's work; an example is the distorted suffragette depicted in his *Cat Woman.* The artist was preoccupied with old age

Following La Route Napoléon

On March 1, 1815, having escaped from a Senate-imposed exile on Elba that began in April 1814, Napoléon, accompanied by a small band of followers, landed at Golfe-Juan. The deposed emperor was intent on marching northward to reclaim his throne as emperor.

Though the details of his journey have been obscured by time, there are two versions of a local legend about one of his first mainland encounters. The first version claims that shortly after landing at Golfe-Juan, Napoléon and his military escort were waylaid by highwaymen unimpressed by his credentials. The other turns the story around, claiming that Napoléon's men, attempting to build a supply of money and arms, waylaid the coach of the prince de Monaco, whose principality, stripped of independence during the Revolution, had just been restored by Louis XVIII. When the prince told Napoléon that he was on his way to reclaim his throne, the exiled emperor stated that they were in the same business and bid his men to let the coach pass unhindered.

Napoléon's return was far from triumphant. He was met by sullen rejection at the garrison in Antibes where he wished to spend the night. This lack of enthusiasm was echoed throughout the region; still fresh in the minds of the citizenry was a series of international blunders that had isolated France from the rest of Europe and alienated Napoléon's bourgeois followers. On being denied a bed at Antibes, he moved on to Cannes for the night. This cool reception didn't dampen his determination, but it was a key factor in his deciding that travel north should be along rough mule paths carved through the hinterlands, avoiding large population centers. It was a sound plan, and by March 19 he was back in the Tuileries in Paris. But there was little time to savor this victory—only 100 days later he met his defeat at the Battle of Waterloo. He was

in both men and women, and admired chivalry and dignity in man as represented by Don Quixote—to whom he likened himself. Clews died in Switzerland in 1937, and his body was returned to La Napoule for burial. Marie Clews later opened the château to the public as a testimonial to the inspiration of her husband.

Bd. Henry-Clews. ✆ **04-93-49-95-05.** Admission 4.60€ adults, 3€ students ages 5–15, free for children under 5. By guided tour only (both French and English) Mar–Oct Wed–Mon 2 and 4pm; additional tour July–Aug at 5:30pm. Closed Nov–Feb.

WHERE TO STAY

Ermitage du Riou ★★ This old Provençal hotel is the most tranquil choice at the resort. It borders the Riou River and the Cannes-Mandelieu international golf club. The good-size rooms are furnished in Provençal style with genuine furniture and ancient paintings. Bathrooms have toiletries and thick towels. Views are of either the sea or the golf course.

Av. Henry-Clews, 06210 La Napoule. ✆ **04-93-49-95-56.** Fax 04-92-97-69-05. www.ermitage-du-riou.fr. 41 units. 170€–301€ double; 341€–529€ suite. AE, DC, MC, V. Free parking. **Amenities:** Restaurant; bar; pool; sauna. *In room:* A/C, TV, minibar, hair dryer.

finally and absolutely banished to the isolated island of St. Helena, where he died on May 5, 1821.

In the 1930s, the French government recognized Napoléon's positive influence on internal affairs by building Route 85, **La Route Napoléon,** to roughly trace the steps of the exiled emperor in search of a throne. It stretches from Golfe-Juan to Grenoble, but the most scenic stretch is in Provence, between Grasse and Digne-les-Bains. The route is well marked with commemorative plaques sporting an eagle in flight, though the "action" documented south of Grenoble revolves around simple stops made for food and sleep along the way.

The **Office de Tourisme** at place du Tour, St-Vallier-de-Thiey (✆ **04-93-42-78-00**), can provide you with a detailed account of the trek, a map of the three campsites where Napoléon and his men slept, and a map indicating where the road deviates from Napoléon's actual route, now maintained as a hiking trail where you can follow in his footsteps. The office is open Monday through Friday from 9am to noon and 2:30 to 5:30pm, and Saturday from 10am to noon.

After embarking from Cannes on the morning of March 2, the group passed through Grasse and halted just beyond St-Vallier-de-Thiey, spending the night. From this point to our end destination at Digne-les-Baines, the route touches only a handful of small settlements; the most notable is Castellane and the village of Barrème, where an encampment was set up on the night of March 3. The next day, the group stopped for lunch in Digne-les-Bains before leaving the region to continue north toward the showdown at Grenoble. Although the relais where he dined is long gone, you can stop at **Bourgogne,** 3 av. Verdun (✆ **04-92-31-00-19**), our choice for dining in the town, where tasty fixed-price menus cost 16€ to 40€.

La Calanque *Value* The foundations of this charming hotel date from the Roman Empire. The present hotel, run by the same family since 1942, looks like a hacienda, with salmon-colored stucco walls and shutters. Register in the bar in the rear (through the dining room). Bedrooms range from small to medium, each with a comfortable mattress. Those who take the bathless units will find the corridor bathrooms adequate and well maintained. Aside from a phone, in-room amenities in all units are a bit scarce. The hotel's restaurant spills onto a terrace and offers some of the cheapest meals in La Napoule.

Av. Henry-Clews, 06210 La Napoule. ✆ **04-93-49-95-11.** Fax 04-93-49-67-44. 17 units. 87€–120€ double. Rates include half-board. MC, V. Closed Nov to mid-Feb. **Amenities:** Restaurant; bar.

Sofitel Mandelieu Royal Casino ★★★ This Las Vegas–style hotel owned by the Accor group is on the beach near a man-made harbor, about 8km (5 miles) from Cannes. This was the first French hotel to include a casino and the last (just before the building codes changed) to be allowed to have a casino directly on the beach. The interior is dramatically contemporary, with plush touches, warm shades, and lots of marble. About 80% of all bedrooms were completely renovated and upgraded in 1998, with the remainder fixed up in

2000. Most of the attractive modern rooms are angled toward a view of the sea. Those facing the street are likely to be noisy in spite of soundproofing. The restaurant, Le Féréol, is recommended under "Where to Dine," below.

605 av. du Général-de-Gaulle, 06212 Mandelieu La Napoule. ✆ **800/221-4542** in the U.S. or Canada, or 04-92-97-70-06. Fax 04-93-49-51-50. www.royal-hotel-casino.com. 213 units. 179€–399€ double; 630€–1,800€ suite. AE, DC, MC, V. Parking 12€. **Amenities:** 3 restaurants; 4 bars; nightclub; 2 tennis courts; exercise room; sauna; Turkish bath; limited room service; babysitting; laundry service; dry cleaning. *In room:* A/C, TV, minibar, hair dryer.

WHERE TO DINE

Note that the restaurant in **La Calanque** (see above) is open to nonguests.

Brocherie II SEAFOOD/TRADITIONAL FRENCH The way this restaurant curves along the shoreline gives the impression that you're riding out to sea on a floating houseboat. You'll enter its precincts by crossing a gangplank lined with flaming torches. Specialties include virtually every fish that can be found in local waters—the freshest and best are grilled and served as simply as possible. Your choices of sauce include a rich hollandaise or béarnaise, or an herb-flavored version of white wine, butter, or vinaigrette. There's also a heady version of bouillabaisse, priced at 40€ per person, and a selection of (very expensive) lobsters from the establishment's bubbling holding tank. Meat dishes include succulent brochettes of Provençal lamb with rosemary and red wine.

Au Port. ✆ **04-93-49-80-73.** Reservations recommended. Main courses 12€–17€; fixed-price menu 32€ MC, V. Daily 9am–10pm. Closed Jan.

Le Féréol ★ MODERN FRENCH This well-designed restaurant services most of the culinary needs of the largest hotel (and the only casino) in town, the Royal Hôtel Casino (above). Outfitted in a nautical style that includes some of the seagoing accessories of an upscale yacht, it offers one of the most impressive lunch buffets in the neighborhood. At night the place is candlelit and elegant, and the view through bay windows over the pool is soothing. Menu items include foie gras, scampi tails fried with ginger, zucchini flowers with mousseline of lobster, mignon of veal with Parma ham and tarragon sauce, sole braised with shrimp, and an émincé of duckling baked under puff pastry with cèpes. The dessert buffet lays out a wide array of sophisticated pastries, some light and fruity summer dishes, and others designed as irresistible temptations for chocoholics.

In the Royal Hôtel Casino, 605 av. du Général-de-Gaulle. ✆ **04-92-97-70-00.** Reservations recommended. Main courses 20€–27€; fixed-price menus 32€ lunch, 40€ dinner. AE, DC, MC, V. Daily noon–2:30pm (to 3:30pm July–Aug) and 7–10:30pm (to 11pm July–Aug).

L'Oasis ★★★ FRENCH This is one of the great dining rooms along the Western Riviera. At the entrance to the harbor of La Napoule, in a 40-year-old house with a lovely garden and an unusual re-creation of a mock-medieval cloister, this restaurant became world-famous under the now-retired Louis Outhier. Today chef Stéphane Raimbault prepares the most sophisticated cuisine in La Napoule. Presumably, Raimbault has learned everything Outhier had to teach him and charts his own culinary course. Because Raimbault cooked in Japan for 9 years, many of his dishes are of the East-meets-West variety. In summer, meals are served in the shade of the plane trees in the garden. Menu choices might include roasted saddle of monkfish and risotto of squid with an ink sauce; medallions of veal and duck in a muscat wine and grape sauce; and a roasted Dover sole with parsley scorzonera. The wine cellar houses one of the finest collections of Provençal wines anywhere. Regrettably, there can be rocky moments here, thanks to a staff that's a lot less helpful than it could be.

Rue Honoré-Carle. ✆ **04-93-49-95-52.** Reservations required. Main courses 40€–50€; fixed-price menus 48€ lunch, 82€–140€ dinner. AE, DC, MC, V. Daily noon–2pm and 7:30–10pm. Closed Jan 28–Feb 13.

7 Cannes ★★★

905km (562 miles) S of Paris; 164km (101 miles) E of Marseille; 26km (16 miles) SW of Nice

When Coco Chanel came here, got a suntan, and returned to Paris bronzed, she startled the milk-white ladies of society. Today the bronzed bodies—in nearly nonexistent swimsuits—that line the sandy beaches of this chic resort continue the trend started by the late fashion designer.

Cannes is at its most frenzied during the International Film Festival at the Palais des Festivals on promenade de la Croisette. On the seafront boulevards, flashbulbs pop as the stars and wannabes emerge and pose and pose and pose. For wannabes (particularly female), *outrageous* is the key word. The festival's stellar activities are closed to most visitors, who are forced to line up in front of the Palais des Festivals. Known as "the bunker," this concrete structure is the venue for premières that draw some 5,000 spectators. With paparazzi shouting ("Brad, Jennifer, over here!") and shooting away, and a guard of gendarmes holding back the fans, the guests parade along the red carpet into the building, perhaps stopping for a moment or two to strike a pose and chat with a journalist. *C'est Cannes!*

International regattas, galas, *concours d'élégance,* and even a Mimosa Festival in February—something's always happening at Cannes, except in November, traditionally a dead month.

ESSENTIALS

GETTING THERE Cannes is connected to each of the Mediterranean resorts, Paris, and the rest of France by rail and bus lines. **Trains** arrive frequently throughout the day. Cannes is only 15 minutes by train from Antibes and only 35 minutes from Nice. The TGV from Paris going via Marseille also services Cannes. (Transit from Paris to Cannes via TGV takes only about 6 breathless hr.) For rail information and schedules, call ✆ **08-36-35-35-35.**

The Nice **international airport** (✆ **08-20-42-33-33**) is a 20-minute drive northeast. **Buses** pick up passengers at the airport every 40 minutes during the day, delivering them in Cannes at the Gare Routière, place de l'Hôtel de Ville (✆ **04-93-45-20-08**). Service to Cannes is also available from Antibes, with one bus every half-hour.

By car, Cannes can be easily approached by two cities along the Riviera. From Marseille, take A51 north to Aix-en-Provence, continuing along A8 east to Cannes. From Nice, follow A8 southwest to Cannes.

VISITOR INFORMATION The **Office de Tourisme** is in the Palais des Festivals, esplanade Georges-Pompidou (✆ **04-93-39-24-53;** www.cannes.fr).

SPECIAL EVENTS The **International Film Festival** at the Palais des Festivals on promenade de la Croisette attracts not only film stars, but seemingly every photographer in the world. You've got a better chance of being named prime minister of France than you do of attending one of the major screenings. (Hotel rooms and tables at restaurants are equally scarce during the festival.) But the people-watching is fabulous. If you find yourself here at the right time, you can join the thousands of others who line up in front of the Palais des Festivals, aka "the bunker," where the premieres are held. You might also be able to get tickets for some of the lesser films, which play 24 hours. For information, see "Provence Calendar of Events" in chapter 2 or access **www.festival-cannes.fr**.

Cannes

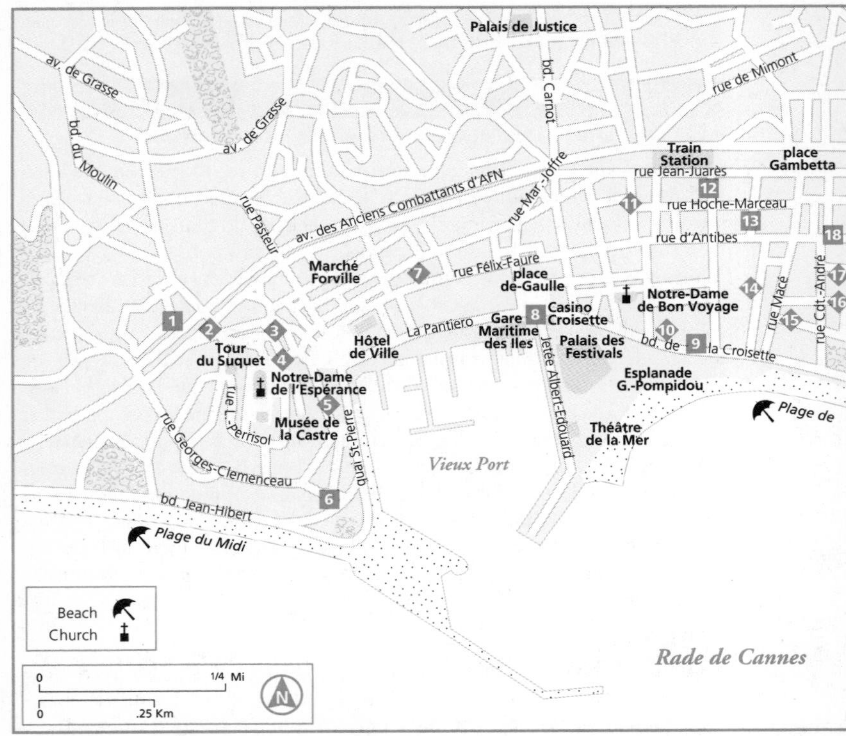

SEEING THE SIGHTS

For many, Cannes consists of only one street, **promenade de la Croisette** (or just La Croisette) ★★, curving along the coast and split by islands of palms and flowers. It's said that Edward, Prince of Wales (before he became Edward VII) contributed to its original cost. But he was a Johnny-come-lately to Cannes. In 1834, Lord Brougham, a lord chancellor of England, set out for Nice and was turned away because of an outbreak of cholera. He landed at Cannes and liked it so much that he decided to build a villa here. Returning every winter until his death in 1868, he proselytized it in London, drawing a long line of British visitors. In the 1890s, Cannes became popular with Russian grand dukes (it's said that more caviar was consumed here than in all of Moscow). One French writer claimed that when the Russians returned as refugees in the 1920s, they were given the garbage-collection franchise.

A port of call for cruise liners, the seafront of Cannes is lined with hotels, apartment houses, and chic boutiques. Many of the bigger hotels, some dating from the 19th century, claim part of the beach for the private use of their guests. But there are also public areas. Above the harbor, the old town of Cannes sits on Suquet Hill, where you'll see a 14th-century tower, the **Tour du Suquet,** which the English dubbed "the Lord's Tower."

Nearby is the **Musée de la Castre** ★, in the Château de la Castre, Le Suquet (© **04-93-38-55-26**), containing paintings, sculpture, examples of decorative arts, and a section on ethnography. The latter includes relics and objects from

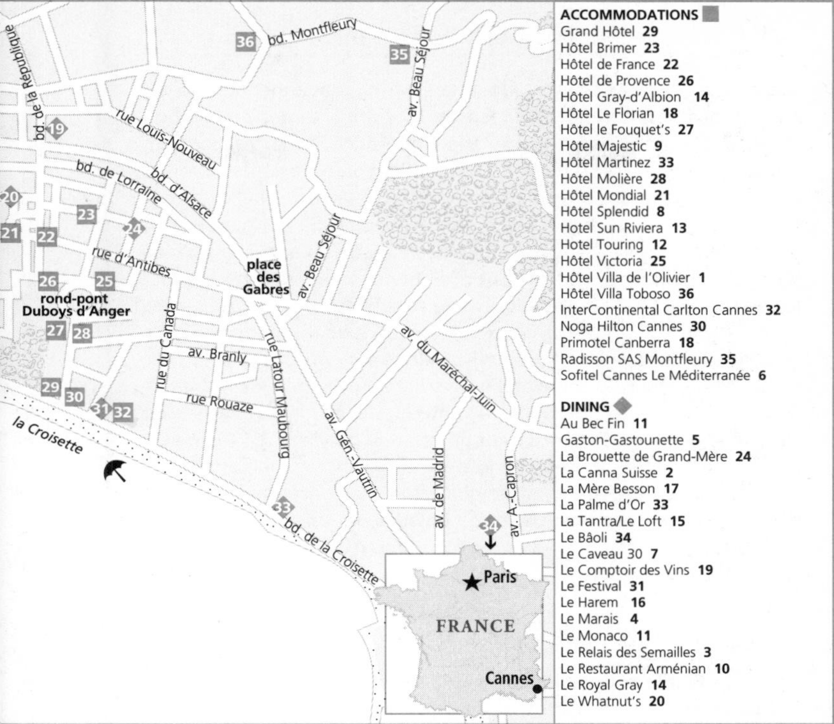

everywhere, from the Pacific islands to Southeast Asia, to South American Peruvian and Mayan pottery. There's also a gallery devoted to relics of ancient Mediterranean civilizations. Five rooms are devoted to 19th-century paintings. The museum is open Wednesday through Monday April through June from 10am to noon and 2 to 6pm, July through September from 10am to noon and 3 to 7pm, and October through March from 10am to noon and 2 to 5pm. Admission is 1.50€ and free for students and children.

Though nobody plans a trip to Cannes to see churches, the city does contain some worthy examples. The largest and most prominent is **Notre-Dame de Bon Voyage,** square Mérimée, near the Palais des Festivals; it was built in a *faux* Gothic style in the late 19th century. The most historic church, **Notre-Dame de l'Espérance,** place de la Castre (✆ **04-93-99-55-07**), was built between 1521 and 1627 and combines both Gothic and Renaissance elements. The town's most unusual church is the **Eglise Orthodoxe Russe St-Michel Archange,** 36–40 bd. Alexandre-III (✆ **04-93-99-03-26**), built in 1894 through the efforts of Alexandra Skripytzine, a Russian in exile; it's capped with a cerulean-blue onion dome and a gilded triple cross. Be warned that it's usually locked, except for services on Saturday at 5pm and Sunday between 9:30am and noon.

A DAY AT THE BEACH

Beachgoing in Cannes has more to do with exhibitionism and voyeurism than with actual swimming.

Seeing Cannes from a Petit Train

One of the best ways to get your initial bearings in Cannes (and to get an idea of the difference between the city's new and old neighborhoods) is to climb aboard one of the white-sided *Petits Trains touristiques de Cannes.* Diesel-powered, and rolling on rubber tires through the streets of the city, they operate year-round (except Nov) every day from 9:30am to between 7 and 11pm, depending on the season. Two itineraries are offered: For views of glittery modern Cannes, board the train at a designated spot in front of either of the town's two casinos for rides along La Croisette and its side streets. For a ride through the relatively narrow streets of Vieux Cannes (Le Suquet), board the train at a clearly designated site along La Croisette on its seaward side, immediately opposite the Hotel Majestique. Both tours depart every hour; each lasts between 30 and 40 minutes, depending on traffic; and each costs between 5€ and 6€ for adults, and between 2.50€ and 3€ for children under 10, depending on the tour. (The tour of the old town is the less expensive.) A combination ticket granting access on both of the two tours (which can be enjoyed on separate days, if you prefer) costs 8€ for adults and 5€ for children under 10. For details, call ✆ **06-14-09-49-39.**

Plage de la Croisette extends between the Vieux Port and the Port Canto. The beaches along this billion-dollar stretch of sand aren't private; in the strictest sense, they're *payante,* meaning you must pay from 15€ to 44€. You don't need to be a guest of the Noga Hilton, Martinez, InterContinental Carlton, or Majestic to use the beaches associated with those hotels, though if you are, you'll usually get a 50% discount. Each beach is separated from its neighbors by a wooden barricade that stops close to the sea, making it easy for you to stroll from one to another.

Why should you pay a fee at all? Well, it includes a full day's use of a mattress, a chaise longue (the seafront isn't sandy or even soft, covered as it is with pebbles and dark-gray shingles), and a parasol, as well as easy access to freshwater showers and kiosks selling beverages. There are also outdoor restaurants where no one minds if you appear in your swimsuit.

For nostalgia's sake, our favorite beach is the one associated with the **InterContinental Carlton** (p. 241)—it was the first beach we went to, as teenagers, in Cannes. The merits of each of the 20 or so beaches vary daily, depending on the crowd. And since every beach allows topless bathing (keep your bottom covered), you're likely to find the same forms of décolletage along the entire strip.

Looking for a free public beach where you'll have to survive without rentable chaises or parasols? Head for **Plage du Midi,** sometimes called Midi Plage, just west of the Vieux Port (✆ **04-93-39-92-74**), or **Plage Gazagnaire,** just east of the Port Canto (no phone). Here you'll find greater numbers of families with children and lots of caravan-type vehicles parked nearby.

OUTDOOR PURSUITS

BICYCLING & MOTOR-SCOOTERING Despite the roaring traffic, the flat landscapes between Cannes and satellite resorts like La Napoule are well

Ferrying to the Iles de Lérins

Across the bay from Cannes, the **Lérins Islands** ★★ are the most interesting excursion from the port. Ferryboats depart at 30-minute intervals throughout the day, from 7:30am to sundown. The largest of the ferryboat companies is **Compagnies Estérel-Chanteclair** (© **04-93-39-11-82**), but other contenders include **Cie Horizon 4** (© **04-93-99-15-09**); **Compagnie Maritime Cannoise** (© **04-93-38-66-33**); and **Trans-Côte d'Azur** (© **04-92-98-71-30**). Departures are from the Gare Maritime des Îles, 06400 Cannes. Round-trip passage costs 8.35€ per person.

ILE STE-MARGUERITE The first island is named after St. Honorat's sister, Ste. Marguerite, who lived here with a group of nuns in the 5th century. Today it is a youth center whose members (when they aren't sailing and diving) are dedicated to the restoration of the fort. From the dock where the boat lands, you can stroll along the island (signs point the way) to the **Fort de l'Ile,** built by Spanish troops from 1635 to 1637. Below the hill is the 1st-century B.C. Roman town where the unlucky man immortalized in *The Man in the Iron Mask* was imprisoned.

One of French history's most perplexing mysteries is the identity of the man who allegedly wore the ***masque du fer,*** a prisoner of Louis XIV who arrived at Ste-Marguerite in 1698. Dumas popularized the legend that he was a brother of Louis XIV, and it has even been suggested that the prisoner and a mysterious woman had a son who went to Corsica and "founded" the Bonaparte family. However, the most common theory is that the prisoner was a servant of the superintendent, Fouquet, named Eustache Dauger. He might have earned his fate by aiding Fouquet in embezzling the king's treasury. At any rate, he died in the Bastille in Paris in 1703.

You can visit his cell at Ste-Marguerite, where it seems that every visitor has written his or her name. As you stand listening to the sound of the sea, you realize what a forlorn outpost this was.

Musée de la Mer, Fort Royal (© **04-93-38-55-26**), traces the history of the island, displaying artifacts of Ligurian, Roman, and Arab civilizations, plus the remains discovered by excavations, including paintings, mosaics, and ceramics. It's open Wednesday through Monday July through September from 10:30am to 12:15pm and 2:15 to 6:30pm; October through June, it closes at sundown (4:30–5:30pm). Admission is 2€ for adults and free for students and youth ages 17 and under.

ILE ST-HONORAT Only a mile long, but richer in history than any of its sibling islands, the Ile St-Honorat is the site of a working monastery whose origins go back to the 5th century. Today the **Abbaye de St-Honorat,** les Iles de Lérins, 06400 Cannes (© **04-92-99-54-00**), boasts a combination of medieval ruins and early-20th-century ecclesiastical buildings, inhabited by a permanent community of about 30 Cistercian monks. If space is available, outsiders can visit, for prayer and meditation only, and spend the night. However, most visitors come to wander through the pine forests on the island's western side and sun themselves on its beaches.

suited for riding a bike or motor scooter. At **Cycles Daniel,** 2 rue du Pont Romain (✆ **04-93-99-90-30**), *vélos tout terrain* (mountain bikes) cost 15€ a day. Renters of motorized bikes and scooters will pay 35€ per day and must be at least 14 years old. For the larger of the scooters, potential renters must present a valid driver's license. Another purveyor of bikes is **Mistral Location,** 4 rue Georges Clémenceau (✆ **04-93-39-33-60**), which charges 11€ per day.

BOATING Several companies can rent you a boat of any size, with or without a crew, for a day, a week, or a month. An outfit known for its short-term rentals of small craft, including motorboats, sailboats, and canoes, is **Elco Marine,** 110 bd. du Midi (✆ **04-93-47-12-62**). For access to larger boats, including motor-driven and sailing yachts and craft suitable for deep-sea fishing, try **MS Yachts,** 57 La Croisette (✆ **04-93-99-03-51**), or **Mediterranée Courtage** (Agence Y.P.), 22 quai Port Marseille (✆ **04-93-38-30-40**).

GOLF One of the region's most challenging courses, **Country-Club de Cannes-Mougins,** 175 av. du Golf, route d'Antibes, Mougins (✆ **04-93-75-79-13**), 6.5km (4 miles) north of Cannes, was a 1976 reconfiguration by Dye & Ellis of a course laid out in the 1920s. Noted for the olive trees and cypresses that adorn a flat terrain, it has many water traps and a layout loaded with technical challenges. It has a par of 72 and since 1981 has hosted the Cannes-Mougins Open, an important stop on the PGA European Tour. The course is open to anyone (with proof of handicap) willing to pay greens fees of 100€, depending on the day of the week. An electric golf cart rents for 45€, and golf clubs can be rented for 24€. Reservations are recommended.

SWIMMING Cannes probably has more privately owned swimming pools per capita than anywhere else in France, so if your hotel isn't equipped with one, consider an excursion to the **Piscine Pierre de Coubertin,** av. P. de Coupertin (✆ **04-93-47-12-94**). Its length of almost 23m (75 ft.) makes it ideal for swimming laps. Because it's used for a variety of civic functions, including practices for local swim teams, hours are limited, so call ahead. Entrance costs 2€ for adults and 1€ for children 3 to 15.

TENNIS At least some of the resorts in Cannes maintain their own tennis courts. But if your lodgings don't provide them, the city of Cannes maintains a half-dozen tennis courts (one made from synthetic resins and five clay-topped) that cost between 9.50€ and 12.50€ per hour, depending on the court and the time of day you want to play, plus 4€ per hour for lighting. They're located at **Tennis Municipal de la Bastide,** 220 av. Francis Tonner, 06400 Cannes (✆ **04-93-47-29-33**). And if those courts are already taken, consider heading for the five clay-topped courts at **Tennis Municipal Aérodrome,** Aérodrome de Cannes Mandelieu, 06400 Cannes (✆ **04-93-47-29-33**), also maintained by the municipality, which charges the same rates.

SHOPPING

Cannes competes more successfully than many of its neighbors in a highly commercial blend of resort-style leisure, luxury glamour, and media glitz. So you're likely to find branch outlets of virtually every stylish Paris retailer.

There's every big-name designer you can think of (Saint Laurent, Rykiel, Hermès) as well as big-name designers you've never heard of (Claude Bonucci, Basile, and Durrani)—but, more important, there are real-people shops, resale shops for gently worn star-studded castoffs, two flea markets for fun junk, and a fruit, flower, and vegetable market.

ANTIQUES In the Casino Croisette (also called the Palm Beach Casino) on La Croisette, Cannes hosts one of France's most prestigious **antiques salons,** conducted biannually in mid-July and late December or early January. Its organizers refuse to include low- or even middle-bracket merchandise. This is serious—not for the gilt-free crowd—with lots of 18th- and early-19th-century stuff. Admission is 10.65€ per person. A bevy of services is available for crating, freighting, and flying whatever you buy to wherever you want it. For dates and information, call or write the **Association des Antiquaires de Cannes,** 6 rue de Foresta, 06300 Nice (✆ **04-93-26-11-01**).

Looking for top-notch antiques dealers whose merchandise will wow you? One of the city's most noteworthy dealers is **Hubert Herpin,** 20 rue Macé (✆ **04-93-39-56-18**). Within this store, you'll find a wide selection of bronze and marble statues, marquetry, and 18th- and 19th-century furniture.

BOOKS A year-round bookstore, **Ciné-Folie,** 14 rue des Frères Pradignac (✆ **04-93-39-22-99**), is devoted entirely to films. It's called *La Boutique du Cinema.* The outlet is the finest film bookstore in the south of France and also sells vintage film stills and movie posters.

CHOCOLATE & JELLIED FRUITS There are several famous chocolatiers in Cannes—try **Maiffret,** 31 rue d'Antibes (✆ **04-93-39-08-29**)—but the local specialty is *fruits confits* (jellied fruits, also called crystallized fruits), which became the rage in the 1880s. Maiffret sells these, especially in summer, when the chocolates tend to melt. Patés and confits of fruit, some of which decorate cakes and tarts, are also sold. Look for the Provençal national confection, *calissons,* crafted from almonds, a confit of melon, and sugar. A block away is **Chez Bruno,** 13 rue Hoche (✆ **04-93-39-26-63**). Opened in 1929 and maintained by a descendant of its founder, the shop is famous for *fruits confits* as well as its *marrons glacés* (glazed chestnuts), made fresh daily.

DEPARTMENT STORES Near the train station in the heart of Cannes, **Galeries Lafayette** has a small branch at 6 rue du Maréchal-Foch (✆ **04-97-06-25-00**). It's noted for the upscale fashion in its carefully arranged interiors.

DESIGNER SHOPS Most of the big names in fashion, for both men and women, line **promenade de la Croisette,** known as **La Croisette,** the main drag facing the sea. These stores are in a row, stretching from the InterContinental Carlton almost to the Palais des Festivals, with the best names closest to the **Gray-d'Albion,** 17 La Croisette (✆ **04-92-99-79-79**), both a mall and a hotel (how convenient). The stores in the Gray-d'Albion mall include **Hermès.** The mall is broken into two parts; you go outdoors from the first part of the building and then enter again for the second part. It serves as the shopper's cutaway from the primary expensive shopping street, La Croisette, to the less expensive shopping street, **rue d'Antibes.**

FLEA MARKETS Cannes has two regular flea markets. Casual, dusty, and, to an increasing degree, filled with the castaways of estate sales, the **Marché Forville,** conducted in the neighborhood of the same name, near the Palais des Festivals, is a stucco structure with a roof and a few arches but no sides. Between Tuesday and Sunday, it's the fruit, vegetable, and flower market that supplies dozens of grand restaurants. But Monday is *brocante* day, when the market fills with offhanded, sometimes strident antiques dealers selling everything from grandmère's dishes to bone-handled carving knives.

On Saturday, a somewhat disorganized and busy **flea market** is held outdoors along the edges of the allée de la Liberté, across from the Palais des Festivals.

Hours depend on the whims of whatever dealer happens to haul in a cache of merchandise, but it usually begins around 8am and runs out of steam by around 4:30pm. ***Note:*** Vendors at the two flea markets might or might not be the same.

FOOD Of the many streets that will attract with rustic and authentic Provençal allure, the most appealing, and the one lined with the greatest density of emporiums selling wine, olives, herbs, and oils, is the **rue Meynadier.**

A charmingly old-fashioned shop, **Cannolive,** 16–20 rue Vénizelos (✆ **04-93-39-08-19**), is owned by the Raynaud family, who founded the place in 1880. It sells Provençal olives and their by-products—*tapenades* (purées) that connoisseurs refer to as "Provençal caviar," black "olives de Nice," and green "olives de Provence," as well as three grades of olive oil from regional producers. Oils and food products are dispensed from no. 16, but gift items (fabrics, porcelain, and Provençal souvenirs) are sold next door.

MARKETS At the edge of the Quartier Suquet, the **Marché Forville** is the town's primary fruit, flower, and vegetable market. On Monday it's a *brocante* market. See "Flea Markets," above.

PERFUME The best shop is **Bouteille,** 59 rue d'Antibes (✆ **04-93-39-05-16**), also the most expensive. Its prices are high because it stocks more brands, has a wider selection, and gives away occasional samples. A selection of other shops dots rue d'Antibes. Any might feature your favorite fragrance in a promotional deal. A final option for the reasonably priced perfumes is the boutiques associated with the Hôtel Gray-d'Albion.

SWIMWEAR If you want to shock the photographers along the Riviera with daring swimwear, the place to go is **Maison Janine,** 27 La Croisette (✆ **04-93-39-11-95**). This is the best of the dozens of swimsuit emporiums in Cannes, a true bikini shop for those who want to reveal what they've got.

WHERE TO STAY

VERY EXPENSIVE

Hôtel Majestic ★★★ At the west end of La Croisette, the Majestic stands for glamour and has done so since 1926. Like the InterContinental Carlton (see below), it is a favorite with celebs during the annual film festival. Constructed around an overscale front patio, the hotel opens directly onto the esplanade and the sea. Inside, the setting is one of marble, crystal chandeliers, Oriental carpets, Louis XV silk furniture, and potted palms. The guest rooms are furnished with more of the same. All rooms are fitted with bedside controls and luxury amenities; the most special of the lot are 16 sea-view units with private terraces. The spacious, bright corner accommodations offer the best value. Bathrooms are sumptuous, with deluxe toiletries.

14 bd. de la Croisette, 06407 Cannes. ✆ **04-92-98-77-00.** Fax 04-92-98-77-60. 287 units. 200€–840€ double; 800€–4,590€ suite. AE, DC, MC, V. Parking 33€. **Amenities:** 2 restaurants; bar; pool; salon; 24-hr. room service; laundry service; dry cleaning. *In room:* A/C, TV, minibar, hair dryer, safe.

Hôtel Martinez ★★ Only the Majestic and the Carlton are slightly more luxurious. When this landmark Art Deco hotel was built in the 1930s, it rivaled any along the coast in sheer size alone. Over the years, however, it has fallen into disrepair and closed and reopened several times. But in 1982, the Concorde chain returned the hotel and its restaurants to their former luster, and today it competes with the Carlton and Noga Hilton. Despite its grandeur, the hotel is a little too convention-oriented for our tastes, but the rooms remain in good shape. The aim of the decor was a Roaring Twenties style, and all units boast marble bathrooms, wood furnishings, tasteful carpets, and pastel fabrics. The hotel also offers a private stretch of beach and a water-skiing school.

73 bd. de la Croisette, 06400 Cannes. © **04-92-98-73-00.** Fax 04-93-39-67-82. www.hotel-martinez.com. 397 units. 240€–760€ double; from 975€ suite. AE, DC, MC, V. Parking 27€. **Amenities:** 2 restaurants; bar; pool; 7 tennis courts; 24-hr. room service; laundry service; dry cleaning. *In room:* A/C, TV, minibar, hair dryer, safe.

InterContinental Carlton Cannes ★★★ This is the Riviera's most celebrated hotel. Cynics say that one of the most amusing sights in Cannes is the view from under the vaguely Art Deco grand gate of the Carlton. Here you'll see vehicles of every description pulling up to drop off huge amounts of baggage and vast numbers of oh-so-fashionable guests. The epitome of luxury, the hotel has become such a part of the city's heartbeat that to ignore it would be to miss the resort's spirit. The twin gray domes at either end of the facade are often the first things recognized by starlets planning their grand entrances in the hotel's public and private rooms.

Shortly after it was built in 1912, the Carlton attracted Europe's *haut monde,* including royalty. They were followed decades later by battalions of important screen stars. Today the hotel is more democratic, hosting conventions and motorcoach tour groups; however, in summer (especially during the film festival) the public rooms are still filled with all the voyeuristic and exhibitionistic fervor that seems so much a part of the Riviera. The guest rooms were renovated in 1990. Double-glazing, big bathrooms, and luxurious appointments are standard. The most spacious rooms are in the west wing, and many of the upper-floor rooms open onto balconies fronting the sea.

58 bd. de la Croisette, 06400 Cannes. © **04-93-06-40-06.** Fax 04-93-06-40-25. 338 units. 370€–750€ double; from 1,070€ suite. AE, DC, MC, V. Parking 36€. **Amenities:** 3 restaurants; 2 bars; indoor pool; health club; 24-hr. room service; laundry service; dry cleaning; nonsmoking rooms. *In room:* A/C, TV, minibar, hair dryer, safe.

Noga Hilton Cannes ★★ Opened in 1992, the Hilton was the first major palace hotel to open in Cannes since the 1930s. This six-story deluxe place, with massive amounts of exposed glass, boasts a contemporary design mimicking the best aspects of its older twin, the lakefront Noga Hilton in Geneva. You register in a soaring lobby sheathed in semitranslucent white marble. The guest rooms are stylish, with impeccable soundproofing and all the electronic accessories you'll ever need. Since all rooms are equivalent, the difference in rates is determined by exposure to the sea. Many of the appointments evoke a 1930s aura; all have balconies and bedside controls. The Prestige Rooms have very large beds and elegant carpeting. Other units, less desirable, are called "city-view" and "garden-view" accommodations. There are six rooms for persons with disabilities, and 21 are reserved for nonsmokers.

50 bd. de la Croisette, 06414 Cannes. © **800/445-8667** in the U.S. or Canada, or 04-92-99-70-00. Fax 04-92-99-70-11. www.hilton.com. 234 units. 230€–580€ double; 320€–880€ suite. AE, DC, MC, V. **Amenities:** 2 restaurants, 2 bars; outdoor pool; health club; business center; shopping arcade; 24-hr. room service; babysitting; laundry service; dry cleaning; nonsmoking rooms. *In room:* A/C, TV, minibar, hair dryer, safe.

Fun Fact

The twin cupolas of the InterContinental Carlton were modeled on the breasts of the most fabled local courtesan, **La Belle Otéro.** The hotel's main restaurant also carries her name.

EXPENSIVE

Grand Hôtel ★ This hotel is graced with a garden with tall date palms and a lawn sweeping down to the waterfront esplanade. A recently renovated structure of glass and marble, it is part of a complex of adjoining apartment-house wings and encircling boutiques. Eleven floors of rooms (with wall-to-wall picture windows) open onto tile terraces. Vibrant colors are used throughout: sea blue, olive, sunburst red, and banana. The bathrooms are lined with colored checkerboard tiles and have matching towels and rows of decorative bottles. Those rooms with sea views are the most expensive; the hotel's private beach is below.

45 bd. de la Croisette, 06400 Cannes. ✆ **04-93-38-15-45.** Fax 04-93-68-97-45. 78 units. 277€ double. AE, MC, V. Parking 11€. Closed Nov–Dec 14. **Amenities:** Restaurant; bar; pool; limited room service; babysitting; laundry service; dry cleaning. *In room:* A/C, TV, minibar, hair dryer.

Hôtel Gray-d'Albion ★★ The smallest of the major hotels is not on La Croisette, but its pastel-colored rooms are outfitted with all the luxury a modern hotel can offer. Groups form a large part of its clientele, but it also caters to the individual guest. Rooms on the eighth and ninth floors have views of the Mediterranean. All bedrooms are fairly standardized and medium in size, blending both contemporary and traditional furnishings along with such extras as bedside controls. Each room has a balcony, but the views aren't notable. Bathrooms are well equipped and clad in marble and granite, each with a set of deluxe toiletries and make-up mirrors. Dining selections include Le Royal Gray, one of the best in Cannes (see below), and a beach-club restaurant.

38 rue des Serbes, 06400 Cannes. ✆ **04-92-99-79-79.** Fax 04-93-99-26-10. www.lucienbarriere.com. 189 units. 185€–405€ double; 510€–1,450€ suite. AE, DC, MC, V. Bus: 1. **Amenities:** 2 restaurants; bar; salon; 24-hr. room service; babysitting; laundry service; dry cleaning. *In room:* A/C, TV, minibar, hair dryer, safe.

Radisson SAS Montfleury ★★ This is a classical, contemporary hotel that has carved out a good market for itself among independent travelers, although it can't compete with the big guns reviewed above. Although it seems distant from the crush of Cannes, it's actually only a short but winding drive away. The modern palace shares a 10-acre park with a sports complex. The magnificent curved pool has a sliding roof and is surrounded by palms. The guest rooms are stylishly filled with all the modern conveniences, including bedside controls, luxury mattresses, and well-appointed bathrooms.

25 av. Beauséjour, 06400 Cannes. ✆ **800/333-3333** in the U.S. and Canada, or 04-93-68-86-86. Fax 04-93-68-87-87. www.radisson.com. 182 units. 99€–369€ double. AE, DC, MC, V. From Cannes, follow the signs to Montfleury or the blue-and-white signs to the Radisson SAS Montfleury. **Amenities:** 2 restaurants; 2 bars; pool; 24-hr. room service; babysitting; laundry service; dry cleaning. *In room:* A/C, TV, minibar, hair dryer, safe.

Sofitel Méditerranée ★★ On the harborfront of Cannes, with views that extend over some of the most expensive private yachts in the Mediterranean, this is a seven-story chain hotel. It has surrounding balconies and an open-air lounge on its top floor. A remake of an older hotel, it has a well-designed, bright interior, offering a well-trained staff and contemporary-looking upscale bedrooms, some with views over the sea, and well-designed bathrooms.

2 bd. Jean-Hibert, 06400 Cannes. ✆ **800/221-4542** in the U.S., or 04-92-99-73-00. Fax 04-92-99-73-13. www.sofitel.com. 149 units. 245€–360€ double; from 394.90€ suite. Rates include breakfast. AE, DC, MC, V. Parking 16€. Bus: 1. **Amenities:** Restaurant; bar, lounge; pool; 24-hr. room service; laundry service; dry cleaning. *In room:* A/C, TV, minibar, hair dryer, safe.

MODERATE

Hôtel Brimer On a quiet street about 4 blocks from the seafront, this small hotel occupies the second floor of a four-story building constructed in the

1970s. In 1998, it was renovated and upgraded by owner Brice Guëlle, who runs a tight ship. Bedrooms are well maintained, are furnished unpretentiously but comfortably, and are relatively affordable in high-priced Cannes. Breakfast is the only meal served, although there are many bistros in the neighborhood.

6 rue Lecerf, 06400 Cannes. ✆ **04-93-38-69-54.** Fax 04-92-98-68-30. www.brimer.fr. 15 units. 70€–105€ double; 120€–160€ suite. AE, DC, MC, V. Parking free on street. **Amenities:** Laundry service; dry cleaning. *In room:* TV, minibar, hair dryer.

Hôtel le Fouquet's ★ *Finds* This is an intimate hotel drawing a discreet clientele, often from Paris, who'd never think of patronizing the grand palace hotels. Very "Riviera French" in design and decor, it's several blocks from the beach. Each of the cozy-looking bedrooms is outfitted differently, just a bit, from its neighbor. Each has pastel colors and contemporary furniture, and the personality of the owner, who's often on-site, is very palpable, making it feel a bit like an intimate B&B. Bathrooms, although small, are efficiently organized.

2 rond-point Duboys-d'Angers, 06400 Cannes. ✆ **04-92-59-25-00.** Fax 04-92-98-03-39. 10 units. 115€–190€ double. AE, DC, MC, V. Parking 12€. Closed Nov to mid-Mar. Bus: 1. **Amenities:** Limited room service; laundry service; dry cleaning. *In room:* A/C, TV, minibar, hair dryer, safe.

Hôtel Mondial This modern hotel on a commercial street, with stores on its lower floor, is about a 3-minute walk from the beach. Three-quarters of its rooms have views of the water, and the others overlook the mountains and a street. The soft Devonshire-cream facade has a few small balconies. The attractive rooms are the draw here, with matching fabrics for the comfortable beds and draperies, and sliding mirror doors on wardrobes. Bathrooms, though small, are neatly organized.

77 rue d'Antibes and 1 rue Teïsseire, 06400 Cannes. ✆ **04-93-68-70-00.** Fax 04-93-99-39-11. 49 units. 130€–155€ double; 225€–295€ suite. AE, DC, MC, V. **Amenities:** Babysitting; laundry service; dry cleaning. *In room:* A/C, TV, minibar, hair dryer, safe.

Hôtel Splendid This is a good, conservative choice—a favorite of academicians, politicians, actors, and musicians. Opened in 1871, it's one of the oldest hotels at the resort. An ornate white building with sinuous wrought-iron accents and an old-fashioned staff, the Splendid looks out onto the sea, the old port, and a park. The rooms boast antique furniture and paintings as well as videos. The more expensive rooms have sea views. Each comes with a small but efficient bathroom.

Allée de la Liberté (4 and 6 rue Félix-faure), 06400 Cannes. ✆ **04-97-06-22-22.** Fax 04-93-99-52-02. hotel.splendid.cannes@wanadoo.fr. 64 units. 119€–246€ double; 199€–250€ suite. Breakfast 15€. AE, MC, V. Parking 8€. **Amenities:** Room service (breakfast only). *In room:* A/C, TV.

Hotel Sun Riviera ★ This is a genteel, polite hotel that's less well known than the blockbuster mega-hotels nearby. But the fact that it's a demure, less-well-known choice, with relatively reasonable prices and a limited number of amenities, almost guarantees a healthy roster of bookings throughout the summer and throughout the film festival. Cheerful, stylish, and welcoming, with an image that's deliberately set a notch or two below what you might have expected at, say, the Carlton or the Majestic, it offers a discreetly opulent decor in the public rooms, and medium-sized bedrooms that are comfortably outfitted with conservative good taste. It's set in the heart of Cannes, near most of the important shops and downtown bars and restaurants.

138 rue d'Antibes, 06400 Antibes. ✆ **04-93-06-77-77.** Fax 04-93-38-31-10. 42 units. 185€–230€ double; 410€ suite. AE, DC, MC, V. **Amenities:** Bar; babysitting; laundry service; dry cleaning. *In room:* A/C, TV, minibar.

Hôtel Victoria The Victoria is a stylish modern hotel in the heart of Cannes. Nearly half the rooms have balconies overlooking the small park; the best rooms have terraces. Period reproductions, bedspreads of silk, and padded headboards evoke a boudoir quality in the rooms. Those facing the park cost a little more but are well worth it.

Rond-point Duboys-d'Angers, 06400 Cannes. ✆ **04-92-59-40-00.** Fax 04-93-38-03-91. www.hotelvictoria.com. 25 units. 95€–145€ double. AE, DC, MC, V. Parking 14€. Closed Nov–Dec. **Amenities:** Bar; pool. *In room:* A/C, TV, minibar.

Hôtel Villa de l'Olivier ★ Small, charming, and personalized, with a low-key management by the Schildknecht family, this is a well-positioned hotel that was once a private villa. In the 1960s, it was transformed into a hotel, and a six-unit annex was built in the garden. Today you'll find structures with lots of glass that overlook a kidney-shape swimming pool, and a decor that has aspects of the French colonial tropics, with lots of potted plants and a breezy indoor-outdoor motif that is appealing and relaxing. Bedrooms are outfitted with fabric-covered walls, in different colors and patterns, with lots of Provençal accessories. Bathrooms are small but tidily maintained.

5 rue des Tambourinaires, 06400 Cannes. ✆ **04-93-39-53-28.** Fax 04-93-39-55-85. www.hotelolivier.com. 24 units. 120€–140€ double; 244€ suite. AE, DC, MC, V. Parking 10€. Closed 3 weeks in Dec. **Amenities:** Pool; room service (for drinks only); laundry service. *In room:* A/C, TV.

Primotel Canberra *Finds* This hotel occupies a marvelous location between the deluxe InterContinental Carlton and the Palais des Festivals, but it seems little known. It's often booked during the festival by independent producers hoping to hit the big time. The rooms are well maintained, a blend of traditional and modern; those with southern exposure are sunnier and cost more. Size ranges from small to medium, but each comes with a good mattress. Breakfast is the only meal served, and limited parking is available by the hotel's small garden.

120 rue d'Antibes, 06400 Cannes. ✆ **04-97-06-95-00.** Fax 04-92-98-03-47. 41 units. 121€–161€ double; 267€ suite. AE, DC, V. Parking 13€. **Amenities:** Bar; limited room service; babysitting; laundry service; dry cleaning. *In room:* A/C, TV, minibar.

INEXPENSIVE

Hôtel de France ★ *Value* This centrally located hotel is 2 blocks from the sea. This is one of the best of the affordable hotels in Cannes. The rooms are functional but well maintained and reasonably comfortable, with good mattresses. You can sunbathe on the rooftop.

85 rue d'Antibes, 06400 Cannes. ✆ **04-93-06-54-54.** Fax 04-93-68-53-43. www.h-de-france.com. 33 units. 80€–136€ double. AE, DC, MC, V. Closed Nov 20–Dec 25. **Amenities:** Bar; lounge; babysitting; laundry service; dry cleaning. *In room:* A/C, TV, hair dryer, safe.

Hôtel de Provence Built in the 1930s and renovated into its present uncluttered format in 1992, this small-scale, unpretentious hotel is a distinct contrast to its intensely stylish, huge competitors. Most of the rooms have private balconies, and many overlook the carefully tended shrubs and palms of the hotel's walled garden. Bedrooms are showing their age but still offer fine comfort, and, for Cannes, the place is a remarkable bargain. Each unit comes with quality mattresses and good linen on twin or double beds, and a small bathroom. In warm weather, breakfast is served under the vines and flowers of an arbor.

9 rue Molière, 06400 Cannes. ✆ **04-93-38-44-35.** Fax 04-93-39-63-14. www.hotel-de-provence.com. 30 units. 63€–98€ double. AE, MC, V. Parking 10€. Closed mid-Nov to mid-Dec. **Amenities:** Bar. *In room:* A/C, TV, minibar, hair dryer, safe.

Hôtel Le Florian This hotel is set on a busy but narrow, densely commercial street that leads directly into La Croisette, near the beach. It has been maintained by three different generations of the Giordano family since the 1950s. Basic but comfortable, most rooms are rather small but have compact bathrooms with renovated plumbing. No meals are served other than breakfast.

8 rue Commandant-André, 06400 Cannes. ✆ **04-93-39-24-82.** Fax 04-92-99-18-30. 28 units. 50€–74€ double. AE, MC, V. Parking 14€ per night nearby. Closed Nov 18–Jan. Bus: 1. **Amenities:** Breakfast room. *In room:* A/C, TV, hair dryer.

Hôtel Molière ★ *Finds* Although it dates from around 1990, this hotel gives the distinct impression that it's one of the solidly established old-timers in a town loaded with venerable competitors. The hotel lies just 100m (328 ft.) from the Croisette; your approach will be through a long, verdant garden studded with cypresses and flowering shrubs, in which tables and chairs are set out for gossip and contemplation. The neighborhood it occupies is quieter than you expect, just behind both the Noga Hilton and the Carlton. Bedrooms are outfitted with lots of fabric, in tones of champagne, pink, and, in some cases, teal blue, giving an overall impression of well-upholstered comfort without a lot of decorative flair. Staff works hard and is generally polite and cooperative.

5-7 rue Molière, 06400 Cannes. ✆ **04-93-38-16-16.** Fax 04-93-68-29-57. www.hotel-moliere.com. 24 units. 93€–115€ double; 130€–146€ suite. AE, MC, V. Closed Nov. **Amenities:** Limited room service. *In room:* A/C, TV, hair dryer, safe.

Hotel Touring Simple, sparsely decorated, and uncomplicated, this hotel occupies the premises of what was built around 1900 as a beaux arts–style villa, within about a minute's walk from the railway station and a 5-minute walk from the beach. Inside you'll find a wide assortment of rooms and room sizes, with the biggest having soaring ceilings and a sense of monumental spaciousness, and the smallest being cramped but with serviceable beds. This is the type of place where you'll do little more than sleep. Around seven of the rooms have tiny balconies overlooking the street. Expect a polite staff and a clientele that includes about 40% gay men and—to a lesser extent—women, many of whom are involved, in one way or the other, with aspects of the film industry.

11 rue Hoche, 06400 Cannes. ✆ **04-93-38-34-40.** Fax 04-93-38-73-34. 26 units. 59€–71€ double. AE, MC, V. Closed 2 weeks in Nov–Dec. **Amenities:** Limited room service. *In room:* TV, fridge, hair dryer, safe.

Hôtel Villa Toboso Adjacent to the largest sports center in Cannes, this former private villa is now a small, homey hotel. (In a romantic outburst, the former owner named it after the city in Spain where Cervantes's Don Quixote is said to have met Dulcinea.) The main lounge has a concert piano, and dancers from the neighboring Rosella Hightower School often frequent the place. Most of the personalized bedrooms have windows facing the garden, and some have terraces and kitchens. Beds have comfortable mattresses, and bathrooms are well kept.

7 allée des Olivers (bd. Montfleury), 06400 Cannes. ✆ **04-93-38-20-05.** Fax 04-93-68-09-32. 15 units. 56€–118€ double. AE, DC, V. Free parking. **Amenities:** Pool; limited room service; babysitting; laundry service; dry cleaning. *In room:* A/C, TV, hair dryer, safe.

WHERE TO DINE

VERY EXPENSIVE

La Palme d'Or ★★★ FRENCH This is one of the great restaurants along the Riviera. When the Taittinger family (of champagne fame) renovated their hotel, one of their primary concerns was to establish a restaurant that could rival the tough competition in Cannes. And they've succeeded. The light wood–paneled

Art Deco marvel has bay windows, a winter garden theme, and outdoor and enclosed terraces overlooking the pool, the sea, and La Croisette. Your meal will be artfully handled by Vincent Rouard, maître d'hôtel, and the Alsatian-born chef Christian Willer. Menu items change with the seasons but are likely to include warm foie gras with fondue of rhubarb; filets of fried red mullet with a beignet of potatoes, zucchini, and an olive-cream sauce; or a medley of crawfish, clams, and squid marinated in peppered citrus sauce. A modernized version of a Niçois staple includes three parts of a rabbit with rosemary sauce, fresh vegetables, and chickpea rosettes. The most appealing dessert is wild strawberries from nearby Carros, with a Grand Marnier–flavored nage and a "cream sauce of frozen milk." The service is sensitive, sophisticated, and worldly, without being stiff.

In the Hôtel Martinez, 73 bd. de la Croisette. ✆ **04-92-98-74-14.** Reservations required. Main courses 45€–120€; fixed-price menus 47€–140€ lunch Mon–Sat, 70€–135€ dinner. AE, DC, MC, V. Wed–Sun 12:30–2pm and 7:30–10:30pm (also Tues 7:30–10:30pm mid-June to mid-Sept). Closed Nov 15–Dec 20.

EXPENSIVE

Gaston-Gastounette ★ TRADITIONAL FRENCH This restaurant opens onto the best views of the marina from its location in the old port. It has a stucco exterior with oak moldings and big windows, and a sidewalk terrace surrounded by flowers. You can choose from three different bouillabaisses: from full-blown authentic stewpots that are meals in their own right to an appetizer version. Other choices include baby turbot with hollandaise sauce; filets of John Dory with wild mushrooms; an unusual broth composed in a style reminiscent of Japan, flavored with monkfish, saltwater salmon, and chives; and a succulent platter of fried mixed fish served with basil-flavored butter sauce. Profiteroles with hot chocolate sauce make a memorable dessert.

5 quai St-Pierre. ✆ **04-93-39-47-92.** Reservations required. Main courses 25€–47€; fixed-price menus 31€ lunch, 35€ dinner. AE, DC, MC, V. Daily noon–2pm and 7–11pm. Closed Dec 1–20.

La Tantra/Le Loft FRENCH/ASIAN An enduring favorite on the city's dine-and-then-dance circuit is this duplex-designed restaurant and disco on a side street that runs directly into La Croisette. On the street level, you'll find a Tao-inspired dining room, artfully simple and outfitted in a way that, if it wasn't filled with chattering and gossiping diners, might inspire a meditation or a yoga class. Menu items focus on a French adaptation of Asian cuisine, with lots of sushi, tempura that includes a succulent combination of deep-fried banana slices, zucchini flowers, shrimp, and lobster; a Japanese-style steak of Kobe beef marinated in teriyaki, soy, and garlic; and deep-fried noodles dotted with chunks of shrimp and lobster. Be warned in advance that the 9pm seating is relatively calm; the 11pm seating is more linked to the disco madness going on upstairs. There, in a venue lined with plush, *puta-scarlet* sofas and exposed stone, you'll witness all the gyrations and mating games of a scantily clad crowd of all kinds of hipsters, from across the wide, wide range of social types inhabiting Cannes.

13 rue du Dr. Monod. ✆ **04-93-39-40-39.** Reservations recommended. Main courses 20€–40€. AE, DC, MC, V. Daily 9–11pm; dance club (no cover charge) nightly 11pm–4am.

Le Bâoli FRENCH/JAPANESE One of the ultimate hipster joints in Cannes occupies a waterfront site outfitted like a temple garden in Thailand, complete with lavishly carved doorways, potted and in-ground palms, and hints of the Spice Trade scattered artfully in the out-of-the way corners. There's room here, either indoors or on a terrace overlooking the twinkling lights of La Croisette, for up to 350 diners at a time, and plenty of room after the end of the dinner service for a dance club venue where at least some of the clients might be dancing frenetically, in scantily clad giddiness, on the tables. Menu items include Japanese-inspired teppanyaki dishes prepared tableside by a samurai-style chef, as well as French dishes that feature tartare of tuna spread on toasts, crisp ravioli stuffed with shrimp, lobster in citrus sauce with a confit of tomatoes, filet of sea wolf with fennel, and a particularly elegant version of macaroni that's "perfumed" with an essence of lobster. Vegetarians appreciate the availability of such dishes as risotto with green asparagus, broccoli, and fava beans. The name of the restaurant, incidentally, derives from a well in Indonesia with reputed mystical powers.

Port Canto, bd. de la Croisette. ✆ **04-93-43-03-43.** Reservations recommended. Main courses 20€–43€. AE, MC, V. Daily 8pm-midnight; disco (no cover charge) nightly midnight–4am. Closed Nov–Mar.

Le Festival TRADITIONAL FRENCH Screen idols and sex symbols flood the front terrace of this place during the film festival. Almost every chair is emblazoned with the name of a movie star (whose bottoms might or might not have graced it), and tables here are among the most sought-after in town. You can choose from the Restaurant or the less formal Grill Room. Meals in the Restaurant might include bourride Provençale, *soupe des poissons* with rouille, simply grilled fresh fish (perhaps with aïoli), bouillabaisse with lobster, pepper steak, and sea bass flambéed with fennel. Items in the Grill are more in the style of an elegant brasserie, served a bit more rapidly and without as much fuss but at more or less the same prices. An appropriate finish in either section might be a smoothly textured peach Melba, invented by Escoffier.

55 bd. de la Croisette. ✆ **04-93-38-04-81.** Reservations required. Main courses 27€–35€; fixed-price menu from 40€. AE, DC, MC, V. Daily 11:30am–3pm and 7:30–10pm (till 11pm during film festival and July–Aug). Closed Nov 18–Dec 26.

Le Royal Gray ★★ MODERN FRENCH This restaurant manages to be both cozy and grand, replete with leather chairs, late-19th-century colors of brown and bordeaux, and warm lighting. Michel Bigot's cuisine is subtle and sometimes surprisingly simple, not aiming for the cutting-edge cerebrality of the place's more innovative competitors. Examples are terrines of foie gras, smoked salmon with a "bouquet" of shrimp and sweet-and-sour quenelles, fricassée of lobster with creamy tarragon sauce, roasted filets of John Dory with olives and baby mushrooms, and grilled filet of beef with béarnaise sauce. In 2000, a dish created in the kitchens of this restaurant won the "Prix de Cannes" and, as such, has been broadly copied by other restaurants along the Coast: roasted filet of *pagre* (sea bream) served with olive oil, fennel, celery, and artichoke hearts.

In the Hôtel Gray-d'Albion, 38 rue des Serbes. ✆ **04-92-99-79-79.** Reservations required. Main courses 19€–29€; fixed-price menus 42€. AE, DC, MC, V. Daily 12:30–2pm and 8–10:30pm.

MODERATE

La Canna Suisse ★ *Finds* SWISS Two sisters own this small-scale 30-year-old restaurant in Vieux Cannes that's decked out like a Swiss chalet and that specializes in the cheese-based cuisine of Switzerland's high alps. Since its cuisine is so closely geared to cold weather dining, the restaurant wisely opts to close during the crush of Cannes' midsummer tourist season, doing a landmark business in autumn, winter, and early spring. The menu features only two kinds of fondue—a traditional version concocted from six kinds of cheese and served in a bubbling pot with chunks of bread on skewers, plus another that adds either morels or cèpes to the blend, depending on your wishes. The only other dining options here include raclette and a recipe for *tartaflette* (an age-old recipe that combines boiled potatoes with fatback, onions, cream, herbs, and Reblochon cheese) that are equally savory. There's a long list of (mostly white) French and Swiss wines, which usually taste wonderful when served with any of these ultratraditional dishes.

23 rue Forville (le Suquet). ✆ **04-93-99-01-27.** Main courses 13€–19€. AE, MC, V. Mon–Sat 7:30–10:30pm. Closed June to mid-Aug.

La Mère Besson ★ TRADITIONAL FRENCH The culinary traditions of the late Mère Besson, who opened her restaurant in the 1930s, are carried on in one of Cannes's favorite places. Dishes are served up in great steaming portions; all are prepared with respect for Provençal traditions and skill. Most delectable is *estouffade Provençal* (beef braised with red wine and rich stock flavored with garlic, onions, herbs, and mushrooms). You can also sample an old-fashioned platter with codfish, fresh vegetables, and dollops of the famous garlic mayonnaise (aïoli) that Provence produces by the tubful. Other specialties are fish soup, a *bourride Provençale* (a form of thick fish and vegetable stew), and shoulder of lamb with Provençal herbs and purée of garlic.

13 rue des Frères-Pradignac. ✆ **04-93-39-59-24.** Reservations required. Main courses 17.50€–30€; fixed-price menu 25€–30€ dinner. AE, MC, V. Mon–Sat 7:30–10pm. Bus: 1.

Le Caveau 30 FRENCH/SEAFOOD The emphasis in this place, specializing in fine cuisine, is fresh seafood. Begin with a seafood platter and follow with one of the chef's classic dishes, pot-au-feu "from the sea" or shellfish paella. Bouillabaisse is the most popular dish, of course, but you might prefer a *filet au poivre* (pepper steak) or even fresh pasta. The 1930s decor, air-conditioning, and terrace all make dining a pleasant experience.

45 rue Félix-Faure. ✆ **04-93-39-06-33.** Reservations required. Main courses 17.30€–30€; fixed-price menus 22€–30€. AE, DC, MC, V. Daily noon–2:15pm and 7–11pm.

Le Harem ★ *Finds* MEDITERRANEAN Set in the heart of Cannes, midway between la rue d'antibes and La Croisette, this is the hippest, most popular, and most sought-after "new Moroccan" restaurant in Cannes, as proven by the bevy of soccer, pop music, and cinema stars who have visited it since its opening in 2002. It contains a trio of dining rooms, each lavishly outfitted *à la Marocaine,* with chastened brass coffeepots, tribal carpets from the sub-Saharan desert, geometrically carved panels, and leatherwork. If you opt for a meal here, don't expect just another ethnic restaurant in the souk, as this one contains a well-defined postmodern twist, both in its decor and its cuisine.

The menu acknowledges the cuisines of Morocco, Tunisia, Algeria, Spain, and Italy. There are at least a half-dozen *tagines* (clay pots in which chicken, lamb, fish, and vegetables are spiced, slow-cooked, and made savory) and at least three different versions of couscous (a traditional version with only lamb; a *royale* version containing merguez sausage, chicken, lamb, and beef; and a super-deluxe seafood version, priced at 70€ per person, that's loaded with lobster and shellfish). Other divine dishes, not deriving from North Africa, include tuna fried with Iberian cured ham in the Basque style, a salad of chickpeas with coriander and mint, and an Andalusia-inspired tomato-based gazpacho.

15 rue des Frères Pradignac. ✆ **04-93-39-62-70.** Reservations recommended. Main courses 18€–70€. AE, DC, MC, V. Daily 8pm–midnight.

Le Marais FRENCH This is the most successful gay restaurant in Cannes, with a crowd of mostly gay men from the worlds of fashion and entertainment, sometimes with their entourages. The setting is a warm and appealing mix of Parisian and Provençal, with paneled walls and a bustling terrace that is one of the most sought-after outdoor venues in town. Menu items include sea bream filet with olive-based tapenade sauce, and a "triptych" of meats that includes magret of duck, beef filet, and shoulder of lamb with mint sauce. Know in advance that this is primarily a restaurant and doesn't cater to a crowd of folk coming in just to drink.

9 rue du Suquet. ✆ **04-93-38-39-19.** Reservations recommended. Main courses 17€–30€; fixed-price menu 27€–32€. MC, V. Tues–Sun 7:15–11pm (and Mon during film festival).

Le Relais des Semailles TRADITIONAL FRENCH This long-enduring favorite is reason enough to visit Le Suquet, Cannes's old town. The casual atmosphere is complemented by the food, based on available local ingredients. Stuffed pigeon and roasted slices of foie gras are typical dishes, and the vegetables are always beautifully prepared. Try, if featured, the salad of wild greens *(mâche)* with truffles—sublime. The grilled sea bass is perfectly fresh and aromatically seasoned with herbs. Depending on what looked good at the market that day, the chef might be inspired to, say, whip up a rabbit salad with tarragon *jus.* The setting is intimate, offering casual dining out on the terrace or in air-conditioned comfort.

9 rue St-Antoine. ✆ **04-93-39-22-32.** Reservations required. Main courses 27€–32€; fixed-price menus 33€–51€. AE, DC, MC, V. Daily 7:30–11:30pm.

Le Restaurant Arménian ★ *Finds* ARMENIAN/TURKISH/GREEK Cannes has always been one of the most cosmopolitan cities along the Riviera, and the success of this Armenian culinary outpost seems to prove it. There's no menu here, although once your experience here is finished, you'll know a lot more about the cuisines of Armenia, Turkey, and Greece than you did before. For a set price, you'll experience an abundant medley of dishes that will be brought to your table in quantities you might find staggering. Expect about 20 cold plates, at least a dozen warm plates, enough vegetables to warm the heart of the most fanatical vegetarian, and at least 5 different desserts. There are lots of braised eggplants, tomatoes (both stewed and raw), an emphasis on cracked wheat in the form of such dishes as *kechgeg* (stewed beef served on a bed of cracked wheat), cabbage stuffed with mint, grilled meatballs with fresh herbs, and many others. According to owners Christian and Lucie Panossian, about 80% of the dishes served here are steamed rather than fried, establishing this place as one of the most health-conscious eateries in town. You'll find this place directly on the coastal boulevard, a short walk from the Hôtel Martinez.

82 La Croisette. ✆ **04-93-94-00-58.** Reservations required for lunch, recommended for dinner. Fixed-price menu 42.50€. DC, MC, V. Tues–Sun noon–2pm and 8pm–midnight; July–Aug daily.

Le Whatnut's TRADITIONAL FRENCH Sophisticated, urbane, and permissive, this restaurant also features a bar and a dance floor where patrons can dance and drink till long after the usual dinner hour, and even arrive for a meal long after everything else is closed. The interior has *trompe l'oeil* and ornate plaster ceilings, and the outdoor terrace is accented with decorative columns and the scent of night-flowering vines. The menu isn't terribly long but is well chosen. Examples are a diet-conscious array of grilled fish, such as sea bass, a platter with shrimp and scallops, and filets of beef garnished with morels or foie gras. If you opt for just a drink, expect to pay from around 5.50€ for a beer and from around 7€ for a whiskey and soda.

7 rue Marceau. ✆ **04-93-68-60-58.** Reservations recommended. Main courses 16€–25€; fixed-price menu 27€. AE, DC, MC, V. May–Sept daily 8–11:30pm; Oct–Apr Wed–Sun 8–11:30pm; bar open till 2:30am.

INEXPENSIVE

Au Bec Fin *Value* TRADITIONAL FRENCH On a street halfway between the train station and the beach, this is an 1880s bistro. It has little decor—sometimes red carnations are brought in from the fields to brighten the tables—but offers especially good food. A typical meal might include salade Niçoise, the house specialty; then *caneton* (duckling) with cèpes; and finally a choice of cheese and dessert.

12 rue du 24-Août. ✆ **04-93-38-35-86.** Reservations required. Main courses 12€–19€; fixed-price menu 15€–24€. AE, DC, MC, V. Mon–Sat noon–2:30pm and 6–10:30pm. Closed Dec 15–Jan 15.

La Brouette de Grand-Mère *Finds* TRADITIONAL FRENCH Few other restaurants in Cannes work so successfully at establishing a cozy testimonial to the culinary skills of old-fashioned French cooking. Owner Christian Bruno has revitalized the recipes that many of the chic and trendy residents of Cannes remember from their childhoods (or from an idealized version of their childhoods). Memories are evoked, in a way that Proust might have appreciated, through dishes that include a savory meat-and-potato stew known as *pot-au-feu,* roasted quail served with cream sauce, and chicken casserole cooked with beer. Traditional starters might include sausage links, terrines, and baked potatoes stuffed with smoked fish roe and served with a small glass of vodka. Set in the heart of town just behind the Noga Hilton and the InterContinental Carlton, the place offers two dining rooms, each outfitted in Art Deco–style in tones of deep red and soft violet, and an outdoor terrace.

9 bis rue d'Oran. ✆ **04-93-39-12-10.** Reservations recommended. Fixed-price menu, including apéritif and unlimited wine, 32.70€. MC, V. Mon–Sat 7:30–11pm. Closed June 25–July 10 and Nov to mid-Dec.

Le Comptoir des Vins TRADITIONAL FRENCH The origins of this place are from 1995, when its owners established a wine shop with bottles from between 450 and 500 wine producers from throughout France, some of them very obscure. Soon afterward, a restaurant was established in the back of the store that quickly caught on as a dining attraction in its own right. Part of its allure derives from white marble tables, bistro-style chairs, and sunlight flooding in from an overhead skylight. You can order any of 10 kinds of wine by the glass, but if you're really intrigued by anything you see in the store, the restaurant will uncork it for you for a surcharge of 6.50€ more than what you paid for the bottle, retail, in the shop. Menu items include an extensive selection of *charcuteries* and cheeses, piled high upon olivewood planks, as well as a savory collection of meats, fish, and vegetarian dishes. All of these are designed to go well with wines, and with a vast inventory of vintages to choose from, the composition of a savory meal here is ripe with gastronomic possibilities.

13 bd. de la République. ✆ **04-93-68-13-26.** Reservations recommended. Main courses 12€–18.50€; fixed-price menu 25€. MC, V. Mon–Sat noon–2pm; Thurs–Sat 7:30–10pm. Closed 2 weeks in Feb.

Le Monaco ★ *Finds* FRENCH/ITALIAN Restaurant tabs on La Croisette often resemble the annual budget of an Ivory Coast country. But believe it or not, pricey Cannes has working people who have to eat, and they often go to Le Monaco, a blue-collar place with great food served bistro-style. The likeable ambience features closely placed tables, clean napery, and a staff dressed in bistro-inspired uniforms. Menu choices include *osso buco* with sauerkraut, spaghetti bolognese, paella, couscous, roast rabbit with mustard sauce, mussels, trout with almonds, and minestrone with basil. Another specialty is grilled sardines, which many restaurants won't serve anymore, considering them too messy and old-fashioned.

15 rue du 24-Août. ✆ **04-93-38-37-76.** Reservations required. Main courses 10€–24€; fixed-price menu 20€. MC, V. Mon–Sat noon–2:30pm and 7–10:30pm. Closed Nov 10–Dec 10.

CANNES AFTER DARK

Public perceptions of Cannes are invariably associated with permissiveness, filmmakers celebrating filmmaking, and gambling. If gambling is your thing, there are a pair of world-class casinos within Cannes, each loaded with addicts, mere voyeurs, and everyone else in between. The better established of the two is the **Casino Croisette,** in the Palais des Festivals, 1 jetée Albert-Edouard (✆ **04-92-98-78-00**). Run by the Lucien Barrière group, and a well-respected fixture in town since the 1950s, it's a direct competitor of the newer **Palm Beach Casino,** place F.D. Roosevelt (Pointe de la Croisette; ✆ **04-97-06-36-90**), which lies on the southeast edge of La Croisette. Originally inaugurated in 1933 and rebuilt in 2002 by the Partouche group, it features three restaurants, Art Deco decor, and a format that's glossier, newer, and a bit hungrier (and trying harder) for new business. Both casinos maintain slot machines that operate daily from 11am to 5am and suites of rooms devoted to les grands jeux (blackjack, roulette, and chemin de fer) that are open nightly from 8pm to 5am. Both charge 11€ for access to les grands jeux, where presentation of a passport or an identity card is required.

In the cellar of the Hotel Grey d'Albion is the long-term nightlife staple, the disco, **Jane's,** 38 rue des Serbes (✆ **04-92-99-79-79**). It isn't considered ultra-hip or even particularly cutting edge, but you can have a lot of fun here merely because of the exoticism of the diverse crowd of occasionally single people who mill through the place. There's a cover of between 10€ and 15€, depending on the night of the week, and a policy of allowing women in free every Friday and Saturday before midnight. At the Casino Croisette is the nightclub **Jimmy's** (✆ **04-92-98-78-78**), with a 16€ cover.

The hippest and most consistently in-demand club is **Le Cat-Corner,** 22 rue Macé (✆ **04-93-39-31-31**), where a multicultural blend of night owls, most under 35, come to dance, drink, talk, and flirt. It opens every night from 11:30pm till 4am and charges 16€ for admission. Catering to a hip crowd of heterosexuals, it has one floor, a *faux*-baroque decor, a color scheme of Bordeaux and orange, and lots of cozy places to sit.

The aptly named **Bar des Stars,** in the Hotel Majestic Barrière, 14 La Croisette (✆ **04-92-98-77-00**), is where deals are made during the film festival. Directors, producers, stars, would-be stars, press agents, film writers, and various wannabes waiting to be discovered crowd in here at festival time. Even when there's no festival, it's a lively place for a drink with its scarlet decor evocative of some Art Deco oriental fantasy.

Gays and lesbians will feel comfortable in **Le Vogue,** 20 rue du Suquet (✆ **04-93-39-99-18**), a mixed bar open Tuesday through Sunday from 7:30pm till 2:30am. Another gay option is **Disco Le Sept,** 7 rue Rouguière (✆ **04-93-39-10-36**), with two shows, each lasting 2 hours, that begin nightly at 1:30am and at 3am. Entrance is free. A lot of straights go here, too.

Le Divan, 3 rue Rouguière (✆ **04-93-68-73-70**), is set in a vaulted cellar designed to look much older than it really is. Ringed with mirrors, this is one of Cannes's major watering holes. Its almost-as-new competitor, also catering to a clientele of mostly gay men, is **Le Hype,** 4 rue Jean-Jaurès (✆ **04-93-39-20-50**), which combines a restaurant function with its drinking and flirting.

One of the newest nightlife options is gay and mixed disco, **Diabolica,** 48 bd. de la République (✆ **04-93-68-23-23**). Established in 2001, it appeals to high-energy dance enthusiasts, thanks to a big dance floor, frequent references to the film festival, and the kind of recently released house, garage, and Latino music you might have expected in Los Angeles. It's open Thursday through Sunday and charges a cover of up to 13€, depending on the night of the week.

A discreet hushed ambience prevails at **Zanzibar,** 85 rue Félix Faure (✆ **04-93-39-30-75**), with its dark wood paneling. A bartender confided to us, "If a gay man wants to meet a French version of Brad Pitt, especially at festival time, this is the place." The mixed bar is open all night and caters to all sexual persuasions. At dawn the doors open and the last of the drag queens stagger out.

8 Grasse ★★

906km (563 miles) S of Paris; 18km (11 miles) N of Cannes; 10km (6 miles) NW of Mougins

Grasse, a 20-minute drive from Cannes, is the most fragrant town on the Riviera, though it *looks* tacky modern. Surrounded by jasmine and roses, it has been the capital of the perfume industry since the days of the Renaissance. It was once a famous resort, attracting such royalty as Queen Victoria and Princess Pauline Borghese, Napoléon's promiscuous sister. Today some three-quarters of the world's essences are produced here from foliage that includes violets, daffodils, wild lavender, and jasmine.

ESSENTIALS

GETTING THERE **Buses** pull into town at intervals of between 30 and 60 minutes every day from Cannes (trip time: 45 min.). The one-way fare is 4€. There are also about 30 buses every day arriving from Nice (trip time: around 1 hr.). The one-way fare costs around 6€. The buses disembark at the Gare Routière, avenue Thiers (✆ **04-93-36-35-35**), a 10-minute walk north of the town center.

Visitors arriving by **car** take A8, which funnels in traffic from Monaco, Aix-en-Provence, and Marseille.

VISITOR INFORMATION The **Office de Tourisme** is in the Palais des Congrès on place du Cours (✆ **04-93-36-66-66;** www.ville-grasse.fr).

SEEING THE SIGHTS

A market for fruits and vegetables from the surrounding hills, **Marché aux Aires,** is conducted in the place aux Aires every Tuesday through Sunday from 8am to noon.

PERFUME FACTORIES

Parfumerie Fragonard One of the best-known perfume factories, it's named after the famous 18th-century French painter. This factory is the best one to visit. An English-speaking guide will show you how "the soul of the flower" is extracted. After the tour, you can explore the museum of perfumery, which displays bottles and vases that trace the industry back to ancient times. Of course, if you're shopping for perfume and want to skip the tour, that's okay.

20 bd. Fragonard. ✆ **04-93-36-44-65.** www.fragonard.com. Free admission. Daily 9am–6:30pm (Nov–Jan closed noon–2pm).

Parfumerie Molinard Another popular place is this firm, well known in the United States; its products are sold at Saks, Neiman Marcus, and Bloomingdale's. In the factory, you can witness the extraction of the essence of the flowers, and the process of converting flowers into essential oils is explained in detail. You'll discover why turning flowers into perfume has been called a "work of art," and

Fun Fact **Pricey Petals**

It takes 10,000 flowers to produce 2.2 pounds of jasmine petals; almost a ton of petals is needed to distill 1½ quarts of essence. These figures are important to keep in mind when looking at that high price tag on a bottle of perfume.

you can admire a collection of antique perfume-bottle labels as well as see a rare collection of perfume *flacons* (bottles) by Baccarat and Lalique.

60 bd. Victor-Hugo. ✆ **04-93-36-01-62.** Free admission. May–Sept daily 9am–6:30pm; Oct–Apr daily 9am–12:30pm and 2–6pm.

MUSEUMS

Musée d'Art et d'Histoire de Provence This museum is in the Hôtel de Clapiers-Cabris, built in 1771 by Louise de Mirabeau, marquise de Cabris and sister of Mirabeau. The collection includes paintings, four-poster beds, marquetry, ceramics, brasses, kitchenware, pottery, urns, and archaeological finds.

2 rue Mirabeau. ✆ **04-93-36-01-61.** Admission 5€ adults, 3€ children 8–16, free for children under 8. June–Sept daily 10am–7pm; Oct–May Wed–Mon 10am–12:30pm and 2–5:30pm.

Musée International de la Parfumerie This museum will teach you even more than you might want to know about perfume—for example, you learn that it takes a metric ton of flowers to make 1 gram of fragrance. You can also see interesting, often bizarre exhibits relating to the perfume industry. One of the most fascinating on the second floor displays a 3,000-year-old mummy's perfumed hand and foot. Apparently, the flesh stayed preserved over the centuries because of the perfuming process. In the fourth-floor greenery, you can smell some of the base elements that go into the creation of celebrated perfumes. Was that Elizabeth Taylor we saw whiffing and sniffing, perhaps trying to come up with some new exotic fragrance?

8 place de Cours. ✆ **04-93-36-80-20.** Admission 4€ adults, 2€ children. Oct–May Wed–Mon 10am–12:30pm and 2–5:30pm; June–Sept daily 10am–7pm.

Villa Fragonard Jean-Honoré Fragonard was born in Grasse in 1732. The villa's collection includes his paintings as well as the paintings of other members of his family—his sister-in-law, Marguerite Gérard; his son, Alexandre; and his grandson, Théophile. The grand staircase was decorated by Alexandre.

23 bd. Fragonard. ✆ **04-93-36-01-61.** Admission 5€ adults, 3€ children 8–16, free for children under 8. June–Sept daily 10am–7pm; Oct–May Wed–Mon 10am–12:30pm and 2–5:30pm.

WHERE TO STAY

Hôtel La Bellaudière This hotel is in a stone-sided farmhouse whose foundations go back 400 years, 3km (2 miles) north of the town center. The cost-conscious, completely unpretentious hotel is run by Fréderique and Phillippe Maure. Bedrooms are simple but severely dignified, outfitted with Provençal motifs and accessories. Each has a medium-quality but comfortable mattress and a tiled bathroom. There's a view of the sea from many of the bedrooms, a garden terrace lined with flowering shrubs, and a sense of friendly cooperation from the hosts.

78 route de Nice, 06130 Grasse. ✆ **04-93-36-02-57.** Fax 04-93-36-40-03. 17 units. 35€–64€ double. AE, DC, MC, V. Free parking. **Amenities:** Restaurant. *In room:* TV.

Hôtel Panorama Built in 1984 in the commercial center, this hotel lies behind a facade in a sienna hue that its owners call "Garibaldi red." The more expensive rooms have balconies, southern exposures, and views of the sea. Furnishings are basic and simple, although all the mattresses are reasonably comfortable. Tiled bathrooms are small and well kept. There is no bar or restaurant, but the staff is cooperative and hardworking.

2 place du Cours, 06130 Grasse. ✆ **04-93-36-80-80.** Fax 04-93-3692-04. 36 units. 69€–95€ double. AE, DC, MC, V. **Amenities:** Limited room service; laundry service; dry cleaning. *In room:* A/C, TV, nonalcoholic minibar.

WHERE TO DINE

La Bastide St-Antoine (Restaurant Chibois) ★★★ FRENCH/PROVENÇAL The renown that this restaurant has enjoyed since it opened in 1996 is viewed with amazement and envy by every restaurateur in France. It occupies a 200-year-old Provençal farmhouse surrounded by 2.8 hectares (7 acres) of stately trees and verdant shrubberies. In the 1950s, the Kennedy family rented it as their summer retreat. What intrigued the French press was the elevation to superstardom of Jacques Chibois, formerly employed in the dining room of Cannes's Hôtel Gray-d'Albion. His fame came in 1997 with awards lavished on him by the controversial Gault-Millau group.

With a hardworking team directed by the maître d'hôtel Hervé Domenge, the restaurant serves a sophisticated array of dishes that aren't so much composed as "harmonized"—at least, according to Domenge. To begin, you might try a salad of red snapper with parsley, Provençal vegetables, and olive oil; or a slice of braised foie gras with a "pyramid" of artichokes and a dollop of terrine of foie gras. Main courses to look for are butterflied crawfish with a chiffonnade of basil, a pan-fried medley of exotic mushrooms and truffles, red mullet with *chayote* (a confit of lemons and fresh thyme), and an exotic recipe for veal chops cooked in laurel leaves and flavored with sherry and a *pain perdu* of eggplant and dried flap mushrooms. Dessert might be sliced apples in puff pastry with a caramel sauce or frozen rhubarb flavored with oranges, wild strawberries, and rhubarb sorbet.

In 1998, the owners added eight rooms and three suites, outfitted in a whimsical and idiosyncratic Provençal style. Each has upscale furnishings and exceptionally comfortable beds. Doubles cost 243€ to 268€, and suites cost 370€ to 434€.

48 av. Henri-Dunant. ✆ **04-93-70-94-94.** Reservations required. Main courses 40€–70€; fixed-price menus 45€–135€ lunch Mon–Sat, 107€–135€ dinner. AE, DC, MC, V. Daily noon–2pm and 8–9:30pm.

Restaurant Amphitryon FRENCH/SOUTHWESTERN Many of the buildings that line this street, including the premises of this restaurant, were stables in the 19th century. Today, amid fabric-covered walls and soothing grays and off-whites, you can enjoy the flavorful cuisine of Michel André. The food is inspired by southwestern France, with plenty of foie gras and duckling, as well as lamb roasted with thyme. A ragout of fish in red wine has in recent years become one of the chef's most popular dishes. Also recommendable are the Mediterranean fish soup with Provençal rouille and virtually any of the autumn dishes enhanced with seasonal fresh mushrooms.

16 bd. Victor-Hugo. ✆ **04-93-36-58-73.** Reservations recommended. Fixed-price menus 25€–32€ lunch, 35€ dinner. AE, DC, MC, V. Mon–Sat noon–1:30pm and 7:30–9:30pm. Closed Aug 1–Sept 1 and Dec 23–Jan 2.

9 Mougins ☆

903km (561 miles) S of Paris; 11km (7 miles) S of Grasse; 8km (5 miles) N of Cannes

This once-fortified town on the crest of a hill provides an alternative for those who want to be near the excitement of Cannes but not in the midst of it. Picasso and other artists appreciated these rugged, sun-drenched hills covered with gnarled olive trees. Picasso arrived in 1936 and, in time, was followed by Jean Cocteau, Paul Eluard, and Man Ray. Picasso decided to move here permanently, choosing as his refuge an ideal site overlooking the Bay of Cannes near the Chapelle Notre-Dame de Vie, which Winston Churchill once painted. Here he continued to work and spent the latter part of his life with his wife, Jacqueline. Fernand Léger, René Clair, Isadora Duncan, and even Christian Dior have lived at Mougins.

Mougins is the perfect haven for those who feel that the Riviera is overrun, spoiled, and overbuilt. It preserves the quiet life very close to the international resort. The wealthy come from Cannes to golf here. Though Mougins looks serene and tranquil, it's actually part of the industrial park of Sophia Antipolis, a technological center where more than 1,000 national and international companies have offices.

ESSENTIALS

GETTING THERE The best way to get to Mougins is to **drive.** From Nice, follow E80/A8 west and then cut north on route 85 into Mougins. From Cannes, head north of the city along N85. From La Napoule-Plage, head east toward Cannes on N7 and then north at the turnoff to Mougins up in the hills.

There's no rail station in Mougins, but there's daily **bus** service into Mougins from Cannes aboard the bus that travels from Cannes to Grasse. En route to Grasse, it stops in Mougins at Val de Mougins, about a 10-minute walk from the center. Fares from Cannes to Mougins are about 4€ each way. For information about departure times and schedules, call **Rapides-Côte-d'Azur** at ✆ **04-93-99-00-07.** Given the complexities of a bus transfer from Cannes, it'll invariably be a lot easier just to pay about 19€ for a **taxi** to haul you and your possessions northward from Cannes.

VISITOR INFORMATION The **Office de Tourisme** is at 15 av. Jean-Charles-Mallet (✆ **04-93-75-87-67**).

SEEING THE SIGHTS

For a look at the history of the area, visit the **Musée Municipal,** place du Village (✆ **04-92-92-50-42**), in the St. Bernardin Chapel. It was built in 1618 and traces area history from 1553 to the 1950s. It's open December through October Monday through Friday from 10am to noon and 2 to 6pm; admission is free.

You can also visit the **Chapelle Notre-Dame de Vie,** chemin de la Chapelle, 1.5km (1 mile) southeast of Mougins. The chapel, once painted by Churchill, is more famous for the priory next door where Picasso spent his last 12 years. It was built in the 12th century and then reconstructed in 1646; it was an old custom to bring stillborn babies to the chapel to have them baptized. The priory is still a private home occupied intermittently by the Picasso heirs. Alas, because of a series of break-ins, the chapel is open only during Sunday Mass between 9 and 10am.

Musée de l'Automobiliste ☆ This museum is ranked seventh in the list of cultural sights on the Côte d'Azur. Founded in 1984 by Adrien Maeght, this ultramodern concrete-and-glass structure houses temporary exhibitions, but also owns one of Europe's most magnificent collections of original and prestigious automobiles—more than 100 vehicles from 1894 to the present.

Aire des Bréguières. ✆ **04-93-69-27-80.** Admission 7€ adults, 5€ children 11 and under. Oct and Dec–Mar daily 10am–6pm; Apr–Sept daily 10am–7pm.

WHERE TO STAY

Note that **Le Moulin de Mougins** (see "Where to Dine," below) offers charming rooms and suites.

Manoir de l'Etang ★★ *Finds* Housed in a 19th-century Provençal building in the midst of olive trees and cypresses, this is a choice place to stay. It boasts all the romantic extras, including "love goddess" statuary in the garden and candlelit dinners, but it still charges reasonable rates. The rooms are bright and modern—you'll feel almost as if you're staying in a private home, which this place virtually is. Some rooms are extremely spacious. Bathrooms are well maintained, with adequate shelf space. In winter, meals are served around a wood-burning fireplace. The chef bases his menu on the freshest ingredients available in any season.

Aux Bois de Font-Merle, allée du Manoir, 06250 Mougins. ✆ **04-92-28-36-00.** Fax 04-92-28-36-10. www.manoir-de-letang.com. 16 units. 92€–153€ double; 206€–245€ apt. AE, MC, V. Closed late Oct to Feb. **Amenities:** Restaurant; bar; pool; laundry service. *In room:* A/C, TV, minibar.

Mas Candille What was once a 2-century-old Provençal farmhouse is today a cozy hotel of charm and comfort. The public rooms contain many 19th-century furnishings, and some open onto the gardens. The renovated guest rooms are cozy and tranquil, with traditional Provençal furnishings. Bathrooms, though compact, are tidily maintained. The family managers are always willing to provide you with whatever you need to make your room more comfortable.

The dining room has elegant stone detailing and a massive fireplace with a timbered mantelpiece. The food is exceptional. Typical dishes are *soupe de poissons,* stuffed zucchini flowers, and braised sweetbreads with mushrooms. Fresh salads and light meals are available throughout the day. In good weather, lunch is served on the terrace; dinner is served on the terrace in summer only.

Bd. Rebuffel, 06250 Mougins. ✆ **04-92-28-43-43.** Fax 04-92-28-43-40. www.lemascandille.com. 41 units. 304€–395€ double; 625€ suite. AE, DC, MC, V. **Amenities:** Restaurant; 2 outdoor pools; 3-hole golf course; spa; 24-hr. room service; laundry service. *In room:* A/C, TV, minibar, hair dryer, safe.

WHERE TO DINE

Brasserie de la Méditerranée FRENCH/PROVENÇAL This outfit adds a much-needed informality to the restaurant scene of a town noted for hyper-upscale gastronomy. Set within a modern building overlooking the village's main square, and outfitted in tones of pink and salmon, it specializes in the kind of cuisine you'd expect in a bustling brasserie in Lyons, but with a Provençal accent. Menu items include scallops with a balsamic vinaigrette; superb lobster served with a *barigoule* of artichoke hearts; sliced turbot in a white butter sauce; and veal saltimbocca (with ham).

Place de la Mairie. ✆ **04-93-90-03-47.** Reservations recommended. Main courses 13.50€–32.30€; set menus 24€–40.30€. AE, DC, MC, V. Daily noon–2:30pm and 7–10:30pm. Closed Jan 10–Feb 10.

L'Amandier de Mougins Café-Restaurant ★ *Value* NIÇOISE/PROVENÇAL The illustrious founder of this relatively inexpensive bistro is the world-famous Roger Vergé, whose much more expensive Moulin de Mougins is described below. Conceived as a mass-market satellite to its exclusive neighbor, this restaurant serves relatively simple platters in an airy stone house. The specialties are usually based on traditional recipes and might include a terrine of the elusive Mediterranean hogfish with lemon; a tartare of fresh salmon and a ceviche of tuna with hot spices; magrêt of grilled duckling with honey sauce and lemons, served with deliberately undercooked polenta; rack of lamb served with a risotto of zucchini flowers; and filets of farm-raised sea bass on a Moroccan-inspired ragoût of vegetables and saffron-flavored potatoes.

Place du Commandant-Lamy. ✆ **04-93-90-00-91.** Reservations recommended. Main courses 25€–30€; fixed-price menu 28€–34€. AE, DC, MC, V. Daily noon–2pm and 7–9:30pm.

Le Feu Follet *Value* FRENCH/PROVENÇAL Beside the square in the old village, this restaurant offers two roughly plastered rooms that always seem cramped and overcrowded, but the quality of the cuisine (and the affordable prices) make it a worthy choice. Only top-quality ingredients, the best in the market, go into the cooking. One longtime habitué, describing the Provençal vegetables served here, claimed they were "filled with the sun." Fancy sauces and overpreparation of dishes are never a factor, and the fresh herbs of Provence are used effectively. Typical dishes are baked filet of beef in red wine and butter, crawfish in lemon juice, and snails in garlic cream.

Place de la Mairie. ✆ **04-93-90-15-78.** Reservations required. Main courses 22€-26€; fixed-price menu 32€. AE, MC, V. Tues–Sat noon–2pm and 7–10pm; Sun 2:30–7pm.

Le Moulin de Mougins ★★★ TRADITIONAL FRENCH This place is the kingdom of Roger Vergé, the *maître cuisinier de France,* and is among France's top 20 restaurants. It's 6km (4 miles) from Cannes. A stone oil vat, 3m (10 ft.) wide with a wooden turnscrew and a grinding wheel, sits near the entrance. Monsieur Vergé's specialties include *filets de rougets* (red mullet) with artichokes; *noisettes d'agneau* (lamb) de Sisteron with an eggplant cake in thyme-flavored sauce and *poupeton* (zucchini flowers) stuffed with a mixture of truffles and pulverized mushrooms; fricassée of lobster with sweet wine, cream sauce, and sweet peppers; and pepper steak "à la Mathurin," with grapes, pepper, and brandy. Dessert might be a lemon soufflé. His forté is fish from the Mediterranean, bought fresh each morning. Monsieur Vergé lists a lot of fantastic, even historic wines but also has a good selection of local vintages.

The mill offers four suites and three rooms, all air-conditioned and decorated with French antiques. They rent for 183€ to 320€.

Notre-Dame de Vie, 06250 Mougins. ✆ **04-93-75-78-24.** Fax 04-93-90-18-55. Reservations required. Main courses 32€–68€; fixed-price menus 47€–120€ lunch, 94€–122€ dinner. AE, DC, MC, V. Tues–Sun noon–2:15pm and 8–10pm. Closed Dec 12–Jan 12.

10 Golfe-Juan ★ & Vallauris

913km (567 miles) S of Paris; 6km (4 miles) E of Cannes

Napoléon and 800 men landed at Golfe-Juan in 1815 to begin his Hundred Days. Protected by hills, Golfe-Juan was also the favored port for the American navy, though today it's primarily a family resort known for its beaches. It contains one notable restaurant: Chez Tétou.

The 2km (1¼-mile) R.N. 135 leads inland from Golfe-Juan to Vallauris. Once merely a stopover along the Riviera, Vallauris (now noted for its pottery) owes its reputation to Picasso, who "discovered" it. The master came to Vallauris after World War II and occupied a villa known as "The Woman from Wales."

ESSENTIALS

GETTING THERE You can **drive** to Golfe-Juan or Vallauris on any of the three east-west highways along the Riviera. Although route numbers are not always indicated, city names are clear once you're on the highway. From Cannes or Antibes, N7 east is the fastest route. From Nice or Biot, take A8/E80 west.

There's a sleepy-looking rail station in Golfe-Juan, on avenue de la Gare. To get here, you'll have to transfer from a **train** in Cannes. The train from Cannes costs 2€ each way. For railway information, call ✆ **08-36-35-35-35.** Alternatively, a flotilla of **buses,** operated by RCA (Rapides Côte-d'Azur; ✆ **04-93-39-11-39**), makes frequent transits from Cannes; the 20-minute trip costs 2.10€ each way. From Nice, the 60-minute trip costs 5.80€ each way.

VISITOR INFORMATION There's an **Office de Tourisme** at av. de Frère Roustan (✆ **04-93-63-73-12**) and another on square 8-Mai in Vallauris (✆ **04-93-63-82-58**).

SEEING THE SIGHTS

Landlocked Vallauris depends on the sale of tourist items and ceramics. Merchants selling the colorful wares line both sides of **avenue Georges-Clemenceau,** which begins at a point adjacent to the Musée Picasso and slopes downhill and southward to the edge of town. Some of the pieces displayed in these shops are in poor taste. In recent years, the almost-universal emphasis on the traditional rich burgundy color has been replaced with a wider variety geared to modern tastes.

On the place du Marché in Vallauris, near the site where Aly Khan and Rita Hayworth were married, you'll see Picasso's **Homme et Mouton (Man and Sheep).** The town council of Vallauris had intended to ensconce this statue in a museum, but Picasso insisted that it remain on the square "where the children could climb over it and the dogs water it unhindered."

Bordering place de la Liberation is a chapel of rough-hewn stone, shaped like a Quonset hut, containing the **Musée Picasso La Guerre et La Paix** ★ (✆ **04-93-64-16-05**), and also the entrance to the 16th-century **Château de Vallauris** (same phone). Inside the château is a two-in-one museum, **Musée Alberto Magnelli** and the **Musée de la Céramique Moderne.** This trio of museums developed after Picasso decorated the chapel with two paintings: *La Paix* (Peace) and *La Guerre* (War), offering contrasting images of love and peace on the one hand, and violence and conflict on the other. In 1970, a house painter gained illegal entrance to the museum one night and, after whitewashing a portion of the original, substituted one of his own designs. When the aging master inspected the damage, he said, "Not bad at all." In July 1996, the site was enhanced with a permanent exposition devoted to the works of the Florentine-born Alberto Magnelli, a pioneer of abstract art whose first successes were acclaimed in 1915 and who died in 1971, 2 years before Picasso. The third section showcases ceramics, both traditional and innovative, from potters throughout the region. All three museums are open October through March Wednesday through Monday from 10am to noon and 2 to 6pm. April through September, they're open Wednesday through Monday from 10am to 6:30pm. Admission costs 4€ for adults and 2€ for students and children 15 and under.

A DAY AT THE BEACH

Because of its position beside the sea, Golfe-Juan developed long ago into a warm-weather resort. The town's twin strips of beach are **Plages du Soleil** (east of the Vieux Port and the newer Port Camille-Rayon) and **Plages du Midi** (west of those two). Each stretches 1km (a half-mile) and charges no entry fee, with the exception of small areas administered by concessions that rent mattresses and chaises and offer access to kiosks dispensing snacks and cold drinks. Regardless of which concession you select (on Plage du Midi, they sport names like Au Vieux Rocher, Palma Beach, and Corail Plage; on Plage du Soleil, they're Plage Nounou and Plage Tétou), you'll pay 13€ for a day's use of a mattress. Plage Tétou is associated with the upscale Chez Tétou (see "Where to Dine," below). If you don't want to rent a mattress, you can cavort unhindered anywhere along the sands, moving freely from one area to another. Golfe-Juan indulges bathers who remove their bikini tops, but, in theory, it forbids nude sunbathing.

SHOPPING IN VALLAURIS

A shop that rises far above its neighbors is the **Galerie Madoura,** av. de Georges et Suzanne Ramié, in Vallauris (✆ **04-93-64-66-39**); it's the only shop licensed to sell Picasso reproductions. It's open Monday through Friday from 10am to 12:30pm and 2:30 to 7pm (to 6pm Oct–Mar). Some of the reproductions are limited to 25 to 500 copies. Another gallery to seek out is the **Galerie Sassi-Milici,** 65 bis av. Georges-Clemenceau (✆ **04-93-64-65-71**), displaying works by contemporary artists.

Market day at Vallauris takes place every day except Monday from 7am to 12:30pm, at **place Isnard,** with its flower stalls and local produce. For a souvenir, you might want to visit a farming cooperative, the **Cooperative Nérolium,** 12 av. Georges-Clemenceau (✆ **04-93-64-27-54**). It produces such foods as bitter-orange marmalade and quince jam, and scented products like orange flower water. Another unusual outlet for local products is the **Parfumerie Bouis,** 50 av. Georges-Clemenceau (✆ **04-93-64-38-27**).

La Boutique de l'Olivier, 46 av. Georges-Clemenceau (✆ **04-93-64-66-45**), is a specialist in objects made of olive wood. These include pepper mills, salad servers, cheese boards, free-form bowls, and bread-slicing boxes. **Terres à Terre,** 58 av. Georges-Clemenceau (✆ **04-93-63-16-80**), is known for its culinary pottery, made of local clay. This is an excellent outlet for picking up terra-cotta pottery. Gratin dishes and casseroles have long been big sellers here.

WHERE TO STAY

Hotel Beau-Soleil Set on a quiet cul-de-sac, within a 5-minute walk from the center of the town or the beach, this pink-and-white, boxy-looking hotel was built in 1973. The angles of the architecture might remind you of a modern-day adaptation by a 1920s-era cubist painter. Bedrooms are outfitted in Provence-inspired colors, with small-scale crystal chandeliers, big windows overlooking either the hotel's shaded terrace or the faraway hills, a writing table, and neat bathrooms with showers. The social center is the shaded terrace, dotted with potted plants.

Impasse Beau-Soleil, 06220 Golfe-San-Juan (Vallauris). ✆ **04-93-63-63-63.** Fax 04-93-63-02-89. www.hotel-beau-soleil.com. 30 units. 91€–130€ double. MC, V. Parking free. **Amenities:** Restaurant; bar; pool; nearby golf courses; tennis court. *In room:* A/C, TV, hair dryer, minibar, safe.

WHERE TO DINE

Auberge du Relais Imperial FRENCH/PROVENÇAL On a narrow, antique-looking street running parallel to the harbor front, this is an all-Provençal, cheerful restaurant that's outfitted with old-fashioned paneling and a scattering of regional antiques. It's a well-managed alternative to the high prices and off-hand grandeur of the also-recommended Chez Tétou. Menu items are savory and well prepared, including foie gras "with five perfumes," Breton lobster in an herb-flavored crust, minced shrimp fried with parsley and garlic, and a roster of fresh fish such as *rascasse* (hogfish), monkfish, and sea bass. Bouillabaisse can be prepared for two for about half the price of its counterpart at Chez Tétou—if it's ordered a day in advance.

21 rue Louis Chabrier. ✆ **04-93-63-70-36.** Reservations recommended. Main courses 12.50€–34.20€. MC, V. Thurs–Tues noon–2pm and 7:30–10pm; during July and Aug Thurs–Tues noon–2pm and daily 7:30–10pm. Closed Nov to mid-Mar.

Chez Tétou ★★ SEAFOOD In its own amusing way, this is one of the Côte d'Azur's most famous restaurants, capitalizing on the glittering *beau monde* who frequented it during the 1950s and 1960s. Retaining its Provençal earthiness despite its incredibly high prices, it has thrived in a white-sided beach cottage for more than 65 years. It still serves a bouillabaisse often remembered years later by diners. Other items on the deliberately limited menu are grilled sea bass with tomatoes Provençal, sole meunière, and several preparations of lobster—the most famous of which is grilled and served with lemon-butter sauce, fresh parsley, and a bed of basmati rice. Appetizers are limited to platters of charcuterie (cold cuts) or several almost-perfect slices of fresh melon since most diners order the house specialty, bouillabaisse. Your dessert might be a special powdered croissant with "grandmother's jams" (winter) or a homemade raspberry and strawberry tart (summer).

Av. des Frères-Roustand, sur la Plage, Golfe-Juan. ✆ **04-93-63-71-16.** Reservations required. Main courses 50€–60€; bouillabaisse 68€–85€. No credit cards. Thurs–Tues noon–11:30pm and 8–10:30pm. Closed Nov to Mar 10.

11 Juan-les-Pins ★★

913km (567 miles) S of Paris; 10km (6 miles) S of Cannes

This suburb of Antibes is a resort that was developed in the 1920s by Frank Jay Gould. At that time, people flocked to "John of the Pines" to escape the "crassness" of nearby Cannes. In the 1930s, Juan-les-Pins drew a chic crowd during winter. Today it attracts young Europeans from many economic backgrounds in pursuit of sex, sun, and sea, in that order.

Juan-les-Pins is often called a honky-tonk town or the "Coney Island of the Riviera," but anyone who calls it that hasn't seen Coney Island in a long time. One newspaper writer called it "a pop-art Monte Carlo, with burlesque shows and nude beaches"—a description much too provocative for such a middle-class resort. Another newspaper writer said that Juan-les-Pins is "for the young and noisy." Even F. Scott Fitzgerald decried it as a "constant carnival." If he could see it now, he'd know that he was a prophet.

ESSENTIALS

GETTING THERE Juan-les-Pins is connected by **rail** and bus to most other Mediterranean coastal resorts, especially Nice (trip time: 30 min.). For rail information and schedules, call ✆ **08-36-35-35-35.** There are also **buses** that arrive from Nice and its airport at 40-minute intervals throughout the day. A bus leaves for Juan-les-Pins from Antibes at place Guynemer (✆ **04-93-34-37-60**) daily every 20 minutes and costs 1.50€ one-way (trip time: 10 min.). To **drive** to Juan-les-Pins from Nice, travel along N7 south; from Cannes, follow the signposted roads. Juan-les-Pins is just outside of Cannes.

VISITOR INFORMATION The **Office de Tourisme** is at 51 bd. Charles-Guillaumont (✆ **04-92-90-53-05;** www.riviera.fr/tourisme.htm).

SPECIAL EVENTS The town offers some of the best nightlife on the Riviera, and the action reaches its height during the annual jazz festival. The **Festival International de Jazz** is held in mid-July for 10 to 12 days, attracting jazz masters and their fans. Concerts are presented within a temporary stadium custom-built for the event within Le Parc de la Pinède. Tickets range from 18€ to 30€ and can be purchased at the Office de Tourisme.

A DAY AT THE BEACH

Part of the reason people flock here is that the town's beaches actually have sand, unlike many of the other resorts along this coast, which have pebbly beaches. **Plage de Juan-les-Pins** is the town's most central beach. Its subdivisions, all public, include **Plage de la Salis** and **Plage de la Garoupe.** If you don't have your own beach chair, go to the concessions operated by each of the major beachfront hotels. Even if you're not a guest, you can rent a chaise and mattress for 12€ to 18€. The most chic of the lot is the area maintained by the Hôtel des Belles-Rives. Competitors more or less in the same category are La Jetée and La Voile Blanche, both opposite the tourist information office. Topless sunbathing is permitted, but total nudity isn't.

WATERSPORTS

If you're interested in scuba diving, check with your hotel concierge or one of these companies: **Club de la Mer,** Port Gallice (✆ **04-93-61-26-07**); or **EPAJ,** embarcadère Courbet (✆ **04-93-67-52-59**). A one-tank dive costs 40€, including all equipment. **Water-skiing** is available at virtually every beach in Juan-les-Pins, including one outfit that's more or less permanently located on the beach of the Hôtel des Belles-Rives. Ask any beach attendant or bartender, and he or she will guide you to the water-skiing representatives who station themselves on the sands. A 10-minute session costs about 24€.

WHERE TO STAY

EXPENSIVE

Belles-Rives ★★★ This is one of the Riviera's fabled addresses, on a par with the equally famous Juana, though the Juana boasts a superior cuisine. Once it was a holiday villa occupied by Zelda and F. Scott Fitzgerald, so it was the scene of many a drunken brawl. In the following years, it hosted the illustrious—the duke and duchess of Windsor, Josephine Baker, and even Edith Piaf. A certain 1930s aura still lingers. A major restoration was concluded in 1990, with less comprehensive upgrades at 2-year intervals since. Double-glazing and a new air-conditioning system help a lot. As befits a hotel of this age, rooms come in a variety of shapes and sizes, ranging from small to spacious, but each is highly comfortable with a double bed or set of twins. All the tiled bathrooms are spotlessly maintained and have deluxe toiletries.

The lower terraces are devoted to garden dining rooms. Dinners are served in the romantic setting at "La Terrasse" with a panoramic bay view. Lunches are stylish but somewhat less formal and offered in a setting overlooking the beach. Also on the premises are a private beach and a landing dock.

33 bd. Baudoin, 06160 Juan-les-Pins. ✆ **04-93-61-02-79.** Fax 04-93-67-43-51. www.bellesrives.com. 45 units. 180€–500€ double; 545€ suite. AE, DC, DISC, MC, V. Free parking. Closed mid-Oct to Mar. **Amenities:** Restaurant; bar; courtesy car; limited room service; babysitting; laundry service; dry cleaning. *In room:* A/C, TV, minibar, hair dryer, safe.

Hôtel Juana ★★★ This balconied Art Deco hotel, owned by the Barache family since 1931, is separated from the sea by the park of pines that gave Juan-les-Pins its name and that was so beloved by F. Scott Fitzgerald. The hotel has a private swimming club where you can rent a "parasol and pad" on the sandy beach at reduced rates. Nearby is a park with umbrella tables and shady palms. The hotel is constantly being refurbished, as reflected in the attractive rooms with mahogany pieces and large bathrooms in marble or tile imported from Italy. The rooms also have such extras as balconies.

La Pinède, av. Gallice, 06160 Juan-les-Pins. ✆ **04-93-61-08-70.** Fax 04-93-61-76-60. www.hotel-juana.com. 40 units. 215€–425€ double; from 460€ suite. MC, V. Parking 15€. Closed Nov–Mar. **Amenities:** Restaurant; 2 bars; heated outdoor pool; bike rental; concierge; secretarial services; 24-hr. room service; massage; babysitting; laundry service; dry cleaning. *In room:* A/C, TV, minibar, hair dryer, safe.

MODERATE

Hôtel des Mimosas *Value* This elegant 1870s-style villa sprawls in a tropical garden on a hilltop. The hotel is set, California style, amid huge palm trees. Michel and Raymonde Sauret redesigned the interior with the help of an architect who trained in the United States. The decor is a mix of high-tech and Italian-style comfort, with antique and modern furniture. Rooms range in size from small to medium, and each comes with a compact tiled bathroom. All have balconies. The hotel is fully booked in summer, so reserve far in advance.

Rue Pauline, 06160 Juan-les-Pins. ✆ **04-93-61-04-16.** Fax 04-92-93-06-46. 34 units. 100€–120€ double. AE, MC, V. Free parking. Closed Sept 30–Apr 30. From the town center, drive a half-kilometer west, following N7 toward Cannes. **Amenities:** Pool; dry cleaning. *In room:* TV, minibar, safe

Hôtel Le Pré Catelan In a residential area near the town park, this Provençal villa from around 1900 offers a garden with rock terraces, towering palms, lemon and orange trees, large pots of pink geraniums, trimmed hedges, and outdoor furniture. The atmosphere is casual; the setting is uncomplicated and unstuffy. The more expensive rooms have terraces; furnishings are durable and rather basic. Nonetheless, there is fine comfort here, with bathrooms that are tidily maintained and equipped with showers. Despite the setting in the heart of town, the garden here manages to provide a sense of isolation. No meals are served other than breakfast because the place closed its faltering restaurant in 1996.

22 av. des Palmiers, 06160 Juan-les-Pins. ✆ **04-93-61-05-11.** Fax 04-93-67-83-11. www.precatelan.com. 24 units. 96€–130€ double; 148€ suite. AE, DC, MC, V. **Amenities:** Pool. *In room:* TV, minibar.

INEXPENSIVE

Hôtel Cecil Located 5m (17 ft.) from the beach, this small, well-kept hotel is one of the best bargains in Juan-les-Pins. The owner/chef Michel Courtois provides a courteous welcome and good meals. The rooms are well worn, yet clean. Mattresses are still comfortable after much use; bathrooms are small. In summer, you can dine on a patio.

Rue Jonnard, 06160 Juan-les-Pins. ✆ **04-93-61-05-12.** Fax 04-93-67-09-14. www.hotelcecilfrance.com. 21 units. Apr–Sept 40€–70€ double. AE, DC, MC, V. Parking 8€. Closed Oct–Mar. **Amenities:** Restaurant; bar. *In room:* TV.

Hôtel Le Passy Centrally located, Le Passy opens onto a wide flagstone terrace. The other side faces the sea and coastal boulevard. The furnishings are Nordic modern, and the newer rooms have little balconies. Those that overlook the sea carry the higher price tag. Most rooms are small but have comfortable beds; each bathroom is compact and tidily maintained. In high-priced Juan-les-Pins, this is considered one of the more affordable choices, even though it's a bit sterile.

15 av. Louis-Gallet, 06160 Juan-les-Pins. ✆ **04-93-61-11-09.** Fax 04-93-67-91-78. 35 units. 78€–101€ double. AE, DC, MC, V. Parking 11€. **Amenities:** Lounge; 24-hr. room service; babysitting. *In room:* A/C, TV, safe.

WHERE TO DINE

EXPENSIVE

La Terrasse ★★★ FRENCH/MEDITERRANEAN Bill Cosby loves this gourmet restaurant so much that he's been known to fly chef Christian Morisset and his Dalí mustache to New York to prepare dinner for him. Morisset, who trained with Vergé and Lenôtre, cooks with a light, precise, and creative hand. His cuisine is the best in Juan-les-Pins. The setting is lively and sophisticated, with a conservatively modern decor overlooking the verdant garden, and a glassed-in terrace whose roof opens for midsummer ventilation and a view of the stars. Menu items are steeped in flavors of Provence and are served in a setting that's airy, sun-flooded, and chic. Examples include giant ravioles (Morisset is very specific and refers to them as *ravioles,* not *raviolis*) stuffed with fresh crawfish and an olive-flavored essence of shellfish, and a rack of lamb from the salt marshes of Pauillac cooked in a clay pot from nearby Vallauris, served with stuffed zucchini flowers and Provençal herbs. Dessert might include a Napoléon *(mille feuille)* of wild strawberries with a mascarpone cream sauce.

In the Hôtel Juana, La Pinède, av. Gallice. ✆ **04-93-61-20-37.** Reservations required. Main courses 40€–65€; fixed-price menus 48€ lunch, 80€–107€ dinner. AE, MC, V. July–Aug daily 12:30–2pm and 7:30–10:30pm; Apr–June and Sept–Oct Tues and Thurs–Sun 12:30–2pm, Thurs–Mon 7:30–10:30pm. Closed Nov–Mar.

Le Bijou Plage FRENCH/PROVENÇAL This upscale brasserie flourishes beside the seafront promenade and has done so for about 80 years. The marine-style decor includes lots of varnished wood and bouquets of blue and white flowers in a mostly blue-and-white interior. Windows overlook a private beach whose sands are much less crowded than those of the public beaches nearby. Menu items are sophisticated and less expensive than you'd expect. Examples are an excellent version of bouillabaisse, grilled sardines, risotto with John Dory and truffled butter, steamed mussels with *sauce poulette* (frothy cream sauce with herbs and butter), grilled John Dory with a vinaigrette enriched by a tapenade of olives and fresh basil, and a super-size *plateau des coquillages et fruits de mer* (shellfish). Don't confuse this informally elegant place with its beachfront terrace, open only April through September daily from noon to 4pm.

Bd. du Littoral. ✆ **04-93-61-39-07.** Reservations recommended. Main courses 28€–70€; fixed-price menus 22€–45€ lunch, 28€–48€ dinner. AE, DC, MC, V. Daily noon–2:30pm and 7:30–10:30pm (to 11:30pm June to mid-Sept).

MODERATE

Le Perroquet PROVENÇAL The cuisine is well presented and prepared, and the restaurant's ambience is carefully synchronized to the resort's casual and carnival-like summer aura. It's across from the Parc de la Pinède, and it's decorated with depictions of every imaginable form of parakeet, the restaurant's namesake. Look for savory versions of fish, at its best when grilled simply with olive oil and basil, and served with lemons. A worthwhile appetizer is the *assortiment Provençale,* which includes tapenade of olives, marinated peppers, grilled sardines, and stuffed and grilled vegetables. Steaks might be served with green peppercorns or béarnaise sauce, and desserts include three types of pastries on the same platter.

Av. Georges-Gallice. ✆ **04-93-61-02-20.** Reservations recommended. Main courses 14€–26.10€; fixed-price menus 26€–30.50€. MC, V. Daily noon–2pm and 7–11pm. Closed Nov–Dec 26.

INEXPENSIVE

La Romana FRENCH/INTERNATIONAL Behind the town's casino, this is an aggressively unpretentious restaurant that successfully caters its trade to the thousands of budget-conscious holiday makers who flood the town every season. Don't expect grande cuisine, as the venue is too simple, too informal. What you'll get—amid a generic 1930s-style decor accented with touches of wrought iron—is pizzas, meal-size salads, fried fish and fried scampi, grilled steaks with french fries, and *plats du jour* whose composition change every day.

21 av. Dautheville. ✆ **04-93-61-05-66.** Pizzas and pastas 10€–12€; main courses 12€–25€. DC, MC, V. Daily noon–2:30pm and 7–11pm.

JUAN-LES-PINS AFTER DARK

For starters, visit the **Eden Casino,** boulevard Baudoin, in the heart of Juan-les-Pins (✆ **04-92-93-71-71**), and try your luck at the roulette wheel or at one of the slot machines. The area containing slot machines doesn't charge admission. It's open every day from 10am to 5pm. The area containing *les grands jeux* (blackjack, roulette, and *chemin de fer*) is open daily from 9:30pm to 5am and charges 12€ per person. An ID card with photo is required.

For a more faux-tropical experience, head to **Le Pam Pam,** route Wilson (✆ **04-93-61-11-05**), where you can sip rum drinks in an ambience created and celebrated by reggae, Brazilian, and African performances of music and dance.

If you prefer some high-energy reveling, check out the town's many discos, the best of which are **Whisky à Gogo,** boulevard de la Pinède (✆ **04-93-61-26-40**), with its young trendsetters and rock beat. In summer it fills up with the young, restless, and horny. Between October and Easter, it's open only on Friday and Saturday nights. **Le Village,** 1 bd. de la Pinède (✆ **04-93-61-18-71**), boasts an action-packed dance floor and DJs spinning the latest from the international music scene. The cover charge is a stiff 15€.

For a more relaxed evening, go to the British pub **Le Ten's Bar,** 25 av. du Dr.-Hochet (✆ **04-93-67-20-67**), where you'll find 50 brands of beer and a sociable crowd of young and old merrymakers. **Le Madison,** 1 av. Alexandre-III (✆ **04-93-67-83-80**), features the town's best jazz and blues.

12 Antibes ★★ & Cap d'Antibes ★★

913km (567 miles) S of Paris; 21km (13 miles) SW of Nice; 11km (7 miles) NE of Cannes

On the other side of the Baie des Anges (Bay of Angels), across from Nice, is the port of Antibes. This old Mediterranean town has a quiet charm unique on the Côte d'Azur. Its little harbor is filled with fishing boats and pleasure yachts, and in recent years it has emerged as a new "hot spot." The marketplaces are full of flowers, mostly roses and carnations. If you're in Antibes in the evening, you can watch fishers playing the traditional Riviera game of boules.

Spiritually, Antibes is totally divorced from Cap d'Antibes, which is a peninsula studded with the villas and pools of the super-rich. In *Tender Is the Night,* F. Scott Fitzgerald described it as a place where "old villas rotted like water lilies among the massed pines." Photos of film and rock stars lounging at the Eden Roc have appeared in countless magazines.

ESSENTIALS

GETTING THERE **Trains** from Cannes arrive at the rail station, on place Pierre-Semard, every 20 minutes (trip time: 10 min.), at a one-way fare of 3€. Trains from Nice arrive every 30 minutes (trip time: 18 min.), charging a one-way fare of around 4€. For rail information, call ✆ **08-36-35-35-35.** There's also a **bus** station, La Gare Routière, on place Guynemer (✆ **04-93-34-37-60**), which receives buses from throughout Provence.

If you're **driving,** take E1 east from Cannes, taking the turnoff to the south for Antibes, which leads to the historic core of the old city. From Nice, take E1 west until you come to the turnoff for Antibes. From the center of Antibes, follow the coastal road, boulevard Leclerc, south until you come to Cap d'Antibes.

VISITOR INFORMATION The **Office de Tourisme** is at 11 place du Général-de-Gaulle (✆ **04-92-90-53-00;** www.antibesjuanlespins.com).

SEEING THE SIGHTS

Musée Picasso ★ Housed in the ancient Château Grimaldi on the ramparts above the port is one of the world's greatest Picasso collections. Picasso came here after his bitter war years in Paris and stayed in a small hotel at Golfe-Juan until the museum director at Antibes invited him to work and live at the museum in 1946. Picasso spent a year painting here. When he departed, he gave the museum all the work he had done—24 paintings, 80 ceramics, 44 drawings, 32 lithographs, 11 oils on paper, 2 sculptures, and 5 tapestries. There is also a gallery of other modern artists—Léger, Miró, Ernst, and Calder, among others. Be warned in advance that some of these works might be in storage when you visit, based on whether a temporary exhibition is being displayed. Allow up to 2 hours for your visit.

Place du Château. ✆ **04-92-90-54-20** for recorded message, or 04-92-90-54-20 for an attendant. Admission 4.60€ adults, 2.30€ students and persons under 26, free for ages 6 and under. Oct–May Tues–Sun 10–noon and 2–6pm (June–Sept Tues–Sun 10am–6pm).

Musée Naval et Napoléonien Anyone interested in the meteoric career of Napoléon Bonaparte should be intrigued by this museum. Its interesting collection of Napoleonic memorabilia includes naval models, paintings, and mementos. A toy soldier collection depicts various uniforms, including one used by Napoléon in the Marengo campaign. A wall painting on wood shows Napoléon's entrance into Grenoble; another tableau shows him disembarking at Golfe-Juan on March 1, 1815. In contrast to the Greek-god image of Napoléon in the famous paintings by Canova in the Louvre, a miniature pendant by Barrault reveals the Corsican general as he really looked, with pudgy cheeks and a receding hairline. In the rear rotunda is one of the many hats worn by the emperor. The museum is in a 17th- to 18th-century stone-sided fort and tower; the view of the coast from the top of the tower is worth the admission price.

Batterie du Grillon, bd. J.-F.-Kennedy. ✆ **04-93-61-45-32.** Admission 3€ adults; 1.50€ students, youth 12–25, and seniors; free for ages 11 and under. Mon–Fri 9:30–noon and 2:15–6pm; Sat 9:30–noon.

WHERE TO STAY

VERY EXPENSIVE

Hôtel du Cap–Eden Roc ★★★ Legendary for the glamour of both its setting and its clientele, this Second Empire hotel, opened in 1870, is surrounded by 10 splendid hectares (25 acres) of gardens. It's like a great country estate, with spacious public rooms, marble fireplaces, scenic paneling, chandeliers, and richly upholstered armchairs. F. Scott Fitzgerald immortalized the hotel as Hotel des Etrangers in his classic *Tender Is The Night,* and over the years it has attracted the glitterati of the 20th century, including Hemingway, Picasso, the Windsors, Valentino, Marlene Dietrich, and even Churchill, DeGaulle, Eisenhower, and John F. Kennedy.

Rooms are among the most sumptuous on the Riviera, each a statement of the deluxe tastes of another era. Some guest rooms and suites have regal period furnishings. Beds are lush and plush, with elegant appointments. Marble bathrooms are roomy and offer deluxe toiletries. Know in advance that there is much emphasis on clothing and style here, especially in the evening. The staff is well rehearsed, but regardless of how important you are, they can always claim they've dealt with bigger and more famous names. The world-famous Pavillon Eden Roc, near a rock garden apart from the hotel, has a panoramic Mediterranean view. Venetian chandeliers, Louis XV chairs, and elegant draperies add to the drama. Lunch is served on an outer terrace, under umbrellas and an arbor. Dinner specialties include bouillabaisse, lobster Thermidor, and sea bass with fennel.

Bd. J.-F.-Kennedy, 06600 Cap d'Antibes. ✆ **04-93-61-39-01.** Fax 04-93-67-76-04. www.edenroc-hotel.fr. 140 units. 420€–510€ double; 670€–1,100€ suite. No credit cards. Free parking. Closed mid-Oct to Apr. Bus: A2. **Amenities:** Restaurant; 2 bars; pool; fitness club; sauna; secretarial service; 24-hr. room service; massage; babysitting; laundry service; dry cleaning. *In room:* A/C, TV, hair dryer, safe.

Hôtel Imperial Garoupe ★★ One of the Riviera's newest upscale hotels, it is run by Gilbert Irondelle (son of the director of Antibes' Hôtel du Cap), who transformed it into a low-key and very charming pocket of posh that's a bit less intimidating than the hyper-chic, hyper-expensive hotel run by his father. A one-story building designed around a landscaped patio, with architectural elements that evoke both Tudor England and the deserts of Morocco, the hotel offers luxurious and comfortable bedrooms filled with oversize contemporary furnishings and lots of padded upholsteries. Marble or tile bathrooms have plenty of deluxe toiletries. The hotel, set within 5m (17 ft.) of the beach, is the centerpiece of a 1.4-hectare (3½-acre) park whose lovely rows of pines nevertheless block some of the sea views.

770 chemin de la Garoupe, 06600 Cap d'Antibes. ✆ **800/525-4800** in the U.S., or 04-92-93-31-61. Fax 04-92-93-31-62. www.imperial-garoupe.com. 34 units. 470€–800€ double; 490€–1,000€ suite. AE, DC, MC, V. Free parking. Bus: A2. **Amenities:** Restaurant; bar; heated outdoor pool; 24-hr. room service; babysitting; laundry service; dry cleaning. *In room:* A/C, TV, minibar, hair dryer.

EXPENSIVE

Hôtel Royal Built 90 years ago, this is the oldest hotel in Antibes. The famous guests of yesterday, like novelist Graham Greene, have long since checked out, and celebrities now go elsewhere. But the Royal has done a good job of staying abreast of changing times. All of its bedrooms have been modernized. The furniture is undistinguished, but the good mattresses are firm. The hotel also has a private stretch of beach for guest enjoyment. Even if you're not staying at the hotel, you can enjoy a meal at Le Dauphin, one of the hotel's two restaurants.

Bd. du Maréchal-Leclerc, 06600 Antibes. ✆ **04-93-34-03-09.** Fax 04-93-34-23-31. 37 units. 164€–190€ double. Rates include half board. AE, DC, MC, V. Parking 8€. Closed Nov 2–Dec 18. Bus: A2. **Amenities:** Restaurant; bar; 24-hr. room service. *In room:* A/C, TV, hair dryer.

La Baie Dorée Set between the sea and the coastal road, this hotel appears to rise from the water like a series of boxy, interlocked rectangles, each capped with a terra-cotta roof and ringed with strategically positioned balconies and terraces. From its base, a pier jutting out to sea allows guests to swim and boat, despite the lack of a sandy beach nearby. Public areas are dignified modern spaces with high ceilings; rectilinear lines; simple, summery furnishings; and big windows that seem to flood the interior with views of the nearby sea, almost as if you were aboard a yacht. Each room has a private terrace and a neatly kept bathroom. The upper-tier rooms have Jacuzzis.

579 bd. de la Garoupe, 06160 Cap d'Antibes. ✆ **04-93-67-30-67.** Fax 04-92-93-76-39. www.baiedoree.com. 17 units. 200€–300€ double; 400€–680€ suite or duplex. Extra bed 40€. AE, MC, V. Closed Nov to mid-Dec. **Amenities:** Restaurant; 2 bars; 24-hr. room service; babysitting; laundry service; dry cleaning. *In room:* A/C, TV, minibar, hair dryer, safe.

MODERATE

Auberge de la Gardiole ★ *Finds* Monsieur and Madame Courtot run this country inn with a delightful personal touch. The large villa, surrounded by gardens, is in an area of private estates. The charming rooms are on the upper floors of the inn and in the little buildings in the garden. They come in a variety of shapes and sizes, each furnished with a certain charm and an eye to comfort. Bathrooms are small. The cheerful dining room has a fireplace and hanging pots and pans, and in good weather, you can dine under a wisteria-covered trellis. The owners buy the food and supervise its preparation; the cuisine is French/Provençal.

Chemin de la Garoupe, 06160 Cap d'Antibes. ✆ **04-93-61-35-03.** Fax 04-93-67-61-87. www.hotel-lagaroupe-gardiole.com. 17 units. 90€–130€ double; 165€–200€ suite. AE, MC, V. Closed Nov–Mar. Bus: A2. **Amenities:** Restaurant; bar; pool; limited room service; laundry service. *In room:* A/C in most units, TV, minibar, safe.

Castel Garoupe We highly recommend this Mediterranean villa, on a private lane in the center of the cape, because it offers spacious, tastefully furnished rooms, some equipped with kitchenettes. Bedrooms are exceedingly comfortable and have well-maintained, compact bathrooms. The hotel has private balconies, shuttered windows, and a tranquil garden.

959 bd. de la Garoupe, 06160 Cap d'Antibes. ✆ **04-93-61-36-51.** Fax 04-93-67-74-88. www.castel-garoupe.com. 20 units. 118€–146€ double; 140€–168€ studio apt w/kitchenette. AE, MC, V. Closed Nov to mid-Mar. Bus: A2. **Amenities:** Outdoor pool; exercise room; limited room service; babysitting. *In room:* A/C, TV, kitchenette, fridge, hair dryer, safe.

Hôtel Beau Site This white stucco villa with a tile roof and heavy shutters is surrounded by eucalyptus trees, pines, and palms. Located off the main road, a 7-minute walk from the beach, it has a low wall of flower urns and wrought-iron gates. The interior is like a country inn, with oak beams and antiques. The guest rooms are comfortable and well maintained, and bathrooms are small.

141 bd. J.-F.-Kennedy, 06150 Cap d'Antibes. ✆ **04-93-61-53-43.** Fax 04-93-67-78-16. www.hotelbeausite.net. 30 units. 72€–120€ double. AE, DC, MC, V. Bus: A2. **Amenities:** Bar; pool; 24-hr. room service; babysitting; laundry service; dry cleaning. *In room:* A/C, TV, hair dryer.

INEXPENSIVE

Le Cameo On a historic square, this 19th-century Provençal villa is in the center of town. The rooms are old-fashioned and admittedly not for everyone—perhaps they are typical of the kind of place where Picasso might have stayed when he first hit town. Mattresses are well worn but still have comfort in them. Locals gather in the home-style dining room, with its bouquets of flowers and crowded tables. Look for a simple setting here and a goodwilled welcome from the accommodating staff.

Place Nationale, 06600 Antibes. ✆ **04-93-34-24-17.** Fax 04-93-34-35-80. 9 units, 5 with bathroom, 4 with shower only. 57€ double with shower; 59€ double with bathroom. DC, MC, V. Parking 5.30€. Closed Jan–Feb. Bus: A2. **Amenities:** Restaurant; bar, lounge. *In room:* TV.

WHERE TO DINE

La Bonne Auberge ★ TRADITIONAL FRENCH Its heyday as one of the Riviera's greatest restaurants is but a memory, although this long-established favorite is still a worthy choice. For many years after it opened in 1975, this was the most famous restaurant on the French Riviera. In 1992, when its founder, Jo Rostang, died, his culinary heir, Philippe Rostang, limited its scope and transformed it into a worthwhile but less ambitious restaurant. The fixed-price menu offers a wide selection. Choices vary but might include a Basque-inspired *pipérade* with poached eggs, sea wolf with soya sauce, savory swordfish tart, chicken with vinegar and garlic, and perch-pike dumplings Jo Rostang. Dessert might be an enchanting peach soufflé.

Quartier de Brague, route N7. ✆ **04-93-33-36-65.** Reservations required. Fixed-price menu 35€. DC, MC, V. Wed–Sun noon–2pm; Tues–Sat 7–10pm. Closed mid-Nov to mid-Dec. Take coastal highway N7 east 4km (2½ miles) from Antibes.

La Taverne du Saffranier PROVENÇAL Earthy, irreverent, and firmly entrenched in a century-old building in the Provençal motif, this cost-conscious brasserie trots out a changing medley of local specialties for a local clientele. Portions are savory and generous, and locals find it replete with associations from their real or imagined Provençal childhood. Examples include a platter of stuffed vegetables *(petits farcis),* ceviche or cold raw fish in hot sauce (particularly refreshing on a hot day), a savory version of fish soup, and grilled fish with only a dash of fresh lemon. The kitchens can also prepare their own version of bouillabaisse, but they require a day's advance notice.

Place du Saffranier. ✆ **04-93-34-80-50.** Reservations recommended. Main courses 12€–25€; fixed-price menu 15€. No credit cards. Tues–Sun noon–12:30pm; Tues–Sat 7–10:30pm.

Les Vieux Murs *Value* FRENCH/SEAFOOD This charming Provençal tavern is imbued with a raffish kind of chic. It occupies a room inside the 17th-century ramparts that used to fortify the old seaport, not far from the Musée Picasso (p. 265). The space contains soaring stone vaults and a simple white-painted decor, with a glassed-in front terrace that offers a pleasant view of the water. Menu specialties are a warm salad of mullet, sophisticated arrays of crudités that reflect the bounty of the local harvest; artichoke hearts with a confit of tomatoes; and fresh filets of daurade, hogfish, sole, salmon, and red mullet prepared dozens of ways. Especially appealing is the roast chapon, a local sea fish, with a simple but ultrafresh fricassée of fresh vegetables and olive oil. Suzanne and Georges Romano often have more hungry diners than tables, so try to book early. Their fixed-price menu is one of the best values on the coast.

Promenade de l'Amiral-de-Grasse. ✆ **04-93-34-06-73.** Reservations recommended. Main courses 24.50€–32.60€; fixed-price menu 35.50€–67€. AE, MC, V. Daily noon–2pm and 7:30–10pm. Closed Mon Oct–Apr. Bus: A2.

Restaurant de Bacon ★★★ SEAFOOD In a posh area set on a rocky peninsula, this restaurant enjoys a panoramic coast view. Bouillabaisse aficionados claim that Bacon offers the best version in France of this fish stew, conceived centuries ago as a simple fisher's supper and translated into one of the world's great dishes. In its deluxe version, saltwater crawfish float atop the savory brew, but we prefer the simple version, where a waiter adds the finishing touches at your table. You can also try the fish soup with traditional garlic-laden rouille sauce, fish terrine, sea bass, John Dory, or one of the exotic collection of fish unknown in North America—these include sar, pageot, and denti, prepared several ways. Fish dishes are priced by the gram (like lobster in America).

Bd. de Bacon. ✆ **04-93-61-50-02.** www.restaurantdebacon.com. Reservations required. Main courses 16€–110€; fixed-price menu 45€–65€. AE, MC, V. Wed–Sun noon–2pm and Tues–Sun 8–10pm. Closed Oct–Jan.

6

The Eastern Riviera: From Biot to Monaco to Menton

At Biot, the Riviera continues east through a string of upscale resorts that embody the glamour of the **Côte d'Azur.** Several have been home to the 20th century's great writers and artists. Biot is no exception, with its museum dedicated to the art and life of long-time resident Fernand Léger. Set back from the coast, nearby Villeneuve-Loubet pays tribute to another art in the haute cuisine of Auguste Escoffier, the greatest chef ever to man a kitchen in a nation with a rich culinary heritage.

Farther into the foothills, many artisans live and work in Tourrettes-sur-Loup, where they sell their wares in small shops. Nearby Vence boasts Matisse's Chapelle du Rosaire, adorned by the masterful painter in his twilight years. The great artist is represented side by side with his contemporaries in St-Paul-de-Vence's Fondation Maeght, a museum as modern as the art it houses. Along the coast, Cagnes-sur-Mer continues the region's list of who's who in the 20th century—it was once home to Simone de Beauvoir, and it contains Les Collettes, Renoir's final home.

Nice, the Riviera's capital and largest city, is one of the few budget-oriented resorts on the coast, making it a good base for exploring the region. It features no less than five worthy museums and is filled with noteworthy architecture. Its residents have included Matisse, Stendhal, Nietzsche, George Sand, and Flaubert.

East of Nice is Villefranche-sur-Mer, a fishing village and naval port where small houses climb the hillside; these were once the residences of notables like Aldous Huxley, Katherine Mansfield, and Jean Cocteau. If you can't afford to stay at the ultrachic St-Jean-Cap-Ferrat, you can at least sample the lifestyle at the Musée Ile-de-France, former home of a Rothschild heir, Baronne Ephrussi. Beaulieu is another pocket of posh, featuring a replica of an ancient Greek residence. Eze attracts with its garden of exotic plants, and the Roman ruins at La Turbie ensure a never-ending stream of visitors. Peillon is a scenic foothill village, seated 300m (1,000 ft.) above the nearby shore.

The tiny principality of Monaco is awash with rumors of royal romance and indiscretion, glamorous nightlife, and gambling. Just inland, northeast of Monaco, is the tranquil medieval mountain village of Roquebrune. Cap-Martin is another spot associated with the rich and famous ever since Empress Eugénie wintered here in the 19th century. And sleepy Menton, 8km (5 miles) east of Monaco, is more Italianate than French as it stands right at the border with Italy at the far eastern extremity of the Côte d'Azur.

1 Biot ★

917km (570 miles) S of Paris; 10km (6 miles) E of Cagnes-sur-Mer; 6km (4 miles) NW of Antibes

Biot has been famous for its pottery ever since merchants began to ship earthenware jars to Phoenicia and destinations throughout the Mediterranean. Biot was first settled by Gallo-Romans and has had a long, war-torn history. The potters and other artists still work at their ancient crafts today. Biot is also the place Fernand Léger chose to paint until the day he died.

ESSENTIALS

GETTING THERE Biot's **train station** is 3km (2 miles) east of the town center. There's frequent service from Nice and Antibes. For rail information and schedules, call ✆ **08-36-35-35-35.**

The **bus** from Antibes is even more convenient than the train. For bus information and schedules, call ✆ **04-93-34-37-60** in Antibes. In Biot, buses pull into, and depart from, the place Guynemer.

To **drive** to Biot from Nice, take N7 west. From Antibes, follow N7 east.

VISITOR INFORMATION The **Office de Tourisme** is at 46 rue St-Sebastien (✆ **04-93-65-78-00**).

EXPLORING THE TOWN

To explore the village, begin at the much-photographed **place des Arcades,** where you can see the 16th-century gates and the remains of the town's former ramparts. The **Eglise de Biot,** place des Arcades (✆ **04-93-65-00-85**), dates from the 15th century, when it was built by Italian immigrants who arrived to resettle the town after its population was decimated by the "black death." The church is known for two stunning 15th-century retables: the red-and-gold *Retable du Rosaire* by Ludovico Bréa, and the recently restored *Christ aux Plaies* by Canavesio. The church is open daily from 8am to 7pm between May and June. And usually, but not always, on Friday or Saturday at 9pm, it's the site of Les Heures Musicales, wherein a series of classical concerts makes the ceiling vaults resonate with the sounds of classical music.

Musée d'Histoire Locale et de Céramique Biotoise This museum displays the historical and contemporary work of local glassblowing artists, potters, ceramists, painters, and goldsmiths of the area. The museum, which can be visited in less than an hour, is mainly of interest to the serious collector. At least it helps you understand why Biot is the capital of glassblowing on the Riviera. You learn that the local soils provide the best sand for glassblowing. Since 1956 the old methods of making oil lamps and carafes have been revived. Look for the narrow-spouted *pontons* from which a jet of liquid such as wine can be poured straight into one's mouth.

Place de la Chapelle. ✆ **04-93-65-54-54.** 2€ adults, 1€ children 6–16, free for children under 6. Wed–Sun 2:30–6pm.

Musée National Fernand-Léger ★★ The greatest collection of Léger's work is in this museum, opened in 1960. It's on the eastern edge of town, beside the road leading to Biot's train station. The collection was assembled by the artist's widow, Nadia Léger, who donated its contents to the French government. The stone-and-marble facade is enhanced by Léger's mosaic-and-ceramic mural. On the grounds is a polychrome ceramic sculpture, *Le Jardin d'Enfant.* The collection includes gouaches, paintings, ceramics, tapestries, and sculptures, showing the development of the artist from 1905 until his death.

Chemin du Val-de-Pome (on the east edge of town, beside the road to Biot's rail station). ✆ **04-92-91-50-30.** Admission 4€ adults, students and persons under 18 receive a 40% discount, free for children 6 and under. Open Wed-Mon as follows: July–Sept 10am–6pm; Oct–Mar 10am–12:30pm and 2–5pm; Apr–June 10am–12:30pm and 2–6pm.

SHOPPING

Glass, pottery, and other crafts are what to look for in Biot. In the late 1940s, glassmakers created a bubble-flecked glass known as *verre rustique.* It comes in brilliant colors like cobalt and emerald and is displayed in many store windows on the main shopping street, **rue St-Sebastien.** Many interesting stores are also found in the pedestrian zone in Biot's historic center. Stroll along some of the oldest streets, like the **rue des Tines** and the **place des Arcades.** Most of the glassworks, and many shops selling glass, are at the lower (southern) side of town, beside the **Route de la Mer.**

The best place to watch the glassblowers and buy glass is **Verreries de Biot,** 5 chemin des Combes (✆ **04-93-65-03-00**), at the edge of town. Established in 1956, it was the first, and remains the largest, of the many glassblowing establishments. Have a look at one-of-a-kind collector pieces at the Galerie International du Verre, where the beautifully displayed glass is for sale, often at exorbitant prices. Hours are Monday through Saturday from 9am to 6:30pm. You can also visit the showroom on Sunday from 10:30am to 1pm and 2:30 to 6:30pm.

The namesake of the **Galerie Jean-Claude Novaro** (also known as Galerie de la Patrimoine), place des Arcades (✆ **04-93-65-60-23**), is known as the "Picasso of glass artists." His works are pretty and colorful, though sometimes lacking the diversity and intellectual flair of the artists displayed at the Galerie International du Verre.

La Poterie Provençale, 1689 Rte. de la Mer (✆ **04-93-65-63-30**), almost adjacent to the Musée Fernand-Léger, about 3km (2 miles) southeast of town, is one of the last potteries in Provence to specialize in the tall, amphoralike containers known as *jarres.* The place refers to itself as *une jarrière* because of its emphasis on the containers.

WHERE TO STAY

Domaine du Jas Set at the base of the hill on which sits medieval Biot, this well-managed and intimate inn was built in the early 1990s in the form of three villa-inspired low-rise buildings clustered within a palm-studded garden around a rectangular swimming pool. Each unit has its own terrace or balcony, views of the pool or garden, and, in some cases, panoramas of medieval Biot rising dramatically on the slopes above. Color schemes, both around the pool and within the bedrooms, reflect the ochres, strong yellows, and verdant greens of Provence; throughout, floors are sheathed with slabs of flagstones. The Mascella-Torgoman family (Cherif and Christine) maintain this place much like a private home where friends of the family happen to drop in for extended stays. There's no reception desk, *per se,* but rather, an informal ambience that might remind you of a private house party.

No formalized restaurant or bar (that is, with a full-time waitstaff or bartender) is on the premises, but drinks and light luncheon platters and salads are served informally around the pool.

625 route de la Mer, 06410 Biot. ✆ **04-93-65-50-50.** Fax 04-93-65-02-01. www.domainedujas.com. 19 units. 132€–235€ double. AE, DC, MC, V. Free parking. Closed Nov 15–Mar 15. **Amenities:** Pool; limited room service; babysitting; laundry service. *In room:* A/C, TV, hair dryer, safe.

WHERE TO DINE

Les Terraillers ★★★ MEDITERRANEAN This stone-sided restaurant is about half a mile south of Biot, in what was built in the 1500s as a studio for the production of clay pots and ceramics. The cuisine of chef Claude Jacques and his staff changes with the seasons and is more sophisticated and appetizing than those of many competitors. Examples are a platter containing two preparations of pigeon (thigh and breast cooked in different ways) served with a corn galette and the pigeon's own drippings; roasted scallops with saffron and mussel-flavored cream sauce and a leek confit; a tart with artichoke hearts and tomatoes en confit with lobster salad; braised John Dory Provençal style, with olive oil and a fricassée of zucchini, artichokes, tomatoes, and olives; and ravioli filled with panfried foie gras served with essence of morels and mushroom duxelle.

11 route du Chemin-Neuf. ✆ **04-93-65-01-59.** Reservations required, as far in advance in possible. Main courses 28€–33€; fixed-price menus 29€–60€ lunch, 42€–60€ dinner. MC, V. June–Sept Fri–Wed noon–2pm and 7–10pm; Oct–May Fri–Tues noon–2pm and 7–10pm. Closed Nov. Take route du Chemin-Neuf, following the signs to Antibes.

2 Tourrettes-sur-Loup ★

929km (577 miles) SE of Paris; 29km (18 miles) W of Nice; 6km (4 miles) W of Vence; 21km (13 miles) NE of Grasse

Often called the "City of Violets" because of the small purple flowers cultivated in abundance beneath the olive trees, Tourrettes-sur-Loup sits atop a sheer cliff overlooking the Loup valley. Though violets are big business for the town (they're sent to the perfume factories in Grasse, made into candy, and celebrated during a festival held each Mar), you'll probably find the many shops lining the streets much more interesting. These small businesses are often owned by artisans who sell their own art—most notably hand-woven fabrics and unique pottery. Even if you're not interested in buying, walking through the old town is worth the trip up the hill.

The unusual city was built so that the walls of the outermost buildings form a rampart; three towers rising above the village give it its name. A rocky horseshoe-shape path leads from the main square and then loops back again; follow it for a pleasant tour of the medieval village. Along the way, you'll pass the Chapelle St-Jean, with naïve frescoes that tell biblical stories, weaving in the traditions of local life. Also in the village is a 12th-century church that has paintings by the school of Brea. Immediately adjacent is a ruined 1st-century pagan shrine in honor of the Roman god Mercury. Access to these monuments is erratic and whimsical, depending on a local representative of the nearby **town hall** (✆ **04-93-59-30-11**). In theory, the sites can be visited Monday through Friday from 9am to 5pm, but to make sure, consult the town hall.

ESSENTIALS

GETTING THERE The nearest rail junction is at Cagnes-sur-Mer; buses run about every 45 minutes from Cagnes to Vence, where you must change to another bus to arrive in Tourettes (about six a day; trip time: 10 min.). There is no bus station; the bus disembarks in the place du Village, in front of the Café des Sports. For **bus schedules** and information, call ✆ **04-93-85-61-81.** To go from Cagnes to Tourrettes takes about an hour—it's more convenient to take a taxi (✆ **04-93-24-18-87**) from Cagnes (they line up at the train station), around 22€ each way.

VISITOR INFORMATION The **Office de Tourisme** is at 2 place de la Libération (✆ **04-93-24-18-93**).

SHOPPING

Tourrettes-sur-Loup boasts more crafts studios than any other town its size in Provence. Nearly 30 artisans, including a handful of noted ones from as far away as Paris, have set up their studios and outlets, often in stone-sided buildings facing the town's main street, **Grand'Rue.** The best way to sample their offerings is to wander and window shop (the town's small size makes this feasible). Here's a list of recommendable artisans:

You'll find jewelry, in designs ranging from old-fashioned to contemporary, at **La Paësine,** 14 Grand'Rue (✆ **04-93-24-14-55**). Original clothing—sometimes in silk—for men and women, as well as draperies, bed linens, and tablecloths, usually in creative patterns, is available at the **Atelier Arachnée,** 8 Grand'Rue (✆ **04-93-24-11-42**). Ceramics crafted from local clay in patterns inspired by the many civilizations that have pillaged or prospered in Provence are sold at **Poterie Tournesol,** 7 Grand'Rue (✆ **04-93-59-35-62**). **Isette L'Amoureux Fonderie d'Art,** 73 Grand'Rue (✆ **04-93-24-11-74**), sells very unusual bronzes, some authorized by well-known masters of the modernist movement. For a view of canvases by painters inspired by the colors and traditions of Provence, head for **Comet Galerie,** 51 Grand'Rue (✆ **04-93-24-11-12**), where the featured artist and owner is someone named Macha, a situation that could easily change by the time of your visit.

Looking for a pick-me-up after a day of shopping? Head for one of the region's best candy shops, **Confiserie des Gorges du Loup,** rue Pont St. Loup (✆ **04-93-59-32-91**), where age-old techniques are used to layer fresh fruit with sugar. The result is an ultrachewy, ultrasweet confection that gradually melts as it explodes flavor into your mouth—the taste has been called "angelic." Sample chocolate-covered orange peel, rose-petal jam, and sugar-permeated sliced apricots, tangerines, plums, cherries, and grapes. Even the local violets are transformed into edible, sugary treats.

WHERE TO STAY

Auberge Belles Terrasses This hotel offers views of the faraway peninsula of Antibes and the sea beyond. Its boxy shape and terra-cotta roof were inspired by an architect's fantasy of an old Provençal manor house, and it was named after the terraces that are angled for maximum exposure to the view. The rooms are simple, traditional, and comfortable, but not particularly stimulating. Bathrooms are small. Much of the allure of this place is its restaurant. Menu items include civet of roast suckling pig, young hen with freshwater crawfish, roast wild hare with mustard sauce, Provençal frogs' legs with garlic-and-butter sauce, and assorted game dishes.

1315 Rte. de Vence, 06140 Tourrettes-sur-Loup. ✆ **04-93-59-30-03.** Fax 04-93-59-31-27. 15 units. 38€–60€ double. MC, V. Closed mid-Nov to mid-Dec. From town, drive about a kilometer, following the signs toward Vence. **Amenities:** Restaurant. *In room:* TV.

Le Mas du Soleil ★ *Finds* This low-slung, rustic-looking villa was created from a family's 1950s private home; an Olympic-size pool was added as a means of encouraging the previous owners' daughter in her career as a competitive swimmer. In the late 1990s, it was acquired by Philadelphia-based retirees Curt and Barbara Wible, who maintain it as a discreet and upscale B&B. Each of the three available units has its own entrance and private terrace, with views that sweep out over the surrounding hills, and a cozy, personalized decor. Each room comes with a private midsize bathroom. In most cases, guests are not invited into the main body of the house, and other than dispensing lots of information about local sightseeing options and restaurants (the center of Tourrettes sur Loup is about 60m/200 ft. away), very few hotel-style services are actually provided here. (The Wibles are quick to point out that this is not a conventional hotel, per se, but rather, a private home that accepts overnight adult guests.) During your stay here, you might enjoy rambling around this establishment's garden, which is artfully divided into a series of flat, carefully maintained terraces.

641 Route de Vence, 06140 Tourrettes sur Loup. ✆ **04-93-24-14-23.** Fax 04-93-24-16-73. www.masdusoleil.com. 3 units. 145€–160€ double. Rates include breakfast. MC, V. No children under 12 are allowed. **Amenities:** Pool. *In room:* TV, hair dryer.

WHERE TO DINE

Auberge Belles Terrasses (see "Where to Stay," above) is also recommended for its cuisine, except on Monday, when it's closed to nonguests.

If you're looking for a head-on view of everyday Provençal life, consider either a *plat du jour,* a glass of pastis, or *un petit café* at the most colorful and animated pub in town, **Le Café des Sports,** 1 Rte. de Vence/place de la Libération (✆ **04-93-59-30-26**). Its paneled interior is representative of old-fashioned Provence. It's open for drinks and coffee every day from 6:30am to 11pm, although the generous *plats du jour,* priced at 8€ (no credit cards), are trotted out only between noon and 2:45pm. There's recorded music every day after around 7pm, when it's everybody's favorite hangout for gossip, chitchat, and local scandal-mongering.

Le Petit Manoir TRADITIONAL FRENCH There are only about 25 seats in the simple dining room of this 17th-century building in an all-pedestrian zone in the heart of town. The cuisine is based on traditional French recipes with an occasional modern twist. The flavorful and appetizing dishes include old-fashioned staples like cured ham braised with herbs, foie gras of duckling with acacia-scented honey, roast rack of rabbit stuffed with basil, and a marmite of fish with aromatic herbs.

21 Grande'Rue, Tourrettes-sur-Loup. ✆ **04-93-24-19-19.** Reservations recommended. Main courses 10.20€–23€; fixed-price menus 16€–39.25€. AE, MC, V. Thurs–Tues noon–2pm and 7:30–10pm (closed Sun night). Closed 2 weeks in Nov and 2 weeks in Feb.

3 St-Paul-de-Vence ★★

925km (575 miles) S of Paris; 23km (14 miles) E of Grasse; 27km (17 miles) E of Cannes; 31km (19 miles) N of Nice

ESSENTIALS

GETTING THERE The best way to get to St-Paul is to **drive.** From Nice, take A8 to Cagnes-sur-Mer and then follow the signs and the Route de la Colle (RD 436) to St-Paul-de-Vence. The drive from Nice to St-Paul takes about 35 to 40 minutes.

The nearest **bus** stop is located on the Route de Vence, ¼-mile from the town ramparts. Buses leave frequently from Nice (31km/19 miles from St-Paul) and the neighboring town of Cagnes-sur-Mer (6km/4 miles from St-Paul). The bus from Nice (no. 400 and 410) costs about 8.75€, and the bus from Cagnes-sur-Mer costs 4.10€. Call the bus company **Cie SAP** at ✆ **04-93-58-37-60** for the schedule.

The closest **train** station is in Cagnes-sur-Mer, 6km (4 miles) away. The train from Nice to Cagnes-sur-Mer takes about 7 minutes and costs 4.10€. For train schedules, call © **08-36-35-35-35.**

VISITOR INFORMATION The **Office de Tourisme** is at Maison de la Tour, 2 rue Grande (© **04-93-58-06-38**).

EXPLORING THE TOWN

Except for local residents and service-related deliveries (such as dropping your luggage off at your hotel), driving a car within the center of St-Paul's old town is prohibited. The pedestrian-only **rue Grande** is the most interesting street, running the entire length of St-Paul. Most of the stone houses along it are from the 16th and 17th centuries, many still bearing the coats-of-arms placed here by the original builders. Today most of them are antiques shops, art-and-crafts galleries, and souvenir and gift shops—some are still artists' studios.

Near the church is the **Musée d'Histoire de St-Paul,** place de Castre (© **04-93-32-53-09**), a museum in a 16th-century village house. It was restored and refurnished in a 1500s style, with artifacts illustrating the history of the village. It's open daily from 10am to noon and 1:30 to 5:30pm. Admission is 4€ for adults, 2.50€ for students and children under 12, and free for children under 5.

Fondation Maeght ★★ The most important attraction of St-Paul-de-Vence lies outside the walls. It is one of the most modern art museums in Europe. On a hill in pine-studded woods, the avant-garde building houses one of the finest collections of contemporary art along the Riviera. Nature and the creations of people blend harmoniously in this unique achievement of the architect José Luís Sert. A stark Calder rises like some futuristic monster on the grassy lawns. In a courtyard, the elongated bronze works of Giacometti form a surrealistic garden, creating a hallucinatory mood. Sculpture is also displayed inside, but it's at its best in a natural setting of surrounding terraces and gardens. The museum is built on several levels, its many glass walls providing an indoor-outdoor vista. The foundation, a gift "to the people" from Aimé and Marguerite Maeght, also provides a showcase for new talent. Exhibitions are always changing. Everywhere you look, you see 20th-century art: mosaics by Chagall and Braque, Miró ceramics in the "labyrinth," and Ubac and Braque stained glass in the chapel. Bonnard, Kandinsky, Léger, Matisse, Barbara Hepworth, and many other artists are well represented.

There are a library (open only to scholars and only by appointment), a cinema, and a cafeteria here. In one showroom, you can buy original lithographs by artists like Chagall and Giacometti, and limited-edition prints.

Outside the town walls. © **04-93-32-81-63.** Admission 9€ adults, 7.50€ students and ages 10–25, free for children under 10. July–Sept daily 10am–7pm; Oct–June daily 10am–12:30pm and 2:30–6pm.

La Collégiale de la Conversion de St-Paul The church was constructed in the 12th and 13th centuries, though it was much altered over the years. The Romanesque choir is the oldest part, containing some remarkable stalls carved in walnut in the 17th century. The bell tower was built in 1740, but the vaulting was reconstructed in the 1800s. Although the facade today isn't alluring, the church is filled with art, notably a painting of Ste-Cathérine d'Alexandrie, attributed to Tintoretto and hanging to the left as you enter. The Trésor de l'Eglise is one of the most beautiful in the Alpes-Maritimes, with a spectacular ciborium. Look also for a low relief of the Martyrdom of St-Clément on the last altar on the right. In the baptismal chapter is a 15th-century alabaster Madonna.

Place de l'Eglise. No phone. Free admission. Daily 9am–6pm (till 7pm July–Aug).

SHOPPING

Climb down some steep steps to a 14th-century wine cellar to visit La Petite Cave de St-Paul, 7 rue de l'Etoile (✆ **04-93-32-59-54**), which stocks an excellent selection of regional wine. Among the shop's most prized wines are bottles from Le Mas Bernard, the winery owned by the Maeght Foundation, which owns only 3 hectares (7.4 acres) of vineyards west of St-Paul. The wine from Le Mas Bernard is very good and unavailable in the United States because of the small production.

The village streets are chock full of expensive boutiques and galleries. Some top galleries include Atelier/Boutique Christian Choisy, 5 rue de la Tour/Ramparts Ouest (✆ **04-93-32-01-80**); and Galerie Lilo Marti, à la Placette (✆ **04-93-32-91-22**). Jewelry lovers will want to check out Nicola's Tahitian Pearl, 47 rue Grande (✆ **04-93-32-67-05**).

WHERE TO STAY

La Colombe d'Or (p. 278) also rents deluxe rooms.

VERY EXPENSIVE

Le Mas d'Artigny ★★★ This hotel, one of the Riviera's grandest, evokes a sprawling Provençal homestead set in an acre of pine forests. It was built in 1973 to evoke a sprawling Provençal *mas.* In the lobby is a constantly changing exhibition of art. Each of the comfortably large rooms has its own terrace or balcony, and private suites with a private pool are on a slope, with hedges for privacy. For such an elegant Relais & Châteaux establishment, the restaurant is a bit lackluster in decor and has a staff that isn't always too alert, but it does have great views of the garden. Chef Francis Scordel regales you with his flavors of Provence—everything tastes as if it were ripened in the sun. Only quality ingredients are used to shape this harmonious and rarely complicated cuisine. The wine cellar deserves a star for its vintage collection, but watch those prices!

Route de la Colle et des Hauts de St-Paul, 06570 St-Paul-de-Vence. ✆ **04-93-32-84-54.** Fax 04-93-32-95-36. www.mas-artigny.com. 85 units. 280€–460€ double; 640€–990€ suite. Rates about 30% lower in the off season. AE, DC, MC, V. Free parking. From the town center, follow signs west about 2km (1¼ miles). **Amenities:** Restaurant; bar; pool; tennis court; exercise room; sauna; bike rental; 24-hr. room service; laundry service; dry cleaning. *In room:* A/C, TV, minibar, hair dryer, safe.

EXPENSIVE

Hôtel Le St-Paul ★★ Converted from a 16th-century Renaissance residence and retaining many original features, this Relais & Châteaux hotel is in the heart of the medieval village. The rooms, decorated in a sophisticated Provençal style, have many extras. Beds are quite sumptuous, with elegant fabrics, deluxe mattresses, and quality linen. Bathrooms are maintained in state-of-the-art condition. Many rooms enjoy a view of the valley with the Mediterranean in the distance. One woman wrote us that while sitting on the balcony of room 30, she understood why Renoir, Léger, Matisse, and even Picasso were inspired by Provence. The restaurant has a flower-bedecked terrace sheltered by the 16th-century ramparts as well as a superb dining room with vaulted ceilings. Menus might include locally inspired dishes like cream of salt cod with a thin slice of grilled pancetta, risotto of crawfish and broadbeans, roast veal chop with morels and barley, and a delightful crème brûlée with a hint of rosemary.

86 rue Grande, 06570 St-Paul-de-Vence. ✆ **04-93-32-65-25.** Fax 04-93-32-52-94. www.relaischateaux.fr/stpaul. 19 units. 170€–290€ double; 220€–560€ suite. AE, DC, MC, V. Free parking. Closed Dec to mid-Jan. **Amenities:** Restaurant; 3 tennis courts; limited room service; babysitting; laundry service; dry cleaning. *In room:* A/C, TV, minibar, hair dryer, safe.

Hôtel Les Vergers de Saint-Paul ★ *Finds* This is a small *hôtel de charme,* as the French say, lying just outside this medieval walled village. Completely renovated in 2002, the hotel lies only 900m (2952 ft.) from the center of the village in an idyllic setting surrounded by greenery. Near the famous Maeght Foundation, the hotel is beautifully modern, opening onto a large pool. Bedrooms are tasteful, comfortable, and elegantly refined. All the accommodations come with a balcony or a terrace overlooking the pool.

940 Route de la Colle, 06570 St-Paul-de-Vence. ✆ **04-93-32-94-24.** Fax 04-93-32-91-07. www.stpaulweb.com/vergers. 17 units. 135€–175€ double; 225€–245€ suite. AE, MC, V. **Amenities:** Bar; lounge; pool; limited room service; babysitting. *In room:* A/C, TV, hair dryer, safe.

Villa St. Maxime ★★ *Finds* An elegant discovery, this is one of the most charming of the small boutique hotels along the Riviera. Set on beautifully landscaped grounds, the hotel contains a large panoramic terrace, a beautiful garden, and an Olympic-size pool. The location is beneath the ramparts of this old fortified town. Antiquity is combined with modern luxuries here. The town is ancient, but the villa is like a work of contemporary art, built with Provençal stone sculpted in bold lines, with a retractable and glass-enclosed reception atrium. Vaulted and pillared halls are architectural grace notes, as is the sleek marble flooring. There are views from almost every window, even of the faraway Mediterranean. The best room is the largest suite with a trip of separate rooms; it contains the most luxurious bathroom in the hills of Nice. Other rooms are also a delight. Accommodations open onto private balconies or terraces.

390 Route de la Colle, St-Paul-de-Vence, 06570. ✆ **04-93-32-76-00.** Fax 04-93-32-93-00. www.villa-st-maxime.com. 6 units. 145€–170€ double; 200€–300€ suite. AE, MC, V. **Amenities:** Bar; pool; babysitting. *In room:* A/C, TV, minibar, hair dryer.

MODERATE

Auberge Le Hameau ★ This romantic Mediterranean villa is on a hilltop on the outskirts of St-Paul-de-Vence, on the road to Colle at Hauts-de-St-Paul. Originally built as a farmhouse in the 18th century, and enlarged and transformed into a hotel in 1967, it contains high-ceilinged, comfortable bedrooms outfitted in conservatively modern furniture. You get a remarkable view of the surrounding hills and valleys, and most of the comfortable whitewashed rooms overlook a vineyard. There's also a sunny terrace with fruit trees and flowers. The setting attracted the keen eye of Marc Chagall, who stayed here on his visit.

528 Route de la Colle (D107), 06570 St-Paul-de-Vence. ✆ **04-93-32-80-24.** Fax 04-93-32-55-75. 15 units. 90€–134€ double; from 157€ suite. MC, V. Closed Jan 6–Feb 15 and Nov 16–Dec 22. From the town, take D107 about a kilometer, following the signs south of town toward Colle. **Amenities:** Pool. *In room:* A/C, minibar.

Auberge Les Orangers ★ *Finds* Monsieur Franklin offers a beautiful "living oasis" in his villa. The scents of roses, oranges, and lemons waft through the air. The main lounge is impeccably decorated with original oils and furnished in a provincial style. Expect to be treated like a guest in a private home. The rooms, with antiques and Oriental carpets, have panoramic views and neatly kept bathrooms with shower stalls. On the sun terrace are banana trees and climbing geraniums.

Chemin des Fumerates, Route de la Colle (D107), 06570 St-Paul-de-Vence. ✆ **04-93-32-80-95.** Fax 04-93-32-00-32. 5 units. 120€–140€ double; 183€ suite. Rates include breakfast. MC, V. Free parking. From the town center, follow the signs to Cagnes-sur-Mer for a kilometer south.

INEXPENSIVE

Les Bastides St-Paul This hotel is in the hills outside town, a kilometer or so south of St-Paul and 4km (2½ miles) south of Vence. Divided into three buildings, it offers clean and comfortably carpeted rooms, each accented with regional artifacts, and a terrace and garden. Bedrooms are small to medium in size, each with a fine mattress, giving you a good night's sleep. On the premises is a pool shaped like a cloverleaf, a cozy breakfast area, and a sensitive management staff headed by the long-time hoteliers Marie José and Maurice Giraudet. Breakfast is served anytime you want it.

880 route des Blaquières (route Cagnes-Vence), 06570 St-Paul-de-Vence. ✆ **04-92-02-08-07.** Fax 04-93-20-50-41. www.bastides.fr.fm. 19 units. 84€–125€ double. AE, DC, MC, V. From the town center, follow the signs toward Cagnes-sur-Mer for 1.5km (1 mile) south. **Amenities:** Pool; limited room service. *In room:* A/C, TV, minibar, hair dryer upon request, safe.

WHERE TO DINE

La Colombe d'Or ★★ MODERN FRENCH "The Golden Dove" has for decades been St-Paul's most celebrated restaurant, famous for its remarkable art collection: You can dine amid Mirós, Picassos, Klees, Dufys, Utrillos, and Calders. In fair weather, everyone tries for a seat on the terrace to soak up the view. You won't find cutting-edge cuisine or wildly exotic experiments. Begin with smoked salmon or foie gras from Landes if you've recently won at the casino. Otherwise, you can count on a soup made with the fresh seasonal vegetables. The best fish dishes are poached sea bass with mousseline sauce and sea wolf baked with fennel. Tender beef comes with *gratin dauphinois* (potatoes), or you might prefer lamb from Sisteron. A classic finish to any meal is a soufflé flambé au Grand-Marnier.

The guest rooms (16 doubles, 10 suites) are scattered among three areas: the original 16th-century stone house, a more recent wing that stretches into the garden adjacent to the pool, and an even more modern annex, built in the 1950s and upgraded several times since. Some have exposed stone and heavy ceiling beams; all are very comfortable.

1 place du Général-de-Gaulle, 06570 St-Paul-de-Vence. ✆ **04-93-32-80-02.** Fax 04-93-32-77-78. www.la-colombe-dor.com. Reservations required. Main courses 15€–37.50€. AE, DC, MC, V. Daily noon–2pm and 7:30–10pm. Closed Nov–Dec.

4 Vence ★

925km (575 miles) S of Paris; 31km (19 miles) N of Cannes; 24km (15 miles) NW of Nice

Travel up into the hills northwest of Nice—across country studded with cypresses, olive trees, and pines, where carnations, roses, and oleanders grow in profusion—and Vence comes into view. Outside the town, along boulevard Paul-André, two olive presses carry on with their age-old duties. But the charm lies in the Vieille Ville. Visitors invariably have themselves photographed on place du Peyra in front of the urn-shape Vieille Fontaine, a background shot in several motion pictures. The 15th-century square tower is also a curiosity.

ESSENTIALS

GETTING THERE Frequent **buses** (no. 400 and 410) originating in Nice take about an hour to reach Vence and cost 4.50€ each way. For bus information, contact the **Compagnie SAP** at ✆ **04-93-58-37-60** for schedules. The nearest **rail station** is in Cagnes-sur-Mer, about 7km (4½ miles) from Vence. From here, about 20 buses per day make the trip to Vence. For train information, call ✆ **08-36-35-35-35.** To **drive** to Vence from Nice, travel along N7 west to Cagnes-sur-Mer and then connect to D236 north to Vence.

VISITOR INFORMATION The **Office de Tourisme** is at 8 place du Grand-Jardin (✆ **04-93-58-06-38**).

EXPLORING THE TOWN

If you're wearing the right kind of shoes, the narrow, steep streets of the Old Town are worth exploring. Dating from the 10th century, the cathedral on place Godeau is unremarkable except for some 15th-century Gothic choir stalls. But if it's the right day of the week, most visitors quickly pass through the narrow gates of this once-fortified walled town to where the sun shines more brightly.

Chapelle du Rosaire ★★ Just outside Vence, Matisse created this masterwork for the Dominican nuns of Monteils, partly as a gesture of thanks for Sister Jacques-Marie, a member of the order, who nursed him back to health after a debilitating illness. From the front, you might find it unremarkable and pass it by—until you spot a 12m (40-ft.) crescent-adorned cross rising from a blue-tile roof.

Henri Matisse was 77 when, after a turbulent introspective time, he set out to design and decorate this "culmination of a whole life dedicated to the search for truth." Matisse wrote: "What I have done in the chapel is to create a religious space . . . in an enclosed area of very reduced proportions and to give it, solely by the play of colors and lines, the dimensions of infinity." The light picks up the subtle coloring in the simply rendered leaf forms and abstract patterns: sapphire blue, aquamarine, and lemon yellow. In black-and-white ceramic, St. Dominic is depicted in just a few lines. Most remarkable are the black-and-white tile Stations of the Cross, with Matisse's self-styled "tormented and passionate" figures. The bishop of Nice came to bless the chapel in the late spring of 1951 when the artist's work was completed. Matisse died 3 years later.

The price of admission includes entrance to L'Espace Matisse, a gallery that documents the way Matisse handled the design of the chapel during its construction (1949–51). It also shows lithographs and religious artifacts that concerned Matisse in one way or another.

Av. Henri-Matisse. ✆ **04-93-58-03-26.** Admission 2.50€ adults, 1€ persons 16 and under; contributions to maintain the chapel are welcomed. Dec–Sept Tues and Thurs 10–11:30am and 2–5:30pm; Mon, Wed, and Sat 2–5:30pm. Sun Mass at 10am, followed by visit at 10:45am.

WHERE TO STAY

VERY EXPENSIVE

Le Château du Domaine St-Martin ★★★ This is the grandest address in the hills above Nice. This château, in a 14–hectare (35-acre) park, was built in 1936 on the grounds where the Golden Goat treasure, a legendary stash of gold, was reputedly buried. A complex of tile-roofed villas with suites was built in the terraced gardens. You can walk through the gardens on winding paths lined with tall cypresses, past the ruined chapel and olive trees. The exceedingly spacious guest rooms are furnished in elegant taste. State-of-the-art bathrooms are equipped with dual basins and luxury toiletries. The restaurant has a view of the coast and offers superb French cuisine. In summer, many guests prefer the poolside grill.

Av. des Templiers BP102, 06142 Vence. ✆ **04-93-58-02-02.** Fax 04-93-24-08-91. www.chateau-st-martin.com. 40 units, 5 cottages. 240€–790€ double; 315€–1,525€ suite. AE, DC, MC, V. Closed Nov to mid-Feb. From the town center, follow the signs toward Coursegoules and Col-de-Vence for 1.5km (1 mile) north. **Amenities:** Restaurant; bar; 24-hr. room service; laundry service; dry cleaning. *In room:* A/C, TV, minibar, hair dryer, safe.

Exploring the Gorges du Loup

After paying your respects to Matisse at the Chapelle du Rosaire in Vence, you can take D2210 through some of the Riviera's most luxuriant countryside. The **Gorges du Loup** isn't as dramatic as the Grand Canyon du Verdon (see chapter 4) but still features a scenic 13km (8-mile) drive that loops along the eastern and western edges. This drive showcases waterfalls, most notably the **Cascades des Demoiselles,** with its partially fossilized plant life, and the 39m (130-ft.) **Cascade de Courmes.** There are also jagged glacial holes best exemplified by the **Saut du Loup** at the valley's northeastern end.

Gourdon, the only village along the gorge's western rim, with a year-round population of only 59 but a larger summer population, functions as a tourist trap. If you stop here, ignore the souvenir shops and visit the immense 13th-century **Château de Gourdon** (© **04-93-09-68-02**). It houses two museums: The **Musée Historique** features a Rembrandt self-portrait, Marie Antoinette's writing desk, and an assortment of armor, arms, and torture instruments. The **Musée de Peinture Naïve** offers a small Rousseau portrait, among other works. The magnificent 17th-century formal garden is graced with topiaries often photographed by gardening magazines. The museums are open June through September daily from 11am to 1pm and 2 to 7pm, and October through May Wednesday through Monday from 2 to 6pm. A combined ticket to the garden and the museums is 3.80€. Tickets to one or the other aren't available.

On the southeastern edge of the gorge, at Pont-du-Loup, go to **La Confiserie des Gorges du Loup,** rue Principale (© **04-93-59-32-91**), where you can sample sweets while watching the confectioners sugar-coat tangerines or chocolate-dip orange peels. Less than a kilometer

MODERATE

Le Floréal On the road to Grasse is this pleasant, comfortable hotel with a view of the mountains and a refreshing lack of pretension. Many of the well-furnished rooms look out into the garden, where orange trees and mimosa add fragrance to the breezes. Most accommodations are medium-size, and each is most comfortable, with quality mattresses and fine linen. Bathrooms are compact and tiled.

Av. Rhin-et-Danube, 06140 Vence. © **04-93-58-64-40.** Fax 04-93-58-79-69. 42 units. 60€–196€ double (prices increase over Christmas). AE, DC, MC, V. Free parking. **Amenities:** Restaurant; bar; pool; sauna; 24-hr. room service; babysitting; laundry service; dry cleaning. *In room:* A/C, TV, hair dryer.

Relais Cantemerle ★★ One of the most appealing places in Vence is this artfully designed cluster of accommodations that resembles an old-fashioned compound of Provençal buildings. It surrounds a verdant lawn dotted with old trees. Public areas are stylishly outfitted with Art Deco furniture and accessories; they include a flagstone terrace that's the site of sun-flooded meals. Accommodations aren't overly large, but they contain unusual overscaled Art Deco armchairs, louvered wooden closet doors, and balcony-style sleeping lofts. The bathrooms are beautifully kept.

farther south, the 15th-century Gothic church at Le Bar-sur-Loup features a morbid ***Danse Macabre,*** a 15th-century painting of fallen and dancing humans whose souls are being wrested away by black demons and then weighed by St. Michael before being tossed into the pits of hell. Speculation links the anonymous work of art to the plague.

After taking in this sober vision, backtrack to Pont-du-Loup and travel 8km (5 miles) east to **Tourrettes-sur-Loup,** where you can find accommodations in an unspoiled medieval village on a rocky bluff high above a violet-filled valley (see earlier in this chapter).

If you're coming from Cannes, take A85 for 21km (13 miles) northwest to Grasse, and then travel east for 6km (3¾ miles) on Route 2085, where you'll turn north at Magagnosc, following D3 for 8km (5 miles) north to Gourdon, at the edge of the gorge. To come from Nice, take E80 for 3km (2 miles) west to Route 2085, and then drive 26km (16 miles) west to Magagnosc, to follow the same path north to Gourdon. Once in Gourdon, you can continue north on D3 along the western rim of the gorge; after 6km (4 miles), turn right onto D6 to return south along its eastern lip. Turn east on D2210 at Pont-du-Loup for a 8km (5-mile) drive to Tourrettes-sur-Loup, or continue on to Vence, another 3km (2 miles) along, where you can turn south on Route 36 for a 9km (5½-mile) drive back to the coast.

For information, contact the **Office de Tourisme,** 22 cours Henri-Cresp, 06130 Grasse (✆ **04-93-36-03-56**); place Grand-Jardin, 06140 Vence (✆ **04-93-58-06-38**); or 2 place de la Liberation, 06140 Tourrettes-sur-Loup (✆ **04-93-24-18-93**).

258 chemin Cantemerle, 06140 Vence. ✆ **04-93-58-08-18.** Fax 04-93-58-32-89. www.relais-cantemerle.com. 19 units. 153€ double; 184€ 1-bedroom duplex for 2; 46€ additional bed. 30€ supplement for half-board. AE, MC, V. Closed mid-Oct to mid-Apr. **Amenities:** Restaurant; bar; limited room service; laundry service. *In room:* A/C, TV, minibar, hair dryer.

INEXPENSIVE

Auberge des Seigneurs (Inn of the Noblemen) This 400-year-old stone hotel gives you a historic taste of Provence. Inside is a long wooden dining table, in view of an open fireplace with a row of hanging copper pots and pans. The cuisine of François I is served in an antique atmosphere with wooden casks of flowers and an open spit for roasting and grilling. Fascinating decorative objects and antiques are everywhere.

Guest rooms are well maintained, though management gives priority to the restaurant, which generates far more revenue. Bedrooms have lots of exposed paneling and beams. Twin or double beds are fitted with firm mattresses. The compact tiled bathrooms have adequate shelf space.

Place du Frêne, 06140 Vence. ✆ **04-93-58-04-24.** Fax 04-93-24-08-01. 6 units. 72€ double. AE, DC, MC, V. Closed Nov–Mar 15. **Amenities:** Restaurant; limited room service. *In room*: Hair dryer.

Hôtel Villa Roseraie ★★ *Finds* This charming small hotel, a 5-minute walk from the historic center of Vence, lies in a totally renovated 19th-century manor house. Marc Chagall lived for many years on a hill across from the hotel. It's an easy walk from the Matisse Chapel. Monica and Maurice Garnier are among the most charming hosts in Vence, and they've furnished their home with old-fashioned pieces, often antiques. The garden offers perfect southern exposure. The "Rose Garden" (its English name) is studded with magnolias, yucca, eucalyptus, banana trees, palms, and, of course, roses. Rooms no. 4, 5, and 8 have balconies; no. 12, 14, 15, and 16 have ground-floor patios. Bathrooms contain showers and are decked in Provençal tiles from neighboring Salernes. There's no better way to start the day here than by sampling one of the fresh house-baked croissants.

Av. Henri-Giraud, route de Coursegoules, 06140 Vence. ✆ **04-93-58-02-20.** Fax 04-93-58-99-31. 16 units. 85€–132€ double. AE, MC, V. From the town center, drive less than a half-kilometer, following the signs toward Col-de-Vence. **Amenities:** Pool; limited room service; babysitting. *In room:* TV, minibar, hair dryer, safe in some units.

WHERE TO DINE

Auberge des Seigneurs (see above) is an excellent place to dine at reasonable prices.

Jacques Maximin ★★★ MODERN FRENCH This deluxe dining room is justly hailed as one of the Riviera's grandest restaurants. The setting is an artfully rustic 19th-century manor house that was transformed in the mid-1980s into the private home of culinary superstar Jacques Maximin. Today it's the target of pilgrimages by foodies and movie stars venturing north from the Cannes Film Festival, including Hugh Grant, Elizabeth Hurley, and Robert De Niro. You can sample a menu firmly entrenched in the seasonal produce of the surrounding countryside. Stellar examples are salads made with asparagus and truffles, Canadian lobster, or fresh scallops; pigeon breast with cabbage with lentil cream sauce; peppered duck; and some of the best beef dishes in the region. Expect surprises from the capricious chef, whose menu changes virtually every day.

689 chemin de la Gaude. ✆ **04-93-58-90-75.** Reservations required. Main courses 28€–59€; fixed-price menus 40€–87€ lunch, 60€–89€ dinner. AE, DC, MC, V. Tues–Sun 12:30–2pm; Tues–Sat 7:30–10pm. Closed Nov 12–Dec 12 and daily for lunch July–Aug. From the historic core of Vence, drive sourthwest for 4km (2½ miles), following the signs to Cagnes-sur-Mer.

La Farigoule PROVENÇAL In a century-old house that opens onto a rose garden, where tables are set out during summer, this restaurant specializes in Provençal cuisine prepared by skilled English-speaking chef Patrick Bruot, formerly a resident of New York. Menu items include a conservative but flavorful array of dishes that feature a bourride Provençal; shoulder of roasted lamb with a ragout of fresh vegetables, served with fresh thyme; aïoli; and such fish dishes as dorado with a confit of lemons and fresh aromatic coriander.

15 rue Henri-Isnard. ✆ **04-93-58-01-27.** Reservations recommended. Fixed-price menu 22€–43€ at lunch, 28€–43€ at dinner. Thurs–Mon noon–2pm and 7:30–10pm.

5 Cagnes-sur-Mer ★/Le Haut-de-Cagnes ★

917km (570 miles) S of Paris; 21km (13 miles) NE of Cannes

Cagnes-sur-Mer, like the Roman god Janus, has two faces. Perched on a hill in the "hinterlands" of Nice, **Le Haut-de-Cagnes** is one of the most charming spots on the Riviera. Naomi Barry of the *New York Times* wrote that it "crowns the top of a blue-cypressed hill like a village in an Italian Renaissance painting." At the foot of the hill is an old fishing port and rapidly developing beach resort called **Cros-de-Cagnes,** between Nice and Antibes.

For years, Le Haut-de-Cagnes attracted the French literati, including Simone de Beauvoir, who wrote *Les Mandarins* here. A colony of painters also settled in—Renoir stated that the village was "the place where I want to paint until the last day of my life."

The racecourse is one of the finest in France.

ESSENTIALS

GETTING THERE The train depot, **Gare SNCF,** lies in Cagnes-Ville at avenue de la Gare, receiving trains that run along the Mediterranean coast, with arrivals every hour from both Nice and Cannes. For rail information, call ✆ **08-36-35-35-35. Buses** from Nice and Cannes stop at Cagnes-Ville and at Béal/Les Collettes, within walking distance of Cros-de-Cagnes. For information, call ✆ **04-93-20-45-05** in Cannes or **04-93-85-61-81** in Nice. The climb from Cagnes-Ville to Haut-de-Cagnes is very strenuous, so year-round a free minibus runs about every 30 minutes from place du Général-de-Gaulle in the center of Cagnes-Ville to Haut-de-Cagnes. By **car,** from any of the coastal cities of Provence, follow the A8 coastal highway, exiting at CAGNES-SUR-MER/CROS-DE-CAGNES.

VISITOR INFORMATION The **Office de Tourisme** is at 6 bd. Maréchal-Juin, Cagnes-Ville (✆ **04-93-20-61-64;** www.cagnes-tourisme.com).

SPECIAL EVENTS The **Festival International de Peinture (International Festival of Painting)** is presented by Cagnes's Town Hall and the Musée d'Art Moderne Méditerranéen during July and August in the Château Musée, 7 place Grimaldi. Painters from about 40 nations participate in the exposition and promotion of their works. For information, call ✆ **04-93-22-19-25.**

SEEING THE SIGHTS

The orange groves and fields of carnations of the upper village provide a beautiful setting for the narrow cobblestone streets and 17th- and 18th-century homes. Drive your car to the top, where you can enjoy the view from place du Château and have lunch or a drink at a sidewalk cafe.

While in Le Haut-de-Cagnes, visit the **fortress** on place Grimaldi. It was built in 1301 by Rainier Grimaldi I, a lord of Monaco and a French admiral (see the portrait inside). Charts reveal how the defenses were organized. In the early 17th century, the dank castle was converted into a more gracious Louis XIII–style château.

The château contains two interconnected museums, the **Musée de l'Olivier (Museum of the Olive Tree)** and the **Musée d'Art Moderne Méditerranéen (Museum of Modern Mediterranean Art),** 7 place Grimaldi (✆ **04-93-20-87-29**). The modern art gallery displays works by Kisling, Carzou, Dufy, Cocteau, and Seyssaud, among others, with temporary exhibitions. In one salon is an interesting trompe-l'oeil fresco, *La Chute de Phaeton.* From the tower, you get a panoramic view of the Côte d'Azur. The museums are open Wednesday through Monday: May through September from 10am to noon and 2 to 6pm, and October through April from 10am to noon and 2 to 5pm. Admission to both museums is 3.50€ for adults and 1.75€ for students and children under 12. The Festival International de la Peinture (see above) takes place here.

A DAY AT THE BEACH

Cros-de-Cagnes is known for 4km (2¼ miles) of seafront evenly covered with light-gray pebbles (the French refer to it as *galet*) that've been worn smooth by centuries of wave action. These beaches are collectively identified as the **Plages de Cros-de-Cagnes.** The expanse is punctuated by five concessions that rent beach mattresses and chaises for around 15€. The best, or at least the most centrally located, are **Tiercé Plage** (✆ **04-93-20-13-89**), **Le Cigalon** (✆ **04-93-07-74-82**), and **La Gougouline** (✆ **04-93-31-08-72**). As usual, toplessness is accepted, but full nudity isn't.

A NEARBY ATTRACTION

Musée Renoir & Les Collettes ★ Les Collettes has been restored to what it looked like when Renoir lived here from 1908 until his death in 1919. He continued to sculpt here, even though he was crippled by arthritis. He also continued to paint, with a brush tied to his hand and with the help of assistants.

The house was built in 1907 in an olive-and-orange grove. There's a bust of Madame Renoir in the entrance room. You can explore the drawing room and dining room on your own before going up to the artist's bedroom. In his atelier are his wheelchair, easel, and brushes. From the terrace of Madame Renoir's bedroom is a stunning view of Cap d'Antibes and Haut-de-Cagnes. On a wall hangs a photograph of one of Renoir's sons, Pierre, as he appeared in the 1932 film *Madame Bovary.* Although Renoir is best remembered for his paintings, it was in Cagnes that he began experimenting with sculpture. The museum has 20 portrait busts and portrait medallions, most of which depict his wife and children. The curators say they represent the largest collection of Renoir sculpture in the world.

19 chemin des Collettes. ✆ **04-93-20-61-07.** Admission 4€ adults, 2€ children, free for children under 12. May–Sept Wed–Mon 10am–noon and 2–6pm; Oct–Apr Wed–Mon 10am–noon and 2–5pm. Ticket sales end 30 min. before the lunch and evening closing hours.

WHERE TO STAY

IN CAGNES-SUR-MER

Hôtel Le Chantilly *Value* This is the best bargain for those who prefer to stay at a hotel near the beach instead of an inn in the hills. It won't win any architectural awards, but the owners have landscaped the property and made the interior as homey and inviting as possible, using Oriental rugs and potted plants, including dwarf palms, as grace notes. Everything was freshly painted and upgraded in 1999. Bathrooms are compact and tiled. In fair weather, you can enjoy breakfast, the only meal served, on an outdoor terrace. The rooms, for the most part, are small but cozily furnished and well kept, often opening onto balconies. The owners, Monique and Jean-Claude Barran, will direct you to nearby restaurants.

Chemin de la Minoterie, 06800 Cagnes-sur-Mer. ✆ **04-93-20-25-50.** Fax 04-92-02-82-63. 20 units. 45.60€–59.30€ double. MC, V. Free parking. **Amenities:** Lounge. *In room:* TV, minibar.

IN LE HAUT-DE-CAGNES

Note that **Le Grimaldi** (see "Where to Dine," below) also rents rooms.

Le Cagnard ★★ Several 13th-century houses were joined together in the 1960s to form this complex, a glamorous Relais & Châteaux property. The dining room is covered with frescoes, and there's a vine-draped terrace. The rooms and salons are furnished with antiques, such as provincial chests, armoires, and Louis XV chairs. Each room has its own style: Some are duplexes; others have terraces and views of the countryside. The luxurious bathrooms are spacious, with tub and shower combinations. The cuisine of chef Jean-Yves Johany is reason enough to make the trip. Fresh ingredients are used in the delectable dishes placed on one of the finest tables set in Provence. The hotel is open year-round, but the restaurant closes from November to December 15, and is closed Tuesday and Thursday at lunch.

Rue du Pontis-Long, Le Haut-de-Cagnes, 06800 Cagnes-sur-Mer. ✆ **04-93-20-73-21.** Fax 04-93-22-06-39. www.le-cagnard.com. 25 units. 150€–200€ double; 230€–400€ suite. AE, DC, MC, V. Parking 12€. **Amenities:** Restaurant; bar; limited room service; laundry service; dry cleaning. *In room:* A/C, TV, minibar, hair dryer, safe.

WHERE TO DINE

IN LE HAUT-DE-CAGNES

Josy-Jo ★★ TRADITIONAL FRENCH Sheltered behind a 200-year-old facade covered with vines and flowers, this restaurant lies on the main road to the château. It used to be the home and studio of Modigliani and Soutine, when they borrowed it from a friend during their hungriest years. Today it functions as a cheerful and often bustling dining enclave. Everything is kept running smoothly by the good-natured Bandecchi family. The cuisine is divine, fresh, and excellent, featuring grilled meats and a roster of fish. You can enjoy brochette of gigot of lamb with kidneys, four succulent varieties of steak, calves' liver, a homemade terrine of foie gras of duckling, and an array of salads.

8 place du Planastel. ✆ **04-93-20-68-76.** Reservations required. Main courses 27€–34€. AE, MC, V. Mon–Fri noon–2pm and 7:30–10pm; Sat 7:30–10pm.

Le Grimaldi TRADITIONAL FRENCH Here you can dine under bright umbrellas on the town's main square or in a dining room built during the Middle Ages. Run by the same hardworking family since 1963, the restaurant serves specialties like salade Niçoise, *lapin* (rabbit) *chasseur,* a savory version of bouillabaisse, mussels Provençal, and trout with almonds. A noteworthy specialty is escalope of veal "Grimaldi" that's prepared with cheese, crème fraîche, and port.

The hotel also offers six simply furnished rooms, usually with original, roughly hewn ceiling beams, a wash basin, and a bidet. The price is 34.20€ for a single or double, plus 8€ for overnight parking. None has a toilet or shower, although shared facilities are accessible via the upstairs corridors.

6 place du Château. ✆ **04-93-20-60-24.** Reservations recommended. Main courses 10.50€–22€; fixed-price menus 20€–29.50€. AE, DC, MC, V. Daily noon–3pm and 7:30–11pm. Closed Jan 15–Feb 15.

IN CROS-DE-CAGNES

Loulou (La Réserve) ★★ TRADITIONAL FRENCH Run by the Campo family, this place is named for a famous long-departed chef. Brothers Eric and Joseph Campo prepare dishes that include spectacular versions of calamari and octopus salad; fish soup; shrimp steamed and then served with fresh ginger and cinnamon; and grilled, very fresh versions of what local suppliers have brought in that day. These are served as simply as possible, usually with just a drizzling of olive oil and balsamic vinegar. Meat dishes include a flavorful version of veal kidneys with port sauce, usually featured in autumn and winter, and delectable grilled steaks, chops, and cutlets. Everything here is solid, intelligent, and reliable, with a staff that isn't afraid to be gutsy and creative, and flavors that are inherent in virtually every dish. In front is a glassed-in veranda that's a prime spot for people-watching.

91 bd. de la Plage. ✆ **04-93-31-00-17.** Reservations recommended. Main courses 25€–37€; fixed-price menu 38€. AE, MC, V. Mon–Fri noon–1:30pm and 7–9:45pm; Sat 7–9:45pm. Closed for lunch July 14–Aug 31.

6 Nice ★★★

929km (577 miles) S of Paris; 32km (20 miles) NE of Cannes

The Victorian upper classes and tsarist aristocrats loved Nice in the 19th century, but it's solidly middle class today, and far less glamorous and expensive than Cannes—the least expensive of any resort. It's also the best excursion center on the Riviera, especially if you're dependent on public transportation. For example, you can go to San Remo, "the queen of the Italian Riviera," and return to Nice by nightfall. From the Nice airport, the second largest in France, you can travel by bus along the entire coast to resorts like Juan-les-Pins and Cannes.

Nice is the capital of the Riviera, the largest city between Genoa and Marseille. It's also one of the most ancient, having been founded by the Greeks, who called it "Nike," or Victory. Because of its brilliant sunshine and relaxed living, it has attracted artists and writers. Among them were Dumas, Nietzsche, Apollinaire, Flaubert, Victor Hugo, George Sand, Stendhal, Chateaubriand, and Mistral. Henri Matisse, who made his home in Nice, said, "Though the light is intense, it's also soft and tender." The city has, on the average, 300 days of sunshine a year.

ESSENTIALS

GETTING THERE Nice is a major transportation hub and a convenient base from which to explore the region. The **Aéroport International Nice–Côte d'Azur** (✆ **08-20-42-33-33**) is France's second busiest airport, with up to 45 planes per day flying from Paris to Nice; there's also a flight from New York to Nice. EasyJet (✆ **0870/6000-000** in London; www.easyjet.com), a European budget airline, offers a flight from London to Nice. The airport, with two terminals, is 7km (4⅓ miles) from the city center. Terminal 1 is used for international flights. For information about public transportation, and also to summon a taxi to any point within Nice, call ✆ **04-93-21-43-84.** A taxi takes 20 minutes and costs about 25€ to 30€. A bus leaves the airport every 30 minutes for the town center and SNCF train station, costs 3.50€, and takes 30 minutes. An equivalent bus, with roughly the same frequency and charging the same fares, departs from the airport for the *Gare Routière* (Municipal Bus Station).

From Paris's Gare de Lyon, the **TGV train** takes 6½ hours to get to Nice's Gare S.N.C.F. and affords beautiful views along the coast—particularly from Cannes to Nice. There are two trains per day from October to May and three per day from June to September. The train from Paris costs 89€. The slow trains that travel along the coast of the Riviera stop in Nice, so there is frequent service to Cannes, Monaco, and Antibes, among others. For train information, call ✆ **08-36-35-35-39.** Trains arrive in the center of the modern part of the city on avenue Thiers.

Gare Routière de Nice is the bus station at promenade de Paillon (✆ **04-93-85-61-81**). Buses are a cheap and practical way to visit nearby villages and towns.

VISITOR INFORMATION Nice maintains three tourist offices, the largest and most central of which is at 5 promenade des Anglais (✆ **08-92-70-74-07**), near place Massena. Additional offices are in the arrivals hall of the **Aéroport Nice–Côte d'Azur** (✆ **04-92-14-48-00**) and the railway station on avenue Thiers (✆ **04-92-14-48-00**). Any can make a hotel reservation (but only for the night of the day you happen to show up), charging a modest fee that varies according to the classification of the hotel you book.

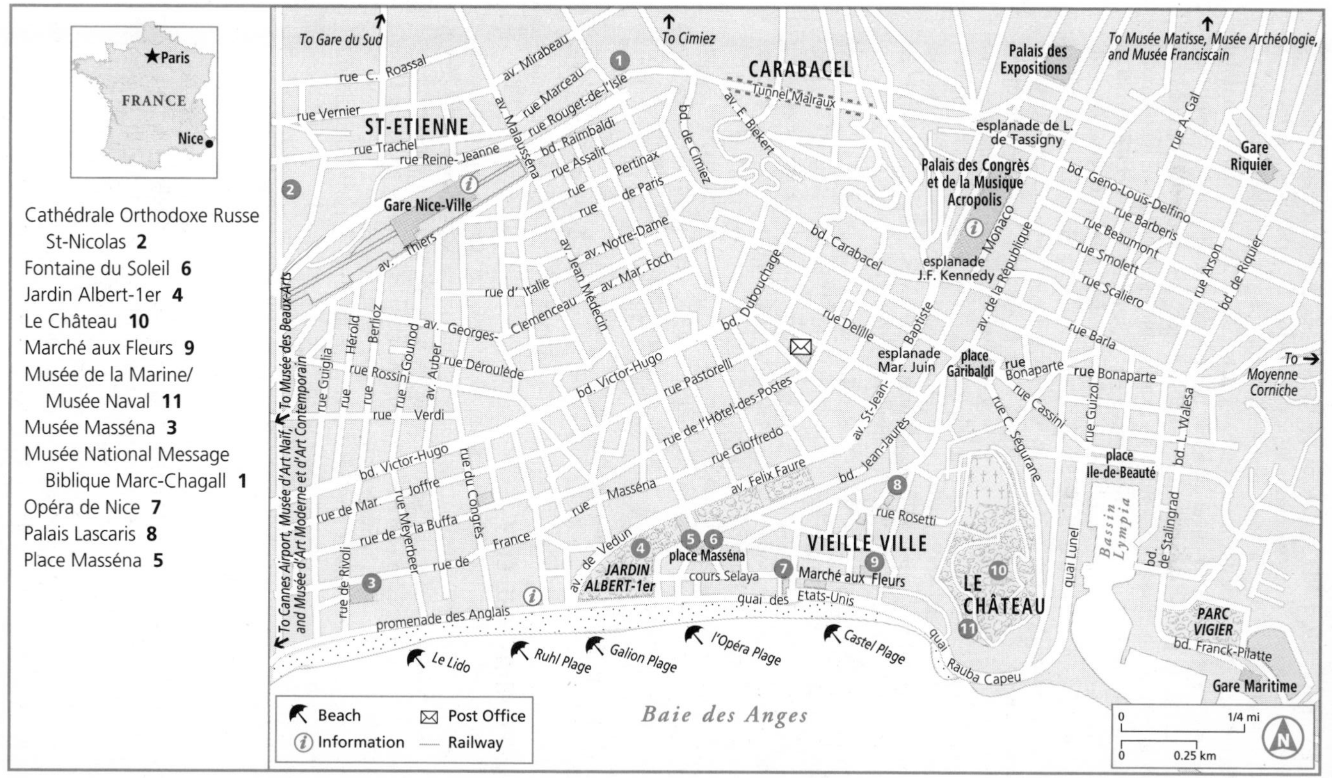

Cathédrale Orthodoxe Russe St-Nicolas 2
Fontaine du Soleil 6
Jardin Albert-1er 4
Le Château 10
Marché aux Fleurs 9
Musée de la Marine/ Musée Naval 11
Musée Masséna 3
Musée National Message Biblique Marc-Chagall 1
Opéra de Nice 7
Palais Lascaris 8
Place Masséna 5
FRANCE
Paris
Nice
Beach
Information
Post Office
Railway
0 1/4 mi
0 0.25 km
N
ST-ETIENNE
CARABACEL
VIEILLE VILLE
LE CHÂTEAU
JARDIN ALBERT-1er
PARC VIGIER
Gare Nice-Ville
Gare Riquier
Gare Maritime
Palais des Expositions
Palais des Congrès et de la Musique Acropolis
place Masséna
place Garibaldi
place Ile-de-Beauté
Bassin Lympia
Baie des Anges
Le Lido
Ruhl Plage
Galion Plage
l'Opéra Plage
Castel Plage
promenade des Anglais
quai des Etats-Unis
quai Rauba Capeu
To Gare du Sud
To Cimiez
To Musée Matisse, Musée Archéologie, and Musée Franciscain
To Moyenne Corniche
To Musée des Beaux-Arts
To Cannes Airport, Musée d'Art Naïf, and Musée d'Art Moderne et d'Art Contemporain

GETTING AROUND Most of the local buses in Nice create connections with one another at their central hub, the **Station Central,** 10 av. Félix-Faure (✆ **04-93-13-53-13**), a very short walk from the place Masséna. Municipal buses each charge 2€ for a ride within Greater Nice. To save money, consider buying a five-ticket carnet for 12.85€. Bus nos. 2 and 12 make frequent trips to the beach. Long-distance buses making the trek, say, between Nice and such destinations as Monaco, Cannes, St-Tropez, and other parts of France and Europe depart from the **Gare Routière,** 5 bd. Jean-Jaurès (✆ **04-93-85-61-81**).

The best place to rent bikes and mopeds in Nice is from **Cycles Arnaud,** 5 rue François 1e (✆ **04-93-87-88-55**), just behind the place Grimaldi. Open Tuesday through Saturday from 9am to noon and 2 to 7pm, it charges 15€ per day for both bikes and mopeds, and requires a deposit of at least 304€ or more, depending on the value of the machine you rent. Somewhat less appealing, but useful for the days when Cycles Arnaud is closed, is **Nicea Rent,** 12 rue de Belgique (✆ **04-93-82-42-71**), which charges about the same rates, but whose staff isn't always on the premises. (They maintain a somewhat erratic mobile phone service at ✆ **06-12-44-15-37.**) It's open daily from 9am to 6pm.

SPECIAL EVENTS The **Nice Carnaval** draws visitors from all over Europe and North America to this ancient spectacle. This "Mardi Gras of the Riviera" begins sometime in February, usually 12 days before Shrove Tuesday, celebrating the return of spring with 3 weeks of parades, *corsi* (floats), *veglioni* (masked balls), confetti, and battles in which young women toss flowers. Only the most wicked throw rotten eggs instead of carnations. Climaxing the event is a fireworks display on Shrove Tuesday, lighting up the Baie des Anges (Bay of Angels). King Carnival goes up in flames on his pyre but rises from the ashes the following spring. For information, contact the tourist office (see above).

Also important is the **Nice Festival du Jazz,** taking place during a week in mid-July, when a roster of jazz artists performs in the ancient Arène de Cimiez. For information, contact **Salle Nikaia,** route de Grenoble (✆ **08-20-02-04-06**).

EXPLORING THE CITY

In 1822, the orange crop at Nice was bad and the workers faced a lean time, so the English residents put them to work building the **promenade des Anglais** ★★, a wide boulevard fronting the bay. Split by "islands" of palms and flowers, it stretches for about 6km (4 miles). Fronting the beach are rows of grand cafes, the **Musée Masséna,** villas, and hotels—some good, others decaying.

In the east, the promenade becomes **quai des Etats-Unis,** the original boulevard, lined with some of the best restaurants in Nice, all specializing in bouillabaisse.

Tips Taking the Train Touristique

To tour Nice the easy way, take the **Train Touristique de Nice** (✆ **06-16-39-53-51**), which departs from the Jardin Albert-1er. Rolling on rubber wheels, it makes a 40-minute sightseeing transit past many of Nice's sites—place Masséna, promenade des Anglais, quai des Etats-Unis, and the graveyard. With departures every 30 to 60 minutes, the train operates daily from 10am to 5pm (until 6pm in Apr, May, and Sept; until 7pm June–Aug). There's no service between mid-November and mid-December and during most of January. Train rides last about 45 minutes. The price is 6€ per person.

Rising sharply on a rock is the site known as **Le Château,** the spot where the ducs de Savoie built their castle, which was torn down in 1706. All that remains are two or three stones—even the foundations have disappeared in the wake of Louis XIV's deliberate destruction of what was viewed at the time as a bulwark of Provençal resistance to his regime. The steep hill has been turned into a garden of pines and exotic flowers. To reach the panoramic site, you can take an elevator. The park is open daily from 8am to dusk.

At the north end of Le Château is the famous old **graveyard** of Nice, visited primarily for its lavishly sculpted monuments that make their own enduring art statement. It's the largest in France and the fourth largest in Europe.

In the Tour Bellanda is the **Musée de la Marine/Musée Naval,** Parc du Château (✆ **04-93-80-47-61**), sitting on "The Rock." The tower stands on a precariously perched belvedere overlooking the beach, the bay, the old town, and even the terraces of some of the nearby villas. Of the museum's old battle prints, one depicts the exploits of Caterina Segurana, the Joan of Arc of the Niçois. During the 1543 siege by Barbarossa, she ran along the ramparts, raising her skirt to show her shapely bottom to the Turks as a sign of contempt, though the soldiers were reported to have been more excited than insulted. The museum is open June through September Wednesday through Sunday from 10am to noon and 2 to 7pm. Admission is 2.30€ for adults and free for students and children under 16.

Continuing east from "The Rock," you reach the harbor, where the restaurants are even cheaper and the bouillabaisse is just as good. While sitting here lingering over an apéritif at a sidewalk cafe, you can watch the boats depart for Corsica (perhaps take one yourself). The port was excavated between 1750 and 1830. Since then, an outer harbor—protected by two jetties—has also been created.

The "authentic" Niçois live in **Vieille Ville** ★, the old town, beginning at the foot of "The Rock" and stretching out from place Masséna. Sheltered by sienna-tiled roofs, many of the Italianate facades suggest 17th-century Genoese palaces. The old town is a maze of narrow streets, many of them teeming with local life. Some, including the rue Masséna, the rue Droite, and the rue Pairolière, are reserved exclusively for pedestrians. On these narrow streets, you'll find some of the least expensive restaurants in Nice. Buy *la pissaladière* (an onion pizza) from one of the local vendors. Many of the old buildings are painted a faded Roman gold, and their banners are multicolored laundry flapping in the sea breezes.

While here, try to visit the **Marché aux Fleurs,** the flower market at cours Saleya. The vendors start setting up their stalls Tuesday through Sunday from 8am to 6pm in summer, and from 8am till between 2 and 4pm in winter. A flamboyant array of carnations, violets, jonquils, roses, and birds of paradise is hauled in by vans or trucks and then displayed in the most fragrant market in town.

Nice's commercial centerpiece is **place Masséna,** with pink buildings in the 17th-century Genoese style and the **Fontaine du Soleil** (Fountain of the Sun) by Janoit, from 1956. Stretching from the main square to the promenade is the **Jardin Albert-1er,** with an open-air terrace and a Triton Fountain. With palms and exotic flowers, it's the most relaxing oasis at the resort.

MUSEUMS

There's a higher density of museums in Nice than in many comparable French cities. If you decide to forgo the beach and devote your time to visiting some of the best-respected museums in the south of France, you can buy from the local tourist office a **Carte Passe-Musée** costing 15€ for 3 days or 25€ for 7 days. It allows you admission into seven of the city's largest museums. There are no reductions for students or children. This pass is sold at any of the municipal museums. For more information, call ✆ **04-97-03-82-20.**

Musée d'Art Moderne et d'Art Contemporain ★★ French and American avant-garde art from the 1960s until the 21st century is displayed here in a museum composed of a quartet of square towers with rooftop terraces. Each section is linked by a glass passageway. We know of no other museum that so dramatically reveals the growth of parallel art movements in two countries, evolving at the same time. In the '60s it was called American pop art, whereas on the Riviera it was known as Nouveau Réalisme, but the results are very similar. Pop artists such as all the big names, including Andy Warhol, Roy Lichtenstein, and Robert Rauschenberg are featured, of course. One entire section of the museum is devoted to the French artist Yves Klein (1928–92). His two major works, *Garden of Eden* and *Wall of Fire,* can be seen on the rooftop terraces. Some of the outstanding works displayed are by artists of the Nice School, including Sacha Sosno, Robert Malavaal, and Jean-Claude Fahri.

Promenade des Arts. ✆ **04-93-62-61-62.** 4€ adults, 2.50€ students, free for ages 17 and under. Tues–Mon 10am–6pm. Bus: 1, 2, 3, 5, 6, 16, or 25.

Musée des Beaux-Arts ★★ The collection is housed in the former residence of the Ukrainian Princess Kotchubey. There's an important gallery devoted to the masters of the Second Empire and Belle Epoque, with an extensive collection of the 19th-century French experts. The gallery of sculptures includes works by J. B. Carpeaux, Rude, and Rodin. Note the important collection by a dynasty of painters, the Dutch Vanloo family. One of its best-known members, Carle Vanloo, born in Nice in 1705, was Louis XV's premier *peintre.* A fine collection of 19th- and 20th-century art is displayed, including works by Ziem, Raffaelli, Boudin, Renoir, Monet, Guillaumin, and Sisley.

33 av. des Baumettes. ✆ **04-92-15-28-28.** Admission 3.80€ adults, 2.30€ students, free for children under 18. Tues–Sun 10am–6pm. Bus: 3, 9, 12, 22, 23, or 38.

Musée International d'Art Naïf Anatole-Jakovsky (Museum of Naïve Art) ★ This museum is housed in the beautifully restored Château Ste-Hélène in the Fabron district. The collection was once owned by the namesake of the museum, for years one of the world's leading art critics. His 600 drawings and canvases were turned over to the institution and made accessible to the public. Artists from more than two dozen countries are represented here—from primitive painting to contemporary 20th-century works.

Av. Val-Marie. ✆ **04-93-71-78-33.** Admission 3.80€ adults, 2.30€ students and seniors, free for children 18 and under. Wed–Mon 10am–6pm. Bus: 9, 10, or 12; the walk from the bus stop takes 10 min.

MORE SIGHTS

Cathédrale Orthodoxe Russe St-Nicolas à Nice Ordered built by none other than Tsar Nicholas II, this is the most beautiful religious edifice of the Orthodoxy outside Russia and is the perfect expression of Russian religious art abroad. It dates from the Belle Epoque, when some of the Romanovs and their entourage turned the Riviera into a stamping ground (everyone from grand dukes to ballerinas walked the promenade). The cathedral is richly ornamented and decorated with lots of icons. You'll easily spot the building from afar because of its collection of ornate onion-shape domes. Church services are held on Sunday morning.

Av. Nicolas-II (off bd. du Tzaréwitch). ✆ **04-93-96-88-02.** Admission 2.50€ adults, 2€ students, free for children under 12. May–Sept daily 9am–noon and 2:30–6pm; Oct–Apr daily 9:30am–noon and 2:30–5:30pm. It's closed to purely touristic visits on Sun mornings. From the central rail station, head west along av. Thiers to bd. Gambetta; then go north to av. Nicolas-II.

Palais Lascaris *Kids* The baroque Palais Lascaris in the city's historic core is intimately linked to the Lascaris-Vintimille family, whose recorded history predates 1261. Built in the 17th century, it contains elaborately detailed ornaments. An intensive restoration undertaken by the city of Nice in 1946 brought back its original beauty, and the palace is now classified a historic monument. The most elaborate floor is the *étage noble,* retaining many of its 18th-century panels and plaster embellishments. A pharmacy from around 1738, complete with many of the original Delftware accessories, is on the premises. Every Wednesday between 2 and 4pm, the museum focuses attention on children of any age: Various craftspeople are invited to show the details of how they accomplish their art forms through live demonstrations.

15 rue Droite. ✆ **04-93-62-72-40.** Free admission. Tues–Sun 10am–noon and 2–6pm. Bus: 1, 2, 3, 5, 6, 14, 16, or 17.

NEARBY SIGHTS IN CIMIEZ

In the once-aristocratic hilltop quarter of **Cimiez** ★, Queen Victoria wintered at the Hôtel Excelsior and brought half the English court with her. Founded by the Romans, who called it Cemenelum, Cimiez was the capital of the Maritime Alps province. Recent excavations have uncovered the ruins of a Roman town, and you can wander among the diggings. The arena was big enough to hold at least 5,000 spectators, who watched contests between gladiators and wild beasts shipped in from Africa. To reach this suburb, take bus no. 15 or 17 from place Masséna.

Monastère de Cimiez (Cimiez Convent) The convent embraces a church that owns three of the most important works from the primitive painting school of Nice by the Bréa brothers. See the carved and gilded wooden main altarpiece. In a restored part of the convent where some Franciscan friars still live, the Musée Franciscain is decorated with 17th-century frescoes. Some 350 documents and works of art from the 15th to 18th centuries are displayed, and a monk's cell has been re-created in all its severe simplicity. See also the 17th-century chapel. In the gardens, you can get a panoramic view of Nice and the Baie des Anges. Matisse and Dufy are buried in the cemetery.

Place du Monastère. ✆ **04-93-81-00-04.** Free admission. Museum daily 10am–noon and 3–6pm; church daily 8am–7pm.

Musée Matisse ★ This museum honors the great artist who spent the last years of his life in Nice; he died here in 1954. Seeing his nude sketches today, you'll wonder how early critics could have denounced them as "the female animal in all her shame and horror." The museum has several permanent collections, most painted in Nice and many donated by Matisse and his heirs. These include *Nude in an Armchair with a Green Plant* (1937), *Nymph in the Forest* (1935/1942), and a chronologically arranged series of paintings from 1890 to 1919. The most famous of these is *Portrait of Madame Matisse* (1905), usually displayed near a portrait of the artist's wife by Marquet, painted in 1900. There's also an ensemble of drawings and designs *(Flowers and Fruits)* he prepared as practice sketches for the Matisse Chapel at Vence. The most famous are *The Créole Dancer* (1951), *Blue Nude IV* (1952), and around 50 dance-related sketches he did between 1930 and 1931.

In the Villa des Arènes-de-Cimiez, 164 av. des Arènes-de-Cimiez. ✆ **04-93-53-40-53.** Admission 3.80€ adults, 2.30€ students, free for ages 18 and under. Wed–Mon 10am–6pm. Closed Jan 1, May 1, and Dec 25.

Musée National Message Biblique Marc-Chagall ★★ In the hills of Cimiez above Nice, this handsome museum, surrounded by shallow pools and a garden planted with thyme, lavender, and olive trees, is devoted to Marc Chagall's treatment of biblical themes. Born in Russia in 1887, Chagall became a French citizen in 1937. The artist and his wife donated the works—the most important collection of Chagall ever assembled—to France in 1966 and 1972. Displayed are 450 of his oils, gouaches, drawings, pastels, lithographs, sculptures, and ceramics; a mosaic; 3 stained-glass windows; and a tapestry. A splendid concert room here was decorated by Chagall with brilliantly hued stained-glass windows. Temporary exhibitions are organized each summer featuring great periods and artists of all times.

Av. du Dr.-Ménard. ✆ **04-93-53-87-20.** Admission 6.70€ adults, 5.20€ students, free for children under 18. Wed–Mon 10am–6pm.

OUTDOOR PURSUITS

THE BEACH Nice's seafront offers at least seven public beaches. None of them has sand; they're covered with gravel (often the size of golf balls). The rocks are smooth but can be mettlesome to people with poor balance or tender feet. Tucked in between the public beaches are the private beaches of hotels such as the Beau Rivage. Most of the public beaches are divided into two sections: a free area and an area where you can avail yourself of the chaise longues, mattresses, parasols, changing cabanas, and freshwater showers. For the privilege, you'll pay 10€ to 12€ for a half day and 12€ to 15€ for a full day. Nude sunbathing is prohibited, but toplessness is common. Take bus no. 9, 10, 12, or 23 from the center of town to get to the beach.

GOLF The oldest golf course on the Riviera is about 16km (10 miles) from Nice: **Golf Bastide du Roi** (also known as the Golf de Biot) is at avenue Michard Pellissier, Biot (✆ **04-93-65-08-48**). Open daily, this is a flat, not particularly challenging sea-fronting course. (Regrettably, it's necessary to cross over a highway midway through the course to complete the full 18 holes.) Tee times are 8am to 6pm; you can play until the sun sets. Reservations aren't necessary, though on weekends you should probably expect a delay. Greens fees are 40€ for 18 holes; club rental is 10€.

HORSEBACK RIDING **Club Hippique de Nice,** 368 Rte. de Grenoble (✆ **04-93-71-24-34**), rents 15 of its horses. About 5km (3 miles) from Nice, near the airport, it's hemmed in on virtually every side by busy roads and highways, and conducts all activities in a series of riding rinks. Riding sessions should be reserved in advance; they last about an hour and cost 14€.

SCUBA DIVING The best outfit is the **Centre International de Plongée de Nice,** 2 ruelle des Moulins (✆ **06-09-52-55-57** or 04-93-55-59-50), adjacent to the city's old port, between quai des Docks and boulevard Stalingrad. A *baptême* (initiatory dive for first-timers) costs 24€, and a one-tank dive for experienced divers, equipment included, is 30€; a license is required.

TENNIS The oldest tennis club in Nice is the **Nice Lawn Tennis Club,** Parc Impérial, 5 av. Suzanne-Lenglen (✆ **04-92-15-58-00**). It's open daily from 8:30am to 9:30pm (mid-Oct to mid-Apr) and charges 19€ per person for 2 hours of court time, or a reduced rate of 55€ per person for unlimited access to the courts for 1 week. The club contains a cooperative staff, loyal clientele, 13 clay courts, and 6 hard-surfaced courts. Reserve a court the night before.

SHOPPING

You might want to begin with a stroll through the streets and alleys of Nice's historic core. The densest concentrations of boutiques are along **rue Masséna, place Magenta, avenue Jean-Médecin, rue de Verdun,** and **rue Paradis,** as well as on the streets funneling into and around them. Shops of note include **Gigi,** 7 rue de la Liberté (© **04-93-87-81-78**), which sells sophisticated-looking clothing for women; and **Georges Rech Homme,** 10 rue de la Liberté (© **04-93-87-53-96**), an emporium for menswear.

Opened in 1949 by Joseph Fuchs, the grandfather of the present English-speaking owners, the **Confiserie Florian du Vieux-Nice,** 14 quai Papacino (© **04-93-55-43-50**), is near the Old Port. The specialty here is glazed fruits crystallized in sugar or artfully arranged into chocolates. Look for exotic jams (rose-petal preserves or mandarin marmalade) and the free recipe leaflet as well as candied violets, verbena leaves, and rosebuds. One of the oldest chocolatiers in Nice, **Confiserie Auer,** 7 rue St-François-de-Paule (© **04-93-85-77-98**), was established five generations ago, in 1820, near the opera house. Since then, few of the original decorative accessories have been changed. The shop specializes in chocolates, candies, and confit de fruit, all those Provençal goodies.

Façonnable, 7–9 rue Paradis (© **04-93-87-88-80**), is the original site that sparked the creation of several hundred branches around the world. This is one of the largest, with a wide range of men's suits, raincoats, overcoats, sportswear, and jeans. The look is youthful and conservatively stylish, for relatively slim (French) bodies. Whereas the branch at 7–9 rue Paradis specializes in menswear, there's an outlet for women's clothing and sportswear (Façonnable Femmes/Façonnable Sport) directly across the street at 10 rue Paradis (© **04-93-88-06-97**).

If you're thinking of indulging in a Provençale *pique-nique,* **Nicola Alziari,** 14 rue St-François-de-Paule (© **04-93-85-76-92**), will provide everything: from olives, anchovies, and pistous to aïolis and tapenades. It's one of Nice's oldest purveyors of olive oil, with a house brand that comes in two strengths: a light version that aficionados claim is vaguely perfumed with Provence, and a stronger version suited to the earthy flavors and robust ingredients of a Provençal winter. Also look for a range of objects crafted from olive wood.

If you're looking for arts and crafts, head to the **Atelier Contre-Jour,** 3 rue du Pont Vieux (© **04-93-80-20-50**), for handcrafts in painted wood, painted furniture, picture frames of painted wood, and silk lampshades. Visit **Plat Jérôme,** 34 rue Centrale (© **04-93-62-17-09**) for varnished pottery. Many artists' studios/galleries are located on side streets near the cathedral in the Old Town.

Other shopping recommendations are **La Couquetou,** 8 rue St-François-de-Paule (© **04-93-80-90-30**), selling *santons,* the traditional Provençal figurines. The best selection of Provençal fabrics is found at **Le Chandelier,** 7 rue de la Boucherie (© **04-93-85-85-19**), where the designs of two of the region's best-known producers of cloth, Les Olivades and Valdrôme, are modeled on the burnt yellows and cerulean tones of Provence.

Lovers of olives and olive oil flock to **Huilerie Alziara** ★★, 14 rue St-Francois-de Paule (© **04-93-85-76-92**), a hole-in-the-wall filled with Provençal goodies ranging from olive oil soap to sacks of dried lavender and *herbes de Provence.* The best perfume is sold at **Aux Parfums de Grasse,** 10 rue St-Gaétan

(© **04-93-85-60-77**). More than 75 scents from Provence, especially the area around Grasse, are sold here.

Nice is also known for its street markets. In addition to the flower market, **Marché aux Fleurs** (see "Exploring the City," above), there's the main Nice flea market, **Marché à la Brocante,** also at cours Saleya, which takes place every Monday from 8am to 5pm. There's another flea market on the port, **Les Puces de Nice,** place Robilante, open Tuesday through Saturday from 9am to 6pm.

The local antiques market, **Marché d'Art des Antiquaries** ★, is staged Tuesday through Saturday from 9am to 5:30pm, overflowing on the streets of Vieux Nice, especially rue Emmanuel-Philibert, rue Catherine-Segurane, and rue Antoine-Gauthier.

WHERE TO STAY

VERY EXPENSIVE

Hôtel Négresco ★★★ The Négresco is one of the Riviera's many superglamorous hotels, though it's not sited for tranquillity—the Négresco stands in the heart of noisy Nice. Jeanne Augier has taken over the place and has triumphed. This Victorian wedding-cake hotel is named after its founder, Henry Négresco, a Romanian who died franc-less in Paris in 1920. It was built on the seafront, in the French château style, with a mansard roof and domed tower; its interior decorators scoured Europe to gather antiques, tapestries, paintings, and art. Some of the guest rooms are outfitted in homage to the personalities who stayed at the hotel during its long and illustrious history: the Coco Chanel Room, for example. Others are fancifully modeled after literary or musical themes, like La Traviata. Each was renovated sometime during the mid- to late 1990s, and in 1998, most of the bathrooms were upgraded into well-engineered, state-of-the art affairs, usually with pink or white marble. Suites and public areas are even grander, as is the case with the Louis XIV salon, reminiscent of the Sun King himself, or the Napoléon III suite, where swagged walls, a leopard-skin carpet, and a half-crowned canopy in pink create an undeniable sense of majesty. The most expensive rooms with balconies face the Mediterranean. The staff wears 18th-century costumes. Reasonably priced meals are served in La Rotonde, but the featured restaurant—one of the Riviera's greatest—is Chantecler (p. 302).

37 promenade des Anglais, 06000 Nice CEDEX. © **04-93-16-64-00.** Fax 04-93-88-35-68. www.hotel-negresco-nice.com. 150 units. 213€–460€ double; 585€–1,410€ suite. AE, DC, MC, V. Parking 24€. **Amenities:** 2 restaurants; bar; fitness center; secretarial service; 24-hr. room service; massage; babysitting; laundry service; dry cleaning; private beach. *In room:* A/C, TV, minibar, hair dryer.

La Pérouse ★★ *Finds* Once a prison, La Pérouse is now a unique Riviera hotel. Set on a cliff, it overlooks the sea and is entered through a lower-level lobby, where an elevator takes you up to the gardens. There's no hotel in Nice with a better view over both the old city and the Baie des Anges. Many people stay here for the view alone. In fact, La Pérouse is built right into the gardens of an ancient château-fort. Inside, the hotel is like an old Provençal home, with low ceilings, white walls, and antiques. Most of the lovely rooms have loggias overlooking the bay. Medium-size guest rooms are fairly standardized but evoke the tropics in their use of rattan and bamboo along with floral fabrics. Some of the pieces are in a cheap veneer, but the mattresses are first-rate, and added features include spacious closets and often balconies.

11 quai Rauba-Capéu, 06300 Nice. © **04-93-62-34-63.** Fax 04-93-62-59-41. 59 units. 220€–395€ double; 660€ suite. AE, DC, MC, V. Parking 15€. Bus: 6, 9, or 10. **Amenities:** Restaurant; bar; pool; exercise room; sauna; Jacuzzi; limited room service; laundry service; dry cleaning. *In room:* A/C, TV, minibar, hair dryer, safe.

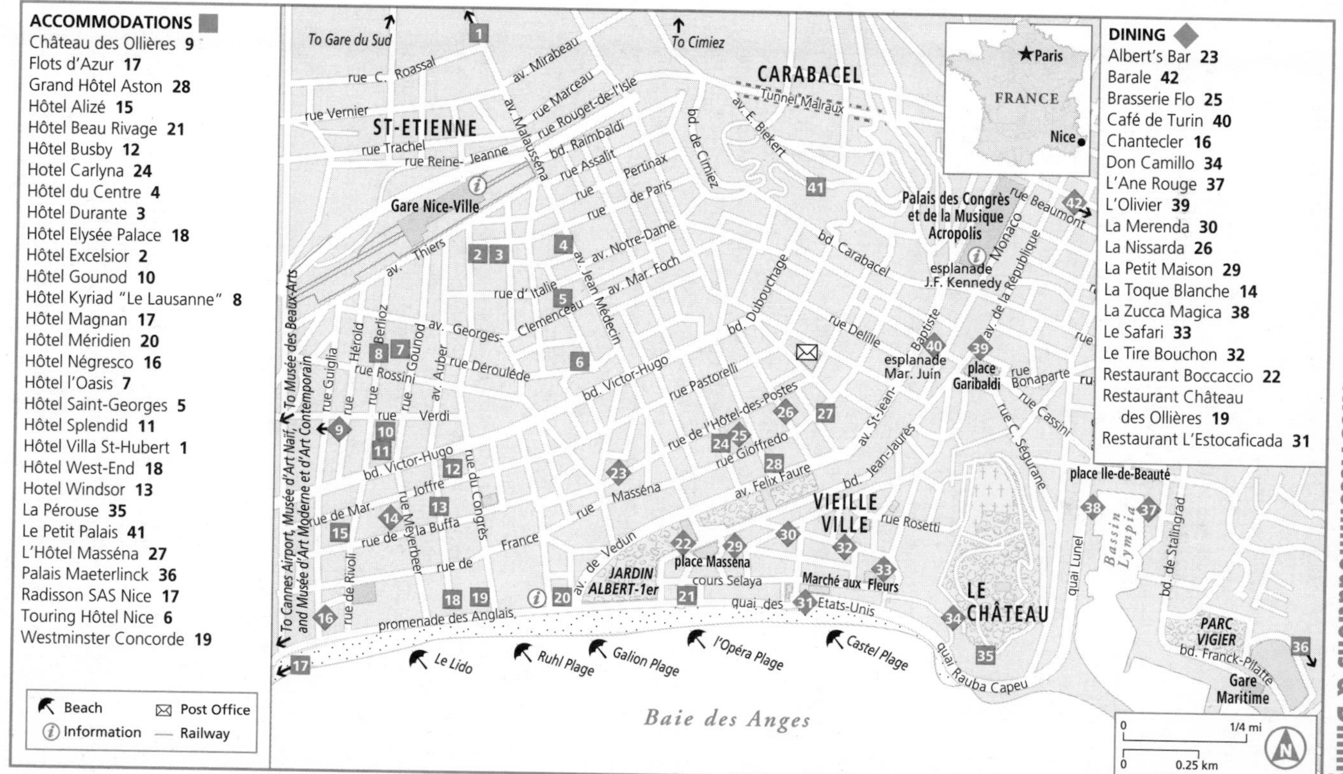
ACCOMMODATIONS
Château des Ollières 9
Flots d'Azur 17
Grand Hôtel Aston 28
Hôtel Alizé 15
Hôtel Beau Rivage 21
Hôtel Busby 12
Hotel Carlyna 24
Hôtel du Centre 4
Hôtel Durante 3
Hôtel Elysée Palace 18
Hôtel Excelsior 2
Hôtel Gounod 10
Hôtel Kyriad "Le Lausanne" 8
Hôtel Magnan 17
Hôtel Méridien 20
Hôtel Négresco 16
Hôtel l'Oasis 7
Hôtel Saint-Georges 5
Hôtel Splendid 11
Hôtel Villa St-Hubert 1
Hôtel West-End 18
Hotel Windsor 13
La Pérouse 35
Le Petit Palais 41
L'Hôtel Masséna 27
Palais Maeterlinck 36
Radisson SAS Nice 17
Touring Hôtel Nice 6
Westminster Concorde 19
Beach
Information
Post Office
Railway
DINING
Albert's Bar 23
Barale 42
Brasserie Flo 25
Café de Turin 40
Chantecler 16
Don Camillo 34
L'Ane Rouge 37
L'Olivier 39
La Merenda 30
La Nissarda 26
La Petit Maison 29
La Toque Blanche 14
La Zucca Magica 38
Le Safari 33
Le Tire Bouchon 32
Restaurant Boccaccio 22
Restaurant Château des Ollières 19
Restaurant L'Estocaficada 31
FRANCE
Paris
Nice
0 1/4 mi
0 0.25 km
N
To Gare du Sud
To Cimiez
ST-ETIENNE
CARABACEL
VIEILLE VILLE
LE CHÂTEAU
PARC VIGIER
Gare Maritime
Gare Nice-Ville
Palais des Congrès et de la Musique Acropolis
esplanade J.F. Kennedy
esplanade Mar. Juin
place Garibaldi
place Massena
place Ile-de-Beauté
Marché aux Fleurs
JARDIN ALBERT-1er
Bassin Lympia
Baie des Anges
Le Lido
Ruhl Plage
Galion Plage
l'Opéra Plage
Castel Plage
promenade des Anglais
quai des Etats-Unis
quai Rauba Capeu
quai Lunel
bd. de Stalingrad
bd. Franck-Pilatte
bd. de Cimiez
av. E. Biekert
Tunnel Malraux
bd. Carabacel
bd. Dubouchage
av. Jean Médecin
av. Malausséna
bd. Victor-Hugo
rue de France
rue de Rivoli
rue Meyerbeer
rue du Congrès
av. de Verdun
rue Masséna
To Cannes Airport, Musée d'Art Naïf, and Musée d'Art Moderne et d'Art Contemporain
To Musée des Beaux-Arts

Palais Maeterlinck ★★★ This deluxe hotel occupies a fin-de-siècle villa inhabited between the World Wars by the Belgian writer Maurice Maeterlinck, winner of the Nobel Prize for Literature. The location is high on a cliff 3km (2 miles) from the center of Nice. While many visitors find the setting sumptuous, the service and experience of the staff pale in comparison to the Négresco's. But on the plus side, since it's calmer and more tranquil than the hotels in more central locations, it enjoys the allure of verdant terraces and a large outdoor pool, set amid banana trees, olive trees, and soaring cypresses. A funicular will carry you down to the rock-strewn beach and marina. Each elegant guest room is outfitted in a different monochromatic color scheme and neoclassical Florentine styling, all with terraces opening onto views of Cap d'Antibes and Cap-Ferrat, and with deluxe bathrooms containing tubs and showers. Le Mélisande is a gastronomic hideaway with a neo-Renaissance decor.

Basse Corniche, 06300 Nice. ✆ **04-92-00-72-00.** Fax 04-92-04-18-10. www.palais-maeterlinck.com. 40 units. 245€–500€ double; 415€–2,600€ suite. AE, DC, MC, V. Drive 6.5km (4 miles) east of Nice along the Basse Corniche. **Amenities:** 2 restaurants; bar; 24-hr. room service; health club and spa; pool; laundry service; dry cleaning. *In room:* A/C, TV, minibar, hair dryer, safe.

EXPENSIVE

Château des Ollières ★ *Finds* The most appealing and unusual place to open in Nice in many years made its debut as a hotel in 1996. The setting is a 10-minute walk from the Négresco and the Promenade des Anglais, in a 1.2-hectare (3-acre) park loaded with exotic trees and shrubs. Its centerpiece is a beaux-arts villa built in the 1850s by a Russian prince. Inside you'll find a noteworthy collection of oil paintings and "neo-Napoléonienne" and Empire-inspired antiques, including a set custom-made for the dining room at the time of the villa's construction. Bedrooms are outfitted in the same high-ceilinged, ornate style as the public areas. Bathrooms are elegant, including bidets and deluxe toiletries.

39 av. des Baumettes, 06000 Nice. ✆ **04-92-15-77-99.** Fax 04-92-15-77-98. www.chateaudesollieres.com. 34 units. 140€–370€ double; 180€–500€ suite. AE, MC, V. Bus: 38. **Amenities:** Restaurant; bar; limited room service; babysitting; laundry service; dry cleaning. *In room:* A/C, TV, minibar, hair dryer, safe.

Grand Hôtel Aston ★ One of the most alluring in its price bracket, this is an elegantly detailed 19th-century hotel that has been radically renovated. Bedrooms are outfitted in monochromatic color schemes. Price scales vary according to view: the street, the splashing fountains of the place Masséna, or the panorama of the coastline from the top floor. On summer evenings, you can relax at the bar in the garden, which sometimes plays dance music. The hotel is associated with Holland's Golden Tulip chain.

12 av. Félix-Faure, 06000 Nice. ✆ **04-92-17-53-00.** Fax 04-93-80-40-02. www.hotel-aston.com. 155 units. 197€–278€ double. AE, DC, MC, V. Parking 16€. Bus: 12. **Amenities:** Restaurant; bar; rooftop pool; 24-hr. room service; babysitting; laundry service; dry cleaning. *In room:* A/C, TV, minibar, hair dryer, safe.

Hôtel Beau Rivage ★ This hotel across from the beach is famous for having housed both Matisse and Chekhov during its heyday around the turn of the 20th century. It was radically renovated in the early 1980s, and today the interior has a bland but tasteful modern decor and a staff that seems to make a point of appearing overworked regardless of how few guests there might be. The soundproof rooms are vaguely Art Deco and rather small, with contemporary bathrooms. For dining, Le Bistrot du Rivage is relatively formal and very appealing. Its specialties are meats and fish prepared on a large grill. Between May and September, tables are set on a terrace.

24 rue St-François-de-Paule, 06300 Nice. ✆ **04-92-47-82-82.** Fax 04-93-80-55-77. www.nicebeaurivage.com. 118 units. 180€–200€ double; 305€ suite. AE, DC, MC, V. Bus: 1, 2, 5, or 12. **Amenities:** Restaurant; bar; limited room service; babysitting; laundry service; dry cleaning. *In room:* A/C, TV, minibar, hair dryer, safe.

Hôtel Elysée Palace ★★ Views sweep out over the sea from most of the rooms of this hotel. Decor is conservative and contemporary, and the amenities in the rooms are typical. The seafront rooms, of course, are the more desirable. Rooms on the fifth, sixth, and seventh floors overlook the Mediterranean. Bathrooms are clad in marble with bidets, but you have to request robes and hair dryers from reception. The hotel has its own private beach a short walk from its premises.

59 promenade des Anglais, 06000 Nice. ✆ **04-93-97-90-90.** Fax 04-93-44-06-55. 143 units. 245€–375€ double; 320€–375€ suite. AE, DC, MC, V. Parking 15€. Bus: 9, 10, or 12. **Amenities:** 2 restaurants; bar; pool; 24-hr. room service; babysitting; laundry service; dry cleaning. *In room:* A/C, TV, minibar, safe.

Hôtel Méridien ★ One of Nice's largest hotels, this one rises five floors above the junction of the promenade des Anglais and a small formal park, the Jardin Albert-1er. Built in the 1960s by Air France in an angular design with lots of shiny metal and glass, it was later acquired by Britain's Forte group and hosts many organized tours from Britain and northern Europe. Two escalators carry you up through a soaring, impersonal atrium to the reception area. The recently renovated guest rooms are modern and standardized, many with sea views. The seafront rooms, though desirable for the view over the hotel's private beach, are actually the smallest in the hotel; space has been sacrificed to make way for terraces or balconies. Bathrooms are well equipped. There's a zesty restaurant, Le Colonia Café, that celebrates the late-19th-century overseas conquests of France and England—the emphasis is on spicy, sometimes curried international cuisine.

1 promenade des Anglais, 06046 Nice. ✆ **04-97-03-44-44.** Fax 04-97-03-44-45. www.lemeridien.com. 318 units. 280€–420 double; from 670€–1370€ suite. Discounts of around 15% during selected dates Oct–Apr. AE, DC, MC, V. Bus: 8, 9, 10, or 3. **Amenities:** 2 restaurants; bar; pool; health club; 24-hr. room service; massage; babysitting; laundry service; dry cleaning. *In room:* A/C, TV, minibar, hair dryer, safe.

Hôtel Splendid ★ This is one of Nice's best modern hotels, on the corner of a wide boulevard lined with shade trees, 4 blocks from its private beach. Built on the site of the Hôtel Splendid (ca. 1881), it was heralded as a new era in French hotels. Frequent renovations have kept the place fresh. The rooms usually have terraces or balconies, and several floors are reserved for nonsmokers. Accommodations come in various shapes and sizes, but all have private safes, electronic locks, and soundproofing. Beds are a bit narrow, but the mattresses are first-class. Bathrooms are tiled and well equipped.

50 bd. Victor-Hugo, 06048 Nice. ✆ **04-93-16-41-00.** www.splendid-nice.com. 127 units. 210€ double; from 315€–330€ suite. AE, DC, MC, V. Parking 19€ Bus: 9 or 10. **Amenities:** Restaurant; bar; pool; health club; sauna; steam room; limited room service; babysitting; laundry service; dry cleaning. *In room:* A/C, TV, minibar, hair dryer.

Hôtel West-End A Belle Epoque monument whose flowering terrace overlooks the sea, this Best Western is named after London's theater district. Though the ornate facade and the stately lobby were retained in honor of the original construction, the guest rooms were streamlined during several modernizations, yet are comfortable and well furnished. The best units are found on the fifth and sixth floors. Other rooms are more standardized and commercial, often filled with business travelers. All come with comfortable mattresses, most often on twin or double beds; many offer sea views. You can enjoy drinks on the terrace near a restaurant serving French and international cuisine. Because of the hotel's relatively large size, the staff can often appear a bit overworked, but overall it's a worthy choice.

31 promenade des Anglais, 06000 Nice. ✆ **800/528-1234** in the U.S., or 04-92-14-44-00. Fax 04-92-17-53-65. www.hotel-westend.com. 126 units. 206€–245€ double; 470€–600€ suite. AE, DC, MC, V. Parking 18€. Bus: 8. **Amenities:** Restaurant; bar; 24-hr. room service; laundry service; dry cleaning. *In room:* A/C, TV, minibar, hair dryer.

Radisson SAS Nice ★ Set alongside the major beachside thoroughfare of Nice, this streamlined and tastefully contemporary hotel has undergone more name and ownership changes than any other major hotel in town. In 1998, it was acquired by the Radisson chain, which inaugurated renovations to the public areas and bedrooms. Many business travelers come here. Standardized accommodations come with built-in furniture, double glazing, and comfortable beds. Overall, there's a sense of bustle, with an alert staff that's hip to the goings-on in Nice and along the Côte d'Azur—a feel of Paris-on-the-beach. Visitors enjoy soft piano music in the sophisticated lobby. Les Mosaiques offers a gastronomic French cuisine.

Promenade des Anglais 328, 06200 Nice. ✆ **04-93-37-17-17.** Fax 04-93-71-21-71. www.radissonsas.com. 329 units. 250€–330€ double; 352€-502€ suite. AE, DC, MC, V. Parking 18€. Bus: 8. **Amenities:** Restaurant; bar; pool; health club; sauna; 24-hr. room service; massage; babysitting; laundry service; dry cleaning. *In room:* A/C, TV, minibar, hair dryer.

Westminster Concorde ★ This 1860 hotel stands prominently along the famous promenade. Its elaborate facade was restored in 1986 to its former grandeur, and many renovations were made, including the installation of air-conditioning. The contemporary rooms have soundproof windows; a few open onto balconies. Accommodations range in size from medium to spacious, running the gamut from period styling to contemporary. Often they have high ceilings, antique mirrors, French windows, and brass beds. Bathrooms are tiled or marble, with generous shelf space.

27 promenade des Anglais, 06000 Nice. ✆ **04-92-14-86-86.** Fax 04-93-82-45-35. www.westminster-nice.com. 100 units. 145€–255€ double; from 335€ junior suite. AE, DC, MC, V. Parking 20€. Bus: 9, 10, or 11. **Amenities:** Restaurant; bar; limited room service; laundry service; dry cleaning. *In room:* A/C, TV, minibar, hair dryer.

MODERATE

Hôtel Busby This place should please you if you want a nostalgic hotel of faded early-20th-century grandeur. The Busby family, who were the original owners, refer to its ornate facade as "style Garibaldi" and have retained the balconies and the shutters on the tall windows. Renovated at regular intervals, yet looking a bit tired, the guest rooms are dignified; some contain mahogany twin beds and white-and-gold wardrobes. Mattresses are a bit worn, but there is still comfort here. Likewise, the tiled bathrooms are a bit cramped but have adequate shelf space.

36–38 rue du Maréchal-Joffre, 06000 Nice. ✆ **04-93-88-19-41.** Fax 04-93-87-73-53. www.busby-hotel.com. 80 units. 114€–124€ double. AE, DC, MC, V. Closed Nov 15–Dec 20. Bus: 9, 10, 12, or 22. **Amenities:** Bar; lounge; 24-hr. room service; babysitting; laundry service; dry cleaning. *In room:* A/C, TV, hair dryer.

Hôtel Excelsior Its ornate corbels and chiseled stone pediments rise grandly a few steps from the railway station. This 19th-century, much renovated hotel has a pleasantly modern decor with durable rooms that have seen a lot of wear but are still serviceable. Mattresses are middle grade, on twin or double beds. Furnishings, for the most part, are functional and conservative; units were last renovated in 1998. Bathrooms are small. The beach is a 20-minute walk through the residential and commercial heart of Nice.

190 av. Durante, 06000 Nice. ✆ **04-93-88-18-05.** Fax 04-93-88-38-69. 45 units. 86€–121€ double. MC, V. Bus: 1, 2, 5, 12, 18, 23, or 24. *In room:* TV.

Hôtel Gounod ★ This is our favorite hotel in this price range in Nice, built around 1910 in a neighborhood where the street names honor composers. The Gounod *(un petit Négresco)* boasts ornate balconies, a domed roof, and an elaborate canopy of wrought iron and glass. The attractive lobby and adjoining lounge are festive and stylish, with old prints, copper pots with flowers, and antiques. The high-ceilinged guest rooms are quiet and usually overlook the gardens of private homes on both sides. There are comfortable mattresses and neatly kept bathrooms.

3 rue Gounod, 06000 Nice. ✆ **04-93-16-42-00.** Fax 04-93-88-23-84. www.gounod-nice.com. 46 units. 135€ double; 200€ suite. AE, DC, MC, V. Parking 11€. Closed Nov 20–Dec 20. Bus: 8. **Amenities:** Room service; massage; babysitting; dry cleaning. *In room:* A/C, TV, minibar, hair dryer.

Hotel Kyriad "Le Lausanne" This is a solid, middle-bracket hotel with a central location in a commercial neighborhood in the heart of Nice. It was radically renovated in the mid-1990s and does not retain very much of its original architectural embellishments. Views from the windows look out over the street, and its efficient bedroom furnishings are standard for the well-respected Clarine chain. Rooms have comfortable mattresses, tiled bathrooms, and adequate shelf space. Overall, this is a reliable, although not particularly exciting, hotel choice. No meals are served other than breakfast.

36 rue Rossini, 06000 Nice. ✆ **04-93-88-85-94.** Fax 04-93-88-15-88. 35 units. 62€–150€ double. MC, V. Parking 11€. Bus: 8. **Amenities:** Lounge; babysitting. *In room:* A/C, TV, hair dryer.

Hotel Windsor ★ *Finds* One of the most arts-conscious hotels in Provence, it's in a *maison bourgeoise,* built by disciples of Gustav Eiffel in 1895, near the Hotel Négresco and the Promenade des Anglais. A one-of-a-kind series of frescoes adorns each of the bedrooms. The heir of the long-time owners, the Redolfi family, is responsible for commissioning these paintings, based on Gustav's mystical visions following his extensive travels in Africa and South America. About 40 of the rooms were frescoed by the since-deceased Antoine Bodoin, who was a talented decorator rather than an artist. The rest of the paintings were arranged for by Christian Bernard, a museum curator in Belgium who sent a series of well-known artists here on long-term residencies, including American Richard Barry, British Glenn Baxter, and French-born François Morellet. These artists have left an enduring creative legacy on the walls of the rooms you might inhabit. Bedrooms here have good mattresses and small bathrooms that are tidily maintained. Amid the Zen-inspired public areas are more mythical frescoes. The garden contains scores of tropical and exotic plants, and the recorded sounds of birds singing in the jungles of the Amazon. There's a deeply rooted sense of total immersion in the priorities and politics of southern France's world of contemporary gallery-goers. Whether it's wonderful or *de trop* will depend on you.

11 rue Dalpozzo, 06000 Nice. ✆ **04-93-88-59-35.** Fax 04-93-88-94-57. www.hotelwindsornice.com. 57 units. 90€–136€ double. MC, V. Parking 10€. Bus: 9, 10, or 22. **Amenities:** Restaurant; bar; pool; health club; sauna; steam room; limited room service; babysitting; laundry service; dry cleaning. *In room:* A/C, TV, minibar, safe.

L'Hôtel Masséna ★ Few other hotels evoke the Belle Epoque as gracefully or as authentically as this stone-and-wrought-iron monument to the architecture of the early 20th century. In 1999, the new owners of this place radically upgraded the bedrooms, transforming the hotel into a well-orchestrated bastion of calm and comfort. Many of the rooms are now upholstered in fabrics depicting the olive tree or olive branches. The most expensive rooms are airy, spacious, and outfitted in tones inspired by the colors of Provence, especially peach and soft green. Less expensive rooms are altogether comfortable, albeit somewhat smaller. Although all units have soundproofing, the ones that are the quietest are those overlooking the hotel's back side, or its interior courtyard.

58 rue Gioffredo, 06000 Nice. ✆ **04-93-85-49-25.** Fax 04-92-47-88-89. www.hotel-massena-nice.com. 106 units. 100€–190€ double. Extra bed 30€. AE, DC, MC, V. Parking 15€. Bus: 15. **Amenities:** Bar; 24-hr. room service; babysitting; laundry. *In room:* TV, minibar, hair dryer, safe.

INEXPENSIVE

Flots d'Azur This three-story villa-hotel is next to the sea, a short walk from the more elaborate and pricier promenade hotels. While the rooms vary in size and decor, most of them have good views and sea breezes. The largest rooms are on the ground, but they don't open onto views. If available, ask for one of the top floor rooms, three in all. They have large windows with a panoramic sweep and a small balcony. Double-glazed windows were recently added to cut down on the noise. There's a small sitting room and sun terrace in front, where a continental breakfast is served. Parking is free in the hotel's small driveway, but a free space disappears quickly.

101 promenade des Anglais, 06000 Nice. ✆ **04-93-86-51-25.** Fax 04-93-97-22-07. www.flotsdazur.com. 21 units. 45.74€–103.67€ double. MC, V. Bus: 8. **Amenities:** Laundry service; dry cleaning. *In room:* A/C, safe.

Hôtel Alizé *Value* Right on the promenade des Anglais and boulevard Gambetta, this modest hotel, near the chic and pricey Négresco, is a real bargain. Breakfast is the only meal served, but there are many restaurants nearby. Each of the small to medium-size bedrooms comes with a good mattress; the decor often features bright, inviting colors. There were extensive renovations in 1998 and 1999, and the accommodations are much improved, as are the bathrooms.

65 rue Buffa, 06000 Nice. ✆ and fax **04-93-88-99-46.** 11 units. 45€–65€ double. MC, V. Parking 20€ Bus: 8. **Amenities:** Lounge. *In room:* A/C, TV, hair dryer.

Hotel Carlyna Built "sometime before 1940," and positioned in the commercial heart of Nice, midway between two popular restaurants, this hotel offers a format of simple, well-scrubbed functionality at relatively reasonable rates. The Bouvet family has owned the place since 1998 and has made many improvements. Each of the bedrooms is different from its neighbors, each outfitted in soft tones of either red or blue and accessorized with cheerful fabrics. The spacious bathrooms are tiled and often equipped with hand-held Danish-style showers.

8 rue Sacha-Guitry, 06000 Nice. ✆ **04-93-80-77-21.** Fax 04-93-80-08-80. 24 units. 57€–64€ double. AE, DC, MC, V. Bus: 1, 4 ,7. **Amenities:** Room service (breakfast only); laundry service. *In room:* A/C, TV.

Hôtel du Centre Near the train station, this simple but clean hotel welcomes a clientele that is almost 100% gay. The uncomplicated rooms are very close to the attractions of downtown Nice. Mattresses are well worn but still comfortable. Bathrooms are small and standardized. The hotel is peaceful, with nearly no amenities. The staff is a useful source of inside information for whatever you might be seeking.

2 rue de Suisse, 06000 Nice. ✆ **04-93-88-83-85.** Fax 04-93-82-29-80. www.nice-hotel-centre.com. 28 units. 45€–55€ double. AE, MC, V. Parking 6€. Bus: 23. *In room:* TV.

Hôtel Durante A comfortable and much modified building dating from around the turn of the 20th century, this hotel is very popular with producers, actors, and directors during the nearby Cannes Film Festival. Many rooms face a quiet courtyard. The furnishings have known better days, but the beds are still quite comfortable. The owner dispenses both charm and information about local cinematic events. There's also a private garden.

16 av. Durante, 06000 Nice. ✆ **04-93-88-84-40.** Fax 04-93-87-77-76. 24 units. 71.50€–86.60€ double. MC, V. Closed Nov 8–Feb 8. **Amenities:** Bar; babysitting. *In room:* A/C, TV, kitchenette, fridge, hair dryer, safe.

Hôtel l'Oasis ★ *Finds* The strongest memories that remain with clients of this establishment involve its semitropical garden, where antique fountains were filled in long ago with verdant plants, and where you can imagine the ghosts of the influential people who stayed here during the first half of the 20th century, when the place was a boardinghouse with goodly numbers of Russians. They included Anton Chekhov, who composed part of *Three Sisters* here, and Lenin, who spent a holiday here in 1911. Although an air of old-fashioned manners remains intact, bedrooms have been modernized many times since, most recently in a contemporary, vaguely Provençal motif. Bathrooms are tiled and well scrubbed; accommodations are well maintained. The location, about a 12-minute walk from the railway station, is convenient to virtually everything in Nice.

23 rue Gounod, 06000 Nice. ✆ **04-93-88-12-29.** Fax. 04-93-16-14-40. www.hotel-oasis-nice.com.fr. 38 units. 80€–98€ double. AE, DC, MC, V. Parking 6€. **Amenities:** Bar service in garden; limited room service; babysitting. *In room:* A/C, TV, hair dryer.

Hôtel Magnan This well-run modern hotel is from 1945 but has been renovated frequently during its long and busy life. It's a 10-minute bus ride from the heart of town but only a minute or so from promenade des Anglais and the bay. Many of the simply furnished rooms have balconies facing the sea. The look is a bit functional, but for Nice this is a good price, considering how comfortable the beds are. Don't expect much from the bathrooms other than a shower stall. The owner, Daniel Thérouin, occupies the apartment on the top floor, guaranteeing close supervision. Breakfast can be served in your room. Aside from that, amenities are very scarce.

Square du Général-Ferrié, 06200 Nice. ✆ **04-93-86-76-00.** Fax 04-93-44-48-31. hotelmagnan@wanadoo.fr. 25 units. 54€–70€ double. AE, MC, V. Parking 6.50€. Bus: 12, 23, or 24. *In room:* TV, minibar.

Hotel Saint-Georges Originally built during the grand days of Niçois tourism, this hotel dates from around 1900 and still retains a few of its original architectural grace notes. A verdant patio and garden are the site of clusters of iron chairs and tables, where breakfast is served, and which many clients select as a spot for afternoon reading. Inside the motif is less nostalgic—angular and contemporary, it has mirrored, sometimes stark walls and efficient modern furnishings. Most bedrooms have high ceilings and casement doors that open onto tiny porches hemmed in with wrought-iron railings. The rooms are fairly small, but each comes with a firm mattress and compact tiled bathrooms.

7 av. Georges Clemenceau, 06000 Nice. ✆ **04-93-88-79-21.** 35 units. 65.06€ double. MC, V. Bus: 1. **Amenities:** Lounge. *In room:* A/C, TV, hair dryer.

Hôtel Villa St-Hubert ★ *Value* Set 5 blocks inland from the seacoast and the beach, this hotel consists of an interconnected pair of early-20th-century town houses. Today they're the property of the Chevalier family, who maintains clean, well-appointed bedrooms, each with a different color scheme. Bedrooms are medium in size, with firm mattresses and well-maintained bathrooms. One of the hotel's most appealing corners is the ivy-covered, geranium-filled courtyard, the site of morning breakfast and afternoon teas. No meals are served other than breakfast, but in light of the many nearby restaurants, no one seems to care.

26 rue Michel-Ange, 06100 Nice. ✆ **04-93-84-66-51.** Fax 04-93-84-70-96. 13 units. 57€–68€ double. AE, DC, MC, V. Parking 7€. **Amenities:** Lounge; limited room service. *In room:* A/C in some, TV, kitchenette in some, minibar, hair dryer, safe.

Le Petit Palais ★ *Finds* This whimsical hotel occupies a mansion built around 1890; in the 1970s, it was the home of the actor/writer Sacha Guitry, a name that's instantly recognized in millions of French households. It lies about a 10-minute drive from the city center in the Carabacel residential district. Much of its architectural grace remains, as evoked by the Florentine moldings and friezes and the Art Deco/Italianate furnishings. The preferred rooms, and the most expensive, have balconies for sea views during the day and sunset watching at dusk. Accommodations are generally small to medium, each with a firm mattress and a neatly organized bathroom.

10 av. Emile-Bieckert, 06000 Nice. ✆ **04-93-62-19-11.** Fax 04-93-62-53-60. www.guide-gerard.com. 25 units. 95€–124€ double. AE, DC, MC, V. Parking 10€. **Amenities:** Room service; laundry service. *In room:* TV.

Touring Hôtel Nice Set within a century-old building, this hotel evokes a severely dignified town house in Tuscany. It was built during the height of France's railway-building frenzy. In 2000, the venerable building was acquired by two couples, the Jean dit Gautiers and the Einaudis, who brought years of hotel experience in some of the grandest hotels of Monaco to their new enterprise. Today this is one of the best-managed hotels in Nice in its price range, with a staff that's a lot more sophisticated and worldly than what you might have expected in such an unpretentious setting. Bedrooms are simple, durable, soundproofed, and comfortable, and breakfast is served in what was originally conceived as a rather grand, full-scale restaurant, with many of the original architectural adornments still in place.

5 rue de Russie, 06000 Nice. ✆ **04-93-88-70-15.** Fax 04-93-87-91-06. www.touring-hotel-nice.com. 18 units. 57€ double. Children under 10 stay free in parent's room. MC, V. Bus: 1, 2, or 12. **Amenities:** Alcohol-free bar. *In room:* TV.

WHERE TO DINE

VERY EXPENSIVE

Chantecler ★★★ MODERN FRENCH This is Nice's most prestigious restaurant and one of the best in all of France, perhaps in the world. In 1989, a massive redecoration sheathed its walls with panels removed from a château in Puilly-Fussé, a Regency-style salon was installed for before- or after-dinner drinks, and a collection of 16th-century paintings, executed on leather backgrounds in the Belgian town of Malines, was imported. A much-respected chef, Alain Llorca, revised the menu to include the most sophisticated and creative dishes in Nice. Dishes change almost weekly but might include filet of turbot served with a purée of broad beans, sun-dried tomatoes, and fresh asparagus; roasted suckling lamb served with beignets of fresh vegetables and ricotta-stuffed ravioli; and a melt-in-your-mouth fantasy of marbled hot chocolate drenched in an almond-flavored cream sauce.

In the Hôtel Négresco, 37 promenade des Anglais. ✆ **04-93-16-64-00.** Reservations required. Main courses 43€–65€; fixed-price menus 45€–55€ lunch, 90€–130€ dinner. AE, MC, V. Daily 12:30–2pm and 8–10pm. Closed mid-Nov to mid-Dec. Bus: 8, 9, 10, or 11.

EXPENSIVE

Barale ★ FRENCH/ITALIAN This is the hearty domain of Catherine-Hélène Barale, the grand mère of Nissarda cuisine, a unique blend of Italian and French cookery. For decades, it has reigned as the most offbeat choice in Nice. Everything depends on the whim of Madame Barale, who might or might not take a liking to you. If she doesn't like you, she might show you to the door. Yet in spite of her eccentricities, even her refusal to define precise prices on her menu, this remains an enduring favorite, at least for some; others might feel that one dinner here is enough. It's certainly not a conventional restaurant. Filled with antiques, it is usually crowded with diners who seek old-time flavors that have largely disappeared from many menus. Madame Barale was born here, and she has learned the family secrets well. Her menu is listed on a blackboard hung with garlic pigtails, and it depends on her shopping that day. However, she almost always sells squares of the Nice pizza called pissaladière and, of course, the classic salade Niçoise. For a second course, try gnocchi or green lasagna. Main courses often include *pieche*—poached veal stuffed with fresh Swiss chard, cheese, ham, eggs, and rice—which is superb. We recommend the fresh fruit tart for dessert.

39 rue Beaumont. ✆ **04-93-89-17-94.** Reservations required. Meals 34€–47.50€. No credit cards. Tues–Sun 8:30pm–midnight. Closed Aug.

Restaurant Château des Ollières TRADITIONAL FRENCH Few other restaurants in Nice provide such an opportunity for insights into the Belle Epoque life of grandeur and ease. You might find yourself coming here as much for the beauty of the setting as for the food. A Russian prince built the château in the 1870s for the French woman whose marriage he ended. The restaurant is in a new wing with architecture matching the original, added in the late 1990s. At this writing, the only dining option is a fixed-price menu that consists of "amuses-gueules" of the chef: a starter, a fish (sea bass or turbot) or meat (rack of lamb is an excellent choice), and a dessert. Know in advance that although the food is delicate and very well prepared, the real allure of this restaurant is its beauty, its collection of antiques, and its many references to yesteryear.

In the Château des Ollières hotel, 39 av. des Baumettes. ✆ **04-92-15-77-99.** Reservations recommended. Fixed-price lunch 42€; fixed-price dinner 47€. AE, DC, MC, V. Daily noon–1:30pm and 8–9:30pm.

MODERATE

Don Camillo ★★ PROVENÇAL Named in the 1950s after its founder, Camille, a Niçois patriot (who preferred the Italian version of his name), this nine-table restaurant promises (and delivers) some of Nice's most authentic Provençal food. Off Cours Saleya, the dining room is adorned with pleasant, light colors and the modern paintings of the Niçois painter Laurent Gerbert. Franck Cerutti, assisted by his wife, Véronique, applies the gilded training he learned during stints at some of the grand restaurants of the Côte d'Azur. Staples of the menu are fava beans, Swiss chard, goat cheese, stockfish, cuttlefish, and a medley of herbs produced on the region's dry hillsides. Every dish bears the mark of a master chef who's almost guaranteed to become much better known among Provence's gastronomes. At the end of your meal, do your best to sample the selections from the cheese tray. Each derives from a small local farm, with many fermented from sheep's or goat's milk.

5 rue des Ponchettes. ✆ **04-93-85-67-95.** Reservations recommended. Main courses 12€; fixed-price menus 31.20€. AE, MC, V. Mon 8–9:30pm; Tues–Sat noon–1:30pm and 8–9:30pm. Bus: 8.

La Merenda ★★ *Finds* NIÇOIS Since there's no phone, you have to go by this place twice: once to make a reservation and once to dine. However, it's worth the extra effort—this is the best bistro in Nice. Forsaking his crown at the renowned Chantecler (see above), Dominique Le Stanc opened up this tiny bistro serving a sublime cuisine. "A no-star hole in the wall," the press screamed. But that's what Le Stanc wanted. Born in Alsace, his heart and soul belong to the Mediterranean, the land of black truffles, seasonal wild morels, fat sea bass, and plump asparagus. His food is rightly called a lullaby of gastronomic unity, with texture, crunch, richness, and balance. "I've known my days of glory in the gastronomic world. Now I'm doing family cooking, which is what I always like to eat." Le Stanc never knows what he's going to serve until he goes to the market. Look for his specials on a chalkboard. Perhaps you'll find stuffed cabbage, fried zucchini flowers, or oxtail flavored with fresh oranges. Lamb from the Sisteron is cooked until it practically falls from the bone. Raw artichokes are paired with a salad of *mâche.* Service is discreet and personable. We wish we could dine here every day.

4 rue Terrasse. No phone. Reservations required. Main courses 28€–38€. No credit cards. Mon–Fri noon–2pm and 7–9:30pm. Closed Aug 4–18, Dec 24–Jan 4, and Feb 16–22. Bus: 8.

L'Ane Rouge ★★ PROVENÇAL Facing the old port and occupying an antique building with its original ceiling beams and stone walls is one of the city's best-known seafood restaurants. In one of the pair of cozy modern dining rooms, you can enjoy traditional and time-tested specialties like bouillabaisse; bourrides; filet of John Dory with roulades of stuffed lettuce leaves; mussels stuffed with chopped parsley, breadcrumbs, and herbs; and salmon in wine sauce with spinach. Service is correct and commendable.

7 quai des Deux-Emmanuels. ✆ **04-93-89-49-63.** Reservations required. Main courses 21€–53€; fixed-price menus 24€ lunch, 32€–56€ dinner. AE, DC, MC, V. Fri–Tues noon–2pm and Thurs–Tues 8–10:30pm. Closed 2 weeks in Feb. Bus: 30.

La Toque Blanche *Value* FRENCH/SEAFOOD La Toque Blanche has only about a dozen tables amid its winter-garden decor. The owners, Gilles and Diana Houbron, pay particular attention to their shopping and buy only very fresh ingredients. The cuisine is skillfully prepared—try the sea bass roasted with citrus juice, sautéed sweetbreads with crawfish, or salmon prepared with fresh shrimp. The fixed-price menus are a particularly good value.

40 rue de la Buffa. ✆ **04-93-88-38-18.** Reservations not required. Main courses 13.50€–23.60€; fixed-price menus 24€-30€. MC, V. Tues–Sat 12:30–2pm and 7–9:30pm; Sun 12:30–2pm. Closed Jan 10–20. Bus: 8.

Restaurant Boccaccio MEDITERRANEAN Adjacent to place Masséna, in a pedestrian zone that enhances the desirability of its streetfront terrace, this restaurant boasts worthy cuisine and a devoted local following. Bouillabaisse is reasonably priced here, and the range of fresh fish (grilled with lemon-butter or baked in a salt crust) is broad and well prepared. The paella might remind you of Spain, and desserts like cappuccino tiramisú and crêpes suzettes round out meals nicely. There's a large dining room upstairs, inspired by the interior of a yacht, if the outdoor terrace doesn't appeal to you.

7 rue Masséna. ✆ **04-93-87-71-76.** Reservations recommended. Main courses 13.50€–32.60€; fixed-price menu 33€; bouillabaisse 54€ per person. AE, DC, MC, V. Daily noon–2:30pm and 7–11pm. Bus: 4, 5, or 22.

INEXPENSIVE

Albert's Bar FRENCH/PROVENÇAL/ITALIAN Set on a pedestrian-only street in the heart of Nice, this restaurant (ca. 1960) took on a new lease after its acquisition in 1995 by hardworking entrepreneur Jacqueline Harroch. Inside you'll find a pair of air-conditioned dining rooms lined with important-looking paintings and a flowering terrace. There are no freezers anywhere within the kitchens here. Instead, everything is bought and served fresh daily, as part of a regime where ultrafresh produce is one of the cardinal tenants. A superb starter is the salad of artichoke hearts, served with a dollop of grated Parmesan, splashes of olive oil, fava beans, and chopped chives. Grilled fish, especially sea bass, John Dory, octopus, and squid, is served piping hot from a grill, and desserts such as figs in a caramel sauce with vanilla ice cream will have you singing the praises of this so-called "bar," which is actually a supremely well-organized and successful restaurant.

1 rue Maurice Jaubert. ✆ **04-93-87-30-20.** Reservations recommended. Main courses 16€–32.50€. AE, DC, MC, V. Daily noon–3pm and 7pm to midnight.

Brasserie Flo FRENCH/ALSATIAN In 1991, a restaurant chain based in France (the Jean-Paul Bucher group), noted for its skill at restoring historic brasseries, bought the premises of a faded turn-of-the-20th-century restaurant near place Masséna and injected it with new life. Its high ceilings are covered with their original frescoes; the place is brisk, stylish, reasonably priced, and fun. Menu items include an array of grilled fish, *choucroute* (sauerkraut) Alsatian style, steak with brandied pepper sauce, and fresh oysters and shellfish. (Flo isn't associated with Le Florian, above, though they are frequently confused.)

2–4 rue Sacha-Guitry. ✆ **04-93-13-38-38.** Reservations recommended. Main courses 15€–30€; fixed-price menus 29€; children's menu 15€. AE, DC, MC, V. Daily noon–2:30pm and 7pm–midnight. Bus: 1, 2, or 5.

Café de Turin ★★ CONTINENTAL/SEAFOOD The origins of this place began in 1900, when it served glasses and carafes of wine to local office workers and laborers. In the 1950s, it added a kitchen to its premises, and ever since, it's churned out the kinds of hearty, bistro-style platters that go well with wines and beer. Much of the energy of the place is expressed outside, under the arcades of the central plaza (place Garibaldi) where it's located, where local hipsters strut their stuff as part of the passing parade, people jump to their feet to table-hop, and harassed but well-intentioned waiters do their best to keep the food and beverages flowing. The place is celebrated for its *coquillage* (raw shellfish), attracting the likes of Princess Caroline, who drives over from Monaco. Other items include whatever species of grilled fish is available that day: patés, terrines, salads, pastas, and a satisfying selection of ice creams and pastries.

5 place Garibaldi. ✆ **04-93-62-29-52.** Reservations recommended weekends at night; otherwise, not necessary. Main courses 15€–23€. MC, V. Bus: 9 or 10.

La Nissarda ★ NIÇOIS Set in the heart of town, about a 10-minute walk from place Masséna, this restaurant is maintained by a Normandy-born family (the Adam Pruniers) that works hard to maintain the aura and (some of) the culinary traditions of Nice. In an intimate (40-seat) setting lined with old engravings and photographs of the city, the place serves local versions of ravioli, spaghetti, carbonara, lasagna, and fresh-grilled salmon with herbs. A handful of Norman-based specialties also manages to creep into the menu, much to the appreciation of diners lonely for northern France, including escalopes of veal with cream sauce and apples. Ceiling fans spin overhead as you dine.

17 rue Gubernatis. ✆ **04-93-85-26-29.** Reservations recommended. Fixed-price menu 16€–21€. MC, V. Mon–Sat noon–2pm and 7–10pm. Closed Aug.

La Petite Maison ★★ Finds FRENCH/PROVENÇAL This bustling and noisy tavern is set in the heart of the old town, within what was originally conceived in the 19th century as a grocery store, beneath vaulted ceilings. Locals guard the address, hoping it won't be mobbed by tourists. Those regulars include Elton John and his longtime companion, who live in a villa a few miles away. It's usually packed with diners wanting to taste this array of Niçois cuisine, the authenticity of which is virtually unequalled in the city. Try the world's finest zucchini blossom fritters and the earthy Niçois blood sausage called *trulle,* and finish with a dessert that will send you rushing to the phone to call *Gourmet* magazine—homemade ice cream flavored with pine nuts and candied orange blossoms.

11 rue St-Francois de Paule. ✆ **04-93-85-71-53.** Reservations recommended. Main courses 10.50€–21€. AE, V. Mon–Sat noon–2:30pm and 7:30pm–midnight.

La Zucca Magica (The Magic Pumpkin) ★ Finds VEGETARIAN ITALIAN Bustling, energetic, and charming, this is one of the most successful vegetarian restaurants along the Riviera, serving a roster of all-vegetarian pastas, salads, and casseroles that changes every day. Owner Marco Folicardi was once hailed as the finest vegetarian chef in Rome before heading for Nice, where he opened this tavern in a spot on the Old Port close to the post office and the port's only church. There are only 18 tables in this joint, a cozy tavern decorated with different shapes and sizes of pumpkins. Menu items change every day, according to whatever is in season at the time. Try his lasagna with ricotta, fresh asparagus, and a flavor of lemon zest; or his open ravioli of tomatoes, leeks, and goat cheese; and most definitely his cheese and eggplant "meatballs." Dessert might include fresh cherry flan with homemade vanilla ice cream and wild strawberries. Don't come here expecting a wine list. Folicardi serves only one house wine, and the staff's opinion will have a strong influence on what you end up eating. But few go away disappointed. In fact, your lunch might be your most fondly remembered in Nice.

4 bis quai Papacino. ✆ **04-93-56-25-27.** Reservations recommended. Menus 16€ at lunch, 25€ at dinner. No credit cards. Tues–Sat 12:30–2:30pm and 7:30–10:30pm.

Le Safari ★★ PROVENÇAL/NIÇOIS The decor couldn't be simpler: a black ceiling, white walls, and an old-fashioned terra-cotta floor. The youthful staff is relaxed, sometimes in jeans, and always alert to the waves of fashion. Look for mobs here, many of whom prefer the outdoor terrace overlooking the Marché aux Fleurs and all of whom appreciate the earthy, reasonably priced meals that appear in generous portions. Menu items include a pungent *bagna cauda,* where vegetables are immersed in a sizzling brew of hot oil and anchovy paste; grilled peppers bathed in olive oil; *daube* (stew) of beef; fresh pasta with basil; an omelet with *blettes* (tough but flavorful greens); and the unfortunately named *merda de can* (dogshit), which, as a gnocchi stuffed with spinach, is a lot more appetizing than it sounds.

1 cours Saleya. ✆ **04-93-80-18-44.** Reservations recommended. Main courses 16€–26€; fixed-price menu 26€. AE, MC, V. Daily noon–3pm and 7:30–10:30pm. Closed Mon Nov–Mar. Bus: 1.

Le Tire Bouchon ("The Corkscrew") SOUTHWESTERN FRENCH Set in the heart of the old city, this is a cozy restaurant with a Bordeaux-tinged color scheme, two dining rooms, an old-fashioned decor, and an allegiance to the rich and hearty cuisine of France's southwest. Menu items reflect the kind of conservative cuisine that hasn't changed very much since the days when its clients might have been children. The best examples include onion soup with a crusty top, cassoulet (the earth pork-and-bean stew of Toulouse), andouillettes (chitterling sausages), confit of duckling, scallops in white-wine sauce, and various forms of fish. The place attracts a bevy of local residents, many of whom have been coming regularly since the place was established more than a decade ago.

19 rue de la Préfecture. ✆ **04-93-92-63-64.** Reservations recommended. Main courses 15€–23€. DC, MC, V. Daily 7-8:30pm. Bus No. 9 or 10.

L'Olivier PROVENÇAL/SICILIAN Established in 1989, this charming restaurant lies beneath the arcades of place Garibaldi, in the heart of Old Nice, just in back of the Museum of Modern Art. Named in honor of the premises' former occupant (an old-style shop selling olives, olive oil, and anchovies), the restaurant serves an original and sometimes unique cuisine based on modern versions of local culinary traditions. Flavorful and well-prepared items include smoked slices of foie gras; deboned sea bass stuffed with shellfish and herbs and served with a crabmeat sauce; lasagna made with a *daube joues de boeuf;* and a Sicilian-inspired medley of eggplant, olives, olive oil, and herbs combined into a southern Italian ratatouille. Dessert might be a gratin of frozen and caramelized lemons, or black-chocolate truffles.

3 place Garibaldi. ✆ **04-93-26-89-09.** Reservations recommended. Main courses 10€–16€. AE, DC, MC, V. Daily noon–2:30pm; Thurs–Tues 7:45–10pm. Closed 1 week in Aug.

Restaurant L'Estocaficada *Value* NIÇOIS *Estocaficada* is the Provençal word for stockfish, the ugliest fish in Europe. You can see one for yourself—there might be a dried-out, balloon-shape version on display in the cozy dining room. Brigitte Autier is the owner/chef, and her busy kitchens are visible from everywhere in the dining room. Descended from a matriarchal line (since 1958) of mother-daughter teams who have managed this place, she's devoted to the preservation of recipes prepared by her Niçois grandmother. Examples are gnocchis, beignets, several types of *farcies* (tomatoes, peppers, or onions stuffed with herbed fillings), grilled sardines, or bouillabaisse served as a main course or in a miniversion. As a concession to popular demand, the place also serves pizzas and pastas.

2 rue de l'Hôtel-de-Ville. ✆ **04-93-80-21-64.** Reservations recommended. Main courses 12€–18€; fixed-price menu 17€, 21€, and 25€. AE, MC, V. Tues–Sat noon–2pm and 7–9:30pm. Bus: 1, 2, or 5.

NICE AFTER DARK

Nice has some of the most active nightlife along the Riviera, with evenings usually beginning at a cafe. At kiosks around town, you can pick up a copy of *La Semaine des Spectacles,* which outlines the week's diversions.

The major cultural center on the Riviera is the **Opéra de Nice,** 4 rue St-François-de-Paule (✆ **04-92-17-40-40**), built in 1885 by Charles Garnier, fabled architect of the Paris Opéra. A full repertoire is presented, with emphasis on serious, often large-scale operas. In one season you might see *Tosca, Les Contes de Hoffmann,* Verdi's *Macbeth,* Beethoven's *Fidelio,* and *Carmen,* as well as a *saison symphonique,* dominated by the Orchestre Philharmonique de Nice. The opera hall is also the major venue for concerts and recitals. Tickets are available (to concerts, recitals, and full-blown operas) up to about a day or two before any performance. You can show up at the box office (Tues–Fri 10am–5:30pm) or buy tickets in advance with a major credit card by phoning ✆ **04-92-17-40-40.** Tickets run 10€ for nosebleed (and we mean it) seats to 60€ for front-and-center seats on opening night.

If you speak French, **Théâtre de Nice/Centre Dramatique National Nice-Côte d'Azur,** promenade des Arts (✆ **04-93-80-52-60**), offers a dramatic and busy season running from October to April, with tickets costing 8€ to 30€. Box office hours are Tuesday through Saturday from 1 to 7pm. A series of concerts and recitals are held at the mammoth **Acropolis,** 1 esplanade Kennedy (© **04-93-92-83-00**), the convention center and concert hall. Tickets range from 14€ to 50€. Most concerts are presented from November to April. Box office hours are Monday through Saturday from 10am to 5pm.

Near the Hôtel Ambassador, **L'Ambassade,** 18 rue des Congrès (© **04-93-88-88-87**), was designed in a mock-Gothic style that includes the wrought-iron accents you'd expect to find in a château; it has two bars and a dance floor. At least 90% of its clients are straight and come in all physical types and age ranges. The cover is 15€ to 16€ and includes the first drink.

One of the most charming discos in Nice is **Niel's Club,** 10 rue Cité du Parc (© **04-93-80-49-84**), in a location on an all-pedestrian zone just inland from the quai des Etats-Unis. The setting is a 19th-century cellar whose stone and brick vaulting used to shelter horses, goats, and sheep. Since 2002, its walls have been painted a shade of mauve, and it's been filled with hipster music much appreciated by the crowds of extroverted Niçoise who pile in here for drinking and dancing. Expect to pay a cover charge of up to 11€, which includes the first drink, especially on its busiest nights, Friday and Saturday. No one shows up before 10pm, and the place rocks on till dawn.

For a hot live music venue, **Chez Wayne,** 15 rue de la Prefecture, off place Rossetti in Vieux Nice (© **04-93-13-46-99**), presents live rock and often jazz bands, with the music beginning at 9pm nightly. An on-site bar and restaurant is open nightly from 3 to 11pm.

Cabaret du Casino Ruhl, in the Casino Ruhl, 1 promenade des Anglais (© **04-97-03-12-77**), is Nice's answer to the cabaret glitter that appears in more ostentatious forms in Monte Carlo and Las Vegas. It includes just enough flesh to titillate; lots of spangles, feathers, and sequins; a medley of cross-cultural jokes and nostalgia for the old days of French *chanson;* and an acrobat or juggler. The cover of 16€ includes the first drink; dinner and the show, complete with a bottle of wine per person, costs 46€. Shows are presented every Friday and Saturday at 10:30pm. No jeans or sneakers.

The casino contains an area exclusively for slot machines, open daily from noon to 4am, entrance to which is free. A more formal gaming room (jacket required, but not a tie), with blackjack, baccarat, chemin de fer, and 21 tables, is open nightly at a fee of 11€ per person every Monday through Friday from 8pm to 4am and every Saturday and Sunday from 5pm to 5am.

Le Relais, in the Hotel Négresco, 37 promenade des Anglais (© **04-93-16-64-00**), is the most beautiful bar in Nice, filled with white columns, an oxblood-red ceiling, Oriental carpets, English paneling, Italianate chairs, and tapestries. It was once a haunt of the actress Lillie Langtry. With its piano music and white-jacketed waiters, the bar still attracts a chic crowd.

Nice has many bars in the Old Town where Americans will feel right at home, including the **Scarlett O'Hara Irish Pub,** on the corner of rue Rosetti and rue Droite (© **04-93-80-43-22**); **Wayne's,** 15 rue de la Préfecture (© **04-93-13-46-99**); and **William's Pub,** 4 rue Centrale (© **04-93-62-99-63**), which has live music. If you'd rather hang out with French people, try **La Civette,** a popular spot for aperitifs at 29 rue de la Préfecture (© **04-93-62-35-51**). **Butterfly,** 2 quai des Etats-Unis (© **04-93-92-27-31**), is a hip nightclub with dancing right across from the beach; the cover is 8€.

You can also make a night of it (or several nights of it) at the following establishments: **Latinos,** 6 rue Chauvain (✆ **04-93-85-01-10**), for "tapas"; **Café Chris,** 3 rue Smolett (✆ **04-93-26-75-85**), a bustling cafe; and **Le C.D. Restaurant and Salad Bar,** 22 rue Benoit Bunico (✆ **04-93-92-47-65**), where you can people-watch while you munch.

7 Villefranche-sur-Mer ★

935km (581 miles) S of Paris; 6km (4 miles) E of Nice

According to legend, Hercules opened his arms and Villefranche was born. It sits on a big blue bay that looks like a gigantic bowl, large enough to accommodate U.S. Sixth Fleet cruisers and destroyers. Quietly slumbering otherwise, Villefranche takes on the appearance of an exciting Mediterranean port when the fleet is in.

Once popular with such writers as Katherine Mansfield and Aldous Huxley, it's still a haven for artists, many of whom take over the little houses—reached by narrow alleyways—that climb the hillside. Two of the more recent arrivals who have bought homes in the area are Tina Turner and Bono.

ESSENTIALS

GETTING THERE **Trains** arrive from most towns on the Côte d'Azur, especially Nice (every 30 min.), but most visitors **drive** via the Corniche Inférieure (Lower Corniche). For more rail information and schedules, call ✆ **08-36-35-35-35.** There's no formalized **bus** station in Villefranche.

VISITOR INFORMATION The **Office de Tourisme** is on Jardin François-Binon (✆ **04-93-01-73-68;** www.villefranche-sur-mer.com).

EXPLORING THE TOWN

The vaulted **rue Obscure** is one of the strangest streets in France (to get to it, take rue de l'Eglise). In spirit it belongs more to a North African casbah. People live in tiny houses, but occasionally there's an open space, allowing for a courtyard.

One artist who came to Villefranche left a memorial: Jean Cocteau, the painter, writer, filmmaker, and well-respected dilettante, spent a year (1956–57) painting frescoes on the 14th-century walls of the Romanesque **Chapelle St-Pierre,** quai de la Douane/rue des Marinières (✆ **04-93-76-90-70**). He presented it to "the fishermen of Villefranche in homage to the Prince of Apostles, the patron of fishermen." One panel pays homage to the gypsies of the Stes-Maries-de-la-Mer. In the apse is a depiction of the miracle of St. Peter walking on the water, not knowing that an angel supports him. Villefranche's women in their regional costumes are honored on the left side of the narthex Cocteau. The chapel, which charges 2€ admission for everyone (adults, children, and students), is open Tuesday through Sunday June through August from 10am to noon and 4 to 8pm; September through November 15 from 9:30am to noon and 2 to 6pm; December 15 through February from 9:30am to noon and 2 to 5:30pm; and March through May from 9:30am to noon and 3 to 3pm. (It's closed Nov 17–Dec 15.)

WHERE TO STAY

Hôtel Versailles Several blocks from the harbor and outside the main part of town, this three-story hotel gives you a perspective of the entire coast. The hotel offers comfortably furnished rooms and suites (suitable for up to three) with big windows and panoramas. Guests can order breakfast or lunch under an umbrella on the roof terrace. Rooms are clean and bright, with comfortable mattresses and tiled bathrooms.

Av. Princesse-Grace-de-Monaco, 06230 Villefranche-sur-Mer. ✆ **04-93-76-52-52.** Fax 04-93-01-97-48. www.hotelversailles.com. 46 units. 110€–130€ double; 190€ suite. AE, DC, MC, V. Free parking. Closed Nov-Jan. **Amenities:** Restaurant; lounge; pool; limited room service. *In room:* A/C, TV.

Hôtel Welcome ★ The Welcome was a favorite of Jean Cocteau, who'd probably still check in if he were still around because it's the best hotel at the port. In this six-floor villa, with shutters and balconies, everything has recently been modernized and extensively renovated. Bedrooms are mostly medium in size, each comfortably appointed with a firm mattress resting on a twin or double. Bathrooms are tiled and small. Try for a fifth-floor room overlooking the water. The sidewalk cafe is the focal point of town life.

1 quai Courbet, 06231 Villefranche-sur-Mer. ✆ **04-93-76-27-62.** Fax 04-93-76-27-66. www.welcomehotel.com. 37 units. 128€–179€ double. AE, DC, MC, V. Closed Nov 15–Dec 20. **Amenities:** Restaurant; bar; babysitting; self-service laundry. *In room:* A/C, minibar, safe.

WHERE TO DINE

Chez Michel's FRENCH/PROVENÇAL This bustling and animated brasserie is owned and managed by the husband-and-wife team Michel and Michelle. The setting is a cozily unpretentious dining room lined with Provençal landscapes. Well-prepared menu items made with fresh ingredients include dishes such as a filet of beef Rossini (layered with foie gras), grilled sea bass with a tapenade of olives, rack of lamb with Provençal herbs, and a roster of fresh char-grilled fish of the day that is usually served either with a basil-flavored vinaigrette or with lemon-flavored butter sauce.

Place Amélie Pollonais. ✆ **04-93-76-73-24.** Reservations recommended. Main courses 12.50€–17€. AE, MC, V. Wed–Mon 12:30–3:30pm and 5:30–11:30pm.

La Mère Germaine ★ FRENCH/SEAFOOD Plan to relax here over lunch while watching fishers repair their nets—this is the very best of a string of restaurants on the port. The cuisine is prepared by the grandson (the likable Thierry Blouin) of the matriarch, Mère Germaine, who opened the place in the 1930s. It's popular with U.S. Navy officers, who've discovered the bouillabaisse made with tasty morsels of freshly caught fish and mixed in a cauldron with savory spices. We recommend the grilled loup (sea bass) with fennel, salade Niçoise, sole Tante Marie (stuffed with mushroom purée), and beef filet with three peppers. The perfectly roasted *carré d'agneau* (lamb) is for two.

Quai Courbet. ✆ **04-93-01-71-39.** Reservations recommended. Main courses 23€–35€; fixed-price menu 38€; bouillabaisse 60€. AE, MC, V. Daily noon–2:30pm and 7–10pm. Closed Nov 12–Dec 24.

La Trinquette ★ PROVENÇAL/SEAFOOD Charming and traditional, in a pre-Napoleonic building a few steps from the harbor front, this restaurant prides itself on the excellence of its fish and bouillabaisse. The fish is brought out from a back room if anyone is skeptical enough to ask to see the actual fish before it's cooked. You can choose from among 15 to 20 kinds, prepared any way you specify, with a wide variety of well-flavored sauces. Bouillabaisse is an enduring favorite—much cheaper here than at many other places. There's even a roasted version of *chapon de mer,* served with a Provençal sauce. How do the hardworking owners, Paul and Monique Osiel, recommend their fresh John Dory? Roasted as simply as possible, served only with a hint of beurre blanc. Alternatives for this or any of the other offerings include aïoli, the region's garlic-enriched mayonnaise.

Port de la Darse. ✆ **04-93-01-71-41.** Reservations recommended. Main courses 10€–23.50€; bouillabaisse 40€; fixed-price menus 20€–30€. No credit cards. Thurs–Tues noon–2:15pm and 7–10pm. Closed Dec–Jan.

8 St-Jean-Cap-Ferrat ★

938km (583 miles) S of Paris; 10km (6 miles) E of Nice

This place has been called "Paradise Found"—of all the oases along the Côte d'Azur, none has quite the snob appeal of Cap-Ferrat. It's a 15km (9-mile) promontory sprinkled with luxurious villas, outlined by sheltered bays, beaches, and coves. The vegetation is lush. In the port of St-Jean, the harbor accommodates yachts and fishing boats.

ESSENTIALS

GETTING THERE Most visitors drive or take a **bus** or **taxi** from the rail station at nearby Beaulieu. Buses from the station at Beaulieu depart at hourly intervals for Cap-Ferrat. There's also bus service from Nice. For bus information and schedules, call ✆ **04-93-85-64-44.** By **car,** St-Jean-Cap-Ferrat is best reached from Nice by driving along N7 east.

VISITOR INFORMATION The **Office de Tourisme** is on avenue Denis-Séméria (✆ **04-93-76-08-90;** www.riviera.fr/tourisme.htm).

SEEING THE SIGHTS

One of the ways to enjoy the scenery here is to wander on some of the public paths. The most scenic goes from **Plage de Paloma** to **Pointe St-Hospice,** where a panoramic view of the Riviera landscape unfolds.

You can also wander around **St-Jean,** a colorful fishing village with bars, bistros, and inns. The beaches, although popular, are pebbly, not sandy. The best and most luxurious belongs to the Grand Hôtel du Cap-Ferrat (see below). It's open to nonguests, who pay 15€ to rent a mattress and an umbrella.

Everyone tries to visit the **Villa Mauresque,** avenue Somerset-Maugham, but it's closed to the public. Near the cape, it's where Maugham spent his final years. When tourists tried to visit him, he proclaimed that he wasn't one of the local sights. One man did manage to crash through the gate, and when he encountered the author, Maugham snarled, "What do you think I am, a monkey in a cage?"

Once the property of King Leopold II, of Belgium, the **Villa Les Cèdres** lies west of the port of St-Jean. Although the villa can't be visited, you can go to the **Parc Zoologique,** boulevard du Général-de-Gaulle, northwest of the peninsula, near Villa Les Cèdres (✆ **04-93-76-04-98**). It's open daily April through October from 9:30am to 5:30pm (to 7:30pm May–Sept). Admission is 10.20€ for adults, 8.50€ for students, and 7€ for ages 3 to 10 years. This private zoo is in the basin of a now-drained lake and was Leopold's domain. It houses a wide variety of reptiles, birds, and animals in outdoor cages. Six times a day, there's a chimps' tea party, which explains Maugham's remark.

Musée Ile-de-France ★★ The museum offers a chance to visit one of the Côte d'Azur's most legendary villas, an Italianate villa built by Baronne Ephrussi de Rothschild. She died in 1934, leaving the stately building and its magnificent gardens to the Institut de France on behalf of the Académie des Beaux-Arts. The wealth of her collection is preserved: 18th-century furniture; Tiepolo ceilings; Savonnerie carpets; screens and panels from the Far East; tapestries from Gobelins, Aubusson, and Beauvais; original drawings by Fragonard; canvases by Boucher; rare Sèvres porcelain; and more. Covering 4.8 hectares (12 acres), the gardens contain fragments of statuary from churches, monasteries, and torn-down palaces. One entire section is planted with cacti.

Av. Denis-Séméria. ✆ **04-93-01-33-09.** Admission 10€ adults, 7.50€ students and children 7–18. Nov–Feb Mon–Fri 2–6pm and Sat–Sun 10am–6pm; Mar–Oct daily 10am–6pm.

WHERE TO STAY

VERY EXPENSIVE

Grand Hôtel du Cap-Ferrat ★★★ One of the best features of this turn-of-the-20th century palace is its location at the tip of the peninsula in the midst of a 5.6-hectare (14-acre) garden of semitropical trees and manicured lawns. It has been the retreat of the international elite since 1908 and occupies the same celestial status as the Réserve and Métropole in Beaulieu (see the next section). Its cuisine even equals the Métropole's. The building has open loggias and big arched windows, and a terrace over the sea where you can enjoy the views. Guest rooms are conservatively modern, with dressing rooms. For the most part, they look as if the late Princess Grace might settle in comfortably at any minute. They are generally spacious and open to sea views, with thick carpets and elegant fabric wall coverings. Bathrooms are state-of-the-art, with robes, bidets, and power showerheads. The beach is accessible via funicular from the main building.

Bd. du Général-de-Gaulle, 06230 St-Jean-Cap-Ferrat. ✆ **04-93-76-50-52.** Fax 04-93-76-04-52. www.grand-hotel-cap-ferrat.com. 53 units. 580€–1,100€ double; 1,680€–2,550€ suite. Rates include breakfast. AE, MC, V. Indoor parking 75€; outdoor parking free. Closed Jan–Feb. **Amenities:** 2 restaurants; 2 bars; Olympic-size heated pool; 2 tennis courts; sauna; bike rental; 24-hr. room service; babysitting; laundry service; dry cleaning. *In room:* A/C, TV, minibar, hair dryer, safe.

La Voile d'Or ★★★ The "Golden Sail" is a brilliant tour de force offering intimate luxury in a converted villa. As a deluxe hotel, it's absolutely equal to the Grand Hôtel, though its cuisine isn't quite as superb. It's owned by an antiques collector turned hôtelier, Jean R. Lorenzi, and stands at the edge of the little fishing port and yacht harbor, with a panoramic view of the coast. The guest rooms, lounges, and restaurant open onto terraces. Rooms are individually decorated with hand-painted reproductions, carved gilt headboards, baroque paneled doors, parquet floors, antique clocks, and paintings. Each has a sense of intimacy you'd expect in a private home.

31 av. Jean-Mermoz, 06230 St-Jean-Cap-Ferrat. ✆ **04-93-01-13-13.** Fax 04-93-76-11-17. www.lavoiledor.fr. 45 units. 215€–710€ double; 435€–815€ suite. Rates include continental breakfast. AE, MC, V. Parking 22€. Closed Nov to late Mar. **Amenities:** Restaurant; bar; 2 outdoor saltwater pools; exercise room; sauna; limited room service; babysitting; laundry service; dry cleaning. *In room:* A/C, TV, minibar, hair dryer.

EXPENSIVE

Hotel Royal Riviera ★★ Rising five graceful stories above the thin line that separates the quietly prestigious towns of St.-Jean and Beaulieu, this hotel evokes the Riviera's gilded age, having been constructed in 1904. Fans of Zelda and F. Scott Fitzgerald know they frolicked here in the '30s, creating pages that might have been torn from *Tender Is the Night.* In 1988, an unfortunate modernization destroyed much of the Belle Epoque charm of the palace, before Grace Leo-Andrieu, one of France's most inventive hoteliers, arrived from Paris to help the hostelry regain its old reputation. She can't help the location near the train tracks, which makes some of the front rooms noisy, but she's done everything else in her power to make this a pocket of posh that's becoming increasingly chic by the minute. It occupies a .4-hectare (1-acre) tract with a beach of its own, to which tons of sand are added at regular intervals. Bedrooms are posh and plush, with big windows, private balconies, deep sofas, and fruitwood armoires. The largest and most appealing are the corner units (any room ending in "16"). Regardless, each is charming, elegant, chic, and modern. Bathrooms are fairly routine but well equipped, with robes.

3 av. Jean Monnet, 06230 Saint-Jean-Cap-Ferrat. ✆ **04-93-76-31-00.** Fax 04-93-01-23-07. www.royal-riviera.com. 95 units. 105€–135€ double; 520€–1,070€ suite. Rates include half board. AE, DC, MC, V. Free parking. **Amenities:** 2 restaurants; bar; pool; 24-hr. room service; babysitting; laundry service; dry cleaning. *In room:* A/C, TV, minibar, hair dryer, safe.

MODERATE

Hôtel Brise Marine ★ This villa (ca. 1878) with a front and rear terrace is on a hillside. A long rose arbor, beds of subtropical flowers, palms, and pines provide an attractive setting. The atmosphere is casual and informal, and the rooms are comfortably but simply furnished, with small tiled bathrooms. You can have breakfast in the beamed lounge or under the rose trellis.

58 Av. Jean-Mermoz, 06230 St-Jean-Cap-Ferrat. ✆ **04-93-76-04-36.** Fax 04-93-76-11-49. www.hotel-brisemarine.com. 18 units. 125€–140€ double. AE, DC, MC, V. Closed Nov–Jan. **Amenities:** Bar. *In room:* A/C, TV, hair dryer, safe.

Hôtel Clair Logis ★ *Finds* A rare find here, this hotel is in a 19th-century villa surrounded by .8 hectares (2 acres) of semitropical gardens. The pleasant rooms are scattered over three buildings. The hotel's most famous guest was de Gaulle, who lived in a room called *Strelitzias* (Bird of Paradise) during many of his retreats from Paris. Each room is named after a flower. The most romantic and spacious accommodations are in the main building; the seven rooms in the annex are the most modern but have the least character and tend to be smaller and cheaper. Rooms were renovated in 1998, and each has a neatly kept bathroom with a shower.

12 av. Centrale, 06230 St-Jean-Cap-Ferrat. ✆ **04-93-76-51-81.** Fax 04-93-76-51-82. www.hotel-clair-logis.fr. 18 units. 110€–125€ double. AE, DC, MC, V. Closed Jan 10 to mid-Mar and Nov–Dec 15. *In room:* TV, minibar, hair dryer.

Hôtel Le Panoramic *Value* This hotel, built in 1958 with a red-tile roof and much style and glamour, is one of the more affordable choices here. You'll reach the hotel by passing over a raised bridge lined with colorful pansies. The well-furnished rooms have a sweeping view of the water and the forest leading down to it. Accommodations are a bit small, but each is fitted with fine linen, plus a compact tiled bathroom. Breakfast is the only meal served.

3 av. Albert-1er, 06230 St-Jean-Cap-Ferrat. ✆ **04-93-76-00-37.** Fax 04-93-76-15-78. www.hotel-lepanoramic.com. 20 units. 103€–140€ double. AE, DC, MC, V. Closed mid-Nov to Dec 26. **Amenities:** Limited room service; laundry service; dry cleaning. *In room:* TV.

WHERE TO DINE

Capitaine Cook ★ PROVENÇAL/SEAFOOD Next door to the fancy Hôtel La Voile d'Or (see above), a few blocks uphill from the center of the village, this restaurant specializes in seafood served in hearty portions. You get a panoramic view of the coast from the restaurant's terrace, and inside the decor is rugged sea shanty style. Oysters, served simply on the half shell or in several creative ways with sauces and herbs, are a specialty. While roasted catch of the day is the mainstay, the filet mignon is also popular. The staff speaks English.

11 av. Jean-Mermosz. ✆ **04-93-76-02-66.** Main courses 21€–24€; fixed-price menus 21€–26€. MC, V. Fri–Tues noon–2pm; Thurs–Tues 7:30–9:30pm. Closed mid-Nov to Dec.

Le Provençal ★ FRENCH/PROVENÇAL With the possible exception of the Grand Hôtel's dining room, this is the grandest restaurant of this very grand resort area. Near the top of the resort's highest peak, it has a panoramic view, with sightlines that on good days sweep as far away as Menton and the Italian border. Many of the menu items are credited directly to the inspiration of "the Provençal" in the kitchen—in this case, the well-trained Jean-Jacques Jouteux. No stranger to the fine art of catering to an upscale clientele, he's assisted by an attractive staff. Menu items include marinated artichoke hearts presented beside half a lobster, a tarte fine of potatoes with undercooked foie gras, rack of lamb with local herbs and tarragon sauce, and crawfish asparagus and black-olive tapenade. The best way to appreciate the desserts is to order the house sampler, *"les cinq desserts du Provençal"*—a potpourri of five petits desserts that usually includes macaroons with chocolate and crème brûlée. With the passage of years here, the cooking seems more inspired than ever.

2 av. Denis-Séméria. ✆ **04-93-76-03-97.** Reservations required. Main courses 40€–56€; fixed-price menu 68€. AE, MC, V. Apr–Sept daily noon–2:30pm and 7:30–11pm; Oct–Mar Wed–Sun noon–2:30pm and 7:30–11pm.

Le Sloop MODERN FRENCH The most popular and most reasonably priced bistro in this very expensive area, it sits directly at the edge of the port, outfitted in blue and white inside and out. The best of regional produce is handled deftly. A meal here might begin with a salad of flap mushrooms steeped *"en cappuccino"* with liquefied foie gras, or perhaps a sautéed panful of flap mushrooms served with grated Parmesan cheese. This might be followed with a filet of deboned sea bass served with a red ("Bandols") wine sauce, or a mixed fish fry of three kinds of Mediterranean fish, bound together with olive oil and truffles. Dessert might include a custom-baked *("à la minute")* tarte with red plums, or any of about seven other desserts, each based on "the red fruits of the region." The regional wines are reasonably priced.

Au Nouveau Port. ✆ **04-93-01-48-63.** Reservations recommended. Main courses 25€–30€; fixed-price menu 32€. AE, MC, V. June–Sept Wed 7–9:30pm, Thurs–Tues noon–2pm and 7–11pm; closed Tues lunch and Wed lunch July–Aug.

9 Beaulieu ★

938km (583 miles) S of Paris; 10km (6 miles) E of Nice; 11km (7 miles) W of Monte Carlo

Protected from the cold north winds blowing down from the Alps, Beaulieu-sur-Mer is often referred to as "La Petite Afrique" (Little Africa). Like Menton, it has the mildest climate along the Côte d'Azur and is especially popular with the wintering wealthy. Originally, English visitors staked it out. Beaulieu is graced with lush vegetation, including oranges, lemons, and bananas, as well as palms.

ESSENTIALS

GETTING THERE Most visitors **drive** from Nice via the Moyenne Corniche or the coastal highway. **Trains** connect Beaulieu with Nice, Monaco, and the rest of the Côte d'Azur. For rail information, call ✆ **08-36-35-35-35.**

VISITOR INFORMATION The **Office de Tourisme** is on place Georges-Clemenceau (✆ **04-93-01-02-21;** www.ot-beaulieu-sur-mer.fr).

EXPLORING THE TOWN

Villa Kérylos ★, rue Gustave-Eiffel (✆ **04-93-76-44-09**), is a replica of an ancient Greek residence, painstakingly designed and built by the archaeologist

Theodore Reinach. Inside the cabinets are filled with a collection of Greek figurines and ceramics. But most interesting is the reconstructed Greek furniture, much of which would be fashionable today. One curious mosaic depicts the slaying of the minotaur and provides its own labyrinth (if you try to trace the path, expect to stay for weeks). It's open from February 3 to November 3 daily from 10am to 6pm; July and August daily 10am to 7pm; and from November 4 to February 2 Monday through Friday from 2 to 6pm, and Saturday and Sunday from 10am to 6pm. Admission is 7€ for adults, 5.50€ for seniors and children 7 to 18, and free for children under 7.

Casino de Beaulieu, avenue Fernand-Dunan (© **04-93-76-48-00**), built in the Art Nouveau style in 1903, was revitalized with new management in 1997. The main part of the casino where the blackjack, roulette, and chemin de fer tables are housed is open every night from 8pm to dawn. The ambience is glamorous, and men are required to wear jacket and tie. Entrance is 15€. For a more casual spot of gambling, the casino has a separate area reserved for slot machines only. Entrance is free and there is no dress code. This area is open daily from 11am to 4am. There are also a bar and a disco on the premises.

The town boasts an important church, the late-19th-century **Eglise de Sacré-Coeur,** a quasi-Byzantine, quasi-Gothic mishmash at 13 bd. du Maréchal-Leclerc (© **04-93-01-18-24**). With the same address and phone is the 12th-century Romanesque chapel of **Santa Maria de Olivo,** used mostly for temporary exhibits of painting, sculpture, and civic lore. Both sites are open daily from 8am to 7pm.

As you walk along the **seafront promenade,** you can see many stately Belle Epoque villas that evoke the days when Beaulieu was the very height of fashion. Although you can't go inside, you'll see signs indicating Villa Namouna, which once belonged to Gordon Bennett, the owner of the *New York Herald,* who sent Stanley to Africa to find Livingstone; and Villa Léonine, former home of the marquess of Salisbury.

MEMORABLE STROLLS

For a memorable 90-minute walk, start directly north of boulevard Edouard-VII, where a path leads up the Riviera escarpment to **Sentier du Plateau St-Michel.** A belvedere here offers panoramic views from Cap d'Ail to the Estérel. A 1-hour alternative is the stroll along **promenade Maurice-Rouvier,** beginning at a point adjacent to the sea and the Royal Riviera hotel. The promenade runs parallel to the water and stretches between Beaulieu and the old port of St-Jean de Cap Ferrat. Expect a walk of about 30 minutes each way, although you might opt to prolong the experience with a *cafe* or drink in Cap Ferrat once you get there. As you walk, you'll see some of the region's most elegant mansions, set within manicured gardens overlooking the blue sea and the curving shoreline of the French Riviera.

A DAY AT THE BEACH

Don't expect soft sands. Some seasons might have more sand than others, depending on tides and storms, but usually the surfaces are covered with light-gray gravel that has a finer texture than beaches at other resorts nearby. The longer of the town's two free public beaches is **Petite Afrique,** adjacent to the yacht basin; the shorter is **Baie des Fourmis,** beneath the casino. **Africa Plage** (© **04-93-01-11-00**) rents mattresses for 14€ to 16€ per day. It also sells snacks and drinks.

WHERE TO STAY

VERY EXPENSIVE

La Réserve de Beaulieu ★★★ One of the Riviera's most famous hotels, this pink-and-white fin-de-siècle palace is on the Mediterranean. Here you can sit having an apéritif watching the sun set over the Riviera, while a pianist treats you to Mozart. A number of the public lounges open onto a courtyard with bamboo chairs, grass borders, and urns of flowers. Social life centers on the main drawing room, much like the grand living room of a country estate. The hotel has been rebuilt in stages, so the rooms range widely in size and design; however, all are deluxe and individually decorated, with beautiful views of mountains or the Mediterranean. Some even have their own private balconies. Accommodations are sumptuous—read that, gorgeous. Luminous tile bathrooms come with deluxe toiletries and dual basins. In 1998, the hotel joined the ranks of Europe's Relais & Châteaux.

5 bd. du Maréchal-Leclerc, 06310 Beaulieu-sur-Mer. ✆ **04-93-01-00-01.** Fax 04-93-01-28-99. www.reservebeaulieu.com. 38 units. 188€–953€ double; 668€–2,287€ suite. AE, DC, MC, V. Parking 23€. Closed mid-Nov to Dec 25. **Amenities:** Restaurant; bar; outdoor pool; 24-hr. room service; massage; babysitting; laundry service; dry cleaning. *In room:* A/C, TV, minibar, hair dryer, safe.

Le Métropole ★★★ This Italianate villa offers some of the most luxurious accommodations along the Côte d'Azur and, as a hotel, is on equal rank with the fabled Réserve. It's a Relais & Châteaux property and is set on .8 hectares (2 acres) of grounds, discreetly shut off from the traffic around Beaulieu. You'll enter a world of polished French elegance: balconies opening onto sea views, marble, Oriental carpets, and polite staff members. Guest rooms are furnished in tasteful fabrics and flowery wallpapers. Bathrooms are elegantly spacious, most often tiled, and have double sinks.

15 bd. du Maréchal-Leclerc, 06310 Beaulieu-sur-Mer. ✆ **04-93-01-00-08.** Fax 04-93-01-18-51. www.le-metropole.com. 42 units. 220€–690€ double; 610€–790€ suite. Half board 60€ per person. Rates include half board. AE, DC, MC, V. Closed Oct 20–Dec 20. **Amenities:** Restaurant; bar; outdoor pool; 24-hr. room service; laundry service; dry cleaning. *In room:* A/C, TV, minibar, hair dryer, safe.

MODERATE

Inter-Hôtel Frisia Most of the Frisia's rooms, decorated in a modern style, open onto views of the harbor. Expectedly, sea-view rooms are the most expensive. Public areas include a sunny garden and inviting lounges. English is widely spoken here, and the management makes foreign guests feel especially welcome. Breakfast is the only meal served, but many reasonably priced dining places are nearby.

Bd. Eugène-Gauthier, 06310 Beaulieu-sur-Mer. ✆ **04-93-01-01-04.** Fax 04-93-01-31-92. www.frisia-beaulieu.com. 34 units. 55€–115€ double. AE, MC, V. Closed Nov 12–Dec 13. **Amenities:** Bar; babysitting; laundry service; dry cleaning. *In room:* TV, minibar, hair dryer, safe.

INEXPENSIVE

Hôtel Le Havre Bleu In what used to be a private Victorian villa, the hotel lies behind one of the prettiest facades of any inexpensive hotel in town, with arched, ornate windows and a front garden dotted with flowering urns. Guest rooms are functional and, as befits a house of this age, vary in shape and size. All come with comfortable mattresses and tiled bathrooms. Breakfast is the only meal served.

29 bd. du Maréchal-Joffre, 06310 Beaulieu-sur-Mer. ✆ **04-93-01-01-40.** Fax 04-93-01-29-92. 22 units. 45.60€–53.20€ double. AE, DC, MC, V. **Amenities:** Lounge.

Hôtel Marcellin *Finds* A good budget selection in an otherwise high-priced resort town, the turn-of-the-20th-century Marcellin rents restored rooms with homey luxuries, all with a southern exposure. It has been run by the same family since 1938. Ranging from small to medium, rooms have first-rate mattresses. Bathrooms are a bit cramped. The hotel stands amid the town's congestion, near its western periphery, a 5-minute walk to the beach. Its only breathing space consists of a small outdoor terrace. Despite that, it's a pleasant, well-maintained place to stay. Breakfast is the only meal served, but many restaurants are nearby.

18 av. Albert-1er, 06310 Beaulieu-sur-Mer. ✆ **04-93-01-01-69.** Fax 04-93-01-37-43. 21 units. 58€–62€ double. MC, V. Closed Nov 11 to Christmas. *In room:* TV.

WHERE TO DINE

The African Queen INTERNATIONAL Named by its movie-loving founders after the Hollywood classic, this hip and popular restaurant is filled with posters of Hepburn and Bogie and has a jungle-inspired decor. Much influenced by the United States (its sophisticated maître d' lived in Miami for 6 years), it has welcomed stars like Jack Nicholson, Raymond Burr, Robert Wagner, and Diana Ross during the nearby Cannes Film Festival. Menu specialties are a *dégustation de bouillabaisse,* African curry of lamb or beef and served like a rijstaffel with about a dozen condiments, or any of an array of steaks, fish, or shellfish. Less expensive are the seven or eight kinds of pizza, which even visiting Italians claim are very good. No one will mind if you stop in for only a strawberry daiquiri or piña colada. The check is presented in a videocassette case labeled—what else?—*The African Queen.*

Port de Plaisance. ✆ **04-93-01-10-85.** Reservations recommended. Main courses 13€–24.50€; pizzas 8€. MC, V. Daily noon–midnight.

La Pignatelle FRENCH/PROVENÇAL Even in this super-expensive resort town, you can find an excellent and affordable Provençal bistro. Despite its relatively low prices, La Pignatelle prides itself on the fact that all the products that go into its robust cuisine are fresh. As a result, it's usually crowded. Specialties are salade Niçoise; a succulent version of *soupe de poissons,* for which someone has labored to remove the bones; cassolette of mussels; monkfish steak garnished only with olive oil and herbs; scampi Provençal; tripe Niçoise; and a *"petite friture du pays,"* which incorporates very small fish with Provençal traditions that are many hundreds of years old.

10 rue de Quincenet. ✆ **04-93-01-03-37.** Reservations recommended. Main courses 9.50€–22.90€; fixed-price menu 12€–23€. MC, V. Thurs–Tues noon–2pm and 7–10pm. Closed Nov.

Le Catalan *Value* FRENCH/CATALAN/INTERNATIONAL This place is endlessly popular, and endlessly busy, thanks to relatively low prices and succulent food. You'll dine within any of three separate dining rooms or on a terrace overlooking the sea. A sought-after menu item is pizza, which comes in at least a dozen varieties here and is baked to bubbling perfection in a wood-burning beehive oven. More substantial fare involves such dishes as paella and zarzuela, pasta with shellfish, and a full roster of grilled meats and fish. Everybody from dock workers in grimy clothes to plumb society matrons from Paris dine here virtually elbow to elbow in an establishment that's acclaimed for its *égalité.*

52 Bd. Général Leclerc. ✆ **04-93-01-02-78.** Reservations recommended. Pizzas 7€–12€; main courses 13.60€–22.50€. MC, V. Tues–Sat noon–2:30pm and 7–11pm.

Les Agaves ★ FRENCH/PROVENÇAL One of the most stylish restaurants in Beaulieu is housed within a turn-of-the-20th-century villa across the street from the railway station. Inside, within an ambience of richly grained paneling and high ceilings, you'll enjoy the kind of food that such U.S.–based publications as *Bon Appetit* have praised as delectable. Of particular note is curry-enhanced scallops served with garlic-flavored tomatoes and parsley, lobster salad with mango, chopped shrimp with Provençal herbs, and several different preparations of foie gras. Filet of sea bass with truffles and champagne sauce is particularly delectable.

4 av. Maréchal Foch. ✆ **04-93-01-13-12.** Reservations recommended. Main courses 18€–32€; fixed-price menu 30€. AE, MC, V. Daily 7:30–10pm. Closed Nov.

10 Eze & La Turbie ★

941km (585 miles) S of Paris; 11km (7 miles) NE of Nice

The hamlets of Eze and La Turbie, though 6.4km (4 miles) apart, have so many similarities that most of France's tourist officials speak of them as if they were one. Both boast fortified feudal centers high in the hills overlooking the Provençal coast, built during the early Middle Ages to stave off raids from corsairs. Clinging to the rocky hillsides around these hamlets are upscale villas, many of which were built since the 1950s by retirees. Closely linked, culturally and fiscally, to nearby Monaco, Eze, and La Turbie each has a full-time population of fewer than 3,000.

ESSENTIALS

GETTING THERE Eze (also known as Eze-Village) is accessible via the Moyenne (Middle) Corniche road; La Turbie is accessible via the Grande (Upper) Corniche. Signs are positioned along the coastal road indicating the direction motorists should take to reach either of the hamlets.

VISITOR INFORMATION The **Office de Tourisme** is on place du Général-de-Gaulle, Eze-Village (✆ **04-93-41-26-00**).

EXPLORING THE TOWNS

The medieval cores of both towns contain art galleries, boutiques, and artisans' shops that have been restored. Two art galleries of particular note within Eze are **Galerie Sevek,** rue du Barri (✆ **04-93-41-06-22**), and **Galerie Doussot,** rue Principale (✆ **04-93-41-01-62**).

The leading attraction in Eze is the **Jardin Exotique,** boulevard du Jardin-Exotique (✆ **04-93-41-10-30**), a lushly landscaped showcase of exotic plants at the pinnacle of the town's highest hill. Entrance is 2.30€ for adults and free for children 11 and under. In July and August, it's open from 9am to 8pm; the rest of the year, it opens between 8:30 and 9am and closes between 5 and 7:30pm, depending on the time of sunset.

La Turbie boasts a ruined monument erected by the ancient Roman emperor Augustus in 6 B.C., the **Trophée des Alps** (also called by locals "La Trophée d'Auguste"). It rises near a rock formation known as La Tète de Chien, at the highest point along the Grand Corniche, 450m (1,500 ft.) above sea level. The monument, restored with funds donated by Edward Tuck, was erected by the Roman Senate to celebrate the subjugation of the people of the French Alps by the Roman armies. A short distance from the monument is the **Musée du Trophée des Alps,** rue Albert-1er, La Turbie (✆ **04-93-41-20-84**), a minimuseum containing finds from archaeological digs nearby and information about the monument's restoration. It's open daily April through June from 9am to 6pm, July through September from 9am to 7pm, and October through March from 9:30am to 5pm. Entrance is 4€ for adults, 2.50€ for students and youths 12 to 25, and free for children 11 and under. It's closed January 1, May 1, November 1, and December 25.

WHERE TO STAY & DINE

Auberge Eric Rivot This straw-yellow stucco villa is a few steps from the Basse Corniche. It has a quiet rear terrace, and the decor features rattan chairs, exposed brick, and lots of brass. The simply furnished doubles draw mainly a summer crowd, though the inn is open most of the year. Bedrooms are small but decently furnished with beds containing middle-grade mattresses. Bathrooms are tiled and compact. Half board is a good deal here—the meals are satisfying and wine is included.

44 av. de la Liberté, 06360 Eze-Bord-de-Mer. ✆ **04-93-01-51-46.** Fax 04-93-01-58-40. 10 units. 57€ double. Half board 52€ per person extra. AE, DC, MC, V. Closed mid-Nov to Dec 1. **Amenities:** Restaurant; lounge. *In room:* TV, minibar, hair dryer.

Château Eza ★★★ This château is the former Riviera home of Prince William of Sweden. It stands at the edge of a cliff at 396m (1,300 ft.) looking out over the resort of St. Jean-Cap-Ferrat. This is one of the Riviera's great pockets of posh. Entered on a narrow cobblestone street, it offers sumptuous bedrooms, a celebrated gourmet cuisine, and service fit for royalty. The elegant bedrooms are spread over a cluster of restored buildings dating from the Middle Ages. Each of the guest rooms is reached by walking under stone passageways past cavelike shops. Although the setting is ancient, the rooms are thoroughly modernized, with private bathrooms, charming fireplaces, and private balconies opening onto panoramic views. Canopied beds, art objects, beautiful carpets, and valuable tapestries set the tone. This is as close as the Riviera gets to fantasy living.

Moyene Corniche, Eze Village, 06360. ✆ **04-93-41-12-24.** Fax 04-93-41-16-64. http://hotelsdeluxe.com/chateaueza. 10 units. 380 € double; 630€ suite. AE, DC, MC, V. Closed Dec–Mar. **Amenities:** Restaurant; bar; lounge; limited room service; babysitting; laundry service; dry cleaning. *In room:* A/C, TV, minibar, hair dryer, safe.

Hostellerie du Château de la Chèvre d'Or ★★★ This is a miniature village retreat built in the 1920s in neo-Gothic style, but without a beach. On the side of a stone village off the Moyenne Corniche, this Relais & Châteaux property is a complex of village houses, all with views of the coastline. The owner has had the interior of the "Golden Goat" flawlessly decorated to maintain its old character while adding modern comfort. Great care is taken to maintain deluxe mattresses and the elegant bathrooms. Even if you don't stop in for a meal or a room, try to visit for a drink in the lounge, which has a panoramic view.

Rue du Barri, 06360 Eze-Village. ✆ **04-92-10-66-66.** Fax 04-93-41-06-72. www.chevredor.com. 33 units. 320€–700€ double; from 600€ suite. AE, MC, DC, V. Closed mid-Nov to Mar. **Amenities:** 3 restaurants; bar; outdoor pool; limited room service; laundry service; dry cleaning. *In room:* A/C, TV, minibar, hair dryer, safe.

11 Peillon ★★

19km (12 miles) NW of Nice

This fortified medieval town is the most spectacular "perched village" along the Côte d'Azur. At 300m (1,000 ft.) above the sea, it's also unspoiled, unlike so many other perched villages that are filled with day-trippers and souvenir shops.

The main incentive to visit Peillon is the town itself, with its semifortified architecture, which makes you feel that even today it could lock its doors, bar its windows, and keep any intruder at bay. Specific sites of interest include the town's severely dignified parish church, the **Eglise St-Sauveur,** open daily from 8am to around 6pm. Built in a simple country-baroque style, it's the site of many marriages, baptisms, and wedding ceremonies. Another site of interest is the 15th-century **Chapelle des Pénitents Blancs,** on place August-Arnuls. It's usually locked, so visits require that you first drop by the town hall (**La Mairie;** place de la Mairie; ✆ **04-93-79-91-04**), where an employee—if it's convenient and if he or she isn't otherwise occupied—will accompany you with a key and wait for you while you admire the interior. The service is free, but a gratuity is appreciated. If you plunk .30€ into a machine near the gate, lights will illuminate the interior's noteworthy frescoes. Painted in 1491 by Jean Cannavesio, they represent the eight stages of the passion of Christ.

The narrow streets radiate outward from the town's "foyer," **place Auguste-Arnuls,** which is shaded by rows of plantain trees centered around a fountain that has splashed water from its basin since 1800. Some of the streets are enclosed with vaulting and accented with potted geraniums and strands of ivy.

If you're in the mood for walking, consider a 2-hour, 12km (7½-mile) northward hike across the dry and rocky landscape to Peillon's remote twin, Peille, a smaller version of Peillon.

ESSENTIALS

GETTING THERE Few other towns in Provence are as easy to reach by **car** and as inconvenient to reach by public transportation. Peillon is an easy 20-minute drive (depending on traffic) northeast from Nice; take D2204 to D21.

Only two **trains** a day stop near Peillon at St-Techle, an antiquated station connecting Nice with Coni, a town across the border in Italy. For rail information and schedules, call ✆ **08-36-35-35-35.** You'll find lots of dilapidated local color at the railway station of St-Techle. There are no taxis waiting and no bus service to carry you on to Peillon. If you can find a phone in St-Techle, the phone number of the best local **cab service** is ✆ **04-93-27-00-83.** You can also contact the company's cellphone by dialing ✆ **06-13-43-89-29.** Transit from the railway station at St-Techle to Peillon costs about 7.60€ each way. Most backpackers continue into Peillon by hitchhiking.

The Santa Azur bus line operates four buses a day from Nice, with multiple stops en route (trip time: around 25 min.). Don't expect it to be convenient—you'll be dropped off about 3km (2 miles) from Peillon's center, at a tiny crossroads known as Le Moulin. Many hardy souls opt to continue on to the center by foot because there's no transport into Peillon. For **bus information,** call ✆ **04-93-85-61-81.**

VISITOR INFORMATION The **Tourist Office** in Nice (✆ **04-93-79-92-04**) is responsible for supplying information about Peillon. But a more likely bet for on-the-spot tourist information is to chat with the staff at **Auberge de la Madone** (see below) or to informally contact anyone at Peillon's **Town Hall** (✆ **04-93-79-91-04**).

WHERE TO STAY & DINE

Auberge de la Madone ★★ This hotel, with its well-recommended restaurant, is the leading choice and has been since it opened back in the 1930s. The oldest section of the stone-sided complex of buildings dates from the 12th century. Evocative of a sprawling *mas Provençal,* it gives you a real glimpse of a

Provence from long ago. It's capped with terra-cotta tiles and draped with a small version of the hanging gardens of Babylon. On the opposite side of place Auguste-Arnuls from the rest of the village, it boasts a wide terrace offering a great view of the town's vertical, angular architecture. The guest rooms are comfortable and rustic, outfitted with Provençal themes and fabrics. In 1998, the hotel built an annex within a 5-minute walk, with seven additional rooms—the annex's accommodations are much simpler than those in the main building; rates depend on the plumbing and views. Bathrooms are generally small.

The hotel restaurant is by far the most formal in town, serving lunch and dinner every day except Wednesday and during the annual closing noted below. Menu items are based on cuisine that developed over the centuries and include unusual dishes like *tourton des pénitents,* a salty tart enriched with 17 herbs, almonds, eggs, and cream; suckling lamb with garlic mashed potatoes and a tapenade of olives; farm-raised guinea fowl with a confit of pears; and a pot au feu, a savory kettle of seafood served with aïoli. A recipe that was specifically praised early in 1999 by the American edition of *Bon Appetit* for its originality and subtle flavors was a white beet tart capped with a "petal" of foie gras.

06440 Peillon. ✆ **04-93-79-91-17.** Fax 04-93-79-99-36. 20 units. Main building 85€–180€ double; 99€–220€ suite. Annex 40€–67€ double. MC, V. Free parking. Closed Jan 7–31 and Oct 20–Dec 20. **Amenities:** Restaurant (closed Wed); bar, lounge. *In room:* TV, hair dryer.

12 Monaco ★★★

954km (593 miles) S of Paris; 18km (11 miles) E of Nice

The outspoken Katharine Hepburn once called Monaco "a pimple on the chin of the south of France." She wasn't referring to the principality's lack of beauty, but rather to the preposterous idea of having a little country, a feudal anomaly, taking up some of the choicest coastline along the Riviera. Hemmed in by France on three sides and facing the Mediterranean, tiny Monaco staunchly maintains its independence. Even Charles de Gaulle couldn't force Prince Rainier to do away with his tax-free policy. As almost everybody in an overburdened world knows by now, the Monégasques do not pay taxes. Nearly all their country's revenue comes from tourism and gambling.

Monaco—or rather, its capital of Monte Carlo—has for a century been a symbol of glamour. Its legend was further enhanced by the 1956 marriage of the man who was at that time the world's most eligible bachelor, Prince Rainier III, to the American actress Grace Kelly. She had met the prince when she was in Cannes for the film festival to promote *To Catch a Thief,* the Hitchcock movie she made with Cary Grant. A journalist friend arranged a *Paris Match* photo shoot with the prince—and the rest is history. The Monégasques welcomed the birth of daughter Caroline in 1957 but went wild at the birth of Albert, a male heir, in 1958. According to a 1918 treaty, Monaco will become an autonomous state under French protection if the ruling dynasty becomes extinct. However, the fact that Albert is still a bachelor has the entire principality concerned. The third royal daughter, Stephanie, was born in 1965.

Though not always happy in her role, Princess Grace soon won the respect and adoration of her people. In 1982, a sports car she was driving, with her daughter Stephanie as a passenger (not as the driver, as was viciously rumored), plunged over a cliff, killing Grace but only injuring Stephanie. The Monégasques still mourn her death.

Monaco became a property of the Grimaldi clan, a Genoese family, as early as 1297. With shifting loyalties, it has maintained something resembling independence ever since. In a fit of impatience the French annexed it in 1793, but the ruling family recovered it in 1814; however, the prince at that time couldn't bear to tear himself away from the pleasures of Paris for "dreary old Monaco."

ESSENTIALS

GETTING THERE With no border formalities, Monaco is easy to get to by car, bus, or train. There's frequent **train service** (every half-hour) to and from Cannes, Nice, Antibes, and Menton. Trips from Nice to Monaco cost 4€ and take 25 to 30 minutes. From Paris, departing from the Gare de Lyon, there are at least two trains per day, each requiring between 6 and 6¾ hours each way, sometimes requiring a change of equipment and a brief stopover in Nice. One-way fares cost around 80€ per person. For train schedules, call ✆ **93-10-60-01** in Monaco or 08-36-35-35-35 in France.

In late 1999, Monaco opened an enormous train station a quarter mile east of the old station. This station has three exits on three levels, and if you don't know which exit to use, you might have trouble finding your hotel. Monaco is a confusing place to navigate, so you might want to pick up a free map at the station's tourist office (open daily June–Sept 8:30am–7:30pm). Arriving at the Monaco train station after 9pm is like arriving on Wall Street after 9pm—it's desolate, and there's not a soul on the street. On the bright side, Monaco restaurants serve dinner late, so you can usually get a full meal at least until 11 pm.

There's frequent **bus service** (every 15 min.) to Nice, Beaulieu, and Menton on line no. 100 of the French bus company Rapides Côte d'Azur (✆ **04-93-85-64-44**). The trip from Nice to Monaco by bus takes a half-hour and costs 6€ round-trip or 3€ one-way. The times and prices are the same to Menton. The easiest place to catch a bus is in front of the gardens that preface the Casino, but it also stops in front of the port (on boulevard Albert-1er at the Stade Nautique stop) and at several other spots around town.

If you're **driving** from Nice to Monaco, take N7 northeast. The 19km (12-mile) drive takes about 35 minutes because of heavy traffic; Cannes to Monaco requires about 55 minutes. If driving from Paris, follow A6 to Lyon. In Lyon, take A7 south to Aix-en-Provence and A6 to Monaco.

VISITOR INFORMATION The **Direction du Tourisme** office is at 2A bd. des Moulins (✆ **92-16-61-66;** www.monaco.net).

GETTING AROUND The best way to get around Monaco is by **bus,** and you can buy bus cards, which cost 1.30€ per ride, directly on the bus. Bus stops are set up every few blocks on the main streets in town, including boulevard Albert-1er, avenue St-Martin in Monaco Ville, and boulevard des Moulins in Monte Carlo. Buses go to all the major tourist sights; just look at the front of the bus to see the destination.

For a **taxi,** call ✆ **93-15-01-01.** There are taxi stands in front of the Casino on avenue de Monte-Carlo, at place des Moulins in Monte Carlo; at the Port de Monaco on avenue Président J. F. Kennedy; and in front of the Poste de Monte-Carlo on avenue Henry-Dunant. There's a **Hertz** car rental office at 27 bd. Albert-1er (✆ **93-50-79-60**), and an **Avis** office at 9 av. d'Ostende (✆ **93-30-17-53**).

SPECIAL EVENTS Some of the most-watched **car-racing events** in Europe are held in January (Le Rallye) and May (the Grand Prix). Mid-April witnesses one of the Riviera's most famous **tennis tournaments.** For 1 week every June,

Monte Carlo is home to a week-long convention that attracts media moguls from virtually everywhere: **Le Festival International de la Télévision,** wherein the winning shows from all over the world are broadcast and judged on their individual merits. For information and further details, write or call Festival International de la Télévision, 4 bd. des Jardins Exotiques (© **93-10-40-60**).

EXPLORING THE PRINCIPALITY

The second-smallest state in Europe (Vatican City is the tiniest), Monaco consists of four parts. The old town, **Monaco-Ville,** on a promontory, "The Rock," 60m (200 ft.) high, is the seat of the royal palace and the government building, as well as the Oceanographic Museum. To the west of the bay, **La Condamine,** the home of the Monégasques, is at the foot of the old town, forming its harbor and port sector. Up from the port (walking is steep in Monaco) is **Monte Carlo,** once the playground of European royalty and still the center for wintering

Tips Number, Please: Monaco's Telephone System

Since 1996, Monaco's phone system has been independent of France.

To call Monaco from within France, dial **00** (access code for international long-distance calls placed from mainland France), followed by Monaco's country code, **377,** and then the eight-digit local phone number. To call Monaco from North America, dial the international access code, **011,** followed by Monaco's country code, **377,** plus the local eight-digit Monaco number.

If you're calling France from within Monaco, dial **00** (the international access code), **33** (the country code for France), **4** (the area code, without the zero), and the eight-digit number. To call locally within Monaco, dial all eight digits of the phone number.

wealthily, the setting for the casino and its gardens and the deluxe hotels. The fourth part, **Fontvieille,** is a neat industrial suburb.

Ironically, **Monte-Carlo Beach,** at the far frontier, is on French soil. It attracts a chic crowd, including movie stars in scanty bikinis and thongs. The resort has a freshwater pool, an artificial beach, and a sea-bathing establishment.

No one used to go to Monaco in summer, but now that has totally changed—in fact, July and August tend to be so crowded that it's hard to get a room. Furthermore, with the decline of royalty and multimillionaires, Monaco is developing a broader base of tourism (you can stay here moderately—but it's misleading to suggest that you can stay cheaply). The Monégasques very frankly court the affluent visitor. And at the casinos here, you can also lose your shirt. "Suicide Terrace" at the casino, though not used as frequently as in the old days, is still a real temptation to many who have foolishly gambled away family fortunes.

Life still focuses on the **Monte Carlo Casino** ★, which has been the subject of countless legends and the setting for many films (remember poor Lucy Ricardo and the chip she found lying on the casino floor?). High drama is played to the fullest here. Depending on the era, you might have seen Mata Hari shooting a tsarist colonel with a jewel-encrusted revolver when he tried to slip his hand inside her bra to discover her secrets—military, not mammary. The late King Farouk, known as "The Swine," used to devour as many as 8 roast guinea hens and 50 oysters before losing thousands at the table. Richard Burton presented Elizabeth Taylor with the obscenely huge Koh-i-noor diamond here. Surrounded by cultivated gardens, the casino stands on a **panoramic terrace** ★★, offering one of the grandest views along the entire Riviera.

SEEING THE SIGHTS

Collection des Voitures Anciennes de S.A.S. le Prince de Monaco

Prince Rainier III has opened a showcase of his private collection of more than 100 exquisitely restored vintage autos, including the 1956 Rolls-Royce Silver Cloud that carried the prince and princess on their wedding day. It was given to the royal couple by Monaco shopkeepers as a wedding present. A 1952 Austin Taxi on display was once used as the royal "family car." Other exhibits are a Woodie, a 1937 Ford station wagon once used by Prince Louis II when on hunting trips, and a 1925 Bugatti 35B, winner of the Monaco Grand Prix in 1929.

Other outstanding autos are a 1903 De Dion Bouton and a 1986 Lamborghini Countach.

Les Terrasses de Fontvieille. ✆ **92-05-28-56.** Admission 6€ adults, 3€ students and children 8–14, free for children under 8. Daily 10am–6pm. Closed Nov.

Les Grands Appartements du Palais ★ The Italianate home of Monaco's royal family, the Palais du Prince, dominates the principality from "the Rock." The palace was built in the 13th century, and part dates from the Renaissance. When touring Les Grands Appartements, you're shown the Throne Room and allowed to see some of the art collection, including works by Brueghel and Holbein, as well as Princess Grace's stunning state portrait. You're also shown the chamber where England's George III died. The ideal time to arrive is 11:55am to watch the 10-minute Relève de la Garde (changing of the guard).

In a wing of the palace, the **Musée du Palais du Prince** (Souvenirs Napoléoniens et Collection d'Archives) (✆ **93-25-18-31**), contains a collection of mementos of Napoléon and Monaco itself. When the royal residence is closed, this museum is the only part of the palace the public can visit.

Place du Palais. ✆ **93-25-18-31.** Combination ticket 6€ adults, 3€ children 8–14, free for children under 8. Palace June–Sept daily 9:30am–6:30pm; Dec–May 10:30am–12:30pm and 2–5pm. Museum June–Sept daily 9:30am–6:30pm; Oct to Nov 11 daily 10am–5pm; Dec 17 to May Tues–Sun 10:30am–12:30pm and 2–5pm. Closed Nov 12–Dec 16.

Jardin Exotique Built on the side of a rock, the gardens are known for their cactus collection. They were begun by Prince Albert I, who was a naturalist and a scientist. He spotted some succulents growing in the palace gardens, and knowing that these plants were normally found only in Central America or Africa, he created the garden from them. You can also explore the grottoes here, as well as the **Musée d'Anthropologie Préhistorique** (✆ **93-15-80-06**). The view of the principality is splendid.

Bd. du Jardin-Exotique. ✆ **93-15-29-80.** Admission to garden 6.50€ adults, 3.20€ children 6–18, free for children under 6. Mid-May to mid-Sept daily 9am–7pm; mid-Sept to mid-May daily 9am–6pm.

Musée National de Monaco ★ In a villa designed by Charles Garnier (architect of Paris's Opéra Garnier), this museum houses one of the world's greatest collections of mechanical toys and dolls. See especially the 18th-century Neapolitan crib, which contains some 200 figures. This collection, assembled by Madame de Galea, was presented to the principality in 1972; it stemmed from the 18th- and 19th-century trend of displaying new fashions on doll models.

17 av. Princesse-Grace. ✆ **93-30-91-26.** Admission 5€ adults, 3.50€ students and children 6–14, free for children under 6. Easter–Sept daily 10am–6:30pm; Oct–Easter daily 10am–12:15pm and 2:30–6:30pm.

Musée de l'Océanographie ★★ This museum was founded in 1910 by Albert I, great-grandfather of the present prince. In the main rotunda is a statue of Albert in his favorite costume—that of a sea captain. Displayed are specimens he collected during 30 years of expeditions aboard his oceanographic ships. The aquarium—one of the finest in Europe—contains more than 90 tanks.

Prince Albert's collection is exhibited in the zoology room. Some of the exotic creatures here were unknown before he captured them. You'll see models of the oceanographic ships aboard which he directed his scientific cruises from 1885 to 1914. The most important part of its laboratory has been preserved and reconstituted as closely as possible. The cupboards contain all the equipment and documentation necessary for a scientific expedition. Skeletons of specimens are on

The Shaky House of Grimaldi

Monaco, according to Somerset Maugham, is 149 sunny hectares (370 acres) peopled with shady characters. According to a 1918 treaty, Monaco must maintain an ongoing stream of male heirs to retain its independence from France. The tax-free principality is the oddest fiscal and social anomaly in Europe, a blend of Las Vegas hype and aristocratic glitter whose luster has been sorely tarnished since the demise of Princess Grace ("a snow-covered volcano," said Alfred Hitchcock).

The marriage of the world's most eligible bachelor and the Hollywood golden goddess dominated headlines in April 1956. However, like Grace and Rainier themselves, the marriage did not age gracefully. Rainier's snide public assessments of his celebrity wife's accomplishments showed an unpleasant rivalry. In turn, Grace, beneath her cool veneer, was a lonely and frustrated woman who sought solace in a string of affairs.

The children of this ill-fated union have rebelled against the strictures imposed on them by their less-than-noble parents. More at home in the watering holes of big-city Paris than in the claustrophobic and judgmental homeland, they take turns being the one most likely to shock the multinational residents of their tax-free domain.

The most obviously disaffected is Stephanie, whose tantrums as a 13-year-old were duly noted by scads of journalists and whose sexual insouciance has contributed, according to local wits, to the ill health of her not particularly serene father. Her affairs have included the sons of both Jean-Paul Belmondo and Alain Delon, also children of second-generation fame. For a time, she moved to Los Angeles, where she tried to build a show-business career. Promising beginnings in Stephanie's fertile roster of career options were stymied by maneuvering from the Grimaldi fortress. Her ambitions have mostly collapsed, as have her attempts to become a model or pop singer. In 1995, Stephanie married a former palace guard, Alain Ducruet, by whom she bore two children; however, a year later she divorced him because he had been caught cavorting naked with Miss Bare Breasts of Belgium. In 1998, Stephanie continued to make headlines by staying mum about her new baby's dad—Camille Marie Kelly was Stephanie's third child born out of wedlock. One palace guard summed up Stephanie's affairs and babies: "In these times, it's not a question of morals. A princess can do what she likes." "From Tiaras to Trailer Parks" blares the headlines in the world press today. Princess Stephanie now spends her days traveling with the circus in Europe, with her companion, Franco Knie, owner of the caravan.

Everyone in his prospective kingdom constantly urges Albert, now in his 40s, to take a bride and produce the male heir necessary to preserve

the main floor, including a giant whale that drifted ashore at Pietra Ligure in 1896—it's believed to be the same one the prince harpooned earlier that year. The skeleton is remarkable for its healed fractures sustained when a vessel struck the animal as it was drifting asleep on the surface. An exhibition devoted to the

the principality's independence. He has publicly denied rumors of homosexuality and has cavorted with an assortment of famous faces, from Brooke Shields to Donna Rice to Claudia Schiffer. As a local commentator has said, "It's one thing for him to marry a bimbo; it's another to marry someone like his mother." At the moment (subject to change at any minute), Albert continues to play the field, finding no replacement to fill the shoes of Princess Grace.

Caroline, mother of three, has done her royal part. She would if she could, according to observers, force a power struggle with Albert for the right of succession. Her first husband, the much older businessman/boulevardier Philippe Junot, was the sort of man every mother hopes her daughter will not marry—which is probably why Caroline did. After she announced that she was divorcing womanizing Junot, the Vatican was called in to annul the marriage (which it finally did in 1992). Within a year of her mother's death, Caroline met and fell deeply in love with 27-year-old Stefano Casiraghi, son of an Italian industrialist. She was 4 months pregnant when they married in 1984, and she and Stefano had two more children (who remained "illegitimate" until 3 years after their father's death). In 1989, Stefano died in a speedboating accident and Caroline went into severe mourning, chopping off her hair and withdrawing from her duties. Eventually, she and her children moved to France and she returned to her position as "First Lady of Monaco." On January 23, 1999, her 42nd birthday, Caroline took a new husband, Prince Ernst of Hanover, who had been married to her best friend. Oddly, by marrying Ernst, she fulfilled the wishes of her late mother, who always wanted her to marry him. The couple will not be poor: Ernst is reportedly worth $800 million.

On May 31, 1997, Prince Rainier and his family marked the 700th anniversary of Grimaldi rule—6,600 Monégasques showed up for an open-air ceremony at place du Palais. With all their troubles and scandals, the clan has come a long way since January 8, 1297—that's when a political refugee from Genoa, Francesco Grimaldi, accompanied by some cronies in monks' clothing, persuaded the defenders of the local castle to give him shelter. Once he and his men penetrated the defenses, they ripped off their hoods and took the castle by force. The Principality of Monaco was born, and it's been in Grimaldi hands ever since.

One Monégasque summed up the Grimaldi situation well: "I go to church every morning to pray for the Prince and his family. I pray God will keep them safe and sane. Because that is my security. Without the Grimaldis, we would be merely hors d'oeuvres for France."

discovery of the ocean is in the physical-oceanography room on the first floor. Underwater movies are shown continuously in the lecture room.

Av. St-Martin. ✆ **93-15-36-00.** Admission 11€ adults, 6€ children 6–18, free for children under 6. Apr–June and Sept daily 9am–7pm; July–Aug daily 9am–8pm; Oct–Mar daily 10am–6pm.

OUTDOOR PURSUITS

A DAY AT THE BEACH

Just outside the border, on French (not Monacan) soil, the **Monte-Carlo Beach Club** ★ adjoins the Monte-Carlo Beach Hotel, 22 av. Princesse-Grace (✆ **04-93-28-66-66**). Permeated with intricate social rituals that might not be immediately visible to first-timers, the beach club has thrived for years as an integral part of Monaco's social life. You'll find a beach whose sand is replenished at regular intervals, two large pools (one for children), beach cabanas, a restaurant, a cafe, a bar, and memories of Princess Grace, who used to come here in flowery swimsuits, greeting her friends and subjects with humor and style. As the Celsius reading lowers in late August, expect the beach to close for the winter. The admission charge, 40€for the day, grants you access to the public changing rooms, toilets, the restaurants, and the bar. A day's use of a private cubicle, which you'll use to change and to lock up your street clothes, costs an additional 15€. And a full day's rental of a mattress for sunbathing costs 16€. As usual, topless is acceptable for both genders, but bottomless isn't.

Monaco, in its role as the quintessential kingdom by the sea, also offers sea bathing at its most popular beach, the **Plage de Larvetto,** off avenue Princesse-Grace (✆ **04-93-30-63-84**). There's no charge for bathing on this strip of beach, whose sands are frequently replenished with sand hauled in by barge. The beach is open to public access at all hours.

OTHER OUTDOOR ACTIVITIES

GOLF The **Monte Carlo Golf Club,** route N7, La Turbie (✆ **04-93-41-09-11**), on French soil, is a par-72 golf course with ample amounts of prestige, scenic panoramas, and local history. Certain perks (including use of electric golf buggies) are reserved for members. Before they're allowed to play, nonmembers are asked to show proof of membership in another golf club and provide evidence of their handicap ratings. Greens fees for 18 holes are 85€ Monday through Friday and 100€ Saturday and Sunday. Clubs can be rented for 15€. The course is open daily from 8am to sunset.

SPA TREATMENTS In 1908, the Société des Bains de Mer launched a seawater (thalassotherapy) spa in Monte Carlo. It was inaugurated by Prince Albert I himself. However, in World War II, it was bombed and only reopened in 1996. **Les Thermes Marins de Monte-Carlo,** 2 av. de Monte-Carlo (✆ **92-16-40-40**), is one of the largest spas in Europe and the only one in Monaco. Spread over four floors are a gigantic pool, a Turkish haman, a health food restaurant, a juice bar, two tanning booths, a fitness center, a beauty center, and private treatment rooms.

SWIMMING The stupendous **Stade Nautique Rainier-III,** quai Albert-1er, at La Condamine (✆ **93-15-28-75**), an outdoor pool that overlooks the yacht-clogged harbor, was a gift from the prince to his loyal subjects. It's open May through October daily from 9am to 6pm (open till midnight July–Aug). Admission for a one-time visit costs 5.20€ per person; discounts are available if you plan to visit it 10 times or more. Between November and April, it's transformed into an ice-skating rink. If you want to go swimming in winter, try the indoor **Piscine du Prince Héréditaire Albert,** in the Stade Louis II, at 7 av. de Castellane (✆ **92-05-42-13**). It's open Monday, Tuesday, Thursday, and Friday from 7:30am to 2:30pm; Saturday from 2 to 6pm; and Sunday from 9am to 1pm. Admission is 3.50€.

TENNIS & SQUASH The **Monte Carlo Country Club,** in France on avenue Princesse-Grace, Roquebrune-St-Roman (© **04-93-41-30-15**), has 23 tennis courts (21 clay and 2 concrete). Payment of the 36€ entrance fee provides access to a restaurant, a health club with Jacuzzi and sauna, a putting green, a beach, and squash courts, as well as the well-maintained tennis courts. Plan to spend at least half a day, ending a round of tennis with use of any of the other facilities. It's open daily from 8am to 8 or 9pm, depending on the season.

SHOPPING

Rising costs and an increase in crime have changed women's tastes in jewelry, perhaps forever. **Bijoux Cassio,** 10 bd. des Moulins (© **93-25-55-10**), sells only imitation gemstones. They're rather shamelessly copied from the real McCoy sold by Cartier and Van Cleef & Arpels. Made in Italy of gold-plated silver, the fake jewelry costs between 10€ and 300€ per piece, many thousands of francs less than the authentic gems.

Boutique du Rocher, 1 av. de la Madone (© **93-30-91-17**), is the largest of two roughly equivalent boutiques opened in 1966 by Princess Grace as the official retail outlets of her charitable foundation. The organization merchandizes Monégasque and Provençal handcrafts: carved frames for pictures or mirrors; housewares; gift items crafted from porcelain, textiles, and wood; toys; and dolls. On the premises are workshops where local artisans produce the goods for sale. It's a short walk from place du Casino; a second branch is at 25 rue Emile de Loth, in Monaco-Ville (© **93-30-33-99**).

Brett Merrill, 17 bd. des Moulins (© **93-50-33-85**), is a menswear store aiming at the solid middle-bracket man who simply wants to dress appropriately and look good. You can pick up a swimsuit, shorts, slacks, a blazer, and a pair of socks to replace the ones you ruined by too many walking tours, at prices that won't require that you remortgage your house.

You don't have to be Princess Caroline to be able to afford to shop in Monaco, especially now that **FNAC** (© **93-10-81-81**), a member of the big French chain that sells records, CDs, tapes, and books, has opened in the heart of town at the Centre Commercial Le Métropole, 17 av. des Spélugues in the Jardins du Casino, alongside the Hôtel Métropole and across from the casino.

If you insist on ultrafancy stores, you'll find them cheek by jowl with the Hôtel de Paris and the casino, and lining the streets leading to the Hôtel Hermitage or across from the gardens at the minimall Park Palace. Look for **D. Porthault,** the luxury French linen maker, at 26 av. de la Costa (© **93-50-16-28**), and **Chanel,** on place de la Casino at allée Serge-Diaghilev (© **93-50-55-55**). **Allée Serge-Diaghilev** is just that: an alley, but a very tiny one filled with designer shops.

However, to get a better perspective on upper-middle-class shopping, visit the **Galaxie de Metropole,** 17 av. des Spélugues. It has a few specialty shops worth visiting (especially if you aren't going into France). Check out **Geneviève Lethu** (© **93-50-09-41**) for colorful and country tabletop design, or **Manufacture de Monaco** (© **93-50-64-63**) for glorious bone china and elegant tabletop design. If the prices send you to bed, two doors away is a branch of the chic but often affordable French linen house **Yves Delorme** (© **93-50-08-70**).

Royal Food (© **93-15-05-04**) is a tiny gourmet grocery store down a set of curving stairs hidden in the side entrance of the mall; here you can buy food items from France, Lebanon, and the U.S.A., or stock up for *le pique-nique* or for your day trips. This market is open Monday through Saturday from 9am to 8pm.

For real-people shopping, stroll **rue Grimaldi,** the principality's most commercially minded street, near the fruit, flower, and food market (below), and **boulevard des Moulins,** closer to the casino, where glamorous boutiques specialize in international chic. There's also an all-pedestrian thoroughfare with shops less forbiddingly chic: **rue Princesse-Caroline** is loaded with bakeries, flower shops, and the closest thing you'll find to funkiness in Monaco. Also check out the **Formule 1 shop,** 15 rue Grimaldi (© **93-15-92-44**), where everything from racing helmets to specialty key chains and T-shirts celebrates the roar of high-octane—and, outside the racetrack, utterly impractical—racing machines.

Should you be looking for the heart and soul of the real Monaco, get away from the glitz and head to **place des Armes** for the fruit, flower, and food market held daily from 9am to noon. It has an indoor and an outdoor market complete with a fountain, cafes, and hand-painted vegetable tiles set beneath your feet. While the outdoor market packs up promptly at noon, some dealers at the indoor market stay open to 2pm. If you prefer bric-a-brac, there's a small but very funky (especially for Monaco) flea market, **Les Puces de Fontvieille,** held Saturday from 10am to 5pm at the Espace Fontvieille, a panoramic open-air site near the heliport in Monaco's Fontvieille district.

WHERE TO STAY

VERY EXPENSIVE

Hôtel de Paris ★★★ On the resort's ornate main plaza, opposite the casino, this is one of the world's most famous hotels and most spectacular beaux-arts monuments. Linked with the sybaritic, high-spending image of Monte Carlo, it's the principality's choice address, more famous and legendary even than the Hermitage (see below). At least two-dozen movie companies have used its lobby as a background. The ornate facade has marble pillars, and the impressive lounge has an Art Nouveau rose window at the peak of the dome. The hotel is furnished with a dazzling decor that includes marble pillars, statues, crystal chandeliers, sumptuous carpets, Louis XVI chairs, and a wall-size fin-de-siècle mural.

The guest rooms are fashionable and, in many cases, sumptuous. The rooms opening onto the sea aren't as spacious as those in the rear. Rooms come in a variety of styles, with elaborate period decor or a fashionably contemporary one. Some of the rooms are so large that if Edward VII were still alive, he would no doubt find plenty of living space for his corpulent body. Elegant tasteful fabrics, rich carpeting, and classic accessories make this a continuing favorite among the world's discerning guests who go to sleep at night in some of the most luxurious beds on the Riviera. Bathrooms are commodious, clad in marble with plenty of room for your stuff, with dual basins, robes, and deluxe toiletries.

Place du Casino, 98000 Monaco. © **92-16-26-26.** Fax 93-16-38-50. www.monte-carlo.mc/lodging-monaco. 197 units. 365€–685€ double; from 680€–5,370€ suite. Breakfast 30€–35€. AE, DC, MC, V. Parking 25€. **Amenities:** 3 restaurants; bar; large indoor pool; fitness center; Thermes Marins spa, offering complete cures of thalassotherapy under medical supervision; 2 saunas; concierge; salon; 24-hr. room service; babysitting; laundry service; dry cleaning; valet parking. *In room:* A/C, TV, hair dryer, safe.

Hôtel Hermitage ★★★ Picture yourself sitting in a wicker armchair, being served drinks under an ornate stained-glass dome with an encircling wrought-iron balcony. The cliff top Hermitage, with its "wedding cake" facade, was the creation of Jean Marquet (who invented marquetry). Large brass beds anchor every room, and decoratively framed doors open onto balconies. Even the smallest rooms are medium in size. Large mirrors, spacious lighted closets, elegant fabrics and upholstery, and sumptuous beds make living here idyllic. The newest rooms are in the Coasta and Excelsior wings. They lack tradition, but they equal the accommodations in the main building, which many guests still prefer because of its old-fashioned French decor and street-front exposure. Clad in marble, bathrooms are roomy and well appointed, with plenty of shelf space, robes, deluxe toiletries, and dual basins. The stylish dining room has Corinthian columns and chandeliers and serves a refined modern cuisine. High-season rates are charged during Christmas, New Year's, Easter, and July and August.

Square Beaumarchais, 98005 Monaco CEDEX. ✆ **92-16-40-00.** Fax 92-16-38-52. www.monte-carlo.mc/lodging-monaco. 300 units. 365€–685€ double; from 680€ suite. AE, MC, V. Parking 25€. **Amenities:** Restaurant; bar; indoor pool; health club; spa; sauna; 24-hr. room service; babysitting; laundry service; dry cleaning. *In room:* A/C, TV, minibar, hair dryer, safe.

EXPENSIVE

Hôtel Mirabeau ★ Only the five lowest floors of this 30-story skyscraper are devoted to a hotel—the remainder houses upscale private apartments. Set in the heart of Monte Carlo next to the casino, and known for its La Coupole restaurant, it's a sophisticated hybrid with many functions. Each of the rooms boasts conservatively modern, rather elegant furnishings, and many contain terraces with a romantic view overlooking the pool and Mediterranean seascape. The rooms facing the sea are the most sought after, but units facing traffic are soundproof. Bedrooms are well appointed, with walk-in closets and two large beds. Bathrooms are spacious and contain deluxe toiletries and plush towels. La Coupole is highly praised for its inventive yet classical cooking (closed Aug). Between May and September, the poolside Café Mirabeau provides an attractive setting for relaxed breakfasts, casual buffet lunches, and upscale dinners.

1 av. Princesse-Grace, 98000 Monaco. ✆ **377/92-16-65-65.** Fax 377/93-50-84-85. www.montecarloresort.com. 103 units. 250€–425€ double; from 600€ suite. AE, DC, MC, V. Parking 21€. **Amenities:** Restaurant; bar; pool; limited room service; babysitting; laundry service; dry cleaning. *In room:* A/C, TV, minibar, hair dryer, safe, robes.

Le Métropole Palace ★ In the heart of Monaco, this hotel is rebuilt on the site of the original Métropole, on Monte Carlo's "golden square." The hotel is superb in every way and has an array of handsomely furnished and beautifully decorated rooms. Each includes a radio, hypoallergenic pillows, and a full line of toiletries. Spaces are generous and furnishings are classical, including occasional antiques; all come with double glazing and soothing pastel color schemes. Marble bathrooms have robes and often a shower with a whirlpool tub. The upscale Le Jardin serves splendid French and international cuisine.

B.P. 19, 4 av. de la Madone, 98007 Monaco. ✆ **93-15-15-15.** Fax 93-25-24-44. www.metropole.mc. 152 units. 340€–390€ double; 495€–575€ suite. AE, DC, MC, V. Parking 25€. **Amenities:** Restaurant; bar; pool; 24-hr. room service; babysitting; laundry service; dry cleaning. *In room:* A/C, TV, minibar, hair dryer.

Le Monte Carlo Grand Hotel ★★ Originally conceived and built by the Loews Corporation, this is a glittering modern palace hotel that was bought and renamed late in 1998 by local investors. It hugs the seacoast from a position below the terraces that support the famous casino—on one of the most valuable pieces of real estate along the Côte d'Azur. Architecturally daring when it was completed in 1975 (some of its foundations were sunk directly into the seabed, and some of the principality's busiest highways roar beneath it), the resort is now viewed as an integral part of Monégasque life. It contains Monaco's highest concentration of restaurants, bars, and nightclubs—it's somewhat like Las Vegas with a Gallic accent. Many celebrities have been attracted here, including Walter

Cronkite and Peter Ustinov. Guest rooms are tastefully, even conservatively, furnished in a style somewhere between Los Angeles and Miami, and are flooded with light from big windows, with views over the town or the sea. Each has a summery, pastel-colored decor, well-designed bathrooms, and a sense of well-upholstered modern comfort. Touches of glitter and flash are consistent with its status as the site of one of the principality's casinos.

12 av. des Spélugues, 98007 Monaco CEDEX. ✆ **93-50-65-00.** Fax 93-30-01-57. www.montecarlograndhotel.com. 619 units. 275€–465€ double; 550€–2,000€ suite. AE, DC, MC, V. Parking 20€. **Amenities:** 3 restaurants; bar; outdoor pool; health club. *In room:* A/C, TV, minibar, hair dryer, safe.

Monte-Carlo Beach Hotel ★★★ Despite its name, this hotel is in France, not Monaco. Built in 1928, it was known for years as the "Old Beach Hotel" until the Société des Bains de Mer decided that was too unglamorous a title for such a luxury retreat. Tons of money later, it emerged with a new name and vastly improved rooms and facilities. The most pampered guest always asks for the most beautiful accommodation in the house, the spacious circular unit above the lobby. Eva Peron stayed here in 1947 during her infamous Rainbow Tour of Europe, and Princess Grace came here almost every day in summer to paddle around the pool, a rendezvous for the rich and beautiful. Though Roquebrune/Cap-Martin is its postal address in France, the hotel is located not there, but at the border of Monaco. All of the rooms are identical, each having a sea view. The hotel's last major renovation occurred in 1995, when virtually everything—furniture, mattresses, carpets—was replaced with conservative-looking modern furnishings. The bathrooms are elegant.

Av. Princesse-Grace, Monte-Carlo Beach, 06190 Roquebrune/Cap-Martin. ✆ **92-16-25-25.** Fax 92-16-26-26. www.montecarloresort.com. 45 units. 250€–600€ double; 1,000€–1,600€ suite. AE, DC, MC, V. Free parking. Closed Nov–Mar. Located on the France-Monaco border. **Amenities:** 4 restaurants; 2 bars; outdoor pool; 24-hr. room service; babysitting; laundry service; dry cleaning. *In room:* A/C, TV, minibar, hair dryer, safe.

MODERATE

Columbus Hotel ★ *Value* Beneficiary of a $10 million upgrade of a 10-year-old hotel in 2000, this nine-story hotel offers good value and lots of style from a location in the residential community of Fontvieille, a 5-minute drive from the glitter of Monte Carlo. Bedrooms are airy, champagne-colored, and outfitted with minimalist ("very cool") furniture. In many cases, they open onto small balconies. This is the flagship of a chain of chic, midprice hotels founded by British investor Ken McCulloch. Don't be confused by recent name changes associated with this place, including the Abela Monaco and the S.M.H. Hotel Monaco.

23 av. des Papalins, 98000 Monaco. ✆ **92-05-90-00.** Fax 92-05-91-67. www.columbushotels.com. 181 units. 200€–295€ double; 350€–450€ suite. AE, MC, V. Parking 23€. **Amenities:** Restaurant; bar; outdoor pool; fitness room; business center; salon/barber; 24-hr. room service; babysitting; laundry service; dry cleaning. *In room:* A/C, TV, minibar, hair dryer, safe.

Hôtel Alexandra This hotel is in the center of the business district, on a busy and often-noisy street corner. Its comfortably furnished guest rooms don't generate much excitement, but they're reliable and respectable. Rooms are small to medium in size, each quite comfortable with a firm mattress and fine linen. Bathrooms are tidily organized, with adequate shelf space. The Alexandra knows it can't compete with the giants of Monaco and doesn't even try. But it attracts those who'd like to visit the principality without spending a fortune. Don't expect too many amenities.

35 bd. Princesse-Charlotte, 98000 Monaco. ✆ **93-50-63-13.** Fax 92-16-06-48. 56 units. 120€–135€ double. AE, DC, MC, V. Parking 7€. *In room:* A/C, TV, hair dryer.

Hôtel Balmoral ★ This is one of the most solidly dependable choices in the moderately priced field. This hotel was built in 1898 by the grandfather of the present owner, Jacques Ferreyrolles. On a cliff halfway between the casino and the Palais du Prince, it boasts eight floors of rooms and lounges with sea views. The rooms are like the public rooms—homey, immaculate, and quiet. You get comfort here but not necessarily a lot of space to spread out. Mattresses are firm, and white, crisp linen is used. Bathrooms are small and tiled. The Balmoral is so inviting that guests often extend their stays.

12 av. de la Costa, 98006 Monaco. ✆ **93-50-62-37.** Fax 04-93-15-08-69. www.hotel-balmoral.mc. 66 units. 110€–180€ double; 150€–300€ suite. AE, DC, MC, V. Parking 8€. **Amenities:** Restaurant; bar; limited room service; babysitting; laundry service; dry cleaning. *In room:* A/C, TV.

INEXPENSIVE

Hôtel Cosmopolite Bargains and Monaco rarely go together, but this hotel is an exception to the expensive rule. When it was built in the 1930s, this hotel was sited in the then-fashionable neighborhood a few steps downhill from the railway station. Today it's an appealingly dowdy Art Deco monument with three floors, no elevator, and comfortable but anonymous-looking rooms. Madame Gay Angèle, the English-speaking owner, is proud of her "Old Monaco" establishment. Her more expensive rooms have showers, but the cheapest way to stay here is to request a room without a shower—there are adequate facilities in the hallway. Mattresses are a bit thin, but there is still reasonable comfort, especially at these prices.

4 rue de la Turbie, 98000 Monaco. ✆ **93-30-16-95.** Fax 93-30-23-05. 26 units, 7 with bathroom. 60€–85€ double without bathroom; 70€–160€ double with bathroom. No credit cards. Free parking on street. Closed Dec–Jan 3. Bus: 1 or 2. *In room:* Hair dryer.

Hôtel de France Not all Monégasques are rich, as a stroll along this street will convince you. Here you'll find some of the cheapest places to stay and eat in this high-priced principality. This 19th-century hotel, 3 minutes from the rail station, has modest furnishings but is clean and comfortable. Bedrooms are small but well organized, with firm mattresses, plus tiny tiled bathrooms.

6 rue de la Turbie, 98000 Monaco. ✆ **93-30-24-64.** Fax 92-16-13-34. www.monte-carlo.MC/france. 26 units. 87€–110€ double. Rates include breakfast. MC, V. Parking 10€. *In room:* TV.

WHERE TO DINE

VERY EXPENSIVE

Le Grill de l'Hôtel de Paris ★★★ MODERN FRENCH In the flood of publicity awarded to this hotel's street-level restaurant, Le Louis XV (see below), it's been easy to overlook the equally elegant contender on the rooftop. The view alone is worth the expense, with the turrets of the fabled casino on one side and the yacht-clogged harbor of Old Monaco on the other. The decor is gracefully modern, with an ambience somewhat less intense than that in the self-consciously cutting-edge Ducasse citadel downstairs. Despite that, the place is undeniably elegant, with a two-fisted approach to cuisine that includes every imaginable sort of grilled fish (sea wolf, monkfish, sole, salmon, mullet, cod, or turbot) and meat such as Charolais beef and lamb from the foothills of the nearby Alps. In fair weather and in summer, the ceiling opens to reveal the starry sky. The fine cuisine is backed up by one of the Riviera's finest wine lists, with some 20,000 bottles; the wine cellar is carved out of the rock below. Service is faultless but never intimidating or off-putting.

In the Hôtel de Paris, place du Casino. ✆ **92-16-29-66.** Reservations required. Main courses 34€–140€. AE, DC, MC, V. Daily noon–2:15pm and 8–10:15pm. Closed Jan 6–31 and at lunch in summer.

Le Louis XV ★★★ FRENCH/ITALIAN On the lobby level of the Hôtel de Paris, Louis XV offers what one critic called "down-home Riviera cooking within a Fabergé egg." Despite the place's regal trappings (or as a reaction against them?), the culinary star chef/namesake Alain Ducasse creates a refined but not overly adorned cuisine, which is served by the best staff in Monaco. Everything is light, attuned to the seasons, with an intelligent and modern interpretation of both Provençal and northern Italian dishes. The chef commands the finest ingredients in Europe, and his menu is ever changing to take advantage of what is best in any season. The service is superb. Ducasse is now dividing his time between this glittering enclave and his restaurant in Paris.

In the Hôtel de Paris, place du Casino. ✆ **92-16-30-01.** Reservations recommended. Jacket and tie required for men. Main courses 80€–92€; fixed-price menus 160€–180€ dinner. AE, MC, V. Thurs–Mon 12:15–1:45pm and 8–9:45pm. Also open Wed at lunch during July–Aug.

EXPENSIVE

Baccarat ★ ITALIAN Established late in 2002 as one of Monaco's newest upscale and elegant restaurants, this is a sedate and elegant testimonial to the flavors and presentations of Italy, with a special emphasis on Sicily, birthplace of its owner and chef, Carmelo Gulletta. Within a vaguely Art Deco ambience of high-backed cardinal-red chairs, a not particularly riveting view over the street, and off-white walls lined with the avant-garde paintings of Monégasque painter Clérissy, you'll enjoy a cuisine that the owners say is more Italian and less Monésgasque than anything else in Monaco. The dining room is supervised by Guletta's France-born, English-speaking wife, Patricia. The antipasti selection is the best in the principality, ranging from steamed asparagus with hollandaise to an Andalusian gazpacho. The chefs turn out risottos as good as anything found in Italy, along with Monaco's most enticing pastas, especially a savory spaghetti with little baby clams. Fish dishes such as sole meunière in general are better than the meat and poultry offerings.

4 bd. des Moullins. ✆ **93-50-66-92.** Reservations recommended. Main courses 13€–30€. AE, MC, V. Sun–Fri noon–2:30pm; daily 7–10:30pm.

Bar et Boeuf ★ INTERNATIONAL This restaurant is one of the many jewels in the crown of super-chef Alain Ducasse, who is, according to many culinary critics, both a culinary genius and the orchestrator of an assembly line that cranks out predictably upscale, predictably expensive food in dozens of chic outlets around the world. Gael Greene has referred to him as "Robo-Chef," and a small but increasingly vocal number of critics are complaining about "franchise sprawl." You can still get a genuinely good meal here, even if none of it is prepared, or even supervised, by Ducasse himself. Come here for a Gallic and very upscale reinvention of a surf-and-turf restaurant, where the only fish used is *bar* (sea bass) and where the beef might be the most cosseted and fussed-over pieces of meat in France. Examples include filets of sea bass with a citrus marmalade and an assortment of different species of braised celery; filet steak with Sicilian herbs; beef Wellington; and beef with a sauté of *taggiasche* (Italian) olives and a soja glaze, served with fried spiny artichokes. The most lavish and expensive dish on the menu—priced at 50€ per person—is tournedos Rossini layered with foie gras and truffles, and served with a *tartare* of truffled foie gras and exotic pan-fried mushrooms.

In the Sporting d'Eté Monte Carlo, av. Princess Grace. ✆ **377/92-16-60-60.** Reservations recommended. Main courses 25€–50€. AE, DC, MC, V. Late May to late Sept 7:30–11pm.

Le Café de Paris ★ TRADITIONAL FRENCH Its *plats du jour* are well prepared, and its location encourages a front-seat view of the comings and goings on Monte Carlo's nerve center—the plaza adjacent to the casino and the Hôtel de Paris. But to our tastes, this re-creation (ca. 1985) of old-time Monaco is a bit too theme-ish, too enraptured with the devil-may-care glamour of Monte Carlo's yesteryears, and a bit too claustrophobic to be really comfortable. Despite that, the Café de Paris continues to draw an active crowd of patrons who appreciate the materialistic razzmatazz and upscale format the French refer to as a *brasserie de luxe.* Menu items change frequently, and platters, especially at lunchtime, are popular with local office workers because they can be served and consumed relatively quickly. Adjacent to the restaurant, you'll find (and hear) a jangling collection of slot machines and a cliché-riddled cluster of boutiques selling expensively casual resort wear and souvenirs.

Place du Casino. ✆ **92-16-20-20.** Reservations recommended. Main courses 16€–49€. Breakfast daily for 15€. AE, DC, MC, V. Daily 7am–1am.

Monte Carlo L'Argentin ★ STEAKS/GRILLS Conceived with panache, L'Argentin is a generous, stylish international restaurant. It's one of the largest in town, banked with windows facing the sea, and has the most impressive grill setup. Uniformed chefs tend three blazing fires, from which diners are protected by a thick sheet of glass. The decor was inspired by the Argentinian pampas and has gaucho accessories, like cowskin-draped banquettes. All the beef served here is imported from the American Midwest; menu choices include a mixed grill called parillada Argentine, Mexican-style flank steak, many kinds of grilled fish, and a perennial favorite, standing rib of American beef grilled over a wood-burning fire. The restaurant remains open, albeit with a limited menu, from 1 to 4am, mimicking the hours of the roulette wheels in the hotel's nearby casino.

In the Grand Hotel, 12 av. des Spélugues. ✆ **93-50-65-00.** Reservations recommended. Main courses 36.50€–59.75€; fixed-price menu 63.50€. AE, DC, MC, V. Daily 7:30pm–4am.

Rampoldi ★ FRENCH/ITALIAN Rampoldi is closely linked to the charming but somewhat dated interpretation of *La Dolce Vita.* Established in the 1950s and staffed with a complementary mix of old and new, it has a spirit more Italian than French. It also serves some of the best cuisine in Monte Carlo from an agreeable location at the edge of the Casino Gardens. Menu items include a succulent array of pastas like tortellini with cream and white truffle sauce, sea bass roasted in a salt crust, ravioli stuffed with crawfish; chateaubriand with béarnaise sauce, and veal kidneys in Madeira sauce. Crêpes suzette make a spectacular finish.

3 av. des Spélugues. ✆ **93-30-70-65.** Reservations required. Main courses 25€–40€; fixed-price menu 23€–45€. AE, MC, V. Daily 12:15–2:30pm and 7:30–11:30pm. Closed Feb 3–18.

Restaurant du Port ★ ITALIAN/FRENCH Set in a big-windowed restaurant directly on one of the quays overlooking the old port, this is a seafood restaurant that's a bit tough but glamorous, with a sometimes hysterically busy staff that might remind you of the dockyards of Genoa. The venue is very much macho Italian. Menu items might include a selection of elegant pastas (tagliatelle with smoked salmon and spaghetti with lobster), antipasti, and meat dishes like filet of beef aux délices, mignon of veal in orange sauce, rack of lamb with Mediterranean herbs, and a full array of Italian and French wines. Other excellent courses from across-the-border Italy include spaghetti with seafood and a superb filet of veal with porcini mushrooms. The very fresh fish of the day is grilled to perfection. Dessert? Why not a *cassata siciliana,* a Sicilian dessert made with ricotta cheese, lots of candied fruit, sponge cake, almond paste, and liqueur? In summer, the restaurant expands onto an outdoor terrace overlooking the yachts of the harbor.

Quai Albert-Ier. ✆ **93-50-77-21.** Reservations recommended. Main courses 16.20€–35€; set lunch 27.50€; set dinner 30€. Daily noon–2:30pm and 8–10:30pm. Closed Nov 1–15.

INEXPENSIVE

Le Texan TEX-MEX These Tex-Mex specialties sometimes attract even the most discriminating French taste buds. There are a handful of outdoor tables, a long bar, a roughly plastered dining room draped with the flag of the Lone Star State, and a scattering of Mexican artifacts. You'll find Le Texan on a sloping residential street leading down to the old harbor—a world away from the glittering casinos and nightlife of the upper reaches. Menu items include T-bone steak, barbecued ribs, pizzas, nachos, tacos, a Dallasburger (with guacamole), and the best margaritas in town.

4 rue Suffren-Reymond. ✆ **93-30-34-54.** Reservations recommended. Main courses 12€–22€. AE, DC, MC, V. Daily noon–midnight.

Pizzeria Monégasque FRENCH/ITALIAN This *pizzeria de luxe* offers four dining rooms and an outdoor terrace. Almost anyone might arrive—in a limousine or on a bicycle, in all kinds of garb that could quickly convince you that Monaco is actually a rather small and gossipy town. The owner has grown accustomed to seeing all the follies and vanities of this town pass through his door; he serves pizzas, fish, and grilled meats to whoever shows up. Specialties are magret du canard (duckling), grilled steaks, carpaccio, and beef tartare. Of the 10 kinds of pizza, the most popular are pizza Terrazzini (it includes cheese and pistou) and the "special" version that's served with Tunisian-style *merguez.*

4 rue Terrazzani. ✆ **93-30-16-38.** Pizzas 7.50€–12€; main courses 11€–19€; fixed-price menu 21.50€. AE, MC, V. Mon–Sat noon–2:30pm and 7:30–11pm (till midnight Fri–Sat). Closed Dec 25–Jan 1.

Stars 'n Bars *Kids* AMERICAN This place revels in the cross-cultural differences that have contributed so much to Monaco's recent history. Modeled on the sports bars popular in the States, it features two distinct dining and drinking areas devoted to American-style food, and a third-floor space, The Club—a sports bar with memorabilia donated by athletes of note. There is even a disco after 10:30pm (sometimes with live performances). Try an Indy 500 or a Triathlon salad, a Wimbledon or a Slam Dunk sandwich, or a Breakfast of Champions (eggs and bacon and all the fixings). If your children happen to be in tow and are feeling nostalgic about the ballpark back home, order a Little Leaguer's platter (for those under 12). Unless an artist of international note appears, there's never a cover charge.

6 quai Antoine-1er. ✆ **97-97-95-95.** Reservations recommended. Dinner salads and platters 10.50€–24€; sandwiches 8€–14€. AE, DC, MC, V. Tues–Sun 11am–midnight. (June–Sept, it's also open Mon 11am–midnight). Bar open till 3am.

MONACO AFTER DARK

Sun Casino, in the Monte Carlo Grand Hotel, 12 av. des Spélugues (✆ **93-50-65-00**), is a huge room filled with one-armed bandits. It also features blackjack, craps, and American roulette. For those who want to gamble with a wider view of the sea, additional slot machines are available on the roof starting at 11am. The casino is open daily from 5pm to 4am. Admission is free.

A speculator, François Blanc, developed the **Monte Carlo Casino,** place du Casino (✆ **92-16-21-21**), into the most famous in the world, attracting the exiled aristocracy of Russia, Sarah Bernhardt, Mata Hari, King Farouk, and Aly Khan (Onassis used to own a part interest). The architect of Paris's Opéra Garnier, Charles Garnier, built the oldest part of the casino, and it remains an extravagant example of the 19th century's most opulent architecture. It's rather schizophrenically divided into areas—one devoted to the casino and others for different kinds of nighttime entertainment, including a theater (see below) presenting opera and ballet.

Unlike the jaded roués whose presence here became a cliché during the Belle Epoque, the new grand dukes are likely to include fast-moving international businesspeople on short-term vacations and a crowd that's more varied than in days of yore. Baccarat, roulette, and chemin-de-fer are the most popular games, though you can play *le craps* and blackjack as well.

The **Salle Américaine,** containing only Las Vegas–style slot machines, opens at noon, as do doors for roulette and *trente-quarente.* A section for roulette and chemin-de-fer opens at 3pm. Most of the facilities inside are operational by 4pm, when additional rooms open with more roulette, craps, and blackjack. The gambling continues until very late/early—the closing depends on the crowd. To enter the casino, you must carry a passport, be at least 21, and pay an admission of between 8€ and 17€, depending on where you want to go. In lieu of a passport, an identity card or driver's license will suffice. After 9pm, the staff insists that gentlemen wear jackets and neckties for entrance into the private rooms.

The premises also contain a **Cabaret** in the Casino Gardens. An orchestra plays before the show. A sexy cabaret featuring lots of feathers, glitter, jazz dance, ballet, and Riviera-style seminudity is presented at 10pm Tuesday through Sunday from mid-September to the end of June. If you want dinner as part of the show, service begins at 9pm and, with the show included, costs 68.40€ per person. If you want to see just the show, your drinks will cost from 45€ each. For reservations, call ✆ **92-16-36-36.**

In the casino's **Salle Garnier,** where lots of gilt and Belle Epoque accents evoke the l9th-century opera house of Paris, concerts are held periodically. For information, contact the tourist office (✆ **93-41-26-00**) or the Atrium du Casino (see below). The music is usually classical, featuring the Orchestre Philharmonique de Monte Carlo.

The casino also contains the **Opéra de Monte-Carlo,** whose patron is Prince Rainier. This world-famous house, opened in 1879 by Sarah Bernhardt, presents a winter and spring opera repertoire that traditionally includes Puccini, Mozart, and Verdi. It was here that the legendary Les Ballets Russes de Monte-Carlo was first introduced in 1918 by Serge Diaghilev, starring Karsavina and the immortal Nijinsky, and choreographer Michel Fokine. The national orchestra and Les Ballets de Monte Carlo appear here. Tickets might be hard to come by; your best bet is to ask your hotel concierge. You can make inquiries about tickets on your own at the **Atrium du Casino** (✆ **92-16-22-99**), open Tuesday through Sunday from 10am to 7pm. Standard tickets are 25€ to 105€.

CLUBS & BARS

Tiffany, avenue des Spélugues (✆ **93-50-53-13**), is a favorite of the 25- to 40-year-old crowd who likes a glamorous modern setting

More high-energy and hip than Tiffany is **Le Box,** 39 av. Princesse Grace (✆ **93-30-15-22**), where the young, the restless, the beautiful, and Princess Stephanie wannabes dance, drink, flirt, and carouse until the wee hours. It's open nightly from 11pm till dawn. The entrance fee of 13.70€ includes the first drink.

Finally, for an insight into the terribly fashionable, terribly blasé, and terribly jaded nocturnal pleasures of the Monégasques, consider dropping into **Jimmy'z,** in Le Sporting Monte Carolo, 26 av. Princesse-Grace (© **92-16-22-77**). Recently acquired from queen of the night, Régine, by Monaco's Société des Bains de Mer, it boasts metallic walls, dozens of potted plants, deep upholsteries, a decorative lagoon, and a roof that opens wide during warm weather for a view of the moon and stars. Entrance is free, but once you're inside, you'll be strongly encouraged to order a drink, or perhaps several, with whisky priced at 39€ each. It's open nightly from 11pm to around 4am. Between October and May, it's closed every Monday and Tuesday. Men are encouraged to wear jackets, or at least long-sleeved shirts.

13 Roquebrune ★★ & Cap-Martin ★★

953km (592 miles) S of Paris; 5km (3 miles) W of Menton

Roquebrune, along the Grande Corniche, is a charming mountain village with vaulted streets. It has been restored, though some critics have found the restoration "artificial." Today its rue Moncollet is lined with artists' workshops and boutiques with inflatedly priced merchandise.

Five kilometers (3 miles) west of Menton and 2km (1½ miles) west of Roquebrune, Cap-Martin is a satellite of the larger resort, associated with the rich and famous since Empress Eugénie wintered here in the 19th century. In time the resort was honored by the presence of Sir Winston Churchill, who came here often in his final years. Two famous men died here—William Butler Yeats in 1939 and Le Corbusier, who drowned while swimming off the cape in 1965. Don't think you'll find a wide sandy beach—you'll encounter plenty of rocks, against a backdrop of pine and olive trees.

ESSENTIALS

GETTING THERE To **drive** to Roquebrune and Cap-Martin, follow N7 east for 26km (16 miles) from Nice. Cap-Martin has **train** and bus connections from the other cities on the coast, including Nice and Menton. For more **railway** information and schedules, call © **08-36-35-35-35.** To reach Roquebrune, you'll have to take a **taxi.** You can take a bus, but there's no formal bus station in Roquebrune; you get off on the side of the highway. For more information about **bus** routes, contact the Gare Routière in Menton (© **04-93-28-43-27**).

VISITOR INFORMATION The **Office de Tourisme** is at 218 av. Aristide-Briand in Roquebrune (© **04-93-35-62-87**).

EXPLORING ROQUEBRUNE

It will take you about an hour to explore the site of this hill village. You can stroll through its colorful covered streets, which still retain their authentic look even though the buildings are now devoted to handcrafts, gift and souvenir shops, or art galleries. From the parking lot at place de la République, you can head for place des Deux-Frères, turning left into rue Grimaldi. Then head left to **rue Moncollet** ★, the town's most interesting street dating back to the 10th century. This long, narrow street is covered with stepped passageways and filled with houses that date from the Middle Ages, most often with barred windows.

Rue Moncollet leads into rue du Château, where you might want to take time to explore the **Château de Roquebrune** ★ (© **04-93-35-07-22**). The only one of its kind, the château was originally a 10th-century Carolingian castle—the present structure dates in part from the 13th century. It houses a historic museum. The castle is dominated by two square towers, from both of which there is a panoramic view along the coast to Monaco. The castle gates are open daily July through August from 10am to 12:30pm and 3 to 7:30pm; April through June and September from 10am to 12:30pm and 2 to 6:30pm; October, February, and March from 10am to 12:30pm and 2 to 6pm; and November through January from 10am to 12:30pm and 2 to 5pm. Admission is 4.50€ for adults, 3€ for seniors, 2€ for students and children 7 to 11, and free for ages 6 and under.

Rue du Château leads to place William-Ingram. After crossing this square, you reach rue de la Fontaine. Take a left. This will lead you to the **Olivier Millénaire** (millennary olive tree). This olive tree is said to be one of the oldest in the world, having survived for at least 1,000 years.

Back on rue du Château, you can reach the 12th-century **Eglise Ste-Marguerite** (no phone), which hides behind a relatively ordinary baroque facade. The interior is of polychrome plaster. Look for two paintings by a 17th-century local artist, Marc-Antoine Otto—a Crucifixion (the second altar) and a Pietà (above the entrance door). The church is open every afternoon from 2 to 5:30pm, and for religious services on Sunday morning from around 8am to 3pm.

EXPLORING CAP-MARTIN

Cap-Martin is a rich town. At the center of the cape is a feudal tower, used today as a telecommunications relay station. At its base you can still see the ruins of the **Basilique St-Martin,** the only remains of a priory constructed here by the monks of the Lérins Islands in the 11th century. After repeated pirate raids in the 15th century, it was destroyed and abandoned. If you follow the road (by car) along the eastern shoreline of the cape, you'll be rewarded with a view of Menton set against a backdrop of mountains. In the far distance looms the coastline of the Italian Riviera, and you can see as far as the resort of Bordighera.

You can take one of the most interesting walks along the Riviera here, but be aware that it's a 3-hour trek. If you have a car, you can leave it in the parking lot at avenue Winston-Churchill. The coastal path, called **Sentier Touristique** ★★, leads from Cap-Martin to Monte-Carlo Beach. The path is marked by a sign labeled PROMENADE LE CORBUSIER. As you go along, you can take in a view of Monaco set in a natural amphitheater. In the far distance, you'll see Cap-Ferrat and even Roquebrune, with its château. The scenic path comes to an end at Monte-Carlo Beach.

You can also take a scenic 6-mile drive that takes about an hour. Leave by D23, following the signs to **Gorbio,** a perched village standing on a hill. Along the way on the narrow, winding road, you'll pass homes of the wealthy in a verdant setting of pines and silvery olives. The site of the village is wild and rocky, the buildings having been constructed as a safe haven from pirate attacks. The most interesting street is **rue Garibaldi,** which leads past an old church to a panoramic belvedere.

WHERE TO STAY

Hôtel Victoria This rectangular low-rise building is set behind a garden in front of the beach. Built in the 1970s, it was renovated in the mid-1990s in a neoclassical style that weds tradition and modernity. It's the "second choice" in town for those who can't afford the lofty prices of the more spectacular Vista

Palace (see below). Bedrooms are well appointed, with comfortable beds. Rooms open onto balconies fronting the sea. Bathrooms are small but well organized. Breakfast is the only meal served.

7 promenade du Cap, 06190 Roquebrune/Cap-Martin. ✆ **04-93-35-65-90.** Fax 04-93-28-27-02. www.hotelmenton.com/hotel-victoria. 32 units. 68€–119€ double. AE, DC, MC, V. Parking 8€. **Amenities:** Bar. *In room:* A/C, TV, minibar, hair dryer.

Hôtel Vista Palace ★★★ This extraordinary hotel/restaurant stands on the outer ridge of the mountains running parallel to the coast, giving a spectacular "airplane view" of Monaco. And the design of the Vista Palace is just as fantastic: Three levels are cantilevered out into space, so every room seems to float. Nearly all have balconies facing the Mediterranean. Bedrooms are spacious and elegantly appointed, and you'll find good-size bathrooms in marble or tile, each with luxury toiletries. If you don't want to stay here, at least consider stopping by for a meal—it's expensive but worth it. Le Vistaero features Mediterranean cuisine envied by the region's other restaurateurs.

Grande Corniche, 06190 Roquebrune/Cap-Martin. ✆ **04-92-10-40-00.** Fax 04-92-10-40-40. www.vistapalace.com. 68 units. 203€–350€ double; 400€–1,400€ suite. AE, DC, MC, V. Parking 20€ in garage. **Amenities:** 3 restaurants; bar; outdoor pool; health club; sauna; 24-hr. room service; massage; babysitting; laundry service; dry cleaning. *In room:* A/C, TV, minibar, hair dryer, safe.

WHERE TO DINE

Au Grand Inquisiteur ★ *Finds* TRADITIONAL FRENCH This culinary find is a miniature restaurant in a two-room cellar near the top of the medieval mountaintop village of Roquebrune. On the steep, winding road to the Château de Roquebrune, this climate-controlled building is made of rough-cut stone, with large oak beams. The cuisine, though not the area's most distinguished, is quite good; try the chef's duck special or scallops meunière. Most diners opt for one of the fresh fish choices. The wine list is exceptional—some 150 selections, most at reasonable prices.

18 rue du Château. ✆ **04-93-35-05-37.** Reservations required. Main courses 14€–27€; fixed-price menu 25€–37€. MC, V. Wed–Sun noon–1:30pm and 7:30–10pm. July–Aug closed for lunch; also closed Mon for dinner. Closed Nov–Dec 26.

Hippocampe TRADITIONAL FRENCH Opened in 1963, this fine restaurant along the seafront offers a full view of the bay and even the Italian coastline. Made safe by a thick stone wall, its terrace is shaded by five crooked pines. The "Sea Horse" is a stone-and-glass garden house with a tile roof and scarlet and pink potted geraniums. Specialties include filets de sole en brioche, coq au vin (chicken cooked in wine), terrine of salmon in basil sauce, and duck with peaches.

44 av. Winston-Churchill. ✆ **04-93-35-81-91.** Reservations required. Main courses 30€–58€; fixed-price menus 30€–38€. AE, DC, MC, V. Tues–Wed and Fri–Sat noon–1:45pm and 7:30–9:30pm; Thurs and Sun noon–1:45pm. Closed Nov 1-Jan 15.

'Idee-Fixe TRADITIONAL FRENCH This well-managed, unpretentious restaurant with a hardworking staff is in an antique building in the heart of the old town. Food is well prepared; you can order an *omelet soufflé* garnished with crabmeat, a tart but savory appetizer of fried St-Marcellin cheese served with slices of golden apples, or a tartare of salmon. Pastas include gnocchi and tagliatelle with either Roquefort cheese or salmon. Main courses feature such delights as filets of red snapper with a lemon-flavored mousse, sea bass with Provençal herbs, and filet of beef sandwiched between slices of foie gras and flambéed in cognac. There's both a terrace and a small balcony for outdoor dining.

1 rue de la Fontaine. ✆ **04-93-28-97-25.** Reservations recommended. Main courses 14.20€–22€; fixed-price menu 25€. MC, V. Wed–Mon 7–10:30pm.

Le Roquebrune TRADITIONAL FRENCH Few other restaurants along the Cote d' Azur give as authentic or charming a picture of old-fashioned French manners and cuisine as this one. According to the family matriarch, Laurence Marinovich, "We've been doing the same thing for years; it's just that we've suddenly become fashionable again." None of this is lost upon such luminaries as Alain Ducasse, who dines here discreetly whenever he wants to escape the microcosm of his hyper-chic restaurant in nearby Monte Carlo. It's positioned 4.8km (3 miles) east of the center of Roquebrune, in a house (ca. 1925) that belonged to the ancestors of the present owners, the above-mentioned Laurence and her daughters Marine and Patricia. One of the family's secrets involves the use of utterly fresh ingredients, especially the vegetables and the fish, which is unloaded directly from the boats of fishermen working the nearby sea. Bouillabaisse and its simpler cousin, *soupe de poisson,* are works of culinary art here, and the single most expensive item on the menu (lobster salad) contains a lot more meat than you might have expected, as well as a tempting array of ultrafresh greens. Pasta with clams is a winner, as are any of the other grilled fish that are prepared and served with gusto by the polite and hardworking staff.

100 Avenue Jean-Jaurès (Basse Corniche). ✆ **04-93-35-00-16.** Reservations recommended. Main courses 12-84€; fixed-price menu 60€. AE, DC, MC, V. June–Sept Sat–Sun noon–2pm; daily 7–10pm. Oct–May Thurs–Mon 7–10pm.

14 Menton ★★

959km (596 miles) S of Paris; 63km (39 miles) NE of Cannes; 8km (5 miles) E of Monaco

Menton is more Italianate than French. Right at the border of Italy, Menton marks the eastern frontier of the Côte d'Azur. Its climate is the warmest on the Mediterranean coast, and in winter it attracts a large, rather elderly British colony. The impact of these seniors on the population of 130,000 has earned Menton the sobriquet "the Fort Lauderdale of France."

According to a local legend, Eve was the first to experience Menton's glorious climate. When she and Adam were expelled from the Garden of Eden, she tucked a lemon in her bosom, planting it at Menton because it reminded her of her former stamping grounds. Lemons still grow in profusion here, and the fruit is given a position of honor at the Lemon Festival held over a 2-week period in February. Actually, the oldest Menton visitor might have arrived 30,000 years ago. He's still around—or, at least, his skull is—in the Musée de Préhistoire Régionale (see below).

Don't be misled by all those "palace-hotels" studding the hills. They are no longer hotels—they've been divided up and sold as private apartments. Many of these turn-of-the-20th-century structures were erected to accommodate elderly Europeans, English and German, who arrived carrying a book written by one Dr. Bennett in which he extolled the joys of living at Menton.

ESSENTIALS

GETTING THERE Many visitors arrive by **car** on one of the corniche roads. Specifically, you can follow N7 east from Nice and arrive in 45 minutes.

There are good **bus and rail connections** that make stops at each resort along the Mediterranean coast, including Menton. Two trains per hour pull in from

Nice (trip time: 35 min.), and two trains per hour come from Monte Carlo (trip time: 10 min.). For rail information and schedules, call ✆ **08-36-35-35-35.** Two local bus companies, **Autocars Broch** (✆ **04-93-31-10-52**) and **RCA** (✆ **04-93-85-64-44**), run buses between Nice, Monte Carlo, and Menton, usually around two per hour, for a round-trip fee of 5.50€ from Nice.

VISITOR INFORMATION The **Office de Tourisme** is in the Palais de l'Europe, 8 av. Boyer (✆ **04-92-41-76-76;** www.villedementon.com).

SEEING THE SIGHTS

Menton is situated on the Golfe de la Paix (Gulf of Peace) on a rocky promontory that divides the bay in two. The fishing town, the older part with its narrow streets, is in the east; the tourist zone and residential belt are in the west.

The filmmaker, writer, and artist Jean Cocteau liked this resort, and in the **Musée Jean-Cocteau,** Bastion du Port, quai Napoléon-III (✆ **04-93-57-72-30**), you can see his death portrait, sketched by MacAvoy. Some of the artist's memorabilia is here—stunning charcoals and watercolors, brightly colored pastels, ceramics, and signed letters. The museum is open Wednesday through Monday from 10am to noon and 2 to 6pm. Admission is 4.20€.

At **La Salle des Mariages,** in the Hôtel de Ville (town hall), rue de la République (✆ **04-92-10-50-00**), Cocteau painted frescoes depicting the legend of Orpheus and Eurydice, also the subject of his film *Orphée.* A tape in English helps explain them. The room, with its red-leather seats and leopard-skin rugs, is used for civil marriage ceremonies. It's open Monday through Friday from 8:30am to 12:30pm and 1:30 to 5pm. Admission is 2€. Advance reservations are necessary.

Musée de Préhistoire Régionale, rue Lorédan-Larchey (✆ **04-93-35-84-64**), presents human evolution on the Côte d'Azur for the past million years. It contains the 25,000-year-old head of the *Nouvel Homme de Menton* (sometimes known as "Grimaldi Man"), found in 1884 in the Baousse-Rousse caves. Audiovisual aids, dioramas, and videocassettes enhance the exhibition. The museum is open Wednesday through Monday from 10am to noon and 2 to 6pm. Admission is free.

Musée des Beaux-Arts, Palais Carnoles, 3 av. de la Madone (✆ **04-93-35-49-71**), contains 14th-, 16th-, and 17th-century paintings from Italy, Flanders, Holland, and the French schools, as well as modern paintings by Dufy, Valadon, Derain, and Leprin—all acquired by a British subject, Wakefield-Mori. The museum is open Wednesday through Monday from 10am to noon and 2 to 6pm. Admission is free.

A DAY AT THE BEACH

Menton's beaches stretch for 3.2km (2 miles) between the Italian border and the city limits of Roquebrune and are interrupted only by the town's old and new ports. Collectively, they're known as **La Plage de la Promenade du Soleil** and, with rare exceptions, are public and free. Don't expect soft sands or even any sand at all: The beaches are narrow, are covered with gravel (or, more charitably, big pebbles), and are notoriously uncomfortable to lie on. Don't expect big waves or tides, either. Who goes there? In the words of one nonswimming resident, mostly Parisians or residents of northern France, who are grateful for any escape from their urban milieux. Topless bathing is widespread, but complete nudity is forbidden.

Unlike Cannes, where thousands of chaises pepper the beaches, there are few options in Menton for renting mattresses and parasols (most people bring their own). Two exceptions are **Le Splendid Plage** (✆ **04-93-35-60-97**) and **Les Sablettes** (✆ **04-93-35-44-77**), both charging around 15€ for use of a mattress. They're immediately to the east of the Vieux Port.

WHERE TO STAY

Hôtel Aiglon A nugget along the coast, this hotel was converted from a stately Riviera villa. In a large park filled with Mediterranean vegetation, it offers an intimate and homey environment. Rooms are tastefully furnished and contain elegant beds. Bathrooms are small and tiled. The magnet of the hotel is a heated pool around which is a 1900s veranda. The garden setting is beautifully maintained. Other facilities include a solarium and a children's game area. An excellent Provençal and international cuisine is offered, with windows opening onto the pool and garden.

7 av. de la Madone, 06500 Menton. ✆ **04-93-57-55-55.** Fax 04-93-35-92-39. www.aiglonhotel.com. 29 units. 50€–65€ double; 135€–195€ suite. AE, DC, MC, V. Free parking. **Amenities:** Restaurant; bar; pool; limited room service; babysitting; laundry service. *In room:* A/C, TV, minibar, hair dryer, safe.

Hôtel Chambord This hotel is located on the main square next to the **Casino de Menton,** 1 Avenue Félix Faure (✆ **04-92-10-16-16**). It is well maintained, with rows of balconies and awnings. The comfortable guest rooms have generous space and are neatly organized, with streamlined modern furniture. Bathrooms are well maintained. Breakfast is the only meal served.

6 av. Boyer, 06500 Menton. ✆ **04-93-35-94-19.** Fax 04-93-41-30-55. 40 units. 100€–110€ double. AE, DC, MC, V. Parking 8€. **Amenities:** Lounge. *In room:* A/C, TV, minibar, hair dryer, safe.

Hôtel Le Dauphin This affable hotel lies just off the beach. The double-insulated rooms are bright and uncluttered, each with a balcony opening onto the mountain range or the sea. Small to medium in size, they are tidily maintained. The small tiled bathrooms have adequate shelf space. The multilingual owner/director Jacques Ridés is a classical-music buff who has created an unusual hotel feature: two acoustically inviting practice studios—the Apollo, with a grand piano, and the Dionysos, with a baby grand, for 'round-the-clock rehearsal. The attentive staff is welcoming. Three meals per day are served, featuring many specialties of Provence.

28 av. du Général-de-Gaulle, 06500 Menton. ✆ **04-93-35-76-37.** Fax 04-93-35-31-74. 28 units. 85€–98€ double; 120€ triple. Rates include continental breakfast. AE, MC, V. Closed Nov 12–Dec 20. **Amenities:** Restaurant. *In room:* A/C, TV, minibar, hair dryer, safe.

Hôtel Méditerranée This white-and-salmon hotel is 3 short blocks from the sea. A raised terrace with a view of the water, chaise lounges, and potted plants are on the premises. The rooms are attractively decorated and include private balconies opening onto the sea. Most are spacious, with comfortable beds (usually twins). The hotel also has a restaurant, which offers a veranda for dining in fair weather.

5 rue de la République, 06500 Menton. ✆ **04-93-28-25-25.** Fax 04-92-41-81-82. 90 units. 93€ double. Children 4 and under stay free in parents' room. AE, DC, MC, V. Parking 7€. **Amenities:** Restaurant; bar; laundry service; dry cleaning. *In room:* A/C, TV, minibar, hair dryer, safe.

Hôtel Napoléon On a palm tree–shaded avenue, this recently renovated hotel features a pool set in a small garden and stone terrace. The main lounge and bar, furnished with 18th-century English and Italian pieces, is really like a large living room. The guest rooms, decorated in vivid colors, have mahogany furniture, comfortable beds, and balconies overlooking the sea and the old town. There are a rooftop terrace and an air-conditioned restaurant with great views. Nonguests are welcome to visit for lunch or dinner. The staff here is particularly attentive and helpful.

29 Porte de France, 06503 Menton. ✆ **04-93-35-89-50.** Fax 04-93-35-49-22. 40 units. 86€–114€ double. AE, DC, MC, V. Free parking. Closed Nov 1–Apr 18. **Amenities:** Bar; lounge; pool; babysitting; limited room service; laundry service; dry cleaning. *In room:* A/C, TV, minibar, hair dryer, safe.

Hôtel Princesse et Richmond ★ At the edge of the sea near the commercial district, this hotel boasts a facade of warm Mediterranean colors, with a sunny garden terrace. The owner rents comfortable soundproof rooms with modern and French traditional furnishings and balconies. They range from small to medium in size, each with a comfortable bed. Drinks are served on the roof terrace, where you can enjoy a view of the curving shoreline. The staff organizes sightseeing excursions.

617 promenade du Soleil, 06500 Menton. ✆ **04-93-35-80-20.** Fax 04-93-57-40-20. www.princess-richmond.com. 46 units. 78€–112€ double; 145€–185€ suite. AE, DC, V. Parking 10€. Closed Nov 4–Dec 18. **Amenities:** Pool; Jacuzzi; exercise room. *In room:* A/C, TV, minibar, hair dryer.

Hotel Riva This hotel is adjacent to a verdant park, a few steps from the beach. Its design is conservative and angular-looking. It has many of the luxuries and much of the feeling of a hotel you would find along the coast of southern Florida. Its modern design includes lots of balconies and multileveled terraces for sunbathing and drinking cocktails. Bedrooms are small to medium in size but are elegantly furnished with quality mattresses and fine linen. High-quality materials such as marble and granite are used throughout, complementing dignified beechwood furniture. Other than breakfast and brunch, no meals are served, but considering the proximity of many restaurants, no one seems to mind.

600 promenade du Soleil, 06500 Menton. ✆ **04-92-10-92-10.** Fax 04-93-28-87-87. www.rivahotel.com. 40 units. 80€–110€ double. AE, MC, V. Parking 8€. **Amenities:** Bar; lounge; sauna; Jacuzzi; babysitting; laundry service; dry cleaning. *In room:* A/C, TV, minibar, hair dryer, safe.

WHERE TO DINE

La Calanque ★ FRENCH/SEAFOOD Informal and earthy in a charming, rustic Provençal way, this restaurant provides a waterside view and well-prepared food. In fair weather, tables are set under shade trees in full view of the harbor. We recommend the spaghetti napolitaine, tripe Niçoise, *soupe de poissons* (fish soup), and fresh sardines (grilled over charcoal and very savory), with the focus on locally harvested seafood. Two specialties are bouillabaisse and *barba giuan,* small biscuits cooked in olive oil after having been stuffed with a variety of local greens.

13 square Victoria. ✆ **04-93-35-83-15.** Main courses 12€–21€; fixed-price menu 20€–26€. MC, V. Tues–Sat noon–2pm and 7:15–9:30pm; Sun noon–2pm.

L'Albatros ★ *Finds* FRENCH/PROVENÇAL This charming little bistro along the port specializes in fish dishes from the Mediterranean. On the second floor and on the terrace, you can enjoy a view over the old harbor and bay while sampling fresh fish purchased directly from Menton fishers. Menu items are conservative but savory, with lots of emphasis on Provençal interpretations of fish and seafood. Examples include a succulent bouillabaisse, prepared for a minimum of two diners and priced at 30.40€ per person. There's also a *cassoulet des pécheurs,* a stewpot brimming with herbs, saffron, and fish; and a thick and juicy charolais of beef with béarnaise sauce. Everything here is fresh, unpretentious, and low-key.

31 quai Bonaparte. ✆ **04-93-35-94-64.** Reservations recommended. Main courses 20€–30€; fixed-price menu 27€. MC, V. Tues–Sun noon–3pm and 7:30–11pm (till 10pm in off-season).

Petit Port FRENCH/PROVENÇAL Small and charming, employing many members of an extended family, this restaurant serves well-prepared fresh fish in a century-old house near the medieval port. Everything is homemade, even the bread. Specialties are grilled sardines (increasingly difficult to find), fish soup, several kinds of grilled meats and fish, and (in honor of the northern France origins of its owner) tripe in the style of Caen. The place prides itself on its location—less than a mile from the Italian border.

1 place Fontana. ✆ **04-93-35-82-62.** Reservations recommended. Main courses 22-30€. AE, MC, V. Thurs–Tues noon–3pm and 7pm–midnight.

Rocamadour FRENCH/PROVENÇAL This pleasant restaurant overlooks the port. You dine at tables set under a canopy where colored lights are turned on at night. Some specialties offered by the chef are from the Périgord region, including foie gras. *Magret de canard* (duckling) is another specialty. But basically the cookery is grounded in the rich tradition of the Côte d'Azur, with an emphasis on very fresh fish. The restaurant was founded almost a century ago by a chef from Rocamadour, and the name of that town has stayed with the place.

1 square Victoria. ✆ **04-93-35-76-04.** Reservations recommended. Main courses 7.50€–24€; fixed-price menu 17.50€. AE, MC, V. Thurs–Tues noon–2:30pm and 7:30–10pm.

Appendix: The South of France in Depth

Though **Provence** is hardly the region author Edith Wharton and others discovered long ago, this legendary area today has more museums and attractions than ever, along with better hotels and a great increase in the number of chefs earning Michelin stars. So it hasn't been irretrievably spoiled. It's true that its overpopularity and overbuilding, together with the summer hordes descending on such cities as Avignon and on the French Riviera, have made parts of the province undesirable—especially if you're caught driving behind a mile-long line of cars in summer heat. The once-sweet disposition of its citizens is a bit taxed, too, by endless tourist pressure. But there's the vast hilly hinterland to explore, where you'll find old traditions intact and old men playing a leisurely game of boules on a hot afternoon, preferably under shade trees.

One of the major joys of visiting Provence is seeking out the scenery and locations depicted in the canvases of Cézanne, van Gogh, and other painters. A trail of modern artists attracted to the brilliant light of the Côte d'Azur have left a rich heritage: Matisse at a chapel at Vence, Cocteau at Menton and Villefranche, Picasso at Antibes, Léger at Biot, Renoir at Cagnes, and Bonnard at Le Cannet.

Every habitué has a favorite oasis along the **Riviera** and will try to convince you of its merits: Some say "Nice is passé." Others maintain that "Cannes is queen." Others shun both in favor of Juan-les-Pins, and still others winter only at St-Jean-Cap-Ferrat. If you have a large bankroll, you might prefer Cap d'Antibes, but if money is short, you can try the old port of Villefranche. Each resort on the Côte d'Azur offers its own special flavor and special merits. Glitterati and eccentrics have always been attracted to this narrow strip of fabled real estate only 201km (125 miles) long between the Mediterranean and the mountain ranges.

The corniches of the Riviera stretch from Nice to Menton. The Alps here drop into the Mediterranean, and roads were carved along the way. The lower road, about 32km (20 miles) long, is the Corniche Inférieure. Along this road are the ports of Villefranche, Cap-Ferrat, Beaulieu, and Cap-Martin. The Moyenne Corniche, or Middle Road, 31km (19 miles) long, also runs from Nice to Menton, winding spectacularly in and out of tunnels and through the mountains. We can thank Napoléon for the panoramic Grande Corniche that he ordered built in 1806—La Turbie and Le Vistaero are the principal towns along the 32km (20-mile) stretch, which reaches more than 480m (1,600 ft.) in elevation at Col d'Eze.

The landscape, cuisine, lifestyle, history, and architecture of **Languedoc** are similar to that of its neighbor, Provence. The mighty Rhône marks the dividing line between the region of Provence and the Côte d'Azur and that of Languedoc-Roussillon. The city of Nîmes, for example, seems very Provençal in character, though officially it's in Languedoc. You'll find Languedoc both less touristed than Provence and more affordable. You'll find outstanding museums like the Toulouse-Lautrec museum at Albi and the Goya museum at Castres, and unique landscapes like the Camargue. The ancient city of Toulouse, with its medieval monuments, is today an important center of France's high-tech industry.

1 History 101: A Few Thousand Years in Provence

THE GREEKS ARRIVE

During the Bronze Age, Provence was inhabited by primitive tribes whose artistic legacy, in the form of etched pottery, dates from around 6000 B.C. By around 700 B.C., traders from Greek-speaking areas around the Aegean established colonies at Antipolis (Antibes), Nikaia (Nice), and Massilia (Marseille). Mediterranean wines, grains, and ceramics were exchanged for pewter and livestock from west-central France.

The Greeks even sailed up the Rhône, trading with the Celtic and Ligurian tribes and influencing them with their sophisticated ways. They introduced the grape and the olive—both would play vital roles in the Provençal economy for millennia to come.

In 600 B.C., Protis, captain of a group of Greek traders, was the guest of honor at a Provençal celebration in honor of Gyptis, the daughter of a local tribal leader. So charmed was she by her father's guest that she selected Protis for her husband. Her dowry included the harbor front of what is now Marseille, the gateway through which massive amounts of materiel, ancient warriors, and weapons later poured.

Around the same time, waves of migration from the Celtic north added to the non-Mediterranean population. The Celts intermarried easily with the native Ligurians and eventually formed a fierce force that opposed the expansionist efforts of the Greeks. In 218 B.C., some tribes supported Hannibal in his advance on Rome across the Alps, an alliance that Rome would severely punish several generations later. As the local forces faced off against the Greeks in the south, tensions grew to the point that the Greeks called on the rapidly emerging Roman state to subdue the threat to their colonial power. The resulting genocide helped define the future racial and cultural makeup of Provence.

THE ROMANS TAKE OVER

Because of the need for a buffer between Rome and the "savages" of Gaul—and also because of the area's fertility—the Romans considered the Mediterranean coastline one of its most treasured provinces. They named their new possession Provincia Transalpina—later it was bastardized into "Provence." Gallia Narbonensis (Narbonne) was the administrative center. By 55 B.C., Julius Caesar had conquered all of Gaul and even invaded Britain, an act that suddenly diminished Provence's importance in the context of the Roman Empire.

Few Roman regions received such a concentrated dose of Romanization as did this area. Evidence remains in the ruins of grandiose construction: amphitheaters, bathhouses, temples, and stadiums at Arles, Orange, Nîmes, Glanum (near St-Rémy), Fréjus, and Cimiez. The Pont du Gard—a masterpiece of civil engineering and one of France's most frequently photographed sites—was completed in 19 B.C. Marseille, whose pedigree predated that of virtually every other site in Provence, was bypassed during this explosion of Roman building because of its alliance with the losing side in the civil war between Pompey and Caesar.

Later, as the scope of the empire diminished and its far reaches became frayed and tattered, Provincia Narbonensis remained staunchly Roman. Even after the empire's east-west schism and long after Paris and the Rhône valley became centerpieces for Frankish resistance, Provence remained a beneficiary of the empire.

ROME COLLAPSES

The conversion of the emperor Constantine to Christianity marked the beginning of the end for Rome. Although Constantine's attention was mainly directed to the Middle East and he ruled from Constantinople rather than Rome, he declared Arles his favorite city in the western empire and built a palace there—ironically, faced with the pressures of his position, he rarely visited it. In A.D. 400, the short-lived emperor Honorius gave Arles a fleeting role as the capital of the Three Gauls (Britain, Spain, and France). Meanwhile, the spread of the inflammatory new religion, Christianity, reached Provence. You can see some of the earliest evidence of this in Marseille in the oft-repaired Basilique St-Victor.

Arles's brief preeminence served it poorly after the empire's collapse. In A.D. 471, it was sacked by the Visigoths, and a few years later, along with other important Provence settlements, it was sacked by other tribes. From A.D. 600 to 800, the area was devastated by the Saracens (Moors) and by Charles Martel himself, one of the patriarchs of modern France. Between A.D. 736 and 740, he led his Frankish troops in orgies of appalling brutality. The only relief came with the brief ascendancy of the Merovingians around A.D. 500.

Charlemagne passed through Provence en route to Rome, where he was crowned Emperor of the West by the pope. After Charlemagne's death, his empire was split among three feuding grandsons; Provence was bequeathed to Lothair, the eldest. Lothair placed his own son, Charles, on the throne of Provence, designating it a kingdom in its own right. By A.D. 879, Provence was ruled jointly with Burgundy by the medieval ruler Boson, brother-in-law of Charles the Bald.

CULTURAL FLOWERING

In 1032, with its capital at Aix-en-Provence, the eastern half of Provence joined the Holy Roman Empire, a loose configuration of duchies and kingdoms unified mainly by fear and loathing of the Moors. The area west of the Rhône came under the control of the comtes de Toulouse. During a period of almost 300 years, architecture, poetry, and music flourished. This cultural high point was marked by the songs and poetry of the troubadours, who traveled from castle to castle, and by the beginnings of literature and popular entertainment as we know them today.

By around 1125, the comtes de Toulouse and the comtes de Barcelona controlled Provence. For a time, it appeared that they might have united their kingdoms against their enemy, the French. By 1246, however, control of Provence tipped in favor of the French kings, thanks to marriages between the family of Louis IX (St. Louis) and the rulers of Barcelona. Today the village of Barcelonette derives its medieval name from the influence of these counts.

The Paris-based kings understood Provence's strategic importance as a starting point for conquests of other Mediterranean kingdoms. St. Louis ordered the construction of one of the most remarkable sites in southern France, the fortified town of Aigues-Mortes, as a bulwark against the Moors. In 1248, he set sail with his army on the Seventh Crusade, only to die en route in Tunis.

POPES & PLAGUES

In 1307, the French-born pope Clement V fled Rome, causing one of the most bizarre political imbroglios in European history. Fearful of the instability in Rome, he decided to move the official seat of the papacy to Avignon. And surrounded by an army of courtiers, priests, soldiers, and purveyors of luxury goods, the papacy remained for 70 years under the protection of the kings of France and the comtes de Provence. At one point there were actually two popes, one in Rome and one in Avignon. During this period, Avignon became a vibrant and prosperous city, a center of wealth and culture. Eventually, after much contention, the papacy was returned to Rome, and Avignon's importance collapsed.

Plagues decimated the population of Provence in 1348 and 1375. At the same time, extortion, plundering, and highway robbery by small-time feudal despots, especially the rulers of the much-dreaded Les Baux, added to a general sense of confusion, unrest, and despair.

By 1409, however, things were looking up. The University of Aix was founded as southern France's answer to the thriving Sorbonne in Paris, and in 1434, René d'Anjou was designated count of an independent Provence. He fostered economic development and supported the arts. Shortly after René's death, his nephew and heir signed a pact with the wily French king Louis XI, who immediately used it to annex Provence.

WARS OF RELIGION

Provence's first religious war was a result of a heresy that spread rapidly over Europe in the 13th century. The Cathars, or the "Pure Ones," also known as Albigenses, were a highly ascetic sect who believed the material world was the incarnation of evil and should be rejected in favor of a mystical union with Christ. Most Cathari strongholds were in Languedoc, but many adherents lived in Provence. The heresy was an excuse for the French monarchs and the Church to attack and seize the area. The rallying cry of the French forces as they slaughtered the Cathars—"Kill them all, and God will decide who is guilty"—lives in infamy even today. The Albigensian Crusade, begun in 1208, not only violently obliterated the heresy but also destroyed medieval Provençal culture and ensured the ascendance of French as spoken in the northern part of France over the French of Provence.

The second religious war began in the 1500s, when the Reformation changed Europe forever. Influenced by the thriving community of Protestants under John Calvin, whose stronghold lay in Geneva, Huguenots (Protestants) in Provence grew in number and power. One of the most extreme of these sects was the Vaudois. Founded in the 1200s by a wealthy merchant, Valdès or Vaudès, from Lyon, the sect rejected the idea of an ecclesiastical hierarchy, preached the virtues of poverty, and denied the authenticity of the sacraments. Memories of the Cathari might have fueled this movement, which was greeted with horror by the church. When in 1545 the Vaudois responded to their persecutors by attacking several Catholic churches near their stronghold in the Luberon hills, the armies of François I massacred more than 3,000 of them over a 4-day period and sent 600 into the French navy as slaves.

However, Protestantism continued to flourish in Orange, Uzès, and especially Nîmes. For 40 years beginning in 1560, religious battles occurred regularly. Chief of state Richelieu, whose obsession was the unification of all aspects of French society into a form approved by Paris, eventually suppressed or destroyed Huguenot communities throughout France. The bloodiest of these skirmishes was in the Atlantic coast port of La Rochelle, but also destroyed were the Provençal strongholds at Uzès and Les Baux.

REVOLUTIONARY TIMES

In 1720, a devastating plague was imported through the harbor of Marseille, killing what is conservatively estimated at 100,000 people. Despite this and other setbacks, Provence had become one of France's wealthiest regions. An aesthetic had developed that was distinct to the region and is imitated today around the world. Majestic town houses were built in the towns, along with *mas,* estates in the country.

As revolutionary fervor swept over France in 1789, Provence made its contribution. One of the most articulate and inflammatory members of Paris's Etats-Généraux—the radical committee that controlled the Revolution in its early stages—was the Comte de Mirabeau, elected as representative by Aix-en-Provence. In 1792, a corps of volunteers from Marseille, singing a call to arms written by Rouget de Lisle, marched through the streets of Paris toward the Tuileries. The song's original name was "L'Hymn de Bataille de l'Armée du Rhin" ("Battle Hymn of the Army of the Rhine"), but that was later changed to "La Marseillaise."

It was at Golfe-Juan, a minor seaport near Cannes, that Napoléon Bonaparte began his Hundred Days, his last bid for power. The enthusiasm that welcomed his armies in Provence set a pattern for his reception along the route of his march to Paris. The route he followed—now Route N85 through Dignes and Sisteron—has been known ever since as "La Route Napoléon."

In 1790, an act of the Revolutionary government had a permanent impact on Provence. France was divided into a labyrinth of political districts *(départements)* that shattered both the country's medieval boundaries and its political networks. In the process, the once-autonomous region of Provence was carved into three, and later five, subdivisions.

THE 19TH CENTURY

Partly because of its strategic dominance of more than half of France's Mediterranean ports, Provence gained enormous prosperity during the 19th century.

In 1864, a railway line linked Provence with the rest of France, encouraging increased travel. The 1869 opening of the Suez Canal and the expansion of French influence into Morocco, Algeria, Tunisia, and Egypt thrust Provence's ports into international prominence and helped develop Marseille as one of the greatest seaports in the world.

The development of Nice and the Riviera into international resorts was largely a result of the unemployment caused by the phylloxera epidemic in Provençal vineyards and the collapse of the silkworm industry. Tourism was a logical answer to the economic deprivation. In 1822, the expatriate British colony in Nice helped finance its namesake promenade. In 1830, Lord Brougham bought an estate in Cannes and promoted Cannes in Britain as a suitably hedonistic place for the upper classes to escape from the fog, the cold, and the Victorian repressions of England. In 1860, the region around Nice, whose administration by the House of Savoy represented an anachronistic holdover from the feudal age, was fully integrated into France. Then, a few years later, the ruler of one of western Europe's least prosperous territories, Monaco, built the most opulent casino in the world. Thanks to the patronage granted to the site by the haut monde, profits came pouring in.

In the mid–19th century, a group of cultural luminaries, fearing a total demise of Provençal language and culture, founded Félibrige, an organization devoted to the restoration of Provence's medieval literary forms. Five years later, the artistic patriarch Frédéric Mistral published his Provençal poem *Mirèio,* which was met with widespread acclaim.

WORLD WARS & POSTWAR

Fortunately for Provence, most of the destruction of World War I occurred in other areas of France. During World War II, Provence and Languedoc were part of the territory controlled by the collaborationist Vichy government, which initially meant some protection from the Nazi rule in the rest of France. In 1940, after Nazi-dominated North Africa fell to the Allied forces, the Nazis retracted their pledge not to occupy the zones controlled by Vichy and moved into Provence with heavy artillery. Two years later, when they moved to confiscate the French navy's warships, French saboteurs sank most of the Mediterranean fleet in the harbor at Toulon.

On August 15, 1944, Allied forces landed successfully on the Provençal coast between St-Raphaël and St-Tropez, and within 14 days, all of Provence was liberated.

Few other regions of the world have zoomed into the international consciousness the way Provence has since 1945. In 1947, Cannes began its role as Europe's film capital with its first film festival, grown since to almost mythic proportions. Farming and industry were modernized, and tourism took a giant leap forward. Celebrity watching seemed to go hand in hand with voyeurism and exhibitionism, as the Riviera's topless beaches caused a stir as far away as Chicago and as stars like Brigitte Bardot elevated St-Tropez to its role as sybaritic capital of the most sybaritic country.

In 1953, the socialist Gaston Defferre, a pivotal figure in the region's politics, was elected mayor of Marseille, a post he held for 33 years. His ardent appeals for the semiautonomy of Provence finally came to fruition in 1981 with Mitterrand's approval of a limited form of self-government.

In 1962, the collapse of the French government in Algeria introduced a new element—a flood of newly impoverished, newly homeless French citizens who arrived by the thousands. Mainlanders contemptuously called them *pieds-noirs* (blackfeet). The wave of anti-immigrant sentiment would have repercussions for years to come and would move the traditional leftist political scene sharply to the right.

In 1970, the opening of the A6/A7 high-speed autoroute between the French capital and Marseille made access to the region much easier. Between 1970 and 1977, two major national parks (Parc Naturel Régional de la Camargue and Parc Naturel Régional de Lubéron) were created for the preservation of Provence's native ecology. And in 1981, the high-speed Train à Grande Vitesse (TGV) was launched between Paris and Marseille, reducing transit time to less than 4 hours.

However, anti-immigrant sentiment has been growing, and in 1985 voters supported Jean-Marie Le Pen's anti-immigration platform, Le Front National. In some French minds, North Africans were unwelcome, regardless of their French citizenship. The event that brought about a more generous attitude was France's win in the World Cup in 1998. Zinedine Zidane, who scored the winning goals, is the son of Algerian immigrants. President Chirac pinned Legion of Honor ribbons on Zidane and his teammates. But expecting Zidane to lead France into its multicultural future is a bit much to ask, even for a World Cup hero. Anti-immigrant fever still remains a social problem in France, especially in Provence, which has seen a huge influx of people from North Africa and is viewed as a stronghold for Jean-Marie Le Pen, the leader of the National Front. In a runoff in the 2002 presidential elections, Jacques Chirac easily swept to victory, but Le Pen beat out Socialist leader Lionel Jospin, winning some 18% of the vote, regarded as one of the biggest upsets in French electoral history.

In mid-June 2001, the south of France became even more closely linked to Paris with the launch of a new TGV Med train, bringing the trip time from Paris to the beaches of Marseille to just 3 hours and promising a major boost for the economy of the country's "second city." The link cost $3.25 billion and took 12 years to complete. Other southern towns along the train route, including Avignon and Aix-en-Provence, are also expected to benefit economically.

The creation of a Euro-Mediterranean free-trade zone by the year 2010, announced in 1995 in Barcelona, together with a vast financial aid program funded by European Union loans, bodes well for Marseille and other ports of Provence just when it seemed that decay was inevitable. This massive development should have enormous impact on the region.

2 A Taste of Provence

LA CUISINE DU SOLEIL

Pungent and earthy, Provençal cuisine is generally high in vitamins and fiber and low in saturated fat. The flavors of southern France incorporate the liberal use of olive oil; herbs like basil, garlic, rosemary, and sage; and a sophisticated blend of products from the mountain areas, such as lamb from the Alpilles, and the bounty of the Mediterranean. This is *la cuisine du soleil,* infused with warmth and sunshine, based on a wealth of produce and raw ingredients that spring from soil whose richness is belied by its parched, often stony surface.

THE BOUNTY OF PROVENCE

Because much of the allure of Provençal cuisine derives from its raw ingredients, menus are likely to state the source of what you're about to consume. To see this wealth firsthand, head for any of the open-air markets where vast amounts of meat, cheese, produce, wine, and herbs with evocative names like purple hyssop and *sarriette* (summer savory) are sold from simple kiosks.

FRUITS & VEGETABLES Strawberries from the village of Carpentras or the district of Bouches-du-Rhône have a special cachet. Melons, especially ogen melons, from the town of Cavaillon were so famous that in 1864, civic leaders opted to present a dozen perfect melons each year to the French novelist Alexandre Dumas *père* as a sign of their ongoing respect. He later wrote that he hoped that the readers of Cavaillon would always find his books as charming as he found their melons. Apricots are delicious anywhere, but if they're from the slopes of the Roussillon, your menu will usually let you know. *Mousserons,* one of many varieties of wild mushrooms you'll see in local markets, evoke *frissons* among gastronomes when they're from the Ardèche, west of the Rhône. Lots of species of onions are for sale; one of the most intriguing is the banana-shape *échalotes-bananes.*

OLIVES Along with bread and wine, olives were practically the staff of life for many centuries in Provence. Look for varieties like *olives cassées* from Les Baux and fennel-flavored *picholines du Gard.* Any resident of Nice might rebel at the idea of making a *salade Niçoise* with anything other than nut-brown *olives de Nyons.*

CHEESE Sophisticated gastronomes consider a well-selected cheese tray to be one of the symbols of civilization, and in the south of France you could spend hours choosing among the varieties of *chèvre* alone. A Provençal folk saying likens goats to "the poor man's cow," but over the centuries, goat-milk cheese has attained gourmet status. Merchants who deal in the creamy delicacies are proud of the variety and will provide details about any cheese's origin. Looking for something esoteric? Ask for a rare tomme de Camargue, a firm but creamy cheese that combines milk from both goats and sheep and whose disclike surface is embedded with sprigs of rosemary. There's also *Banon vrai,* a goat-milk cheese made in the hamlet of Banon in northern Provence. During its fermentation, it's marinated in *eaux de vie,* aged in clay pots on dried chestnut leaves, and wrapped with raffia string. Equally delicious is *lou pevre,* a goat cheese whose pungency is enhanced by a black-pepper coating.

BREAD Almost as varied as the cheeses are the shapes and ingredients of the bread. You can buy it as long, thin *ficelles,* marvelously crusty, and as *gibassiers,* baked with a dollop of olive oil for flavor. These aren't to be confused with *pain d'olives,* with the flesh of the olive in the dough; *pain de raisins,* flavored with dried raisins; *pain à l'anis,* aniseed bread; and earthy *pain au levain,* sourdough bread. In Aix, you'll find a regional recipe for *pain d'Aix,* a double-mounded staple that resembles women's breasts. The most democratic of Provençal breads is *pain d'égalité,* developed in response to an edict during the Revolution declaring that only one kind of bread, composed of one part rye flour and three parts wheat, could be consumed in an egalitarian society. Today this is scorned as something akin to generic supermarket bread, but it's still occasionally available in Provençal markets. Beware of Provençal witches, who, according to legend, will come to dance on any loaf of bread that's turned upside down.

PASTRIES & SWEETS As far as pastries go, southern France is expert at turning out *calissons,* rectangular sweets concocted from almond paste; they invariably taste best when baked in Aix-en-Provence. There are more recipes for *nougat,* honey-sweetened chewy candy flavored with either almonds or pistachios, than anyone could possibly document—nougat from the industrial-looking town of Montelimar seems to have a slight edge. A variety of almond-and-honey cookies, *croque moines* (crusty monks), were named for the monks who baked them to raise money for their causes. *Une galette Provençale,* a tartlet filled with pralines, almond cream, and grated orange zest, is a perennial childhood favorite in Arles and St-Rémy.

A MENU OF CHOICES

CASSOULET & BOUILLABAISSE What dish should you especially look for in the southwest? The magic word is cassoulet, not to be confused with a *cassolette,* a fancy word for a small stewpot and whatever ingredients someone might be tempted to throw into it. *Cassoulet* is to Toulouse what bouillabaisse is to Marseille, a succulent mixture of slow-cooked white beans flavored with an herbed combination of roasted lamb, mutton, goose, sausages, duck, and various forms of pork.

Bouillabaisse is Provence's most famous dish. Traditionally, it combines a trio of fish: rascasse, grondin, and congre (the spiny red hogfish, gurnet, and conger eel). The original recipe from Marseillaise kitchens actually called for a dozen kinds of fish, including fielan, rouquier, and sard. Increasingly, mussels or, to make it elegant, spiny lobsters are added. The kettle of fish is cooked rapidly in bouillon and flavored with olive oil and various seasonings (bay leaf, saffron, onion, and fennel). We always toss in some cognac or white wine. A paste of Spanish peppers, called a rouille, sharpens the sauce, giving it an extra reddish color. The cooking time is 10 minutes.

VEGETARIAN DISHES Provence has a delightful emphasis on vegetarian dishes, which seem to have a transcendent earthiness from deep within the soil. Examples are succulent grilled eggplant with basil-tomato sauce, and grilled vegetables garnished with zucchini flowers (stuffed with a purée of zucchini and herbs, coated with batter, and deep-fried). No one denies the international

The Pleasure of Pastis

The proper start to a Provençal meal is a glass or two of the unpretentious local apéritif, *pastis,* a translucent yellow liqueur that becomes cloudy when you add water or ice. Although it's usually associated with truck drivers and dockyard laborers in Marseille, you might really appreciate it once you develop a taste for it. It's scented with anise, fennel, mint, and licorice, but in the case of France's most popular brand name Ricard (beneficiary of millions of francs' worth of ad campaigns) or its sweeter rival, Pernod, it contains some additional secret ingredients.

appeal of room-temperature *ratatouille,* the soothing combination of eggplant, onions, peppers, and herbs slowly stewed in olive oil.

The perfect accompaniment for any of these dishes is *aïoli,* the garlic-laced mayonnaise that's the appropriate foil for fish, grilled vegetables, and plain or toasted bread. Incidentally, aïoli can also refer to an entire meal composed of poached salt cod, boiled vegetables, and (in some cases) roasted snails; the garlic mayonnaise binds the disparate ingredients together.

Also look for specialties like *pissaladière,* a doughy form of onion pizza; *mesclun,* assorted wild greens that make divine salads; and *pistou,* a rich basil-infused soup similar to minestrone.

GOOSE & DUCK Southwestern France is the world's headquarters of dishes boasting fattened goose and duck. The appreciation of *foie gras* from either bird has been elevated to something approaching a cult, and many dishes gain a noteworthy unctuousness when fried in *graisse d'oie* (goose fat). Thighs of both species are cooked in large quantities of their own ample fat to create tender *confits,* and the breast of ducks *(magrets)* are often grilled over charcoal or oak fires. *Aiguillettes* (long, thin strips carved from the duck's back) are prepared according to a varied repertoire of techniques. Patés made from the by-products of duck, and sometimes studded with truffles, figure high on everyone's favorite appetizer list. Goose, at least in Gascony, might be flambéed in Armagnac and then slowly braised with wine and vegetables for the classic *daube d'oie.*

HEARTY STEWS A specialty remembered (sometimes fondly, sometimes not) from many Provençaux childhoods is *pieds et paquets,* a combination of mutton or lamb tripe and lambs' feet cooked with cured, unsmoked pork, garlic, wine, and tomatoes. This classic is much appreciated by adventurous gastronomes. An equally prized variation is a *gratin de pieds de porc aux truffes* (gratin of pigs' feet with truffles). *Civet de lapin* is wild rabbit stewed with herbs and red wine, with rabbit blood added to the stew at the last minute as a thickener. *Daube de boeuf à la provençale* is an unusual combination of stewed beef marinated in garlic purée with red wine. *Bourride,* a succulent fish stew, is Languedoc's answer to the world-famous bouillabaisse of Provence. *Baudroie* is a simple but flavorful mix of monkfish, thin-sliced potatoes, garlic, onions, herbs, and an unexpected ingredient—the zest of navel oranges.

GAME If you're planning a trip to the deep south in autumn, you'll discover many game dishes at your disposal. These include *perdreau* (partridge), *sanglier* (wild boar), *chevreuil* (venison), *faison* (pheasant), and *lièvre* (wild hare). Often the meat will be marinated in herbs and wine, roasted with acute care by experts, and served with vibrant red wine from grapes grown in the Rhône Valley.

BULL Throughout the south, but especially in the flat wetlands and bull-raising terrain of the Camargue, look for *gardiane de taureau.* Concocted from tough and somewhat fibrous bull flesh and flavored with olives and red wine, it's invariably served with *riz de Camargue*—rice from the lowlands of the delta of the Rhône.

LES VINS DE PROVENCE

For winemaking purposes, Provence is defined as the area between Cannes, not far from the Italian border, and the eastern banks of the Rhône. Although Avignon, Châteauneuf-du-Pape, and Orange are historically and culturally a part of Provence, their wines fall into a distinctly separate district, the Côtes-du-Rhône, which begins at Avignon and extends about 225km (140 miles) northward up the valley of the Rhône to just south of Lyon, near Côte Rotie. Wine produced west of the Rhône, within an area that extends about 64km (40 miles) north of the Mediterranean coast all the way to the Spanish border, belongs to a still different entity, Languedoc-Roussillon.

Most of the wines from these three districts are red and tend to be strong, solid, and flavorful, usually with a potent level of alcohol (a by-product of the high sugar content of the grape varieties that thrive in the heat and constant sunlight).

The pleasure of Provence's wine is undeniable. However, the threat of inadequate rainfall in a region known for its droughts keeps local vintners perennially insecure. Consequently, vintners have traditionally relied on a complicated blending of grapes. Since the phylloxera epidemic of the late 19th century, these grape blends have included varietals from Italy and Spain. The result, according to many connoisseurs enamored with the more aristocratic vintages of Burgundy and Bordeaux, is an occasional inconsistency in the way the wines might age.

In 1923, a distinguished Provençal landowner, Baron Le Roy de Boiseaumarie, inaugurated a series of quality controls from his lands near Châteauneuf-du-Pape. His efforts were instrumental in imposing standards on vintners and helped launch what later evolved into the national Appellations d'Origine Contrôllées (A.O.C.).

Despite the appeal of southern French wines as an accompaniment for strongly flavored foods like anchovies, sardines, and bouillabaisse, the region has a lower percentage of wines that oenophiles call "great" than do more temperate regions. So pride is taken by vintners with lands in designated A.O.C. districts, and massive investments in recent years have helped elevate many of the region's vintages to international repute. While it's no guarantee of quality, looking for A.O.C. labels is a beginning point for newcomers who want to distinguish prestigious vintages from ordinary *vin de table.* Many A.O.C. designations are relatively new—upstarts compared to the more venerable designations in Burgundy and Bordeaux. Côtes du Provence, producer of more than 100 million bottles annually, was designated A.O.C. as recently as 1977.

Impressions

An optimistic description of Provence wines always mentions the sun-baked pines, thyme, and lavender, and claims that the wine takes its character from them. This is true of some of the best of them. . . . Others get by on a pretty colour and a good deal of alcohol. 'Tarpaulin edged with lace' is a realistic summing up of one of the better ones.

—Hugh Johnson, *World Atlas of Wine*

The two best Provençal whites are produced near Aix, most notably the delicate Cassis and the more forthright Palette. Bellet, a relatively small wine-growing district in the hills above Nice, produces fashionable reds, whites, and rosés.

Particularly strong reds are Gigondas and Vacqueras, whose alcohol content sometimes exceeds 13%. Names to look for on a wine list are Côtes de Provence (Pierrefeu and Château Minuty are two important producers) from the dry hills north of Toulon, Côtes du Rhône Villages, Côtes du Vivarais, and Châteauneuf-du-Pape, the only wine in the world that's allowed to bear the crest of the long-ago popes of Avignon. Because of the vagaries of rainfall and the growing season, any bottle of this last wine might be composed of more than a dozen grapes from around the district. A memorable sweet wine from the Côtes du Rhône, favored by pastry chefs as a foil for their concoctions, is Baumes de Venise.

The two most famous rosés of the south are Tavel, a name that's been used by several novelists as the wine of choice of their dashing heroes; and Bandol, a worthy producer of which is Château Simone. A recent contender rapidly growing in repute is Listel, a cloudy rosé produced on the sun-baked plains of the Camargue.

The vineyards of Languedoc-Roussillon represent more than a third of France's total acreage devoted to grapes. The fields around Nîmes, Béziers, and Narbonne produce rivers of ordinary table wine, which, thanks to newfangled methods of cultivation and harvesting, have of late been more favorably regarded by wine scholars. Aristocratic vintages from Languedoc include unusual sweet wines like Banyuls and Muscat de Rivesaltes and the reds from towns on the eastern foothills of the Pyrénées, Côtes de Roussillon.

SAMPLING THE VINTAGES

A cost-effective means of trying ordinary table wines is bringing your own container (usually a plastic jug sold on the premises or in hardware stores) to a large-scale producer. At bargain-basement prices, they'll use a gas pump–inspired nozzle to pump wine from enormous vats directly into your container. In a restaurant, such a vintage would be sold in a glass carafe or ceramic *pichet* at a low price. If you're driving through the vineyards and see one of the many signs announcing *vente au détail,* it means that you'll be able to buy estate-bottled wine by the bottle, invariably at lower prices than in retail wine shops.

If you opt to visit some of Provence's vineyards, don't be disappointed by the overuse of the word *château.* Only in rare instances will you discover baronial homes or showcase architecture. In unpretentious rural Provence, most of the wine is produced by small or medium-size farms on plots family-owned for many generations. In fact, nearly half the wine of southern France is produced by cooperative wineries. However, most of the places described in "The Best Vineyards," in chapter 1, just happen to have an impressive château associated with their land.

Index

See also Accommodations and Restaurant indexes, below.

General Index

Accommodations

Restaurants

Frommer's® Complete Travel Guides

Alaska
Alaska Cruises & Ports of Call
Amsterdam
Argentina & Chile
Arizona
Atlanta
Australia
Austria
Bahamas
Barcelona, Madrid & Seville
Beijing
Belgium, Holland & Luxembourg
Bermuda
Boston
Brazil
British Columbia & the Canadian Rockies
Brussels & Bruges
Budapest & the Best of Hungary
California
Canada
Cancún, Cozumel & the Yucatán
Cape Cod, Nantucket & Martha's Vineyard
Caribbean
Caribbean Cruises & Ports of Call
Caribbean Ports of Call
Carolinas & Georgia
Chicago
China
Colorado
Costa Rica
Cuba
Denmark
Denver, Boulder & Colorado Springs
England
Europe
European Cruises & Ports of Call
Florida
France
Germany
Great Britain
Greece
Greek Islands
Hawaii
Hong Kong
Honolulu, Waikiki & Oahu
Ireland
Israel
Italy
Jamaica
Japan
Las Vegas
London
Los Angeles
Maryland & Delaware
Maui
Mexico
Montana & Wyoming
Montréal & Québec City
Munich & the Bavarian Alps
Nashville & Memphis
New England
New Mexico
New Orleans
New York City
New Zealand
Northern Italy
Norway
Nova Scotia, New Brunswick & Prince Edward Island
Oregon
Paris
Peru
Philadelphia & the Amish Country
Portugal
Prague & the Best of the Czech Republic
Provence & the Riviera
Puerto Rico
Rome
San Antonio & Austin
San Diego
San Francisco
Santa Fe, Taos & Albuquerque
Scandinavia
Scotland
Seattle & Portland
Shanghai
Sicily
Singapore & Malaysia
South Africa
South America
South Florida
South Pacific
Southeast Asia
Spain
Sweden
Switzerland
Texas
Thailand
Tokyo
Toronto
Tuscany & Umbria
USA
Utah
Vancouver & Victoria
Vermont, New Hampshire & Maine
Vienna & the Danube Valley
Virgin Islands
Virginia
Walt Disney World® & Orlando
Washington, D.C.
Washington State

Frommer's® Dollar-a-Day Guides

Australia from $50 a Day
California from $70 a Day
England from $75 a Day
Europe from $70 a Day
Florida from $70 a Day
Hawaii from $80 a Day
Ireland from $60 a Day
Italy from $70 a Day
London from $85 a Day
New York from $90 a Day
Paris from $80 a Day
San Francisco from $70 a Day
Washington, D.C. from $80 a Day
Portable London from $85 a Day
Portable New York City from $90 a Day

Frommer's® Portable Guides

Acapulco, Ixtapa & Zihuatanejo
Amsterdam
Aruba
Australia's Great Barrier Reef
Bahamas
Berlin
Big Island of Hawaii
Boston
California Wine Country
Cancún
Cayman Islands
Charleston
Chicago
Disneyland®
Dublin
Florence
Frankfurt
Hong Kong
Houston
Las Vegas
Las Vegas for Non-Gamblers
London
Los Angeles
Los Cabos & Baja
Maine Coast
Maui
Miami
Nantucket & Martha's Vineyard
New Orleans
New York City
Paris
Phoenix & Scottsdale
Portland
Puerto Rico
Puerto Vallarta, Manzanillo & Guadalajara
Rio de Janeiro
San Diego
San Francisco
Savannah
Seattle
Sydney
Tampa & St. Petersburg
Vancouver
Venice
Virgin Islands
Washington, D.C.

Frommer's® National Park Guides

Banff & Jasper
Family Vacations in the National Parks
Grand Canyon
National Parks of the American West
Rocky Mountain
Yellowstone & Grand Teton
Yosemite & Sequoia/Kings Canyon
Zion & Bryce Canyon

Frommer's® Memorable Walks

Chicago
London
New York
Paris
San Francisco

Frommer's® With Kids Guides

Chicago
Las Vegas
New York City
Ottawa
San Francisco
Toronto
Vancouver
Washington, D.C.

Suzy Gershman's Born to Shop Guides

Born to Shop: France
Born to Shop: Hong Kong, Shanghai & Beijing
Born to Shop: Italy
Born to Shop: London
Born to Shop: New York
Born to Shop: Paris

Frommer's® Irreverent Guides

Amsterdam
Boston
Chicago
Las Vegas
London
Los Angeles
Manhattan
New Orleans
Paris
Rome
San Francisco
Seattle & Portland
Vancouver
Walt Disney World®
Washington, D.C.

Frommer's® Best-Loved Driving Tours

Britain
California
Florida
France
Germany
Ireland
Italy
New England
Northern Italy
Scotland
Spain
Tuscany & Umbria

Hanging Out™ Guides

Hanging Out in England
Hanging Out in Europe
Hanging Out in France
Hanging Out in Ireland
Hanging Out in Italy
Hanging Out in Spain

The Unofficial Guides®

Bed & Breakfasts and Country Inns in:
- California
- Great Lakes States
- Mid-Atlantic
- New England
- Northwest
- Rockies
- Southeast
- Southwest

Best RV & Tent Campgrounds in:
- California & the West
- Florida & the Southeast
- Great Lakes States
- Mid-Atlantic
- Northeast
- Northwest & Central Plains
- Southwest & South Central Plains
- U.S.A.

Beyond Disney
Branson, Missouri
California with Kids
Central Italy
Chicago
Cruises
Disneyland®
Florida with Kids
Golf Vacations in the Eastern U.S.
Great Smoky & Blue Ridge Region
Inside Disney
Hawaii
Las Vegas
London
Maui
Mexio's Best Beach Resorts
Mid-Atlantic with Kids
Mini Las Vegas
Mini-Mickey
New England & New York with Kids
New Orleans
New York City
Paris
San Francisco
Skiing & Snowboarding in the West
Southeast with Kids
Walt Disney World®
Walt Disney World® for Grown-ups
Walt Disney World® with Kids
Washington, D.C.
World's Best Diving Vacations

Special-Interest Titles

Frommer's Adventure Guide to Australia & New Zealand
Frommer's Adventure Guide to Central America
Frommer's Adventure Guide to India & Pakistan
Frommer's Adventure Guide to South America
Frommer's Adventure Guide to Southeast Asia
Frommer's Adventure Guide to Southern Africa
Frommer's Britain's Best Bed & Breakfasts and Country Inns
Frommer's Caribbean Hideaways
Frommer's Exploring America by RV
Frommer's Fly Safe, Fly Smart
Frommer's France's Best Bed & Breakfasts and Country Inns
Frommer's Gay & Lesbian Europe
Frommer's Italy's Best Bed & Breakfasts and Country Inns
Frommer's Road Atlas Britain
Frommer's Road Atlas Europe
Frommer's Road Atlas France
The New York Times' Guide to Unforgettable Weekends
Places Rated Almanac
Retirement Places Rated
Rome Past & Present

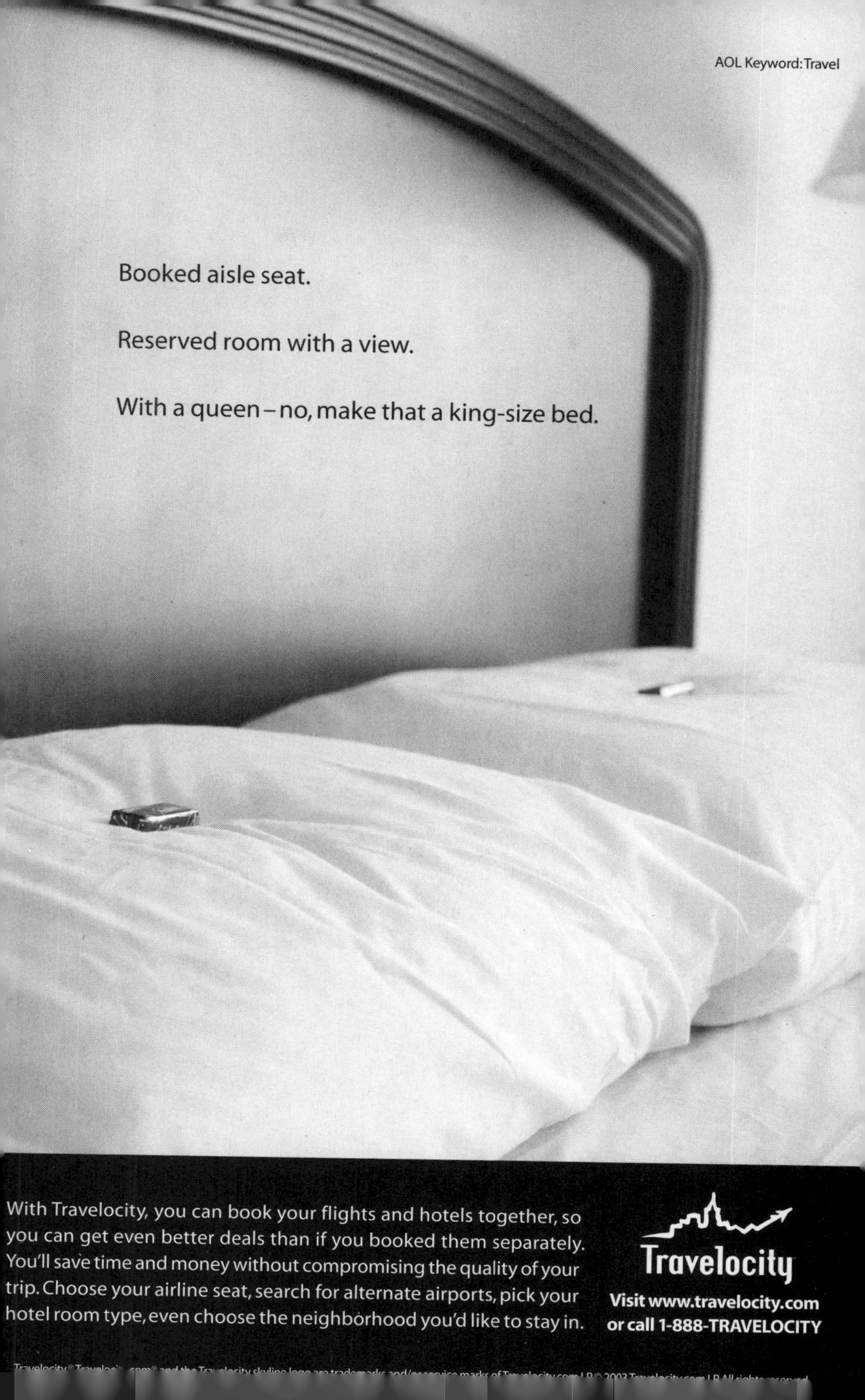
AOL Keyword: Travel
Booked aisle seat.
Reserved room with a view.
With a queen – no, make that a king-size bed.
With Travelocity, you can book your flights and hotels together, so you can get even better deals than if you booked them separately. You'll save time and money without compromising the quality of your trip. Choose your airline seat, search for alternate airports, pick your hotel room type, even choose the neighborhood you'd like to stay in.
Travelocity
Visit www.travelocity.com
or call 1-888-TRAVELOCITY